D1265664

# THE
# MIDDLE
# WAY

*Finding Happiness in a World of Extremes*

## LOU MARINOFF, PH.D.

STERLING

New York / London
www.sterlingpublishing.com

STERLING and the distinctive Sterling logo are registered trademarks of
Sterling Publishing Co., Inc.

Library of Congress Cataloging-in-Publication Data Available

2   4   6   8   10   9   7   5   3   1

Published by Sterling Publishing Co., Inc.
387 Park Avenue South, New York, NY 10016
© 2007 by Lou Marinoff

Distributed in Canada by Sterling Publishing
c/o Canadian Manda Group, 165 Dufferin Street
Toronto, Ontario, Canada M6K 3H6
Distributed in the United Kingdom by GMC Distribution Services
Castle Place, 166 High Street, Lewes, East Sussex, England BN7 1XU
Distributed in Australia by Capricorn Link (Australia) Pty. Ltd.
P.O. Box 704, Windsor, NSW 2756, Australia

Sterling ISBN-13: 978-1-4027-4344-3
ISBN-10: 1-4027-4344-0

For information about custom editions, special sales, premium and
corporate purchases, please contact Sterling Special Sales
Department at 800-805-5489 or specialsales@sterlingpub.com.

# Contents

## Part II: The Extremes and the ABCs

## Part III: The ABCs Here and Now

# Acknowledgments

This book grew out of an essay I wrote during 2003 for *Global Agenda*, the annual magazine of the World Economic Forum.[1] The essay applies the philosophies of Aristotle, Buddha, and Confucius (the ABCs) to the art of modern leadership. I thank Nick Evans for inviting and editing it, and thank Professor Klaus Schwab for inspiring it. The book was further shaped during a dinner in Manhattan, in June 2003. I thank my companions at that dinner—Joelle Delbourgo, Santiago del Rey, and Julian Marinoff—for their impetus and encouragement.

The ABCs stand for Aristotle, Buddha, and Confucius—three of the greatest teachers humanity has ever known. In the process of writing this book, I have drawn not only on their timeless teachings, but also on lessons learned directly from some of their worthy successors. So I offer thanks to esteemed teachers and mentors from Aristotelian, Buddhist, and Confucian traditions alike, including Professor David Bohm; President Daisaku Ikeda; Roshi Robert Kennedy, S.J.; Grandmaster S. M. Li; Professor Elaine Newman; Sogyal Rinpoche; and Professor Klaus Schwab.

I also thank friends and colleagues who were kind enough to read the manuscript and offer their valuable advice: Moshe Denburg, Pierre Grimes, and Michael Grosso. In addition, I thank many other friends and colleagues whose willingness to engage me in dialogue improved my understanding of the issues treated herein: Dr. Ibrahim Abouleish, Professor Dominique Belpomme, Dr. Virginia Bonito, Salvatore Geraci, Ida Jongsma, Dr. Yoichi Kawada, Dr. Patti Knoblauch, Elisa Manzini, Dr. Pamela Mar, William O'Chee, Professor Per Pinstrup-Andersen, Denise Railla, Dr. Frank-Jürgen Richter, Dr. Peter Ritter, Paul Robertson, Guy Spier, Dr. Tan Chin Nam, Matt Taylor, Sundeep Waslekar, Dr. Albert Werckmann, and Masao Yokota, among others.

I thank Stephanie Land for her wonderful work as an editor, Daniel Cortés Coronas for his astute copyedits, and Patty Gift and the team at Sterling for their invaluable final editions.

I also thank many hospitable organizations and helpful people within them, who kindly invited my collaboration and afforded me memorable journeys during the research and writing of this book. They include the Association of Commonwealth Universities and the British Council (UK), De Arbeiderspers (the Netherlands), the Aspen Institute, the Institute for Local Government, and the Omega Institute (USA), Center for Leadership and the Arts (Denmark), Commonwealth Publishing Group (Taiwan), Eco-Festival Bourbon-l'Archambault (France), Ediciones B (Argentina, Chile, Mexico, Spain, Uruguay), ETOR (Spain), Federal Agency for Civic Education (Germany), Keter (Israel), Nuevos Pasos (Argentina), Paideia (Italy), Record (Brazil), SEKEM (Egypt), Soka Gakkai International (Canada, Japan, USA), and the World Economic Forum (China, India, Singapore, Switzerland, USA).

I would like to express particular thanks to President Daisaku Ikeda, of Soka Gakkai International (SGI), for his inspiration, encouragement, and contributions to this book. He is a remarkable teacher, leader, and exemplar of the Mahayana Buddhist tradition. I have either quoted him directly, or referred to his works, throughout these pages.

The ABCs have much to offer, as do their worthy successors. The Middle Way has never been more vital to humanity's well-being than in today's global village. So despite Ecclesiastes' injunction "To the making of many books, there is no end," duty and dharma compel me to share with you some salient ideas from *The Middle Way*. I assume sole responsibility for errors or misunderstandings.

Lou Marinoff
The Global Village, 2006

# List of Illustrations

*Note: The Web pages cited below were extant when the citations were originally made. The author and publisher cannot be responsible for Web pages that have subsequently been discontinued or moved to other URLs.*

# Introduction

You probably realize by now that all of humanity inhabits a place called "the global village," a term coined by Marshall McLuhan during the 1960s. It's a planetary community of billions of people, not all of whom are at peace with themselves or one another on a given day. The growth and evolution of this village is ongoing and apparently unstoppable, but its inhabitants experience many kinds of "growing pains," both acute and chronic. This book's first premise is that much human suffering is caused—or worsened, or prevented from being alleviated—by extremisms of various types, ranging (for example) from religious fanaticism to moral anarchy, from functional illiteracy to deconstructed higher education, from male chauvinism to militant feminism. The second premise is that three great sages of antiquity—namely Aristotle, Buddha, and Confucius, to whom I refer collectively as the ABCs—each taught ways to eliminate needless suffering, to guide human beings toward personal fulfillment, beneficial insight, and social balance. Each of them recognized that extremism is anathema to happiness, health, and harmony: yours, and everyone else's.

The ABCs share something else as well: the supremely important notion that the main purpose of being alive is to lead a good life, here and now. Their varying theories and practices are meant to produce goodness in this moment, and the next, and the next . . . amounting to lasting goodness for you and for others. The ABCs are not concerned with past lives or future ones. They address the heavens and hells we make here on this earth, in every instant. The ABCs teach that by properly exercising the considerable power you hold over this moment in your life, you will make good things manifest for yourself and others. Inversely, they all warn that by carelessly squandering this power, you will make bad things manifest. So you decide: If you prefer fairy tales with "happily ever after" endings, put down this book and pick up Mother Goose. If you prefer to lead a good life now, continue reading.

The book has three parts. Part I looks at civilizational dynamics that drive both cooperation and conflict in the global village, and introduces each of the ABCs themselves. Chapter 1 examines the foundational ideas of four great civilizations whose core beliefs and values are prone to diverge or to conflict, but which are pressured by globalization to converge and commingle. In order to reconcile the extremes within, between, and among these great civilizations—Western, Islamic, Indian, and East Asian—we must decode their "cultural DNA" and find their common ground. Chapter 2 introduces Aristotle's golden mean, a system of virtue ethics rooted in Euclidean geometry, which helps us discover individual excellence en route to personal fulfillment. Chapter 3 introduces Buddha's Middle Way, a most powerful and nonviolent way to unite and align the best interests of individuals and communities alike. Chapter 4 introduces Confucius's Balanced Order, a system of virtue ethics rooted in yin-yang metaphysics, which helps us achieve and maintain harmony in our relationships. Chapter 5 explores the sacred geometry of the ABCs, showing how their symbols reflect their respective philosophies of morality, society, and politics. The chapter also reveals and illustrates surprising geometric links that suggest the ABCs are related by cosmic laws.

Part II looks at some notorious extremes, and explains how the ABCs can help reconcile them, via The Middle Way. Every one of us veers toward some extreme or other at times, and so you may encounter yourself somewhere in this book, indulging in an extreme you possibly mistook for a norm. The Middle Way is for you too, not just for the extremists who live next door, or in the nearby town, or in the neighboring country. Chapter 6 assesses political polarization, particularly in the United States, highlighting the absence of a common good in the bitter cultural struggles between left-wing and right-wing extremists. Can the USA achieve civil and racial harmony? Chapter 7 examines sacred and profane extremes that emerge from religious fanaticism on the one hand, and postmodern anarchy on the other. Can religious fanatics and moral anarchists find common ground? Chapter 8 looks at the paradox of tribal extremes. Natural selection favored demographic dispersion and tribal hostilities for dozens of millennia, whereas globalization now favors and forces the homogenization and commingling of tribes. Chapter 9 opens a Pandora's box of extremes: the politics of human sex difference, and their associated gender wars. Can The Middle Way reconcile perennial conflicts between the sexes? Chapter 10 probes cognitive extremes, examining the roles of four cultural traditions—oral, written, visual, and digital—in both fostering and impairing cognitive development, especially in children. Chapter 11 exposes educational extremes that afflict the illiterate poor in one way and the indoctrinated affluent in another. Chapter 12 examines totemic extremes, from the branding and imposition of toxic McFoods and McDrugs to the banning of demonstrably helpful natural remedies. What does The Middle Way prescribe? Chapter 13 assesses economic extremes, from overabundance to dire dearth of material necessities, and the avarice or desperation they engender. Chapter 14 focuses on the Middle East—a cradle of extremisms, a region where extremism is the norm. One of the great challenges confronting the global village is to find a Middle Way in the Middle East. Chapter 15 looks at terrorism, asking "What is it?" and "What can we do?" and "Where's The Middle Way?"

Part III focuses on what you can do to apply the ABCs to the betterment of your life and the human estate. We are all nodes in a global network, and so each one of us can exert a palpable influence by applying the ABCs to reconcile extremes we encounter on a daily basis, starting on those within ourselves. Chapter 16 suggests ways of applying the ABCs here and now, as soon as you put down this book. Beyond this, a short list of recommended reading is compiled for each chapter. Moreover, since a picture is worth a proverbial thousand words, you may encounter a number of black-and-white illustrations accompanying various chapters. Different editions of this book (in different languages) have reproduced differing numbers of these illustrations. I invite you to view the complete set, in full color, at www.themiddleway.us.

# PART I

## The ABCs

# 1

# GLOBALIZATION AND ITS DISCONTENTS
## Convergence and Conflict of Four Civilizations

*Thus then a single harmony orders the composition of the whole . . .
by the mingling of the most contrary principles.* —Aristotle

*Nothing ever exists entirely alone; everything is in relation
to everything else.* —Buddha

*It is now a very long while since the Way prevailed in the world.*
—Confucius

## More Than Once Upon a Time

ROUGHLY BETWEEN 10,000 and 4,000 B.C.E., four seeds germinated in
the fertile soil of human consciousness. They sprouted into four sapling
civilizations: Hellenic, Abrahamic, Indian, and East Asian. Over
millennia, these saplings rooted and branched, fruited and flowered,
spread and grew into dense civilizational forests. Today, the vast
majority of humanity dwells under their canopies. This book illustrates
how extremisms within and among them have made the world a more
conflicted place than it needs to be, and suggests how The Middle
Way—stemming from the ancient traditions of Aristotle, Buddha, and
Confucius—can be utilized to reconcile these extremes.

If you've been paying attention to the news, any news, even the
distortions and sensationalized half-truths that pass for mainstream

media news, you know that we live in a complex and sometimes seemingly crazy world. Your own life may appear impossibly complicated at times, and you may have witnessed or become embroiled in clashes that seem unresolvable. These struggles and challenges might pertain to your family, your relationships, your career, your creativity, or to fulfilling your aspirations in life. The global village swarms with people buzzing on every conceivable frequency, and we're all being pressured to accomplish more things in less time. On top of this, you're probably aware that some people work incessantly for war, while others strive incessantly for peace. Most of us get caught in cross fires between contending extremisms—Star Wars, Culture Wars, Gender Wars, War on Poverty, War on Drugs, War on Terror—and there are many figurative and literal casualties. Can you resolve your own issues and help reconcile so many extremes? It just so happens that you can accomplish both tasks at once. By following The Middle Way.

Before delving into The Middle Way, I want to set the stage by looking at the "big picture" of the global village. To see this picture, I want you to relax, sit in a comfortable chair, and set aside your own complexities and conflicts for a time. We'll return to them soon enough, I promise. But if you can reduce the buzzing in your mind for just a little while, I'll be able to share with you a spectacular view of Earth from space—not a satellite photograph of planet Earth, but rather a philosophical snapshot of globalization and its discontents. Looking at our terrestrial orb from a satellite's orbit, you can see prominent geographical features: oceans, lakes, rivers, mountains, forests, deserts. Looking at the global village from a philosopher's orbit, you can see prominent civilizational features: politics, religions, cultures, sciences, technologies, arts.

In particular, I draw your attention to four mighty human civilizations, rooted in different geocultural soils, all of which have flourished at different times, in different ways, for different reasons, and with different purposes. The four are Western, Islamic, Indian, and East Asian. They are currently the mightiest civilizations on the planet, and events that unfold within, between, and among them have the greatest impact on the entire global village. Western civilization is based in the European Union (EU), United Kingdom (UK), Scandinavia, and North

America, with outposts in Latin America, Australia, New Zealand, and Israel. Islamic civilization is based in the Middle East, North Africa, Central Asia, Malaysia and Indonesia, with influence in India and the EU and UK. Indian civilization is based in the subcontinent, with offshoots in adjacent nations to the north (e.g., Nepal) and toward Southeast Asia. East Asian civilization is based in China, Korea, and Japan. Each one of these mighty civilizations has more than a billion people living under its vast multicultural canopy. Together, they account for more than 80 percent of the human population.

I have not forgotten sub-Saharan Africa, from which humanity itself may have originated, and from which a fifth great civilization (the United States of Africa? the African Union?) may one day arise. The conspicuous contributions of so many African Americans to Western civilization, especially since their emancipation from the twin yokes of slavery and segregation, speak volumes. In Africa there is extreme affliction of every conceivable kind, yet there is also abundant hope for the success of cooperative initiatives among indigenous peoples and developmental experts, a success that will require The Middle Way. African-American philosopher Kwame Anthony Appiah has called Africa "the greatest challenge" facing globalization.[1] That challenge is a topic for another book entirely.

I haven't forgotten other large nations, such as Turkey, Russia, and Brazil, that play influential roles in the global village as well. Turkey is a pivotal and unique state astride the cusp of the West and the Middle East. Viewed one way, it is Western; another way, non-Western. Russia is a vast nation that touches on and influences all four civilizations, and whose contributions will be vital to the full functionality of the global village. Western Russia shares a common heritage with Europe, while eastern Russia is much more conspicuously Asian. Brazil is the largest and most populous nation in Latin America. Its most affluent echelons are unmistakably influenced by Western culture, yet in many salient respects Brazil remains part of the developing world. Nor have I forgotten many other, smaller nations and peoples. But in this book I will focus on dynamics that drive the four biggest civilizations: Western, Islamic, Indian, and East Asian.

Over centuries, these four mighty civilizations have remained distinct in some ways, and have merged in others. Each has powerfully forged its own version of human identity, yet each one's version has also fallen prey to extremisms of various kinds. These civilizations continually clash within and between their extremes, but they can be united by subscribing to The Middle Way. While 9/11 and its aftermath were the products of one such protracted conflict—1,500 years of intermittent warfare between Western and Islamic civilizations—each of the four great civilizations has the capacity for cooperation, both within itself and with all the others. Part of this book's purpose is to illuminate how.

Before we begin our closer look at each of these civilizations, it's important that I clarify one thing: Every person, and every nation, can be both great and terrible in its own way. My purpose is not to praise, condemn, or judge. Rather, it is to characterize, to articulate the foundational principles that inform their "operating systems," to understand how these principles converge and conflict within and between the civilizations themselves, and to apply The Middle Way to reconciling some of the extremes that lead to the most destructive conflicts.

Let's begin by contemplating a simplified but representative picture of the defining ideas behind each civilization—its "cultural DNA." I call this picture an "ideograph," because it represents core ideas, and some of their interconnections, in graphic form. You can see the entire ideograph in fig. 1.1.

## Western Civilization

We'll start with the West. Its cluster of nations form the "neighborhood" of the global village in which I have spent the most time, and with which I am most familiar. No matter what language you are reading these words in now, know that I am writing them in my native tongue, English, a leading tongue of Western civilization and globalization alike. Yet English is an Indo-European language rooted in Sanskrit, stemming from Indian civilization. The Indo-European family of languages reflects an ancient interconnectedness among peoples, who became geographically, culturally, and politically dispersed over many millennia, but who are now being reconnected, at many levels, as a result of globalization.

Western civilization itself is characterized by a cultural "double helix." One strand is Hellenic philosophy; the other, Judeo-Christian religion. The entwinement of these strands is unique to the West. The Roman, Spanish, French, Dutch, Portuguese, Austro-Hungarian, and British and American empires, whose actions and reactions still resound through global history and current events alike, have been among the chief torchbearers of Western civilization—and every one of them has also borne the cultural double helix: Hellenic philosophy and Judeo-Christian religion.

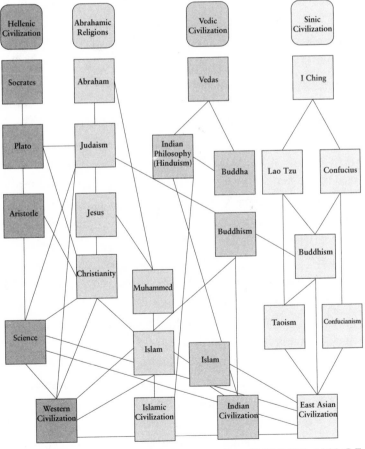

Figure 1.1 Ideograph of Four Civilizations, circa 5000 B.C.E.-1900 C.E.

The Hellenic strand contains the definitive lineage of Western philosophy through Socrates, Plato, and Aristotle. Athens was the prototypical western city-state: democratic, progressive, divisive, capitalistic, corruptible, eccentric, and susceptible to erratic political vacillations. It put Socrates to death, yet allowed his devoted student, Plato, to found the Academy, the model for the world's universities. Plato's best student was Aristotle, who developed logic, science, rhetoric, poetics, ethics, and politics, and who became known in the West—until challenged by the seventeenth-century Early Moderns—as "The Philosopher." To put Aristotle's relevance in perspective, how long can anyone or anything remain "number one"? One immortal 1960s hit—Procol Harum's "A Whiter Shade of Pale"—was number one in France for about two years. (Maybe they were trying to figure out the lyrics.) Pete Sampras, one of the greatest tennis players of all time, was ranked number one for six years, a remarkable accomplishment in men's professional tennis. In chess, Garry Kasparov led the world for about fifteen years, an outstanding feat. How long can any top political leader remain in office? Eight years in the United States, by lawful limit. Longer in some other democracies, and longer still in dictatorships. But only for a few decades, at most. So imagine the towering influence of Aristotle, who has been revered in the West as "The Philosopher" for two thousand years. That's because of his genius and influence in this Hellenic strand, and also because of the amplifying and stimulating interplay between the Hellenic and Judeo-Christian strands themselves.

The Judeo-Christian strand embodies the definitive religion of the West, namely Christianity, the first organized religion to win converts worldwide by intending to "complete" Judaism. Jews still await the Messiah; Christianity began as a radical sect of Jews who accepted Jesus as such. Christians believe that they are "saved" now and forever, by Jesus; and so they want to "save" everybody else too. Jews believe that they will be redeemed eventually, but meanwhile they still are waiting, and trying to preserve themselves in the process. There are more than one billion Roman Catholics, and more than half a billion members of Eastern Orthodox, Protestant, and other denominations: about 1.5 billion Christians, most of them in the West. There are about twelve million

Jews: half in Israel, half still scattered throughout the Roman diaspora that took place around 70 C.E. So there are more than one hundred Christians for every Jew. Judeo-Christianity is hyphenated because of a shared Godhead and scripture, including a shared creation myth in Genesis. The Torah of the Jews consists of the five books of Moses, which became the Pentateuch and—with the books of the Prophets of Israel thrown in—the Old Testament shared by contemporary Jews and Christians.

Thomas Aquinas of the Roman Catholic Church helped enshrine Aristotle, along with Saint Augustine, in his *Summa Theologica.* In this sense Aristotle owes Christianity a great debt for recognizing his genius and preserving his philosophy, even if religious scholars occasionally mistook some of his scientific errors for dogma. But if we expand the context to include Aristotle's teacher, Plato, we find a deeper debt, this time Judeo-Christianity's debt to Hellenism. When Hellenic philosophy first appeared in ancient Israel, it provoked a schism between the Sadducees (who embraced it) and the Pharisees (who rejected it). Meanwhile Plato's trio of eternal forms, their essences, and copies embodying their essences, laid the metaphysical foundation in pagan Western civilization upon which the Trinity of Christianity—The Father, the Son, and the Holy Spirit—fit like a proverbial glove.[2]

This ongoing mutual reinforcement and renewal of the Western double helix, Hellenic philosophy and Judeo-Christian religion, gave rise to unprecedented bursts of creative cultural development, from neo-Platonist revivals to the Italian Renaissance, from the Reformation to the Enlightenment, from the Industrial Revolution to the Cybernetic Age. In their most divine recombinations, J. S. Bach played upon these strands when he composed his music, a reflection of Hellenic geometry, Cabalistic numerology, and Christian liturgy. The pulsating double helix of Western civilization with its interplay of powerfully creative patriarchal lineages—the philosophies of Socrates, Plato, and Aristotle remixed with the legacies of Abraham, Isaac, and Jacob—provided canvasses upon which a pantheon of Western creative geniuses could paint. Above all, the double helix of Western civilization has encouraged and celebrated individual achievement, from the Olympic Games to the

Nobel Prize, which reward excellences of the human body and mind alike, and from Speaker's Corner in London's Hyde Park to the First Amendment of the American Constitution, which enshrine, encourage, and (on a good day) protect freedom of individual expression.

Such love of liberty has translated into a comparatively good life for the average person in the West. Western life is characterized by the highest material standards of living in the world, for the greatest number of citizens, and for the longest duration. And precisely because the average citizen in the West has been so well off—in material affluence, in protection of law, in civil liberty—compared with the average person in the other three civilizations, the average Westerner has been willing to defend his or her hard-won liberties with unprecedented creativity and vigor, supported by the leading edges of science and technology that free-thinking peoples have continuously evolved.

If you consider the amazing inventions that revolutionized and are still transforming the global village, it is not a coincidence that so many of them originated in the West. The partial list includes the printing press, the telescope, microscope, sextant, cotton gin, steam engine, electric battery, lightbulb, internal-combustion engine, automobile, airplane, telephone, telegraph, radio, television, X-ray machine, vaccine, jet engine, rocket engine, transistor, personal computer, Internet, and World Wide Web. These are all products of the fruitful interplay between Aristotelian science and Judeo-Christian religion—with an emphasis on individualism—that characterize Western civilization.

Thanks to the West's unprecedented innovation and sense of individuality, among other reasons, Western armies have also historically tended to defeat non-Western ones in wars, even when vastly outnumbered. From the Greek and Macedonian phalanxes to the Roman legions, from the Norman knights to the Spanish conquistadors, from the British redcoats to the American marines, the West repeatedly repulsed non-Western invaders, subdued non-Western aggressors, aggressively conquered new territories itself, and colonized much of the rest of world. The influence of Rome continues to this day, as her material empire metamorphosed into a spiritual one. Spanish speakers are still the third-largest language group in the world, a legacy of

Spanish conquests in the Americas and the Caribbean. Well into the twentieth century, Britons could claim that the sun never set on their empire. After World War II, America's power dwarfed them all; but like the others, it too will decline in its time.

The history of humanity to date is also, sadly, a history of bloodletting on extravagant scales. From Chinese civilization springs the idea of Tao, and complementarity. Taoists would say that the unrivaled creative power of the West implies an equal and opposite potential for destructiveness. They are correct.

This is most evident if we consider the horrific wars of Western nations against one another. The battlefield carnage of the Napoleonic Wars, the American Civil War, World War I, and World War II are unprecedented, even in the copious annals of human conflict. The most destructive weapons in the world were also invented by the West.

Many societies have experienced the meltdown of their cultures in the face of Western civilization. Native and aboriginal peoples, as well as enslaved Africans and colonized peoples, have experienced the West as a disruptor or destroyer of their more bucolic existences. Yet the world is never simply black-and-white. The truth is that innumerable peoples also made alliances with Western invaders, often because they saw these "white devils" as less oppressive than their indigenous masters. So the Spanish found willing local allies against the Aztecs; the French and Americans found them against the Iroquois and Lakota; and the British found Arabian allies against the Ottoman Turks. The West has also attracted millions of enslaved peoples seeking liberty: political asylum, socioeconomic mobility, and religious tolerance, as well as freedom to practice intolerance in a safe place. Every civilization embodies contradictions and paradoxes. To mention one more: The West is now self-destructing, via the unremitting abuse of its own liberties, a subject we will return to later.

The highly evolved freedoms of the West allow for individual liberty to be guided by any God, any book, or any prophet of one's choosing, or by different ones every day of the week, or by none at all. The West publishes far more books annually than other civilizations, and overall bans far fewer.[3] So the postmodern, post-Christian formula "Any God, any book, any prophet" has become a Western norm. This in turn becomes a source of conflict—both internal and external—with other civilizational formulas, especially the unitary Abrahamic ones.

## Islamic Civilization

The Middle East is a special place in its own right, not least because it gave rise to the third religion in the Abrahamic lineage, namely Islam. Founded by the charismatic Arabian prophet Mohammed in the seventh century C.E., Islam rapidly spread through the Middle East and well beyond, becoming a powerful enough force to unite the fierce, proud, and quarrelsome tribes that have populated the region since the dawn of humanity. The tribal lore from which Arabian Muslims claim direct descent, by both nativity and faith, is identical to that of Jews and Christians. It is the lore of the Patriarchs: Abraham, Isaac, Jacob. The name *Ibrahim*, Arabic for Abraham, is prevalent throughout Islamic cultures. Whenever I greet a friend named Ibrahim (and I know several), I recall that my father's middle name was Abraham, and so I understand that I am greeting a brother, or an uncle, or a cousin. The Jews and the Arabs have a history as old as their Patriarchs, but Islam itself is the youngest of this family of Abrahamic faiths.

I first heard the phrase *Abrahamic faith* as a facilitator of dialogue among prominent religious leaders and spokesmen from each faith. The first purpose of such dialogue was—and is—to search for common values among spiritual leaders. The second purpose is to build on that foundation of common values. But build what? An understanding of some of the misunderstandings that have contributed to the recent spate of clashes between Western and Islamic civilizations. Since these clashes are inflamed by religious as well as political and economic motives, it is essential for peace that the global leadership of the Abrahamic faiths—Judaism, Christianity, Islam—cultivate deeper mutual understanding and a shared version of their history. The third purpose follows from this. If spiritual leaders manage to spread their deeper mutual understanding to their respective flocks, it would exert a dampening force on extremism of every kind, and would conduce to world peace. That's the theory.

But to begin the practice, one has to find a First Common Value—Aristotle's "Prime Mover"—to gather the spiritual leaders all together, to commence the search for more. "One Ring to bind them," as Tolkien would say. They all belong to Abrahamic faiths, so the first Patriarch binds them. So far, so good. But after that, as everyone knows, things get more complicated.

Islam has followed a proselytizing pattern similar to its elder sibling, Christianity. The youngest of the Abrahamic faiths, celebrating its fourteen-hundredth birthday in the twenty-first century, Islam has already amassed a following of 1.5 billion people worldwide and is growing. During its rapid rise from desert tribal origins to a great world religion, Islam encountered, and is still encountering, trials and tribulations similar to those of Christianity, born six hundred years earlier. Like Christianity, Islam has won converts by political coercion, military conquest, and adopted faith. Like Christianity, Islam has seen periods of schism and civil war, expansion and contraction, renaissance and repression, tolerance and intolerance.

The British essayist and mordant wit Thomas Carlyle was an agnostic product of the Enlightenment. Impressed by the advances of Western science, he opined that "the soul is a gas, and the next world, a coffin." Carlyle was a proponent of the "Great Man" theory of history, which holds that momentous historical events are the products of the inspiration and effort of individuals, and of their influence on the masses. Carlyle wrote that "No false man can found a religion." By this he did not mean that he believed any or all religions to be true; instead, he believed the founders of religions to be clear in their own minds, and sincere in their own hearts. They live and die true to themselves, and so others readily follow them, because many people live and die falsely to themselves, and so need the support of truth-livers. Founders of religions inhabit a place that Lao Tzu (who we will meet later in this chapter) called "beyond the region of life and death." Where do they abide? They abide in clarity of mind and authenticity of deed. This was certainly the case with Abraham, Moses, Jesus, and Mohammed. To Carlyle, it accounted for the persistence of the Abrahamic faiths over time.

The Enlightenment taught Carlyle that false ideas cannot indefinitely withstand the tests of human ingenuity, and that truths will prevail. All religions share this sense of prevalent truth, which is more important than the details of their scripture. It is for the anointed ones, and the learned scholars, to dispute interpretations of text. What most religious adherents seek is to bathe regularly in the light of truth, which cleanses and purifies the soul.

One can appreciate the strategic thinking of Mohammed and his successors in the seventh century c.e. They had observed the improbable persistence of Judaism over millennia already, and knew of the successes of Christianity. They must have been struck by the common denominators. The Jews were the inventors of monotheistic religion, the original People of the Book. "One God, one prophet, one book" is a compelling triumvirate—though not as minimal as "No god, no prophet, no book," which we will encounter in East Asia. The Christians had a Trinity too: One Father, one Son, one Holy Spirit. The Arabs understood Christianity as an extension or possible completion of Judaism, but they did not on the whole identify with it, even though there are numerous sects of Christian Arabs (e.g., Maronites), Christian Persians (e.g., Nestorians), and Christian Egyptians (e.g., Copts). But the seventh-century Arabs were impressed by the compelling Hebraic minimalism of "Yahweh, Moses, Torah." So "Allah, Mohammed, Koran" immediately struck a deep chord in Arabia and soon far beyond, as the Islamic rendition of "One God, one prophet, one book."

Like my father and forefathers before him, I have trekked the scalding sands of the Middle East and North Africa, where little enough grows. Even less grew there in the seventh century c.e., when Islam swept across those deserts like a wildfire, fed by exotic spiritual fuel. After absorbing the Berbers and the Moors into its *ummah*, Islam marshaled an army ten thousand strong across the Strait of Gibraltar and onto the Rock itself. In 711 c.e., Islamic conquerors quickly subdued an Iberia grown degenerate under the declining Visigoths, descended from Alaric's barbarians who had sacked Rome three centuries earlier. The Islamic invaders crossed the Pyrenees and pillaged their way toward Paris, desecrating and looting Christian holy places en route. They were checked and reversed by Charles Martel's knights at the battle of Poitiers, in 732 C.E. They retreated to Iberia, where Islamic caliphs and their successors held sway for a good three hundred years before gradually relinquishing all their Iberian gains, city by city, century by century, until the last Moorish stronghold, Granada, fell to Catholic monarchs Ferdinand and Isabella in 1492. In that fateful year, Arabs and Jews alike shared a bitter exodus from Iberia.

But during the Moorish occupation of Spain, and thanks to Moorish influence across North Africa, a golden age had unfolded under Islamic rule. The conquerors were curious about Hellenic and Roman cultures, and so they translated the canon from Greek and Latin into Arabic. Moreover, eager to engage in dialogue with the intellectual successors of Western civilization, who had become an endangered species in Europe as the Western Roman empire crumbled into the Dark Ages, the caliphs sheltered and succored Jewish and Christian scholars and philosophers, and encouraged intellectual ferment in Islamic communities. This kind of tolerance always engenders cross-pollination of ideas, and so there emerged a vast constellation of Islamic philosophers, poets, lawmakers, theologians, scientists, mathematicians, and physicians, alongside non-Islamic intellectuals.

Luminaries of Islam's Golden Age include Mohammed ibn Musa al-Khwarizmi (circa 780–840), whose works form a cornerstone of modern mathematics and from whose books we derive the English words "algebra" and "algorithm"; Avicenna (980–1037), the celebrated physician and philosopher whose works influenced Thomas Aquinas among other seminal Christian theologians; Abu Hamid al-Ghazali (1058–1111), one of the preeminent scholars and mystics of Islam, whose works helped forge its civilizational identity; Moses Maimonides (1135–1204), who fled Cordoba and found refuge in Cairo, where he became court physician to Sultan Saladin, a leading light of the Egyptian Jewish community, and a rabbinical influence on Judaism worldwide; and Leonardo Fibonacci, born in Pisa but educated in North Africa, who discovered a priceless geometric treasure that we will unearth in chapters 2 and 5. Islam was both open and tolerant during its Golden Age, when it became a custodian of and contributor to Western civilization, which in turn helped spur its own development.

Islam swept north and east from Arabia. To the north, it flourished in Constantinople, the capital of Byzantium, and throughout Turkey. The Seljuk period gave rise to one of the greatest Islamic mystics and poets of all time, Jelaluddin Rumi (1207–1273). To the east, Islamic warriors established a base in India in 711 C.E., which inaugurated a centuries-long series of incursion and conquest, plunder and commerce. In other words, they engaged in empire building of the same kind as Western civilization. Large parts of central Asia fell under Muslim sway—Iran, Afghanistan, northern India and, for a time, southern India too. Just as later happened with Christian conquerors in far-off lands, the political dominance of the Islamic invaders eventually waned, but the religious influence of Islam took root and flowered. Islam powerfully pervaded art and architecture, influencing monuments like the Taj Mahal, a wonder of the world, built by seventeenth-century emperor Sha Jehan for his beloved deceased princess. Islam offered a compelling and succoring way of life to indigenous peoples of India, many of whom were condemned by their own caste system or oppressed by despotic princes and corrupt Brahmins.

Islamic traders established outposts along the Silk Road and other East Asian trade routes, and so Islam became rooted in Malaysia and Indonesia, two populous Islamic nations. Lush equatorial rainforests and idyllic Pacific atolls are a far cry from the desolate sands of Arabia, but Islam is there to stay. Again, Islam's unified "way of life" appealed strongly to indigenous Malaysian and Indonesian peoples, who were later colonized by waxing yet still powerful Western nations, oppressed by local satraps and sycophants of empire, and who did not identify with the imperious and commercial versions of Christianity imported by their European overlords. So Islam's many and varied geopolitical constituents—African, Arabian, Turkish, Central Asian, West Asian, Southeast Asian—share a unitary conception of Islamic civilization, with its glorious history, compelling presence, and hopeful future. This premodern Islamic fundamentalist unity (notwithstanding vicious interdenominational hostilities) contrasts strongly with postmodern Judeo-Christian fragmentation of worldviews.

But, like Western societies, Islamic civilization is riven by complex internal religious and tribal factions: Wahabists versus Sunnis versus Shi'ites, just to scratch the surface. In his book *From Beirut to Jerusalem*, Thomas L. Friedman describes how no fewer than fourteen warring factions dismantled Lebanon during the 1980s. And exactly like Christianity, which passed through a Dark Age, oppressing the human spirit with theocracies, Inquisitions, censorship of books, burning alive of "witches" and "heretics" and "infidels," so too do some Islamic peoples and nations traverse a similar stage in their own development. So-called "unbelievers" were burned alive on 9/11 too, by suicidal Saudi Arabian Islamists inflamed with age-old religious hatreds, not dissimilar to those that had fueled the pyres of the Spanish Inquisition and the New England Puritan witch hunts in their time. "When will they ever learn?" sang Pete Seeger in the 1960s. This question still burns.

Conflict between Arabian Islamic sects, and between Islam and the West, are also fueled by oil. Petroleum is still the world's largest industry, and Islamic civilization has been both blessed and cursed by housing the world's largest and most accessible oil fields—notably those in and around the Persian Gulf. The business and politics of oil made both commerce and conflict inevitable between Western and Islamic civilizations. Only when petroleum-based technologies are finally superseded will some aspects of this conflict subside.

The six-hundred-year gap between Christianity and Islam is also a source of much global tension. Just like unreformed Christianity of yore, unreformed Islam is a fundamentalist religion, reluctant to evolve and resistant to change. Yet globalization forces change upon all, and so most Islamic leaders realize that they too must adapt. Many have the will to do so, but their challenge is monumental: They must bridge a centuries-wide chasm in political, philosophical, scientific, and technological development—and make conspicuous progress in mere decades. India and China are doing this now, as we shall next see. But India and China are not governed by the Abrahamic faiths, whose adherents are renowned for being proud and stiff-necked, vengeful and unforgiving. Those qualities may have served a worthwhile purpose during the infancy of human history, but they too must be outgrown for humanity's maturity to unfold.

Let none forget how Western cultural evolution itself has been plagued by both reactionary theocratic suppression and retrograde political intolerance of reliable scientific knowledge and method. Among many examples, one can cite the Roman Church's prohibition of Galilean astronomy, the Anglican and Roman censorship of Hobbesian political theory, the creationist denial of Darwinian evolutionism, the Nazi proscription of "Jewish physics," the Soviet endorsement of Lamarckian agronomy, the allied American antirealist repudiation of science itself.[4] (In Part II, we will expand upon each of these examples.) Yet Western science and technology have proved unstoppable, in spite of—and maybe even because of—repeated suppressions of objective fact by dogmatic faith.

The twin lamps of spiritual truth and religious awe are not extinguished by scientific progress and technological innovation. On the contrary, we illuminate human lives more brightly by acknowledging man's discovery of lawful processes in nature, and by implementing technologies that further spiritual practice and sustain religious community. Science and religion are not incompatible. Western civilization became preeminent by furthering their coexistence through its double helix. Islamic civilization can do the same. If it does, it will become that much greater, and will add future chapters to human history that will rival and eclipse its past glories. But meanwhile, Islamic civilization has fallen far behind the West and East Asia, in terms of modernization and economic productivity. This is both a cause and an effect of religious extremism becoming a way of life.

True to the heritage of the Abrahamic faiths, the Middle East is the birthplace of Islam, and Saudi Arabia remains its spiritual home. Mecca, Saudi Arabia, is Islam's holiest site, and the hajj (pilgrimage to Mecca) is a spiritual duty of all Muslims. If Saudi Arabia reforms, perhaps all Islam will reform. The British gave the Arabs Lawrence of Arabia, who fomented Arab nationalism. While this political tactic helped the British defeat the Ottoman Turks during World War I, it also made them exacerbate and inherit the impossible politics of the Middle East (which we will revisit in chapters 14 and 15). Meanwhile, Western and Middle Eastern nations are both cooperating yet still clashing, and into this centuries-old fray is drawn the whole of Islamic and Western civilizations.

The Jews may have a unique role to play, as commentators on—if not arbiters of—this global dispute. The Jews are the first nation of the Abrahamic lineage and have obeyed God's injunction to "be fruitful and multiply," though in surprising and unpredictable ways. The Abrahamic "descendents" of that command amount to some three billion Christians and Muslims. Jews can appreciate both Christians and Muslims, in some ways better than Christians and Muslims appreciate themselves, and certainly better than they understand each other. Over many centuries, Jews have alternately enjoyed prosperity, and endured persecution, under both Christian and Muslim rule. Now perhaps Jews can contribute to the reconciliation of this Christian-Muslim "sibling rivalry," which implicates two mighty civilizations in lethal global conflicts.

Let me suggest to you what I suggested to leaders of the Abrahamic faiths, to abet their noble and courageous search for common values. I paraphrased Leon Trotsky for them. (To the FBI: I am not now, and have never been, a member of the Communist Party.) Trotsky was a Russian Jew, Bolshevik leader, and founder of the Red Army. He was later murdered in Mexico City by the long psychopathic arm of Joseph Stalin. Trotsky had once quipped, "You may not be interested in the dialectic, but the dialectic is interested in you." And the same is true of globalization: You may not be interested in globalization, but globalization is interested in you. This rang true for Jewish, Christian, and Muslim religious leaders, because each of them is keenly aware of large-scale forces exerted by globalization on the lives of their adherents, for good and ill. They all have well-founded concerns about deleterious effects of globalization—a revolution in cybernetics, commercialism, and consciousness—upon the spiritual estate of their flocks. Thus they can unite in their common interest of globalization's interest in them.

Islamist terrorists neither speak nor act for the majority of Muslims. As we will see later, the intelligentsia of Islamic civilization is denouncing terrorism ever more vociferously. Leaders and scholars are carefully reexamining Islam's roots and branches, to see how modernity can best be grafted onto them. Since Judaism and modernity can be compatible, and since Christianity and modernity can be compatible, then Islam and modernity can be compatible too. This is the great challenge facing Islamic civilization: to modernize without losing its identity.

## Indian Civilization

To me as to many others, the captivating Indian subcontinent is the most spiritually affluent place on earth. It needs to be, to counter its crushing material poverty. In Indian philosophy, the telling dualism is not mind and body (as it was for Rene Descartes among so many in the West) but matter and spirit. Matter is regarded as unimportant and transitory, spirit as all-important and enduring. Yet if Western civilization errs on the side of too much materialism, then Indian civilization errs on the side of too much spiritualism. (This too is shifting, as India's middle class grows.) Western intellectuals and authors who visit India, from the insightfully brazen psychiatrist Erik Erickson[5] (Gandhi's posthumous psychoanalyst) to Nobel laureate Elie Wiesel[6] (a witness to and survivor of Nazi horror), record how they are simultaneously awed by India's pervasive spiritual wealth, yet demoralized by her crushing material poverty.

India weaves together an eclectic and almost psychedelic tapestry of religions, cultures, ethnicities, and spiritual practices. Her main ethnoreligious groups are Hindu, Muslim, and Sikh, but Buddhists, Jains, Jews, Christians, and adherents of every belief system under the sun—including Chinese Confucians—can be found there. The dominant ethnoreligious name, Hindu, is a British misnomer that has become so universal that even Indians themselves now utilize it. Alexander the Great applied the name "India" when he arrived there in 325 B.C.E. Subsequent invaders, from Muslim to British, pronounced the name of the Sindhu River valley as "Indus," which mutated to "Hindu."

However you name it, a great civilization took root there perhaps ten thousand years ago, during the late Neolithic revolution. It was composed of the original "Aryans," a name later hijacked by the Nazis for their own diabolical purposes. The civilization of the Indus valley bequeathed humanity an incomparably rich mythology and advanced philosophy, embodied in the voluminous Vedas. Strictly speaking, there is no such thing as "Hinduism." The indigenous Indian religions are social manifestations of schools of Indian philosophy emanating from Vedic lore. Orally transmitted as early as 4,000 B.C.E., then gradually recorded in Sanskrit, the Vedas consist of four sets of writings—Rg, Yajur, Sama, Atharva—about twenty thousand verses in all. Each Veda passed through four different stages of deepening and development: Samhita, Brahmana, Aranyaka, and Upanishad. There are 108 Upanishads, which represent the culmination of Vedic thought and practice, and are collectively known as "Vedanta." "Veda" means knowledge; "Vedanta" the end (as in summit) of knowledge. The earliest Upanishads date from 1,000 to 400 B.C.E., and so were in existence during Buddha's time as well.

In contrast to the Abrahamic faiths, which are paradigms of monotheism (one God, one prophet, one book), the polytheism and pluralism of indigenous Indian philosophies is mind-boggling. "Hinduism" refers to a multitude of schools, sects, and denominations that defy rigid classification, but which share the idea that philosophy and religion are inseparable. Ordinarily there are around nine recognized "traditions" or "schools" in Indian philosophy, six orthodox and three heterodox. The orthodox schools that accept the authority of the Vedas are Nyaya, Vaisesika, Samkhya, Yoga, Mimamsa, and Vedanta. These schools are all interrelated, and enormously complex.[7] Yet their common spirit is shaped and pervaded by a trio of immortal works—the Bhagavad Gita, the Upanishads, and the Yoga Sutras of Patanjali—beacons of spiritual light to all humanity. The heterodox schools, which reject Vedic authority, are Carvaka, Jainism, and Buddhism. Carvaka is a form of materialism, which even Buddha lambasted for its immorality. Jains are renowned for their practice of ahimsa, nonharm to all sentient beings, a practice which many Buddhists also share.

It is fascinating that the orthodox Indian schools regard the so-called "heterodox" schools that reject Vedic authority as part of Vedic tradition nonetheless. Indeed, Vedic scholars can show how the very seeds of heterodoxy are sown in the orthodoxies themselves. If the Vedanta is truly the "end of knowledge"—that is, of knowledge conducive to spiritual progress and reunion with the Godhead—then everything after the Vedas must be contained or presaged in the Vedas. This is why so many Indian faiths, especially in contrast to the Abrahamic ones, are seemingly open to everything. Not confined to "one God, one prophet, one book," they blissfully absorb "all Gods, all prophets, all books."

Only in India can someone who rejects the Vedas still be considered an adherent of the Vedas. This ancient and enchanting openness is reflected in the Bhagavad Gita, when Krishna declares to Arjuna, "By whatever path they follow, they come to me at last." Contrast this open-minded position with the inflexibility of some adherents to other faiths, who insist dogmatically that their particular path is the only way to salvation. Yet only The Middle Way, derived as it is from Indian philosophy, can mediate among all ways, any way, one way, and no way.

Orthodox Indian schools recognize three main gods, the Trimurti: Brahma, Vishnu, and Shiva. They represent the cyclical creation, preservation, and annihilation of all phenomenas, including the cosmos itself. Each deity has many incarnations. Krishna, for example, is the eighth avatar of Vishnu. What happened to the other seven? That's a long story. It takes many lifetimes to learn it, and even more incarnations to relate it. There is no hurry in India, where souls have not only all the time in the world, but also all the time in the universe.

Indian cosmic mythology is a long story too, and is also the one with whose numbers the modern science of cosmology agrees most closely. The *kalpa*, or age of the universe, is of closer order of magnitude to current scientific estimates than any other ancient cosmology. In addition, Indians believe that the universe passes through vast cycles of development, decay, destruction, and rebirth. This is also congruent with much current Western scientific cosmology. Indian insight into the nature of the phenomenal world, the orders of beings it contains, and the laws governing not only their physical but also their soulful interactions, is truly profound. From this cosmology springs a complex theology and nuanced philosophy, possibly the oldest philosophy known to man.

The ancient Indian philosophical system is both highly sophisticated in its grasp of cosmic laws, and yet has proven sustainable over millennia by the masses, even though their lives are largely predetermined by birth and caste. India is awash in paradoxes. Here's another one: The harsh rigidity of the caste system, which has maintained hundreds of millions of people at or below subsistence poverty over centuries, and has made socioeconomic mobility impossible, is counterbalanced by a warm open-mindedness that is optimistic and gymnastic. So Westerners visiting India encounter worn-out beggars dying like dogs in the street, and are appalled; then they encounter beaming, joyful children, and are enchanted. Indeed, I know of no place more enchanting and appalling at the same time, than India. But to digest and experience the Bhagavad Gita (among many great Indian books) as a work of practical wisdom for one's life is also to fall in love with Indian philosophy for life.

Alexander the Great reached and occupied part of India, but left little trace of his teacher's—Aristotle's—philosophical tradition. The Macedonian conqueror came east not to build lyceums, but to destroy the Persian Seleucid dynasty that had almost toppled Athens and the West. But the later Muslim invasion of India met with far greater receptivity, and Islam established a palpable presence in India, some contemporary consequences of which we will revisit later on. Like Hinduism, Islam offered a comprehensive way of life; but unlike Hinduism's caste system, Islam's social fabric was not stratified by unbridgeable classes. This must have tempted many from the lower castes to convert. While they did not escape poverty by their conversion to Islam, they did gain dignity.

When India was finally ready to absorb Aristotle, he appeared in the form of the British Empire. Britain's dominance of global sea lanes, and the docility of millions of Indians in allowing a few white men to rule their subcontinent (for a short while) allowed the British East India

Company to monopolize India's cotton and salt markets, and more notoriously to create a minination of opium addicts in China, coercing Indian farmers to grow the opium poppy. Yet India absorbed the English language, which helped unify its five hundred tongues and innumerable dialects, absorbed the British Civil Service and its Mandarin model of government, and began to absorb Western science, technology, commerce, and education. And India absorbed Jews and Christians in the process. India had long since reabsorbed Buddhism, which had intended to reform Indian philosophy but which instead became an unorthodox school of Indian philosophy itself.

India's capacity to absorb philosophies and religions appears boundless. The all-embracing and nonproselytizing worldview of the Vedas seems effortlessly receptive to "all Gods, all prophets, all books," and remains tolerant of all interpretations of everything, including itself. The nubile Indian mind can thus accept if not reconcile contradictions at the outset, and moreover (like the Chinese but unlike the Western mind) is not obsessed with paradox, an authentic Hellenic heirloom. Indian philosophy views the cosmos as a theatric spectacle, where illusory matter meets playful spirit and where material bodies are but castaway garbs for souls, which skip on stepping stones of lifetimes to their serendipitous immersion in Brahma's sea of light and love. Ideas are the emanations of divine consciousness, not the tokens of academic dispute. So Indians exposed to Western mathematics and science absorbed them with great facility, and began to make significant contributions themselves in the twentieth century, from Srinivasa Ramanujan's representation of $\pi$ to Subramanyan Chandrasekhar's physics of black holes.

The influence of Indian philosophy is significant in the West, and increasingly pervasive. As Aristotelian science gradually outgrew its parent, Athenian philosophy, it became sufficiently advanced (after two thousand years) to mesh with Indian philosophy. And Buddhist philosophy, the child of that prodigious parent, meshes with simply everything.

An Indian named Mohandas Gandhi, trained in British law and Socratic philosophy, and influenced by New England idealist Henry

David Thoreau's treatise on nonviolent civil disobedience, absorbed all these teachings and blended them with some austere Indian practices, including lengthy periods of abstinence from sex. Over decades, Gandhi cultivated enough spiritual force, and attracted sufficient followers, to convince the British to relinquish India pacifically and graciously. He also tried to loosen up India's rigid caste system, and implement land reform. Gandhi's form of militant but nonviolent resistance to oppression—"Satyagraha," or unflinching adherence to truth—was also adapted in the United States by Martin Luther King Jr., who found it equally effective in catalyzing civil rights for African Americans. Both Gandhi and King were assassinated, but their moral influence on the global village is imperishable.

Scattered drops of Indian culture rained on the nineteenth-century West, preceding the twentieth century's monsoon. Arthur Schopenhauer recognized Indian philosophy as a panacea against suffering, while George Ivanovitch Gurdjieff[8] sought mystic revelation in the East. Canadian physician R. M. Bucke embarked on a lifelong spiritual pilgrimage after a spontaneous kundalini experience opened his crown chakra.[9] But when the Indian yogi Vivekananda settled in New England in the early 1900s, he was probably regarded as a cultural freak. It was during this period that Rudyard Kipling predicted of East and West that "never the twain shall meet." As it turned out, Kipling was a far better poet than prophet.

A mere century later, New England, like America coast to coast, abounds with gurus, ashrams, and yoga camps of every kind. The 1960s was the pivotal decade during which Asian philosophies—Hinduism, Buddhism, Taoism—became known to and absorbed by mainstream Western culture, thanks partly to celebrity musicians, poets, and authors who took them up for the sake of their own spiritual development, popularizing them in the process. These practices paid large dividends for their artistic development too.

In pop music, The Beatles and their involvement with Maharishi Mahesh Yogi imported transcendental meditation wholesale into Western public consciousness. On Chicago's legendary South Side, the Paul Butterfield Blues Band recorded their *East-West* album, whose title track blended Dixieland with raga. Sri Chinmoy became the guru of jazz-rock fusion guitarist John McLaughlin. Jazz immortals Wayne Shorter, Herbie Hancock, and Larry Coryell discovered Nichiren Buddhism—a Japanese tradition based on Buddha's Lotus Sutra— which elevated their energy, clarity, and creativity, and inspired their musical evolution. Thanks to the genius of Ravi Shankar, Indian classical music also became well known in the West, attracting the likes of violinist Yehudi Menuhin, whose recordings with Shankar are celebratory meetings of India's ancient and Europe's relatively recent classical traditions. Al Di Meola and L. (Lakshminarayana) Subramaniam further fused Western and Indian forms. Intellectual Richard Alpert reincarnated himself as Ram Dass. A triumvirate of generation-defining Jewish poets—Allen Ginsberg, Bob Dylan, and Leonard Cohen—all flirted with Buddhism, as Indian philosophy's extended family immigrated to the West.

The industry of Indian gurus burgeoned too. The orange-clad *sunsyasin* of Bhagwan Shree Rajneesh, the blissed-out *premies* of Guru Maraji, the Hare Krishna chanters of Swami Prabhupada, along with eclectic dharma bums and die-hard hippies, all received, absorbed, reflected, and transmitted sat-sang into Western thought.

And because Indian philosophy is so well attuned to the fundamental vibrations that create, sustain, and annihilate the cosmos, Western physics and Indian cosmology also merged in the atomic age. When Robert Oppenheimer, the "father" of the atomic bomb, witnessed the first nuclear detonation at Alamogordo, New Mexico, he was moved to think not of Prometheus stealing fire from the gods, but of Krishna metamorphosing into Kali, the goddess of Destruction, and of her terrible words to an awestruck Arjuna: "Now I am become Death, the destroyer of worlds." The next generation of this lineage is more pacific. David Bohm, a student of Oppenheimer's, who subsequently revealed the implicate order and discovered the quantum potential, also teamed up with Indian guru Jiddu Krishnamurti to develop dialogues on education and betterment for a global humanity.

Although Western and Islamic civilizations occupied India, they were both absorbed by her, too. Now India is beginning to stir in response to globalization, to regard her population of more than one billion as a significant cultural voice and huge economic asset in the global village. India is the world's largest democracy, as well as its most traditional and yet anarchic civilization. India is mostly nonaligned in Western conflicts, but has her own conflicts with Islamic states. India and Pakistan possess nuclear weapons and are fighting a cold war—as well as a hot war over Kashmir. Economically, India identifies with burgeoning China, whose economy may soon enough eclipse that of the United States. Indian business leaders would like to emulate Chinese growth rates, and Indians are becoming increasingly competitive in high-tech sectors. India has formed an axis with China, Brazil, and Russia—three populous developing nations, each of which exerts decisive economic influence over its respective geopolitical region. But India and China have also clashed militarily, mostly in the form of border skirmishes. As they continue to flex their growing economic muscles, future conflicts between these two Asian juggernauts are foreseeable, yet hopefully not inevitable.

Indian civilization will make its presence increasingly felt in the global village. But India's greatest export of all may turn out to be its most ancient: Buddhism, to which we will return in chapter 3, and which remains a central theme of this book.

## East Asian Civilization

China is the massive sun of East Asian civilization, in terms of its history, geography, population, economic growth, and waxing influence on the global village. China has many important "planets" in its civilizational orbit, notably Japan, which considers China its parent culture, and whose economic successes China seeks to emulate. China is also mindful of the "Four Tigers"—Singapore, Hong Kong, Taiwan, and South Korea—each of which boasts a prosperous Western-style economy grounded in an Asian ethos. China itself has more than a billion people, even with the "one child per family" restriction that kept its population from exploding. China is the center of East Asian civilization and is poised to become the preeminent power of the global village. The political and cultural dynamics that accompany China's ascent to world power are themselves evolving, and no one yet knows what shapes they will assume. The Chinese leadership is both enthusiastic and cautious—committed to the openness that economic growth demands, yet aware that some conservative constancy is required as a stable background to constructive change.

Like India, China has known ancient civilizations and contending dynasties, both enlightened and despotic. We will touch on some of them when we look more closely at Buddha and Confucius. But unlike India, whose Sanskrit tongue is matriarch to the family of Indo-European languages, China's original written language is ideographic, or pictorial, rather than alphabetical. There is no oral language called "Chinese," only a written one. Speakers of Chinese dialects—like Mandarin, Jin, Jianghuai, Wu, Xiang, Gan, Hakka, Minbei, Minnan, Yue, and Pinghua—are not mutually intelligible, yet they all read the same characters. The only comparable situation in the West, the Middle East, or India is with respect to formal languages, such as logic or mathematics. Physicists from different cultures understand the same written equations, even though they may call the symbols by different names.

Chinese philosophical traditions are also unique, and unprecedented in the West. Tao is one of the most beautiful and profound concepts ever to dawn in the human mind, yet it is by definition inexplicable in any tongue, and was for a long time incomprehensible to the West. I will try to clarify some fundamentals here and in chapter 4. The Tao has also degenerated in China, and is neglected by many Chinese, but there are living Chinese masters who can discourse at great length on Tao, and can illustrate its direct applications to many and varied arts: from calligraphy to Tai Chi, from acupuncture to herbal medicine. The Tao is one philosophical strand of a triple braid, along with Confucianism and Buddhism, that defines the cultural DNA of East Asian civilization.

Japan adds one further formidable strand: Bushido, originally the unwritten code of its samurai. Influenced by Shinto, Confucius, and Buddha, Bushido engenders an ethos of chivalry whose noblest manifestations surpass even the flower of Western knighthood. Just as chivalry's influence persists in the West, so Bushido continues to infuse the spirit of Japan.

Returning to the mystery of Tao: That no one can define it highlights its singular importance. Mastery of Tao—a Chinese philosopher's stone—is what Confucius sought, and so it turns out that Taoist teachings are readily transmissible by Confucian methods. Confucius himself declared, "I transmit. I do not innovate." East Asian cultures preserved their integrity for centuries on end by means of Confucian transmission of Confucian philosophy itself. But Confucian methods are also ideal for transmitting Tao, and are linked to Buddhism via Tao, as we shall see. Lao Tzu and Confucius were at odds on many issues (as were Plato and Aristotle in the West), but shared a common philosophical origin (the *I Ching*). This situates Confucius's approach to Tao as among the more stable and less reckless routes to the summit of the ineffable.

Since words are the everyday tokens of human thoughts, we also tend to think as we speak and write. It is clear that Chinese and Japanese systems of highly contextualized pictorial written language engendered unique possibilities for sophisticated patterns of abstract thought. When politically permitted to do so, East Asian cultures have acquired and mastered Western languages, philosophy, science, technology, medicine, and arts with considerable acumen. By contrast, and absent political impediments, how many Westerners have acquired—let alone mastered—Chinese or Japanese languages, philosophy, medicine, or arts? The question is rhetorical: very few indeed. East Asian civilization has proved adept at studying and learning from the West; but Western civilization has not proved as adept at studying and learning from East Asia. What does this mean? Perhaps that East Asian civilization has the capacity to overtake Western civilization and to become the next dominant power in the global village.

The populousness of India and East Asia is mind-boggling to most Westerners, myself included, who upon visiting feel swallowed whole by teeming masses. The individual can sustain an inflated sense of importance in the West; in Asia, the individual is a drop in the ocean. Consider the trading bloc of the Association of South East Asian Nations (ASEAN), founded in 1967 to further mutual economic and cultural growth. Indonesia, Malaysia, Philippines, Singapore, and

Thailand were the original members, and the group now includes Brunei Darussalam (1984), Vietnam (1995), Laos and Myanmar (1997), and Cambodia (1999). The current ten-nation ASEAN region has a population of about five hundred million—larger than North America and comparable to the expanding EU—but has less than half the population of China, and far less than half of China's economic potential. This huge conglomerate of ASEAN, a giant by many world standards, is a dwarf compared with China.

Much like India, but not to the same extreme, China herself is a patchwork of indigenous tribes and cultures, gradually unified over sometimes turbulent centuries of contending dynastic rule. Unconquered by non-Asian powers, China was nevertheless brought to heel by the feared and fearless Mongol hordes of Genghis Khan and his grandsons, notably Kublai Khan, who founded the Yuan dynasty. And also like India, China has been relatively modest in its territorial acquisitions, with the glaring exceptions of its occupation of Tibet and role in the Korean War. China has not been an aggressor on the scale of past Western, Islamic, or Japanese military expansions. The supreme arts of self-defense—the so-called "martial arts"—which originated in China, and branched out all over East Asia, are based upon self-preservative and defensive principles, rather than destructive and offensive ones.

China's military strength, like Russia's, consists in defense and counterattack, rather than aggressive offense. Spacious countries have geography on their side, and one must never neglect geography's influence on the formation of national character. Russia stalled the invading armies of Napoleon Bonaparte and Adolf Hitler with little more defense than the Russian winter. China itself is so vast that it simultaneously underwent a civil war between Western-supported Chiang Kai-shek and Mao Tse-tung's Marxist-Leninist revolutionaries, along with a Japanese occupation of Manchuria.

One of the man-made wonders of the world is the Great Wall of China, a 3,728-mile fortification begun in the seventh century B.C.E., and extended and renovated into the sixteenth century C.E. The Mongols alone managed to breach it. Contrary to urban legend, the Great Wall is not visible from orbital space, but is the only wonder of the world to attract such a claim. It's also a witness with lengthy testimony to China's conspicuously defensive mentality. Livy claimed that the Romans conquered the world in self-defense, which translates into the contemporary American athletic maxim that the best defense is a great offense. Notwithstanding Roman circuses, and lionized superstars of contemporary Western civilization's professional sports, great defense is crucial to winning the trophy of civilizational survival. Even the British, who swaggered off sailing ships and blustered their way to mastering much of Asia, made no more than a dent in Chinese culture. India was the jewel in their crown; China was the treasury they bankrupted with opium. But China survived British narco-trafficking, too.

The Chinese famously invented both paper and gunpowder, using them for calligraphic arts and fireworks displays. The later printing press and firearm were signature Western applications for these inventions. Ancient Chinese cosmologists observed eclipses and other astronomical events. Chinese doctors accurately mapped acupuncture meridians, developed herbal remedies, and compiled more than two thousand books on medical arts and sciences, only one of which—*The Yellow Emperor's Book of Chinese Medicine*—survived the compulsive book burnings of rapacious warlords. Nonetheless, the most important philosophical works and practices—the core teachings of Taoism, Confucianism, and Buddhism—survived and thrived. They spread to Korea, and to Japan, and many centuries later, to the West.

Again I emphasize the special relationship between Japan and China. Japan combined the fiercely independent spirit of an uninvaded island people (reminiscent of the British) with the defensive ethos of the Chinese model, and so were a closed book to the world for centuries, until the West began to embroil them in oceanic commerce. The Jesuits, who arrived in Japan as missionary soldiers of Christ in the sixteenth century, were the first Westerners to study Japanese language and culture. They also found Japan in a state of pristine medieval feudalism, with warlords and samurai armies contending for power, and beneath them a subservient pyramid of serfs and fisherfolk. However, within two centuries of exposure to the West, Japan began to industrialize and develop Western-style military capabilities. By the first half of the twentieth century no Asian nation could withstand Japan's military onslaught. The British Empire was by then a spent military force in Asia, so the unenviable job of containing and reversing Japan's occupation and domination of Asia fell to the United States. Maoist China knew how much Japan had achieved by grafting Western limbs onto its Confucian trunk, but (like the Stalinist Soviet Union) China could not attain comparable results using inherently flawed Marxist-Leninist models. Contemporary China, however, is now beginning to adopt the Western capitalist formula for economic success.

So consider that after Japan's unconditional surrender to the United States in 1945, which ended World War II, a pacified, democratized, and industrialized Japan swiftly became the world's second-largest economic power, and remained so for decades. Japan consists of four main islands and thousands of smaller ones, poor in natural resources, with a population that numbered 127 million at the end of the twentieth century—about 10 percent of the population of China, or India, or Islamic civilization—and an area about the size of Italy. How did Japan become the world's second-largest national economy? It did so by harnessing Western models of democratization and industrialization to Confucian philosophical traditions of virtue ethics and social organization.

Now the Chinese are undertaking a similar process, but with a population ten times larger than Japan's, an area more than twenty times larger than Japan's, and with an abundance rather than a dearth of natural resources. So as China follows in the footsteps of its "progeny culture" Japan, it may dominate the world economically in the twenty-first century, to an even greater extent than the United States did in the twentieth century.

The foundational practical philosophy that underpins Chinese and Japanese civilizations is Confucian, and derives from his application of the Tao. Just as Aristotle became "The Philosopher" of the West, so Confucius became "The Philosopher" of East Asia. He drew upon the Tao, as did his elder contemporary, the civil servant Lao Tzu. In essence, Taoism is a secular metaphysical view of the universe that brings human existence into harmony with natural process. There is no Godhead in Taoist thought; neither in Confucius's *Analects* nor in Lao Tzu's *Tao Te Ching* (*The Way and Its Power*). There is, however, a Way: not a God to be worshipped; rather a path to be followed. Yet it is, paradoxically at times, the path of no path.

Just as with Indian philosophy, the twentieth century saw a convergence of East Asian philosophy and Western science, which blossomed in Western intellectual culture. Fritjof Capra's *The Tao of Physics* was a huge best-seller and gave rise to a publishing mania for books entitled The Tao of . . . (everything from *Health*, *Sex*, and *Longevity* to *Pooh*). Gary Zukav's *The Dancing Wu Li Masters* was a milestone in synthesizing modern particle physics and ancient Chinese philosophy. Dozens of new translations of the *I Ching* appeared. Robert Pirsig's *Zen and the Art of Motorcycle Maintenance* catapulted Japanese Buddhism into the literary limelight. One of the most important historical works of the twentieth century, and possibly of all time, was Arnold Toynbee's *A Study of History*, which traced the rise and fall of great civilizations as a function of the Chinese metaphysics of yin and yang. Additionally, Chinese medical practices, especially acupuncture, have made serious inroads into Western medicine.

The absence of a foundational deity or deities in Chinese and Japanese civilizations is distinctive of East Asia. As we have seen, Islamic civilization (like the Abrahamic religions from which it springs) adheres to "one God, one prophet, one book." Polytheistic Indian civilization absorbs "all Gods, all prophets, all books." Western civilization offers its citizens free choice among "any God, any prophet, any book." East Asian civilization, notwithstanding its converts to Christianity and Islam, and its worshippers of Buddha as a god, is nonetheless epitomized by atheistic Tao and Confucianism, which impart secular ethics but adhere to "no God, no prophet, no book." The people themselves observe Confucian rituals and practice Confucian virtues, but do not worship Confucius, who would have been horrified to be deified.

And this is precisely why Buddhism, although born in India and sequestered as a monastic religion for centuries in Tibet, became deeply rooted in the secular Confucian cultures of China, and later Japan. China and Japan have thus played pivotal roles in cultivating and then disseminating Buddhism worldwide.

East Asian civilization, geographically and culturally the most remote from the West, was the last to be encountered by it. Alexander reached India in the fourth century B.C.E. Islam reached Europe in the eighth century C.E. But the first Western delegation to China, a Venetian commercial and Christian missionary expedition that included Marco Polo, reached the Court of Emperor Kublai Khan in Beijing only in the thirteenth century C.E. Western contact with aloof Japan came even later: Portuguese Jesuits first settled there in the sixteenth century C.E. In that same century the French voyaged west, seeking new trade routes to the exotic Orient. They sailed up the Saint Lawrence River to the extinct volcanic island of Mount Royal (Montreal), which to this day boasts a suburb optimistically named "Lachine"—French for "China." The sixteenth-century French were slightly ahead of their time; Chinese food, for example, finally became available in Lachine some four centuries later.

East Asia has often appeared inscrutable to Westerners, and for good reason: East Asian philosophy, language, and culture evolved in distinctively non-Indo-European and non-Abrahamic pathways. The Way (Tao) is omnipresent too, however invisible and elusive. Globalization has opened East Asia to Western science, technology, and commerce, and has opened the West to East Asian philosophy, language, and culture. A Chinese master, venerable S. M. Li, observed that the two end points of any length of string are the most remote from each other, yet they also touch when the loop is closed. Chinese philosophy and Japanese Buddhism are now touching Western minds in this very way, via the closed loop of globalization.

### Convergence at Ground Zero: From Locality to Globality

Globalization is a process that, by definition, is more powerful than any of the four great civilizations described in this chapter. Globalization is rapidly melting down the boundaries and borders—political, religious, geographic, ethnic, tribal, cultural, philosophical—that to varying degrees have separated and differentiated these four civilizations, and their myriad subcultures, along with the rest of humanity. The Internet epitomizes globality: Your physical location is vital to postal mail yet irrelevant to e-mail. You are a transient node in a virtual global network. Cyberspace cannot be "colonized" or "occupied" by any conquering civilization, nor can it be "sealed off" or "walled off" indefinitely by any defensive one. Cyberspace is the cybernetic Commons, shared by all with connectivity, irrespective of civilizational, political, religious, geographic, ethnic, or tribal identity.

The potential of globalization is far nobler than perhaps intended by its initiators, who were rightly but primarily concerned with economic development. Globalization's further promise is to provide a context for reuniting the human species as a whole—notwithstanding all the differences that divide us. Globalization makes palpable the ancient Buddhist idea that we are all connected. But as globalization reaches out to everyone on the planet, weaving us into its tapestry of networks, it necessarily highlights human differences in the very process of transcending them.

The term *Ground Zero* originally meant the point where a bomb detonated. After Hiroshima and Nagasaki (August 6 and 9, 1945), it came to mean the zone of total devastation at the epicenter of a nuclear detonation. Since 9/11, Ground Zero also refers to the vast pit, emptied of debris, from which the twin towers of the World Trade Center rose in 1970, and into which they imploded in 2001. There is an ironic connection here too: The top-secret development of the atomic bombs later dropped on Japan was code-named "The Manhattan Project." The death toll and devastation at Hiroshima and Nagasaki were incomparably greater than that of 9/11, and yet the effect of visiting Hiroshima's or Nagasaki's Ground Zero is not so very different from the effect of visiting Manhattan's Ground Zero. All three are places where thousands of civilians perished suddenly and violently, in deliberate conflagrations caused by weapons that were viewed as morally repugnant by the target cultures and morally justifiable by the wielders.

My intention here is to illustrate a significant difference between Ground Zero at Hiroshima and Manhattan: not in terms of how many were killed (over one hundred thousand versus three thousand), but in terms of their civilizational identities. World War II was a devastating and total war, pitting the entire resources—civilian and military alike—of nation-states against one another. It was also a war whose immediate origins are susceptible to lucid testimony: Hitler's Nazified Germany and Tojo's Imperial Japan were ruthless and savage aggressor-states, full of well-intended civilians ruled by merciless militaristic regimes, which conquered, brutalized, enslaved, and murdered millions of people in dozens of nations beyond their borders.

The civilians killed at Hiroshima were almost all Japanese, casualties of a total war between Japan and the United States, which Japan herself had provoked by attacking Pearl Harbor. It was a horrific characteristic of World War II that civilian populations—in dozens of cities—would be among the first, as well as the last, to pay the ultimate price for conflicts initiated by maniacal and implacable adventurer-conquerors. The civilians of Hiroshima suffered horribly from the A-bomb, and only they are qualified to tell us what nuclear weapons feel like at the receiving end. Yet these civilians were also part of a Japanese war machine that had murdered more than fifteen million Asians and others outside Japan—men, women, children, POWs—even though the citizens of Hiroshima probably did not know this at the time. Alas, a state of ignorance is not a state of innocence. Civilians of Dresden and Hamburg also perished—a hundred thousand at a time—in firestorms caused by massive conventional bombings, and German civilians who suffered and died in this way perhaps did not know that their Nazi government had likewise cruelly murdered more than fifteen million people during its reign of aggressive terror. But a state of general ignorance or tacit compliance among German civilians was not a state of innocence either.

In stark contrast, the civilians killed on 9/11 came from more than ninety-one different nations, representing every major civilization and world religion. Jews, Christians, Moslems, Hindus, Sikhs, Jains, Buddhists, and Confucians, from every continent and half the world's nations, died on 9/11. They were not condemned by any sovereign government's orders; rather, by nonstate actors as much opposed to their own government in Arabia as to the government of the United

States. Unlike Pearl Harbor, 9/11 was not an attack on one sovereign nation by another; rather, it was an attack on the chamber of commerce of the global village, and on citizens of the global village itself, by outlaws hostile to and fearful of globalization, and violently opposed to its transcendent possibility of uniting humanity in a pacific and prosperous global community. The attack on the Pentagon itself (as well as the intended attack of Flight 93, probably on the White House) was none other than a declaration of war on the United States, but not by a state: rather, by the extremist fringe of a civilization.

Globalization connects us all, for better or worse. Human discontents once confined to relatively isolated places are now being destructively manifested in highly accessible ones: New York skyscrapers, Balinese nightclubs, Madrid train stations, London subways, Tel Aviv cafés, Egyptian hotels, Iraqi infrastructures. Once again, locality vanishes in the face of globality. No places and no peoples are isolated anymore. We are all interconnected. So please realize that Ground Zero is no longer confined to Hiroshima and Nagasaki, or for that matter to Lower Manhattan: Ground Zero is under your very feet. Whether you're sitting or standing or lying down; whether you're walking or riding or flying; whether you're gardening or commuting or vacationing—Ground Zero is always there. It is part of the human condition in the global village. Whether this shadow lengthens or recedes depends partly upon what you yourself do or don't do about it. At the very end of this book, I will summarize what the ABCs would advise you to do once you put the book down.

Globalization is commingling the four great civilizations and dissolving their boundaries in historically unprecedented ways. Each of these civilizations is converging, as well conflicting, with the others. The conflict that led to 9/11, and that inspired Samuel Huntington's influential book *The Clash of Civilizations*, tells part of this story. Huntington explored dynamics of the clash between Western and Islamic civilizations. But clashes between the other pairs of civilizations need to be understood as well.

Western and Indian civilizations also clash, generally in terms of economics. Dire poverty in India and its neighboring states, afflicting hundreds of millions of people, is proving inescapable not only because of endemic corruption and socioeconomic rigidity in these nations. But in addition, enormous agricultural subsidies paid to farmers in the affluent West, in tandem with prohibitive tariffs imposed on produce from developing nations, impede many of our Indian counterparts from bettering their lives. So the West's affluence depends partly but far from wholly on India's poverty. Yet this is a wholly undesirable state of affairs.

Western and East Asian civilizations clash, too, in economic and military spheres. China's economy, however you measure it, may overtake the United States's within a century (if not mere decades), and as a result Americans will have to pay more for necessities, and low-income earners will be able to afford fewer luxuries. Americans are already steeped in denial regarding the internal deficiencies contributing to their nation's decline—not only in global public opinion, but crucially in cultural assets—which means they're not prepared to reverse the damage. There are also two regional flashpoints for war between the West and East Asia: North Korea and Taiwan. North Korea is, at this writing, a rogue state whose nuclear capacities destabilize the entire East Asian region. Even Japan is rearming in the face of possible North Korean aggression. Taiwan, where Gen. Chiang Kai-shek took refuge after conceding China's civil war to Mao Tse-tung, maintains a precarious U.S.-backed independence from mainland China. Beijing is patient but immovable on this point: Sooner or later, Taiwan will rejoin China.

Islamic and Indian civilizations clash as well. Pakistan and India both possess nuclear weapons, and both appear proud contributors to the next chapter in "the book" on nuclear deterrence. The odds that deterrence will fail get shorter as the book on deterrence gets longer. Like the clash between the West and the Middle East, the clash between democratic Hindu India and autocratic Muslim Pakistan affects other nations in the region—such as Nepal, Kashmir, Afghanistan— condemning them to become battlegrounds in the subsidiary conflicts that deterrence always foments to blow hot steam off cold war.

Indian and East Asian civilizations are economic competitors whose clashes may emerge as competitions heighten. India wants to emulate China's economic growth and regards its own vast population increasingly as an asset in globalized markets. India and China contain half the world's people, and may become direct competitors in many sectors. They have already experienced shooting wars along their borders, and the buffer states between them may become casualties as these two Asian juggernauts flex their growing muscles.

Last but not least, East Asian and Islamic civilizations may also clash in Asia. Malaysia and Indonesia are populous Islamic nations (about twenty-five million and two hundred million respectively) and suffer from the similar challenges to economic development as their Middle Eastern and other Islamic counterparts. Insufficient separation between mosque and state—plus indigenous poverty, endemic corruption, and crony capitalism—inhibit socioeconomic mobility, modernization, and distributive justice. These conditions also sustain a breeding ground for Islamist terrorism—evidenced in the bombing of a popular Balinese nightclub, calculated to drive Western tourists out of Indonesia, which depends greatly on tourism. If Islamist terrorists ever make the mistake of attacking Confucian targets, their countries of origin could suffer reprisals that make regime changes in Afghanistan and Iraq look like mild diplomacy.

## Happily Ever After, or a Good Life Now?
I would love to be able to claim with conviction and finality that this tale of four great civilizations has a happy ending. I am rather more convinced that the tale never ends, and that any moment of it can be serendipitous or catastrophic. My purpose in writing this book is really twofold. First, I would like to apply the ABCs to reconciling some of the extremes that drive global conflicts. Second, I would like to persuade you to apply the ABCs to reconciling your own conflicts, which may appear more important and more immediately relevant to you than the clashes of civilizations. But if you appreciate one moral of this chapter—that nothing is local, everything is global—then you should also appreciate that your own problems are not local or isolated either; rather, they are shared and networked globally. How you handle your issues affects how others handle theirs. Handle your conflicts wisely and you will not only resolve them, you will also set an example that others can follow. Handle

them foolishly and you will not only exacerbate them, you will also create a ripple effect that worsens conditions for other people too. So as I said in the introduction: If you prefer fairy tales with "happily ever after" endings, put down this book and pick up a collection of nursery rhymes. If you prefer to lead a good life now, continue reading.

Refer again to fig. 1.1, an ideogram of the four great civilizations, the different strands of thought that subtend them, and some of the many interconnections among them. Prior to globalization, it was possible for inhabitants of each of these civilizations to regard themselves as separate or distinct from all the others. But in reality that has rarely been the case; most people were simply ignorant of their interconnections. The forces of globalization began to draw these civilizations much closer together in the twentieth century.

Consider this revealing account of "An American at Breakfast," written by anthropologist Robert Linton in the 1960s:

"On his way to breakfast, he stops to buy a paper, paying for it with coins, an ancient Lydian invention. At the restaurant a whole new series of borrowed elements confronts him. His plate is made of a form of pottery invented in China. His knife is of steel, an alloy first made in southern India, his fork a medieval Italian invention, and his spoon a derivative of a Roman original. He begins breakfast with an orange, from the eastern Mediterranean, a cantaloupe from Persia, or perhaps a piece of African watermelon. With this he has coffee, an Abyssinian plant, with cream and sugar. Both the domestication of cows and the idea of milking them originated in the Near East, while sugar was first made in India. After his fruit and first coffee he goes on to waffles, cakes made by a Scandinavian technique from wheat domesticated in Asia Minor. Over these he pours maple syrup, invented by the Indians of the eastern woodlands. As a side dish he may have the egg of a species of bird domesticated in Indo-China, or thin strips of the flesh of an animal domesticated in Eastern Asia which may have been salted and smoked by a process developed in northern Europe . . . When our friend has finished eating he settles back to smoke, an American Indian habit, consuming a plant domesticated in Brazil in either a pipe, derived from the Indians of Virginia, or a cigarette, derived from Mexico. If he is hardy enough he may even attempt a cigar, transmitted to us from the Antilles by way of Spain. While smoking he reads the news of the day, imprinted in characters invented by the ancient Semites upon a material invented in China by a process invented in Germany. As he absorbs the accounts of foreign troubles he will, if he is a good conservative citizen, thank a Hebrew deity in an Indo-European language that he is 100 percent American."[11]

You see? Humanity has always been interconnected, but mostly unaware. Nowadays we are interconnected not only by tools, symbols, and products that diffuse across civilizational boundaries, but also by our immediate contact with people of all cultures, owing to the dissolution of those very boundaries, along with the dissolution of our ignorance of connectedness itself.

However, human beings require shared contexts in which to assemble and commingle. By the transcendence of economic and technological forces (which connect people as well as divide them) over political and religious forces (which divide people as well as connect them), globalization has succeeded in assembling and commingling all the different strands of cultural DNA, along with all their conflicting core

| CIVILIZATION | CULTURAL DNA | CORE FORMULA |
| --- | --- | --- |
| Indian | Vedic philosophy | all Gods, all books, all prophets |
| East Asian | Confucian & Taoist philosophy | no Gods, no books, no prophets |
| Islamic | Abrahamic (primarily Islamic) religion | one God, one book, one prophet |
| Western | Hellenic philosophy & Abrahamic (primarily Judaeo-Christian) religion | any Gods, any books, any prophets |

Figure 1.2 Four Civilizations: Cultural DNA and Core Formulas

formulae, in one great melting pot. (See fig. 1.2.) What globalization has not yet provided is a global human context for reconciling the extremes of difference that lead to conflict. The ABCs provide precisely this.

What context can accommodate one God, no God, any God, every God? One prophet, no prophet, any prophet, every prophet? One book, no book, any book, every book? What way contains one way, no way, any way, every way?

The Middle Way.

# 2

## ARISTOTLE'S GOLDEN MEAN
### Attaining Excellence and Happiness amid Unreason

*Moral excellence is a mean . . . between two vices, the one involving excess, the other deficiency.* —Aristotle

### "The Philosopher"

ARISTOTLE WAS BORN in 384 B.C.E. in Stagyra, a Thracian seaport colonized by the Greeks. His father, Nichomachus, was court physician to the Macedonian King Amyntas, so Aristotle had a privileged beginning in life. At age seventeen he was sent to Plato's Academy in Athens, then the intellectual center of the West, where he studied for the next twenty years. After Plato's death in 347 B.C.E., Aristotle left Athens. Although he had been Plato's most outstanding student, Aristotle had also diverged from his teacher in some key respects, and so was not selected to succeed Plato as head of the Academy. He accepted an invitation from King Philip of Macedonia to tutor his son Alexander (the future Alexander the Great), which Aristotle did for five years. After Philip's death, Alexander embarked on his legendary conquests, and

Aristotle returned to Athens to open his own school: the Lyceum. There he taught for the next thirteen years, giving advanced lectures for his more accomplished students, and talks for the general public. He married twice, and his second wife, Herpyllis, bore a son, Nicomachus, for whom he wrote the endearing *Nicomachean Ethics*. When Alexander died in 323 B.C.E., political sentiment in Athens shifted against all things Macedonian, and Aristotle's life became endangered. He fled to Chalcis so that, in his own words, "the Athenians might not have another opportunity of sinning against philosophy as they had already done in the person of Socrates." Aristotle died there, in 322 B.C.E.

Aristotle was the third philosophical patriarch of the remarkable Athenian lineage that forms one strand of Western civilization's double helix. His teacher, Plato, had recorded and dramatized Socratic dialogues, giving the Western world unprecedentedly powerful insights into thought itself. Platonic philosophy revivified Judaism in postbiblical Jerusalem, laid the metaphysical foundations for Christianity in late Imperial Rome, and bequeathed the West a version of idealism that was condemned in 1948—by Viennese-Jewish philosopher Sir Karl Popper, the only philosopher of the twentieth century elected to the Royal Society—for laying the totalitarian foundations for the political excesses of Nazi Germany and Soviet Russia.

Plato's teacher, Socrates, invented philosophical methods of inquiry and applied them to questions of knowledge, ethics, laws, love, beauty, justice, and more—raw verbal gemstones that Plato polished into written philosophical jewels. Socrates himself had been tried on charges of corrupting Athenian youth, trumped-up by vengeful political enemies, and had allowed himself to be martyred in Athens while remaining true to his principles—rather than permitting well-connected friends to smuggle him out alive, to exile in Thebes.

If you doubt for one moment the depth and duration of Platonic and Socratic political influence on the West, read for example Dr. Martin Luther King Jr.'s "Letter from a Birmingham Jail."[1] There you will rediscover the cultural double helix of Hellenic philosophy and Judeo-Christian religion, writ large in America's civil rights movement of the 1950s and 1960s, by the man who led his people to freedom using a judicious blend of Mosaic and Socratic traditions, descended to him via Thoreau and Tolstoy, with Gandhi between the lines.

The magnitude of Aristotle's contributions, beyond those of Socrates and Plato, won him such preeminence that the following quotation is found throughout cyberspace:

"Aristotle, more than any other thinker, determined the orientation and the content of Western intellectual history. He was the author of a philosophical and scientific system that through the centuries became the support and vehicle for both medieval Christian and Islamic scholastic thought: until the end of the 17th century, Western culture was Aristotelian. And, even after the intellectual revolutions of centuries to follow, Aristotelian concepts and ideas remained embedded in Western thinking."[2]

The very curriculum of the modern university was forged in the crucible of Aristotle's formidable mind. Subjects that he invented or reinvented include logic, physics, astronomy, meteorology, zoology, ethology, theology, psychology, politics, economics, rhetoric, and poetics. He also invented taxonomy, the art and science of classification. From foodstuffs in supermarkets to books in libraries, from stars and galaxies to flora and fauna, from elements of the periodic table to ads in newspapers: All are *classified*, thanks to Aristotle. He was also the first to formulate laws of binary and syllogistic logic, laws of thought that complemented the theorems of plane geometry catalogued by Euclid. Aristotle is a link to digital computing too. Both TTL logic of hardware, and formal programming languages of software, are direct extensions of Aristotle's formalization of logic and reasoning. Aristotle was also the first to engage systematically in what we today call "scientific inquiry," making observations of particular phenomena—from astronomical to zoological—and attempting to infer from them universal laws. Of course most of his science has been superseded, but such is the nature of scientific progress. Much twentieth-century science been superseded too.

The so-called "social sciences"—social psychology, cultural anthropology, sociology, economics, and political science—are fuzzy extensions of Aristotelian natural science (physics, chemistry, biology). They gradually extended Western civilization's reliable knowledge of nature into human realms, allowing Western nations to nurture political and socioeconomic structures—for good and for ill, as always—that accommodated the evolving theories and technologies of natural science. The Industrial Revolution was unprecedented in human history, and could not have occurred anywhere else in the world at the time, thanks again to the West's cultural double helix.

The Romans built roads and marched legions down them, bringing their imperial versions of law, order, and progress—and later, Christianity—to what they regarded as an uncivilized world. Fast-forward to the nineteenth century: The British controlled the sea lanes and sailed fleets up and down them, bringing their imperial version of civilization to what they similarly regarded as an uncivilized world. In the late twentieth and early twenty-first centuries, the United States controls global air space and influences global economies, exporting McDonald's and MTV (the American view of civilization, encapsulated in its brands) to what Americans regard as an uncivilized world. In each case, the West reached the rest of the world before the rest of the world reached the West, owing largely to brazen initiatives of rebellious freethinkers, rugged individualists, fearless explorers, and ambitious pioneers, armed with civil liberties, Promethean arsenals, and Christian Bibles.

The American Indians, so Hollywood informs us, poetically called the locomotive an "iron horse." The architects of trans-American railways were pragmatists, not poets, who in the spirit of Western materialism would have called a horse a "hay-burning locomotive." Western civilization prevailed time and again over indigenous peoples precisely because the West developed dynamic social sciences in tandem with potent natural ones, and regularly updated its religious and political operating systems accordingly, albeit not without bitter and sanguinary strife. Dynamic cultures dance rings around static ones, pave roads through them, and build Wal-Marts among them—for better and for worse.

Aristotle knew this too, and was the first to name man "*homo politicus*"—the political animal—taking into account that every human activity is susceptible to politicization, while implying that politics is not susceptible to every humane act. And Aristotle was the first in the West to develop a form of virtue ethics, transposing the golden mean of geometry into a moral compass for humanity. For these reasons among others, Aristotle deservedly reigned as "The Philosopher" for two thousand years.

## Happiness, Reason, and Proportion

For Aristotle, happiness is an end in itself, the only thing worth attaining in this human life. "Happiness then is the best, noblest, and most pleasant thing in the world," he says in his *Ethics*. If you are not as happy as you'd like to be, then maybe Aristotle's wisdom can be of help to you. Aristotle believed strongly in purpose: Everyone has a purpose in life, and lasting happiness comes through fulfilling it. Everybody has capacities and talents, and by cultivating them virtuously we become fulfilled. It is also the duty of family, and the responsibility of government, to cocreate environments conducive to the cultivation of excellence and the practice of virtue, which "needs the external goods as well; for it is impossible, or not easy, to do noble acts without the proper equipment." Disordered families, dysfunctional cultures, and despotic regimes are profoundly un-Aristotelian, as are belief systems that sacrifice the real potential of this life for the uncertain reward—or oblivion—of the next.

So Aristotle advocated a life of reason as the first step, but not the last, on the road to happiness. Absent the exercise and application of reason, we would subsist in a late Stone Age, with a lifestyle described by Thomas Hobbes as "solitary, poor, nasty, brutish, and short." For Aristotle, the purpose of reason is not just to theorize for its own sake, but to guide our actions into virtuous channels.

Aristotle claimed that it is both desirable and possible to be happy in this life. His ethics teach us how to recognize and avoid extremes in life, for it is extremes, or a desire for extremes, that so often causes unhappiness. Not eating enough will make you emaciated, unhappy, and prematurely dead, while eating too much will make you overweight, unhappy, and prematurely dead. What is true of food is also true of work, money, sex, and almost everything else that people pursue, produce, or consume in the normal course of their lives. As Aristotle explains,

> "Both excessive and defective exercise destroys the strength, and similarly drink or food which is above or below a certain amount destroys the health, while that which is proportionate both produces and increases and preserves it. So too is it, then, in the case of temperance and courage and the other virtues."[3]

Aristotle teaches us to find a balance between dearth and excess, a Middle Way between not enough and too much. Lasting happiness arises from finding and maintaining this balance, which is the golden mean, while unhappiness is a product of venturing too far toward either extreme.

The world we inhabit is not always fair or just or reasonable. Half the world's population lacks the basic necessities for a decent life. Even people who enjoy decent lives or very good lives suffer from imperfections in themselves, in others, and in the nature of things. People in the developing world dream of having the opportunities enjoyed by more affluent societies. In the developed world, even the most affluent or successful people express frustration with their careers, their families, their fulfillment.

If the universe is a fundamentally or ultimately orderly place, then why is the human world so disorderly at times? And if the universe is a fundamentally chaotic or ultimately disorderly place, then what can we do to maximize order in human realms? One thing we can do is use our powers of reason. While reason alone cannot redress all poignant human problems and cannot resolve all our dilemmas, lack of reason will certainly contribute to our woes, not to their management or resolution.

When people find others unreasonable, or find the world unfair, they are really saying that certain priorities or events seem out of order. According to what order should values, persons, and systems be arranged? This is a fundamental question posed by, and to, our powers of reason. As Aristotle cautions in his *Nicomachean Ethics*,

"To entrust to chance what is greatest and most noble would be a very defective arrangement."

## The Golden Mean

Why did Aristotle borrow so conspicuously from geometry, a deductive art and a measurement science, to provide a framework for his ethics? First, because he saw the natural world as a place of lawfulness and orderliness, and wanted the human world to be as lawful and as orderly as nature. Human preoccupation with these twin notions is ongoing, as witnessed by the long-running TV series *Law and Order*. Second, Aristotle perceived the aesthetic beauty of nature and knew it to be based on "correct" proportions. He then had the brilliant insight that morally commendable human behaviors ought also to be based on "correct" proportions.

Aristotle understood that human nature harbors potential for both good and evil, and we are made by nature to acquire habits—for better or worse. Good habits are virtues; bad habits, vices. In the course of a lifetime, most people experience both. The practice of virtuous habits conduces to happiness; of vicious habits, to unhappiness. And so Aristotle wrote: "Neither by nature, then, nor contrary to nature do the virtues arise in us; rather we are adapted by nature to receive them, and are made perfect by habit."

Virtues cannot be imposed by legislated laws or political orders. Man-made laws can be bent and broken, can be unjust on their face or in their application, can become outmoded or superseded; and so man-made laws cannot be allowed to constitute the basis of moral behaviors. Obversely, we legislate against vices that we do not wish to see practiced in civil society, yet each individual decides whether to obey or to flout the laws. The laws we follow should reflect, but cannot dictate, our morals.

Aristotle knew, too, that moral order could not be imposed on a society, any more than it could be legislated. For the imposition of moral order can only take place in tandem with the suppression of individual development and the restriction of personal choice. Western morality rests squarely on each person's choice, and depends upon a majority's preference for better over worse thoughts, words, and deeds. To impose

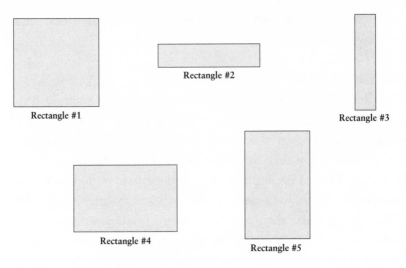

Figure 2.1 Assorted Rectangles

morality is an affront to its very meaning. It can be done, but only by political tyranny. And Aristotle knew that tyrants did not usually embark on campaigns of moral edification. Benevolent despots are few and far between.

So Aristotle turned to geometry, as he had already done for his physics. He got the physics wrong, but got the ethics right. Virtues are analogous to well-proportioned shapes; vices, to ill-proportioned ones. Aristotle's virtue ethics are a geometry of morality. His use of the golden mean is not at all gratuitous. Now let us see where he acquired it.

Suppose I ask you to imagine or draw a rectangle. Do you know its definition? It's a figure that encloses four right angles in the plane. Consider five different rectangles, depicted in fig. 2.1, Which have better, and which have worse, proportions? Rectangle #1 is a very special rectangle, whose sides are all equal. We call it a square. It's not representative of the infinity of possible rectangles, nor is it the one you're likely see if you ask a lot of people to draw rectangles. Similarly, of infinite possible societies, there is not one in which everyone's moral behaviors are exactly the same. If there were, it would be called "square," Beatnik slang for "closed to creative possibility." That's what the uninhibited French sometimes call the overinhibited English: "*têtes-*

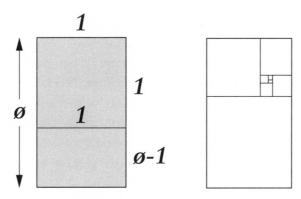

Figure 2.2 The Golden Ratio

*carrées*," or "square-heads."[4] Human relationships, like larger human society, becomes open to creative possibility because of differences between people, which can flourish in many and varied ways. We may demand equality before the law, but we do so as individuals with differing tastes and varying preferences.

How about rectangle #2? It's definitely a rectangle and not a square, but is it well proportioned? Most people think that it's too long and not tall enough. Rectangle #3 has the same proportions as #2, only it's rotated ninety degrees. Consistently, most people think it's too tall and not wide enough. How about #4 and #5? Most people think they are much "better proportioned," more like the figure they would produce if asked to imagine or draw a rectangle. Now it just so happens that #4 and #5 are close to the proportions of the golden ratio. This is a very special ratio, called $\varphi$ (Greek letter "phi").

The golden ratio is special because $\varphi = 1/(\varphi-1)$. This allows us subdivide any golden rectangle into a square and another golden rectangle, or to add a square to a golden rectangle and produce a larger golden rectangle. You can continue either process indefinitely, but only with this golden ratio, as fig. 2.2 depicts.

Aristotle knew that $\varphi$ was special, but he could not have known how much more so it has proved to be. It permeates architecture and art, from Classical Greece to the Italian Renaissance to French Impressionism, and far beyond—into realms of personal identification, business, and global commerce. Leonardo da Vinci proportioned Mona Lisa's face to fit precisely in a golden rectangle. Legions of architects, sculptors, and painters have similarly utilized φ, but for copyright reasons we cannot reproduce their images here. You can view some full-color illustrations at www.themiddleway.us. Take a closer look at your Social Security card, driver's license, business cards, and credit cards: They all approximate golden rectangles. Fig. 2.3 reveals φ in the Parthenon, a cursory glimpse of its deep and pervasive embeddedness.

But this only skims φ's surface, beneath which φ networks with nature too. The golden ratio gives rise to the celebrated Fibonacci series, {0, 1, 1, 2, 3, 5, 8, 13, 21, 34, 55, . . . ,} discovered by Leonardo Pisano Fibonacci (1170-1250). Each term in the series is the sum of the previous two terms. How does this arise from φ? Fig. 2.4 shows how it happens. Start with a unit square, and add another unit square to it. Now add a square whose side is as long as the previous two squares together. Now just keep adding squares according to this rule (you

Figure 2.3 Faces of the Golden Ratio

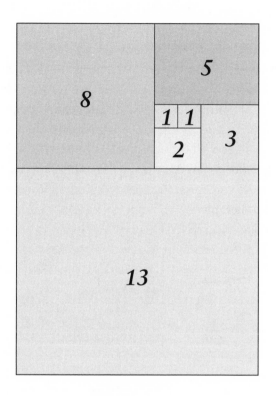

Figure 2.4
The Fibonacci Series
via Geometry

$$\emptyset^2 = \quad \emptyset + 1$$
$$\emptyset^3 = \quad 2\emptyset + 1$$
$$\emptyset^4 = \quad 3\emptyset + 2$$
$$\emptyset^5 = \quad 5\emptyset + 3$$
$$\emptyset^6 = \quad 8\emptyset + 5$$
$$\emptyset^7 = \quad 13\emptyset + 8$$
$$\emptyset^8 = \quad 21\emptyset + 13$$

Figure 2.5
The Fibonacci Series via Algebra

might find the concept easier to grasp by looking at fig. 2.4), and you will get closer and closer to the proportions of the golden rectangle. This amounts to saying that successive ratios of Fibonacci numbers approximate the golden ratio: The series 2/1, 3/2, 5/3, 8/5, . . . , converges to φ. If you prefer algebra to geometry, see fig. 2.5.

There is more. If you now trace an arc through each of the blocks in fig. 2.4, you will get a Fibonacci spiral, as in fig. 2.6. This spiral is one of nature's favorite templates for constructing patterns far and wide. From spiral shells and spiral galaxies to spiraling leaves, branches, and kernels of innumerable flora, from tree forks to forked tongues of lightning, the Fibonacci series is everywhere in nature. For examples, see figs. 2.7–2.10. Fibonacci is also found in the keys of a piano, and in

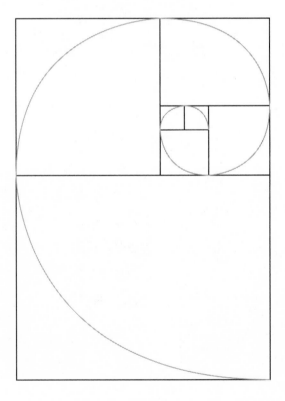

Figure 2.6 The Fibonacci Spiral

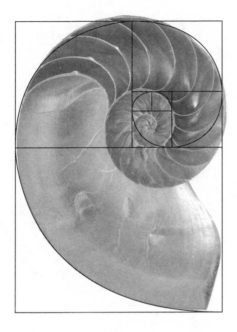

Figure 2.7 The Fibonacci Spiral in a Nautilus Shell

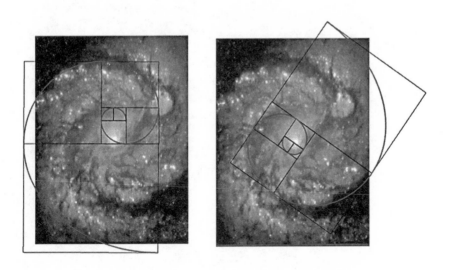

Figure 2.8 The Fibonacci Spiral in Spiral Galaxy M100

Figure 2.9 The Fibonacci Spiral in a Cauliflower

Figure 2.10 The Fibonacci Spiral in a Shrimp Cocktail

Mozart's compositions. Philosophy, geometry, music, and nature are all intertwined, and in more ways than anyone knows. We'll look at a few ways in chapter 5.

Meanwhile it is clear that elegant geometric patterns underlie natural formations, music, and aesthetics alike. In the late twentieth century, psychologists discovered the "geometry of beauty." Infants instinctively recognize and spend more time looking at faces that most adults consider more "beautiful," and less time looking at faces that most adults consider less "beautiful." Beauty and its recognition are innate human attributes, independent of race or ethnicity or even age. Beauty turns out to be a matter of proportion. People who undergo cosmetic surgery to improve their "looks" are actually adjusting the proportions of one or more smaller features, to enhance the overall proportion of their visage. The discovery of the geometry of beauty also reinforces Aristotle's golden mean of morality, since ethics and aesthetics have often been lumped together and relegated to the domain of pure subjectivity, with no purchase in the world of objective measurement. A geometry of beauty is depicted in fig. 2.11.

Figure 2.11 Geometry of Beauty
"Standards of beauty may be related to natural mathematical proportions which have captivated humans across cultures since the beginning of time, such as the golden ratio." http://www.ocf.berkeley.edu/~wwu/psychology/attraction.shtml

### Imprecision and Moderation; Terrorism and Tolerance

Aristotle realized that we cannot measure moral qualities with the same precision as physical ones: "Thus a master of any art avoids excess and defect, but seeks the intermediate and chooses this—the intermediate not in the object but relatively to us." We should all eat and drink and sleep in moderation, but the fine-tuning of proportions—locating the virtuous "intermediate"—is up to each individual. The moral golden mean is attained by steering a course between two extremes: excess and dearth, too much and not enough. But as we all have different tastes, preferences, and capacities, no two people will chart exactly the same intermediate course.

Rather than viewing good and evil as opposing cosmic forces locked in a perpetual titanic struggle (a view that endures from ancient Persia's Zoroastrians to modern Hollywood's *Star Wars*), and rather than viewing "goodness" as an essence emanating from the pure form of "The Good" (as Plato taught), Aristotle suggested that goodness results from practicing virtues, and that most virtues are practiced by following a golden mean between two vicious extremes.

A classic virtue is temperance, which commonly means exercising moderation in what we consume. For example, how much alcohol should you drink? There are different ways of approximating a golden mean. One way is by averaging what you imbibe. For example, you might drink no alcohol during the week, then go out on a bender every weekend. This amounts to alternating the vice of abstention with the vice of overindulgence, yet producing an average amount of consumption that appears virtuous overall. You might also drink moderate amounts of alcohol on a daily basis, consuming a glass of beer or wine with dinner. Either way, you are avoiding the real extremes that Aristotle would call vices: The extreme of alcoholism on the one hand, and the extreme of abstemiousness on the other.

People who for one reason or another become substance abusers, or addicts, cannot indulge in moderation and so should abstain. This gives rise to the saying "abstention is addiction"—which in some cases is true. Alcoholics cannot imbibe one drink; nicotine addicts cannot smoke one cigarette; gambling addicts cannot buy one lottery ticket. Once they get started, they can't stop. So they mustn't get started.

Aristotle also accounted for this kind of case, in which we cannot find a golden mean, so are obliged to choose what he famously called "the lesser of two evils." The extreme of abstention is usually a lesser vice than the extreme of addiction (as sins of omission are lesser than those of commission) yet abstention is still an extreme.

Cultures often attempt to prohibit what they call "vices," by imposing abstention—usually through criminalization or religious proscription of feared substances or practices. In Aristotelian terms such behavior can become vicious itself, not least by preventing people from finding their own virtuous golden mean. Prohibition in the United States was one such example, in which a minority of teetotalers manipulated the federal government into criminalizing the manufacture and sale of alcohol, thereby driving it (predictably) into the hands of organized crime. (Prohibition was repealed in 1934.)

At the other vicious extreme, however, intoxicated people get behind the wheels of their vehicles, and drunken drivers irresponsibly destroy lives. There are more than fifty thousand fatalities per year on America's roads, and many of these deaths involve impaired drivers. Driving while intoxicated (DWI) is a criminal offense in America, a vicious abuse of personal liberty that puts others at needless risk, but more emphasis is placed on prosecution than prevention. A golden mean eschews both extremes—prohibition and lack of inhibition—and consists of the responsible consumption of moderate amounts of alcohol.

Exactly how much one drinks, between these two extremes, is once again up to the individual. As Aristotle explains, "By the intermediate in the object I mean that which is equidistant from each of the extremes, which is one and the same for all men; by the intermediate relatively to us that which is neither too much nor too little—and this is not one, nor the same for all." So, for example, if we seek a compass point that lies intermediate between zero degrees and ninety degrees, we will all agree that it is forty-five degrees. But if we all consume alcohol moderately in the course of a week, no two of us will drink precisely the same amounts or exactly the same beverages. The virtue of moderation applies to us all, but the fine-tuning of habits differs with each individual.

So what about religions that preach or compel various kinds of abstention? Islam prohibits drinking alcohol; Hinduism prohibits eating beef; Judaism and Islam prohibit eating pork; some Buddhist sects prohibit taking any intoxicant, including pain-relieving medication; Jehovah's Witnesses prohibit blood transfusions; some Christian (among other) holy orders prohibit marriage. Religious proscription is a contentious topic, and the Hellenes were well aware of it too: They cremated their dead, and were horrified to encounter other tribes who ate their dead. As Herodotus said, "custom is king."

Those who travel from one neighborhood of the global village to another regularly confront apparently irreconcilable extremes of this kind. One April I found myself in Cairo, a city of more than twenty million, where the consumption of alcohol is mostly confined to one tiny quarter which has a few European-style restaurants with bars. Later that month I ended up in New Orleans, a city where alcohol once flowed more copiously than the mighty Mississippi (and I hope will again soon). It's extremely difficult to find a drink in Cairo at any time of day, and extremely difficult *not* to find one in New Orleans 24/7.

To reconcile these extremes, we must appeal to another virtue, namely tolerance. The voice of tolerance says three things: First, I should be free to choose to abstain from alcohol, but not free to impose my choice on you. Second, I should be free to choose to drink too much (provided I do not endanger others), but not free to impose my choice on you. Third, I should be free to choose to drink in moderation, but not free to impose my choice on you.

Among many modern metropoli, New York City evidences all kinds of tolerant extremes. You can visit fundamentalist Muslim neighborhoods in which no alcohol is sold or consumed; yet these neighborhoods do not produce intolerant extremists who blow up alcoholics to protest overconsumption, or blow up liquor stores to protest moderation. You can also visit skid rows, where tormented residents base their lives on the constant consumption of alcohol. Yet these alcoholics do not accost Muslims in the street, trying to foist drinks on them. You can also visit thousands of restaurants and millions of homes in which alcohol is moderately consumed, but not imposed. Many if not a majority of New

Yorkers drink moderately, but do not impose moderation on anyone. Moderation is freely chosen, and can be responsibly practiced. It is much more difficult to practice extremism responsibly, yet tolerant extremes are much less harmful than intolerant ones.

Alcoholics inherit or impose on themselves a devastating illness, becoming slaves of alcohol, and so cannot be trusted to act responsibly until they start recovering. Alcoholics can destroy themselves, damage their families, and kill people if they get behind the wheel. But they do not impose alcoholism on anyone, nor blow themselves up in Muslim neighborhoods to protest abstinence, nor in public places to protest moderation. Yet extremes of religious and political authority do impose abstinences on everyone, precisely because they will not tolerate moderation. That is why al-Qaeda did not target the French Quarter of New Orleans on 9/11. They were not attacking their opposite extreme, namely excess consumption of alcohol; they were attacking something much more important, namely the culture of moderation, which tolerates both extremes.

The virtue of moderation tolerates extremes that are voluntarily chosen, but which do not seek to impose themselves forcibly on others. But moderation cannot tolerate those who use moderation as a weapon against itself. Extremists do not attack our vices; rather, our virtues, such as moderation in the liberty, trust, and tolerance we accord to our fellow travelers. Moderation and tolerance themselves were the primary targets on 9/11, as they are in all such suicide bombings, big or small.

Practitioners of Buddhism from Tibet, Southeast Asia, and Japan have sought and found political refuge and creative possibility in the moderate and tolerant West. In one way (The Middle Way), Buddhism is the complement of terrorism: It views human life as a precious gift, not a vehicle of suicidal murder. In every capital city of the moderate and tolerant West—Washington, D.C.; Ottawa; London; Paris; Madrid; Lisbon; Amsterdam; Berlin; Rome; and Jerusalem among many others—you can find Buddhists chanting daily for peace. When you can find Buddhists chanting daily for peace in Casablanca, Algiers, Tripoli, Khartoum, Cairo, Damascus, Ramallah, Amman, Baghdad, Riyadh, Teheran, Islamabad, and Kabul among other places, you will know that chanting will have served more of its ultimate purpose—namely, world peace. Meanwhile, the tolerant moderation of the West owes Aristotle's golden mean a ponderable debt.

The central process in Aristotle's ethics, as mentioned, is attaining happiness by developing your potential and cultivating your excellence in accordance with moderation. This is also a hallmark of Western individualism, for it presupposes that each of us has different talents and skills, and that we attain fulfillment in life by developing our unique talents and honing our particular skills, once again in accord with virtue. Aristotle's vision of individual fulfillment necessitates tolerance of nonuniformity, and even of nonconformity in a given society, in order that people may express their individuality. He wrote: "For a carpenter and a geometer investigate the right angle in different ways; the former does so insofar as the right angle is useful for his work, while the latter inquires what it is or what sort of thing it is; for he is a spectator of the truth." How alluring are Aristotle's *Ethics*: He invites us to behold the greatest show on earth, namely truth.

Both carpenters and geometers can become fulfilled, but as their talents and interests differ, so do their instruments vary. The carpenter needs to form right angles using wood, so that he can fabricate furniture or dwellings, while the geometer needs to understand the abstract properties of right angles using ideas, so that he can fabricate theorems and proofs. The carpenter and the geometer are equal in moral worth, yet the ways in which they practice virtues differ.

## Movement Toward Moderate Reform

If Aristotle were alive today, and if he studied Western history, he would notice a gradual movement in most world religions spanning centuries, a movement from orthodoxy toward reform, from less tolerance toward more, from lesser individual liberties toward greater ones. Religious fundamentalists—of any religion—prefer to interpret their doctrines and observe their laws in strict or ultraorthodox ways. This is not a problem, as long as their liberty to do so is guaranteed by a secular political authority that also obliges them to be tolerant of religious orthodoxies different from their own, and to be tolerant of reformed believers in their own faith as well. In this context of tolerance, religious fundamentalism is orthodox but not fanatical.

It is primarily religious (and also political) fanatics who cannot tolerate beliefs that differ from their own. Fanatics are dangerously and sometimes violently intolerant of others' beliefs, while fundamentalists are passionately wed to their own beliefs but normally pose no threat to others who believe differently. I live in a county of New York State that contains communities of fundamentalist Jews, fundamentalist Christians, and fundamentalist Muslims, along with rank-and-file moderates as well as agnostics, none of whom disturb or threaten or harm the others in any way. They greet one another with respect and tolerance in public places. Beyond that, some are good neighbors to all. Aristotle would say that this is not because they are answerable to their gods in the next world; rather, because they are accountable to secular political authorities in this one, authorities whose laws grant them decent lives in this world, so they can (if they wish) consecrate themselves in peace and security to preparing for the next.

Religious reform itself has now reached the other extreme in the West, whose societies—from South America to North America to Europe—have become so liberalized that millions now have no religious faith whatsoever. This leaves them extremely vulnerable to moral anarchy on the one hand, and to political crusades on the other. Aristotle would have deplored this extreme as strongly as the other.

### Everything in Moderation?

Is every human behavior subject to Aristotle's golden mean? Does Aristotle sanction anything, provided that it's done in moderation? Of course not. After stating his rule of the golden mean, Aristotle immediately points out a number of exceptions to it—acts that can never be virtuous, even if performed moderately. Murder, theft, robbery, calumny, and adultery are among the acts proscribed by Aristotle's virtue ethics. Destroying lives in moderation, stealing or robbing in moderation, lying in moderation, committing adultery in moderation cannot be ethical in Aristotle's system. Notice how

Aristotle has anticipated or reinvented some of the rules that characterize the codes of conduct of the Abrahamic faiths, among other organized religions. The main difference is that in Aristotelian ethics—just as in Buddhist and Confucian ethics—these laws are not ordained by God, but discovered by man. This illustrates an important overlap between matters of reason and matters of faith.

Western science initiated by Aristotle, and Western religion initiated by the Abrahamic faiths, have been both allied and embattled during their long development. Christian fanaticism has time and again impeded scientific progress in Europe and America alike, and yet the alliance between the Judeo-Christian and Hellenic strands of Western civilization have produced unprecedented scientific and technological developments, unequaled by the other great civilizations. This reflects the Taoist truth that profession of strong faith and exercise of skeptical inquiry are complementary in the human being.

Cultures that place too much emphasis on religion and too little on science do not develop in pathways that permit the fullest human development. This is a problem that greatly afflicted fanaticized Christian cultures a few centuries ago in Europe, just as it afflicts fanaticized Islamic cultures today. Then again, too much emphasis on science and too little on religion produces a different kind of imbalance, resulting in exaggerated materialism and stunted spirituality. Aristotle would surely praise the alliance of faith and reason that animated the scientific genius of Isaac Newton, Charles Darwin, and Albert Einstein—each of whom believed devoutly, if increasingly unfashionably, in a higher power than human intellect. Once again, the golden mean is a useful guide to balancing these two powerful forces—faith and reason—that are always at work and often at odds in human consciousness.

Meanwhile, the virtue ethics of the ABCs coincide with the religious morality of the Abrahamic faiths in condemning harmful acts such as murder, theft, and adultery. Defining the corresponding moral rules, and their exceptions, is no easy matter.

## Fulfillment, Excellence, and Work

Aristotle's golden mean provides a moral compass by which individuals can navigate in daily life. What is the destination of such a voyage? For Aristotle, the ultimate purpose of practicing virtues is this: They help us to lead a fulfilled life. In fact, Aristotle, Buddha, and Confucius all agree on this vital point. Unlike plants and other animals, human beings have a unique capacity to attain fulfillment—a capacity beyond photosynthesizing sunlight as plants do, and satisfying appetites as animals do. But we are also capable of achieving lasting happiness, of a kind unknown to flora and fauna. In Aristotle's terms, there is a kind of "sustainable" or enduring happiness that is not dependent on external things or other persons, rather upon the refinement of personal excellence though the practice of virtue. Aristotle's word for this sustainable happiness is "eudemonia."

This kind of sustainable happiness cannot be taken from you. You can lose your family, your job, your house, your car, your possessions, even your very life itself. But you cannot lose your fulfillment. If you die fulfilled, then you have led a good life—the best life possible, according to Aristotle.

If you contemplate more shallow and transient forms of happiness, you will better appreciate Aristotelian fulfillment. If you think "happiness" means pleasure or euphoria, you are guaranteed to learn a lot about unhappiness in a short time. Most people who seek happiness through the pursuit of pleasure or euphoria become increasingly miserable. This is demonstrable in many different ways. Psychologists and economists, for example, understand it as a law of diminishing returns. Suppose you eat your favorite food for supper. It tastes great, and makes you happy. Suppose you eat it again the next night. It will taste a little less great, and make you a little less happy. If you continue in this way, your "favorite" food will soon produce no happiness at all, even though it still satisfies your physical appetite. You feel full, but unfulfilled. Beyond this, you may even start to dislike your formerly favorite food, and develop an aversion to it, because it no longer satisfies your expectations. Note that this food has not changed at all: It is your desire for it that has changed into aversion, your pleasure that has changed into displeasure, ironically through being satisfied. The moral is that getting what you want can make you very unhappy indeed.

This is also true of erotic love, and its expression in the endless cycle of human relationships that can begin so beautifully and end so badly. It is equally true of ambition, or avarice, or any appetite that needs to be sated by some means external to yourself. Temporary pleasure or euphoria can be attained this way, but it never lasts for long. Why? Because, Aristotle would explain, people who seek happiness outside themselves cannot become fulfilled in this way. Momentary pleasure is not the same as sustainable joy.

The United States is the world's most affluent nation, and yet contains some of the world's most chronically unhappy people. Why? Primarily because the American conception of happiness is profoundly non-Aristotelian. In the oft-quoted Preamble to the Constitution, Americans are guaranteed inalienable rights to "life, liberty, and the *pursuit of happiness.*" I have italicized this phrase to emphasize its flaw. Happiness is not a goal that can be pursued, any more than it's a quarry that can be hunted. On the contrary, people who pursue happiness end up catching unhappiness. Virtue and excellence lie within you, not outside you. Your fulfillment flows from cultivating these attributes, and not from chasing the mirage of happiness. Moreover, and in contrast to providential religions, the ABCs all teach that fulfillment is attainable in this life. Heaven and hell are here on earth, and in any instant you can experience the joy and peace of sustained fulfillment—or, if you prefer or insist, the torment and conflict of sustained dissatisfaction.

Being an optimist, Aristotle focused on the importance of virtuous habits, although he knew (from Socrates via Plato) that any talent can be enlisted for helpful or harmful purposes. Talent alone does not guarantee goodness. Criminals can be very skillful in the commission of hurtful crimes; for example, serial killers or mass murderers are experts in the taking of lives. But their expertise is channeled in harmful pathways. Their "expertise" is morally deplorable and usually depraved—the opposite of Aristotle's notion of *arête*—excellence and virtue.

As we have seen, Aristotle is quasi-egalitarian about this: He asserts that everyone has some talent, some excellence that can be cultivated, although he naturally realizes that no two people share exactly the same gifts, nor manifest similar talents in precisely the same ways. For example, you may be athletically inclined. If so, then Aristotle would counsel you to play a sport, or sports, in which your athletic talent can come to its fullest fruition. If you are a superbly gifted athlete, then you may find your *arête* by playing professional sports, or competing in the Olympic Games. And note the diversity of athleticism: There are many sports and games from which to choose, each reflecting a particular combination of athletic skills. Even if you are a talented amateur, you can experience fulfillment by cultivating your athletic abilities to the full. The vast majority of people who engage in sports and games are not world-class professional or Olympic athletes, yet they still experience fulfillment as talented amateurs, hobbyists, or "weekend warriors."

The same reasoning applies to any field—music, mathematics, medicine, midwifery, movie making, mowing grass, or mixing cement. While there are differences in the kinds of talents required to do these things well, there is no difference in the experience of fulfillment that comes from doing them well. It is true that Aristotle ranks the contemplative life as most conducive to sustainable happiness, and this has parallels in both Buddhist and Confucian traditions. At the same time, the ABCs all emphasize that no job is demeaning in and of itself. For example, Aristotle would value cleanliness as a virtue, and would seek a golden mean in keeping one's person groomed and one's house tidy. Living in an unkempt condition, in filthy and squalid surroundings, is a vice at one extreme. Engaging in compulsive hand washing and in constant cleaning of one's house is a vice at the other extreme. If you are fortunate enough to have a bathroom—which half the world's people still lack—then it's an Aristotelian virtue to keep it reasonably clean. Buddhists and Confucians share this view as well. Cleaning your home and taking out your trash is also meaningful work, and can be done poorly or well, carelessly or mindfully. A virtuous person strives to do things well, and mindfully.

Virtue does not lie in your job title; it lies in good performance of your job. Whatever work you undertake, you should strive to do it well. And if you are fortunate enough to love your work—that is, if the work you do draws upon and engages your particular talents—then you cannot fail to combine excellence and virtue in the performance of your duties.

Yet I meet so many people, especially in Western civilization, who say that they "hate" their jobs. This is a tragic state of affairs. Life on this planet, in human form, is largely consecrated to work. Idleness and laziness afflict rich and poor alike, as well as members of the middle classes, and such habits always produce unhappiness. Forced unemployment, which also afflicts many people from time to time, causes even greater unhappiness, often accompanied by depression or despair. Why? Aristotle would say that every human is here to fulfill a purpose in life, and that each one's purpose can be fulfilled only through cultivation of individual excellence within the shared moral compass of the golden mean. Discovering and cultivating your talent requires work. Similarly, navigating virtuous channels while eschewing vicious extremes also requires work.

So those who wind up in the so-called rat race are people who have become trapped in a system that rewards them monetarily but does not value their work. In supporting this system, they also support the devaluation of their own work. Supporting the devaluation of one's work is the opposite of cultivating one's excellence: It is the cultivation of one's worthlessness. No wonder such people are unhappy. How do people become trapped like this? There are many reasons, but among the most important is the failure to pursue or do what is most meaningful in your life, in exchange for some security or reward that seems at first to compensate you, but which soon shackles or imprisons you to a way of life that is false to your innermost excellence. This lack of fulfillment is bound to make you unhappy, or worse.

It may require considerable courage to cultivate your excellence, especially when doing so leads you to explore unknown pathways, or takes you down roads that diverge from those trod by your family, your community, your peers. For courage means more than showing bravery in times of mortal combat, natural disaster, financial risk, or other imminent danger; it also means being brave enough to be yourself in the face of familial or communal or peer pressure to conform. It requires bravery to lead your own authentic life, instead of a life mapped out for you by others. A fulfilled life is an authentic one.

So it's not an accident that courage is a both a classic virtue, dating from ancient times, and also a contemporary one. Aristotle's prescription for being courageous is to find the golden mean between the two vices on either extreme. At one extreme, a deficiency of courage is what we commonly call "cowardice." At the other extreme, an excess of courage is what we commonly call "rashness." Viewed this way, the virtue of courage really amounts to having a moderate amount of fear. Cowardly people allow themselves to become paralyzed by fear, and so they cannot act when action is necessary. Rash people tend to be fearless, and so they act when action is unwise. Brave people experience fear, but do not let fear prevent them from acting when action becomes necessary. Yet bravery also allows for caution, or prudence, to function as a brake on foolhardy or reckless actions. As Aristotle wrote,

"For the man who flies from and fears everything and does not stand his ground against anything becomes a coward, and the man who fears nothing at all but goes to meet every danger becomes rash."[5]

## The Lesser of Two Evils

Aristotle knew full well that it's not always possible to find the golden mean. Sometimes we are confronted with two options, neither of which is palatable. For example, a woman may find herself in an abusive marriage, where her children as well as herself are the targets. (Men, too, can be abused by their wives, but for the purpose of argument let us speak here of women and children.) A woman in this situation often feels trapped, because both of her main options are unpalatable. On the one hand, she may try to remain in the marriage if it can be salvaged. But then she runs the risk that she and her children will suffer long-term harms from exposure to abuse. On the other hand, she may try to escape from the abusive marriage, seeking refuge for herself and her children. But then she runs the risks of being unable to care for herself and her children, and of enduring the stigma of a failed marriage, or the recriminations of having to seek shelter with her parents.

What is Aristotle's counsel in such situations, when it is not possible to find an immediate golden mean? Naturally, the abused woman could urge her husband to seek help in changing his behavior, and that would be best for all concerned. However, this often proves difficult in practice, because patterns of abuse can be deeply ingrained and resistant to change. And if she wishes to change her situation then she must also change herself, because the abuser always depends on the complicity of the abused, and so there must be something in her character which attracted and encouraged his abuse to begin with. This is usually a two-way street.

So in cases where a golden mean between extremes cannot easily be found, and where the situation more closely resembles a dilemma, on one of whose sharp horns you must impale yourself, Aristotle suggests that you choose the lesser of the two evils. While this strategy is far from ideal, at least it minimizes the harm that you must suffer. The main obstacle to making this choice is finding a way to assess "greater" versus "lesser" evil itself. This can be a daunting prospect. Good and evil cannot be weighed on a scale, like so many fruits and vegetables. So you need to be able to make a qualitative rather than a quantitative assessment of the relative merits and demerits of your situation. To accomplish this, you may benefit from the assistance of a philosophical counselor.[6] While a philosophical practitioner will not tell you what to do, he or she will help you deliberate which choice is indeed the lesser of the two evils, as you construe them.

Now you may well ask: Having been guided to such a fruitful extent by the practice of Aristotelian virtue, are we still bound to find ourselves in situations that compel us to choose a lesser over a greater evil, instead of a greater over a lesser good? If this represents a limit to Aristotle's ethics, can we move beyond it? My answer to you is that we can move beyond this limit, and the way to do so is none other than Buddha's Middle Way, to which we turn in the next chapter.

Like Buddha and Confucius, Aristotle was optimistic about human nature. Even though our genes play dominant roles in determining physical and even psychological traits, it is clear that virtues and vices resemble good and bad habits, respectively. Good habits can be acquired; bad habits can be broken. While this is often easier said than done, it is still worth doing, and Aristotle's philosophy tells us why. As he insisted in his Ethics, "It makes no small difference, then, whether we form habits of one kind or of another from our very youth; it makes a very great difference, or rather all the difference." To what? To your enduring happiness.

## From A to B

As we have just seen, Aristotle's immense influence on Western civilization is situated primarily in the domain of reason and its cognate subjects: logic, mathematics, natural science, social science, ethics, poetics, rhetoric, politics, economics. For Aristotle, the purpose of being alive is to lead a fulfilled life, by a mixture of contemplation (philosophy, or love of wisdom) and application of the golden mean (phronesis, or practical wisdom). The golden mean applies to Aristotle's own philosophy too. Many people do not spend enough time in contemplation—whether because of pressures, duties, laziness, or lack of interest—and so their actions in the world are not always well thought out.

At one extreme of too little contemplation and too much action, I know CEOs of global corporations who work ceaselessly, leading complex organizations of tens of thousands of employees, operating in dozens or hundreds of countries. Several of these CEOs have told me that they want to be philosophers in their next lives. These CEOs are brilliant leaders who have too little time for reflection. And they know it.

But Aristotle also inveighed against the other extreme, an overly theoretical life, which neglects "phronesis," or practical wisdom. He cautioned that people who "take refuge in theory and think they are being philosophers and will become good in this way," are "behaving somewhat like patients who listen attentively to their doctors, but do none of the things they are ordered to do. As the latter will not be made well in body by such a course of treatment, the former will not be made well in soul by such a course of philosophy."[7]

So where is the golden mean between contemplation and action, theory and practice? If your mind is not sufficiently cultivated through informed contemplation, your actions may be ill-considered, and this will bring you trouble. At the other extreme, if your mind is overcultivated by thinking too much, your actions may be impractical, and this will also bring you trouble. If you seek a balance between contemplation and action, philosophy and phronesis, I believe you will find it in Buddha's Middle Way. For it is the human heart that serves to mediate between our thoughts and acts, and Buddhist practice engenders compassion without an agenda. Emotions can inspire or distort our thinking, can ennoble or debase our deeds. Yet without hearts, we would be robots. Buddha's Middle Way fine-tunes the golden mean, allowing us to think more clearly, feel more deeply, and act more wisely.

Daisaku Ikeda, a great Buddhist leader, appreciates and endorses this perspective. He says, "The cyclical application of theory and experiment that forms the basis for the modern western scientific method has indeed done much to enhance and deepen our understanding of the workings of the physical world." At the same time, he asserts that "the methods of Buddhism share a deep commonality with scientific methods." In particular, he conceives that Buddhist theories of human suffering and Buddhist practices conducive to its alleviation "can be seen as analogous to the science of medicine and its applications in clinical practice."[8] Bearing this in mind, let us now turn to Buddha's Middle Way.

# 3

## BUDDHA'S MIDDLE WAY
### Creating Value and Compassion amid Suffering

*Avoiding these two extremes [over-indulgence and asceticism] the Awakened One gains the serendipity of The Middle Way, which produces insight and knowledge, and tends to peace, to wisdom, to enlightenment, to Nirvana.* —Buddha

### Buddhism and the Philosopher's Stone

BUDDHISM CAME TO THE WEST with a long and rich history in tow, having voyaged across centuries and continents before venturing onto Western shores. So Westerners initially viewed Buddhism through the lens of Western philosophies and cultures. Yet it swiftly became a lens through which Westerners can better view their own philosophies and cultures. To begin, let us see how Buddha's Middle Way furthers the Aristotelian golden mean, in terms of perfecting human thought and deed.

There is no end to knowing. Reliable knowledge is like a sphere that grows in volume as human understanding progresses. At any time in history, the surface of our sphere of understanding represents the boundary between the known and the unknown. The more we come to know, the bigger the sphere of reliable knowledge becomes. But then its surface also becomes ever bigger, and touches ever more of the unknown. Therefore the more we come to know, the more we realize how much we don't know. For every question science answers, it raises many more. Clearly, there is no end to knowing. So the human being cannot be completed, or completely fulfilled, through knowledge alone.

The same is true of actions: There is no end to what needs to be done in the world. Once you leave early childhood, you come to realize that you can only accomplish so much in one day. If you look around your home or office, you can always find something that needs to be done. The same is true of your neighborhood, your community, your city, your region, your nation, your continent, and the entire global village. Yet there is an end to every working day. Sooner or later, we have to stop, even if the job is unfinished. And being only human, we cannot work like machines. Yet the work is never done. No one expects that it ever will be, so many people sensibly strive "to make a difference." And one day each of us will retire, and work less than we used to. And one day each of us will expire, and cease working in this world. There is an end to each of us, yet no end to the world's work. So the human being cannot be completed, or completely fulfilled, through action alone—any more than by knowledge alone.

But if fulfillment in the Aristotelian sense is not completely achievable, how can we become fulfilled as human beings in this life? If there is no end to thoughts, no end to actions, and no end to emotions, then where does fulfillment lie? The Abrahamic faiths and the Vedic religions have all answered this question in terms of external powers and future lives. Jews rely on God to help them, and the Messiah to redeem them. Christians rely on God to father them, and Jesus to save them. Muslims rely on Allah to will for them, and Mohammed to guide them. Hindus rely on a pantheon of deities to nurture them, and on the Trimurti to create, sustain, annihilate, reincarnate, and absorb them. Some Buddhists rely on Buddha to liberate them, and on his incarnations to help them. But Buddha himself maintained that each person's complete fulfillment lies within, and is not dependent on any supernatural power or future life. Buddha taught that you hold the keys to your own redemption, salvation, guidance, nurture, absorption, and liberation.

Many Western philosophers have discovered vital pieces of Buddha's puzzle, like so many tiles of a mosaic. Perhaps this helps explain why Buddhism has met with such a warm philosophical reception in the West, for Buddhism assembles these pieces into a coherent whole. Unlike Buddha, most Western philosophers maintained belief in the supremacy of reason alone, and the discovery of reliable knowledge, as the solver of human problems and the arbiter of human conflicts. The power of reason has been indispensable for science and technology, discovery and invention, yet Western philosophers paid insufficient attention to the desires, attachments, and aversions that cloud human thought and haunt human action. By contrast, attentiveness to turbulence in the psyche is a departure point for Indian philosophy. By stilling the turbulent mind, we open gateways to insight and fulfillment. Mind is not stilled by Aristotelian contemplation alone: That requires reliable practice in addition to clear thinking.

So here are but a few fragments of Buddhist thought that one can discern in the works of great Western philosophers. Plato understood that people tend to inhabit dark caves of delusion, and must find ways out of the cave and into the bright light of reality. But Plato gave no reliable method for doing so; his Academy produced the Tyrants of Athens. Epicurus was prominent among the ancients for recognizing philosophy as medicine for the soul; yet he did not hand down the specific formula for making that medicine. Epictetus, the worthy Roman Stoic, rightly observed that "People are not disturbed by circumstances, but by the views they take of them." Yet Epictetus did not teach any reliable method—beyond effective thought—for cultivating a more serene perspective on life's trials and tribulations. The Roman proconsul Boethius wrote *The Consolation of Philosophy* while awaiting execution on death row; yet he could not transport himself into a state of being that needed no consoling. The British empiricist George Berkeley discovered that all existence depends upon a perceiving mind, but did not extend his doctrine to consider the existence and extinction of human suffering. The British empiricist David Hume discovered that personal identity—the "ego" that is central to Freudian psychoanalysis and much Western psychology—is a kind of fiction. Yet

Hume could not apply this discovery to the alleviation of his own personal suffering. The German rationalist Immanuel Kant said that the sole definition of goodness is "a good will." Kant prescribed elegant principles, but no exercises for willing "well" instead of "ill." French existentialists like Jean-Paul Sartre, Simone de Beauvoir, and Albert Camus recognized that our liberty and authenticity require us to assume responsibility for our lives, but they did not describe any concrete practices that would help us "take charge." Postmodern moralist Emmanuel Levinas understood that we are all interconnected, and that the very existence of others imposes moral obligations upon us. Yet Levinas taught no practical exercises that would elevate moral consciousness. The New England transcendentalists, epitomized by Ralph Waldo Emerson and Henry David Thoreau, discovered that communing with nature is an effective way to appreciate the precious gift of life. Yet even they were less than clear about unlocking the full potential of this gift.

So credit Western philosophers for knowing that there is something "out there"—they used to call it the "philosopher's stone"—that can transform the human soul. The Hellenics probably heard of it via India, as did later the Roman Catholic Church, which officially "abolished" the doctrine of reincarnation only in the sixth century C.E. But Christian mystics continued to hunt for the philosopher's stone, and their searches gave rise to alchemy, a very respectable calling at one time. The philosopher's stone was itself transformed into the Holy Grail of the Crusades, which perhaps one knight in a thousand sincerely sought above plunder. But this accounts for the "good sorcerer" in Camelot: Merlin the wizard was an alchemist (and therefore also a philosopher), and tutor to young Arthur. Thomas Hobbes, a philosopher of incandescent wit, wanted for his epitaph, "Here lies the true philosopher's stone." Sir Isaac Newton, renowned for his physics, also wrote a book on alchemy. And so it goes. What were they all seeking? What is this "philosopher's stone"? It might be none other than Buddha's Middle Way.

Buddha's philosophy weaves a tapestry of theory and practice that represents the highest aspirations of humanity. The genius of Buddha is that he saw deeper and went further than any philosopher—Western or Eastern, Aristotelian or Confucian—in developing comprehensible and reliable methods for attaining complete fulfillment in this very life. Unlike the Abrahamic faiths, Buddha taught that the fulfilling power lies within every human being, and not outside them. Unlike the Indian schools that he reformed, Buddha taught that enlightenment—awakening, compassion, serenity—is attainable by anyone. Thus Buddha not only made suffering unnecessary to human existence, he also declared it unnecessary to expect to suffer through ten, a hundred, a thousand, or a million deaths and rebirths before attaining ultimate consciousness, as so many millions have suffered, are suffering, and believe they must suffer.

## Buddha's Reform of Indian Philosophy: The Middle Way 101

Siddhartha Gautama, or Buddha, was himself a kind of extremist at different periods of his life, and he discovered that extremes did not help him become an awakened being. He was born into a ruling family, his father being a raj (or king) of Kapilavastu, in northern India. A soothsayer had warned his family not to allow the young prince to come into contact with aged or infirm people, but he could not be isolated indefinitely within the palace gates. So it came to pass that as a young married man and a father, Siddhartha accidentally encountered an extremely aged woman, bent and disfigured by the ravages of time and illness. (Some say he encountered a corpse.) It suddenly dawned on him that all living beings are born, age, and die, and moreover that we all suffer along the way. Struck by this revelation—"Life is a bitch, and then you die"—Siddhartha aspired to experience a serene consciousness, to get off that carousel of sufferings—strife, sorrow, grief, lamentation, despair, regret, sickness, death—that humans are born riding, and that too many die still riding.

Moreover, Siddhartha was unsatisfied with the explanations he inherited from Indian philosophy and theology, which were already well developed by the fifth century B.C.E. In particular, he did not believe it necessary to cycle through millions of incarnations on that long and winding cosmic road of spiritual development, toward eventual union with the Godhead. Like Aristotle and Confucius, Buddha insisted that the purpose of being alive is fully realizable in this lifetime. Contrary to the deeply ingrained religious conventions in his civilization (which still persist today), Buddha did not see a lifetime of suffering as a necessary or worthy preparation for anything better.

So Siddhartha renounced the extreme comfort and lavish material security of his palace and his princedom and set out on a path of awakening. At first he went from one extreme to the other, from the princely life to that of a wandering pilgrim, a possessionless beggar. Having renounced everything material, he went even further, practicing extremes of ascetic denial: solitude, fasting, penance. He eventually realized that these extremes of renunciation and mortification were bringing him no closer to his goal than had the earlier extremes of luxury and indulgence. Ultimately, by age forty, after years of princely self-indulgence followed by years of arduous religious asceticism, Siddhartha became fully enlightened while sitting under a bodhi tree. "Buddha" means "awakened one." Thus awakened—to the true causes and cures of human suffering—Buddha spent the remaining forty years of his life teaching others the theory and practice of his Middle Way.

In his celebrated sermon at Benares, Buddha asserted that extremes of wealth and of poverty do not conduce, in and of themselves, to attaining enlightenment. Those who spend too much time and expend too much energy accumulating things are likely to be hampered by their accumulation, and to suffer accordingly. Those who spend too much time and expend too much energy renouncing things are also likely to be hampered by their renunciation, and to suffer accordingly. These extremes are richly illustrated in the unhappiness we see in the materialistic West, and among practitioners of fanaticized religions. Materialists who pursue pleasure and profit above all else remain unhappy. Religious fanatics who pursue denial of modernism above all else remain unhappy. American hedonism overproduces and overconsumes; religious fanaticism underproduces and underconsumes. Each accuses the other of evil. Each sees the other's extremism, yet each is blind to its own. Buddha's Middle Way helps us avoid these extremes, by the practice of moderation in our own lives, and of compassion for the sufferings of others. Buddha teaches how not to use our differences as the basis of negative attachments such as hatred.

What is Buddha's Middle Way? It is not, as many Westerners suppose, a weak or "middle-of-the-road" compromise. As Daisaku Ikeda explains, the essence of The Middle Way is "reverence for the sanctity of life—one's own life, the lives of other people, the life of non-human nature and all its extensive and intricate interrelations—coupled with the determination to make this reverence the basis for all one's actions . . . when the value of human dignity and life is accorded this kind of centrality, there can be no question of compromise or accommodation with forces of destruction and divisiveness that would threaten life or undermine our humanity."[1]

So how can we be uncompromising yet nonviolent? As Daisaku Ikeda further explains, "But to be uncompromising does not mean labeling the other as 'enemy' and engaging in open-ended conflict. Rather, it means seeking to identify those specific aspects within a philosophical, religious or cultural tradition that support or justify the denigration or violent destruction of life, and striving to transform those toward nonviolence. The only truly effective means to do this is dialogue, based on a firm recognition of our mutual humanity, and guided by an unflinching commitment to the ideal of harmonious coexistence."[2] Yet to coexist harmoniously with others, you must also "coexist" harmoniously with yourself.

This is why Buddha begins with the Four Noble Truths, which contain the theory and practice of such harmonious coexistence, both personally and interpersonally. These truths differ sharply from religious beliefs. They are not "revealed" truths of scripture, which require faith in supernatural powers, and which immediately divide humanity into endlessly conflicting groups of "believers" versus "unbelievers." On the contrary, Buddha's truths are simple facts of life, that you can reconfirm for yourself in everyday experience, and which unite humanity by identifying the fundamental problem of human existence—namely suffering—and its solution. Buddha's philosophy is both rational and empirical; that is, scientific. So you can test it for yourself.

Buddha's first truth is that life entails suffering. Jews suffer. Christians suffer. Muslims suffer. Hindus suffer. Buddhists suffer. Confucians suffer. Agnostics suffer. Atheists suffer. Men, women, and children suffer. Animals suffer. On every continent, in every region, in every city, town, or village, in every home or office, in every occupation, in every stage of life, and in every mind, you will sooner or later encounter acute or chronic human suffering. Suffering is an undeniable truth of human existence. Yet Buddha does not assert that we are condemned to suffer; he observes that we manage to find ways to suffer nonetheless. Everybody can make a list of their sufferings. Go ahead and make your own list. What are the worst things that you have suffered in the past? What are the worst things that you are suffering now? Have some of the formerly best things in your life ironically become some of the current worst ones? Now expand your mind, and ask some of your family members, friends, or colleagues whether they too can list their sufferings. Of course they can, just as you can. Many people suffer in solitude, or in silence. The First Truth breaks down those barriers, and unites us in our awareness of the universality of human suffering. This prepares us for the next steps: understanding suffering's causes and cures.

Buddha's second truth is that suffering has causes. Man is a supremely rational animal and has always been interested in causes and effects. If you recall your own childhood, or if you have children, or spend time as an educator, you know how fascinated children are by how things work, and curious to know why things are as they are. Attempts to make sense of the world, to deepen our understanding of the causes and effects of all it contains, gave rise to religion and science alike. Whether you believe the universe was created by God, or emerged from the big bang, or both, you maintain that some cause brought about this cosmic effect. The universe is a gargantuan causal nexus, in which we can identify and try to understand myriad causal processes, on every conceivable scale. All phenomena are subject to laws of cause and effect. Each of the cycles of human suffering—strife, sorrow, grief, lamentation, despair, regret, sickness, and death—has its cause.

Buddha's third truth is that the causes of suffering can be removed. Suffering afflicts everyone, yet is neither inevitable nor necessary. That which is born inevitably dies, but does not necessarily suffer. The sufferings to which humans are heir cease when their causes are removed. Not only do they cease; their cessation opens the Way to experiencing their opposites. Cessation of strife makes way for harmony; of sorrow, for happiness; of grief, for joy; of lamentation, for celebration; of despair, for hope; of regret, for fulfillment. Everything is fleeting and impermanent, yet when the causes of suffering are removed, then equanimity endures.

So how do you remove the causes of your suffering? Buddha's fourth truth is a set of explicit practices for accomplishing this task. While the first three truths are somewhat theoretical, the fourth is entirely practical. It is often called the eightfold way, because there are eight interwoven strands of practice for diminishing suffering. These eight are: right view, right intention, right speech, right action, right livelihood, right effort, right mindfulness, right concentration. "Right view" means understanding suffering and its causes and cures. "Right intention" is maintaining good and harmless will, instead of ill and harmful will, toward oneself and others. "Right speech" means understanding the power of our words, for better or worse, upon ourselves and others—slander and gossip and untruth should be especially avoided. "Right action" is doing most things in moderation, but also refraining from taking life, from taking what is not offered, and from taking sexual liberties of various kinds. "Right livelihood" means earning one's living in helpful—rather than harmful—ways. "Right effort" is approaching challenges, opportunities, and obstacles in constructive and not destructive ways. "Right mindfulness" means cultivating presence of mind, alertness and awareness of your body, your emotions, your thoughts, and your environment—the opposite of somnambulating through life. "Right concentration" means developing one's mental powers of attentiveness, visualization, insight, and compassion, which also lead to serenity and equanimity.

Note that the eightfold path neither mentions nor requires belief in supernatural beings (i.e., gods), sacred scriptures, afterlives (e.g., heaven and hell), reincarnations, or rituals. This is Buddha's dramatic reform of the orthodox Indian schools. Buddha reaffirmed the central doctrine that all human suffering originates from cravings and desires, appetites and aversions; yet he denied the necessity of suffering through innumerable lifetimes before attaining liberation. Instead he insisted that anyone could transcend sorrow at any time, via the eightfold way. He taught that all human beings are Buddhas—men and women alike— and that we struggle, persevere, and progress through different stages of awakening. What unites humanity is neither supreme deities nor divine souls: It is our shared capacity to become fully awakened beings.

This is both the most radical and also the most profound statement of human equality ever made, especially in the context of Indian culture. The Indian caste system—in Buddha's day as today—condemns hundreds of millions of people to lead predefined lives, dictated to them at and by birth. A noble birth is supposedly a reward for "good karma"; a lowly birth, an opportunity to serve in a diminished capacity, and so to merit a better birth next time. This Indian perspective is patient, good humored, and long suffering. Orthodox Indian philosophy views millions of reincarnations as the normal journey that a soul makes, as an embodied divinity (atman) seeking reunion with the cosmic oversoul (Brahman). In this process, one mere lifetime, more or less, is utterly negligible. And so in India, one sees hundreds of millions of lives being led in socioeconomic deprivation, and yet with abundant spiritual wealth. It is part of the paradox of India.

Buddha's reform changed the meaning of karma for many Indians, and subsequently for people worldwide. He reinterpreted karma, shifting its focus from fated reincarnation to willed liberation. Orthodox Indian philosophy says: This present life, to which you are fated, is the result of all the past lives you have led. Buddha's philosophy says: This present moment, which you willed for yourself, is the result of all the past moments you have willed. This is a powerful and empowering insight. You can change your thoughts, speech, and deeds—and therefore your life—in this very moment. Making such changes has immediate effects, not only on you, but on others with whom you interact. Of course there are short-term, medium-term, and long-term effects of willing, so making major changes to your life, or to a difficult situation in the world, may require time, effort, and perseverance. But the power of will should never be underestimated. Buddhism contains great practical insight into refining and directing willpower toward benevolent ends.

In the Orthodox Indian system you must passively submit to your fate and do your duty to merit a better life next time. Being dutiful can be noble, and it certainly allows many people to bear enormous hardship cheerfully. But it also exacerbates rather than alleviates suffering. In Buddha's system you actively will your future, by virtue of what you think, say, and do in the present. This is liberating, at least for those who are ready to accept responsibility for their lives and their suffering.

Liberty and responsibility go hand in glove, both in Buddha's ancient philosophy and in modern civic virtue. As long as you are content to blame others for your discontents, as long as you refuse to accept the proper measure of responsibility for your unhappiness, you will not be liberated from your suffering. But as soon as you begin to understand the role that your own view, intention, speech, action, livelihood, effort, mindfulness, and concentration play in the production of your suffering, then you become free to produce the next moment according to your willingness to suffer, or not to suffer. In other words, Buddha's teachings put you in charge of your life. And while that was a radical reform for the sixth century B.C.E., it remains as profound and applicable today as it was then.

This is partly why Buddhism is more than a religion. Every other religion depends upon an external power for salvation or redemption. But Buddhism depends upon no external powers, no immortal souls, no supernatural worlds, no divine interventions. Instead, it mobilizes resources that lie within every human being. Certainly, Buddhism has teachers and sutras to help illuminate The Middle Way. But that Way already lies within you, and Buddhism awakens you to it.

## Theravada and Mahayana; Samsara and Nirvana
Like his contemporaries Socrates and Confucius, Siddhartha wrote

nothing down himself, and depended on devoted students and disciples to record, preserve, and transmit his teachings. This they did, developing and building not only on Buddha's reforms, but also on the rich legacy of Indian yogas, predating Buddha by centuries, that teach effective techniques for regulating breathing, posture, and mental states. This is where Buddha's Middle Way outstrips Aristotle's golden mean and Confucius's balanced order: Buddha's tradition is not focused primarily on rational contemplation or social harmony; rather, it offers a set of effective practices that flow from its theory, that are accessible to all, and that have a demonstrable impact on one's ability to contemplate rationally and socialize harmoniously.

As with the Abrahamic faiths, the religious manifestations of Buddhism are quite sectarian. The main historical bifurcation is between Theravada and Mahayana Buddhists. Theravada is more traditional. It accepts all the foundations of Buddha's teachings, and their elaborations in the Pali Canon—a dozen times more voluminous than the Old and New Testaments together. The goal of Theravada Buddhism is personal liberation from suffering. Its practice gradually assumed the form of a monastic religion, inclining toward the kind of asceticism that Buddha himself decried. Theravada Buddhism is practiced mostly in southern India, Sri Lanka, Thailand, and Myanmar.

Mahayana Buddhism, which developed thanks to Nagarjuna from about the first century C.E. onward, sought to reinterpret and popularize Buddha's teachings, to make them more accessible to all, and more applicable to everyday life. Buddha blazed the trail of The Middle Way; Nagarjuna paved it.[3] For this reason Mahayana has been compared (by some Indian philosophers) to the Protestant Reformation. Mahayana Buddhists assert that personal liberation cannot endure as long there are suffering beings in the world. We are all interconnected, so the more awakened you become the more attuned you become to the sufferings of others. Mahayana Buddhists strive patiently and sincerely to liberate all sentient beings from suffering. Mahayana Buddhism evolved most significantly in Tibet, China, and Japan—and is now spreading throughout the West.

Samsara and nirvana are ancient terms in Indian philosophy that were adopted by Buddha as well. In the twentieth century, these terms penetrated the vocabularies of Western languages too. Samsara is the wheel of suffering, to which unawakened humans are fettered by the cravings of their grasping minds. It is also the sea of sorrow, which must be traversed in order to reach the far shore of liberation. Nirvana is a complement (in the Taoist sense), not a polar opposite, of Samsara. Christians and Theravada Buddhists tend to conceptualize nirvana as a kind of Heaven, to which they must earn admission. Mahayana Buddhism teaches that nirvana is not separate from samsara (there are no separate realities); rather, that it is a state of coolness that results from extinguishing the flames of unwholesome craving.

This concept is not as unfamiliar to Westerners as you might think. In fact, you probably refer to it, indirectly, every day. Being "cool" is good; calling something or someone "cool" is one of the highest compliments that Westerners can pay. "Cool" is not available in stores, or online, at any price. It is not a commodity than you can buy or sell. It is a state of mind that radiates through your physical being and resonates in the minds of others, who receive its vibrations and respond to them. Being cool cannot be forced or contrived. If you try to be cool, you will almost certainly fail. Being cool seems spontaneous and effortless—and it is, once you have done the work. If you practice "cooling" your mind down, you will become cool without even noticing. Buddhist practice is a great way—The Middle Way—and probably the best way to achieve coolness. Very rarely do you see well-practiced Buddhists lose their cool.

Samsara is an overheated state of mind, in which people irradiate themselves and others with selfishness, hatred, turmoil, confusion, conflict, retaliation, and grievance. Entire cultures can become overheated, which causes correspondingly more suffering. But as you become cooler, you reduce your "emissions" from overheated mind-states. Becoming cooler is good for you—health-wise and karma-wise—and has another benefit too. Cooling the mind also warms the heart, and increases one's capacity to love in unselfish and nonpossessive ways. Buddhists develop great compassion. Once you stop transmitting your suffering into your environment, you will become more highly attuned and receptive to the sufferings of others, without being hurt by them yourself. By reducing your dysfunctional Samsaric mode, as an emitter of suffering onto other people, you will enhance your functional nirvanic mode, as an absorber of suffering from other people, without suffering more yourself. You can do yourself and others a power of good right here and now, without hope or fear, without salvation or damnation, without dogma or fanaticism, without souls or gods. You can do it by practicing The Middle Way. Even a few minutes per day of practice will make a huge difference in your life, and in the lives of those around you.

That's why Buddhism is not only more than a religion, and also more than a philosophy: It is in fact a science for living and dying as well as humanly possible. Like every science, Buddhism has theories and methods, akin to scientific hypotheses that can be tested by experiments. And like every reputable science, Buddhism's laws are universal, and the results of its experiments are reproducible by anyone at any time.

## More on The Middle Way

Mahayana Buddhism sprang from the vibrant philosophical culture of India, which had deliberated many of the problems and paradoxes of Western philosophy only centuries earlier. Buddha was well aware of these issues, and found a way to transcend most of them, both through sophisticated dialectics and by effective practices. For example, Western philosophers and theologians have for centuries debated the question of free will versus determinism—as if one negates the other.

What we do with our desires and passions is the key question: Will we channel them constructively or destructively? Harmlessly, or harmfully? By choice, or by fate? Saint Augustine believed that Adam and Eve were made sinful by God, and had no choice but to succumb to temptation in the Garden of Eden. The doctrine of original sin— that human sin originated with Adam and Eve, and all humans are born sinful—still holds sway over more than a billion people. With theological sin comes psychological guilt, and many associated lifelong torments.[4]

Buddha rejected overly deterministic views of human behavior, but accepted necessarily lawful processes in nature. In Buddhist thought, liberty and necessity are connected. This view, rediscovered by modern philosophers in the wake of Aristotelian science, is called "compatibilism," because it holds that free will is compatible with laws of nature. The planets, for example, have no choice in the paths of their orbits. Thanks to discoveries by Johannes Kepler, Newton, and Einstein, we can confidently assert that the solar system's motion is governed by laws of physics. But what about your "orbit"? You may arise and commute to work at approximately the same time every day, but you never traverse precisely the same space in the same amount of time. Your equations of motion are impossible to write down, and not just because of their complexity. It's because you yourself don't know in advance every move you're going to make. You presumably exercise many degrees of freedom, within the regularity and habits of your schedule. Your body obeys biophysical and biochemical laws that you don't even know about, just as the planets obey Kepler's Laws without knowing them.

But you do more than the planets: You make choices. You choose the duration and temperature of your shower, within limits set by the system. You choose what to wear and what to eat for breakfast, again within systemic limits. You choose which route to travel, or which train to catch, again within systemic constraints. But you constantly exercise your will. Anyone can calculate where the planets will be at this exact time in the next millennium. No one can calculate where you will be five minutes from now. That's presumably because you exercise some freedom of choice in the matter, which includes improvisation and spontaneity.

However, freedom of choice does not mean liberty to evade the consequences of choice. Suppose you want to exit a building. You may choose to jump off the roof, but you are not exempt from the laws of gravity. If you choose to jump, you will necessarily fall. The same is true of all our thoughts, words, and deeds: We are free to choose them within our systemic constraints, but not free to evade their necessary consequences. Moreover, as humans we are even free to choose some of our systemic constraints themselves—such as legislated laws, public policies, social mores. Our patterns of thought, speech, and deed are heavily influenced by our cultural conventions and not merely by biological necessities. (We will see many examples of this later.) But what we think, say, and do largely determines our paths through life— and therefore our life experience itself. This is an organic feedback mechanism, for better or worse. More than any human endeavor, more than any career, avocation, profession, or religion, the practice of Buddhism fosters positive feedback loops, and eschews negative ones. Why? Because The Middle Way helps us practice the things that matter most.

If you also happen to believe that there's no such thing as a free lunch, or if you're just a healthy skeptic, you may ask, "So what's the catch? If Buddhism's so great, how come there are relatively few Buddhists in the world?" The broad answers to this question lie in history and cultural evolution. We will turn to some of them soon. The short answers lie in quality and responsibility. Since Buddhism is more than a religion, its success does not depend on the quantity of adherents, but rather on the quality of adherence. A small number of Buddhists can do a lot of good in the world, just as a small number of terrorists can do a lot of harm. But it's not necessarily a bad thing that there aren't more Buddhists in the world. Buddhists themselves don't seem too preoccupied with their numbers. Not one Buddhist has ever knocked on my door unexpectedly, or accosted me on a street corner, trying to convince me to "convert."

Being more than a religion, Buddhism does not need to proselytize to convey its message. It does not need to enlist missionaries to attract a following. Buddhists need only make their music: Dharma (teachings and duties) plays upon the deepest strings of common human experience. As a lighthouse attracts ships trying to navigate treacherous shoals to a safe harbor, so Buddhism attracts adherents similarly trying to navigate life's shoals.

But then (as always) comes "the catch"; not catch-22—more like catch-$\varphi$. You must learn to become your own beacon. The lighthouse is within you, not without you. Many people, perhaps a majority, are not ready to accept that much responsibility for their lives and livelihoods. People who believe they are unaccountable for what they think, say, and do—because they believe in cosmic fate, divine will, or victimology—have the potential to suffer greatly, and to cause great suffering around them. At best they remain unfulfilled, because they are leading someone else's version of their lives. At worst, they wreak havoc on themselves and others. This is a negative feedback loop, caused by *avidya,* or blind ignorance of karmic laws. The biggest havoc wreakers seem to have the smallest understanding of Buddhism. That's not a coincidence. The Middle Way makes people more aware of their accountability for thought, speech, and deed, which leads to better consequences for them, and to everyone who networks with them. This is a positive feedback loop.

Even so, I have been involved with assorted Buddhist communities, in various capacities including retreats, and have observed that a significant proportion of participants are seeking psychological help— often some kind of psychotherapy from the resident lama, roshi, or sensei—as contrasted with the philosophical self-sufficiency that Buddhist practice inculcates. Private audiences with meditation masters are usually occasions for receiving guidance on your current practice, not psychotherapy for your past traumas. Yet it is clear that some people become attracted to Buddhism for the same reasons that they are attracted to organized religions: They seek an "answer" to, or "refuge" from, their psychological issues. I use "answer" in quotes because Buddhist psychology begins where Western psychotherapy ends, so not everyone is ready for it. I use "refuge" in quotes because Buddhism offers no escape whatsoever from human problems; rather, it courageously yet nonconfrontationally meets them and their true causes head-on.

## Impermanence, Momentariness, and Emptiness

Many Westerners seem to find Buddhism quite scary. Why? Because most people sail through life in search of some external lighthouse that will guide them to a safe harbor. People seek safe, solid ground, yet they get shipwrecked on life's shoals and end up in the water. By then it's too late for the lighthouse: They need someone to throw them a life preserver. You can't convince a drowning person that his life preserver is "within." Yet Buddhism makes us aware of the impermanence of all phenomenas—careers, marriages, families, identities, houses, cars, fortunes, American Dreams. None of these things is safe, secure, or solid. So the "search for the safe harbor" is like the "pursuit of happiness"—it cannot be realized. Paradoxically perhaps, but only when you realize that there is no "safe harbor" outside yourself can you find it within.

Even worse, Buddhism also teaches us to experience the momentary nature of all these phenomena. Not only are they impermanent, they also have no continuous existence. Just like quantum particles, neon lights, and Web pages, they flash in and out of being. Some things appear to persist more than others in space and time—a rock lasts longer than a rose—but that is only because the rock changes more slowly than the rose. Neither of them is solid matter—anyone can learn this from physics. Both are flashing in and out of existence—anyone can learn this from Buddhism. It is difficult for us to perceive the empty space that makes up most of the rock. But we humans are uniquely gifted to experience the emptiness between our momentary perceptions of the rock.

If you watch a movie, your perceptual system continuously misinforms you about its discontinuity. The human eye cannot distinguish more than twenty-four frames per second; anything greater appears continuous, even though it is only a sequence of discrete images. If you look at the filmstrip or digital file itself, you will see a sequence of still images, each one slightly different from the previous one. What's between them? Nothing. Nada. Niente. Rien. Emptiness. But without the emptiness between frames, there would be no frames. So the nonexistent and imperceptible parts of the movie are essential to the existent and perceptible parts. Each frame flashes in and out of momentary existence, yet together they appear to tell a continuous story. Where is the apparent continuity? Where is the story? In your mind perhaps, but not in the filmstrip.

Now make the mental transition from film to everyday life, and you can appreciate the same phenomenon at work. Everything you perceive is flashing in and out of momentary existence, subject to laws of change. A bowl of fruit, a landscape, a human life, a galaxy—all are sequences of momentary existences. Each momentary existence is different from the previous one, yet together they appear continuous. Our minds manufacture this apparent continuum, and then project myths and other stories upon it: narratives about the beginnings and endings of things and of beings, and about the changes they go through. Yet by becoming aware of the emptiness between moments of existence, we better understand existence itself. And this is a great benefit of Buddha's Middle Way: It helps us balance existence and nonexistence. Westerners tend to fear nonexistence. But by learning to embrace it, you can manage your existence better too.

The Middle Way goes deeper still: It leads us to understand that experiences themselves are empty.[5] We fill them with emotions, judgments, and other mental formations; we project properties on them that do not belong to them, only to us. For example, suppose you were in a car accident, or survived some other kind of life-threatening accident or illness. Or suppose you attended the funeral of a beloved family member or friend. Or suppose you attended a graduation, or wedding, or performance that featured a beloved family member or friend. Many people describe such experiences as "emotional." Time and again, they use these exact words: "It was an emotional experience." What do they mean? They mean that they felt strong emotions during the experience, or when recollecting it, or that this experience (or its recollection) stimulated strong emotions in them. They may be full of emotions, but the external experience itself is empty. A brush with death might elicit fear, terror, panic, regret, resistance, resignation, exhilaration, celebration, revelation, tranquillity, epiphany, or equanimity. These things are all in us. The external "experience" is empty.

So then what? So then we practice observing our thoughts and feelings, which arise and vanish, flicker in and out of existence, much faster than rocks and roses. They are empty too, just like our self-conceptions. So what remains of us? Only the impartial observer, the one who remains without judgment, who is also empty. And this is what scares intelligent people about Buddhism: that its practice will lead them to confront the impermanence and momentariness of all phenomenas, and ultimately the illusoriness of their cherished "selfhood." Yet it is precisely the maintenance of this illusory self, the "ego" that Western psychology finds so indispensable, that lies near the root of human suffering. Get rid of your ego, and you get rid of your suffering. Most psychotherapies don't help you get rid of your ego; they shelter it and feed it and pet it, like a stray animal. Naturally the ego resists dissolution—it is addicted to being sheltered, fed, and petted, and it clamors most loudly when it is ignored. Buddhist practice dissolves your ego, allowing your Buddha nature to emerge.

Paradoxically, most people are terrified of nothingness. Yet nothing and everything are complements. The "substantial" universe appears to have emerged from nothingness, and most of the energy embedded in the universe today is inaccessible to us, stored in the cosmic vacuum. So even though everything is empty, from this emptiness springs fullness. And from the emptiness of your Buddha nature springs boundless understanding and inexhaustible compassion. But to get in touch with your emptiness, you must be willing to assume the responsibility of seeing through the charade of fullness, permanence, continuity, security, and solidity.

### Where Buddha Went

Every step on the eightfold path is accompanied by a vast body of teachings (sutras) and practices (yogas), developed and reinterpreted over many centuries by great masters from diverse cultures and different civilizations. At every stage of Buddhist practice you will find brilliant texts and sagacious guides to help you. As the Chinese say, "When the student is ready, the teacher will appear." The history of Buddhism is unfinished, and has a long way to go. As we have seen, Buddha himself reformed a deeply philosophical tradition—the combined schools of Indian philosophy—that were already millennia into their own development. But his reforms created something more, a Middle Way that has touched and changed the lives of peoples all over the world.

Unlike the Abrahamic faiths, Buddhism did not and does not rely directly on political conquest to take root and flower. True, the legendary King Asoka apparently converted himself and his realm to Buddhism, just as legions of monarchs later imposed Christianity or Islam upon themselves and their subjects. But Asoka was the exception, not the rule, for Buddhism. And true too, once Buddhism was established as a state or regional religion, its clergy could become corrupted by political power and—just as with all the Abrahamic faiths—could perpetrate or abet deeds that their scriptures forbade and their founders abhorred. This happened for example in thirteenth-century Japan, where corrupted and counterproductive forms of state-sponsored Buddhism were reformed by Nichiren—much as Jesus reformed the Judaism of the Second Temple, and Martin Luther reformed the Roman Catholic Church. In the main, however, Buddhism spread neither via political imposition nor by religious coercion, but by fruitful philosophical transplanting into the soils of diverse cultures. Because of the universality of Buddha's Middle Way and its ability to touch what is truly human in us all, Buddhism is acceptable and palatable to peoples of all religious persuasions, and of none. Because Buddha's Middle Way and its practice does not require enemies or infidels, as so many religions seem to require, Buddhism makes friends and adherents everywhere it travels. It has adapted amazingly well to the soils of many cultures, has transformed them and been transformed by them, and yet retains its essence in them all. The Middle Way is a wonder of the human world.

Buddha's teachings wove themselves back into the rich philosophical tapestry of Indian culture, reacquiring notions that Buddha himself had disparaged—such as reincarnation, idolatry, and other trappings of the supernatural. In its Theravada forms, Buddhism spread throughout southern India, Sri Lanka, and Southeast Asia. It also went north, into Tibet, where it took root and flowered in the indigenous religion of Bon. Tibet eventually became the world's longest-lived Mahayana Buddhist theocracy, ruled by successive Dalai Lamas, whose monastic lineages developed some of the most advanced yogas known to human beings.

Buddhism first arrived in China around 67 C.E. via the trade routes that connected China to India and the Middle East. Buddhism swiftly germinated in the nutritive philosophical matrix of Taoist and Confucian traditions. Much enamored of the Buddhist teachings that had reached them, and their appetites whetted for more, generations of Chinese monks and scholars undertook uncharted, arduous, and perilous journeys to northern India, importing, translating, and reinterpreting sutra upon sutra. So the Chinese patiently, laboriously, and often erroneously pieced together their own versions of the extraordinarily complex jigsaw puzzle of Buddhist theory and practice, further developing them as they went.

The Bodhidharma brought Dhyana Buddhism from India to China in the sixth century C.E. It was called Chan in China, and later Zen in Japan. So profound was the cumulative impact of Buddhism that Chinese civilization vacillated from patronizing to persecuting Buddhists. These vacillations resulted in a wholesale paradigm shift that elevated Buddhism to the status of Confucianism and Taoism, which became known collectively as the "three doctrines" during China's Golden Age of the T'ang dynasty (600–900 C.E.). The most influential of all Chinese Buddhists was T'ien T'ai (or Chih-I, 538–597 C.E.), who interpreted the Lotus Sutra and so laid the foundations for the Golden Age. We will revisit some of his teachings later in this book. Along with other schools, T'ien T'ai's teachings migrated to Korea and then Japan, where it exerted seminal influence on Nichiren.

Buddhism found a true home in Japan. Taking root in the twin soils of Shinto and later Bushido, it flowered as Zen among the samurai, as Pure Land among the feudal peasantry, and in a plethora of monastic sects patronized by assorted warlords and dynastic families. The eclectic and prodigious monk Nichiren ultimately reformed the entire system in the thirteenth century, barely escaping assassination and execution, and surviving a bitter exile in the process. Devoting years to interdenominational study, Nichiren assiduously pieced together all the Buddhist teachings that had percolated from India to China to Japan, until it dawned on him that Buddha's Lotus Sutra represented the summit of Buddhism itself. Daisaku Ikeda has authored (among many books) a brief and beautiful history of Buddhism's remarkable journey from India to China, and its transformation there. As he avers, "China was the great earth that nurtured Buddhism's growth into a world religion."[6]

Indeed, China has played a pivotal role in "exporting" Buddhism to Western civilization, both directly via the occupation of Tibet and expulsion of the Dalai Lama, and indirectly via Japan, where Nichiren's resynthesis of T'ien T'ai's teachings on the Lotus Sutra are now spreading throughout the West, and indeed the world.

So twenty-five centuries after Buddha's lifetime, and during the second half of the twentieth century c.e., the West at long last began to import and absorb Buddhist thought into its mainstream culture. Let us examine a bit more closely three kinds of Mahayana Buddhism best known to Westerners: Tibetan, Zen, and Nichiren Buddhism.

## Tibetan Buddhism

Communist China invaded and occupied Tibet in 1951. Prior to this, the Tibetans had lived in virtual isolation for centuries, evolving many lineages of Buddhism and developing esoteric yogas and secret teachings. Prior to 1951, Westerners knew little about Tibetan culture or Tibetan Buddhism, yet the few isolated works that reached Western minds proved utterly enchanting. James Hilton's utopian novel *Lost Horizon* evoked the paradise of Shangri-la. Heinrich Harrer's *Seven Years in Tibet*, an incredible true story, introduced the fourteenth Dalai Lama and Tibetan culture. Both books were later made into movies. On a more scholarly and also more mystical side, W. Evans-Wentz transmitted four erudite texts, including *The Tibetan Book of the Dead*, with its thought-provoking foreword by Carl Jung.[7] On the completely unbelievable side, Tuesday Lobsang Rampa's tales made Tibetan yogis appear as magicians and supermen.[8] (This was the basis of Hollywood's later movie *The Golden Child*.) Prior to 1951, the aforementioned handful of books was about the sum of available literature in the English language on the elaborate Buddhist culture of Tibet.

The Chinese occupation changed all that. The Dalai Lama and his retinue were recognized in the West as a "government in exile"—though no nation on earth made any move to help them regain their homeland. They were given asylum in India, and still maintain their headquarters at Dharamsala. They established cultural bases in London, New York, and in other friendly Western intellectual centers. They dispatched Chögyam Trungpa (among others) to the United States to network with American "hip culture" and heighten awareness of Tibetan Buddhism. They founded Naropa Institute (near the Colorado Rockies) and Shambhala Press, which began to publish fine translations of Tibetan and eclectic Buddhist works hitherto unknown in Western civilization.

The year of the Tibetan expulsion, 1951, was also the year of my birth. Like many of us baby boomers, the Tibetans in exile also surfed the revolutionary waves of the 1960s, in which hippie counterculture, civil rights, antiwar protest, psychedelia, pop music icons, martial arts, Indian gurus, and Eastern mysticism fused in an unprecedented evolution whose effects are still reverberating today. Tibetans are nowadays more settled in their diaspora, as evidenced by the proliferation of Tibetan boutiques in Greenwich Village and Tibetan monasteries throughout Western civilization. Like so many political and religious exiles before them, the Tibetans are rebuilding their culture in the free West.

The Dalai Lama has been an ambassador of goodwill and an exemplar of Buddhist leadership. He never preached hatred for or retaliation against the Maoist regime that brutally occupied Tibet, ruthlessly suppressed Tibetan culture, razed Tibetan monasteries, and killed Tibetan monks and nuns. Not once has the Dalai Lama ever advocated or condoned violence as a legitimate means to political ends. He has won the minds and hearts of the West through unperturbable endurance of injustice and patient goodwill toward all, including his oppressors. True to the essence of Buddhism, he has no enemies. True to The Middle Way, no Tibetan has ever hijacked an airplane to gain the West's attention to their plight.

The Tibetans have also encountered the Jews, and that experience has been mutually enriching. From the Tibetans, Jews have learned about Buddhism—the world's most powerful antidote to suffering and persecution, areas in which the Jewish people have acquired considerable expertise but few patent remedies in their long history.

From the Jews, Tibetans have learned about diaspora—being scattered from one's homeland, becoming strangers in strange lands, adapting and contributing to local cultures. These have been keys to Jewish survival since the Babylonian diaspora in the eighth century B.C.E., and the Roman diaspora in the first century C.E. Jews have been practicing survival in diasporas even longer than Tibetans have been practicing Buddhism. From the example of Jewish history, Tibetans have derived meaning and purpose of their own exile, reinforcing what they have already been doing according to their lights: Making a gift of their culture to the global village. Jews have a teaching called "tikkun olam," which means "healing the world." To heal the world, one must live in it and indeed throughout it. This is a higher purpose of diaspora, which Jews and lately Tibetans share.[9]

For these among other reasons, it is not surprising that so many Jews are embracing various schools of Buddhism, and in myriad ways. This phenomenon is reminiscent of the Sadducee infatuation with Hellenic philosophy in ancient Israel and has become so widespread that there is even a name for Jews who espouse or practice Buddhism: "Jubus"— short for "Jewish Buddhists."[10] Judaism itself was long ago absorbed by small numbers of Asians—Indians, Chinese, and Japanese alike. Now Western Jews are reabsorbing Buddhism from all regions of Asia.

But why did Mao invade Tibet? It has no political, strategic, or economic importance whatsoever. If you indulge my conspiracy theory, Mao Tse-tung occupied Tibet precisely to expel the Dalai Lama. The Chinese geostrategic game of choice is go, not chess. To win at chess, you must occupy strong squares and maintain strong positions. You must confront, attack, and eliminate opposing pieces. This is also quintessential Western warfare. To win at go, you must induce your opponent to occupy weak intersections and develop weak positions, so you can gradually encircle and envelop opposing pieces. This is quintessential Eastern warfare. So perhaps Mao Tse-tung expelled the Dalai Lama because he surmised that Tibetan Buddhists in exile would penetrate Western civilization and exert a pacific influence, thus weakening the West's resolve to confront China in the future.

## Zen Buddhism

Although Zen appears delightfully if inscrutably Japanese to many Westerners, it originates with Nagarjuna's Madhyamika Buddhism of northern India, which underwent an amazing migration to China, Korea, Japan, and thence to the West. Like Tibetan Buddhism, Zen was for all practical purposes unknown to mainstream Western culture until the mid-twentieth century.

Prior to 1951, the Tibetans were insulated by the Himalayas, the "roof of the world," atop which they dwelled, content for centuries to practice Buddhism in isolation. The Japanese are similarly an insular people, inhabiting four "home islands," and likewise remaining content for centuries to practice an exotic species of feudalism in isolation. But the prodigious Japanese venerated China as their parent culture, and allowed themselves to be influenced by ideas imported from its vast hinterland. So Japanese culture combined its ancestral devotions of indigenous Shinto, its chivalrous samurai code of Bushido, and its poetic arts of haiku and the tea ceremony, with the filial piety of Confucianism and various forms of imported Chinese Buddhism.

Zen entered mainstream Western culture via three main gates: the accessible scholarship of D. T. Suzuki,[11] the writings of pop guru Alan Watts,[12] and the publication of Roshi Philip Kapleau's classic *The Three Pillars of Zen.*[13] Also riding the 1960s wave, Zen settled swiftly into select niches of counterculture. Zen was variously perceived in the West as existential, cool, hip, minimalist, activist, rebellious, and warriorlike. It was also a Buddhism that defied definition: Whatever you said or thought about Zen was bound to be non-Zen. Koans melted down the rational intellect, while the ox-herding pictures turned indescribable mind-states into poetic metaphors. Zen was regarded as both the most incomprehensible but also the quickest way to Satori, or enlightenment. In migrating to America, Zen retained both the religious and the secular aspects it had manifested in Japan, but with a twist.

On the religious side, Japanese Zen masters tend to be abbots of monasteries. On the secular side, Zen's Spartan minimalism made it a natural Buddhism for samurai, who were more than disciplined and inclined enough to sit and breathe and die serenely, and who did not require (and often despised) scholarly exegesis of texts or complex devotional liturgy. But here's the twist: The Jesuits were the first Westerners to live in Japan, as mostly tolerated missionaries. During bouts of intolerance, as in Nagasaki in 1597, the resident Jesuits and their Japanese converts were crucified—but not deterred. The Jesuits are a soldierly as well as a scholarly order. They were ideally suited both to establishing "beachheads" for Christianity in foreign lands, and to learning enough about indigenous cultures to transmit Christianity to them. This backfired delightfully in the twentieth century, when a young Irish Jesuit priest named Robert Kennedy—not to be confused with the American Robert F. Kennedy—was assigned to Japan. There he discovered Zen, and became enamored of it. So beyond his mission of deepening the Japanese experience of Christianity, Robert Kennedy eventually settled in the United States, where he now deepens the Christian experience of Zen Buddhism.[14]

Roshi Kennedy, S.J. received his inkha (seal of dharma succession) from Roshi Bernie Glassman, a Zen Jubu and relentless activist. Roshi Glassman is well known for his compassionate insistence on taking Zen into the "hood": to the homeless, the hapless, the helpless—to those who most need a sip of the milk of human kindness. Thus Zen Buddhism made an improbable journey from the tranquil monasteries of Kyoto to the mean streets of the Bronx. Roshi Glassman, like his successor, Roshi Kennedy, held outdoor retreats at Auschwitz. Sitting in that place brings into starkest possible relief the contrast between Buddhism's nonharm and compassion toward humanity, and Nazism's aggressive harm and murderous indifference toward humanity. Roshi Kennedy, who teaches theology at Saint Peter's College in New Jersey, founded the Morning Star Zendo in Jersey City, which is where I met him.

I fondly recall our rooftop meditations at dawn, the sun rising between the twin towers of the World Trade Center, just a stone's throw across the Hudson River. During lively post-zazen breakfasts, Roshi Kennedy encouraged me to challenge the militant feminists and other radical left-wing political activists that the Morning Star drew into its orbit (along with students, housewives, workers, Christian monks, and Jubus). In truth I needed little encouragement to challenge extremist views. Yet a lasting lesson that Roshi Kennedy taught us every morning, without uttering a word, was that The Middle Way is broad enough to ingather all ways, deep enough to foster dialogue among them, tolerant enough to see beyond our human imperfections—which we all manifest in one way or another—and patient enough to allow our common humanity to surface.

Perhaps Roshi Kennedy's greatest gift is that of Zen Buddhism to Christian holy orders. He conducts Zen exercises within monasteries of many kinds—Benedictine, Trappist, Capuchin—as well as with interfaith religious groups. Amazingly or not, secular Zen Buddhism has the power to rekindle and refresh Christian spiritual devotion.

## Nichiren Buddhism

As we have seen thus far, China is a pivotal culture for Buddhism. As bits and pieces from the vast storehouse of Indian Buddhist teachings gradually accumulated in China, they came to exert a profound effect on the Taoist and Confucian foundations of Chinese culture. In China, Buddhism once again demonstrated its ability to take root and flower in an "alien" cultural soil by speaking meaningfully to the traditions already in place. (In the next chapter, we will sift China's metaphysical soil itself.) As in other regions, Chinese Buddhism evolved into several viable "schools," each of which favored a particular subset of teachings and practices. We have already mentioned T'ien T'ai and Ch'an. Other popular Chinese schools included the "Pure Land," whose followers prayed to the Buddha for salvation, and for rebirth in a kind of Buddhist heaven. So the Pure Land school resembled a Chinese Buddhist version of an Abrahamic faith.

But one school above all painted a most compelling picture of Buddhism, by prioritizing Buddha's teachings, by reconciling distinctions between and among other Buddhist schools, and by juxtaposing Buddhism most compatibly with China's indigenous Taoist and Confucian traditions. This was the school founded by T'ien T'ai. Among its many valuable teachings is the holographic "three thousand states of mind" drawn from the Lotus Sutra, which T'ien T'ai and later Nichiren designated as the summit of Buddhism's voluminous canon.[15]

The guiding idea is that all possible states of mind are simultaneously present in all sentient beings, which means that everyone has the Buddha mind—in addition to all the other states. The question then is how to manifest the more beneficial states, especially the beneficent and compassionate bodhisattva states, and ultimately the fully awakened Buddha-mind state; and at the same time how to diminish the manifestations of more detrimental mind-states, especially those hellish and tormented ones which induce maleficence and harm.

So T'ien T'ai Buddhism is egalitarian and holistic. It asserts that anyone is capable of manifesting any mind-state, that all mind-states are continuously accessible to anyone. T'ien T'ai Buddhism also provides the access keys, which as usual depend on practice—and not on asceticism, prayer, or wishful thinking. No one is excluded by birth or condemned by external forces; we become what we make of ourselves, though naturally we all need salutary and not malign influences to guide us. This Buddhism makes sense to masses of ordinary people, who wish to lead decent and productive lives but do not wish to subject themselves to excesses of denial (such as religious asceticism). It also squares with the Confucian notion that anyone can become a "gentleman" or "gentlewoman" by practicing virtues. It is also consistent with the Taoist maxim of the complementariness of opposites: Every mind-state is alloyed with its complement, which suggests that regular practice is necessary to highlight more wholesome mind-states and keep less wholesome ones at bay. As we will soon see, T'ien T'ai Buddhism is also compatible with the *I Ching*, the foundational but anonymous book that influenced Lao Tzu and Confucius alike. Beyond this, T'ien Tai is a cultural Buddhism, which powerfully mirrors Confucianism's traditional commitments to scholarship, music, and the arts.

All the main schools of Chinese Buddhism gradually migrated to Japan, and settled into Japan's rigid feudal hierarchy. Pure Land was taken up by the serfs, who had no hope of improving their socioeconomic condition, and so were reduced to praying to a Buddhist deity for salvation. Zen was adopted by the samurai, already accustomed to enduring privation and death with stoic resolve and unwavering courage, if not good cheer. The Japanese feudal barons, warlords, and contending dynasties were by and large content to enlist and patronize Buddhism as a means of social and political control, just as the European feudal system enlisted and patronized Christianity. So T'ien T'ai became either neglected or corrupted in Japan, and remained so for centuries, until reformed in the thirteenth century by the scholar-monk Nichiren.

Nichiren reinstated the Lotus Sutra as the pinnacle of Buddhist teaching, and distilled from it a powerful mantra—*nam myoho renge kyo*—which he disseminated to the broad populace as the quickest and surest means of attaining liberation from suffering.[16] Just as Martin Luther reformed papal Catholicism, so Nichiren reformed Japanese Buddhism. But Nichiren Buddhism itself was gradually reabsorbed, returned to the monastery, and recorrupted by the persistent and long-lived Japanese feudal system, which endured until the Meiji restoration of the mid-nineteenth century transformed Japan into a modern state.

Japan emerged in the twentieth century from its centuries-long insularity, initially in the guise of an extroverted and aggressively imperialistic dragon. The ensuing decades-long war fever of Japanese militarism was finally broken in the bloody Pacific theater of World War II, where the United States eventually won an unconditional surrender, and democratized Japan by enforced regime change. But interred within the Japanese war culture of that era, an educational and pacifistic Nichiren Buddhism was reborn, in an organization called Soka Gakkai, which means "Value-Creating Society." We will revisit the courageous and inspiring story of Soka founders in chapter 15, but let us now fast-forward to the latter twentieth century, when Soka Gakkai's Nichiren Buddhism migrated to America.[17]

Soka Gakkai International (SGI) is led by president Daisaku Ikeda, and is chronologically the third major school of Mahayana Buddhism to establish itself in America and throughout the West—arriving after the Tibetans, and also after Zen. Since I have the honor of quoting President Ikeda throughout this book, you can "hear" him speak in his own voice. It has been my privilege to meet Daisaku Ikeda in Japan, and to dialogue with him. I have also studied many of his writings,[18] and have interacted with communities of SGI Buddhists in several countries. SGI has reanimated Nichiren's teachings and disseminated them (along with the Lotus Sutra and much else) to the mainstream populace—true to Nichiren's openly accessible tradition. More than that, SGI has also exemplified and amplified the cultural aspects of the T'ien T'ai school, which influenced Nichiren too. SGI has built schools, universities, culture centers, music libraries, artists' retreats—creating value for humanity while inspiring value within each person.

One of the most potentially damaging experiences for a human being—man, woman, or child—is to be devalued by others. By contrast, one of the most uplifting experiences is to be valued by others, and even better than that is to learn to create value for others. SGI's Nichiren Buddhism excels in value creation.

## From B to C

Daisaku Ikeda has observed that Buddhism was "refined and purified in the rich crucible of Chinese culture."[19] Let us now examine that crucible more closely. Our next two chapters, on Confucius and ABC geometry, will round out this introduction to the ABCs, after which we'll apply them to reconciling life's extremes.

# 4

# CONFUCIUS'S BALANCED ORDER
Restoring Harmony and Virtue amid Discord

*To go beyond is as wrong as to fall short.* —Confucius

## The Aristotle of East Asia

CONFUCIUS (551–479 B.C.E.) IS STILL SYNONYMOUS with East Asian—that is Chinese, Korean, and Japanese—philosophy. Unlike Buddha, who was born into a ruling family, and unlike Aristotle, whose father had political connections with ruling families, Confucius emerged from unassuming origins. His father, a minor magistrate, died when Confucius was only three. Growing up in relative poverty, Confucius worked at a succession of humble jobs—shepherd, cowherd, clerk, bookkeeper—in the course of his philosophical development. Humility was, and remains, a central virtue of Confucian cultures. Also unlike Buddha, Confucius inherited no centuries-old Indian tradition of gymnastic metaphysical debate and esoteric yogic practice. And unlike Aristotle, Confucius was not heir to the formidable and foundational Hellenic legacy of pre-Socratic and Platonic philosophies. Yet like

Aristotle, Confucius rose to a position of magisterial power in his adulthood, persuading more than one warlord that government by virtue is superior to government by coercion. Like Aristotle, Confucius eventually fell from political favor, but not to his death. And like Aristotle and Buddha, Confucius devoted his remaining decades to teaching. He established a remarkable legacy that would define the essential philosophical character of Chinese and neighboring cultures for centuries to come. Confucius's influence on East Asian civilization outweighs even Aristotle's prodigious influence on the West.[1]

What formative written materials did Confucius study? He read the four great works accessible to him: *The Book of Changes (I Ching)*, *The Book of Odes*, *The Book of History*, and *The Book of Music*. From the *Odes* Confucius learned to revere love, both in its poetic and its humanistic manifestations. Loving one's fellow man is a central virtue of Confucian ethics. From the *History*, Confucius learned to venerate ancestry. Honoring one's parents is a mainstay of Confucian cultures. Beyond this, Confucius venerates antiquity by hearkening repeatedly to the half-legendary Dukedom of Chou, a bygone utopia that waxed on the wings of virtue and waned on the molted pinions of virtue's neglect. From the *Music* Confucius learned to attune to the fundamental vibrations that sustain the universe. Just as we play on musical instruments, so the cosmos plays on us. From *The Book of Changes* Confucius learned to follow the Way (Tao)—the sublime Chinese metaphysics of yin-yang, from which he gained insight into natural laws that govern the universe, the earth, the state, the family, and the individual alike.[2] The Confucian project is about understanding these fundamental laws, and applying them to everyday life.

It is Tao above and beneath all, as revealed to Confucius in *The Book of Changes*, that permeated his thought and informed his system of virtue ethics. It is probably not a coincidence that Lao Tzu, the main exponent of Tao who came to be identified with Taoism itself, was an elder contemporary of Confucius and also a civil servant. Lao Tzu's *Tao Te Ching (The Way and Its Power)* is a metaphoric and poetic treatment of The Way, whereas Confucius's *Analects* are literal and practical applications of The Way to everyday life.[3] At the same time, nothing in

Chinese philosophy is simply black-and-white, including the interpenetrating colors of the yin-yang circle that symbolize Tao itself. Both Lao Tzu and Confucius speak of "The Way," yet they often seem to contradict each other. For example, Confucius encourages a commitment to lifelong learning which to this day is taken most seriously in East Asia, for instance by prolific economic powerhouses like Singapore, whose 70 percent ethnic Chinese population is devotedly Confucian. Then again, Lao Tzu counsels us to "do away with learning" in order to understand the deeper meaning of Tao. Is this a contradiction? Let me answer with another apparent contradiction: yes, and no.

Learning, and doing away with learning, appear contradictory only at the most superficial level. "Doing away with learning" does not mean burning books: After all, it's in a book that Lao Tzu offers this advice. Moreover, you cannot do away with learning until you have already learned something. Confucius's message is that we are born to learn, rather than remain in a state of ignorance, while Lao Tzu's message is that language and thinking can mislead us, and have their limits in any case. Surely you have had experiences that words cannot express? Pursuit of knowledge for its own sake can actually close the mind and fail to open the heart. Whether you know a lot or a little, the most important thing is what you do with what you know, in terms of practicing virtue. Some practice virtue by learning; others, by going beyond learning. Lao Tzu's challenge was echoed independently in the seventeenth century by Thomas Hobbes, who said, "If I had read as much as other men, I would know as little." But Hobbes said this after he had already read and written more than most men in his generation. Lao Tzu's (and Hobbes's) point is that you must learn to think for yourself. Paradoxically perhaps, a good way to stimulate thinking for yourself is to acquire some "food for thought" from great minds, which brings us back to Confucius.

Lao Tzu's Taoism can be viewed as esoteric, intended for students of life who have graduated beyond ordinary modes of learning; Confucius's Taoism, as exoteric, intended to guide the vast majority in their practical everyday lives. True to the Tao, which they each espoused in a different way, Lao Tzu and Confucius themselves form a yin-yang complementary pair. The long-standing East Asian penchant for practicality placed emphasis on and loaned impetus to Confucianism, which is really concrete Taoism; while Lao Tzu's abstract Taoism both spawned a tradition of worthy successors (notably Chuang Tzu) yet receded into the cultural background, degenerating into superstition and popular magic. If you seek a Confucian in Beijing, you can talk to anyone on the street. If you seek a true Taoist in Beijing, you must look harder.

Human understanding is best developed via interplay between theory and practice. We need sound theories to inform our practical activities, in order to flourish and not wither as beings. Progress toward Aristotelian excellence and fulfillment, in the science of living as in all other sciences, depends on interplay between hypothesis and experiment. Similarly, persistence in creating value and compassion in Buddhist traditions relies on consistency between theories of the first three Noble Truths and practices of the fourth. Similarly, maintenance of Confucian balanced order depends on harmony between theories of changing circumstances and practice of unchanging virtues.

## Order versus Entropy

A fundamental imbalance between chaos (disorder) and cosmos (order) is woven into the very fabric of the universe, at least in its current phase. It's easier to topple a house of cards than to erect one. A hurricane or tornado can do tremendous damage, destroying in seconds dwellings that took months to build. One act of infidelity or cruelty can ruin a relationship that took months or years to develop. One act of war can swiftly ruin decades of diplomacy and instantaneously destroy lives that took decades to grow and mature.

"Entropy" is the name physicists associate with the second law of thermodynamics, that drives physical systems—whether amoebas or galaxies—from orderly to increasingly disorderly states. It is the nonrecoverable energy one must expend to get anything done, from boiling water to managing organizations. Entropy is cosmically mandated waste—100 percent guaranteed to render all processes less than 100 percent efficient. It is also the basis of Murphy's Law: Whatever can go wrong, will go wrong. Confucius understood moral entropy well enough. He wrote, "This is how the whole scheme of things works. All good things are difficult to achieve; and bad things are very easy to get."[4]

Entropy increases with the forward flow of time, which is why physicist Sir Arthur Eddington called it "time's arrow." Eventually, the universe itself will reach a state of total entropy, or "heat death," in which all molecular motion and even atomic vibration will cease. Finally, peace and quiet will prevail—but maybe not for long. If Vedic cosmology is correct, out of ultimate chaos comes renewed cosmos, and with it another gargantuan cycle of creation, sustenance, and annihilation. As we will see in the next chapter, order does indeed emerge from chaos. The two are also complementary.

Life itself is a highly improbable embodiment of negative entropy. Living beings are much more complexly organized systems than nonliving things. Humans are more complex than other terrestrial beings, but for that reason are also more unstable, ever prone to cruise in entropy's slipstream toward unbalance and disorder. Human families and societies are more complex still, because they combine all the complexities of individuals plus the additional properties of relationships and groups. Life itself somehow evolves, yet individual life-forms all culminate in death, after which their physical matter becomes disordered and scattered by entropy. Every time you draw a breath, you are probably imbibing at least one molecule that used to be part of Aristotle, or Buddha, or Confucius. Unfortunately, their wisdom doesn't come bundled with their ex-molecules: That's entropy at work again. Although Confucius did not study physics or biology as we do today, he nonetheless understood the natural tendency toward disorder in human affairs and human societies, and sought ways of achieving and maintaining as much balance and order as possible, from the individual to the family, from the community to the state.

Confucius would agree with Aristotle that the family is the fundamental unit of the state, as well as a miniature state in itself. For all to be well in the larger state, all must be well in the family. As he said in the *Analects*, "To put the world in order, we must first put the nation in order; to put the nation in order, we must first put the family in order." Disordered families lead to disordered nations; disordered nations, to a disordered world. Confucius's idea that the family is a miniature state anticipates by 2,500 years a special kind of geometry, that of "fractals." As we will see in the next chapter, fractals contain self-similar patterns at every level of magnification. Chinese philosophy brilliantly perceived this phenomenon in human structures, long before Western geometers perceived it in nature. But since Chinese culture had never alienated man from nature as the West has done so decisively—to its growing peril—the Chinese instead reflected on the patterns relating man to nature, which the West is just beginning to rediscover.

Confucius would also agree with the Buddhist view that external conflicts—whether within a family or between nations—are manifestations of unresolved internal conflicts, whether of individual parents or entire cultures. Children inherit not only their parents' genes, but also their prejudices and abuses, along with other psychological baggage. The longer this baggage is carried, the more difficult it becomes to lose, and the more entrenched the conflicts become. "The strength of a nation derives from the integrity of the home," Confucius insisted in his *Analects*. And the weakness of a nation derives from the disintegration of its homes.

"Integrity" has two related meanings, both stemming from the concept of wholeness. First, a person of integrity is whole in the sense that his or her parts are aligned, and not in conflict with one another. "Whole" itself is cognate with "hale"—an older word for "healthy"— as in "hale and hearty." So integrity implies health. Second, as we will see in chapter 5, Hellenic geometry placed great emphasis on the importance of integers, which are "whole numbers." Integrity of number was vital not only to Greek geometry, but also as a link to integrity of persons and polities alike. Aristotle would agree with Confucius, that persons of integrity contribute to an integral home, family, community, and humanity.

It is always ironic, and sometimes tragic, that parenting is life's most important job, yet no one is expected to fulfill any requirements or hold any qualifications to do it. It is Confucius's point, as well as Buddha's, that familial strife results from unresolved parental problems. As

Confucius said in the *Analects,* "To put the family in order, we must first cultivate our personal life; we must first set our hearts right." The ABCs offer myriad ways of setting our hearts right, and each of them provides transformative guidance: Aristotle through contemplation and the golden mean, Buddha through awareness and The Middle Way, Confucius through virtuousness and the Way (Tao) itself.

Yet Confucius and Aristotle differ on a fundamental question, namely who will be favored when the interests of the individual clash with those of the collective—the family, the community, the polity. Their differing answers will emerge again and again as we examine different topics, and will provide interesting food for thought. In a nutshell, it amounts to this: Aristotle thought that the basic goal of every human being is to become happy, or fulfilled. Fulfillment is attained by developing one's excellence in the context of practicing virtues. These Aristotelian goals are realized by, and for, individuals. With Confucius, it's the other way around: The basic goal of every human being is to fulfill the duties and responsibilities demanded by his or her place in the familial, communal, and political order, as ordained by nature. Then individual happiness will follow. Let us delve further into Confucius's conception of balanced order, to see why he gives priority to the collective over the individual.

### Confucius and the *I Ching (The Book of Changes)*
I was given the *I Ching* one day as a gift, when still in my teens. I did not understand it at all at the time—youth being wasted on the young— but within a few short years its precious wisdom became increasingly evident to me. In some of my previous books, which draw upon my experience as a philosophical counselor, I summarized case studies involving *I Ching* and provided brief instructions for its use. This has led to exactly what the Tao predicts, namely complementary reactions: expressions of gratitude from some readers who were ready to receive *I Ching*'s wisdom, and expressions of condemnation from other readers who fancy themselves too "rational" to access the *I Ching* by the recommended "random" means—tossing coins or manipulating yarrow stalks. To edify the critics, I must one day write a book detailing the

intimate relationship between determinism and chance. In fact, there is no such thing as chance, only an inability on our part to explain more fully how and why certain processes appear to us as random. For now, suffice it to say that one who rejects *I Ching*'s wisdom just because it can be "randomly" accessed is like one who refuses to read a message in a bottle, just because the bottle has been washed up at his feet by the "random" motion of the seas.

*I Ching* embodies the metaphysics that inform both Lao Tzu and Confucius alike. Together, this book and these two philosophers define the original "cultural DNA" of East Asian civilization, prior to the arrival of Buddhism from India. The foundational idea is that we encounter in all phenomena the juxtaposition of complements: existence and nonexistence, birth and death, heaven and earth, order and chaos, light and dark, good and evil, justice and injustice, war and peace, male and female, creativity and receptivity, teacher and pupil, leader and follower, sanctity and profanity, joy and sorrow. The key insight of Tao is that these contrasting pairs do not stand in a relation of opposition and mutual exclusion but rather of complementarity and mutual inclusion. In other words, every complementary pair comprises a greater whole, and each complement also contains something of the other. But complementary pairs are never static; they persist in a state of perpetual flux, that we call "change." To manage changes, and to make the best of change's challenges, we must follow Tao, the Way, the line of least resistance, the deepest resonance attainable with changes in our lives.

The generic complements are yin and yang, whose now globally pervasive symbol became familiar to Westerners in the twentieth century. As the Golden Mean of Hellenic geometry was known before Aristotle, so the yin-yang circle of Chinese Tao was known before Confucius. Many books have been written, and many more can be, unpacking the meanings and applications of this symbol. It is depicted in fig. 4.1.

Yin and yang are primordial complements, emanating from Tao. In theory, everything has a complement, except for Tao itself. It is vital to appreciate the distinction between polar opposites and Taoist complements. Again, polarity means opposition and mutual exclusion

Figure 4.1 The Yin-Yang Circle

of pairs—such as north versus south on a compass, positive versus negative poles of a battery, truth versus falsity in Aristotelian logic, manic creativity versus incapacitating depression in human bipolar disorder. Polarity is a Western concept, and has its uses—within limits. By contrast, complementarity means completeness and mutual inclusion of pairs. For example, once you reach the North Pole, any further step you take, in any direction, leads you south. Attaining the "extreme" of one compass point obliges you to move toward the other. So the further north you travel, the closer you get to moving south. North cannot exclude south, only complement it.

And for example, many paradoxes of logic known to the ancient Greeks, and still unresolved today, stem from the eminently reasonable yet ultimately untenable Aristotelian assumption that declarative sentences must be either true or false. Aristotle's logic (unlike his ethics) explicitly excludes The Middle Way. But consider the Liar Paradox: "Epimenides the Cretan said that all Cretans are liars." If the sentence is true, then it is false. Similarly, if it is false, then it is true. (If you don't grasp this paradox, see endnote 5 at the back of this book.) Western philosophers have debated this and kindred paradoxes for more than two thousand years, without resolving all of them conclusively. They insist that reason must dispel paradox, yet it is from reason that paradox emerges.[5]

By contrast, Chinese philosophy accepts paradox as a departure point. For example, *Tao Te Ching* itself begins with a similar paradox: "The true Tao cannot be named." If that is true, then the true Tao has just been named as unnameable. Hence it can be named—a contradiction. And if it is false, then the true Tao can be named—only no one has ever been able to name it, for all names have complements, except for Tao, which is its own complement. This paradox is a departure point for Lao Tzu's book on Tao itself.

Western philosophy—and the logic, mathematics, and sciences that stem from it—begins with reason yet often ends in paradox. Chinese philosophy, by contrast, begins with paradox yet often ends in reason. So Western and Asian philosophy are also complementary in this sense.

Complementarity itself has been appreciated by many great Western minds, including Danish physicist Niels Bohr, Swiss psychologist Carl Jung, and American logician Raymond Smullyan.[6] Niels Bohr is a father of quantum theory. When knighted for his accomplishments in resolving some paradoxes of classical physics by means of even more paradoxical quantum mechanics, the Danish scientist adopted the yin-yang circle for his knightly coat of arms, along with the motto *Contraria Sunt Complementa* ("Opposites Are Complementary").

Indian and Chinese philosophy converged with Western physics in the twentieth century, because these ancient Asian models of thought turn out to be highly congruent with modern scientific understanding of the natural world, which is a much stranger place than most ancient Western philosophers realized. Chinese philosophy applies as well to human society as to nature, for it never saw humans as separate from the natural world, or immune to Tao, which governs all phenomena. And just like the forces of physics, the forces of Tao operate impersonally, without explicitly requiring a Godhead to oversee them. This is another reason why Confucian culture was so receptive to Buddhism, whose laws of dharma and karma also operate impersonally.

From *I Ching*, Confucius learned that everything is subject to laws of change (just as Buddhism asserts that all phenomena are transitory). But change in human beings, and in our mutual relations, is a much more precarious affair than the motions of planets about the sun, or ripening of fruits on the trees. Why? Because humans face more possibilities than planets or fruits. Given more choices than any other being on earth, and also given more mind-states in which to make them, there is also ample opportunity to choose badly (that is, contrary to Tao) and be led astray. In Confucian thought, poor choices lead to personal imbalance and social disorder. In Buddhist thought, they lead to suffering. It is easy to see why Confucian and Buddhist philosophies are in principle so compatible.

There are other reasons too. *The Book of Changes* presupposes that changing circumstances constantly confront you with the necessity of making choices. In any situation in which we ought to pause and reflect before speaking or acting, how many choices do we conceivably face? This is tantamount to asking how many possible interpretations we can make of that given situation. The *I Ching* is organized into hexagrams, each hexagram being composed of six lines. Since each line can be either yin or yang, there are $2^6$ or 64 possible hexagrams. Each has its own name. They range from *The Creative* (Heaven) composed entirely of yang lines, to *The Receptive* (Earth) composed entirely of yin lines, and include every possible combination of lines between these two "pure" states.

If you are mathematically inclined, you have already realized that the *I Ching* uses a binary system of arithmetic, symbolizing "1" as — and "0" as – – . Counting from zero to sixty-three in binary (000000, 000001, 000010, 000011, 000100, 000101, ..., 111010, 111011, 111100, 111101, 111110, 111111) is equivalent to generating the sixty-four hexagrams using yin and yang lines. Why do I mention this? Because the outstanding eighteenth-century German philosopher and mathematician Gottfried Leibniz, who coinvented calculus at the same time as Newton, also "invented" binary numbers. Or so he thought. Why is that important to us? Among other reasons, because the binary system is the basis of digital computing. We are taught the decimal system of arithmetic in school, which is convenient for creatures with ten fingers, but our digital calculators and computers all utilize binary arithmetic internally, although they accept and display decimal numbers for our convenience. So imagine Leibniz's amazement when his friend Father Joachim Bouvet, a Jesuit missionary serving in the court of

Emperor Kang Xi, conveyed to him, from China, the Shao Yung method for generating the *I Ching*'s sixty-four hexagrams. Leibniz took one look at this and realized that his "leading edge" invention of binary numbers had been known to the Chinese for two thousand years.

At the level of the hexagram, the *I Ching* recognizes sixty-four different kinds of situations in which you may find yourself making a choice. But within every hexagram itself, each line may be either "changing" or "nonchanging." This reflects details of our instantaneous situations, in which some elements are more ripe for change while others are less so. That each line may be changing or nonchanging multiplies the possibilities considerably. Each hexagram can contain 0, 1, 2, 3, 4, 5, or 6 changing lines. If no lines are changing, there are just sixty-four possible situations—one situation per hexagram. If one line is changing, then there are six possible new situations within each hexagram, or 6 x 64 = 384 possible situations altogether. If two lines are changing, there are fifteen ways in which this can occur within each hexagram, or 15 x 64 = 960 possible situations altogether. If three lines are changing, there are twenty ways in which this can occur within each hexagram, or 20 x 64 = 1,280 possible situations altogether. The number of possible situations for four changing lines is the same as for two changing lines (960 situations); for five, the same as for one (384 situations); for six, the same as for no changing lines (64 situations). In sum, this means that the *I Ching* describes 64 + 384 + 960 + 1,280 + 960 + 384 + 64 = 4,096 possible situations.

So the *I Ching* tells us that there are 4,096 possible situations of change, in any one of which we may find ourselves at a given instant. And T'ien T'ai Buddhism tells us that there are three thousand simultaneous mind-states, by which we will be guided or misguided at any given instant. The orders of magnitude of complexity of these two systems are the same. The *I Ching* was already deeply ensconced in Chinese thought by Confucius's time (500 B.C.E.), so it is hardly surprising that T'ien Tai's Buddhism met with such receptivity a thousand years later. In many key respects, T'ien T'ai represents a "fine-tuning" of the inner workings of the *I Ching*. Confucius himself had already "fine-tuned" its outer workings. Just as Confucius resolved the external problem of consistently choosing a wise course of action amid so many changing situations, so T'ien T'ai resolved the internal problem of finding and maintaining one-pointedness amid so many mind-states.

Typical of Chinese philosophy, over which it came to exert such compelling influence, I Ching is pragmatic rather than idealistic in its outlook. It does not suppose that we will always act in the best and noblest and most perfect ways—for even if we intend to do so, we are easily led astray by external appearances and internal misjudgments. Rather, I Ching supposes that in every situation we will act either more wisely (according to Tao) or more foolishly (against Tao), and it encourages us to weigh the benefits of wisdom against the detriments of folly. Just as T'ien T'ai and later Nichiren defined a Middle Way to guide us through our three thousand simultaneous mind-states, Confucius defined a set of virtues to guide us through our four thousand changing situations. The practice of Confucian virtues helps us maintain individual balance and social order, thus making life as harmonious as possible. Much human discord on this planet is attributable to conspicuous neglect of Confucian virtues.

## Confucian Virtues

Aristotle and Confucius were the two outstanding virtue ethicists of antiquity. Yet if we compare Aristotelian and Confucian virtues, we discover a fundamental contrast, if not a clash, between them. The so-called "Cardinal Virtues" of the West are—as we should expect from Western civilization's "double helix"—a Judeo-Christian embellishment of Hellenic philosophy. Virtues common to both strands include courage, temperance, justice, and wisdom. Each is located within Aristotle's golden mean, between their respective vices of excess and dearth. Now imagine that you were stranded on a desert island. Which Aristotelian virtues could you practice in isolation? Clearly, you could be courageous, temperate, and wise. You could also exercise justice in the classic Greek sense, in terms of maintaining a balanced soul. Now add to these the cardinal Christian (actually, Abrahamic) virtues of faith, hope, and charity. Once again, you could remain both faithful and hopeful in isolation. To exercise charity, you need beneficiaries. On a desert island, the environment and its flora and fauna could be beneficiaries of your respect and conservation, but probably not of your charity. So the majority of these classic Western virtues—six of seven— are focused on the individual, whether as part of society or isolated from it.

The "desert island" scenario is itself a classic preoccupation of individualized Western civilization. From Daniel Defoe's *Robinson Crusoe* to John Donne's quip that "no man is an Island"; from William Golding's *Lord of the Flies* to Nevil Shute's *On the Beach* (among other apocalyptic novels spawned by the Cold War), and from Friedrich Nietzsche to Sartre to Camus, man is constantly trying to survive his solitude. But as Confucian philosophy recognized early on, what civilized man really needs to survive is not his isolation from others, but rather his immersion with them.

So consider two cardinal virtues that Confucius espoused, and the families of virtues they engender in his system. The two are *ren* and *li*. In the West we will encounter some difficulty as well as difference of opinion in translating these terms, for written Chinese is a pictorial (ideographic) language, of non-Indo-European origin. I do not read Chinese myself but, as with the *I Ching*, I rely on authoritative translators and contemporary Confucian teachers. *Ren* means benevolence, beneficence, goodness, love: an unselfish love of humanity. Confucius believed that all people can attain *ren* by practicing five associated virtues: respect, magnanimity, sincerity, earnestness, and kindness.[7] Applying our "desert island" test, it would be difficult to be magnanimous, sincere, earnest, and kind in isolation. Of course you could respect yourself on a desert island, and venerate your ancestors, and chant for people *in absentia*, but you could not show respect directly to other living beings if they are not present. Confucian respect is not confined to a state of mind: It is what you *show* to others in every aspect of your daily interactions.

This leads to *li*, the other cardinal Confucian virtue. *Li* means propriety, or appropriate conduct. *Li* shapes the interpersonal channels through which *ren* flows from one human being to another. There are five basic kinds of human relationships, and all are governed by *li*: parent and child, husband and wife, friend and friend, old and young, ruler and subject. Returning to the desert island, it is clear that you could not practice *li* at all in isolation, since *li* is concerned exclusively with relations between yourself and others. So in Confucian ethics, only one of ten cardinal virtues can be practiced by the individual alone; nine of ten require a society of persons to be exercised. In classical Western ethics, six of seven cardinal virtues can be practiced by the individual alone.

This is a stark contrast. It illustrates a pervasive difference between Western and East Asian civilization. The West's ethical focus is on the individual; East Asia's, on the social organism. If we seek fundamental explanations for the West's historically outstanding individual achievements, and East Asia's historically enduring social cohesiveness, we find them in these different foundational conceptions of virtue.

*Ren* and *li* form the source and wellspring of Confucian balanced order. Think about it. If you are capable of benevolent love, then you are also capable of remaining balanced—for example, of retaining emotional equilibrium and purpose of will—while enduring what William Shakespeare called "the slings and arrows of outrageous fortune." *Ren* allows you to keep your balance on life's tightrope, whether assailed by internal doubts or buffeted by external forces. *Li* provides, maintains, and restores all-important order to human relationships, which are always prone to relapsing into the primordial chaos from which they spring. *Li* choreographs the dance of linked couples across life's tightropes, ordering their footsteps so that both may cross in safety. In the absence of *li*, one misstep by either causes both to slip. Life's tightrope guarantees no safety net for human relationships; the practice of *li* is the best hedge against any relationship's fatal fall.

It is also plain in Confucian ethics that although *ren* is experienced in similar ways by all human beings, *li* is not. Love of humanity, and the balance it fosters, is egalitarian. The duties in most relationships however, with the tolerable exception of friendships, are experienced in dissimilar ways by human beings, depending on their ordering in the relationship. Duties are therefore inegalitarian. You want an example? I'll give you one from 9/11, whose conflagration elicited *ren* and evoked *li* alike. A brave firefighter, trying to evacuate one of the twin towers before it collapsed, came across a priest administering the last rites to a mortally wounded man who could not be moved. "It's my duty to evacuate this building," said the firefighter to the priest, "so please leave at once." "It's my duty administer the last rites," said the priest, and he remained. The firefighter did his duty and survived to tell the tale. The priest did his duty, and perished. Their unselfish concerns for humanity (*ren*) were equal, and yet their duties (*li*) were different. Both were exemplary Confucians, in circumstances of extreme unbalanced disorder.

In contrast, balanced order produces social harmony, and in this sense it is analogous to musical harmony. For different voices to blend harmoniously, or for different keys on a keyboard to produce a harmonious chord, they must also observe a balanced order. The egalitarian balance of the notes in a chord lies in the evenness of their tonality, their synchronization in time, their equality of volume, of sustenance, of decay. Yet it is the inegalitarian ordering of the notes—that is, each note's different frequency and the way they sound when played together—that produces the harmony itself. If all notes were the same pitch, there could be no harmony at all. Yet their ordering cannot be arbitrary, or random, or based on flawed proportions, or discord will surely result. The intervals between the notes are of supreme importance in the production of harmony. These intervals are determined by geometric ratios fixed by nature and are not subject to vacillating human caprice.

And so it is with *li*. For human relationships to be harmonious, the duties owed to each party by the other are similarly distinguished by social intervals, whose ratios are also fixed by nature. The Confucian idea is to sustain cultural institutions that reinforce and do not undermine the natural order. Undermining the natural order is contrary to the Way (Tao), and invites collapse. Societies that are overly individualistic (like America) see their social fabric frayed and unraveled by rival faction; while societies that are overly egalitarian (like the former Soviet Union) cannot sustain themselves productively. When the natural order of human relationships is violated, individuals become unbalanced as well. Where *li* breaks down, *ren* cannot be expressed. Absent *li* and *ren,* social harmony gives way to societal discord. In such an estate the individual cannot be fulfilled—neither in Confucian nor in Aristotelian terms.

Through this picture window of virtue ethics, we can clearly see the contrast between Aristotelian and Confucian civilizations. The West tends to err on the side of individual rights, strengthening the individual's claims on society while weakening his or her obligations in social relationships. In many American states, it is easier to get a divorce than to cancel a lease on a motor vehicle. The East tends to err on the side of social duties, strengthening the society's claims on the individual while weakening his or her individual rights. In many Asian nations, arranged marriages are still prevalent. Once again, Buddhism provides a fulcrum for balancing the individual's rights with his or her duties toward others. Buddhism embraces both Aristotelian and Confucian strengths, and by doing so diminishes their weaknesses.

## Yin and Yang: "Connected but Different"

African Americans, among others who have endured unjust discrimination, can cite numerous convoluted judgments of American courts prior to the civil rights era. Especially harmful was a notorious attempt both to acknowledge the egalitarianism mandated by the Bill of Rights, yet to sustain a system of racial segregation in the South. This was the "separate but equal" judgment, infamously upheld by an 1896 Supreme Court decision *(Plessy v. Ferguson)*: an impossible juxtaposition of the notion that on one hand people of color enjoyed the same rights as whites, but on the other were obliged to exercise their "identical" rights in separate places: attending "separate but equal" schools, drinking at "separate but equal" water fountains, and running the whole gauntlet of America's "separate but equal" apartheid.

The revelations of I *Ching,* played out in the abstract Tao of Lao Tzu and the concrete Tao of Confucius, lend an ancient and salutary twist to this phrase. Instead of regarding people as "separate but equal," the metaphysics of yin and yang assert that we are all "connected but different." How are we connected? By our shared ability to experience *ren,* and by the inevitability of our social relationships. How are we different? In the different duties and responsibilities assigned to us by nature, manifest in the different ways we experience *li*. Yin and yang are interconnected, in that each contains something of the other. They can never be made separate by man, for they are joined by nature. Yet there is still a boundary between them, permeable though it may be, and some of their conspicuous properties are not at all the same.

It is one error to suppose that we humans are not interconnected; it is another to suppose that our interconnectedness entails sameness. People should all be equal before the law, yet this desirable equality does not erase our differences. We are all equally subject to laws of gravity, but our weights are all different. We are equally subject to laws of karma, but the times required for our actions to ripen are all different. And so forth. However, the two interconnected but different complements of Tao always unite in a greater whole, and so their differences enhance the value of the whole itself. If we speak of "a beautiful couple," we are not focused on their differences, yet we still require difference to appreciate the beauty of their union. Taoist complements are not differences that divide; they are differences that unite. But beyond this, to transcend the differences themselves, we must look to Buddhism.

Night and day are interconnected. They are complements of one whole revolution of the earth upon its axis. Dusk and dawn are periods when one of these complements changes, by imperceptible stages, into the other. Dark and light are also mutually interpenetrating: Even the darkest night contains starlight or moonlight or reflected rays from clouds; while the brightest sunlit day also casts the most darkly contrasting shadows. Yet night and day are unequal, both in their essential characteristics, in their durations, and in the conspicuously different activities that they favor. And so it is with each of the five relationships entailed by Confucian *li*. They are connected but different.

Parents and children are deeply connected, yet have different obligations toward each other. Parents must care for and provide for their offspring, in myriad ways. Children in turn must honor and obey their parents. This reciprocal duty is far more pronounced in Confucian than in Aristotelian cultures, but even so it cannot begin at birth. Parental obligations toward the child are much more onerous during infancy and juvenility, but gradually the child assumes increasing responsibility toward its parents. Eventually the yin-yang cycle complements and completes itself, as the grown-up child cares and provides for its aging parents, who become increasingly childlike in the dependencies of their advancing years. Their love for each other is equal in depth; but their ways of manifesting love are different during each life stage.

Husband and wife are deeply connected, yet have different obligations toward each other and to their marriage. Patriarchs and matriarchs of families play complementary but unequal roles. Yang is the primordial creative male force, which provides for and protects the wife and children. In asserting himself as husband, and by creating the external structures of his career and their shelter, the male's complement of yin receives in turn a home and a family from the female. Yin is the primordial receptive female force, which submits and cleaves to her husband. In yielding herself as wife, the female's complement of yang creates the internal structures of home and family. Man builds the house; woman makes the home. Their roles are perfect complements, yet their duties differ. They honor and love each other equally, yet they contribute differently to the whole they form by marriage.[8]

Old and young are deeply connected, since the old gave rise to the young, and the young will become old in their turn. The young do not always or easily understand this, nor do they necessarily understand their lack of understanding. For this reason alone they must honor and respect their elders, who have acquired the wisdom and patience born of long and deep experience, that serve to temper the rashness and impetuousness of youth. Respecting and revering one's elders is applicable at every age. Parents of middle age receive respect from their children, but give respect to their elderly parents in turn. And this extends to the whole of Confucian society, beyond the family itself. Every person has a duty to honor and respect his and her elders. By paying such respects, the younger one opens a channel to the elder, through which a measure of the elder's experience and wisdom can flow back to the younger. This is the way of cultural continuity and individual growth.

If you are an accomplished student of music, you will sooner or later attend a master class, and perhaps even play for a maestro. By showing respect and attentiveness to the master musician, the student opens a channel and thereby receives a precious gift of the master's experience and wisdom. The audience hears, and the student recognizes, an immediate improvement in her playing. Submitting to this kind of master does not make you a slave; rather, it furthers you on the path of mastery. The same holds true for all of us, who play daily upon the instrument of our lives. Respect for one's elders opens the Way to progress in any endeavor. The old and the young strive equally to experience each moment fully, yet they do so differently.

Ruler and subject are deeply connected, yet their mutual obligations are once again distinctly different. We can readily transpose Confucius's feudal terminology into modern terms: Think about the relation between the leader of a state and its citizens, or between the leader of an organization and its employees, and you have the modern equivalents of ruler and subject. The leader once again embodies yang, the creative: He creates a vision or a goal, inspires others to help attain it, and bears the brunt of the associated responsibilities. The leader's complement of yin is also active: He must remain receptive to the many needs of the followers, and ultimately he receives the lion's share of praise or blame for the outcome. The leader is also a follower, of his own internal vision. The followers of leaders embody yin, the receptive: They receive the leader's vision or goal, and his inspiration for attaining it. Their own individual virtues (in Aristotle's sense) are stimulated by being receptive to the example that the leader creates. The follower's complement of yang is also active: She must create the means for implementing her portion of the strategy or plan that emanates from the leadership. If she too has a strong capacity to lead, then she will demonstrate it by voluntarily assuming more responsibility than was allocated to her, and in this way may climb the leadership ladder. If she has a strong capacity to follow, then she will assume correspondingly less responsibility, and find a suitably comfortable level of participation among the following. The follower is also a leader, recreating the leadership example in her own sector of the organization. Leaders and followers are mutually dependent, yet their roles are very different.

When it comes to friendship, the fifth kind of relationship governed by *li*, we finally encounter a kind of parity that is not immediately evident in the other four. Friendship is perhaps the deepest human connection of all, partly because friends share the same set of mutual obligations, yet do not feel the weight of being obliged. On the contrary, helping a friend is usually more of a joy than a burden. Friendship is such a powerful and unselfish kind of love that it is closest of all to pure *ren*, and so requires that much less of *li* to shape its expression. Whereas relations between parent and child, husband and wife, old and young, leader and follower, may sour under the influence of difficult circumstances, or even collapse under the weight of calamity, friendships tend to ripen and deepen with the passing of time. If you are fortunate to reach an age at which your friendships themselves are forty or fifty or sixty years old, then you know that there is scarcely a more precious gift bestowed upon a person. Lifelong friendship is one of the greatest (some say one of the only) benefits of aging. Exactly like Confucius, Aristotle too extolled the virtues of friendship, recognizing it as the noblest expression of love. There is a kind of *li* that shapes the *ren* of friendship too, but in a complementary sense. Unlike the other forms of human relations, in which one's performance of duty can be justly demanded, friends do not need to make demands on one another. Yet precisely because the performance of duty is not demanded between friends, they can cheerfully go "beyond the call" of duty for one another, and not even consider that they are being more than dutiful.

The equality and parity of friendship complements the inequalities and disparities of the four other kinds of relationships—giving to friends, and receiving from them, feels like one undifferentiated experience, and not like complementary parts of a whole. Yet friendship is also connected to the other relationships in a mysterious way: It is a hardy plant that takes root and flourishes in their soil. Wherever there is *ren*, however expressed via *li*, there too lies the possibility of friendship. So parent and child, husband and wife, elder and younger, ruler and subject, may also become friends, or at least can experience periods or episodes of friendship. Even though their formal relations remain externally shaped by *li*, which keeps them connected but necessarily unequal, they may also enjoy periods of informal and internal friendship, experiencing one another as connected and equal.

Yet even this wonderful complementary possibility—that of formal relationships giving rise to informal friendships—is itself subject to ever-operative laws of balanced order. The Confucian emphasis on the formal aspects of human relations reflects this vital ordering: The formal tends to precede the informal. Parents and children may become friends, but self-evidently they do not begin their relations as friends. The same is true of the other relations. Spouses may eventually become friends, but courtship is very different than friendship. Similarly, although you may end up making friends at work, the hiring process is not in the first instance a search for friends. When this order is reversed, trouble frequently follows. For example, friends who go into business together will soon find their equalities of friendship stressed by the inequitable demands of commercial partnership.

Equalities of friendship aside, the other four dimensions of human relationship are not as separate or distinct as they may at first appear. Their own ordering is not exclusive; rather, each tends to resemble or mirror the other. They all emanate from Tao, which favors or disfavors none. For example, the relation of ruler and subject resembles that of parent and child, in that the adult depends on the leader of the state for authority and guidance, provision, and care, just as the child depends on its parents for these things. The polarity of these roles can also periodically reverse themselves, as in democratic elections, when the followers choose a leader, who then governs with their consent. A child does not normally elect its parents, yet in later life most students gravitate toward particular teachers, from whom they consent to learn. Husbands and wives also experience shifts in polarity, if not constant power struggles. Confucian cultures mirror the natural social order of primates, in which the male is dominant and the female is submissive. Yet Taoists noticed that solvent seas pulverize rigid rocks into sand, that pliable lips protect brittle teeth; that softer ways can overcome and outlast harder ones. And so in some families, "submissive" wives can eventually grind "dominant" husbands into domesticated dust. Externally the man appears to be the family sovereign, or at least its figurehead, but internally, in Confucian as in most cultures, the woman rules the roost at home. In the West, as Emerson judiciously observed, a wife exerts greater influence over her husband—for better or worse— than does the government.

And from our contrasts between Aristotle and Confucius, we can see that they are also Taoist complements, interconnected but different, just like the civilizations they represent. A whole that unites them is Buddhism: The Middle Way within The Middle Way.

## Deference to Yin

I digress to observe that more than chivalry compels the saying "ladies first"—even "liberated" women accept deference when it is offered. If you are a married man and don't defer to your wife often enough, she will let you know. And so the Tao often defers to yin over yang, but not only for the sake of domestic bliss. The principle of wu wei, or action through nonaction, counsels us to rein in our creative natures in certain situations, to refrain from creating uncalled-for thoughts, words, or acts, and instead to exercise yinlike receptivity to circumstances until such time as they favor propitious action.

What situations are these? Primarily, they are the ones in which we aren't quite sure what to do. When you are not sure what to do, you have found the perfect time to do nothing. Why? Because by doing nothing you may fail to do something right, but you will succeed in doing nothing wrong. If your situation is so chaotic that you cannot see a pattern pointing the way to order, then you will probably make things worse by taking action just for action's sake. Once you perceive the Way you can follow it, not before. By doing nothing at the right time you will perceive it immediately, because you will be doing exactly as it suggests: nothing. "Take two nothings, and call me in the morning," is the Tao's prescription in these circumstances. But at other times, for example in the midst of a crisis, you may see with extraordinary clarity precisely what you must do, and so you do it dutifully, beautifully, authentically. Then too have you seen the Way.

Wu wei is also conservative of your vitality, and so safeguards you against wasting energy at times when effort cannot serve to further. And even when effort does further, entropy always exacts transaction costs. Chaos is order's constant companion. So why feed its insatiable appetite unnecessarily? In chess, possibly Persian in origin but most developed in the West, white has an advantage by virtue of moving first. Black must sooner or later wrest the initiative from white. The same is true of tennis, which is like chess at one hundred miles per hour. The server always has the advantage, because the server initiates play. But in Western and "spaghetti Western" movies that make the American Wild West appear more chivalrous than it was, whoever draws first against a master loses. In hockey, the cardinal rule of goaltenders is: Never move first. And in East Asian martial arts, the first move is similarly the losing one. The best defense never moves first: It can afford the luxury of seeing what the other will do, and then of responding appropriately. Like wu wei, defense is conservative. Both defer to inaction over action, stillness over movement; receptivity over creativity; yin over yang.

### Extreme Duties versus Extreme Rights

As I have previously intimated and as we will see, Aristotelian individualism and Confucian collectivism can both be taken to extremes. Western cultures have criticized East Asian ones because they often discount human rights in their dutiful maintenance of conservative social orders, while Confucian cultures have criticized Aristotelian ones because they allow social orders to disintegrate in their zealous crusades for individual rights, which have led to warring cultural factions and the horrors of identity politics (which we will examine soon enough). Both systems have their strengths and weaknesses; tensions between the individual and society are part of the human condition. The Aristotelian emphasis on individual fulfillment and the Confucian emphasis on social order are not directly contradictory, and can themselves be balanced by Buddha's Middle Way, which grants each view its place in the overall scheme of things, and which also relates them through dharma—correct teachings and appropriate practice. Dharma satisfies both Aristotle's pursuit of individual fulfillment by awakening the Buddha within, and satisfies Confucius's maintenance of balanced order by compassionate connectedness with sangha, the community of humankind.

In Daisaku Ikeda's words, "There are important spiritual and ethical cognates between Confucian philosophy, which seeks to create an ideal society through the self-mastery and self-directed transformation of individuals, and Buddhism, with its stress on the processes of refining and elevating our humanity, ultimately transforming the deepest, most essential regions of the inner life. This basic similarity of approach was crucial in facilitating the spread and reception of Buddhism within the Chinese cultural sphere, where Confucianism figured so prominently."[9]

If the Confucian virtue of *li* is pushed to an extreme, it can degenerate from a natural hierarchy of dutiful but loving relationships into a stratified and petrified system of political, economic, and social serfdom, whose constricted channels obstruct *ren*'s flow. If the Aristotelian virtue of fulfillment is pushed to an extreme, it can degenerate from a disciplined dynamism that produces individual merit to a feeding frenzy of rights-crazed radicals, who believe they have entitlements to everything and obligations to nothing. The awakening of human consciousness, the realization of individual potential, and the emancipation of the communal being, are furthered neither through the rigid socioeconomic servitude that has plagued Asian civilization, nor via the political anarchy and moral relativism that sorely afflicts (if not mortally threatens) Western civilization. The Middle Way is a way for all humanity to flourish, East and West alike, regardless of the differing philosophical soils from which their civilizations have sprung.

## The Confucian Legacy

Just as the philosophical issues raised in ancient Hellas spawned a tradition that continues unabated across millennia of Western civilization, and just as these very issues and their parallel tradition unfolded even earlier in Vedic civilization, so the post-Confucians of Sinic civilization engaged in similar debates and dialogues for centuries, until Buddhism arrived to produce its delectable fruits from China's fertile philosophical soil.

For example, the Confucian tradition branched and enriched itself through the philosophers Mencius and Xunzi, more than 1,500 years before Hobbes's and Jean-Jacques Rousseau's divergence on human nature divided Western political opinion between authority and anarchy. Mencius emphasized the inherent goodness of human nature, claiming that the purpose of civilization in general and education in particular is to make implicit human goodness manifest. A stringed instrument produces beautiful music when tuned and plucked by a skillful player; and similarly a human being produces goodness when ethically attuned and morally stimulated by an artful ethos. Xunzi disagreed, claiming that human beings are essentially evil creatures, citing the lamentable record of violence, murder, and crime across the social spectrum—from the extravagant abuses of tyrants to the pettier larcenies of ordinary citizens. So Xunzi argued for a strong and authoritarian government to deter, discourage, curtail, and punish the vindictive wickedness and malicious mischief that lurk in all men's minds and hearts.

These and kindred philosophical conflicts were transformed and reconciled by the arrival of Buddhist teachings. Mahayana Buddhism asserted the normal distribution of moral qualities in human societies, such that some people can always be found who do mostly good deeds, while others can always be found who perpetrate predominantly evil ones. The majority vacillates less radically between these two extremes, in confused or inconsistent frames of mind, capable of doing good at one moment and harm the next. (This is exactly what Socrates taught in Athens too.[10]) Hence the importance of education, role models, and communities to foster The Middle Way—and of correctional measures to contain particularly dangerous persons, and to bestow on them the special education they require.

## From C to Geometry

We have taken a philosophical journey from Aristotle to Buddha, and from Buddha to Confucius. We have seen that A and C are complementary in some respects, and I have suggested that B is both The Middle Way between them, and the whole that unites them. Buddha taught that there is no separate reality. Bearing this in mind, let us now look at the geometry of the ABCs, which reflects even more profound relations among them, as well as their relations to some of nature's fundamental patterns. This also makes the ABCs more relevant to us, by reconnecting humanity to nature, and for reconciling extremes of human nurture, too.

# 5

## ABC GEOMETRY
### Golden Mean, Middle Way, Balanced
### Order Are Deeply Related

*Justice is not a square number.* —Aristotle

*Chaos is inherent in all compounded things.* —Buddha

*If things go amiss, he who knows the harmony
will be able to attune them.* —Confucius

### Measuring the Earth

"GEOMETRY" IS A GREEK WORD meaning "measurement of earth." The importance of geometry itself is immeasurably great. Before demonstrating how the ABCs themselves are related geometrically, let me remind you why geometry is so essential to human beings. The reasons are too numerous to name, but I will briefly mention a few that pertain to our cultural evolution.

First, "measuring the earth" means measuring all that it contains, and especially all the things and properties of things that are necessary or useful to human beings. When prehistoric humans abandoned caves and began to build their own dwellings, from thatched lean-tos to ice-block igloos, from mud huts to animal-skin tents, they had to maintain proportionality among the dimensions and components of each dwelling. If they ignored the proper proportions, their dwellings could not be constructed. How much truer is this of blueprints? Without geometry, we would still be living in caves. Dwellings of so many other animals—from beehives to spiderwebs, from rabbit warrens to coral reefs—all brim with geometry, which these other creatures use instinctively, but which we humans need to learn (or perhaps, as Plato believed, we need merely to recollect).

The earliest humans were hunter-gatherers. To hunt or fish successfully, primitive man needed spears, blowguns, boomerangs, bows and arrows, nets, and snares. These things cannot be fashioned in the absence of measurement. When early humans crafted clothing out of animals skins and other materials, they had to make measurements. And when they gathered fruits or nuts or tubers or vegetation or firewood or water, they had to weave baskets or devise other containers for them, and know how much they could carry at one time, and how far. All this requires measurement. Our earliest ancestors could not have fed and clothed themselves without informal geometry.

At night, they had to protect themselves and their children against predatory animals, including marauding humans. If you dig a moat, how deep and wide should it be? If you build a fence, how high should it be? If you want to keep a campfire burning all night, what volume of wood should you stockpile? All this requires measurement. Early humans could not have protected their encampments and settlements without informal geometry.

Elaborate architecture and reliable navigation require far more sophisticated measurements, which cannot be made without Euclidean geometry and its direct descendents such as trigonometry. With improved science, geometry evolved into chronographic measurement of latitude, telescopic measurement of our solar system, our galaxy, other galaxies, and the very cosmos itself; and to microscopic and microcosmic measurement of cellular, molecular, atomic, and even quantum entities.

It's a remarkable but true fact that we human beings stand precisely midway on our own vast scale of measurement. The scientific term *order of magnitude* denotes a measurement factor of ten. So an object ten times larger than you is said to be "one order magnitude" larger; while an object ten times smaller than you is said to be "one order of magnitude" smaller. Similarly, two orders of magnitude correspond to a factor of $10^2$ or 100; three orders of magnitude, to a factor of $10^3$ or 1,000, and so on. Scientists can currently detect objects twenty-two orders of magnitude distant from us ($10^{22}$ meters distant), and can also detect objects twenty-two orders of magnitude smaller than us ($10^{-22}$ meters smaller). We stand exactly midway on this measurement spectrum, which ranges over forty-five orders of magnitude: from astronomically immense extremes, to subatomically infinitesimal ones. Can you take a cosmic hint? Human beings are nature's geometric embodiments of The Middle Way.

## Geometry, Philosophy, and Music

There are powerful connections between geometry, philosophy, and music—all of which enrich our understanding of The Middle Way. Some examples are instructive. Let's look briefly at key relations between each of the three pairs: geometry and philosophy, philosophy and music, music and geometry. This will better prepare us for the geometry of the ABCs themselves.

Euclid's *Elements*—the theory and construction of figures on flat surfaces—is a paradigmatic book for logic, mathematics, physics, architecture, and aesthetics. In other words, Euclid is a departure point for both the philosophy of geometry and the geometry of philosophy. His *Elements* is also the world's all-time best-selling mathematics book, having been in near-continuous use for more than two thousand years. The West's greatest minds have been nourished, stimulated, and inspired by Euclid's *Elements*, which (among other invaluable treasures) have been jettisoned by postmodernism. Not many university administrators, professors, or students still know the motto that Plato affixed above the entrance to his Academy, the model of our universities themselves: LET NO ONE IGNORANT OF GEOMETRY ENTER HERE. What would Plato or Aristotle say about an education system that is all but bereft of geometry, in which students gauge mainly their "self-esteem"? I leave it to your imagination for now. But I will take no chances, and will return to it later. Suffice it to say that the motto has been changed to: LET NO ONE COGNIZANT OF GEOMETRY GRADUATE HERE.

It's a grand irony: Euclid's *Elements* was the only prerequisite for entry into the West's first and foremost Academy, because an understanding of geometry vouchsafed a foundation for understanding everything else, from poetry to physics, from philosophy to politics. By the late twentieth century, too many Western universities had not only abandoned Euclid as a prerequisite, but also eliminated prerequisites themselves. The result is inevitable: Their graduates' horizons are narrowed instead of broadened. And so the intellectual edifice of Western civilization is imploding, as we will see in chapter 11. A dumbed-down and deconstructed mind politic cannot long sustain the vital functions of its body politic. But far too many Americans and other Westerners don't "get" this, because they no longer "get" Euclid.

Euclid's influence on Western civilization is seminal. Aristotle derived his golden mean—a geometric ethic—directly from Euclid. Galileo, who helped ignite the modern scientific revolution by refuting key errors in Aristotle's physics, used Euclidean geometry to derive the results of his experiments, in which he rolled balls down inclined planes to study their accelerations under gravity. The so-called "Galilean transforms"—his equations of motion—were the departure point for Newton's celebrated laws of motion. The decisive period from Galileo (1564–1642) through Newton (1643–1727) saw swift mathematical developments from geometry to algebra to calculus (to late Baroque music), but all of Newton's epoch-making results can be derived using Euclidean geometry, although it is tedious to do so.

Important contemporaries of Galileo included Hobbes, Baruch Spinoza, and Descartes. The structure of Thomas Hobbes's *Leviathan*, a masterwork and bulwark of Western civilization that founded two modern fields—political science and empirical psychology—was heavily influenced by Hobbes's accidental encounter with Euclid's *Elements*. Spinoza's *Ethics*, one of two core works by that towering figure of Western philosophy, is an attempt to import Euclidean geometry's methods—definition and proposition, deduction and construction—directly into ethical domains. French philosopher and mathematician Rene Descartes invented analytical geometry, which transposed Euclidean geometry into a powerful algebraic system that still bears his name—Cartesian coordinates—a stepping-stone to the later breakthrough in Newtonian calculus.

Carl Friedrich Gauss was a German mathematical genius who discovered—among many things—the "Gaussian distribution," commonly known as the bell-shaped curve, to which we will shortly return. In 1805, Gauss wrote an earthshaking paper that he promptly locked up and kept secret. He feared the condemnation of his peers, or in his words, "the clamor of the Boeotians" (an unruly Greek tribe renowned for its ignorance) if he made his findings public. How did Gauss shake the earth? By daring to wonder whether the geometry of space itself is possibly "non-Euclidean"—that is, not flat.[1]

In 1905, one century after Gauss had concealed the secret, Einstein published his seminal paper on general relativity, which predicted (among other things) that space-time becomes curved in strong gravitational fields. Twenty more years would pass before Eddington confirmed this experimentally, vindicating Einstein and Gauss alike, Boeotians notwithstanding.[2]

Pythagoras was a posthumous contributor to Euclid's *Elements*, renowned for the theorem that still bears his name.[3] Thomas Hobbes became an inveterate geometer when he accidentally read this very proposition in a friend's library, and could not believe it. So Hobbes backpedaled through Euclid until convinced of its truth, which made him "in love with geometry" (as biographer John Aubrey wrote[4]) for the reminder of his long life. No less a figure than Einstein revealed his incipient genius by discovering a new and elegant proof of Pythagoras's theorem while still a teenager—and showing so little interest in prescribed mathematical homework that one teacher called him "a lazy dog who will never amount to anything." Pythagoras himself was fascinated by numbers, and thought the universe was composed of them. He was probably correct.

Pythagoras also discovered a geometric problem latent in music, known as the "Pythagorean comma," whose consequences affect all composers, performers, and piano tuners, as well as discerning listeners. It turns out that the cycle of twelve semitones that comprises a complete octave, and from which all Western musical modes are drawn, do not relate to one another in integral proportions. (Remember integrity, and its relation to wholeness?) This means that no instrument can be perfectly tuned. If you tune the cycle of fifths exactly, the octaves will sound sharp. If you flatten the fifths slightly, the octaves will sound in tune. This has nothing to do with the way instruments are built; it is a property of the geometry of our musical intervals themselves. And so J. S. Bach composed *The Well-Tempered Clavier,* a prelude and fugue in every key, to illustrate just how well even-temperament tuning compensates for the imperfections of the Pythagorean comma.

Now that you see more clearly the importance of geometry, and hence of Plato's emphasis that all his students (including Aristotle) learn it, I can begin to illustrate some deeper relations between geometry, music, and philosophy, and their relevance to The Middle Way. The ancient Greeks, like the ancient Chinese, valued balance and harmony. The Latin word *rational* reflects exactly this, for although it has come to mean "reasonable," it derives from a geometrically more precise term: *ratio,* or integral balance between two (or more) parts of a whole. The Romans got this from Greek geometry. The Greeks optimistically supposed the world to be an orderly place (*cosmos*) and not a disorderly one (*chaos*), and understandably but incorrectly assumed that such order was necessarily reflected in the proportionate balance of all numbers as well. So the Greeks simply assumed that all geometric quantities could be expressed as ratios of whole numbers. Why was this important? Because Euclidean geometry—exactly like music and philosophy—entails both theory and practice. On the one hand, Euclid provided the guiding light for 2,500 years of Western *rational* inquiry by first codifying an elegant system of definitions, axioms, and postulates, then by proceeding to deduce new results from previously established ones, thus building up a whole corpus of reliable knowledge. Euclidean geometry is the original model for what became known as the "hypothetico-deductive" method of Western science.

On the other hand, Euclid also refined the art of geometric construction, which means the drawing of two-dimensional figures in a plane that still bears his name. Such constructions serve two worthwhile purposes. First, they allow us to "illustrate" geometric relations via our powerful and influential sense of vision. A picture is worth not only a thousand words, it can also be worth a hundred lines of proof. If we can illustrate a geometric truth by constructing it, it may become easier to demonstrate that truth via an associated logical deduction. Second, geometric constructions themselves are nothing but blueprints for constructing artistic and architectural works alike—which the Greeks greatly valued, and understood as applied geometry.

Euclidean construction allows us but two instruments: the straightedge and the compass. The sharp end of the compass enables us to make points on the page, while the straightedge permits us to project or connect points with straight lines. The swinging arm of the compass allows us to trace arcs at desired distances from any point, arcs which moreover generate angles of any desired extent, up to and including the 360 degrees that constitute a circle.

These are the "ground rules" of Euclidean geometry, whose challenges are then to construct desired figures (for example, a golden rectangle) or complete desired tasks (for example, bisecting a given angle) using only the straightedge and the compass. Why are these the sole tools permitted? For excellent reasons. They satisfy the elegant demand of universality in constructing figures of any desired ratio, regardless of variable local measures. For example, if you construct a golden rectangle, the ratio of its sides will necessarily be $\varphi{:}1$. If I construct one, its ratio of sides will also be $\varphi{:}1$. This ratio is absolute $\varphi$—in other words, it's universal and unchanging, no matter who undertakes the construction. By contrast, the units of measure that are chosen to represent 1 are local and variable. For example, your 1 may be one inch; my 1 may be one centimeter; somebody else's 1 may be chosen by a random extension of the compass. But our local variability of unit measure makes no difference to the result, which is a figure whose *ratio* of sides is universal and constant, in this case $\varphi{:}1$. This arrangement is both profoundly democratic yet also perfectly rational: It allows the individual considerable latitude in selecting a local measure, but also guarantees universality of the desired ratio.

The connection between geometric ratios, rational individuals, and well-ordered societies ran very deep in the Hellenic mind. If variation in local measures could still produce universal agreement in absolute ratios, in accordance with a greater cosmic order, then perhaps this powerful model of Euclidean geometry could be extended to matters of individual rationality and societal balance. That is, democratic latitude in individual taste and preference could still give rise to well-proportioned or rational citizens, who would then form a harmonious or well-balanced society. Since the universe was by definition an orderly place (a cosmos), whose very fabric was assumed to be woven out of whole numbers (integers), then the Euclidean construction of geometric ratios, the philosophical construction of rational beings, and the political construction of balanced societies were three manifestations of the same principle. This closer analysis of the connection between geometry and politics will enable us to perceive deeper similarities between Aristotle's golden mean and Confucius's balanced order.

So why aren't we inhabiting utopias now? Alas, this elegant idea of the ancient Greeks, which must be accounted as one of the most ennobling seeds ever to germinate in the fertile minds of human beings, unfortunately gave rise to a bitter fruit, namely an inevitable irrationality embedded in the foundations of Euclidean geometry itself. Since infinitely many numbers turn out to be irrational (and worse), it is impossible to express them as ratios of integers. Similarly, since all human beings turn out to be irrational (and worse) in some ways at some times, it is difficult if not impossible to sustain desirable proportions of ethical character, or maintain desirable balance in our relationships with others, at every minute and hour of the day. This suggests that we cannot expect to achieve or maintain perpetually well-ordered societies either. When political pendulums swing into irrational (and worse) domains, they lead to despotism at one extreme and anarchy at the other. Despotic political constructs produce social orders that stifle human possibility or annihilate human flourishing; while anarchic political deconstructions fail to harness human possibility or enable human flourishing at all.

So clearly did the ancient Greeks perceive the connections between Euclidean geometry and utopian democracy that the mathematical elite was both scandalized and demoralized by the discovery by Hippasus of

Metapontum (a student of Pythagoras, born circa 500 B.C.E.) that the square root of two is irrational. When Hippasus proved that the square root of two cannot be represented as a ratio of two integers, he was warned on pain of death not to make this finding public, lest it put paid to utopian political vision so rooted in the supposedly unshakable bedrock of Euclidean construction. Hippasus defied the warning, whereupon the Pythagoreans drowned him in the bay. But his proof still floats. To add insult to their injury, the square root of two is a fairly "common-and-garden" irrational number, whose construction by Euclidean means is child's play. All you need do is construct an isosceles triangle, whose two equal sides are of unit length (you choose the units), and which form an angle of ninety degrees. Applying Pythagoras's theorem, the length of the hypotenuse of that triangle is the square root of two. So simple to construct, and yet impossible to express as a ratio of two integers.

Worse problems followed. It turned out that some "common-and-garden" numbers were so irrational that they could not even be constructed at all, let alone represented as ratios of integers. Take $\pi$, for example. Anyone can draw a circle with a compass, and everyone used to know that the ratio of the circle's circumference to its diameter is $\pi$ again regardless of the relative size of the circle. The ratio itself is universal and constant. Yet however easily one constructs a circle by twirling a compass, it is impossible to construct by Euclidean means a straight line whose length is $\pi$ units. This problem challenged and defeated the finest mathematical minds of the West from Euclid's day until the late nineteenth century, when sophisticated tools of mathematical analysis became available and were used to prove it could not be done at all.[5]

If you were taught in school that $\pi = {}^{22}\!/_{7}$, you were misled. That ratio is an approximation, adequate for constructing Euclidean boxes to contain roughly circular pizzas, but not equal to the true value of $\pi$. We can compute more accurate approximations of $\pi$ to any desired extent—${}^{179}\!/_{57}$, ${}^{289}\!/_{92}$, ${}^{355}\!/_{113}$ are improvements upon ${}^{22}\!/_{7}$—but we can never state $\pi$'s "final" value: It has none. An elegant eighteenth-century series for approximating $\pi$, codiscovered (along with so many other things) by Leibniz, is $\pi/4 = 1 - \frac{1}{3} + \frac{1}{5} - \frac{1}{7} + \ldots$

So I leave this troubling thought to your imagination. If your educators misled you to believe that π = ²²⁄₇, whether intentionally or not, then what else did they mislead you about, particularly in moral and political domains? Perhaps our ABCs can help correct similar inaccuracies and misunderstandings on those more sensitive and also more volatile planes. Notwithstanding the unhappy end met by Hippasus, a great many more people have suffered and died in moral, religious, and political disputes than in mathematical ones. The common denominator, however, is ideology. When confronted by demonstrable truths that run contrary to dogmatic beliefs, people whose power over others depends on falsehoods seem reluctant to embrace truth; they more often attempt to throttle truth by silencing the truth tellers. This is the dark side of the linkage between geometry, ethics, and politics. Now let's step back into the light.

## Linking the Geometries of A and C: The Many Faces of Phi

Next, I would like to show you some vital and beautiful ways in which the geometries of the ABCs are interconnected. First, let's revisit the golden rectangle, from which Aristotle derived his ethics. It's depicted in fig. 5.1. Recall, its sides are in the ratio φ:1. This is the "golden ratio" which, as we have seen, has applications to art, architecture, economics, and ethics—among many things. Kepler called φ "one of geometry's two great treasures."

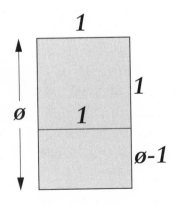

Figure 5.1 The Golden Rectangle

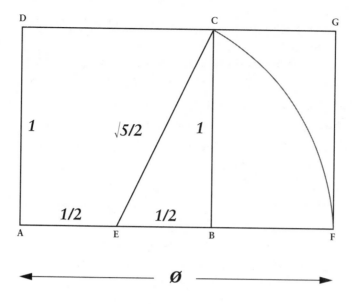

Figure 5.2 Constructing the Golden Rectangle

(The other is Pythagoras's theorem.) The Greeks knew that φ is also irrational: φ = (1 + √5)/2. So how did they construct it? There are many ingenious ways to do so by Euclidean means. Fig. 5.2 illustrates the simplest.[6]

Does the golden rectangle relate to the yin-yang circle? As I pondered this question, it soon became evident that the yin-yang circle also embeds φ in its underlying geometry. How? In plain view. The yin-yang circle is actually composed of five circles: the outermost one, then two smaller and equal inner ones, then two smallest and equal innermost ones. These

Figure 5.3 Five Circles of the Yin-Yang Symbol

five circles are shown in fig. 5.3. In fact, this is exactly how you construct a yin-yang circle by Euclidean means, using only a compass—then maybe a crayon. All you need to know are the ratios of the three different-size circles. Once again these ratios are fixed, regardless of how large or small you choose to make the overall symbol itself.

Suppose we define the outermost circle's diameter as one unit of measure. Then the inner circles each have diameters of half a unit of measure. Now what about the innermost circles? If you measure the yin-yang symbols in common use—they appear everywhere—you will see that the innermost circle's diameters are usually between one-ninth

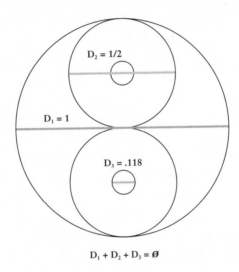

$$D_1 + D_2 + D_3 = \emptyset$$

Figure 5.4 ø in the Yin-Yang Symbol

and one-eighth the size of the outermost circle—that is, between 0.111 and 0.125 units. Their average is 0.118 units. And if you carefully measure the innermost circle of the generic yin-yang symbol, depicted in fig. 5.4, you will also find its diameter to be 0.118 units.

This is very interesting, since $0.118 = \varphi - 1 - \frac{1}{2}$. So if we add the three different diameters used in the construction of the yin-yang circle, their sum is $1 + \frac{1}{2} + (\varphi - 1 - \frac{1}{2}) = \varphi$ units. So $\varphi$ turns out to be the definitive proportion here, just as it is in the golden rectangle. If you use any other ratio for the innermost circles, they will look either too large or too

Generic Yin Yang Symbol          Ø  Yin  Yang  Symbol

Figure 5.5 ø Generates the Yin Yang Symbol

small. But as long as the sum of the three different diameters is φ units, then the yin-yang symbol appears exactly as we are accustomed to seeing it, in the correct aesthetic balance. Compare the two yin-yang symbols in fig. 5.5. I downloaded the generic one from the Web, and constructed the other one using φ. The two are indistinguishable. The golden rectangle and the yin-yang circle are both defined by φ. As we hippies used to say, this is mind-blowing.

While cynics may dismiss this as coincidental, I believe it is not happenstance at all; rather, part of deeper patterns in the world. It is surely not by coincidence that Aristotle and Confucius each came to exert such tremendous influence over their respective civilizations. It is surely not by coincidence that they both saw human beings as subject to natural laws. It is surely not by coincidence that they each understood the significance of ratio and proportion in human affairs. And so it cannot be by coincidence that a special geometric ratio—namely φ—is embedded in symbols that represent Aristotelian and Confucian systems of ethics. I consider it an affirmation of this book's thesis, that the ABCs are fundamental to the evolution of a shared human paradigm in the global village.

Now what about Buddha's symbolism? Since φ is embedded in Aristotelian and Confucian symbols, and if Buddhism is The Middle Way within The Middle Way, then φ ought to be embedded in Buddhist symbolism too. It is, and I am happy to point it out to you. But with Buddhism we encounter a more challenging initial question: What symbol (if any) represents Buddha's Middle Way? With most religions, this is a settled matter. Judaism's symbol is the Star of David; Christianity's, the cross; Islam's, the crescent. Indian philosophy tends to favor either a Ganesh, or a many-armed dancing Shiva, or—as in India's flag—a multi-spoked wheel, representing chakras and the wheel of reincarnation. After deliberating this question, I propose that not one but rather three symbols are typical of Buddhism, one for each Jewel: Buddha (the role model), dharma (the teachings), and sangha (the community).

The symbol of Buddha is Buddha, most often seated in the lotus position. This figure is common to every Buddhist culture. The symbol

Figure 5.6 Stylized Lotus Flowers

of dharma is the lotus flower—symbolic too of the Lotus Sutra, Buddha's ultimate teaching. Some typical stylized lotus flowers are depicted in fig. 5.6. As we will shortly see, the geometry of the lotus embodies both the golden rectangle and the yin-yang circle, just as the dharma embodies both Aristotelian and Confucian ethics.

But what is the symbol of sangha? To my knowledge, sangha has not been generically identified with geometry. What is sangha? The community. What is the community? An aggregation of human beings. Mathematical measurement of aggregates is statistical, not Euclidean, and owes a great debt to a man already mentioned in this context: Gauss. The Gaussian distribution produces a distinctive geometric figure, namely the bell-shaped curve, also known as the "normal distribution." Because sangha embodies the communal norms of Buddhism, this Third Jewel could be represented geometrically by Gauss's normal distribution itself.

## Lessons of the Lotus

The symbol of dharma is the lotus, which itself embodies many metaphorical and allegorical lessons. The lotus flower is surpassingly beautiful, yet Buddhists are fond of reminding us that the lotus sinks its roots into mud. Many people don't regard mud as beautiful—even though some beauty treatments involve the application of mud to one's skin. So the lotus flower represents the interconnectedness of phenomenas, from manifested beauty to unmanifested mud. This parallels the Taoist doctrine of complements: What people regard as "beautiful" (such as flowers) necessarily maintain some connection to what people regard as "unbeautiful" (such as mud). As well, the lotus symbolizes an important Buddhist teaching called "making good causes" or "changing poison into medicine," which we will encounter in different contexts later in this book. The idea is that the lotus plant draws vital nutrients from the unbeautiful mud, which it uses to produce beautiful flowers.

More subtly still, Daisaku Ikeda explains the relation of the lotus plant to karma.[7] Unusually, the lotus plant produces fruit just before it flowers. Would that more humans would do so! Why? Because karma is cause and effect—the ripening fruit of action. If the consequences of our intended actions ripened in our awareness before we performed them, we could refrain from doing harmful things, and manage to do more good things. We all fail to take account of our actions from time to time, yet all our actions are also causes whose effects return to us in a matter of time. The operative question is: When? Dharma teaches us how to shorten the time between cause and effect, making them close to simultaneous. If the fruit of an action has already ripened at the time we perform it, then cause and effect become simultaneous, and the temporal gap between them vanishes. The closing of that gap opens windows in the mind, and doors in the heart.

Among the lotus's many lessons for human beings is that we are all born with the remarkable capacity to draw vital nutrients from the mud of our unhappiest circumstances, which we can use to produce beautiful outcomes. And so the toxic emanations of mind—such as hatred, envy, slander, calumny, betrayal, abuse, oppression—can be transformed into their complements: love, gratitude, praise, truth, trust, support, nurture. How do we change such poisons into medicines? By emulating the lotus in our practice. How do we learn this practice? Coincidentally or not, from the Lotus Sutra.

## Geometry of the Lotus

Now let's create some lotus flowers, both geometrically here and now, and with our vital energies in social contexts. This is not simply for the sake of "arts and crafts." By working with the lotus, you will become more attentive to its sacred geometry, which in turn can have a spiritually transformative effect on you if you are receptive. Philosophy and music can both transform the soul, and we have just explored their intimate connection with geometry, which shares their power.[8] We'll begin our exercise in sacred geometry by constructing a lotus flower in Euclidean space, utilizing a framework of golden rectangles and yin-yang circles. After that we'll examine some amazing lotus flowers in Mandelbrot space, whose images are products of fractal geometry and chaos theory. Here too we will reencounter $\varphi$ and its tireless traveling companion Fibonacci, along with golden rectangles, yin-yang circles, and lotus flowers of astonishing beauty.

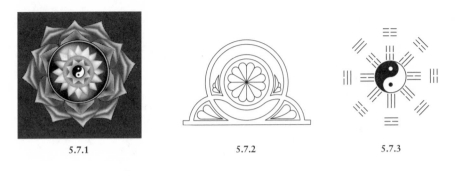

5.7.1          5.7.2          5.7.3

Figure 5.7 The Tao in the Lotus

In case you're wondering, there exist abundant integrations of the lotus flower and the yin-yang circle, illustrating awareness of their interconnectedness. As you might expect, they mostly spring from cultures in which Buddha and Tao are (or at least were at times) happily married. Fig. 5.7.1 is a floral tapestry from Nepal, a handcrafted dyed-in-the-wool Tao in the lotus. Fig. 5.7.2 looks like an Indian lotus, framed in an Islamic motif, set in a golden rectangle. The curvatures of the framework are beginning to bend in a yin-yang direction. Fig. 5.7.3 is the Chinese complement of 5.7.1: the lotus in the Tao. Each of its eight petals is a nuclear trigram, or half a hexagram.

Each of the *I Ching*'s sixty-four hexagrams can be decomposed into two nuclear trigrams. Each trigram simultaneously symbolizes different family members or relationships, different cultural conditions, different geographic features, and different seasons or seasonal transitions. This is the integrated but "fractal" picture of the cosmos from which Confucius derived his ethics. Turning the *I Ching* into a lotus flower is the inspiration of a serene mind. Note also that the trigrams are shaped like golden rectangles. So this lotus explicitly contains both Sinic and Hellenic forms of φ. But instead of incorporating φ as a basic structure, the lotus actually incorporates the structures that incorporate φ.

Like all TV chefs worth their salt, I prepared a lotus dish for you in advance. Two dishes, in fact. Please look again at fig. 5.6. Two of those flowers first bloomed in my experimental digital hothouse. Do you want to guess which ones they are before I tell you? (If yes, stop reading.) They are

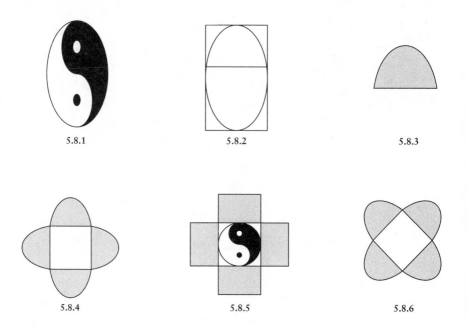

5.8.1    5.8.2    5.8.3

5.8.4    5.8.5    5.8.6

Figure 5.8 Constructing the Phi Lotus

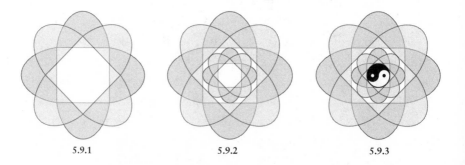

5.9.1    5.9.2    5.9.3

Figure 5.9 Constructing the Phi Lotus

#3 and #8. Now I'll show you how to make #3. We begin by building its framework, which takes five steps. First stretch a yin-yang circle to fit into a golden rectangle, as in 5.8.1 and 5.8.2. Second, remove the petal from the smaller golden rectangle, and color it if you wish. The one in 5.8.3 is golden. Third, conjoin four such golden petals, as shown in fig. 5.8.4.

What you see in 5.8.4 is a module of the framework. But David Bohm showed us how explicit patterns (explicate orders) contain implicit patterns (implicate orders).[9] The implicate order of 5.8.4 is shown in 5.8.5. It is four conjoined golden rectangles, with a yin-yang circle at their center. That is the underlying geometry of the lotus.

The fourth step is to rotate 5.8.4 by forty-five degrees, as in 5.8.6. Fifth, superimpose 5.8.4 and 5.8.6. Now you have the basic framework of this lotus, as in 5.9.1. If you're a minimalist, you're done. If you want to embellish it with a smaller copy of itself in the center, as in 5.9.2, go right ahead. Lotuses are fractals. And if you like it Nepalese style, finish it with a miniature yin-yang circle, as in 5.9.3. You can view or print out any of these lotuses, in living color, from this book's Web site, www.themiddleway.us. Try it out. Show it to some friends, and see if they know what it is. Most Buddhists will recognize a lotus. Ask them what it's made of. Not many may know it's constructed from phi.

Figure 5.10 The Phi Lotus

Fig. 5.10 shows a more elaborate version. Yet curiously enough, it's also more transparent. It has several nested layers, and its color scheme reveals how each golden petal sits on its own golden rectangle. I call it the "Phi Lotus." If you are at all moved by the beauties and symmetries of stylized lotus flowers, and their embodiments of φ, then you have understood something important about sacred geometry. It is nothing but sacred geometry that impelled so much of Hellenic architecture, Renaissance sculpture, Baroque music—and that still informs the esoteric mystical traditions of the world's great religions. Our exercises with the lotus flower illustrate that you need not be Pythagoras, Leonardo da Vinci, or Bach to appreciate the divine proportions of sacred geometry— just as you need not be Aristotle, Buddha, or Confucius to bring your soul into balance and your society into harmony. Now we will shift from Euclidean to fractal lotuses, whose scared geometric features become not only more pronounced, and but also infinitely complex.

## Fractal Geometry of The Middle Way

Fractal geometry and chaos theory are genuinely new developments of the late twentieth century, both abetted by the computer revolution. The number-crunching power and speed of computers, along with their capacity to generate full-color graphical displays, helped geometers visualize and conceptualize fractals, and also helped mathematicians visualize and conceptualize relations between order and chaos. It is not immediately apparent that fractal geometry has anything to do with chaos theory, yet their linkage is undeniable and astounding. Let us briefly illustrate how that linkage is forged, and how it recreates the lotus.

A fractal object is one that embodies self-similarity in its scaled geometric patterns. For example, a deciduous tree is a fractal. Its trunk and main branches form a pattern, and this pattern is repeated in increasingly smaller networks of main branches and sub-branches, down to sub-branches and twigs. But that's not all: The pattern resumes in its leaves. Each leaf has a main stem and branching stems, and so forth, all the way down to its network of veins and capillaries. These are the tree's aboveground patterns. Its underground root system is also fractal.

Figure 5.11 Matryoshka Dolls

You can discover fractals everywhere in nature, if you stay on the lookout for them. The circulatory systems of blood-bearing animals are branching fractals. Spiderwebs and snowflakes are concentric fractals. Coastlines are irregular fractals. Whether you observe their profiles from space, airplanes, mountaintops, rooftops, shoe-tops, or looking through a magnifying glass, you will see characteristic self-similar patterns on every scale of observation. Humans fabricate fractals too, for example sets of nested Russian Matryoshka dolls, as in fig. 5.11.

If we construct fractals by neat and tidy Euclidean methods, they become perfect in symmetry and infinite in scale. Here are two famous fractals from the Euclidean plane: the Sierpinski triangle and the Koch snowflake. As fig. 5.12 illustrates, the Sierpinski triangle commences

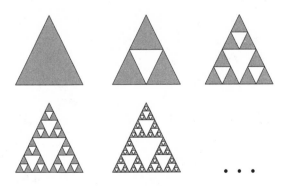

Figure 5.12 The Sierpinski Triangle

with the inscription of the white triangle in the original all-blue one. You can also imagine it as "cutting out" a triangular space from the original. At step two, we repeat the same process in each of the three smaller all-blue triangles. Each step recreates the pattern of the previous step, but also multiplies its number of occurrences and shrinks its scale. The Sierpinski triangle contains an infinite number of triangles, and also an infinite number of identically proportioned patterns. An infinitude of constant proportional patterns is the hallmark of Euclidean fractal objects. The Koch snowflake in fig. 5.13 also belongs to this family, but its patterns are confined to its perimeter instead of its area.

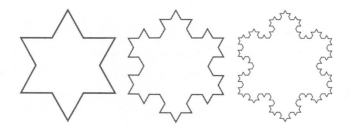

Figure 5.13 The Koch Snowflake

We have already mentioned that the golden rectangle and the yin-yang circle are fractals too, and by now the reasons should be clear. As fig. 5.14 illustrates, golden rectangles of ever-diminishing size are infinitely nestable within any golden rectangle. By the same token, any golden rectangle is itself nestable within an infinite pattern of golden rectangles of ever-increasing size. Similarly, as fig. 5.15 shows, yin-yang circles of ever-diminishing size are infinitely nestable within any yin-yang circle. And once again, any yin-yang circle is itself nestable within an infinite pattern of yin-yang circles of ever-increasing size.

Unlike the Sierpinski triangle and the Koch snowflake, the golden rectangle and the yin-yang circle are more than fractals. Their fractal properties of infinitude and constancy of proportion also lend themselves to ethical and political interpretations. Aristotle's golden mean and Confucius's balanced order—as well as Buddha's Middle Way, which

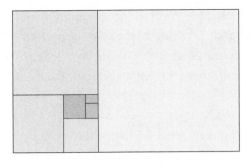

Figure 5.14 The Golden Rectangle Is a Fractal

Figure 5.15 The Yin-Yang Circle Is a Fractal

accommodates them both—apply across space and time, to an infinitude of sentient beings dispersed throughout the universe. These laws formerly applied to beings who were born and who have died; they apply now to beings currently alive who will one day die; and they will apply to beings yet unborn, who will be born and who will die. That is one significance of infinitude: It makes us realize the universality of norms. Similarly, each sentient being who follows these norms in his or her own life, does so on a scale commensurate with his or her position in the nested hierarchies of sentient beings themselves. For instance, a person is not "good" simply by virtue of how much benevolence she creates in the world; rather, a person is "good" by virtue of the proportion of benevolence she creates, relative to her present means to create it. This is the special significance of constant proportionality in the fractals of The Middle Way. Nobody is asking anybody to be perfect. A "passing" grade in benevolence could be as little as one part in φ, or 61 percent. In a democratic election, that's a large measure of confidence.

## Chaos and the ABCs

Like fractal geometry, chaos theory is a late twentieth century development with historically older roots. You can grasp the central ideas of chaos theory without any knowledge of mathematics, even though details of chaos are quite mathematical.[10] I'll eschew all formulae here. The guiding idea is simple to state: In innumerable processes, a slight variation at the beginning leads to a large—and largely unpredictable—variation in the outcome. For example, imagine skiing or snowboarding down a tall mountain, from its summit to its base. Imagine that this mountain has no predefined trails. After you make your first descent, return to the summit and do it again, but this time vary your angle of departure—say by just a few degrees from your previous run. Now where will you end up at the bottom? Possibly miles from the terminus of your earlier descent. A small variation at the top can produce a large and unpredictable variation at the bottom. That is chaos.

If you prefer the beach, imagine tossing a handful of identical wine corks into the surf. They hit the water within a few inches of one another, and start bobbing amid the waves. Within minutes, they become more widely dispersed; within hours or days, they may drift miles apart. Once again, slight variations in their initial positions at the outset lead to large and unpredictable variations in their positions as the process unfolds. That is chaos too.

Chaos is not the same as chance, yet the two are often conflated. But just as with chance, chaos actually comes from order that is too complex for the human mind to grasp, assimilate, or model deterministically. Yet everything that happens in a chaotic process is predetermined by laws of nature. Our astounding gifts of mathematical and physical insight have given us reliable knowledge about many of the dynamical processes of systems. We know how lots of things move, from protons to planets. We can predict with great accuracy the return of Halley's comet every seventy-six years, because it orbits in an ellipse. Greek geometry (conic sections) plus Newtonian celestial mechanics do the trick. But nobody can predict where a single snowflake will land, from the time it leaves the cloud, even though its soft trajectory earthward, accompanied by swirls, drifts, and gyrations, is predetermined by iron laws of nature, just like Halley's comet. So why can't we predict it?

Nature is amenable to our measurements in some respects, and opaque to them in others. Opacity makes us unable to establish what physicists call "initial conditions" in many systems. We cannot apply our iron laws unless we can also supply certain terms—a bushel of them in the snowflake's case, including temperatures, pressures, and wind velocities at every millimeter of the snowflake's descent. Even if we could learn the values of 99.99 percent of all the relevant variables from the instant the snowflake leaves the cloud, and even if we could complete all the computations before it hits the ground, our prediction could still miss by a mile—literally. Why? Because of the variables we need to estimate. If we guess very wrongly, or if there are other variables that we fail to take into account, our equations and computations might be in vain. That's chaos for you: A little bit of it goes a very long way. Meanwhile, the snowflake drifts to earth on a path that only nature knows in advance, which we are able to model but not predict.

The incredible images that chaos theory engenders are snapshots of the trajectory of a single point through a complex Cartesian space, propelled by unlimited iterations of a simple function. This is exactly how we constructed a Sierpinski triangle and a Koch snowflake: by iterations of a simple function. But these fractals were predictable by us, because we knew all the necessary initial conditions prior to each iteration. Fractal geometry isn't chaotic in and of itself; on the contrary, it's highly ordered. What we call "chaos" is partly our inability to predict the surprising emergence of even more highly ordered patterns than Euclidean fractals, out of what we mistakenly supposed (prior to Mandelbrot) to be "random noise." There are complex patterns in the weather, in the news, in the traffic, in our relationships with others, in economic markets, in international affairs, as in all chaotic processes. You may leave home for work every morning, as the snowflake leaves the cloud, and return directly home each night (unlike the snowflake, which does not return directly to the cloud). But what happens between your departure and your return is a combination of order (the patterns you can predict) and chaos (the patterns you can't predict).

Let's look at some highly ordered patterns from classic chaos theory, formed by many iterations of a simple function. Some of the most elegant and well-known patterns to date emerge from what's called a "Mandelbrot set," named after the French geometer, Benoit Mandelbrot, who pioneered

Figure 5.16 The Mandelbrot Set, and Some Details

fractal geometry.[11] There are an infinite number of Mandelbrot sets, from lower to higher algebraic orders, and the pictures I will show you here are from the lower orders only. Each Mandelbrot set, of any order, is infinitely deep and complex. The more iterations we perform, the deeper we can delve into its intricate and intertwined fractals.

Fig. 5.16.1 is a picture of the whole Mandelbrot set; figs. 5.16.2 and 5.16.3 depict its environs as well. Fig. 5.16.4 shows a closer view of the "valley" between two of the main curves. Notice that the "rims" of the valley are populated by increasingly smaller copies of the Mandelbrot set itself—reminiscent of the Matryoshka dolls—in a characteristic fractal pattern. Figs. 5.16.5 and 5.16.6 depict some details of the smaller filaments attached to them. As we magnify these features, we see that each filament is filigreed with infinitely more self-similar Mandelbrot sets. There is no limit to the depth, complexity, and astonishing vistas that emerge as we explore deeper nooks and crannies of the Mandelbrot set. The more we magnify its infinitely elaborate details, the more amazing they appear.

And what about φ? We saw that the golden rectangle and the yin-yang circle are Euclidean fractals, and we utilized them to construct the Phi Lotus. Does φ reemerge from chaos too? It most certainly does. Figs. 5.17.1 and 5.17.2 depict the golden rectangle, along with intricate embellishments, while 5.17.3 and 5.17.4 illustrate the characteristic meeting of yin and yang. Even more astonishing is the higher-order Mandelbrot set depicted in fig. 5.18. Recall how we constructed the yin-yang circle from five circles? This Mandelbrot set accomplishes a similar

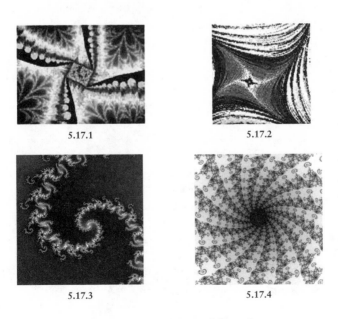

5.17.1

5.17.2

5.17.3

5.17.4

Figure 5.17 φ in the Mandelbrot Set

Figure 5.18 Higher-Order Mandelbrot Set

task, but in its own inimitable fashion—with greater complexity. Among the infinite of patterns that emerge from chaos, φ is well represented.

And what of the lotus flower? It too is embedded in chaos. Fig. 5.19 richly illustrates the variety and beauty of lotus flowers that populate Mandelbrot sets. I have no doubt that every species of lotus flower in the biological universe—not just here on Earth, but on every planet in the cosmos on which the lotus blooms—has its counterpart in Mandelbrot space.

## The Logic of the Lotus

Our rediscovery of φ in the midst of Mandelbrot sets reconfirms that chaos is imbued with special if not sacred order. Are you with me this far? Either way, I will now propose something quite audacious, which

Figure 5.19 Lotus Flowers in and around the Mandelbrot Set

should satisfy both skeptics who delight in denying nature's interconnecting patterns, and attuned ones who revel even more in affirming them. Let me recapitulate. We have contemplated the geometry of the ABCs, and have seen how B (the middle term) incorporates properties of both A and C. We have seen how B's geometry is represented by the lotus flower, which symbolizes dharma and which is also the link (the middle term) between Buddha and sangha.

Now look once more at the bottom row of photos in fig. 5.19, each of which depicts the Mandelbrot set in the center of an exotic lotus. Where did these lotuses come from? They are part of the set of points that lie outside the Mandelbrot set. So what is a Mandelbrot set "doing" in the center of a lotus flower, in the midst of chaos? I propose to you that the Mandelbrot set is none other than a fractal Buddha, seated in the lotus position in the midst of a lotus flower, reminding us that dharma is the link between Buddha and sangha, The Middle Way whereby each human being can experience order amid chaos. The Mandelbrot set symbolizes the vital elements of the ABCs: Aristotle's virtue amid vice, Buddha's serenity amidst confusion, Confucius's harmony amid discord. Look at the computer-generated Mandelbrot sets depicted in fig. 5.20, and at the humanly conceived "Buddha sets" depicted above and beneath them. It is clear to me that these images all represent one and the same thing: The Middle Way. These sets are not inventions of the human mind; rather, patterns of cosmic order embedded in chaos, and reflected in the mirror of the mind.

As I write these words, I can already hear the voices of skeptics, like birds shrilling over a still lake. Those who take Aristotle to an extreme, and err on the side of supposing (contrary to chaos theory) that everything is determinable by independent reason alone, will dismiss me as a "mystic." Those who take Confucius to an extreme, and err on the side of supposing (contrary to human history) that society is sustainable by blind obedience to authority alone, will either accept or reject my assertion, depending on what their authorities instruct them to do. Those who take Buddhism to an extreme, and err on the side of supposing (contrary to Buddha's teachings) that their received image of

Figure 5.20 The Mandelbrot Set as a Fractal Buddha

Buddha must be worshipped as the "one true" idol of Buddha, will accuse me of heresy. Nonetheless, I assert that the Mandelbrot set is a fractal Buddha, whose Middle Way is accessible even—and perhaps especially—near the very heart of chaos. Now look again at fig. 5.16.4 and see how an infinite procession of fractal Buddhas line the limitless crevasse that leads to chaos's core.

I welcome any and all objections to this thesis, especially those that assert that the Mandelbrot set is nothing but a fractal inkblot, not full but rather devoid of meaning, upon which I have projected a fractal Buddha. This is a cogent objection because, as Nagarjuna and others have taught, all dharmas are empty, including these.[12] There is no lotus flower anywhere, nor any Buddha, not even in chaos. "But how can you say it is both full and empty?" the skeptics will ask, as good scientists who use reason to establish the "initial conditions" of a process. But the logic of the lotus is non-Aristotelian; it transcends his rational requirements that a vessel cannot be both full and empty simultaneously. Emptied of water, it is full of air. Emptied of air, it is full of emptiness. Emptied of emptiness, what remains?

I also welcome historical objections. The claim that a Mandelbrot set is a fractal Buddha sounds like something a hippie might have said in 1967, under the influence of LSD and The Beatles. "So how do you know you're not having a flashback?" is a reasonable question, especially since I am lucky enough to be qualified to answer it. Once in a while, back in the 1960s, we really did make connections like this, and they were awesome. But connecting to hallucinogenic images using hallucinogenic channels inhibits retention of the images after the trip. Most hippies who met God in 1967 can barely describe Him today. In my experience, The Middle Way is far superior to LSD. The images it produces with Mandelbrot sets are as mind-expanding as anything that ever came out of Owsley's lab, and you can see them just as often as you like. They are consciousness-altering substances, but not hallucinogenic. Rather than impairing the mind, they improve its functioning.

This completes our brief excursion into the geometry of the ABCs. Remember that the ancient Greeks were profoundly serious in articulating connections among geometry, ethics, and politics. They were certain that by learning to measure the earth, we could also learn to frame our morality, gauge our social relations, and structure our polities—all in accord with universal constants of cosmic (if not sacred) order, such as our friend $\varphi$. Subsequent developments in mathematics, including non-Euclidean geometries, Gaussian distributions, Cantorian transfinite arithmetic, fractals, and chaos theory enrich and reinforce that ancient conviction.

Beyond this, it turns out that these preeminent and perennial symbols of Western and East Asian civilizations are linked by $\varphi$, which undergirds the geometry of the lotus itself. The lotus inwardly accommodates $\varphi$, and outwardly accommodates all civilizations: East Asian, Indian, Islamic, Western, all. Only one way can be so accommodating: The Middle Way.

This also completes Part I, and my brief introduction to the ABCs. Now let's apply the golden mean, Middle Way, and balanced order to reconciling some of life's extremes.

# PART II

# The Extremes and the ABCs

# 6

## POLITICAL EXTREMES
### Polarized America, and the Absence of a Common Good

*Hence it is evident that the state is a creation of nature,*
*and that man is by nature a political animal.* —Aristotle

*Let the aspirant observe not the perversities of others,*
*nor what others have and have not done; rather should he*
*consider what he has done and what he has yet to do.* —Buddha

*A gentleman is proud, but not quarrelsome,*
*allies himself with individuals, but not with parties.* —Confucius

### The ABCs of Politics

ARISTOTLE, BUDDHA, AND CONFUCIUS all acknowledged the importance of politics, each in his own way. Aristotle called man a "political animal" by nature. Even though he held the contemplative life in higher esteem than the life of commercial enterprise and the pursuit of sensual pleasures, he realized that activities and interactions of human groups are ultimately governed by politics. The word itself comes from the Greek "polis"—meaning an independent city-state and its surrounding territory. Athens and Sparta were the two classic "polities" of Hellenic civilization, which destroyed each other during the Peloponnesian War, in whose aftermath Socrates was martyred.

The ancient Greeks experimented with most forms of government, including monarchy (rule by one), oligarchy (rule by nobles), timocracy (rule by the wealthy), democracy (rule by many), and even anarchy (rule by none). Above all, democracy influenced the course of Western civilization, as it is influencing globalization.

Today's metropoli still retain the independent flavor and intellectual ferment of the boisterous Greek polis, even though they are part of larger political entities. Every major metropolis contrasts with the "hinterland" of its respective nation-state: New York with the United States, London with England, Paris with France, and so on. Today's metropolis is a fractal iteration of the ancient Greek polis: bigger and more complex, but containing the same recognizable patterns. The world's great cities concentrate human resources, and tend to be more sophisticated and innovative than environments. Metropoli are hubs and drivers of civilization.

I must also remind you of something Aristotle said about the polis, which still applies to today's metropoli, megalopoli, nation-states, and civilizations. It may surprise you, but Aristotle maintained that the most important factor in the health and sustainability of the polis is a strong middle class. He wrote "that the best political community is formed by citizens of the middle class, and that those states are likely to be well administered in which the middle class is large."[1] This has political and religious implications as well as economic ones, for politics and religion strongly condition economics, and in concert they either sustain or undermine the middle class. The middle class and The Middle Way are also linked, as we shall see. Liberties, opportunities, and hopes (or lack of thereof) that we human beings encounter in life are partly if not largely ordained by the political systems under which we live.

Socrates was convicted and put to death in a hostile political climate that allowed trumped-up charges to be brought against him. His student Plato was encouraged in a supportive political climate to found the Academy—the model for our universities. Plato's Academy became, among other things, a school for training future Athenian leaders (a comparable role played by the American Ivy League in the twentieth century). Aristotle learned from his predecessors that the fate of philosophers depends upon the political climate they inhabit. If this is true for thinkers, whose work is far more independent of material concerns than that of ordinary producers and consumers, it is even more true for producers and consumers themselves. We are all caught in a political web.

Subsequent observations of humans and social animals, down through the centuries, bear this out. We are political animals because we are social animals. Social animals spend considerable time in groups, and groups always give rise to leaders. The process by which groups choose their leaders, or by which leaders choose their groups, or by which would-be leaders compete with one another, drawing their followers into competition too—whether violent or nonviolent—is none other than the political process. Whether you understand politics or not, political forces govern you. You may enjoy the temporary liberty or luxury of abjuring your involvement with politics, but politics never abdicates its involvement with you. To paraphrase Trotsky again: "You may not be interested in political process, but political process is interested in you."

Was Aristotle liberal or conservative in his views? Neither, or rather a mixture of both. For example, Aristotle endorsed what later became core liberal beliefs—freedom and perfectibility of human beings—yet he would dispute the radical liberal corollary that social engineering, government programs, and other external forces conduce to freedom or perfection. Similarly, Aristotle supported what later became core conservative values—legitimate authority and individual responsibility—but he would heartily dispute the orthodox corollaries that we must blindly accept all edicts of authority, and that individuals are solely responsible for what befalls them. Were Aristotle an American, he would vote neither Democratic nor Republican, because the adversarial two-party system is increasingly polarized, and bereft of a common good.

Similarly, Confucian politics were a balanced mixture of liberal and conservative values. While contemporary Asian cultures have retained much (some say too much) Confucian emphasis on subordinating the interests of the individual to those of the collective, this cuts both ways politically. On one hand, absolute obedience was used (or abused) to justify totalitarian political regimes, such as Mao Tse-tung's, which sprang from the revolutionary political left. On the other hand, it was used (or abused) to justify military-industrial feudal systems, such as Imperial Japan's, which grew from the reactionary political right.

Like Aristotle, Confucius believed that the good life is synonymous with the practice of virtue: "He who rules by moral force is like the pole-star, which remains in its place while all the lesser stars do homage to it."[2] Like Aristotle, he prized contemplation, study, and understanding above all else. Confucius also believed that each of us can learn something from anyone we meet: This is an egalitarian, open-minded, and liberal view. Then again, like Aristotle, Confucius believed that a good and strong society requires good and strong leadership, and that the leader's office, from which his authority flows, must be respected. This is a traditional, hierarchical, conservative view.

Confucius even went further than Aristotle, and accorded to each individual a meaningful place in the grand scheme of things (whose source is Tao). Again this is a mixture of conservative and liberal values. On the conservative side, Confucius (like Aristotle) held that there are fixed orders in nature, which are maintained by natural laws. To be harmonious and productive, human society must mirror its proper portion of natural laws. On the liberal side, everyone is accorded a place in society; no one is excluded or marginalized. However, one's place is neither arbitrary nor revolutionary; it is constantly subject to natural constraints. Not everyone is fit to do everything, and thus there can be no perfect equality of outcome. This is a realistic and pragmatic view, shared by Aristotle too.

This Confucian picture presaged an important development in Western civilization; namely, the Elizabethan worldview. Like the Confucian picture, the Elizabethan picture was based on the conception of a great chain of being, and the corollary that everyone contributes to the linkage. In Elizabethan terms, there are four estates, each representing a giant link in the chain: The Divine Estate, where God the king rules over angels and saved souls; the Political Estate, where monarchs rule human subjects; the Animal Estate, where the lion is king (the origin of the "king of beasts") and a top predator in what today we call the food chain; and the Fallen Estate, where Satan the king rules over devils and souls of the damned. Whatever the political shortcomings of a given great chain, it assigns each person a sense of belonging in the cosmos. With this sense of belonging comes a sense of meaning and purpose in life.

Political liberalism in the West, and its ever-increasing emphasis on the claims of the individual over those of collective (except in its Stalinized universities, as we shall see in chapter 11), has given rise to endemic loss of meaning and purpose in life. This loss has been accompanied but not remedied by corresponding increases in mass consumption of psychotherapy and prescription drug use. It also accounts for the growing popularity of philosophical counseling on the one hand, and religious fundamentalisms on the other. Historically, the existentialists were among the first to experience and presage modern man's loss of place and identity. They spoke to and for generations of "liberated" Western intellectuals and activists who are nonetheless—to borrow a phrase and book title from Walker Percy—*Lost in the Cosmos.*[3] As we'll see in chapter 7, postmodernists have revenged themselves upon modernity itself, going to such sublime extremes that the very foundations of Western civilization have now been eroded. Aristotle and Confucius would both caution that if persons are permitted to flout the laws of nature that pertain to human societies— in other words to sunder their links in the Chain of Being—then they will become incapable of being fulfilled as individuals as well.

This is exactly what we observe in the West: pervasive lack of meaning, purpose, and fulfillment. Viktor Frankl, the founder of logotherapy, called it the "existential vacuum." He wrote: "More and more patients are crowding our clinics and consulting rooms complaining of an inner emptiness, a sense of total and ultimate meaninglessness of their lives. We may define the existential vacuum as the frustration of what we may consider to be the most basic motivation force in man, and what we may call . . . the will to meaning."[4] Meaning cannot be supplied by money or mobility alone. It stems from commitments to individual virtue and social stability, which Aristotle and Confucius both regarded as paramount, but which the West has rejected in favor of moral relativism and social instability. Nobody is exempt from natural laws. Whether you believe in gravity or not, if you jump off a roof you will fall, not float. And whether you believe in Tao or not, if your society subverts the Way, it will collapse, not thrive.

What does Buddha have to say about politics? I have good news and bad news for you. The good news is that Buddhism mostly transcends politics. The bad news is that many Buddhists do not. Let me explain.

First, the good news. Buddha's original teachings make it clear that his system is neither a philosophy nor a religion. Rather, it is a set of principles and practices—The Middle Way—which, if followed, reduce suffering and produce happiness, independent of external circumstances. Buddha himself declared it a waste of time and corruption of consciousness to speculate or debate the existence or nonexistence of souls, of Gods, of reincarnation, of afterlives, of supernaturalism, of separate realities, and so forth. But these are the very matters about which all religions, and many philosophies, love to speculate and debate. There is no end to human disputatiousness, and no end to the human suffering spawned by endless speculation and debate. That was Buddha's point, and his reason for eschewing theological and philosophical disputation.

Buddha encouraged his students to transcend their religious superstitions and metaphysical disputes, along with all the other fetters that bind the human being to suffering. And this is why Buddhism transcends politics: because every political system that man or woman has yet devised deeply embeds either religious or philosophical principles (or both) in its very foundations. If you erode those foundational principles, your political edifice collapses; but if you transcend them, you simply don't need the edifice any longer. You have outgrown it by becoming self-governing.

Naturally, given that most people are not self-governing (and that many don't wish to become so), two predictable things happened after Buddha died. First, he was made into a God and worshipped like one, and his teachings were codified into religious practices. So Buddhism ironically became a religion—and even a theocracy, as in Tibet prior to the expulsion of the Dalai Lama. Second, Buddha's teachings traveled around the world, and were adopted and transformed by many cultures. This process is ongoing. One of its consequences is the emergence, in the

West, of a kind of "intellectual Buddhism," whose adherents greatly admire Buddha's teachings from a theoretical standpoint, but who do not practice them as Buddha clearly intended. So Buddhism became a philosophy as well. Rather, the philosophical parts of Buddhism were abstracted from the whole by thoughtful and sincere people, who err on the side of contemplating too much and not practicing enough. I am possibly one of them.

But in fact, Buddhism is so universal, both in its conception of the human being and in the practices that awaken our humanity, that it attracts people from virtually every religious and philosophical background, including mutually incompatible ones. Once people are able to set aside their religious and philosophical differences to experience their humanity in more awakened states, they are able to set aside their political differences as well. That is how and why Buddhism transcends politics.

Now for the bad news: Buddhists themselves don't necessarily transcend politics.

Why not? To begin with, recall Buddhism's Three Jewels: Buddha, Dharma, Sangha (the exemplar, the teachings, the community). That last gem, namely the community, gives rise to both internal and external politics.

Internally, the reasons people share for coming together as a group— even Buddhist reasons—cannot and will not prevent the group from being swayed by fundamental laws of nature. For example, there will always be leaders and followers. There will always be competition among would-be leaders, which causes factions to form that divide the group. There will unfailingly arise ulterior motives, personal conflicts, and interpersonal relations, all of which affect the group's dynamics. So Buddhist groups are prone to political conflicts too, although they may be better than most groups at disguising or mitigating them, if not resolving them.

Externally, we see competition among Buddhist groups—albeit milder than in most other arenas—to recruit new members and even to proselytize their particular doctrines. To Buddhism's political credit, most Buddhists refrain from demonizing non-Buddhists and one another; words like "enemy" or "infidel" or "unbeliever" or "heathen" do not exist in the Buddhist lexicon, as they sadly do in so many of the world's religions. But Buddhists themselves are subject to persecution for political reasons; they do not acquire immunity to external political forces by virtue of transcending them as individuals.

An ancient example is Nichiren, the thirteenth-century Japanese monk who tried to give his interpretation of Buddha's Lotus Sutra to a populace subjugated by warlords who were abetted by a corrupt Buddhist priesthood. Some of these Buddhist priests were complicit in attempted assassinations of Nichiren, and in his eventual political exile. Nowhere are such actions recommended on Buddha's eightfold path. Nichiren was fortunate to have found some political protection, so he could carry on his life's work, which is still valid in this century and will be beyond it.

Long before Nichiren's day, Buddhists had been persecuted in China too, for superficial and deeper reasons. Some who came from India to spread Buddhist teachings were viewed with horror merely because of their shaven pates. Chinese Confucians had banned haircuts, because hair was considered a "gift" from one's parents, and as such had to be treasured. Yet, despite the followers' bald heads, Buddhism soon became established and esteemed in China, owing to its compatibilities with Confucian culture and the greatness of indigenous pioneers like T'ien T'ai in synthesizing the highest ideals of The Middle Way and Tao: universal compassion and universal *ren*. However, subsequent communities of Buddhists were often dissolved and scattered by winds of political change, especially when despotic rulers saw them as subversive threats to Confucian order.

Why were they considered a threat? Because Buddhist practice helps the individual become more self-governing. This sits well enough in Western Aristotelian political systems, which have been individually oriented for centuries, and which tend to view self-governing people as healthy for the body politic. Thoreau epitomized this view. He was not an anarchist; rather, he wanted people to become more self-governing so that governments would need to govern less. However, the notion of self-government is mistakenly perceived as a threat in

Confucian systems, which suppose that self-governing individuals will opt out of the Confucian order and will sever the links of *li* that define their duties to others. Hence Buddhism, which makes people more self-governing by transforming them from within, appears as dangerous to authoritarian political systems as do organized religions, which redirect people's love and dependency from government to other higher authorities, namely deities.

In this context, the expulsion of the Tibetans by the Maoists is part of a much larger political and historical pattern in Confucian Asia. Even though contemporary China's economic flowering is loosening social strictures, Chinese political authorities remain wary of "too much" self-government. Similarly, authoritarian Vietnam has made great economic strides since its reunification, but has also outlawed and persecuted organized religions, including the Theravadan Buddhism that is deeply rooted in its culture. Similarly, reactionary Japanese political parties and their public media have demonized Soka Gakkai's Nichiren Buddhism, precisely because they view it as an emancipating force, and fear erosion of their own political base.

So Buddhists must persevere in trying to transcend politics, both within their own sanghas and as part of the larger polities they inhabit. Buddha himself embodied and reconciled both liberal and conservative political views. His thesis that every human being can become awakened is egalitarian, idealistic, and liberal while his practices that conduce to such awakening are universal, moral, and conservative. This is The Middle Way. If more people walked it, then our political and business leaders would be influenced to walk it too. This would make the world a safer and happier place for all.

## Political Polarization in America

America is a nation of extremists as well as moderates, increasingly polarized and fractured along many axes—political, religious, economic, cultural, educational, racial, sexual, to mention but a few. As a prominent pollster discovered about American public opinion on foreign affairs, "There is no majority stance. Instead, polarized groups of Americans glare at each other across deep chasms."[5] Alas, this is true along all the aforementioned axes. And Americans do more than glare: They actively inveigh against one another with self-righteous intolerances and counterproductive hatreds. The political and social fabric of the nation is increasingly and painfully torn, for want of a Middle Way to bridge extremism's ever-widening chasms.

I travel all over America, and everywhere the chasm of political polarization yawns under my feet. I have many close friends who are liberals, some of them highly influential, and they are overcome with hatred for President Bush and conservatism. They rail against him personally, and against everything he stands for, but they offer few constructive suggestions about how to govern the nation. When I press them on the issue of a common good, or ask them to articulate their political vision for America, their response is consistently the same: "I hate Bush." If I ask about domestic policy, foreign policy, or anything else, I get the same response: "I hate Bush." I am sorry, my liberal friends, but hatred of the opposition is not a wholesome basis for statecraft. I have facilitated more profound discussions of Bush's foreign policy in Cairo than in New York.

I also have many close friends who are conservatives, some of them highly influential, and they are similarly overcome with hatred for Bill Clinton and liberalism. Those with longer memories also hate John F. Kennedy, and the elder statesmen among them even hate Franklin Delano Roosevelt to this very day.

At the extremes of liberalism itself I encounter Marxists and anarchists, who want to bring down Western civilization (and who have already made great strides, as we shall see). At the extremes of conservatism I encounter racists and religious fanatics who are intolerant of human diversity. Too many self-proclaimed "moderate" liberals appear to be in complete ignorance or extravagant denial of the institutionalized reverse racism and totalitarian intolerance of the extreme left; they are too busy hating Bush and conservatism to know or care. Too many self-styled "moderate" conservatives are willing to apologize for or tacitly condone the knee-jerk bigotry and religious intolerance of the extreme right; they are too busy hating Clinton and liberalism to care.

I myself try not to hate anyone or anything, including hatred itself, and that endeavor is greatly furthered by taking refuge in The Middle Way. Hatred is one of three venomous toxins (the other two are greed and envy) that poison the mind, harden the heart, and debase the spirit. Accosted by political extremists everywhere I travel in the United States, and caught in their withering cross fires, I too have finally been driven to an extreme in order to counter them: the extreme center. It's peaceful here, and quiet. That's because in many places I feel like I am practically the only one in this position. Everybody else, it seems, is busy hating one another.

These hatreds run much deeper than mutual disgust with one another's leaders; they have infected the very marrow of the nation, and have fractured the American polity more severely than at any time in American history since the Civil War. The shooting war between the blue-uniformed Yankee states versus the gray-uniformed Confederate ones has metamorphosed into a culture war between the extreme liberal Blue states versus the extreme conservative Red ones. Although the combined area of the Red states is much larger than that of the Blue, their populations are almost equal. So the deadlocked American electorate, split almost evenly in its popular votes, is politically gridlocked. More significantly, the nation is passionately divided over the issues themselves—from the invasion of Iraq to the normalization of gay marriage, from abortion to the death penalty, from stem cell research to medical marijuana, from ultra-orthodox religious indoctrination of the extreme right to postmodern anarchy and moral chaos of the illiberal left. Middle America sorely needs a Middle Way, as does the global village itself.

Even as I write these words, Iran is threatening Israel with nuclear annihilation, while other nations call for Israel's destruction. In response to 9/11, America has changed two retrograde regimes—in Afghanistan and Iraq, both of which have supported, harbored, or cosponsored anti-Israeli, anti-American, and anti-Western terrorism, including 9/11 and countless other acts. Teheran is now declaring that Islam can "win" a nuclear war against Israel, because a few large atomic warheads would obliterate the tiny Jewish state and its six million Jews, whereas any number of retaliatory strikes by Israel (or other Western powers) would fall well short of annihilating the more than one billion Muslims inhabiting dozens of Islamic nations.[6] Therefore, claims the government of Iran, Islam can destroy Israel and lose "only" tens of millions of people in the process, which they claim would be a "victory." This is what my Buddhist friends call "deluded cravings"—on an astronomical scale.

Yet half the global village—along with the extreme left in the United States—considers America the biggest threat to world peace than any other nation in the global village today. I believe that this view is almost as deluded as that of Islamist fanatics who welcome a nuclear holocaust. At the same time, however, it is also true that fanatics of the extreme right in the United States would lose little sleep over American nuclear retaliation against any act of nuclear terrorism. I can see it now, a bumper crop of bumper stickers reading NUKE ISLAM FOR JESUS. The ABCs deplore all these extremes, and of course The Middle Way is the best way to reconcile them.

Yet common sense also deplores aggressors, and—for want of a Middle Way—the global village has become so bereft of common sense that it seems to have forgotten that America was not the aggressor in World War I, was not the aggressor in World War II, was not the aggressor in the Korean War, was not the aggressor in the Cold War, and was not the aggressor on 9/11. Kishore Mahbubani, former Singaporean ambassador to the U.N., current dean of the Lee Kwan Yew School of Public Policy at the National University of Singapore, and a world-class public intellectual, called America "the most benevolent Great Power in history."[7] How history's greatest benevolence metamorphoses into the "greatest threat" to world peace is surely a matter worthy of investigation, no matter whether it is unfolding in objective reality or in subjective fantasy. At the same time, the global village has also forgotten that Israel was not the aggressor in any of the Arab-Israeli Wars, and that violent Palestinian factions have for too long engaged in aggressive terrorism instead of constructive statecraft. Decades of leftist Western denial of Middle Eastern realities have helped engulf the West itself in Islamist terrorism.

Axes that divide America politically are often stereotyped from an extreme rightist viewpoint. The conservative stereotyping of Red versus Blue attitudes portrays "G.I. Joe" versus the "Faerie Queens." We are meant to infer that G.I. Joe is a "regular American"—white, male, heterosexual, God-fearing, patriotic—a defender of liberty, opportunity, and hope, ready to lay down his life to preserve these precious things for everybody, including gays among other peaceniks who despise him. We are also meant to infer that the Faerie Queens are "irregular Americans"—homosexual, atheistic, hedonistic, unpatriotic—currently expanding their civil liberties agenda to include the "right" to marry, while abdicating the responsibility of defending the very liberty and security that allows them to enlarge their frontiers of normalization.

Yet according to the radical liberal dialectic, G.I. Joe is "poor white trash," an ill educated and socioeconomically challenged pawn in the global chess game of the white male heterosexual patriarchal capitalistic Christian fundamentalist hegemonists who shed blood for oil; while the Faerie Queens are well educated, socioeconomically mobile, morally relativistic and agnostic revolutionary "heroes," seeking full emancipation from arbitrary and intolerant but "privileged" norms that have long oppressed the world along the lines of race, class, and gender.

Emergent popular culture completely reverses these stereotypes. For example, consider Pim Fortuyn, an openly gay but politically ultraconservative Dutch politician—a rising star who was leading in the polls until his 2002 assassination by a Dutch environmentalist fanatic. And for example, consider *G.I. Jane,* Hollywood's portrayal of the feminist fantasy that women make just as effective "fighting men" as men themselves—if only they are "permitted." Of course gays can become outstanding politicians, yet this is not a norm; just as women can become outstanding combat soldiers, yet this is not a norm.

From any extreme, the world looks black and white—or these days, Red and Blue. Yet the full spectrum of reality encompasses infinite hues and shades. In defense of "G.I. Joe," it is undeniably true that hundreds of thousands of young American men selflessly laid down their lives in ghastly twentieth-century wars that America did not start, but ended—and did so to preserve the liberty, opportunity, and hope so characteristic of Western civilization. In defense of the "Faerie Queens," it is undeniably true that Christian fundamentalists have wrought prodigious feats of intolerance in the name of a loving God. During the 1990s, I saw a souvenir T-shirt in Provincetown, Massachusetts, that bore the caption JESUS, PROTECT ME FROM YOUR FOLLOWERS.[8] As a philosopher and a Jew, I could readily identify with that message, but my traveling companion dissuaded me from buying the shirt. "Aren't you in enough trouble already?" she reminded me rhetorically.

But now that the global village itself is in more than enough trouble, I am coming out of the closet as a proponent of The Middle Way. In reality, the twentieth and early twenty-first centuries have saddled America with the sometimes impossible and always unenviable job of policing the world. While poets and pacifists aplenty, such as late greats John Lennon and Phil Ochs, were righteous in protesting "police brutality" by the "cops of the world," no city, country, or civilization can survive and thrive in the absence of laws and their enforcement by a justice system—whether municipal, federal, or international—of which the police are a necessary component. At the same time, there are gays in the United States military who undoubtedly serve with courage and distinction, just as there are gays in every walk of life—from Wal-Mart to Wall Street, in every profession from science to the arts to education—and of every religion, color, and ethnicity, who make invaluable contributions to our culture, and whose politics vary across the entire spectrum. The mere statement of a human being's sexual orientation (gay, lesbian, straight, bisexual, celibate) reveals nothing about whether that person is a virtuous citizen, a good neighbor, and a moral human being—whereas how close or far they are from The Middle Way is much more revealing.

We can also find polarization within the Middle Way itself. Consider the self-immolation of Buddhist monks, an extreme way of protesting against violent injustice without physically harming anyone else. Perhaps the most famous twentieth-century example was that of Thich Quang Duc, who lit himself on fire in downtown Saigon in 1963 and burned to death. Quang Duc was not protesting against the Vietnam

War, but against the religious persecution of Buddhists under the corrupt Diem regime, a regime the United States had supported as a "lesser evil" against communism. In contrast, the first-ever Buddhist funeral at America's premier military cemetery—Arlington National— took place in April 2003, where Marine Cpl. Kemaphoom Chanawongse was buried in a hybrid ceremony of saffron robes and dress blues: the Red and the Blue conjoined. Corporal Chanawongse lived in Connecticut, and died in Iraq. His family had immigrated to the United States from Thailand. "They wanted to be in the land of the free," his uncle Kim Atkinson said.[9]

Buddhists freely chant for peace across the United States, yet in reality their freedom to do so is bought and paid for with human blood and human life. As I said in chapter 2 and cannot say often enough: When Buddhists can chant for peace as freely in Baghdad, Kabul, Teheran, Islamabad, Riyadh, and Damascus as they do in New York, Los Angeles, Ottawa, London, Paris, and Berlin, then—ironically— perhaps they will not need to chant so much. Meanwhile, The Middle Way still has a long way to go in reaching polarized Middle America, as it does in reaching the global village's polarization over America itself.

It is the perpetual condition of democracies to squabble incessantly over internal matters as well as foreign affairs, and for their squabbling factions to unite temporarily (if at all) only when confronted by common catastrophe, yet even then only for a short time. But if quarrels between rival factions fail to be reconciled by the shared vision of a common good, then the normal political distribution breaks down, and the body politic becomes polarized. This is an unwholesome and undesirable state of affairs. When the light of common good is permitted to fail, the lurking specters of common ill will stalk its lengthening shadows, and make ready to haunt the approaching dark night of a nation's divided soul.

## Ringing Gaussian Bells

I mentioned Gauss's normal distribution in the previous chapter, and proposed that it be adopted as the geometric symbol of the sangha— The Middle Way for human communities. Let us now look at this distribution more closely. Like the Fibonacci spiral, the bell-shaped curve is found everywhere in nature—and everywhere among humans too, try as they may to dissociate themselves from nature and her underlying patterns.

The bell-shaped curve describes multitudinous properties of aggregations—from atomic to cosmic scales—including many properties of groups of human beings. If you examine a handful of sand on a beach, the masses of the grains are normally distributed. If you examine a stand of trees in a forest, their heights and their numbers of leaves are normally distributed. If you select a group of people at random, their heights, weights, and IQs are normally distributed. If you log the amount of time it takes you to commute to work every morning, these times are normally distributed. Nature adores the Gaussian distribution, at least as much as she adores the golden ratio. The distribution can be approximated by a simple pinball machine, as depicted in fig. 6.1.[10]

Distributions of political opinion are highly susceptible to cultural forces as well as natural ones. In consequence, a culture may tend to reinforce, or undermine, the normal distribution of political opinion.

Toward the left of the spectrum of opinion—corresponding to politically left-wing views—we find social democrats, socialists, and Marxists. Toward the right of the spectrum—corresponding to politically right-wing views—we find social Darwinists, religious fundamentalists, and fascists. The middle of the spectrum contains moderates: Centrists and libertarians are in the middle, and adjacent to them are conservative liberals and liberal conservatives.

Note too that the extreme extremes become indistinguishable. Marxism and fascism, seemingly at the furthest extremes from each other, are each one step removed from totalitarianism. Totalitarianism of the left is virtually indistinguishable from totalitarianism of the right. George Orwell understood this better than most, which is why he observed that a jackboot in the face feels the same, whether it's a left boot or a right boot.

When President Lyndon Johnson referred to the "Great Society" in the 1960s, he was speaking of the moderate American majority of his day, a "moral majority" which, regardless of its leanings toward left or right, still shared a set of common values. But in contemporary America, political opinion is not distributed normally. America is a house increasingly divided, between extremists of the left and the right. It is well documented that the 2004 reelection of President Bush was decided on two issues above all: security and morality. Now, in the aftermath of 9/11, Americans are polarized on the issue of security. The left prefers diplomatic and economic means of countering terrorism, as well as outright appeasement or denial; the right prefers military and political means, including outright armed confrontation and regime change. This is opposition without complementarity. Where is The Middle Way? We shall see. And prior to 9/11, America was in the throes of culture wars, race wars, and gender wars, which have been overshadowed by the priorities of terrorist issues, but which nonetheless continue to divide the body politic within.[11]

The left perceives the right as fundamentalist, dogmatic, repressive, authoritarian, anti-intellectual; while the right perceives the left as deconstructed, radical, promiscuous, anarchic, amoral. Self-righteous extremists on both wings have carved a yawning chasm in American society, across which sanctity and profanity hurl mutual condemnation, fear, and loathing. Once again, we see opposition without complementarity. Where is The Middle Way?

America's political system, like its justice system, is adversarial. This idea is persistent in Western civilization, and was touted by philosophers and statesmen from Cicero in Rome to John Stuart Mill in England. The theory is that contending opinions produce truth, because each side illuminates something larger than itself in the process of making its own case. This was Georg Wilhelm Friedrich Hegel's celebrated idea too: Every thesis has an antithesis, and the pair can always be synthesized to reveal a higher truth.

But the adversarial system can backfire, and mightily. This happens when two contending opinions each illuminate something smaller than themselves, rather than larger. For example, many who favor America's regime changes in the Islamic world assume that Western-style democracy can be imposed militarily, by "hard power," without the essential process of instilling the values required to sustain democracy, via cultural "soft

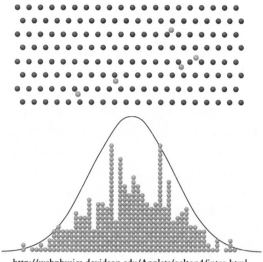

http://webphysics.davidson.edu/Applets/galton4/intro.html

Figure 6.1 The Normal Distribution, Approximated by a Pinball Machine

power." At the same time, many who oppose America's regime changes in the Islamic world have little or no conception of the significance of 9/11, and of the real perils that menace peace, prosperity, and security not only in America, but throughout the global village. Instead of being united by a synthesis of these clashing views, Americans and others are divided by a chasm. Into this yawning chasm plummets truth, and in its place are produced two extreme versions of reality, both of which are skewed away from truth and toward distortion, yet each of which considers itself "normal" and the other "abnormal." Instead of shared normalcy, we get two bitterly contending abnormalities.

America's polarization produces a distribution that's far from normal. It's called "bimodal" or "bipolar." What happened to the Great Society? The moral majority? The average American? They have vanished into the abyss between extremes. Where's The Middle Way? We shall see.

### Lies, Damned Lies, and Statistics
Since Gauss's distribution and related statistics of social science will accompany us throughout this book, it's a good idea to review some

pitfalls of deriving policies from numbers. The branch of mathematics we call statistics was pioneered by Karl Pearson at University College London, near the turn of the twentieth century. Just prior to that, Francis Galton (Charles Darwin's cousin) had published a satirical statistical study in a widely read intellectual gazette of the day, the *Fortnightly Review*, asking whether the power of prayer had any measurable effect.[12] Galton observed that millions of Britons prayed on a daily basis for the health and welfare of the royal family and related aristocrats. He also did a study that revealed that royals had shorter lives, more mental illness (probably due to inbreeding), and more familial dysfunction than nonroyals, on average. So Galton wryly concluded that all the daily prayers were having a negative effect, and he hypothesized that the royal family would be better off if people *stopped* praying for them. To make my point even more bluntly, Benjamin Disraeli, prime minister and caustic wit of that same Victorian era, said, "There are three kinds of lies: Lies, damned lies, and statistics."[13]

A serious point, which I will summarize for you here, underlies these jests. Statistics are correlations, which may or may not be indicative of deeper causal links between the things that are correlated. For example, heavy cigarette smoking is positively correlated with lung cancer and heart disease and is also a cause of these conditions. But being born is even more positively correlated with dying—100 percent of all births end in death, sooner or later—yet no medical examiner ever asserts that birth is a cause of death. The expansion of the universe is positively correlated with increasing life expectancies in some parts of the world, but neither causes the other. My daily loss of brain cells is negatively correlated with the daily increase of cell phones in Asia, but these things are not causally related. Yet social scientists trumpet statistics on a daily basis, and recommend political and social policies on the basis of correlations. This is a pervasive but risky business. Statistics are easy to quote, but even easier to misinterpret—hence Galton's satire and Disraeli's jibe.

## Politics, Race, and the Moral Majority

Since 9/11, the political polarization of America has come to the forefront of domestic and global consciousness. David Brock, a gay intellectual, learned about American polarization the hard way.[14] As a journalism student at Berkeley, Brock sought to express his "classical liberal" viewpoint—reasonable, moderate, principled, tolerant—in Berkeley's radical left-wing student newspaper, which harshly censored him and repudiated his classical liberalism as though he were some kind of fascist. So the neo-Marxists who dictate politically correct thought at Berkeley drove a desperate Brock straight into the equally untender embraces of the extreme right, which employed him as a polemicist against the left until he could no longer abide himself at that extreme either.

Hatred on both wings is fanned and fueled by vindictive media, which control extremist opinions but which are themselves completely out of control, intoxicated by their own power and corrupt beyond conception. To media leaders, from Pat Robertson and Rush Limbaugh to Al Franken and Michael Moore, the consuming masses are like herds of credulous sheep, who daily and unsuspectingly graze their poisoned pastures.

I arrived in the United States in 1994, well before 9/11 rocked and changed the world, and long before the extremist media from both wings seized upon 9/11 to vent their venomous spleens. What the media has temporarily neglected is the biggest single issue that polarized America politically for decades prior to 9/11. I have not forgotten it, because my exposure to it as a new immigrant to the United States left a deep and lasting impression.

In case your memory needs to be refreshed, the 1990s in America was a decade of extreme polarization in race relations. The O. J. Simpson trial captivated Americans, and many feared that a guilty verdict would precipitate the worst race riots since the 1960s. The "even-handed" diplomatic solution of the American justice system—acquit him on criminal charges, then bankrupt him in civil court—did little to mollify emotions at both extremes. White racists and vengeful bigots were already furious because O. J. was rich and famous, and infuriated because he had married and allegedly murdered a white woman. Black racists and guilt-ridden white liberals demanded that O. J. be acquitted because of "historical injustices." So many African Americans had been unjustly accused and convicted—if not lynched by white mobs—that many on the extreme left viewed O. J.'s acquittal as mandatory compensatory justice, a partial "repayment" of a murderous "historical debt."

The 1990s also saw the Rodney King beating and the riots it precipitated in L.A., and the retaliatory Reginald Denny beating, which did not produce riots but which helped entrench white racism. The 1990s saw the publication of Richard Herrnstein and Charles Murray's book *The Bell Curve*, and the misunderstandings it fomented nationwide. Add to this a spate of publications from extreme right-wing think tanks, indicting black and Latino cultures for excessive criminality and violence, countered by a spate of publications from extreme left-wing academics, pinning these problems on "institutionalized racism," "Eurocentric civilization," and "white male heterosexual patriarchal hegemony."

As a then-new immigrant from Canada, my overall impression of America in the 1990s was that of a nation deeply conflicted and bitterly divided—not so much by race, but rather by incessant and extreme politicizations of race. On the one hand, I encountered ordinary Americans of every color and creed getting along just fine, but on the other I was bombarded by continuous racial propaganda from all extremes, emanating mostly from the universities and the mass media. I gradually learned how extremists from both wings profit immensely—in terms of money, power, and prestige—from fomenting, sustaining, and exacerbating these conflicts and divides. I was appalled and horrified by the realization that trials like O. J.'s were not based on evidence and testimony, due process and reasonable doubt. Everything hinged on race, class, and gender—and their politicizations by extremists on both wings. Everywhere in America, streets and schools and monuments are named after Martin Luther King Jr., yet hardly anywhere in America do I see evidence that anyone applies his crowning precept: What's important is not the color of our skin, but the content of our character.[15] America in the 1990s was a nation without a moral majority, a greatly polarized society lacking a Middle Way. Yet my contact with ordinary Americans of all stripes (not to mention all shades) led me to believe that the moral majority was still alive, but faring poorly owing to conspicuous neglect. Nobody was speaking for it, while extremists from both wings—abetted by mass media—were incessantly trying to polarize what remained of it.

## Statistics, Race, and The Middle Way

Although America is politically polarized along many axes, no axis draws more continuous attention—and heavier fire—than the racial one. Partly because of and partly in spite of the successes of the civil rights movement, there are more racial tensions in integrated America today than there were during the segregation era. In America as in the developing world, we see that equal opportunities give rise to disparities of outcome—not only in terms of race but also, as we will see, in terms of gender. Liberal and conservative extremists measure and interpret these disparities differently, using statistics to support their adversarial and mutually incompatible political conclusions. As we saw in the previous chapter, geometry is a way we measure things, to help us understand their underlying patterns and transcendent forms. As we will continue to see, statistics is a way we measure aggregations of things, to correlate one or more variables or properties with one another.

Statistics are a gladiator model of mathematics, and one of relatively few mathematical models that social sciences possess. Because statistics are correlations only, you must continuously bear in mind that even very good correlations are not always or not at all indicative of causal relations. And even where statistical correlations are casual, as between smoking cigarettes and developing lung cancer, the causal relation is always a matter of probability, and never one of necessity. Some people smoke cigarettes and don't get lung cancer. Some people don't smoke cigarettes and do get lung cancer. So when social scientists use statistics to try to persuade you of their pet political biases, they are like gladiators trying to subdue or slay one another's theories with the force of numbers. American circuses of many kinds—academic, broadcast media, film, recording, publishing, and the political arena itself—are full of lustily cheering polarized masses, each throng equally transfixed by the slogans, benedictions, incantations, and statistics that support its prejudices.

So let's employ the adversarial method as it was used by Cicero in Rome, and John Stuart Mill in England: to discover truths that unite us, instead of half-truths that divide us. In this case, as in all cases where moral judgments are used not as balm to heal wounds but as weapons to inflict them, we must try, exactly as the Buddhist teacher Pema Chödrön advises, to transcend the "ordinary morality" of right and wrong.[16]

Each and every "hyphenated" American group has sooner or later found a way to express its greatness. How? All Americans have ancestors who experienced tough times on these shores, one way or another. Some had it a lot worse than others, to be sure. Everybody has paid some dues getting "welcomed" to the United States. The Africans, the Irish, the Germans, the Jews, the Arabs, the Armenians, the Chinese, the Japanese, the Indians, the Latinos—to name but a few groups—have paid dues here. But African Americans have surely paid more dues than the rest.

The greatness of America never lay in the way she welcomed newcomers, nor in the way she conquered the indigenous nations descended from those pioneers who crossed the Siberian land bridge during the last Ice Age. The greatness of America lay in the way she sooner or later invited the survivors of her "welcoming parties" to partake in the American Dream, to draw the waters of their own fulfillment from bountiful wells of American liberty, opportunity, and hope. The wells are far from dry, yet drawing their waters is an increasingly daunting task for many Americans.

Looking at the African-American population, as with any "hyphenated" American population, we can paint a sharply contrasting picture of towering success and appalling failure. On the one hand, we see people of color in virtually every stratum of power, prestige, wealth, influence, celebrity, art, and sport. Having endured and survived slavery in New Rome (that is, America), and having at last been offered the liberties, opportunities, and hopes that come bundled with full American citizenship, innumerable African Americans have become distinguished and valorous New Romans, privileging their nation, their civilization, and the global village with their greatness. From Martin Luther King to James Baldwin, from Colin Powell to Oprah Winfrey, from Condoleezza Rice to Denzel Washington, from Michael Jordan to Toni Morrison, from Herbie Hancock to Thurgood Marshall, from Wynton Marsalis to Spike Lee, we see significant presence, crowning achievements, and enormous contributions of African Americans in the wake of their liberty, opportunity, and hope. Their presence percolates through the whole culture: There are African-American politicians, legislators, judges, mayors, police chiefs, lawyers, doctors, professors, stockbrokers— you name it, they're achieving it. Not only that, they have achieved this sum of greatness in mere decades since their emancipation by the civil rights movement and its aftereffects.

Yet all greatness has its complement, namely terribleness. African Americans also form the largest single component of prison population in the United States, have the largest rate of childbirth out of wedlock, and are the largest group subsisting at the low end of the socioeconomic scale.[17] Like every other hyphenated American group, they span the whole statistical distribution of income. Then again, and unlike every other hyphenated American group, African Americans were brought here against their will, not as seekers and beneficiaries of liberty, opportunity, and hope like most of the rest, but as slaves, to be denied these precious gifts from the outset, and indefinitely. One could easily devote a book to how much African Americans have in common with Jews, including the lasting impact of slavery on individual and collective self-image, and the perilous uncertain journey through diaspora that begins only *after* emancipation. For liberty is only a beginning to a meaningful and decent life, and not an end.

The Jews have still not forgotten their Exodus from Egypt, ancient land of the pharaohs, and the Children of Israel's former house of bondage. The story of the Exodus from Egypt is recounted year after year, century after century, millennium after millennium. The memory of slavery in Egypt, and the emancipation from it, still have an impact on Jews today—four thousand years after the fact. On that basis alone, how can anyone expect African Americans to forget their much more recent enslavement in the New World?

Newly emancipated African Americans faced another difficulty, which the Children of Israel were spared. Moses was both liberator and, necessarily, lawgiver. For as soon as the Children of Israel gained precious liberty from Egyptian bondage, they fell into the other extreme: the self-enslavement of idolatry and similar corruptions. Whereupon Moses gave them the Ten Commandments: laws to funnel their newfound freedoms toward their preservation instead of their self-destruction. Martin Luther King Jr. was quite self-consciously the Mosaic liberator of African Americans, but tragically he fell to an assassin before he could fulfill his secondary but equally vital mission as lawgiver. African Americans became divided early in their emancipation, between those who (like King) upheld the American Constitution and its Bill of Rights, which belatedly but finally applied to them; and those who (like Malcolm X, Angela Davis, Bobby Seale, and many others) rejected the American Constitution and sought political alternatives through violent revolution—whether Islamic, communist, or anarchist.

There was yet another difficulty. The Jews of the Exodus proceeded from their house of bondage toward their Promised Land. But the African Americans' exodus proceeded from one wing of their house of bondage into other wings of that very same mansion. This is a source of African-American "double-consciousness": consciousness of being free Americans, and consciousness of being former slaves.

Meanwhile, as Daisaku Ikeda has observed, bitter racial conflicts in America (as elsewhere) stem from accentuating differences instead of celebrating commonalities. So let me illustrate how differences become fodder for endless political squabbling between extremists from left and right. Afterward, I will contrast that with The Middle Way.

How do extremists account for the disparity between great achievements of African-American individuals, and sore afflictions of the African-American "underclass," as sociologists call it? Both sides use statistics to "prove" their points, which is why I started this section with a cautionary tale from Galton, and an epithet from Disraeli. Statistics are compelling, but also misleading. Interpret them carefully, and wisely.

### Extremism from the Left

Liberal extremists appeal to nationwide and institutional conspiracy. They claim that a few people of color are "favored" by the system, and are put "on show" like Potemkin villages, so that the system can pretend to have succeeded and can offer them up as evidence of its success. But liberal extremists—black and white alike—also claim that the vast majority of black people are still being kept down by institutional racism—operating secretly but powerfully behind the scenes, preventing them from gaining access to equal opportunity and actively persecuting them under the guise of law and order. This is extreme liberalism's explanation for stellar success across the spectrum, as well as high rates of poverty, illegitimacy, and criminal convictions among African Americans.

A typical liberal extremist is Manning Marable, professor of history and political science, and the director of the Institute for Research in African-American Studies at Columbia University. The extremist views he respresents are "politically correct," and enshrined as truth in the mainstream American academy, from coast to coast. As we will see in chapter 11, the American professorate is 95 percent radical liberal, and the 5 percent who profess other views—even moderate, libertarian, or conservative, let alone extreme rightist—are gagged, censored, and persecuted by totalitarian university administrations that have as little regard for the Bill of Rights as did apologists for slavery in the antebellum South.

Professor Marable cites the following statistics: "In New York, a state in which African Americans and Latinos comprise 25 percent of the total population, by 1999 they represented 83 percent of all state prisoners, and 94 percent of all individuals convicted on drug offenses." Turning to black youth, Professor Marable cites these numbers nationwide: "Blacks comprise 44 percent of those detained in juvenile jails, 46 percent of all those tried in adult criminal courts, as well as 58 percent of all juveniles who are warehoused in adult prison." Given that blacks comprise only 12 percent of the United States population overall, these numbers on juveniles are shockingly high. What is Professor Marable's explanation for all this? Institutionalized racism.

"What seems clear is that a new leviathan of racial inequality has been constructed across our country. It lacks the brutal simplicity of the old Jim Crow system, with its omnipresent 'white' and 'colored' signs. Yet it is in many respects potentially far more devastating, because it presents itself to the world as a system that is truly color-blind . . . For Americans who still believe in racial equality and social justice, we cannot stand silent while millions of our fellow citizens are being destroyed all around us. The racialized prison industrial complex is the great moral and political challenge of our time."[18]

I contend that this is partly true, but also partly false. Professor Marable is correct that anti-black racism still exists in the United States. It's not hard to find people of color who can attest to having been made less than welcome in many neighborhoods and organizations, solely and unjustly on the basis of their race. Such injustice persists even in the traditional heartlands of slavery's abolition, like New England. Yet Professor Marable neglects to mention that the most conspicuous form of institutionalized racism in contemporary America is the officially sanctioned party line of the universities themselves, which sponsor open and uncontested vilifications of white males, heterosexuals, and Christians. Jewish males are also considered "white" for the purpose of persecution, exclusion, and demonization; while black and feminist professors are lionized for spewing hate-filled condemnations of Western civilization and its creators from the lecterns and pulpits of the academy (as are gay and lesbian professors rewarded for portraying male heterosexuals as aberrations). Cornel West at Yale, Angela Davis at Berkeley, and Leonard Jeffries at City College of New York are among legion examples of African Americans who openly hate and incite hatred against whites (and especially white males), proudly sponsored by their universities.[19] Led by the Ivy League, North American campuses have become hotbeds of institutionalized anti-white and antimale racist and sexist propaganda, but on this point Professor Marable is regrettably silent. Racism is wrong wherever it occurs, whether against blacks or whites or any other color. Racism is an injustice to humanity, but we must recognize that people of any color (and gender) are capable of becoming racists (and sexists).

Unlike the illiberal left, classical liberals and moderate conservatives have a different view. They assert that individuals themselves, and not some mythical conspiracy, are partly responsible for their successes and failings. There are African Americans who share this view too, notably Thomas Sowell. Yet he is a pariah among illiberal leftists, hated and feared for upholding personal responsibility in an age of collective victimhood.[20] Conservative blacks often observe with sadness and embarrassment that so many African Americans have fallen through "the cracks" of the system.

## Extremism from the Right

Contrary to Professor Marable, right-wing extremists have their own statistics. For example, Jared Taylor (a paleoconservative white nationalist and editor of *American Renaissance*) states:[21]

"Americans as a whole are more violent than Europeans: twice as likely as Frenchmen to commit murder and more than five times as likely as Germans to commit robbery. However, as is clear from the separate calculations for American blacks and whites, it is very high rates of violent crimes by blacks—eight times as high as whites for murder and more than ten times for robbery—that yield this result. These figures actually overstate the white crime rate, since the FBI's Uniform Crime Reports classify Hispanics as 'white.' About 9 percent of the population is Hispanic, and jurisdictions that treat them as a separate category report that they are two to six times as likely as whites to commit murder and robbery . . . This comparison with Europe suggests that the United States has neither a unique 'culture of violence' nor inadequate gun laws. It has a high rate of violent crime because it has a large number of violent black criminals."[22]

(Taylor conveniently forgets that World Wars I and II, among dozens of European wars, were not started by Latinos or blacks; rather, by white Europeans.) Meanwhile, left extremists blame "institutional racism," while right extremists blame "black criminality." These are the two predominant views on race to which Americans have been exposed since the late 1960s. No wonder American culture is so polarized and paralyzed. And no wonder the rest of the world notices it.

En route to The Middle Way, I want to provoke extremists on both wings to think more carefully about their claims. To be sure, America contains both institutional racism and dysfunctional subcultures. However, neither of these things assumes the forms that are claimed, respectively, by left and right extremists. Nor are these things "caused" by the inferences extremists draw from their statistics. Let me explain.

## White Radical Liberal Guilt

A deep and festering guilt pervades white radical liberalism's collective psyche. I was shocked when I first encountered it, soon after my arrival in America, and it took me a while to understand its pernicious effects. Some white radical liberals—including Jews, Christians, and secularists—feel guilty because of America's legacy of slavery, even though they have never owned slaves, nor in most cases are they descended from those who profiteered from slavery. In order to assuage their guilt, they want to "compensate" African Americans for their past oppression. So they have offered all kinds of special programs, initiatives, and incentives to blacks, which sometimes help and sometimes backfire. But these measures do not conduce to recognizing the common humanity of our brothers and sisters of color, as much as they attempt to assuage white liberal guilt. It looks like many white liberals want to apologize for slavery and segregation, and be forgiven by the descendents of those who were enslaved and segregated. But this has mutated into an exercise of arrogance, self-indulgence, delusion, and deceit, and not an exercise of humanism.

According to many influential, successful, astute, socially liberal but fiscally conservative African Americans, being the "beneficiaries" of white guilt translates to being favored, but not really accepted, by white society. These African Americans have stable families, beautiful homes, luxurious cars, prestigious careers, kids in the Ivy League, all the trappings of the American Dream. Yet many still do not feel part of it; rather, they feel patronized and used by white liberals who want to assuage their deep-seated feelings of guilt about slavery and segregation, and nothing more. Ironically, these "favored" people of color are often rejected by less-favored African Americans as well, who accuse them of having sold out, of being "Oreos"—black on the outside but white on the inside. So paradoxically perhaps, some of the most successful African Americans feel most keenly that racism is alive and well in America. Of course they accept the perquisites that come with their achievements—they'd be crazy not to—but they suffer from a sense of hollow or even Pyrrhic victory. And this, they emphasize, is within the liberal camp, where they are supposedly most welcome. In fact, they are economically affluent but politically homeless. This is sad enough for them. Imagine how much sadder it is for a vastly greater number of African Americans who are both economically disenfranchised and politically homeless.

In the antebellum South, on the vast plantations, many slaves were "promoted"—in a sense adopted—by plantation-owning families. They worked and often lived in the owners' mansions, and became indispensable to their masters' families and households. Some of the women also bore children of white paternity. These slaves were well dressed, well fed, well spoken, and well educated. They belonged to a special class: the sophisticated "servant class" that rulers of every civilization have cultivated throughout their empires. But such servants were never accepted as equals. And this is the painful feeling that so many contemporary "Oreo-Americans" carry with them today. Even when they're invited to Washington, D.C., for gala evenings or political confabulations, many feel like tokens of white guilt, which overtly rewards them yet covertly rejects them.[23] And these are their "friends." No wonder some African Americans prefer the brutal honesty of right-wing bigots, who at least possess the candor to express their prejudices openly.

### Guilt versus Shame

It is said that the West is a civilization of guilt, while the East is a civilization of shame. Guilt is internalized torment, carried and transmitted like a disease. People who carry private guilt think they can assuage it by public means, such as by compensating others. That is untrue. Guilt can be expiated by attracting forgiveness from the ones who were wronged (if that is possible in the first instance) and ultimately by forgiving oneself. Absolution alone never works for long, because absolution conditionally assuages guilt while reinforcing the very conditions that make guilt possible. Some people lead their lives consumed by recurrent guilt, which wastes them psychologically just as malaria or any recurrent disease would waste them physically.

Shame is different, and potentially much healthier. Shame is the complement of pride, and both can be good for us—in moderation of course. We feel ashamed publicly, in front of others, and we can expiate shame by first transforming it into humility, and then by performing honorable deeds humbly. You can never expiate guilt in this way. The more you try to compensate for guilt, the more you feed it. Guilt makes us sick; shame makes us well. The Tibetan language, shaped by centuries of Buddhism, has no word for "guilt." Meditate on that.

Whenever I visit Germany, I am relieved to encounter the healthy shame that so many contemporary Germans feel toward the Nazi era of their history. Since most Germans alive today were born after 1945, they have nothing to feel guilty about, even if their own parents were Nazis. Shame is a balm for them: It helps them acknowledge painful truths about their collective past, yet liberates them to do good in the present moment. Contrast this with the guilt of many radical white liberal Americans, which leads them arrogantly to assume responsibility for acts they did not commit, and makes them self-righteously bent on compensating the descendents of the victims at all costs. America's grotesque "culture of compensation" perpetuates nothing but victimhood: It rewards people for being "victims" instead of liberating and cultivating their humanity. Instead of being ashamed of the past and doing good from this moment forward, guilt-ridden white liberals perpetuate both racism and victimhood. Many African Americans are uncomfortable raising this issue publicly, partly because so many of their "benefactors" are too consumed with guilt to acknowledge its devastating effects.

Guilt and bigotry are both forms of self-hatred. As every persecuted people knows, right-wing extremists try to make themselves feel important by demeaning others. Bigoted people lack self-worth. And as every "beneficiary" of tokenism knows, left-wing extremists need to assuage their guilty consciences by compensating others. Guilt-ridden people lack self-worth. Neither the bigoted right nor the guilt-ridden left has compassion for their fellow human beings. Each extreme, after its own fashion, is deluded in ways that render it insensible and heartless.

## The Blues

During Expo '67 in Montreal I spent a lot of time in the American pavilion, a gigantic and capacious multilevel geodesic dome, filled with wondrous displays and marvelous entertainments. A friend of mine was managing the place, so thanks to him I got to meet and jam with some of the musicians. In those days I was a guitar-playing hippie, and I really dug the blues, which had journeyed from the Mississippi Delta to Chicago's South Side, and from there around the world. Hanging out in blues clubs, I heard and met many of the legends, from Sonny Terry and Brownie McGhee to Muddy Waters and Otis Spann, from John Lee Hooker to Howlin' Wolf to Buddy Guy. The blues is one among several related forms of music—gospel, soul, R&B, Motown, jazz—originated by African Americans, and beloved worldwide. The blues touches the heart of life's troubles and woes. White musicians of the 1960s played the blues too—Paul Butterfield, Mike Bloomfield, Johnny Winter, Eric Clapton, Jack Bruce, and John Mayall, among many others. Ultimately, the blues is colorless: Born of unique African-American experience, it nonetheless speaks to the universal human condition of circumstantial sorrow and transcendent hope, of stubborn love and even wry humor in the face of crushing despair.

So one afternoon in the American pavilion, I was jamming blues in the green room with a vintage Mississippi Delta player named Robert Pete Williams. He sang songs about not having any shoes, and how blessed he felt to find a pair. He was an uncomplicated man, with a pure heart and a cherubic countenance. Not an unkind thought furrowed his brow, yet God only knows how much trouble he had seen in his lifetime. He accepted me without demur simply because I was there, and he jammed with me because we both had guitars, and the blues. That was good enough for us both.

From across the room, someone else was looking daggers at me. I could feel his piercing gaze, a lot of enmity behind it. I knew who he was: a South Side Chicago blues legend named Robert Lockwood Jr. Nephew of the immortal Robert Johnson, he had experienced God knows what, having moved from Arkansas to the urban jungles of Chicago. He had a nice pair of shoes—racy Italian leather, better than my holed sneakers or Robert Pete's worn workboots—but his disposition reflected lots of hurt and anger. If certain notorious white executives—renowned for making black blues artists "poor and famous"—hadn't cheated him on recording contracts and royalties, I was certain some other white folks had for sure. He was a complicated man, and his brow was furrowed by life's unfairness and travails. Maybe he mistook me for a spoiled rich white Jewish honky dilettante. Maybe he simply looked at my skin color, and assumed I wasn't black enough to play the blues. He surely didn't know that I pawned guitars to pay my rent, and sometimes even to eat, in those days. I wanted to remind him that we all pay dues—black, white, and even inverse Oreos (black on the inside and white on the outside) too.

Another tragic irony is this: If anything in this world can salve the wounds of suffering on the one hand, and help people recognize their common humanity on the other, it is music. So I wanted to tell Robert Lockwood Jr. about one exotic summer night in downtown Montreal, when some friends and I gave flowers to Sonny Terry and Brownie McGhee, in the warm-up room of Norm Silver's Esquire Show Bar. These two veteran Delta bluesmen thanked us, and joked that it was nice to receive flowers while still alive. I wanted to tell Robert Lockwood Jr. about my pawned Les Paul guitar, sitting in the back of Jack's Pawn Shop. Jack used to let me jack it into a two-hundred-watt Marshall head, driving fifteen-inch Lansing speakers. So one morning I was blasting "Crossroads"—written by Lockwood's illustrious uncle, Robert Johnson himself—in the back of Jack's Pawn Shop, when up pulled a big black limousine, out of which emerged a tall black man in a long black leather coat, who stepped into the shop. He was a rich and famous musician whose tour had apparently hit Montreal. He heard me solo the last twelve bars of "Crossroads," and then and there invited me to join his band. I wanted to tell Robert Lockwood Jr. that there are plenty of black musicians in the world who see the blues as colorless, and who see whites (and even inverse Oreos) as brothers.

Like so many urban bluesmen, Robert Lockwood Jr.'s hardships didn't come from penury in the Mississippi Delta but from liberty in Chicago. He had a real mean case of the urban blues. Yet by understanding and bridging the gulf that separated Robert Pete Williams and Robert Lockwood Jr., we can transcend ordinary morality, and so help reconcile the racial extremes that still polarize America.

### From Ordered Slavery to Chaotic Freedom

Millions of African Americans migrated from the rural South to the urban North during America's "Golden Age" of capitalism. The convulsions of the civil rights movement, which saw black urban ghettoes burn like torches during the 1960s, came hand in glove with a high tide of radical and revolutionary waves of reform churned up by that turbulent decade. The hippies, yippies, Black Panthers, White Panthers, SDS, Weathermen, Chicago Eight, Summer of Love, Woodstock Nation, Bay of Pigs, Vietnam, protests, moon landing—all have conspicuous aftereffects today. During the late 1950s and early 1960s, a literally "black-and-white" American world—black-and-white racial segregation, black-and-white TV, black-and-white kitchen appliances, black-and-white bathroom tiles, black-and-white lifestyles—was transformed out of recognition into vivid living color. America's ultraconservatives of the day, who still weren't comfortable with "Blue Suede Shoes," were suddenly confronted by "Lucy in the Sky with Diamonds." Hippies, rebels, and radicals of the psychedelic left got high on everything under the sun at rock concerts, while evangelical Christian preachers and their zealots got high on Jesus and smashed rock records at revival meetings. The 1960s also gave us black-on-black, as Malcolm X's separatism bashed Martin Luther King's nationalism; and white-on-white, as white cops bashed the skulls of middle-class white kids on international TV. "The whole world is watching, the whole world is watching," chanted the bloodied protesters in Chicago in 1968. The whole world is still watching, but with more disbelief and incomprehension than ever.

While the political left freaked out, the political right closed ranks. They pulled the populace in opposing directions, and American culture has never recovered from that polarization. In the ensuing decades, the Great Society made way for the Great Divide. Millions of African Americans became polarized in that process. They festered in the urban projects, freed from overt slavery and segregation in the racist conservative South, but reenslaved by ideologies from the other extreme in the guilt-ridden liberal North. In their millions, African Americans moved from the Southern frying pan of an unjust but stable order, into the Northern fire of a just but chaotic disorder. They moved from rural apartheid to urban ghettos. They went from one extreme to another.

True, African Americans and their white radical liberal allies wrested precious freedoms from white conservative extremists by means of courageous and nonviolent political protest. But at the same time, other freedoms were foisted on newly emancipated African Americans by the radical liberal left—freedoms not conducive to human fulfillment—and especially at a critical time in their development as an emancipated people. The liberty to self-destruct via teenage motherhood, welfare programs, and quota systems has never been conducive to fulfillment. African Americans were swiftly ushered from the extreme of conservative oppression to the extreme of liberal self-destruction.

The American populace crossed a Rubicon early in the twenty-first century: As of 2004, more than 50 percent of all American children live in homes with fewer than two parents. This is driven by two main factors: increasing divorce rates, and spiraling out-of-wedlock birth rates. African Americans lead the way in the latter category, which averages 50 percent in New York City overall and reaches 80 percent in some neighborhoods. "Forty-five percent of black women managers or professionals have had an illegitimate child, compared to 3 percent of managerial or professional whites."[24] How did this happen? Here's an equation to ponder: Free love + radical feminism + white liberal guilt = sociological catastrophe.

There are recommended sequences for doing things in life, and having a baby out of wedlock in one's teens is premature by our current "best practices" for human development. Yet at the same time, white liberal guilt-driven social policies "reward" teenagers of color who have babies out of wedlock by giving them rent-free apartments and social welfare. This amounts to behavioral reinforcement of self-destruction. These teen mothers were victims to be sure, in this case not of Southern right-wing bigotry, but of Northern left-wing guilt. They had been accorded too much liberty, without a shred of responsibility or proper preparation for exercising it.

On top of this, starting in the late 1960s, American universities capitulated en masse to the demands of neo-Marxist radicals, abolishing standards of literacy and numeracy in order to satisfy preordained admission quotas for African Americans, along with other minorities. As university education became a "right" to be conferred by quotas instead of a privilege earned by scholarly achievement, the K-12 system also lost its incentive to educate. As the Russians say, "A fish rots from the head down." And so the American educational system has rotted.

And what fate befalls a generation of fatherless children? Reread Golding's *Lord of the Flies* and you will rediscover what happens to children bereft of adult authority—and in particular, of paternal authority. Left to their own devices, the fatherless children in Golding's allegory reinvented their own social and political hierarchies—as the ABCs inform us that all humans will naturally do. Only in this case, that hierarchy assumed its most degenerate default form: that of youth gangs, with a modus vivendi of petty violent crime. And in America, that is a big mistake. If you nonviolently swindle masses of gullible citizens out of hundreds of millions of dollars in the United States, the system may slap you on the wrist, fine you a few thousand, and hand you a suspended sentence. But if you rob someone of a few dollars at gunpoint, the system will throw the book at you—precisely because you haven't learned to read it.

In sum, the factor that contributes most to the disproportionate numbers of young black men in American prisons is neither the extreme leftist conspiracy theory of "institutional racism," nor the extreme rightist myth of "black criminality." Rather, it is the absence of a stable, middle-class nuclear family, with a breadwinning father to provide disciplined love and a mature mother to provide unconditional love in a home—and a community of such families to ensure decent education for their children, and to generate structural alternatives to gangs.

## The Middle Way

As African Americans continue their incredible saga—from the ordered injustice of the bigoted South to the chaotic justice of the guilt-ridden North and beyond these extremes toward a transcendent Middle Way— nothing will serve their interests more than the emergence of a strong and solid middle class, which by salutary example and constructive contribution will refute and silence extremists of both the right and the left. As we saw at the beginning of this chapter, that would be the consistent advice of Aristotle and Confucius both. Moreover, such a middle class, once liberated from political extremes, would better perceive and enter The Middle Way.

In a landmark article published by *Tricycle Magazine* in 2004, contributing editor Clark Strand commended Soka Gakkai USA for the conspicuous diversity of its membership, which it has attained (unlike the universities among so many other American institutions) without quota systems, affirmative action, reverse discrimination, political indoctrination, debasement of standards, and all the invidious and insidious measures of the culture wars. Masao Yokota, director of Soka Gakkai International's Boston Research Center, asked Strand to reflect on the reasons for SGI's successful yet uncoerced diversity. Here is Strand's reply.

"The *Lotus Sutra* is the primary reason. There is a theological mandate within the *Lotus Sutra* as practiced by Nichiren Buddhists for embracing diversity. It is found in its teachings of the absolute equality of all human beings. In Japan, where there isn't much cultural or racial diversity, it had remained a theory. But in America, it had a chance to blossom into reality, into a fact. Because when the SGI came here, it encountered for the first time a truly pluralistic society.

"The thing that was finally so fascinating to me about the SGI was that it is in some ways the fulfillment of the American dream. Not just the dream of financial prosperity, but the American dream of freedom and justice for all people. The American dream that expresses religious tolerance and religious plurality. The SGI is not only the only diverse Buddhist organization in America; it might be fair to say it is one of the very few diverse religious organizations of any denomination in America. There are others but they are rare.

"I have heard it said that Sunday is the most segregated day of the week in America, meaning that when people go to their respective religious traditions, their churches, their synagogues, their mosques, they are basically segregated. There is little racial crossover, even within the same faith tradition. For example, the Baptists: There are black Baptists and white Baptist churches, but rarely do the two cross the color line in any significant way."[25]

I share Clark Strand's experience of SGI. Soka Gakkai USA has done a better job than any organization I know in transcending racial strife in the service of humanity and bridging the chasms of a polarized America. Whenever I visit SGI's sanghas, which meet in culture centers from New York to Los Angeles, I am always impressed by two connected phenomena. First, I encounter a racially and culturally diverse group of people, who nonetheless have no racial agendas and need no slogans to celebrate their diversity. Why? Because their sole "agenda" is the celebration of their common humanity, which comes in many "flavors"—male and female, black and white, young and old, liberal and conservative, you name it. But these cosmetic differences amount to nothing among the enlightened, whose Buddha natures have just one taste: the taste of emancipation from suffering, including suffering imposed by political extremisms.

Contrast this humanistic reception accorded by Buddhists, who perceive only human beings, with the dehumanizing reception accorded by American universities, who perceive only race and sex. All applicants to American universities, whether students or faculty, are tracked by Orwellian bureaucracies (in the name of "equality") according to their race and sex, and are obliged (in some states by law) to divulge their racial and sexual identities.[26] What happened to Martin Luther King's exhortation that we be judged not by the color of our skins but by the content of our character? American universities have institutionalized racism and sexism alike, which dehumanizes everyone concerned. Buddhists work above all to unite people on the basis of our shared humanity.

Aristotle teaches that we need to discover and develop our individual excellences to be fulfilled: But fulfillment itself is the goal, not a particular excellence. Confucius teaches that without a stable family structure both the individual and the society will suffer, and such suffering is painfully observable throughout America and the West. Buddha teaches that we need to become awakened to the true causes of suffering, for only then can we alleviate it in ourselves and others. The main cause of suffering in race relations—at both extremes—is the failure to perceive our common humanity.

Right-wing bigots and guilt-ridden liberals alike fail to work for the common good, as do polarized American politicians running for office. During the 2004 election campaign, neither American presidential candidate once mentioned the U.N.'s Millennium Development Goals, which are meant to alleviate suffering and contribute to the common good of the entire global village. The ABCs are concerned above all with achieving common goods; political extremists of both wings are concerned chiefly with fomenting divisive ills. This applies not only to America, but to all who suffer under political extremisms.

When I asked Daisaku Ikeda to account for SGI's noteworthy American successes in bridging political divides including racial ones, he replied: "Buddhism sees in all life the limitless positive possibilities of the Buddha nature; it further discovers in all people—without regard to differences of race, nationality, culture or gender—an equal capacity to realize these potentialities. The impulse to discriminate has deep roots in human life and experience; thus, it can only be met and transformed by a relentless faith in human equality."[27]

Relentless faith in human equality does not spring from bigoted, guilt-ridden, or hateful extremes: Rather, it emerges from The Middle Way. In the next chapter, we will look at more extremes that are related to the political: inflexible religious extremes supported by the political right, and anarchic secular extremes supported by the political left.

# 7

## SACRED AND PROFANE EXTREMES
### Blind Faith versus Deaf Denial

*We should nowhere be more modest than in discussions about the gods*
*. . . lest from temerity or impudence we should make ignorant*
*assertions or knowingly tell lies.* —Aristotle (Fragments)

*Those who take the non-real for the real and the real for the non-real and*
*thus fall victims to erroneous notions, never reach the essence of reality.*
—Buddha

*From a gentleman consistency is expected, not blind fidelity.* —Confucius

### From Religious Fanaticism to Moral Anarchy

HISTORICALLY, THE GROWTH and dominion of Western civilization has unfolded via bitter but ultimately fruitful clashes between religious dogmas of the Judeo-Christian strand, and scientific inquiries of the Aristotelian strand of its cultural DNA. The progress of reliable knowledge—which has paved the way for all the technologies that enable globalization—has been regularly impeded, censored, and suppressed by politically empowered religious extremes that view blind faith as a cultural norm. Step by tortuous step, religious fanaticism grudgingly retreated in the face of the irrepressible advance of science. Then, ironically, by the twentieth century, Western science and technology had developed enough to help strengthen and then to harden political mass movements from both extremes. So fascism and communism both turned against science—for totalitarian states cannot tolerate freedom of thought any better than their theocratic forebears. At great cost and enormous sacrifice, the free West defeated the hard forces of fascist totalitarianism in World War II and communist totalitarianism in the Cold War, only to succumb from within to the relatively soft but venomously lethal profanities of godless neo-Marxism, parricidal feminism, and antirealist postmodernism.

This chapter details the polarization that acutely afflicts America along the axis of reverent versus irreverent belief. At one pole is the sacred religious right, epitomized by the Christian Coalition and its fanatical extremes of evangelical Christianity—apocalyptic faiths that welcome and fuel the civilizational clash with fanatical Islam, and appear equally intolerant of scientific and humanistic sensibilities. At the other pole is the profane sacrilegious left, epitomized by the deconstructed zombies mass-produced on and graduated from the assembly lines of postmodernism's totalitarian factories—the universities. By the time we tour some of these factories in chapter 11, you will be better prepared to confront the sublime surrealism and vicious antirealism that awaits you. On the fanatical extremes of the profane left, militant neo-Marxists and radical feminists have hijacked postmodernism itself, using it as a Trojan horse to smuggle intellectual bankruptcy, moral anarchy, and political chaos into the very soul of Western civilization. On the sacred extreme, we encounter blind faith in supernatural dogma; on the profane extreme, deaf denial as to the nature of reality itself. At both extremes, the ABCs are ignored—and frequently outlawed. The sacred extreme is fixated on heaven and petrified of hell; the profane extreme recreates hell and renames it heaven.

The dichotomy here is neither between faith and reason, nor between doubt and reason. Both the sacred and the profane extremes use their own versions of reason to stimulate powerful emotions, thereby eliciting commitments to unreasonable doctrines that end up paralyzing reason itself. Reason is the enemy neither of faith nor of doubt: It's a good and necessary friend to both. Faith and doubt are, in fact, complements, and as such they coexist in human nature. But extremes of faith or doubt inhibit the exercise of reason. Well-being requires a constant balancing of faith and doubt—but extremists work relentlessly to unbalance people by erring on one side or the other. Sacred religious extremists exaggerate the role of faith, leaving no room at all for doubt. This is unhealthy for all concerned, because doubt (as in "healthy skepticism") is a powerful instrument that impels inquiry and helps discover truth and dispel falsehood.

Equally unbalancing are radical ideologues who exaggerate the role of doubt, critiquing anything and deconstructing everything, and leaving no margin at all for faith. This too is unhealthy, for faith is a powerful instrument that strengthens our capacity to accept situations we may not relish, and to abide in circumstances we may not enjoy. Faith also safeguards us from squandering our energies on people or circumstances we cannot immediately change. Every human being lives with a necessary complement of faith and doubt. Suppress your doubt and you will stunt your humanity; suppress your faith you will depreciate your humanity. Balance the two, and you will maintain your equanimity.

In chapter 1, I mentioned six examples in which sacred or profane extremisms suppressed reasoned inquiry and objective truth: the Roman Church's prohibition of Galilean astronomy, the Anglican and Roman censorship of Hobbesian political theory, the creationist denial of Darwinian evolutionism, the Nazi proscription of "Jewish physics," the Soviet endorsement of Lamarckian agronomy, the allied antirealist (neo-Marxist, feminist, and postmodern) repudiation of science and objective reality itself. Now let's examine each case in a bit more detail.

## Galileo's Inquisition

Galileo was the first man to be threatened with the death penalty for training a telescope on the moon. The Dutch had pioneered the grinding of lenses and the development of microscopes and telescopes. But in the seventeenth century, telescopes were used for military and commercial purposes—from espionage (hence the synonym "spyglass") to early detection of merchant ships approaching harbor. When Galileo looked at the moon through a telescope, he saw a surface crusted with mountains and pitted with craters. But that observation was heresy against the

Church, enough to warrant his burning at the stake. Why? Because Aristotelian physics and cosmology were both based on optimistic but unwarranted assumptions about purpose and perfection of design: "The shape of the heaven is necessarily spherical," wrote Aristotle, "for that is the shape most appropriate to its substance and also by nature primary."[2] This fit well with the Judeo-Christian creation myth of Genesis, and God's perfect works, and so the Roman Catholic Church of the day accepted Aristotle's erroneous assumptions uncritically, and moreover enshrined them as official doctrine. The Pope believed them, and the Pope was supposedly "infallible." Blind faith closes minds, embraces falsehoods, and elevates them to unchallengeable "truths." Anyone who seeks to correct such errors runs the risk of incurring the self-righteous wrath of the closed-minded. Remember poor Hippasus, who paid with his life for circulating his proof that the square root of two is irrational.

Galileo had already exposed a number of Aristotle's errors in physics and favored Copernicus's heliocentric model of the solar system over Ptolemy's geocentric one. So he had become an embarrassing irritant if not a threat to the authority of the regnant Roman Catholic theocrats, who made the usual mistake of trying to suppress truth by silencing the truth teller. The notorious Robert Cardinal Bellarmine, who would soon attract the withering ink of Hobbes's pen, had testified during Galileo's inquisition, "To assert that the earth revolves around the sun is as erroneous as to claim that Jesus was not born of a virgin."[3] Just so. Blind faith—of any faith—is prone to confusing objective facts with subjective articles of faith.

Unlike Hippasus, Galileo had no appetite for martyrdom, and so he accepted a political compromise: He publicly recanted his "heresies" and suffered house arrest, thus avoiding the stake. But the truth was out, the scientific revolution was on, and the replacement of entrenched superstition by testable hypothesis was in. For a while, at least.

### Hobbes's Heresy
Thomas Hobbes was a contemporary of Galileo's, and had met him in Padua while accompanying the sons of the Cavendish family on a grand

tour of Europe, as their tutor. Hobbes was mightily impressed by Galileo's use of experiments with geometry as a way of refuting Aristotle's physics, and by the larger paradigm shift that Galileo's work portended: the emancipation of physics from a branch of theology to a branch of experimental philosophy (as science was originally called) in its own right. When Hobbes returned to England, he resolved to do the same with politics.

And so he did, but not under circumstances that he could have foreseen. Hobbes was unavoidably caught up in the English Civil War. Initially a political conflict, it swiftly developed severe religious overtones as well. The war had begun as a struggle for political power between the absolute authority of King Charles I and the increasing demands of Parliamentarians like Oliver Cromwell for a greater voice in the affairs of state. Taxation without representation was a central issue, just as it would be in the later American Revolution.

The religious quarrel had smoldering roots. King Henry VIII had founded the Anglican Church in 1534 for the purpose of divorcing Catherine of Aragon—which Popes Julius II and later Clement VII had proved reluctant to sanction—and to legally marry Anne Boleyn. Henry and Anne's daughter, Elizabeth I ("Good Queen Bess") established that institution as the Church of England, which was the precipitating cause of the attempted invasion by the Spanish Armada in 1588, the year of Hobbes's birth. The Tudor line had died out with barren Elizabeth and was replaced by the Stuart Kings of Scotland. King James I produced the Bible famously named after him, a mainstay of Anglican liturgy, but his son Charles I married a French Catholic princess, who disquieted both the Anglican aristocracy and Parliament by celebrating Mass openly at court. And when Cromwell's Parliamentarian forces gained ascendancy over King Charles's royalists in Civil War battle, Charles secretly appealed to the Pope for help, and hatched a plot to invade England with Catholic troops from the Continent, from staging areas in Ireland. When Charles lost the war, that treachery among others cost him his head.

Hobbes, whose life in England had become endangered because of his known sympathies for the political authority of the king, was granted safe haven in Paris in 1640, where he accompanied the queen, her son Prince Charles II, and their courtiers. It was during his eleven-year exile in France that Hobbes wrote *Leviathan*, the classic that founded two fields—modern political science and empirical psychology—and drew its author into mortal danger. Why?

Hobbes presented this masterwork in 1651 to young Prince Charles (later King Charles II), whom he had been tutoring in geometry and classics, but to whom he was expressly forbidden to impart instruction in the Aristotelian art of politics. In the notorious thirteenth chapter of *Leviathan*, Hobbes boldly contradicts Saint Augustine's doctrine of original sin, a backbone of both Roman Catholic and Anglican theology. "The desires and other passions of man, are in themselves no sin," Hobbes declared. The entire fourth part of *Leviathan* is a polemic against the Roman Church in general and Bellarmine in particular. Hobbes called the Roman Church a "Kingdom of Darkness," ruled by a "confederacy of deceivers." Rome immediately placed the work on its *Index* of banned books, and French clerics prepared to arraign Hobbes for heresy. At this critical moment Hobbes also lost his diplomatic immunity at court, because the English Catholic contingent came out of their closet long enough to convince the young prince that *Leviathan* was an apology for Cromwell rather than a defense of monarchy. (Indeed, it can be read both ways.) So Hobbes fled back to England, where Cromwell, now Lord Protector of the realm, refrained from persecuting him.

But following the Great Plague and the Great Fire of London, the bishops of London in 1667 moved before Parliament that *Leviathan* be politically condemned. They contended that its blasphemies were the primary causes of London's devastating pestilence and conflagration, which they said the Almighty had visited upon the nation as a punishment for harboring Thomas Hobbes and his philosophy. The bishops' motion was a grand irony, since *Leviathan*'s core thesis is that politics should not be a branch of theology. Parliament sided with Hobbes. They entertained the motion but did not endorse it.

Hobbes's corollary was that humans can truly prosper only in a commonwealth, governed by a secular political authority—whether one man, or an assembly of men. Most of Western civilization now takes that for granted, but in the seventeenth century it was a heresy punishable by death—as it is today in much of Islamic civilization, which still awaits a "Luther of Arabia" to reform its extreme orthodoxies, and an Islamic Hobbes to separate mosque and state. (Kemal Ataturk did just this in Turkey, in the twentieth century, but the Arab world has not followed his lead.)

Nor was Hobbes terribly popular at his alma mater, Oxford. In those days, the university was rigidly controlled by the Anglican Church, and one had to become a prelate or a priest to profess an academic career. In 1684, during a particularly virulent episode of anti-learning, Dean John Fell burned a number of books in a bonfire set in the quad of Christ Church. He used Hobbes's Leviathan to kindle the blaze.

One young student in residence watched in horror as the smoke curled upward, and made ready to flee Oxford's theocratic suppression. While he disagreed with Hobbes on the nature of man, censorship disagreed with him even more. His later political philosophy, including his defense of private property, would come to exert a decisive influence on the framers of the American Constitution. His name was John Locke. And so the torch of political vision in Western civilization, that of free peoples in a prosperous secular commonwealth, was kept alight by Hobbes and handed to Locke, who passed it on to Thomas Jefferson.

But it would require almost two more centuries before the Hobbesian vision of a secularized university came to pass. Jeremy Bentham, the father of utilitarianism, founded University College London (UCL) in 1867. UCL was the first public university in England to admit women, Jews, Catholics, and dissenters, among others previously barred from higher education. Its "sister" institution, New York's famed and infamous City College, was founded earlier, in 1847, but did not admit women until the mid-twentieth century. So just as Galileo freed physics from the yoke of theology, so Hobbes freed politics, psychology, and—indirectly—education alike.

### Darwin's Apostasy

Charles Darwin ignited the ongoing struggle to free biology from theology with his 1859 publication *On the Origin of Species*. By this time Western mathematics, physics, and chemistry were so far advanced that the intelligentsia was ready for a breakthrough in biological theory. It cannot be overemphasized that the greatest mathematicians and scientists of the Enlightenment—including Darwin—still believed fervently in God, but required political freedom from religious dogma to do their work, which lay in the advancement of reliable knowledge of nature and all her products, including humankind.

Darwin never used the word *evolution,* which was introduced posthumously into the sixth edition of the *Origins.* He had written "descent with modification." Nor did he coin the contentious phrase "survival of the fittest"—that was social Darwinist Herbert Spencer's doing, and Darwin never favored it. Moreover, and also contrary to popular misconception, Darwin was neither an atheist nor a materialist. He hypothesized that all life on earth is descended from "one primordial form, into which life was first breathed." While this is incompatible with the myth of Genesis literally interpreted, it implies that a Creator was needed to breathe life into dead matter. Even so, Darwin's prescient insights—which prophesied the science of genetics—raised such a furor among a Western populace of then-predominantly fundamentalist Christians that the wife of the Bishop of Worcester apocryphally remarked, "Descended from apes? Let us hope that it is not true, but if true let us pray that it does not become generally known." Yet as we saw, Darwin's cousin Francis Galton would soon show that prayers are statistically likely to backfire. Darwin's so-called "theory of evolution" became the paradigm of modern biological science, but not without hotly contested debates. Thomas Huxley, grandfather of Aldous, earned the moniker "Darwin's bulldog" for his staunch defenses against the crusading creationist critic Bishop Samuel Wilberforce. In the United States, the state of Tennessee forbade by legal statute in 1925 the teaching of Darwin in all its schools and universities, which led to the notorious Scopes trial.

John Scopes, a Scottish immigrant with a taste for truth, had defied the statute and taught evolution as part of general science in a Dayton, Tennessee, high school, which led to his branding as an infidel and his conviction in a Dayton court. He was defended, albeit in vain, by the renowned Clarence Darrow. Here is the conclusion of H. L. Mencken's coverage of the trial:

"The Scopes trial, from the start, has been carried on in a manner exactly fitted to the anti-evolution law and the simian imbecility under it. There hasn't been the slightest pretense to decorum. The rustic judge, a candidate for re-election, has postured the yokels like a clown in a ten-cent side show, and almost every word he has uttered has been an undisguised appeal to their prejudices and superstitions. The chief prosecuting attorney, beginning like a competent lawyer and a man of self-respect, ended like a convert at a Billy Sunday revival. It fell to him, finally, to make a clear and astounding statement of theory of justice prevailing under fundamentalism. What he said, in brief, was that a man accused of infidelity had no rights whatever under Tennessee law . . .

"Darrow has lost this case. It was lost long before he came to Dayton. But it seems to me that he has nevertheless performed a great public service by fighting it to a finish and in a perfectly serious way. Let no one mistake it for comedy, farcical though it may be in all its details. It serves notice on the country that Neanderthal man is organizing in these forlorn backwaters of the land, led by a fanatic, rid of sense and devoid of conscience. Tennessee, challenging him too timorously and too late, now sees its courts converted into camp meetings and its Bill of Rights made a mock of by its sworn officers of the law."[4]

A kangaroo court is the perfect place for a monkey trial. Precisely because Hobbes's politics had failed to penetrate the American Bible Belt, Darwin's biology was demonized by a court of law that interpreted the American Constitution through the lens of fundamentalist Christianity. This problem continues to haunt the United States into the twenty-first century. At this writing it shows no sign of abatement. A philosopher who accepted a teaching post in the 1990s at a university in the Bible Belt told me how he introduced

Darwinism, and pointed out its strengths and weaknesses as a theory of evolution. The philosopher was soon invited to lunch by a deacon of the church, who suggested that he stop preaching heresy in the classroom. That was in 1995, seventy years after the Scopes trial. Nothing had changed but the actors in the farce.

## Intolerance of "True Believers"

The Enlightenment produced many bright sparks of scientific advancement, all too often by abrading the flint of unyielding fundamentalist faith. The same thing occurs in all fundamentalist religions when fanatics gain political power, and it happens in literary and artistic circles as well as scientific ones. So author Salman Rushdie was sentenced to death by Islamic fanatics for daring to reinterpret the Koran in his novel *The Satanic Verses* while filmmaker Theo van Gogh was murdered in the streets of Amsterdam by an Islamist fanatic for expressing provocative opinions about Islam.

I reiterate that faith and doubt coexist in the human mind, often uneasily. They are complementary, and they must be brought into balance for the human being to attain equanimity. When fundamentalist religions exaggerate blind faith and stifle open-minded doubt, they maintain their followers in a state of imbalance. This is evidenced by their need to proselytize incessantly, among themselves and others. Anyone secure in his faith is also secure in his doubt, so has no need to proselytize. If you accept yourself for what you are, you can accept others for what they are too. But if you are insecure in your faith, it is because you have not accepted your doubts. If you try to bury your doubts with blind faith, then you will need others to profess the same beliefs as you, so you can all pretend together that nobody has any doubts. This is a shared hallucination. But beyond your circle of believers there are yet others who doubt, and their doubt reminds you of your own unresolved doubt, and so you must convert them or silence them in order to restore your collective but nonetheless false sense of security. If you cannot tolerate external doubt, it is because you have neither confronted nor accepted your internal doubt. And even if one proselytizing religion prevailed over all the others, and managed to convert the whole of humanity, then and only then would the real troubles start. With nobody left to convert, each and every "true believer" would have to start confronting his or her own doubts.

This is why "true believers" need desperately to have all the answers. They cannot tolerate one iota of unknowing, not a single shred of doubt. If they allow one doubt to arise, their entire edifice of faith collapses. Such faith is not at all strong but rather transparently weak. Strong faith easily tolerates doubt; only the most fragile faith needs to suppress it. And that is why "true philosophers" have so often been persecuted by "true believers"—philosophers can raise doubts like nobody's business. True philosophers never claim to have all the answers. On the contrary, they have all the questions. If you think you believe something beyond the shadow of a doubt, consult a philosopher, who will find a way to subvert your belief. How? Through inquiry. By questioning your beliefs, a true philosopher can lead you to raise doubts you never dreamed existed. The converse is also true, but much rarer. If you have too many doubts, then a true philosopher can also question them, and through inquiry lead you back to faith.

Peace and progress lie in The Middle Way, which balances faith and doubt. As a philosophical counselor and consultant, I am confronted with human beliefs and doubts of all kinds. There is no limit to human inventiveness, including the varieties of trouble that people invent for themselves by impoverishing their doubt with exaggerated faith at one extreme, or by impoverishing their faith with exaggerated doubt at the other. One of my favorite works of Christian mysticism is *The Cloud of Unknowing*, in which an anonymous monk reinforced his faith by meditating on the unknown and, beyond that, on the unknowable itself. "Of God himself no man can think," he wrote.[5] If God is only half (or any fraction) as great as "true believers" claim, then nobody has ever known, nor can ever know, the contents of God's mind, the workings of God's will, the fulfillment of God's plan. Anyone who claims to know these things truly speaks falsely—whether God exists or not.

People sometimes ask me what I believe. "True believers" love this question, because it's an invitation to proselytize. "True philosophers" consider this a loaded question, because they know that their own beliefs can be subverted, and their own doubts exposed, by an astute inquirer. So when people ask me this question—"What do you believe?"—I usually tell them that "I believe what I doubt, and doubt what I believe." Many find this perplexing. I find it liberating. One advantage of this state of mind is that it confers immunity to sacred extremes, as well as to profane ones. Having looked at some sacred extremes of religious fanaticism and blind faith in the supernatural, let us now turn to the other pole: profane extremes of secular fanaticism and deaf denial of reality.

## Profane Extremes

We have briefly glimpsed three examples of reason's persecution by the sacred extreme of religious fanaticism: Galileo's physics, Hobbes's politics, Darwin's biology, all suffered in this way. There are myriad other examples, but these surely convey the main idea. Let us now look at three examples of reason's persecution by profane extremes of secular fanaticism: the Nazi proscription of "Jewish physics," the Soviet endorsement of Lamarckian agronomy, and the allied antirealist repudiation of reality itself.

While the separation of politics from theology made possible the birth of the modern secular state, secularism soon became vulnerable to profane political extremes, whose horrors were unleashed upon humankind in the twentieth century, on unprecedentedly horrific scales. Religious fanaticism exaggerates faith and suppresses doubt; political fanaticism attenuates faith and prohibits doubt. How? By replacing gods with dictators, and substituting political ideologies for religious doctrines. Our three examples will illustrate how this profane extreme is just as deluded as its sacred counterpart and produces even greater suffering.

## Nazi Proscription of "Jewish Physics"

The Nazis conceived of themselves as the "master race"—so-called pure Aryans—and sought to subjugate or eliminate the rest of European humankind. Hitler's mythology of race, blood, and soil appealed to some of the primal elements in man, and also to the darkest ones. His intention to supplant religious authority with Nazi ideology was transparent. All married couples in the Third Reich, for example, acquired Hitler's *Mein Kampf* as a compulsory wedding present, and were supposed to spend their honeymoon not only conceiving sons for the Fatherland, but also wading through its nine hundred pages of turgid prose. Intruding his political vision into the sacrament of marriage epitomized Hitler's desire to attenuate and fixate religious belief upon the state, and upon himself as its mortal deity. Similarly, all military officers were required to take a personal oath of loyalty—not to God, king, or country—but to the führer. Dictators do not tolerate authorities higher than themselves.

Truth is one such higher authority. Nobody rules truth, yet many make the mistake of trying to legislate it. We have seen scientific truths banned, and truth tellers persecuted or executed, by sacred extremists. The same thing happens at the profane extreme. A core component of Nazi ideology involved demonizing, persecuting, and attempting to annihilate European Jewry. Hitler found it expedient to scapegoat the Jewish people. Upon them he laid blame for Germany's economic ills during the hyperinflation of the Weimar Republic. More broadly still, he accused Jews of masterminding international capitalism, and of plotting incessantly to rule the world (the very thing that Hitler himself was doing). Using the infamous *Protocols of the Elders of Zion* as evidence, and relentless propaganda as reinforcement, he played upon a thousand years of European anti-Semitism to renew and foment deep and violent hatreds of Judaism and all things Jewish.

The Nuremburg Laws of 1935 were a stepping-stone on the road to the Holocaust. They formed the basis for denying Jews citizenship in the Reich, and for disenfranchising Jews of all other trappings of humanity. By the late 1930s the Nazis had confiscated Jewish businesses, forbidden Jewish doctors and lawyers to practice, and expelled Jewish professors from the universities. But European, especially Germanic, Jews had already made outstanding contributions to twentieth-century physics—Albert Einstein, Niels Bohr, Albert Michelson, Wolfgang Pauli, James Franck, and Otto Stern numbered among the Jewish Nobel laureates in physics up to 1945—but their works became anathema to the extremes of Nazi ideology. Werner Heisenberg, a founder of quantum theory and discoverer of the "Heisenberg inequality," was nearly fired from his professorial post merely for mentioning Einstein's name during a lecture. He was exonerated of the crime of promoting "Jewish physics" only because his sister was a friend of Heinrich Himmler's.

It is clear to anyone in his right mind that the laws of physics are not black, white, brown, yellow, Aryan, or non-Aryan. Neither are they Jewish, Christian, Muslim, Hindu, Buddhist, Sikh, agnostic, or atheist. Neither are they Eurocentric, Afrocentric, Democratic, Republican, socialist, communist, libertarian, or anarchist. Laws of physics, like all laws of nature, transcend divisive categories—racial, religious, political—which humans abuse to perpetuate wasteful and harmful conflicts. By elevating Aryanism above all other criteria, and by banning "Jewish physics" (along with Jewish physicists) from the universities, Hitler denigrated truth by making it subservient to racial mythology. Germany paid the inevitable price for its ideological profanity. The exodus of Jewish scientists from fascist Germany and fascist Italy, and later from occupied Europe—and the mass murder of those who could not escape—not only spelled the end of Germany's preeminence in the physical sciences, but also retarded Nazi Germany's development of the atomic bomb. The predicted amount of energy released by nuclear fission is $E = mc^2$, a "Jewish equation" derived by Einstein.

Fear that Hitler would be the first to build and use atomic weapons prompted two Jewish physicists, both refugees from Nazi Europe—Albert Einstein and Leo Szilard—to persuade U.S. president Franklin Roosevelt to initiate the Manhattan Project in 1941.[6] As a result, another Jewish physicist and refugee from Benito Mussolini's fascist Italy—Enrico Fermi—built the first nuclear pile and induced the first contained nuclear chain reaction in the subterranean squash courts of the University of Chicago. The Nazis would never have allowed such a thing, a game of "Jewish squash," played with "Jewish neutrons."

So the Nazi persecution of Jews both abetted Hitler's ascent to power, yet also helped bring about the demise of the Third Reich. What goes around, comes around. This is karma operating on a grand scale.

It also had a decisive effect on the West's victories in both the Cold War and the derivative "space race" against the Soviet Union, about which Western pundits love to quip, "Our German scientists beat their German scientists." That is also a truth, however spoken in jest. Before, during, and after World War II, Germanic scientists fled preferentially Westward, toward liberty, opportunity, and hope. Eastward lay Nazi Germany's left-handed totalitarian twin, Marxist–Leninist–Stalinist Russia. It was a good place to avoid. Just ask Stalin's victims. He murdered twenty to thirty million of his "comrades," surpassing even Hitler's butchery. Why? Partly because he had adopted ideologies of history and economics from the extreme left: Karl Marx's.

### From "Jewish Physics" to "Soviet Biology"

Hitler's Nazi Germany was a totalitarian state, an extreme of the political right. Stalin's Soviet Union was a complementary totalitarian state, an extreme of the political left. Remember the Chinese master who spoke about two ends of a string. The two extremes of a string touch when the loop is closed; and similarly, a left boot in the face is indistinguishable from a right boot in the face. And so wherever laws of nature are subordinated to ideology, whether from the extreme right or the extreme left—the result is the same: political profanity and human suffering.

To appreciate the profanity of the Sovietization of biology, using the example of Trofim Lysenko's Lamarckian agronomy, we must first revisit Charles Darwin and introduce a now well known but then obscure contemporary of Darwin's in London, with whom he enjoyed a brief but pointed correspondence: Karl Marx. I regularly receive letters from readers of my pop-philosophy books, who ask why I have omitted or neglected Marx from consideration as one of the "world's great thinkers." I promise not to neglect him any longer. Bear in mind that, as I write these very words (late in 2005), a BBC survey has declared Karl Marx Britain's most popular philosopher.[7] The top ten philosophers according to the BBC, and the percentage of votes they attracted, were: 1. Karl Marx 27.93%; 2. David Hume 12.67%; 3. Ludwig Wittgenstein 6.80%; 4. Friedrich Nietzsche 6.49%; 5. Plato 5.65%; 6. Immanuel

Kant 5.61%; 7. Thomas Aquinas 4.83%; 8. Socrates 4.82%; 9. Aristotle 4.52%; 10. Karl Popper 4.20%.

This result is indicative of the ongoing and precipitous decline of Western civilization. It is also terrifying for a number of reasons, not least of which is the failure of the British public to recall the name of John Stuart Mill. In the words of Isaiah Berlin, Mill's essay "On Liberty," "to this day remains the most eloquent, the most sincere and the most convincing plea for individual freedom ever uttered."[8] The absence of Mill's name in the top ten, and the prominence of Marx, are highway signs on the low road to enslavement of individuals by collectives.

Karl Marx was a brilliant intellectual and accomplished social misfit, largely unemployable and mostly ostracized by the nineteenth-century Britain that lately so reveres him. He was born into a Jewish-German family of prosperous merchants and professionals, and he came of age during a window of relative European tolerance toward Jews. Notwithstanding the Dreyfus Affair in France and pogroms in Russia, Disraeli was prime minister of the late Victorian British Empire, while Freud was revolutionizing psychology in Vienna. German Jews were permitted to advance themselves if they converted to Christianity. Many took up this offer, including the poet Heinrich Heine and the composer Gustav Mahler. Marx converted too, and married a Protestant woman, whereupon his own family disowned him. Exiled from the Continent owing to his communist activism, Marx settled in London, without money and social connections. He languished in ignominy, peddling journalistic pieces for pennies to feed his starving family while incubating *Das Kapital*, which he wrote in the British Library.

I happened to be writing in that great library myself, a century later, when Mikhail Gorbachev visited Margaret Thatcher in London. She wanted to show him all the sights, from Westminster Abbey to the Crown Jewels, but he only had eyes for the British Library. Gorbachev wanted to see the chair in which Marx had sat to write *Das Kapital*. So they pointed to one, and he was satisfied. In fact, no Londoner knows where Marx had sat. His ideas left by far the more enduring imprint.

Both theoretician and practitioner, Marx strove to destroy Western civilization as we know it, by unraveling both strands of its cultural

DNA and replacing them with his version of communism. He repudiated the Abrahamic faiths with dialectical materialism: No God, one book (*Das Kapital*), one pamphlet (the *Communist Manifesto*), one prophet (Karl Marx). He defied Aristotle by disordering the hierarchy of arts and sciences, and promoting economics *über alles*. He placed politics—and therefore all the other arts and sciences—under central economic control. His economic theory was intended to remedy the grievous wrongs suffered by the working classes during the Industrial Revolution, and was meant to spread worldwide. Capitalism was seen as evil, communism as good.

Marx was not alone in railing against the debilitating, dehumanizing, and rapacious capitalism of the Industrial Revolution. The wretched, squalid and hopeless conditions of the working classes in England, among other places, provoked a romantic rebellion against the mechanization of the human spirit, led by poets like William Wordsworth and Robert Browning, and philosopher Henri Bergson. These conditions engendered a utilitarian concern with maximizing good for the greatest number, led by philosopher-activists Bentham and Mill. They and other activists stimulated reforms of criminal law, so that children would no longer be hanged for theft; and they furthered reforms of slavery, given the bigger picture of British imperialism that embraced the "Triangular Trade." Scathing literary condemnations of urban poverty flowed from the pens of Charles Dickens and Victor Hugo. They loaned impetus to socialism and the trade-union movement that would secure workers' rights, and inspired the *Communist Manifesto* of Karl Marx that called for violent revolutionary overthrow of the governments of the industrialized West.

That said, Marx himself privately envied the lives and lifestyles of the so-called "petty bourgeoisie"—the middle class—whom he accused of complicity in exploiting the proletariat. Having found a friend and benefactor in Friedrich Engels, who himself had inherited factories in England's industrialized Midlands, Marx eventually managed to lead the pampered upper-middle-class lifestyle that he otherwise sought to destroy—in a London town house bought and paid for by the sweat of the workers in Engels' factories.

Nonetheless, Marxism represented the terminus of a widespread romantic and utopian European rebellion against the myriad sufferings of the hapless masses, imposed by successive centuries and layers of feudalism, monarchy, theocracy, mercantilism, imperialism, and industrialization. The ongoing democratic and socialist reforms were not enough for Marx, who sought more rapid and more radical change.

World War I, naively called "the war to end all wars," was the turning point for the communist movement. In the East, Lenin succeeded in deposing and murdering the Russian tsar, removing Russia from the Western alliance against bellicose Germany, ushering in seventy years of Soviet communism, and inspiring Mao Tse-tung's later Marxist–Leninist takeover of China. In the West, an entire generation of young men were mowed down by Maxim machine guns or perished in the pestilential trenches. The Western intelligentsia who managed to survive this unprecedented carnage fingered imperialism and capitalism as the main enemies, and not "the Hun." World War I caused the Western intellectual climate to shift from romantic rebellion to political activism, from gradual reform to swift reformation. Socialism and its more extreme version, namely Marxism, were viewed by well-intended but politically naive intellectuals as an antidote to the excesses of capitalism and a gateway to the universal brotherhood of man. Hope springs eternal, but springs too often from political naivete. Utopian idealists are politically the most dangerous of all extremists, owing to the havoc they wreak on their fellow human beings, whom they falsely accuse and wrongly blame for the failings and failures of their very own doctrines.

Some of the brightest Western intellectuals of that generation, dispossessed and disenfranchised by a world gone mad, became ardent socialists and communists, until their eyes were opened to the true horrors brought about by their misguided movement.

Two such luminaries were Arthur Koestler and George Orwell, intellectual socialists who volunteered and fought in the Spanish Civil War against General Franco's Nazi-backed armies. Orwell found himself betrayed by the very "brotherhood" of socialists whom he had naively mistaken for a utopian political movement. Arthur Koestler's awakening came later, on a trip to Mother Russia herself, where he witnessed firsthand the retrograde horrors of Marx's "dictatorship of the proletariat." Orwell and Koestler soon penned immortal anticommunist literary works, exposing the twisted lies, convoluted doctrines, and mass murders that were needed to sustain Marx's fatally flawed annexation of politics by economics. Orwell's *Animal Farm* satirized Lenin's Bolshevik revolution; Koestler's *Darkness at Noon* exposed Stalin's purge of the Bolsheviks themselves; Orwell's *Nineteen Eighty-Four* captured the living hell of totalitarianism and its ruthless suppressions of the human mind, heart, and spirit.

In a remarkable dialogue between Daisaku Ikeda and Mikhail Gorbachev, these two great leaders recount their formative influences, as well as the horrors each one experienced at the hands of totalitarian extremisms—Ikeda as a youth in Imperial Japan; Gorbachev as a youth in Stalinist Russia. Gorbachev repudiates the evils of collectivization, and what he terms "the lie of totalitarian ideology" in no uncertain terms. Notwithstanding his nostalgia over Marx's pew in the British Library, Gorbachev declares himself "an enemy of authoritarianism and the practice and ideology of the iron hand."[9]

Now let us revisit 1867 London, where Marx had just completed *Das Kapital*, the crucible in which "the ideology of the iron hand" was forged. While desperately poor, hopelessly isolated, and seething with rage against a well-to-do establishment that had no use for him, Marx did not lack the good sense to seek influential friends and supporters of his cause. Like every ambitious author, he wanted powerful and credible endorsers of his book. And so he wrote to none other than Charles Darwin, whose new biological paradigm had propagated across Western civilization, spawned debate wherever it traveled, and fomented a revolution in its own right. Darwin, however, declined Marx's invitation to dedicate *Das Kapital*. "My theories pertain to vegetable and animal kingdoms only," he wrote in his reply to Marx, "and not to political ones."[10] Here too is incontrovertible evidence that Darwin was not a social Darwinist. Ironically, Darwin's rejection of Marx turned out to be reciprocal: Millions of Russians would soon starve to death as a result of the Marxist-Leninist rejection of Darwin's biological theories.

In postrevolutionary Moscow, the Marxist-Leninist-Stalinist "dictatorship of the proletariat" had to determine and dictate a politically correct theory of agricultural science, one that was in keeping with Marx's dialectic, even if it flew in the face of neo-Darwinian genetics, which by then was a nascent science in the West. For Darwin had correctly and brilliantly predicted that overt physical characteristics of plants and animals (today called "phenotypes") were external manifestations of information transmitted by covert means from generation to generation (today called "genotypes"). Social Darwinism had self-servingly but incorrectly extended this doctrine to cultural and political domains, justifying imperialism—along with invidious distinctions of class, race, and gender (and therefore also socioeconomic standing)—on the basis of pseudo-Darwinian "innate superiority." So poor laborers remained poor laborers not because of pitiless industrial serfdom, but because they apparently had "impoverished genes." Social Darwinism was clearly intolerable to Marxism, which sought to eliminate all class distinctions, but unfortunately Stalin's cohorts threw out the baby of Darwinian genetics with the bathwater of social Darwinism. Ironically, a prerevolutionary Russian monk named Gregor Mendel had unknowingly corroborated Darwinian "beanbag genetics" in experiments with garden vegetables.

But the specific agricultural problem later confronting Stalin was to grow a second crop of wheat—so-called "winter wheat"—to feed the newly Sovietized (i.e., collectivized) masses, who were already starving from collectivization itself. The question was: How do you get "summer wheat" to withstand the colder temperatures of the Russian autumn? Neo-Darwinism's answer, and the scientifically correct one, is: You breed hardier strains of wheat by selective genetics. But Darwin was politically incorrect, and so Stalin's minister of agriculture, Lysenko, turned to Darwin's politically correct but biologically incorrect rival: Lamarck.

Jean-Baptiste Lamarck (1744–1829) had presented his masterwork, *Philosophical Zoology*, to Emperor Napoleon in 1805. Lamarckism remained Darwinism's chief rival on the Continent well into the twentieth century, and was especially popular in France, for the compelling patriotic reason that Lamarck was French while Darwin was English. Lamarck's core thesis is that evolution consists of transmitting externally *acquired* characteristics, rather than internally *inherited* ones. So, for example, suppose you want to breed tailless mice. Darwin will tell you to begin by breeding ordinary mice, and to continue breeding only those offspring with shorter-than-average tails, and so forth. Eventually, by breeding selectively for the desired phenotype, you will indirectly select the underlying genotype that gives rise to it. This had already been a successful practice during centuries of plant and animal domestication worldwide—producing fine French wines among many other things in the process—but, until Darwin, had awaited a theory that explained why the practice worked so well.

In stark contrast, Lamarck posed what I call the "French Question" (*La Question Française*): "Selective breeding works in practice, but will it ever work in theory?" Not in France, at any rate. So Lamarck tells you to begin with ordinary mice, but first to amputate their tails before breeding them. If the next generation has tails, amputate them too, and continue breeding and amputating indefinitely. Eventually, avers Lamarck, the mice will "learn" to transmit this acquired characteristic of "taillessness," and will give birth to tailless mice. This outstandingly clever biological fantasy was worthy of Rudyard Kipling's "Just So" stories, but was also perfectly compatible with Marx's outstandingly clever economic fantasy: They both worked quite well in theory, but not at all in practice.

So, true to politically correct Lamarckism, Lysenko proceeded to "teach" the Russian wheat to withstand cold by freezing the entire seed crop, which promptly perished. Millions starved. This anecdote is also holographic: Marx's entire edifice of politically correct falsehoods eventually collapsed under the weight of its grotesque denials and suppressions of scientific, economic, and political reality.

In contrast to the Supreme Soviet, there is also a supreme irony: While social Darwinists were simply wrong about the underlying mechanisms and dynamics of human culture (as Darwin himself knew), Lamarckians would have been absolutely correct to apply their theory to cultural instead of biological evolution, which Lamarck himself partly realized. Lamarck's theory does turn out to be true in a small and special proportion of biological cases. For example, a pregnant woman who acquires HIV or cocaine addiction can pass them along to her offspring while she is gestating—classic Lamarckian cases of the inheritance of acquired characteristics. However, in cultural terms, humans acquire language, customs, innovations, truths, falsehoods, prejudices, hatreds, and all kinds of psychological baggage by external means, which they then transmit to their children. This is Lamarck's theory, writ large across cultural domains.

Juxtaposing Darwin and Lamarck, we arrive at this: Humans are born with big brains—a Darwinian inheritance, via internal genetic means. The human brain is in effect a wetware platform, biologically evolved to load and run cultural software, whose contents vary according to Lamarckian transmission of acquired characteristics. For example, you are biologically "hardwired" (by Darwinian processes) to acquire a first language and a native culture. But languages and cultures are themselves acquired and transmitted precisely by external Lamarckian means. The Darwinian brain is so well adapted in its hardwiring that it can accept and run almost any kind of Lamarckian cultural software. Humans are more biologically egalitarian than many people imagine. A newborn baby of any race, ethnicity, class, or gender will absorb the language and culture to which it is first exposed, regardless of the language and culture into which it is born.

However, not all cultural software is equally conducive to the attainment of that which is best and noblest in the human being: among other things, the virtues of the ABCs. As we will see in the next chapter, cultural software has evolved over millennia to adapt people to particular geopolitical regions. Moreover, some cultural software packages tend also to override our shared humanity and instead impart debilitating prejudices, if not violent hatred. Globalization is now compelling formerly incompatible cultural programs to run side by side, in adjacent and commingled neighborhoods of the global village. We will not end wars and other deadly human conflicts until we modify these cultural operating systems to become mutually compatible instead of mutually conflicting. Fortunately, we can do this by Lamarckian means: By exposing cultures to the ABCs, they can learn to get along better by modifying their operating systems accordingly—especially their political and religious modules, which govern all the rest. And that is a task for humanistic education, not Marxist revolution. Here ends the first lesson on the ideology of Marxism.

## Strange Bedfellows

Sir Winston Churchill and George Orwell (nee Eric Blair) could not have been further apart politically, religiously, or socioeconomically— yet their worldviews were absolutely convergent on one key issue: the profanity of Marxist collectivism (and its merciless annihilation of the individual human mind, heart, and spirit).

Churchill, descended from the Dukes of Marlborough, was born to a station of upper-class privilege and opportunity. He made the most of his circumstances, and history recognizes him as a Renaissance man: statesman, prophet, author, painter, stonemason, acerbic wit, and political visionary. Churchill paid a terrible price for his copious talents, including years of ostracism from British politics when he was a "voice in the wilderness" issuing dire but unheeded warnings to Britain and Europe during the 1930s, as Hitler rearmed the Third Reich in the face of Western weakness, cowardice, and appeasement. Had Britain and Europe listened to Churchill, Hitler's war machine could have been stopped before it got started. But by the time they began listening it was too late for Europe, and Churchill had to lead Britain through its darkest hours. He did so with consummate courage and resolve, single-handedly inspiring the unprepared British to hold out against the war-ready Nazis, until the tide eventually turned. Churchill was the last and possibly greatest prime minister of Imperial Britain. He was certainly the last Briton of the era to rank as an equal beside Harry Truman and Joseph Stalin, as the two emergent superpowers of the United States and the Soviet Union rapidly diverged from alliance against Hitler to mutual enmity during the ensuing Cold War.

George Orwell was born in India. His father was a minor civil servant occupied with the opium trade; his mother, a Burmese tea merchant. Educated in good British schools, including Eton, he developed a deep loathing of the English class system, along with an attraction for the lifestyles of the down-and-out in London and Paris. An aspiring author, he tramped penniless between poorhouses and ventured too among middle-class occupations—policeman in Burma, schoolmaster and shopkeeper in Britain. He gravitated toward socialism and, as we saw, volunteered during the Spanish Civil War—at which conclusion his eyes were opened to the godless profanities of the extreme left. Orwell's greatest works were consecrated to exposing the grotesque injustices of Marxist-Leninist revolution and the Stalinization that inevitably followed.

And this is what Churchill and Orwell had in common: a shared realization of the horrors of Marxism. Although Churchill and Orwell inhabited sectors of the British Empire that were absolutely and mutually remote, and although Churchill vigorously defended its class distinctions while Orwell scathingly repudiated them, both of these great men understood that Marx's "solution" to the social inequities of capitalism was far worse and vastly more abhorrent than the problem itself.

Singapore's founder and visionary Lee Kwan Yew well understands, as few apparently do, that Marxism is an opportunistic cultural virus, prone to infect and tyrannize any sufficiently weakened polity. As Singapore's elder statesman wrote in his *Memoirs*, "when misguided policies based on half-digested theories of socialism and redistribution of wealth were compounded by less than competent government, societies formerly held together by colonial government splintered, with appalling consequences."[11] China, Cuba, Angola, North Korea, Vietnam, and Cambodia have all seen such appalling consequences. If the Maoists win the current civil war in Nepal, they will do exactly what the Khmer Rouge did in Kampuchea: Turn it into an Orwellian state, with cemeteries of killing fields.

And this is exactly what Marxists have done to the life of the mind in the North American universities, as we will see in chapter 11. Marxists are human too, of course, and as such they have Buddha-natures. They are neither more nor less intelligent than anyone else. But their doctrines are more corrosive to humanity than most. Like strong acids, they need to be bottled up and handled with extreme caution.

Believe me, I know by heart the standard objections to my position. Many Marxists will say, "No, no, no, Leninism and Stalinism and Maoism are not Marxism! Marx was a great humanist, and his theories have never been properly applied. If only they were, we'd all be living in utopia." Such enthusiasm is to be commended, but the political myopia that accompanies it is regrettable. Marxism is an ideology that devalues the individual in favor of the collective, that disorders natural hierarchies and levels natural differences, making individual fulfillment and balanced order impossible. As such it is utterly incompatible with the ABCs, and with every version of The Middle Way they espouse.

That said, I must also admit that communism of various kinds can and does work on sufficiently small scales. Many communes have thrived—from the Israeli kibbutz to the Inuit cooperative—and have provided good and meaningful ways of life to their members. Such communes control their own shared resources and determine their own modes of production, independent of any central authority. But to be successful, such communes are inevitably sheltered, protected, and enriched by an overarching umbrella of free markets, and by democratic political institutions that protect individual choice (like joining a commune, or leaving one) and free markets themselves.

## Postmodernism: The Deconstruction of Western Civilization

Even as North America and Western Europe united—perhaps for the last time—against the dire threat of Soviet totalitarianism in Eastern Europe and Maoist totalitarianism in East Asia, Western neo-Marxists never gave up Marx's original mission, that of destroying Western civilization from within. When they failed to accomplish their ends by violent revolution, they discovered a French Trojan horse that allowed them to wreak their profane havoc via cultural infiltration. That horse is called "postmodernism," and it was wheeled into the intellectual fortress and breeding ground of Western civilization—the Academy—by the radicalized Western counterculture of the 1960s. By the end of the twentieth century, the extremists concealed within the horse had accomplished their mission: the deconstruction of the blueprint for Western civilization. Even as globalization proceeds from America's example of liberty, opportunity, and hope, the edifice of American culture is itself imploding from the sabotage of its internal structure by triumphant radicals of the extreme and profane left, who have colonized language, thought, and education, and thereby undermined the foundations of the very civilization that carelessly and effetely afforded them the liberty, opportunity, and hope of doing so.

Please realize that I am not blaming Marxists alone for the cultural collapse of Western civilization, which appears imminent if nothing is done to forestall it. There are many other forces at work, such as globalization itself, and all the conflicts it potentiates as it melts down civilizational boundaries. Another omnipresent force is karma, the ripening fruits of action. As the ancient Chinese knew particularly well, and as the West is just beginning to learn, all empires wax and wane,[12] as do some of the civilizations they help define. So because of the West's continuous waves of expansion that broke over the heads of so many smaller and less dynamic cultures and civilizations, so the West must be swept away by globalization's high tide, or slowly expire in its own ebb tide if it fails to maintain the pace.

Earlier I mentioned the parallel path of violent democratic revolutions, pursued by the United States and France in the late eighteenth century, and now pick up that thread. To understand postmodernism and its deconstruction of Western civilization, we must appreciate the special relationship that exists between the United States and France.

If you read any history of that revolutionary period, you will discover how these two democratic gestations and births (the United States in 1776, France in 1789) informed and reinforced each other. The founding fathers of the United States quite consciously embarked on a political experiment with democracy, inspired by the European Enlightenment that sought to advance knowledge in both natural and social spheres. France had contributed mightily to Enlightenment philosophy, mathematics, sciences, literature—the Aristotelian strand of Western civilization—and France, like the United States but unlike

England and Germany of the day, had freed itself from monarchic rule, in a "utopian" revolution that empowered the murderous Jacobins. Nonetheless, the intellectual elite of America, represented by great minds like Jefferson and Franklin, were also conscious of the relative juvenility and roughness of the New World, compared with the sophistication and style of the Old. They admired France as a kind of elder sibling culture, a model for many things that America was too young to achieve, but not too immature to emulate.[13]

This evolved by stages into a kind of American intellectual hero worship of French language, literature, cuisine, and culture, which persists to this day. In the nineteenth century, a Frenchman named Alexis de Tocqueville painted the definitive "portrait" of American democracy, which is still studied and admired by intellectual historians who remain unpurged by postmodernism.[14] In the twentieth century, between the World Wars, Paris became the romantic and artistic destination of choice for an influential generation of American writers, poets, musicians, composers, dancers, painters, and sculptors. French impressionism, surrealism, and dadaism inspired the neo-Bohemian lifestyle and content of the American "Beat generation" and the pop art of Andy Warhol. French existentialists provided the philosophical model for the quintessential American antihero: James Dean, the rebel without a cause. Even that most prim and proper of New England hostesses, a woman of impeccable Puritan etiquette, namely Julia Child, poured her Anglo-Saxon heart and soul into French cuisine.

Since the era of their twin revolutions, Americans have always had a thing for France. Viewed from an American perspective, the French have historically possessed cultural refinements that many Americans self-consciously lack—including high fashion, haute cuisine, fine wine, poetic language, romantic literature, uninhibited passion, and the ineffable savoir faire in matters of the boudoir, beside which so many Americans feel (not unjustly) like uninitiated Neanderthals at a Hellenic symposium. Indeed, not only the French but also many other Europeans consider "American culture" an oxymoron: a "culture" of neo-Roman bread and circuses transposed into junk food and reality TV, a "culture" of trashy and callow sensationalism, a "culture" of shopping, where everything is instantaneously available and immediately disposable. So the American elite still sends its daughters to Brown to study French literature. France lends Americans who want to transcend themselves a sense of snobbery. Many New Yorkers believe they have attained "high culture" when they are able to butcher a few French phrases over dinner. In any case, many Americans are still hopelessly infatuated with all things French. And so they embraced French postmodernism with even more fervor than Socrates embraced his cup of hemlock, and with even greater adulation than the French embraced Jerry Lewis, by far their favorite American since Benjamin Franklin.

To be sure, the French have also experienced some post–9/11 backlash from the American masses. For instance, in response to French criticism of and lack of support for America's "War on Terror," patriotic spud-eating Americans renamed french fries "freedom fries." But this is purely cosmetic. The deep and possibly mortal wound inflicted by the French on American liberty is ideological. It's called "postmodernism," and the extent of its cultural carnage lies beyond the conception of the consuming masses. The catastrophe of postmodernism cannot be contained or remedied by renaming fried potatoes, just as France's internal clash of postmodern and Islamic cultures cannot be contained or remedied by prohibiting the wearing of religious garb in schools. While cosmetic solutions are fine for cosmetic problems, buying a new hat won't cure a brain tumor. French postmodernism is a tumor of the mind, which has deconstructed modernism's well-ordered picture of reality, replacing it with disordered fantasies. In the process, postmodernism has condemned the very edifice of Western civilization, has demolished its foundational paradigms, and has evicted its gullible citizenry into an ideological void, making them culturally homeless.

## Lyotard's Lexicon

The term *postmodernism* was coined in France by extremist Jean-Francois Lyotard in the 1960s—the same decade in which Canadian media theorist Marshall McLuhan envisioned the "global village," and American inventor Richard Buckminster Fuller launched "spaceship earth." Lyotard had earlier been a devout Trotskyite, agitating for

Trotsky's brand of violent communist revolution in the West. But Lyotard became disenchanted by incessant and vituperative quarreling among rival Marxist factions, who were ever ready to annihilate one another over ideological differences. While every last one of their political variations on Marxism fails dismally in practice, these French academic neo-Marxists bitterly contested (what else?) the "French Question": Which variation works best in theory? Lyotard eventually tired of these fanatical but fruitless conflicts, and sought to transcend them by rejecting everything under the sun, from Marxism to modernity itself. Postmodernism is Lyotard's rejection of all viewpoints: every political theory, every historical perspective, every economic system, every religious faith, every scientific paradigm, every shared human value, and every other conceivable way of understanding the world and our place in it—including The Middle Way.

In Lyotard's lexicon, all these "ways" of looking at things— mythology, history, religion, science, politics, art, philosophy, the ABCs themselves—are called "metanarratives" or "grand narratives." To Lyotard and the generation of postmodernists he and Jacques Derrida spawned, these narratives are nothing but grandiloquent and grandiose tales that we invent to try to make sense of ourselves and the world.

What's wrong with that? Lyotard explains: "In contemporary society and culture—postindustrial society, postmodern culture—the grand narrative has lost its credibility, regardless of what mode of unification it uses, regardless of whether it is a speculative narrative or a narrative of emancipation."[15] So Lyotard denigrates and levels every possible way of looking at things (except his own "anti-way," of course) by calling them "grand narratives" and claiming they have no "credibility." This is the mantra that millions of Western university students have chanted for decades, in their political indoctrinations that pass for higher education in the universities: There is no credible way of understanding or explaining anything. No credo ever coined holds truth and reality in greater contempt than this; no mantra ever minted could mire the human soul more deeply in a bog of confusion and chaos.

In effect, Lyotard is telling every Christian in the world that Christianity has no "credibility," every Muslim that Islam has no "credibility," every Indian that Vedic philosophy has no "credibility," every Confucian that Confucius has no "credibility." Lyotard is telling every Aristotelian scientist that science has no "credibility," every capitalist that capitalism has no "credibilit," every Buddhist that Buddhism has no "credibility," and every citizen of every modern democratic nation that democracy and modernism have no "credibility." Postmodernism demeans every shared perspective, denounces every common aspiration, and shreds every attempt to unite humanity. Lyotard declares: "The sublime feeling is neither moral universality nor aesthetic universalization, but is, rather, the destruction of one by the other in the violence of their differend."[16] The "differend" is a word for the conceptual and linguistic differences that divide people—with a fanatical insistence that no paradigm is "truer" than any other in theory, and that no system works "better" than another in practice.

This sets up Lyotard's not-so-hidden agenda, which consists of singling out the most sophisticated and emancipating paradigms of human history—Western science and Western modernity, the envy of the global village—and accusing them of being the least credible and most evil of all. Lyotard's postmodernism is a metaparadigm of smoke and mirrors, behind which lurks the thwarted but relentless Trotskyite, determined to destroy the West one way or another. So Lyotard denounces the greatest scientific, technological, political, and socioeconomic advancements in human history, calling them "symptoms." And what is the disease? According to Lyotard, "It is the entire history of cultural imperialism from the dawn of Western civilization."[17]

So postmodernism views Western civilization as a "sickness," precisely because all the objective evidence demonstrates conclusively that the modern Western paradigm offers more liberty, opportunity, and hope to its citizens than any other in the world. It is Western modernity that has awakened the formidable creative and purposive powers of the entire global village. It is Western modernity that the other great civilizations, along with many other orbital and pivotal nation-states, are eager to embrace. Western modernity is the engine of globalization itself. But exactly like the looters and parasites in Ayn Rand's towering prophecy *Atlas Shrugged*, postmodernists strive to destroy the very system that nurtures them. Postmodernism is a sickness that, untreated and unchecked, is ravaging the cultural DNA of the West. As Antonio Gramsci among other European Marxists understood so well, one can bring down a civilization without firing a shot, if one commandeers its cultural institutions.

Notwithstanding its problems and shortcomings, modern Western civilization has developed the highest standard of living for the greatest numbers of its citizens as part of the fruition of its evolution. In the process, it also developed manuals of "best practices" for governance of stable democracies, for sustenance of productive economies, and for maintenance of the liberties, opportunities, and hopes they offer to the entire global village. In spite of its many flaws and because of its many virtues, Western civilization has become the envy of the global village, and has produced the blueprint for globalization itself, which so many developing nations and emergent regions seek avidly to implement. It is no coincidence that East Asian civilization, as well as Latin American nations, are progressing to the extent that they are willing and able to adopt that blueprint; while parts of Islamic civilization, South Asia, and the African continent are falling behind to the extent that they are unwilling or unable to adopt it. A synonym for this state-of-the art civilizational blueprint is "modernity."

Lyotard's Marxist sensibilities were deeply disturbed by the notion that one story could possibly be "better" than another, if by "better" one means things like making sense, discovering truth, or delivering results. But remember, to people who pose the "French Question" it's always the theory that counts. So postmodernism takes the extremely and profanely egalitarian view that all metanarratives are equivalent: One story is just "as good as" any other story, and in fact they are all inadequate. Why? Because—according to postmodern theory—all metanarratives mistakenly suppose that the world makes sense to begin with. In fact, asserts postmodernism, nothing makes sense. There is no truth, and therefore no metanarrative can be more—or less—truthful than any other.

I beg to differ. *Forbes* recently published a travel feature, warning Americans and other Westerners away from the fourteen most dangerously unstable, violent, and lawless countries in 2006.[18] They are all failed or failing states, described by journalist Sophia Banay: "From Afghanistan to Zimbabwe, there are nations and peoples being ground under by oppression, terrorism, poverty, and death. These are places where the rule of law is arbitrary, education is an after-thought and life is cheap."[19] Not only do these hell-worlds lack effective government, along with law and order, their economies have also deteriorated, resulting in every conceivable social ill. Citizens suffer not only from violent crime, but also from political corruption, high unemployment, endemic poverty, lack of health care, and high infant mortality. Crumbling infrastructures cannot reliably deliver running water, electricity, or foodstuffs to swelling populations, even in the urban centers. These disintegrating nations subsist at the furthest extreme from Western civilization, precisely because they have rejected, or have proved unable to sustain unaided, the central paradigms of the West. Yet Lyotard and his brainwashed hordes of postmodernists persistently declare that Western civilization is an evil disease.

Declare it to whom? To the students and intelligentsia of the West, upon whom they have feasted since the late 1960s, like ideological parasites. If Western civilization is such an unmitigated abomination, then why don't postmodernists relocate to the fourteen most "non-Western" nations on Earth, from Afghanistan to Zimbabwe? Could it be because they lead incomparably better lives defaming and destroying Western values from within the West itself, which (to its dire peril) affords them the liberty, opportunity, and hope of doing so?

## Derrida's Deconstructions

Lyotard set the stage for Derrida, postmodernism's other "bright light," who developed the tool of "deconstruction" for the purpose of dismantling language and thought. No sooner had Lyotard condemned the edifice of Western civilization, than Derrida arrived to commence its demolition, brick by brick. While words and ideas are not the only means we have of understanding, and not the deepest either, they are nonetheless the means we most naturally and frequently utilize for acquiring and transmitting culture—including manuals of best practices and blueprints for civil society.

Derrida did to words and ideas precisely what Lyotard did to paradigms: He rendered them senseless. For example, Derrida looks at fundamental pairs of words that Aristotle terms opposites and Taoists call complements—such as true/false, object/subject, male/female, reason/emotion, theory/practice, reality/fantasy. He then claims that these "oppositional structures" are dogmatically and violently hierarchical, and are "used" by Western civilization to maintain hierarchies of dominance. So the task of deconstruction is dogmatically and violently to undermine those structures, in any way possible.

To deconstructionists, language has no meaning at all, and refers to things only for the purpose of creating "power structures" through which the creators can exert hierarchical dominance, for example "white male heterosexual patriarchal hegemony." So in the hands of deconstructionists, mathematics becomes an oppressive "social construct," vilified for allegedly maintaining hegemony over women and other "victims" of civilization.

A typical deconstructionist, namely Professor Kevin Kumashiro, is founding director of the Center for Anti-Oppressive Education in Washington, D.C. Like the cadres of deconstructionists ensconced in universities throughout the West, he preaches the following doctrine: "Historically, mathematics has been a tool of colonialism and imperialism. This should not be surprising, given that mathematics has an underlying 'logic of control': mathematizing and quantifying nature and time and space are ways for humans to control not only nature, but also society, since defining 'reason' as, in part, the ability to think 'mathematically' allows certain people (i.e., the 'mathematical' ones) to extend their control over others."[20] Whereas, by redefining "reason" as anything that anyone happens to imagine or emote about anything at any moment, postmodernists have wrested "control" of "others" from "imperialistic" mathematicians, and their "tyranny" of elegant and rigorous insight. Just so. Professor Kumashiro's academic specialties are "queer black youth studies" and "anti-oppressive education." By doing his part to eliminate mathematics, science, and English from American classrooms, replacing them with vulgar politicizations, he will no doubt greatly enhance the educational prospects of all students who fall into his clutches, and not only queer black youths. His Orwellian "anti-oppressive" education guarantees that his students will be oppressed into becoming dysfunctional ignoramuses, instead of functional human beings.

Not surprisingly, then, women have been particular "victims" of mathematics. As we will see further in chapter 9, one well-established sex difference is that females have, on average, less mathematical aptitude than males.[21] So it is not surprising that many women experience mathematics differently than do many men. But this becomes resentful grist for the deconstructionist mill, as evidenced by Prof. Betty Johnston of Sydney's University of Technology: "We found that much of our mathematical experience had been of a dominating practice that alienated us from our own knowledge and the everyday world, separating mind, body and emotion, and prioritizing abstraction and generalization over meaning . . . These hegemonic practices are therefore not the only ones possible; the work that is required to maintain them, in fact, demonstrates the degree to which they can be seen as denials of alternative experiences."[22]

So in the hands of deconstructionists, mathematics (and sciences) are no longer celebrated among our most elegantly refined means of probing deeply and reliably into the inner workings of logical truth and physical reality, and no longer respected among the crowning achievements of human reason; rather, they are "hegemonic practices" that "dominate" women, obliging them to "deny" their "alternative experiences." One consequence of the colonization of our education system by deconstructionists, including militant feminists whose emotionally unfulfilling experiences with mathematics lead them to politicize reason and banish it from the curriculum, is that hordes of their graduates fail to learn how to distinguish reality from fantasy. Another consequence to America, in the real world (which deconstructionists deny), is that the hordes of ill-educated Americans and others under the tutelage of deconstructionists are no longer competitive in the burgeoning intellectual marketplaces of Asia.

Recall the sign that Plato hung outside his Academy, with the message that Aristotle read daily during his decade and a half there, and took to heart for life: LET NO ONE IGNORANT OF GEOMETRY ENTER HERE. Recall that in chapter 5 I outlined the Hellenic connection between mathematics, ethics, and politics. Now, two and a half millennia later, our Academy has fallen into the hands of reason's executioners, who have replaced Plato's sign with its opposite: LET NO ONE COGNIZANT OF GEOMETRY GRADUATE HERE. The effects of deconstruction are pervasive and pernicious. It is not a coincidence that American students are performing increasingly poorly, by international standards, in mathematics and sciences, and not a coincidence that America is losing her global lead in sciences and technologies alike. These cultural strengths of the West have been sapped by the cancer of deconstructionism, which has metastasized throughout Western civilization. The appalling cultural deficits of the American public, including ignorance not only of mathematics and science but increasingly of general knowledge, have not gone unnoticed by the rest of the world. As the authors of *Why Do People Hate America?* write: "Why, people around the world keep asking, is the American public, in a country with the world's most advanced education system and institutions of learning, so exceedingly ignorant of world affairs? They don't know the names of the leaders of other countries, even those of their allies in the West. They don't know where other countries are located. They don't know the history of the world. They apparently don't care, either."[23]

The political extremes that we assessed in the previous chapter unwittingly conspire to grow the vacuum of American ignorance. The extreme right is concerned with religious dogma and corporate profits, and is too myopic and avaricious to fund the necessary educational reforms. The extreme left is obsessed with deconstruction and Marxist ideology, and has parasitized the American education system to the point of cultural collapse. We will revisit these issues in chapters 10 and 11.

All this owes an imponderable debt to the exuberant American adoption of Lyotard and Derrida. France's role as the spawning ground of postmodernism is tragicomic, especially in light of the greatness of French contributions to high culture by the likes of French mathematical geniuses from Blaise Pascal to Jean le Rond D'Alembert, from Pierre-Simon Laplace to Joseph Fourier, from Henri Poincaré to Mandelbrot. But lest we forget, the noble French chemist Antoine Lavoisier was guillotined by the Jacobins, with these words ringing in his ears: "On n'a pas besoin des savants dans notre Republique."[24] So too have generations of Western students been rendered mindless by postmodernism, and its preposterous mantra: There is no truth and no reality; everything is a social construct.

We will revisit the postmodern—and gender feminist—denial of scientific truth in chapter 11. Meanwhile, during the 1990s, NYU physicist Alan Sokal became so incensed by postmodern critics of science that he wrote a spoof entitled "Transgressing the Boundaries: Toward a Transformative Hermeneutics of Quantum Gravity," which was published in *Social Text*, America's foremost postmodern journal. Its publication exposed the blatant fraudulence of postmodernism, whose leading American lights (such as the journal's editor, Professor Stanley Fish) were unable to distinguish their own "authentic" gibberish from the "fake" gibberish of Sokal's satire.[25] Note that the converse does not hold: No postmodern *poseur* can publish anything in a learned scientific journal, because science deals with sophisticated concepts, reliable methods, and universal laws that are anathema to the "social constructs" of antirealism. Lucid scientific expositions are anything but arbitrary strings of meaningless jargon that thinly veil infantile, emotional, or hysterical protests against the brute facts and subtle nuances of reality, including natural law and balanced order.

Postmodernism is the "Emperor's New Paradigm"—and another nail in the coffin of Western civilization. By denying the meaningful structures of language and thought, and by rejecting the objectively ordered world to which meanings refer, deconstructionists have managed to subvert and undermine everything they touch, except their own nonsense. They have brainwashed an entire generation of Western students to parrot the sublime assertion that every conceivable aspect of reality, from geometric proof to scientific law, is a "social construct"—which assertion they ironically take to be an absolute truth. It never occurs to them that the very notion of a "social construct" is itself a social construct.

The myopia of an otherwise erudite political theorist, namely Francis Fukuyama, prompted him to announce "the end of history." He believes that the successes of liberal democracy—beginning with the American and French revolutions, and spreading widely since then—make political history a "finished product" that all nations must sooner or later emulate.[26] Fukuyama appears unaware that deconstructed American and French cultures alike are imploding, and that their fundamental liberties, opportunities, and hopes are being replaced by totalitarian and Orwellian operating manuals. The twenty-first century is likely to witness political horrors that will make the twentieth century seem tame by comparison. Is this "the end of history"? I think not. History will soon enough announce "the end of Fukuyama" (as it does of us all) and simply move on.

Lao Tzu wrote, "What goes against Tao will soon come to an end." Postmodernism goes against Tao, by deconstructing its yin-yang metaphysics. So postmodernism must soon come to an end. My deeper concern is whether postmodernism will bring down Western civilization in its wake. I would not be saying this if postmodernism were just one more eccentric course of extremist studies, camped out on some lunatic fringe of counterculture. On the contrary, postmodernism's debilitating doctrines are ensconced as centrally planned, politically correct, and officially authorized indoctrinations of Western civilization's "higher education" system—from the Poison Ivy League on down—whose brainwashed graduates have spread them far and wide, into every conceivable sector: the media, the publishing industry, the military, the legal system, the corporate culture, and the government, to name but a few.

As George Orwell realized full well, the destruction of language is an essential component of oppression.[27] Western Marxists have deployed and exploited the hapless postmodernists for just this purpose: to destroy language—the essence of reason—which makes way for a Marxist ethos of neo-Stalinist and neo-Maoist oppression in the universities, and from there into the larger culture. I will illustrate this in detail, in chapter 11.

This is a legacy of the 1960s, when postmodernism's "French Question" arrived in America via globalization. While my experience of the 1960s was predominantly via hippie culture—and its expansions of consciousness through mind-altering substances, popular music, Asian philosophy, communal lifestyles, and free love—that turbulent decade also saw the unleashing of structurally violent neo-Marxist revolutionary forces throughout America and the West. In the end, there were so many quarreling factions that the entire left-wing counterculture collapsed. The hippies salvaged and nurtured what peace and love they could, and mostly reverted to recognizable Western norms. As one pundit remarked, "Middle-class values proved stronger than acid"—an endorsement of The Middle Way with which I concur. But the Marxists moved wholesale into the universities, whose administrations capitulated to their every conceivable demand—the more radical, the quicker the capitulation; the more destructive of Western civilization, the deeper the capitulation. Herbert Marcuse, Noam Chomsky, the Frankfurt School—a generation of Marxists took over the academy, and postmodernists became their dupes. The Marxists understood exactly what George Orwell understood: By destroying language, they could enslave an entire generation simply by renaming their enslavement "emancipation." "Freedom is Slavery," wrote Orwell, in his all-too-prescient satire.

This has culminated in the conversion of American higher education from an enterprise that formerly investigated truth and reality, into one that systemically repudiates truth and reality. In the words of one of deconstruction's high prophets of antirealism, philosopher Richard Rorty, "A lot of people now find belief in God immature, and eventually a lot of people may find realism immature."[28] The "maturation" of such antirealism is driving the cultural collapse of the West, exactly as its saboteurs intend. These leading lights of American "intellectual culture" assert that in truth there is no truth, and in reality no reality. An intuitive child would dismiss this laughable paradox as a joke. Yet an entire civilization has allowed itself to be deconstructed by a semantic parlor trick, a transparent sleight of mind.

A politically savvy underground journalist of the 1960s named Julius Lester, himself a former urban guerrilla, broke with the Marxists once he understood their true agenda. In vain he warned, "May 'the people' in whose name we claim to speak be spared our ascendancy to power."[29] Ayn Rand had warned against them too, in the 1940s, in her monumental classic *Atlas Shrugged*, apparently also in vain. And so warned Isaiah Berlin who, like Rand, had fled the collectivized enslavements of Marxist-Leninist Russia for the individual liberties of the West.

If you like sardonic twists, try this: I was naturalized as an American citizen in 2003, and as part of that process had to attest to the following, in writing: "I am not now, nor have I ever been, a member of the Communist Party." This vestige of McCarthyism is soberly administered to millions of immigrants who have sought refuge in America from injustices of totalitarianism, including Marx's version. I myself am a political refugee from Canadian totalitarianism. (Michael Moore forgot to film that part of Canada. I will remedy his omission in chapter 11.) So the U.S. Immigration and Naturalization Service (INS) still screens for "Commies." How dogged of them. I think the INS deserves an award for most time elapsed between locking the barn door after the horse has bolted. Instead of swearing the oath, I wanted to tell the INS agent, "For God's sake, the Commies are running America's universities. I'm part of the solution, not part of the problem." But I was also mindful that, on the eve of his naturalization hearing, Kurt Gödel found a loophole in the American Constitution that would allow a dictator to seize power. He wanted to warn the judge, but Einstein dissuaded him from mentioning it. Had Gödel talked, maybe I would have talked too.

But even the American system, and sometimes especially the American system, beats you up and wears you down. One smart remark to the INS could have cost me two more years. So I sighed and I signed. And unless you want to help me do something more about it, Marx will have the last laugh. After all, what could possibly amuse a hard-core Marxist more than this: The two worst ideas to come out of France in two hundred years—postmodernism and deconstruction—have, thanks largely to America, been permitted to dissolve the blueprint for Western civilization. Perhaps the only thing funnier is America's response to France's recent political estrangement. Yes, the two-hundred-year infatuation might be wearing off, if changing the name of your fried potatoes following a political divergence means anything like changing the name on your mailbox after a divorce. If I were a hard-core Marxist, "freedom fries" might attract my last laugh. This was eerily prophesied by twentieth-century American poet e. e. cummings, who wrote a poem called "as freedom is a breakfastfood."[30]

These profane extremes of postmodern denial, and their dogmatic deafness to reality, are in unrelenting conflict with the sacred extremes of blind religious faith, and their dogmatic assertions of supernaturality. Imposed chaos from the anarchic left clashes daily with ordained mythos from the religious right. The casualties are logos (reason and speech) and ethos (norms). This polarization is tearing America and the West to pieces. Only The Middle Way of the ABCs can restore a semblance of proportion, harmony, and order—and therefore humanity—to an endangered civilization.

Daisaku Ikeda reminds us in his dialogue with Gorbachev what I have tried to show you in this chapter: "History offers many examples of liberals and conservatives alike who, having become apathetic and cynical about truth, have been manipulated by false prophets and charlatans."[31] Sacred and profane extremes are mass movements of ideological tribes. Tribalism was an ancient evolutionary development that once paid large dividends, by furthering our survival as a species. But the agendas and conflicts of contemporary ideological tribes are becoming increasingly inimical to human flourishing. The next chapter probes our primate evolutionary roots of generic tribal extremisms.

# 8

## TRIBAL EXTREMES
Natural Dispersion and Cultural
Commingling in the Global Village

*People regard themselves as noble everywhere, and not only in their own
country; but they deem foreigners noble only when at home.* —Aristotle

*In the sky, there is no distinction of east and west; people create distinc-
tions out of their own minds and then believe them to be true.* —Buddha

*Men are near to each other at birth: the lives they lead sunder them.*
—Confucius

## A Banned Subject

THIS CHAPTER MIGHT ALSO be entitled "Human Sociobiology 101: The
Evolutionary Roots of Tribalism." The twentieth century was one of
unprecedented scientific development, witnessing not only the
furthering of all traditional branches of mathematics and sciences, but
also the emergence of many new branches, as well as fusions of
previously distinct ones. One of these fusions, sociobiology, studies the
biological basis of social behaviors among animals. One of the leading
lights of this new field, E. O. Wilson, published a magnificent seminal
text on the subject in the 1970s.[1] It is undeniable that social behaviors
of animals are influenced by their biology. However, attempts to extend
this field to humans encountered extreme differences of opinion. So
human sociobiology became a battleground for contending political
extremisms of the 1970s—the same extremisms that gave rise to the

culture wars and gender wars that have polarized America. The conservative extreme claims that human social behaviors owe as much to biology as do the behaviors of other animals; in other words, that our nurture is largely determined by our nature. The liberal extreme claims that human social behaviors owe virtually nothing to biology, and almost everything to culture; in other words, that our nurture is not significantly determined by our nature. Since the liberal extreme—and its illiberal postmodern deconstructions of language, truth, science, and reality—has prevailed on the campuses of American universities, human sociobiology is essentially a banned subject. Since I have come to specialize in teaching a number of banned subjects, I am pleased to offer you this introduction to human sociobiology. You won't find it at your local university or community college, I assure you.

The Middle Way asserts that nature and nurture are not polar opposites, but rather Taoist complements. Each contains something of the other, and their interaction often appears seamless. Human beings are at least the sum of their biology plus their culture, and each domain has the power to influence the other. A Middle Way must assert the power of nature and nurture, and must endeavor to understand how they interact. That way lies human liberation from extremes of tribalism that afflict the global village.

In the previous two chapters, we have seen how extremes of political belief, as well as extremes of sacred and profane belief, polarize societies and clash violently across the chasms that their polarizations create. Absent a Middle Way, people must either choose between rival extremisms or else plummet into the abyss between them. Whoever and wherever you are, you know perfectly well that politics and religion are the two time-honored topics guaranteed to produce verbal pyrotechnics, even (or especially) among close friends and tightly knit families. There is simply no end to debates over political and religious matters. Such interminable squabbles are part of the human condition, and can prove salutary as long as they proceed from the standpoint of a common good, or progress toward the discovery of common ground, so that people can agree to disagree within a larger context of a shared humanity, and without inflicting harms—deadly or otherwise—upon one another. The ABCs are particularly effective in providing a universal human context, so that inevitable differences between people, and peoples, need not become the basis of hatred, violence, bloodshed, and the squandering of human life.

The vital common factor that makes political and religious matters the subjects of endless debate and dispute is, in a word, tribalism. Whenever and wherever human groups become bound or united by a myth, totem, flag, party, credo, slogan, ideology, or book, they always experience two things: themselves and others. This "pull-push" pair of "in group" versus "out group" has operated ubiquitously since the dawn of human time. The core social unit is called a "tribe," and it was the fundamental unit of human survival for a very long time. In Darwinian terms the tribe enabled humans to survive for tens if not hundreds of thousands of years, by dispersing them in small bands throughout every conceivable habitat on the planet, but at the corollary cost of inevitable intertribal hostilities. In Lamarckian terms, different tribes acquired and transmitted different tools and symbols, both for sustaining themselves and for competing against others. Wherever nature and nurture complemented each other well, human tribes flourished; where nature and nurture did not complement each other well, human tribes vanished.

Extremes of human geography and caprices of human nature shaped varieties of human tribalism, and for a long time both natural and cultural evolution favored the dispersion of mutually hostile hunting and gathering tribes. These dispersed bands essentially mimicked many definitive social structures that had already proved viable in the biological evolution of our closest living relatives, the great apes and certain Old World monkeys, notably baboons. Since primate social structures represent the very roots of the human "power structures" and "privileged hegemons" that Marxists and postmodernists are obsessed with denouncing and deconstructing—including all the traditional political and religious ones—it behooves us to examine them more closely here.

## Dispersion and Commingling

I will articulate the two overarching and contrasting extremes of this chapter—which I will first enlarge upon, then try to reconcile via The

Middle Way. The prehistoric primate extreme favored the geographic dispersion and competitive enmity of small troops of monkeys, small bands of apes, and small tribes of humans, a time-tested modus vivendi that held sway for about fifteen million years of primate evolution, including the last hundred thousand years of human cultural evolution itself. Ethologists and cultural anthropologists got into the field only in the twentieth century, just in time to observe and study the natural behaviors of social animals and surviving Stone Age humans—most importantly in natural habitats that had not changed for many thousands of years, and that had been cut off from communication with the great civilizations that began to burgeon around ten thousand years ago.

The first modern humans to live among the Inuit of Arctic Canada, the pygmies of the African equatorial rainforest, the Yanomami of the Amazon, the Bushmen of the Kalahari, the Mudmen of New Guinea, or the Aborigines of Australia essentially took a time machine into human prehistory to observe pristine states of static culture—before the neolithic revolution permitted the creation and growth of large permanent settlements, the waxing and waning of empires, and the evolution of dynamic civilizations that have led to globalization. Globalization rapidly and forcibly commingles tribes and peoples whose cultural evolutions, during millennia, had been separate, incompatible, and even mutually hostile.

A long time ago but not very far away, all humans lived in small bands called "dialectical tribes" because the members of each band knew one other on a first-name basis. During their thirty- or forty-year life spans, most early human hunter-gatherers would come to know between two dozen and perhaps two hundred people by name. Static dialectical tribes were prehistoric. They usually lacked a written tradition, and yet were well adapted to nature. They had sophisticated oral traditions—myths, legends, stories, songs—as well as abundant lore on coexisting with their ecosystems. Their tools and symbolic structures were, from our perspective, primitive in the sense of simplicity, but not in the sense of effectiveness. These early humans were great survivors who, despite short life expectancies, high infant mortality rates, Stone Age tools and weapons, rough-cut fashions, and rudimentary dwellings nonetheless had verbal manuals of "best practices" for husbanding their natural resources, and effective if sometimes repressive customs for regulating their social and political conduct. They were not exactly Rousseau's "noble savages," nor were they in a Hobbesian state of nature where life is "solitary, poor, nasty, brutish, and short." These are two extremes—utopia versus dystopia—and critical masses of early humans survived and thrived between them, or we would not be here to make such observations. Hominids had ascended quickly to the top of the food chain, and feared mostly one another. Even so, had human dialectical tribes not been incredibly stable, they could never have survived the hundred thousand or two hundred thousand years it took for the next "great leaps forward"—the neolithic revolution and the founding of large permanent settlements.

As a matter of tragic irony, it remains to be seen whether "historic man" will last as long as "prehistoric man" did, and whether the next hominid waiting on line will shed a tear for either. I could give you the environmental argument, chapter and verse—that human beings now collectively represent the greatest threat to the well-being of our planet than has ever occurred at any time in biological history, which goes back about three billion years.[2] I will instead give you the argument from physical anthropology, in the form of a statistical correlation that both Darwin and his cousin Galton might have found intriguing.

## The Dryopithecine Divergence

Around fifteen million years ago an event known as the dryopithecine divergence took place, when that primordial ape, dryopithecus, appeared—from which the rest of the anthropoid apes, and humans alike, are descended by Darwinian means. An emergent science called "immunological distancing" shows that humans share 98 percent or more of the same genes as chimpanzees, while another new science, molecular anthropology, estimates that about fifteen million years have elapsed since the two species diverged from their common ancestor. Obviously, all humans alive today are genetically one species, and so-called racial or ethnic differences are merely cosmetic. It is human cultural software that determines how we think about and behave toward our fellow humans. Whether we regard them as slaves, oppressors, friends, enemies, heretics, infidels, or Buddhas depends on our cultural arrangements, not our biological ones.

But a funny thing happened on the way to the human zoo: All the other hominid species disappeared. They became extinct, and not in random order. Rather, the life expectancies of hominid species are negatively correlated with (that is, are inversely proportional to) their brain sizes (averaged for the species and proportional to average body weight). In plain English, the smarter primates became, the quicker they became extinct. The australopithecines, who were far smarter and much more humanoid than apes, lasted only a few million years. After them, *Homo habilis* lasted a million years or so. Then came ancient *Homo sapiens*: Cro-Magnon, Java, and Neanderthal, our protohuman forebears, who lasted only several hundred thousand years. Then we appeared. Homo sapiens (or Homo politicus) has been around for only one hundred thousand to two hundred thousand years, and it remains to be seen how long we will last.

Humans are swiftly and surely killing off the remaining great apes, the last five species to survive the dryopithecine divergence: the gorilla, chimpanzee, bonobo, gibbon, and orangutan. Possessing smaller intelligence than the later hominids, our simian cousins nonetheless manifested greater survival skills—which also consisted in avoiding hominids and humans at all costs. The great apes had it good for a long time—millions of years—but they are now falling afoul of globalization's seamy underbelly. Land development and deforestation are rapidly shrinking their habitats, while poaching, petnapping, and allied illegal industries are diminishing their numbers. The apes are not long for this world, but they lasted much longer than their increasingly bigger-brained cousins. That's food for thought.

And here's more: Baboons of the African savannah, who are Old World ground-dwelling monkeys with much smaller brains than the apes, are not at all (or at least not yet) an endangered species. Why? Because their evolved social patterns and behaviors are much better adapted both to nature and to human encroachment on nature. Looking more closely at what conduces to baboon survival, we find the very things that Marxists and deconstructionists alike seek most ardently to jettison: heterosexual male patriarchal hegemony (albeit furry and not at all white). Baboons make social and sexual distinctions aplenty, which is why they may outlast the bigger-brained apes who cleverly deconstruct them. We will revisit the baboons in due course, and probe their survival strategy.

If I were a gambling man, I would wager that the australopithecines were driven to extinction by *Homo habilis*, who in turn was driven to extinction by the Cro-Magnon, and so forth, until Neanderthal was driven to extinction by us. Human beings are now well embarked on the process of driving to extinction more life-forms per day, month, and year than at any time in biological history, including the two most recent mass extinctions of the Jurassic and Late Cretaceous periods. Man is not only a sleeping Buddha, but also a somnambulating ape. He is most benevolent when awake, yet most destructive when asleep—and when man falls asleep at the wheel of globalization, he threatens the planet itself.

But man is something else besides, something that to my knowledge has never been deservingly elaborated. Man is an animal whose modern and postmodern social arrangements are highly variable, but whose longest-lived "survival manual"—which persisted through the Stone Age—was surprisingly consistent among dialectical tribes around the world. Such tribes had survived remotely from one another, yet had evolved in conspicuously parallel and stable pathways. I reemphasize that humanoid and human cultures persisted in such pathways for millions of years; and that our own species did so for at least one hundred thousand years. Our discussions of moral and political philosophy are but a few thousand years old, and only in the twentieth century did women win the vote in Western democracies. Just as big-brained apes are evolutionary experiments whose long-term biological viability has yet to be demonstrated, so democracies are political experiments, whose long-term cultural viability has yet to be demonstrated.

## Dialectical Primatology

Here are three characteristics common to all prehistoric dialectical tribes, pertaining to men, women, and children. With respect to children, there was (and is) a universal capacity to play. With respect to women, there was (and in some cultures still is) a division of labor based strictly on gender. With respect to men, there was (and in most cultures still is) a male dominance hierarchy. Let us review these common characteristics in order, to see what roles they played in primate and human survival.

Anthropologists have observed that play among children is a ubiquitous phenomenon, and psychologists know that play is essential to cognitive development and social maturation. All children play, because it is in their nature to do so. Adults will also play, as well as work, if permitted and not too inhibited to so do. We know that play is a vital and fun activity that fosters learning in human babies and juveniles, and also refreshes adults. We also know that many other animals play regularly and can be readily induced to play with humans too. The list of playful animals (especially when young) includes otters, dogs, cats, hamsters, horses, seals, dolphins, parakeets, parrots, monkeys, and apes. (I have also kept reptiles, and once had a boa constrictor that was capable of rudimentary play.) But human children play so often, so much, and with such enthusiasm that in 1949 the Dutch cultural theorist Johan Huizinga dubbed our species "*Homo ludens*"—the playful animal—on that basis alone.[3]

Anthropologists have also observed a common natural feature among children at play, worldwide: They exhibit a characteristic human "play face," which consists of a slack jaw, open mouth, and relaxed absorption in the game. The game itself is determined by cultural conventions. We all learn games from our parents and our peers, who acquired them and passed them on to us. Play is Darwinian; but its content—the game—is Lamarckian. Such is the complementary relation between nature and nurture. The games themselves may change and evolve, according to the culture in place and the toys available, but the nature of play—both the need to play and the benefits of play—inhere in the human being and are unchanging.

Concerning women, we encounter another phenomenon among hunting and gathering tribes the world over. Independent of climate, habitat, food chain, and available tools, there has been a longstanding and near-ubiquitous sexual division of labor: Men hunted and protected, women gathered and nurtured.[4] This division of labor has profound evolutionary roots. Chimpanzees are now known (thanks largely to Jane Goodall's work[5]) to hunt monkeys and other prey of opportunity for meat—and the hunting chimps are exclusively male. Chimpanzee females and young will eat meat if it is given to them, or more likely if they can snatch a few scraps with impunity from the larger and fiercer adult males. While primates groom one another regularly, which fulfills hygienic needs and deepens social bonds, they do not as a rule share food. Humans as a rule do share food, but traditionally during tens and hundreds of thousands of years of hunting and gathering, the men fished and hunted game while the women gathered water, fruits, nuts, and tubers. The modern equivalent of gathering is shopping. There is no doubt that most women are superior shoppers—they have had a lengthy evolutionary preparation for this activity. Masses of people who today frequent shopping malls, which have become the centerpieces of so-called American culture, do not realize that the shopping mall was conceived as the largest feasible delivery system for lipstick and other cosmetics, whose consumers (and in this case gatherers) are overwhelmingly female.

Hunting and gathering each serve two purposes, without which primates and humans would not have survived even this long, or this briefly, depending on your perspective. The highly structured all-male hunting party is also the council of war. That is, the hunters are not only providers for, but are also defenders and protectors of, the tribe—especially of its most valuable resources, namely the breeding females and their young. And by the same token, the loosely structured all-female gathering circles were the medium for communal mothering and social support groups. Babies were carried in slings, while mobile children walked alongside and helped, leaving the mothers' hands free to forage.

A deeper and more literal evolutionary root of this sexual division of labor is found in human tooth structure. Run your finger along your upper gum line. If you are male, you will immediately discover two oversized bulges, within the gum and just above your incisors. These are the vestigial roots of your formerly prominent "canine" fangs, which male baboons still possess and utilize. If you are female, you lack these vestigial roots, because your female ancestors never possessed the formidable fangs that sprouted from them. Females of many other species do possess such fangs—including felines (from lioness to housecat), canines (from wolf to French poodle), vulpines (foxes), and ursines (bears). All these females hunt game (lapdogs excepted), and so need fangs to spear and shear raw meat. But among the primates, whether monkeys or apes, whether extinct or extant, the female does not possess fangs because she is not evolved to engage in the two occupations that require their use: providing game, and protecting the band. Both these occupations involve violence: drawing blood and taking life.

Like the baboon and the chimpanzee, the human female did not evolve to be a hunter or a warrior, any more than the human male evolved to be a gatherer or a mother. From prehistoric times down to the late nineteenth century, this sexual division of human labor was based on far more than dentition, and ran much deeper than politics. It is a matter that touches our very natures. When prehistoric males set forth to hunt big game, such that a small team of men armed with crude pointed sticks proved willing and able to bring down mammoths and mastodons, or to drive away saber-toothed lions and tigers, they needed the legs, hearts, and brains of warrior-hunters. To risk their lives and to safeguard one another's lives for the sake of providing meat for their dialectical tribe, which unlike other primates they willingly shared with their women and children, the men needed to bond. To do that, they also needed to exclude women from the hunt. And the women were happy to be excluded, for they had evolved to gather and to mother, to be the most valuable resource of the tribe, to merit provision by and protection of men, and to form support groups for those quintessentially female activities.

A terrible problem afflicting Western civilization today stems from its success in transforming the hunt from a literal to a symbolic activity. If you are hunting a paycheck instead of a dangerous animal, your sex may seem irrelevant. Yet the primordial male and female agendas have not themselves been transformed, and—to the extent that they are rooted in nature—cannot be transformed. If you had sent into the field primitive hunting parties composed exclusively of men on the one hand, and of women on the other, what result would you expect? The men would bring back more game and the women less, because the human male evolved to be stronger, swifter, and fiercer than the female, more able to endure the rigors of the hunt. The male has been given far greater stamina, along with greater ability to bond and strategize in life-threatening situations. These capacities, which make men superior hunters, and their complements, which make women superior gatherers, evolved during millions of years, and are deeply ingrained in male and female sex difference, respectively. This is also why boys play preferentially with implements while girls play preferentially with dolls: because of our deeply and divergently evolved social roles. It is not "social constructions" or "privileged hegemons" that ordain these differences. Boys are rehearsing their future roles as providers and protectors, girls as gatherers and mothers. This served primates well for millions upon millions of years, until the Industrial Revolution.[6]

After fifteen million years of primate evolution, tens of thousands of years of cultural evolution, and decades of women's liberation, both men and women now commute daily to work. Organizational cultures are globalization's hunting grounds. Globalized economies depend on women's work as much as on men's work, yet women still earn less than men, on average, in every shared area of employment. Why? As usual, we encounter two extreme answers, both of which are distorted. One extreme—the chauvinistic one—asserts that women do not work as well as men, and so deserve to earn less. That is unfair and untrue. Men and women alike can be lazy and unmotivated, or dedicated and highly motivated. As we will see, in some respects women make finer workers than do men.

However, protection and defense are traditional male primate roles, which have both external and internal facets. The male primate, in addition to being a hunter, has the duty of protecting and defending females and their offspring from external threats—predatory animals in general, and especially marauding male primates from outside the band. The male primate also has the duty of protecting and defending females and their offspring from internal threats—specifically ambitious younger males from within the band, who seek to become dominant and so win access to the female reproductive resources of the band. This dual role—hunter and protector—evolved and sustained the so-called "male dominance hierarchy" that one finds ubiquitously among monkeys, apes, and humans. It is not a "social construct"—it is nature's method, tried and true over millions years, for sustaining the survival of this curious menagerie of big-brained primates.

From the male primate perspective, the females and their offspring are the most valuable resources of the band, troop, or tribe. As such, the capacities that male primates evolved as hunters are identical to those that they utilize as protectors: strength, cunning, stamina, prowess, ferocity, strategy, aggression. But once the female is admitted to the hunt, she becomes both a provider and a competitor of men. Then she no longer needs the male as a provider, and further imagines that she no longer needs him as a protector either. But because the human female is not evolved physically to protect herself as well as a man can protect her, she is not evolved to hunt for herself as well as a man can hunt for her. I am not referring to the few and obvious cases where brilliantly talented women have become fabulously wealthy—such as Oprah—I am making a statistical observation about hundreds of millions of rank-and-file female workers, in every occupation and profession, who earn less than men for doing the same work. The "glass ceiling" is their wake-up call. They have, with the help of complicit males, infiltrated the age-old male dominance hierarchy, which not surprisingly is chilly or inhospitable or offensive precisely because it had evolved to exclude them, in favor of providing, protecting, and defending them so that they in turn could fulfill the roles that nature intended: gatherer, mother, nurturer, homemaker.

To the extent that so-called liberated women have succeeded in usurping this ancient order—the male dominance hierarchy—they have also succeeded in making men irrelevant and making themselves unhappier by far than nature ever intended them to be. Throughout the developed world, women suffer depression more than men, mostly between ages 18–50, where proportions of depressed females are two to three times higher than those of males.[7] Males are more suicidal than females overall—and we will soon see that this statistic has ancient primatological roots. However, female professionals have increasingly high suicide rates, and female doctors now have higher suicide rates than their male counterparts. As one survey concludes, "Women have entered medicine in huge numbers in recent decades, but progress has come at a price."[8] Indeed, this is but one dimension of the price of woman's "emancipation" from primate social orders.

So at one extreme, male chauvinists would exclude women from every nondomestic aspect of human life, which is clearly unfair. The other extreme, the gender feminist one (which is allied to Marxist and postmodern positions) asserts that women face universal discrimination in the workplace, and confront a "glass ceiling" of achievement, through which they can peer but beyond which they cannot progress.

This is partly true and party false. There is no question that when women are "empowered" to intrude into formerly all-male preserves, they violate a deeply evolved sense of maleness, and are bound to provoke primal counterreactions. When women feminize the workplace to make themselves feel more *at home*—often by requiring the institution of speech codes, suppressing humor, and regulating of conduct—they transform the hunting ground into a hen house, often rendering it intolerant of and inhospitable to men in the process. When at last and in spite of all these things women encounter a "glass ceiling," it is because they have gained a privileged perspective from which they can closely observe, for the very first time in human female history, the intimate workings of inner circles of top male predators. It is more difficult for women to break into these circles in the same proportion as men, because of their sexually divergent biological evolution (which we will assess more closely in chapter 9).

Aristotle's teacher, Plato, was in one sense the first equity feminist. In his utopian city-state, which he elaborated in the *Republic*, Plato envisioned a ruling "Guardian" class atop the social pyramid of soldiers, traders, artisans, and farmers that comprised the general population. The Guardians were responsible for the political, military, and educational leadership of the city-state. Since their duty was to govern, Plato wanted them to have no other distractions or conflicts of interest. Hence the Guardians would live communally, owning no private property, and maintaining no separate households. Their children would be raised communally too—never even knowing their biological parents. Plato envisioned the Guardians as an elite community of both men and women, whom he imagined could even wrestle naked in the gymnasium without succumbing to Eros. Plato refrained from mentioning whether the Guardians would have equal numbers of men and women, whether a quota system would be implemented to assure equal numbers, or whether the sex ratio among Guardians would be permitted to fluctuate according to natural ability. Perhaps Plato, in his wisdom, deliberately remained mute on this issue, which is currently being decided in the West by the crudest and most superficial means possible: head counts.

In the West, females comprise about 52 percent of the general population. Thanks to the feminist revolution, that percentage (and higher) of females is currently reflected in college and university enrollments, and will continue to be reflected in many and varied professions, among other career paths, that stem from higher education. In addition, the less-educated working classes also reflect increasing parity of females in the workforce. In fact, since real wages have fallen in the United States since the 1970s, many women are now trapped in the workplace: either because (thanks to spiraling divorce rates) they are the sole breadwinners, or because their families cannot prosper or even survive without two incomes.

However, at the top end of human dominance hierarchies, we do not find proportionately as many women. During the past several years, the number of female CEOs of Fortune 500 companies has averaged about ten. Similarly, the number of female heads of state, out of about two hundred nations, has averaged less than ten. While exceptional women can and do perform as well as exceptional men at the highest levels of corporate and political leadership, evolutionary factors may well account for the reduced proportion of exceptional women compared to that of men. Simply stated, female primates were not evolved to become dominant male primates—just as they were not evolved to become pugilists or Formula One drivers. Given equal opportunity, talented females can excel in business, politics, boxing, and auto racing; yet equal opportunity cannot and does not guarantee equal outcomes. As we will see, social engineering of equal outcomes, to satisfy arbitrary quota systems based on unrealistic expectations, is ruinous to all concerned. But neither glass slippers nor glass ceilings are "social constructs."

It is clearly the case that many women, until about the age of thirty, believe devoutly in the glass slipper. Cinderella may well be a female archetype rather than a fairy tale. Countless women await their rescue by Prince Charming, at least until they are politically indoctrinated by deconstructionists, who assure them that sex difference is a "social construct." Thus they are primed for a rude awakening. Legions of women don pantsuits and ply the organizational hunting ground. When they encounter the glass ceiling instead of the glass slipper, some are unprepared to understand the nature of this barrier. Their "emancipation" allows them to see through the barrier for the first time in history, to peer through a window into the inner world of men. But the barrier is a stark reminder that they themselves are not men, and that all the political fantasies in the world (such as postmodernism's ludicrous assertion that sex difference is "socially constructed") will not change them into men. Professional competence is not gender specific: At any echelon of the organizational hunting ground, women can and do work just as well as men. But it remains to be seen whether women can or will attain the same proportions as men among today's equivalents of Plato's Guardians: political leaders, CEOs, and scientific geniuses. The culture wars are becoming increasingly vicious in these domains—and precisely because the Middle Way is all but absent. Extreme chauvinists are loath to admit that women can break through the glass ceiling on their merits alone, as culture permits; while gender feminists are loath to admit that many women would rather settle for the glass slipper.

But from the perspective of The Middle Way, it is clear that women's contributions to developed economies are essential and invaluable. In many respects, women make finer students and workers than men: They are generally more receptive, more pleasant, more meticulous, more affable, more obedient, more conforming, and more dutiful than men. When they transfer their natural capacities for devotion, fidelity, caring, and giving from domestic scenarios (nature's domains) to academic, professional, or corporate scenarios (nurture's domains), women can indeed become treasures in the workplace, just as they had been in the home.

However, emancipation and empowerment are two different things, which have been wantonly confused of late. To be emancipated is to be given freedom from some kind of bondage—be it slavery or some other form of oppression. To be empowered is to be given opportunity to attain some kind of goal, be it to hunt big game or to earn a big paycheck. What they have in common is this: There is no guarantee that by releasing someone from bondage he will automatically and properly manage his newfound freedom; and similarly there is no guarantee that by giving someone an opportunity to attain a goal she will automatically and responsibly manage her newfound power.

The Middle Way teaches that emancipation and empowerment lie within. Men and women alike free themselves from bondage by discovering their deeper natures. Men and women alike empower themselves through acquiescence, by understanding what they are in the profoundest human sense, which transcends but cannot deconstruct their biology. The lasting personal fulfillment that Aristotle advocates can best be realized through the balanced social order that Confucius advocates. Buddha's Middle Way incorporates the best of both together. Denying human nature, or fantasizing it to be other than it is, or deconstructing it, or trying to dictate changes to it to satisfy political caprice, are all recipes for disaster.

## Dominance Hierarchies

Now let us speak of men and their "male dominance hierarchy." It is partly a virtuous, partly a vicious circle. It is virtuous because men themselves become politically fulfilled by discovering their place in the hierarchy, and bonding accordingly with other men. It is virtuous because women become fulfilled emotionally, maternally, and socially under the provision and protection of a male hierarchy, which affords them the personal security and communal stability they require to be good wives, mothers, and social beings. However, the male dominance hierarchy can also be vicious, because males themselves are capable of sexual abuse and physical violence, both against one another and against others. While women and children need the protection of men, it is against the predations of men themselves that women and children most need protection. The reasons for this are rooted in biology.

Among innumerable species of birds and fishes too, mating is always preceded by displays of ritual courtship by males toward females, which are the natural origins of chivalry, often in tandem with territorial displays by the male. Females of countless species (humans included) respond to the "territorial imperative": from birds to fishes to bipeds, and among a vast variety of species, the most dominant males retain the choicest turf in their given habitats, by defending it in turf wars impelled by instinctive aggression, and geared toward reproductive success. The females of countless species, though they themselves may become victims of male violence, nonetheless are initially sexually attracted to the most dominant (and therefore also the most aggressive and potentially violent) males. The male dominance hierarchy, unique to primates, is like the mythical Worm Ouroboros that swallows its own tail. Violent male hierarchies evolved for internal and external protection. Internally, they are structures intended to channel, restrain, or ritualize the innately violent capacities that nature bequeathed to male primates. Externally, they are meant to protect the troop or band or tribe against the predations of violent males from other troops, bands, or tribes, who would prey on anyone and everyone if unrestrained.

I digress to observe and emphasize that dominance hierarchies in the wider animal kingdom are not exclusively male. There are many mammalian species in which the female is either larger and stronger than the male, and therefore also socially dominant (e.g., hamsters and hyenas), or in which the larger and stronger males are excluded from the society, except during periods of mating (e.g., elephants). Lions themselves are interesting in that the females do most of the hunting. A pack of lionesses is a cunning, cooperative, and deadly unit of predation, which emphatically dispels the myth that females cannot hunt; and yet the pride of lions itself is defended by dominant males.

There are also species such as "social insects" (ants, bees, and wasps) in which absolute authority is vested in the queen, and in which most of the workers are "sisters." The relatively few males in social insect populations are helpless, stingless, short-lived drones, whose sole function is to mate with queens, and whose fate is to perish immediately thereafter. Many other primitive invertebrate species—from spiders to preying mantises—exhibit remarkable evolutionary longevity, maintain no society, and have favored large and dominant females—who more often than not devour the smaller and weaker males after or even during copulation. So there is no "law of nature" that ordains universal male or female dominance; one encounters both throughout. But nothing in nature anticipates the power struggles that now ensue between human men and women over this unsettled question.

Among most herding animals—horses, buffalo, deer, elk, antelope, giraffe, wildebeest, seal, walrus, sea lion—male dominance hierarchies maintain the herd itself, and a majority of females are inseminated by a minority of the most powerful males. Pack animals such as rats are so well organized socially that they continue to compete successfully with humans, and like most humans they mate in pairs yet also sustain male dominance hierarchies. Wolf packs share many features in common with early human hunter-gatherers: Wolves are monogamous and mate for life. Males and females hunt together, but once again, the male wolf is bigger, stronger, and socially dominant, and the pack itself is held together and protected by a male dominance hierarchy.

When we observe our closest living relatives, the primates, we find the male dominance hierarchy particularly pronounced within species that dwell communally. Of the five great apes, the gibbons and the orangutans are rather antisocial. Mature male orangutans live in solitude, coming into contact with females only to mate. Unlike the other apes, orangutans copulate face-to-face, in so-called missionary position—which the missionaries should have called "orangutan position." Gibbons evolved no political hierarchy beyond the nuclear family. The male gibbon is characteristically bigger and stronger than the female, and so remains dominant in the context of the family. Gibbons live and mate like birds, in arboreal nests. They forage for food and do not share it, except with their young. The female attends primarily to caring for the young; the male, primarily to defending the territory. He is running a standard male primate "defender" program; she, a standard female primate "mother" program—exactly the same programs, only with far fewer features and much less sophistication, that human beings run. This is also true of baboons, chimpanzees, and gorillas.

In all primate species, the male is bigger and stronger that the female. She is more attuned to emotions, relationships, her offspring's needs, and to aspects of reality that circumscribe those needs. He is more attuned to protecting the integrity of their territory, defending their lives should intruders threaten, and so to correspondingly different aspects of reality. She looks inward to the home and family, and no doubt derives emotional comfort from her role in this scheme of things. He looks outward to anticipate and ward off threats to their home and family, and no doubt derives emotional comfort from his role too.

Gorillas, for all their intimidating girth, are peaceful vegetarians who mind their own business unless they are interfered with. The dominant male is always a veteran silverback, who maintains a harem of receptive and relatively docile females. They forage and tend their young; he defends their territory against intruders and fights off challenges from younger males, until one day he grows too spent with age and makes way for his successor. The females will immediately curry favor with, appease, deceive, and cuckold their new "master"—a time-tested female primate survival strategy. This arrangement worked well enough for millions of years, in lush volcanic mountain forests long removed from human intrusion. Small bands of gorillas—ten to twenty strong—dotted these remote African regions. Thanks to the pioneering labors of primatologist Dian Fossey, who studied and tried to protect these gorillas until she herself was murdered by poachers, we know that the gorilla is nothing like the monster he is made out to be in *King Kong*. Male gorillas are no match for AK-47s and machetes, and regrettably neither are unarmed primatologists. Poachers, along with allied networks of human consumers of animal trophies and by-products, are driving the gorilla to extinction, just as our ancestors did to other primate species. Fossey, gifted with a marvelous capacity to study the politics and sociology of gorillas, was unable to protect the gorillas or herself against poachers. Some male dominance hierarchies can be held in check, or persuaded to hold themselves in check, only by more powerful male dominance hierarchies. This is as true of the contemporary Middle East (see chapters 14 and 15) as it is of the primordial African rainforest.

I surely need not remind anyone that male dominance hierarchies have waged most of the human wars to date, and invented and used most of the deadliest weapons, including the nuclear variety. Marie Curie's role in man's harnessing radioactivity was vital, yet historically and statistically far fewer women than men have successfully "hunted" the most prized and elusive big game of all: mathematical laws of thought and physical laws of nature. Prior to the twentieth century, women were largely excluded from this hunt. Now, in the wake of their liberation, what Gaussian proportion of women might we expect to see winning Nobel prizes for physics? This contentious question will be addressed in chapter 9. In any case, there is a strong analogy, if not a weak homology, between hunting big game and doing theoretical science. The quarry has evolved to be sure, from corporeal to conceptual, but the qualities required of the hunters are merely transposed from physical to intellectual domains.

My point here is that the roots of human violence are unfortunately evolutionary, and the most violent offences against human beings—whether criminally, religiously, politically, sexually, or insanely motivated—were committed by males in a dominance hierarchy.[9] One of civilization's main challenges has been to channel dominant male hierarchical violence constructively. This has lately become globalization's challenge for all the failed, failing, belligerent, and rogue states.

It is imperative to world security that the primate connection between biology and politics be understood in its proper light. On one hand, human beings have a nature that has not yet and may never be completely "reduced" to biology. So we must ultimately reject the notion that politics can be biologized. On the other hand, human beings have a nurture that can "adduce" any ideology whatsoever to biology, for political reasons alone. So we must also reject the politicization of biology. We will revisit this thorny topic in chapter 9.

Meanwhile, although men are the most violent offenders, they often enjoy the complicity of women, or succumb to the manipulation of women. Charles Manson had female accomplices; Mao's wife instigated the "cultural revolution"; Hitler relied on the emotional support of Eva Braun; and in the biblical equivalent of room service, Salomé ordered John the Baptist's head on a platter.

Thanks largely to the legendary work of Jane Goodall, the "mother" of all primatologists, we can better appreciate the evolutionary connection between chimpanzee and human violence. Chimpanzees, who time and again win both scientific and sentimental contests for the title of our "closest living relative," are also the most promiscuous, sexually abusive, and violent of the apes. They're also the primate precursors of early hominid hunting and warfare. The dominant males rule an unstable and volatile hierarchy that can be best described as balanced disorder, while the females who have mated with them enjoy the greatest protection but also suffer regular abuse. This they willingly pass on, as female chimps with "status" (that is, with a mate and a baby) will abuse less "privileged" females whom they dislike, or younger immature males who irritate them. To retaliate against the abuses of a dominant female is to risk arousing the wrath of her dominant male partner. Chimps love, desire, fear, groom, manipulate, cuckold, and obey other chimps just as humans do other humans. Now chimpanzees are greatly endangered—not by their dominant male hierarchies or their social subordinates, whose cooperation and conflict alike sufficed for chimpanzee adaptation and survival for a dozen million years—but because humans are wiping out their habitats in a headlong rush to dismantle nature and turn jungles into moonscapes or parking lots.

The fifth species of great ape, often confused with chimpanzees but differing significantly from them, are bonobos.[10] Male bonobos have less musculature and aggression than male chimps, but their sexual antics set them apart from all the other apes. Bonobos are bisexual, polymorphously perverse, and orgiastic. They will do anything in any number at any time. They also live in harmony, nonviolently and without dominance hierarchies. In essence, bonobos take free love to a further extreme than even hippies did. They have perpetual peace, but at a price: Bonobos have always been less numerous and more isolated than chimps, against whose aggression they could not compete. Nowadays, their pacific orgiastic ways render bonobos even more endangered than chimps, and globalization will soon make them extinct without even noticing.

Yet so desperate is the global village for solutions to its political, religious, and ideological tribal conflicts that no less a publication than *Foreign Affairs*—the most important quarterly assessment of America's dominant role in current events worldwide—recently published an article devoted to the role of primatology in global politics.[11] The bonobos are described in that article to offer readers at least one example of a great ape that did not require violence or dominance to evolve and sustain a stable society. At the same time, however, the bonobo is now on the verge of extinction. So it would be poor salesmanship, or bad timing, to attempt to convert anyone to "bonoboism." To be sure, humans have a "bonobo nature" as well as a Buddha nature, and you must decide for yourself which one offers a better plan for global peace. As a child of the 1960s, I experienced more than enough bonoboism. But as an adult of the twenty-first century, I have not yet experienced enough Buddhism. So you know where I stand.

## Brown Male Patriarchal Baboonery

The baboons are not yet endangered by man. Why not? Paradoxically perhaps, because their individual intelligence and creativity are markedly weaker than that of apes, while their social order is incomparably stronger. Humans admire the playfulness and inventiveness of chimps and gorillas. Chimps use stones to break open nuts, use leaves as sponges, use twigs to "fish" termites out of their nests. Chimps plainly grieve for their dead as well; a mother will often carry the corpse of a dead baby for days, reluctant to let it go. In captivity, chimps and gorillas have learned to communicate with humans using sign language, and to express themselves in "abstract impressionist" paintings, which may yet make a monkey out of Jackson Pollock. Baboons do none of these things. But the baboons of the

African savannah have evolved to do something that chimps and gorillas cannot do; namely, forage and survive on open ground, where they encountered and competed directly against earlier hominids, and later man.[12]

Humans aside, all the great apes live in or among the trees, which afford immediate avenues of flight from one another, and from external threats. Only the bulkiest gorillas cannot climb trees, and they have nothing to fear (aside from man) on the ground. The forest canopies are ape and monkey highways, and all these primates are fantastically well adapted to climbing, scampering, swinging, leaping, and rapidly traversing considerable distances from branch to branch, and tree to tree. To accomplish this, they required a major evolutionary shift, away from the primacy of olfaction (sense of smell) that serves the lower, ground-dwelling mammalian orders, toward the primacy of binocular vision, like the hunting birds, along with superb hand-eye and foot-eye coordination. In chapter 10, we will examine the unforeseen and potentially catastrophic cultural consequences to humans of the primacy of our sense of sight over all the other external senses.

Humans are not renowned tree dwellers. Human children climb trees better than adults, but as a species we are not evolved to live in them. Rather, the earliest humans inhabited caves, where they could shelter themselves from the elements and, at times more urgently, from other predators, including other humans. It is neither gratuitous nor inaccurate that we refer to the earliest humans as cavemen. But for all primate species, the prospects for variation in diet, along with the diversification of hunting and gathering skills, as well as the establishment of migratory patterns, depend crucially on being able to survive the dangers of living on and moving through open ground. The successful transition from treetops and caves to open ground is the hallmark of two primate species in particular: baboon and man. Baboons accomplished this millions of years ago; man, but a few thousand years ago. Let us therefore look to our evolutionary instructors and see what means they employed to manage this daunting challenge.

African baboons forage across open country, in the presence of many predators, notably big cats (especially leopards), venomous and constricting snakes, and man. Baboons sustain a strict male dominance hierarchy, and maintain a balanced social order that is conspicuous whether one observes them on the march or at rest. Like an early human dialectical tribe, a baboon troop typically contains several dozen members who roam and forage across a territory of several hundred square miles. When moving, baboons deploy in a symmetric column. At the point and the rear of the column are adolescent males, the most reckless and most expendable members of the troop, who are programmed to take death-defying risks in the hopes of earning promotion to a dominant status. As with the other primates, privileges of dominance include reproductive access to females. Female baboons, in turn, are only or mainly receptive to dominant males.

I pause to observe that this phenomenon is replicated precisely, but far more elaborately, in human societies. Even in peacetime, adolescent human males have a much higher death rate than adolescent females, and that is primarily because of their programmed sense of invincibility, which accompanies their strong drive to impress young females with their courage. Many die in the process—from car accidents, toxic alcoholic shock, and other extreme feats—and when these tendencies are harnessed to a war machine, such young men may die in the millions. But since audacity is often the price of victory, whether in war, creativity, or love, so this tactic, adopted wittingly or not from the baboons, works in human contexts just as effectively.

So the young adolescent baboons literally "stick their necks out" to protect the foraging troop: from the front, the rear, and the flanks. Inside them are the next most expendable segment of the population: the adolescent females. Inside them are the dominant males, which represent the last and most formidable line of defense against predators. For the dominant males protect the most valuable resource of the troop: nursing and pregnant females. Adolescent males and the dominant graybeards guard the group, laying down their lives to protect the troop's integrity, and in particular its mature females and young. Most great apes, and most other monkeys, function as individualists within a looser social structure, which in times of severe threat is prone to temporary disintegration. So chimps may take to the trees when threatened, every ape for himself. Baboons, on the other hand, remain in formation and fight. A small number of courageous male baboons, armed with fangs and desperation, may even drive off leopards, which prey on them regularly.

When baboons rest, the column melts into a circle, the circumference guarded by the adolescent males, and whose innermost ring consists of the nursing mothers and pregnant females, guarded and protected by the dominant males. Baboons are ever vigilant and ever disciplined. Although not as playful, inventive, or "human" as the other apes, they are nonetheless far better adapted to open ground, and will survive longer than the other ape species facing human encroachment on their habitats.

You could see the difference for yourself, if you were permitted to conduct the following experiment in one of the "McAfrican Safari Parks" that dot the North American exurbs. If you parked your vehicle in the chimpanzee compound, it would soon need a car wash. If you parked it in the baboon compound, it would soon be stripped of everything removable. Chimps evolved to be party animals, carousing heedlessly in the midst of plenty; baboons evolved to be scavengers, foraging relentlessly amid constant risk and uncertainty.

From the standpoint of psychoprimatology, the chimpanzee lifestyle resembles both the human id and the radical political left: imaginative, erotic, unpredictable, undisciplined, chaotic. By contrast, the baboon resembles the human superego and the orthodox political right: obedient, chaste, predictable, disciplined, orderly. But unlike chimps and baboons, which are evolutionarily fixed in their behaviors, human individuals and cultures show vastly greater malleability, as well as the capacity to shift from one mode of behavior to another as circumstances warrant. Thus a human being or a human tribe may behave like chimps in one scenario, and like baboons in the next. Moreover, some humans behave more like gorillas with respect to minding their own business and maintaining or belonging to harems; others behave more like gibbons or orangutans, mating monogamously or living in solitude, as the case may be.

The howling monkeys are well named for their behavior: Every morning, at dawn, the dominant males venture to the fringes of their territory and howl at the howling monkeys who howl back at them from the fringes of their adjacent territories. This daily "howlfest" reestablishes what pop ethologist Robert Ardrey called the "territorial imperative"—for in these monkeys, as in multitudinous and variegated species the world over, whether airborne, seaworthy, or landlocked, the defense of a territory allows the dominant males to achieve two vital goals: to control a food supply and to attract females.[13]

Female howling monkeys are highly attracted to the most dominant males, because the prospect of male-defended territory is also the promise of a food supply and a measure of protection from predators and invaders, all of which the female needs in order to become sexually receptive and to mother her offspring. So when Mary Wollstonecraft, in her 1790 classic *On the Subjection of Women*, became the first woman on record to denounce marriage as "legal prostitution," an arrangement in which the wife barters sex for economic security, she could scarcely have realized that the evolutionary roots of this phenomenon predate humanity by millions of years, and across thousands of species.[14] And similarly, when political leaders issue undiplomatic statements that offend or scandalize the leaders of neighboring or rival nations and provoke verbal retaliation, threats, and counterthreats via political posturing or "saber rattling"—which in turn get the public media and its hives of consumers buzzing—little do they suspect that they are all running a human version of ancient "howling monkey" software, which still comes bundled with the operating system of the human brain. After all these millions of years, it's probably overdue for an upgrade, namely through the ABCs.

## Dialectical Dispersion and Symbolic Structures

If you now take a step back, or upward, into philosophical orbital space, you can appreciate how ingenious is nature's way of dispersing and equilibrating millions of life-forms into evolving yet relatively stable ecosystems and habitats. Whether we observe coral reefs, equatorial rainforests, undulating savannahs, saltwater marshes, or arid deserts, the same phenomenon is manifest over and over, in myriad ways, in both predator and prey species: Males are programmed to occupy and defend hunting and gathering territories, either individually, against one another, or in groups against other groups, to secure food supplies and attract females. Females are programmed to reproduce, and so are attracted and receptive to males who can provide the best or most supportive environments for themselves and their offspring.

Each ecosystem or habitat contains hundreds or thousands of species, all playing this evolutionary game of survival, adaptation, and reproduction, all coexisting in unstable equilibria, and together constituting the food chain. To maximize opportunities for survival and ensure the continuity of life itself, nature has ingeniously decreed (for all creatures but man) a Middle Way in the population density of a given species in a given territory. For all species except man, nature's Middle Way is called the optimum number—the ideal number for each species that a given territory can support. If the population density of a species (whether ants, frogs, mice, deer, wolves, or monkeys) is too small for a given habitat, they will prosper and breed until they reach their optimum number. If their population density becomes excessive, then normal social behaviors will break down, until either their absolute numbers are reduced or they fission into two groups, one of which migrates to another territory. Either way, their optimum number is restored and, in the latter case, the species disperses further, thus increasing its odds of survival. If a population drops too far below its optimum number, it may become extinct. If a population rises too far above its optimum number, it may overconsume and permanently exhaust the resources in its habitat, and so may also face extinction.

It is through dispersion that flora and fauna come to inhabit every region of the Earth, and settle into their unstable equilibria that fluctuate around nature's Middle Way—the optimum number for each species. Even so, at least 95 percent of all species that ever lived are now extinct. Most of them perished during the cataclysmic extinctions that the biosphere as a whole has experienced, whether precipitated by huge meteorites, or by other forces capable of exerting planetary impact. Human beings themselves have become such a planetary force, and it is a tragedy of globalization that we are destroying natural habitats and wiping out species at a greater rate than any other cataclysm in the history of our planet.

Ironically perhaps, I reiterate that the evolutionary dispersion of primates, hominids, and humans was intended to safeguard them against extinction, by obliging them to occupy far-flung territories and remain out of contact with one another. Yet there are significant differences between monkeys, apes, and men. Howling monkeys define and redefine their territories by the ritual of competitive howling itself, which also means that they need not attack each other or dispute their boundaries by coercive violence. Chimpanzees, who are the "Middle Way" between monkey and man, behave sometimes as monkeys and sometimes as men. Like monkeys, their male dominance hierarchies can often function via displays of power and threats of violence; but like men, they often express their power through violence itself, which extends to neighboring bands of chimps via unprovoked raids, murders, and rapes—the precursors of aggressive human warfare. Humans are capable of behaving in many animal modes. Groups of humans certainly howl at one another like monkeys, except that their howling takes on incomparably richer meanings, most commonly the assertion of political ideologies or religious doctrines. These are human ways of howling. Humans also behave as chimps, and from prehistoric times to the dawn of civilizations they elevated the primate male dominance hierarchy, and the chimpanzee form of unprovoked warfare against neighboring bands, into cultural traditions and art forms. And from the dusk of prehistory until the dawn of globalization, the human female has been a willing accomplice to this way of life, alternately protected and abused by men and their inevitable politics, to whom her programmed desire for babies and motherhood attracted her, and her relatively limited capacity for hunting and defense of territory bound her.

Meanwhile, the evolutionary process of extreme dispersion worked so well that it eventually resulted in the founding and development of permanent settlements, agriculture, animal husbandry, and increasingly sophisticated tools, weapons, and defenses against roaming bands of human marauders and marching armies of adventurer-conquerors. The transitions from dialectical tribe to city-state, from empire to civilization, along with the growth of sustainable civilizations themselves, required more than rudimentary tools, more than primitive technologies, more than oral traditions of myth and lore, more than male dominance hierarchies, more than relentless female reproductive cycles, and more than tribal territorial imperatives. They required the twin developments of political ideologies and religious doctrines, to provide what Hobbes called "a common power to keep them all in awe"—at least long enough for a tribe to endure, or a civilization to coalesce.

Human political systems and organized religions are symbolic cultural structures, which transcend earlier primatological boundaries— geographic as well as tribal. They permit many tribes with diverse customs, and from diverse geographic regions, to become united under one transcendent totem—be it a flag or a book. But most nationalistic politics and transnational religions neither negate nor eradicate the biological and primatological roots of human beings; rather, they create larger arenas in which these ancient influences can fruit and flower. Seen in this way, we can understand that the Cold War was in primatological terms a daily and routine confrontation between gargantuan bands of howling human monkeys of the Soviet Union, and howling human monkeys of the United States. These monkeys, however, had figured out how to arm themselves with nuclear weapons, and so they had to howl just loudly enough to remind each other of this, yet not too loudly for fear of provoking more than howling from the other side. Of course the capitalist monkeys who dominated the United States had a system that offered incomparably more liberty, opportunity, and hope than did the communist monkeys who dominated the Soviet Union, but a visitor from another planet (or a politically naive intellectual from the West) could never have discerned these salient differences merely by listening to both sides howl. Similarly, every tribal war among humans, like every invasion of human adventure-conquerors, has small-scale features that are strongly reminiscent of the "chimpanzee wars" so ably chronicled by Jane Goodall. They also have large-scale features that resemble the rapacious expansions of ant colonies—including slave taking, looting, and annihilation of rival colonies of ants—as observed by pioneering French myrmecologist Auguste-Henri Forel.

That said, Forel had also observed an impressive variety of constructive and cooperative activities in which ants are capable of engaging, as his 1928 inventory reveals: "Among ants we find weavers, butchers, cattle-rearers, masons, road-makers, harvesters, bakers, mushroom farmers, excellent nurses of various kinds, gardeners, warriors, pacifists, slave-makers, thieves, brigands and parasites, but we find no professors, orators, governors, bureaucrats or generals, nor even corporals, nor do we find capitalists, speculators, or mere swindlers."[15] Forel also noticed that ants can modify their behaviors, and he observed that mutually hostile ant species can learn to thrive side by side in friendly neutrality that he called "parabiosis." This led him to muse: "Why then should the selection and mutations of phylogeny have tended to create differences in odours which bring about wars between creatures so capable of peaceful social alliances? . . . If things were not as they are, in principle there would be nothing to prevent a 'universal formicity'."[16]

Indeed, if there could be a universal nesthood of ants, there could also be a universal civilization of human beings. But that would necessitate more humans discovering that which is most noble and ennobling in them, as opposed to reflecting that which is most base and debased alike.

## Man Is Five Thousand Animals

In terms of the evolution and management of human groups, it is more than evident that the human being stands not only atop of the planetary food chain, but also on the top rung of the planetary evolutionary ladder. In consequence, humans are able not only to kill and eat, but also to incorporate essential behavioral features of every other plant and animal species in the biosphere. On any given day, in any human community, you can observe people behaving at different times as ants, bees, termites, rats, sheep, cattle, pigs, dogs, cats, monkeys, apes, sloths, sharks, bears, bulls, hens, roosters, peacocks, parrots, turtles, snakes, eagles, vultures, foxes, jackals, wolves, lambs, rabbits, doves, hawks, worms, and parasites of many kinds. This is more than metaphoric. Some people strongly embody traits of particular animals; others will behave as different animals when they encounter varying situations or experience various mind-states.

Humans also manifest plantlike behaviors, from clinging vines to couch potatoes to other vegetative states. Like flowers, humans also blossom, and fade. These are more than similes.

We have seen from T'ien T'ai Buddhism that humans simultaneously manifest three thousand states of mind. We have seen from the *I Ching* that humans simultaneously face four thousand situations. Now we see from evolutionary considerations that humans simultaneously behave like five thousand life-forms. To be human is to be the sum of all possible flora and fauna—any one of which, and any combination of which, are in themselves less than human. Just as some mind-states are inherently more beneficial than others, and some situations are inherently more desirable than others, so some animals forms are inherently more preferable than others. Which animal form is most preferable for humans? The human one itself, which is more than, as well as other than, the sum of all the rest.

To understand this better, let us look at some circles that circumscribe social insect, rodent, primate, and tribal territories. An ant's "identity" is none other than a particular pheromone—a chemical ID—that identifies it as a member of its nest or formicary (a network of nests). This among other pheromones is produced by the queen, and ants that do not bear it are treated as invaders and killed. Worker ants are hatched from eggs laid uniquely by a queen, and so are spared the sexual conflicts that higher species encounter, and which stem invariably from social consequences of sex difference. The ant's sense of "self" is bound up with her primary social distinction, between "us" (members of her nest or formicary) and "them" (members of other nests or formicaries). This works well enough for ants, which have survived for tens if not hundreds of millions of years, and who will possibly outlast humans.

Rats are a much higher order of being than ants, incomparably more sentient and intelligent. They also use pheromones in their sexual and social transactions. Pheromones, for example, can trigger spontaneous abortions in pregnant female rodents too closely exposed to mature males who are not the sire. Rats rely on a keen sense of smell to maintain order within their pack, and boundaries between rival packs. They wage vicious wars against one another for control of territory, and given abundance of food and absence of predators they breed like (as the expression goes) rats. But if their population density becomes too great, spontaneous abortion is only one of many instinctive population control mechanisms that activate to alleviate overcrowding. They will also practice cannibalism, eating their young and each other alive, to abet decline toward their optimum number.

Resemblances between rats and humans are too numerous to name. Hans Zinsser, the insightful physician who developed the first vaccine against yellow fever, chronicled these resemblances in his brilliant book *Rats, Lice and History.* As Zinsser observes:

"In the first place, like man, the rat has become practically omnivorous . . . It breeds at all seasons and—again like man—is most amorous in the springtime. It hybridizes easily and, judging by the strained relationships between the black and the brown rat, develops social or racial prejudices against this practice . . . Inbreeding takes place regularly. The males are larger, the females fatter. It adapts itself to all kinds of climates. It makes ferocious war upon its own kind . . . Also—like man—the rat is individualistic until it needs help. That is, it fights bravely alone against weaker rivals, for food or for love; but it knows how to organize armies and fight in hordes when necessary . . . Man and rat are merely, so far, the most successful animals of prey. They are utterly destructive of other forms of life. . . . The gradual, relentless progressive extermination of the black rat by the brown has no parallel in nature so close as that of the similar extermination of one race of man by another."[17]

But as we will see in chapter 12, unlike every other species on the planet, humans civilizations have no "optimum number" to check their reproductive fecundity and predatory rapacity. Ultimately, humans may soon overexploit their habitats until nothing consumable remains, and at which time our species will consume itself.

Meanwhile, it should be clear that human collectives—the dialectical tribe, the religious community, the political nation-state, and the multinational corporation—require more than insect pheromones and mammalian olfaction to bind their members. They need totems and taboos, legends and lore, flags and books, a Hobbesian "common power to keep them all in awe." And sadly, many human collectives need enemies as well. We have seen it in racism of every kind, and by all colors. We have seen it in genocides from the Old World to the New, from the northern hemisphere to the southern. We have seen it in religious intolerance, in the periods of rabid persecution and murderous extremism that sooner or later afflict all proselytizing faiths. When will humans ever learn to treat one another as fellow sentient beings, instead of as aliens from inferior planets or subhumans of a lesser species? Perhaps they will learn when they adopt The Middle Way, whose practices cease the feuds that rage within each mind.

We have seen how forces of biological evolution dispersed early human tribes, to give these frail and seemingly hapless hominids a better chance at adaptation and survival. Thus early humans established themselves in a range of remote and mutually isolated habitats, and their cultural evolution proceeded along equally diverse pathways—yet with certain common denominators. Sustained by dominant male hierarchies devoted to provision and protection and by subordinate female support groups equally but differently devoted to gathering and mothering, human tribes gradually evolved into civilizations whose cultural "software"—language and lore, rituals and mores—served the human equivalent of pheromones in ants, of olfaction in rats, and of howling in monkeys to distinguish self from other, "this tribe" from "that tribe," "our turf" from "their turf," "our book" from "their book."

And so, at these extremes of evolutionary dispersion, it becomes possible for some human tribes to fail to recognize the humanity of other human tribes, because their "cultural software" seems to have advantaged them by doing so. But the failure to recognize another's humanity is nothing but the failure to recognize one's own humanity. If humans have evolved on this earth to kill off everything else and eventually themselves, then widespread failure to recognize humanity in oneself and in others is proving to be a useful trait. But if humans have evolved on this planet to understand and appreciate the beauty of nature and the diversity of culture, and the noblest aspirations of sentient life itself, then recognition of humanity, in oneself and others, becomes the paramount human endeavor that must govern and condition all the rest.

Humans by nature embody five thousand animals, as by nature we face four thousand situations in three thousand mind-states. This is what makes us so intriguing, indefinable, and conflicted. When you meet a fellow human, you never know from one moment to the next which animal will manifest which situation from which mind-state. But to attain your full potential as a human being, it is necessary and sufficient to behave as the noblest animal; to manifest the best situation; and to enter the most salutary mind-state. The Middle Way makes this possible.

## Nature's Economies

Three evolutionary developments above all have "painted" human beings into a "corner," from which they (like the other primates) have apparently little room to maneuver, yet from which they can escape by understanding their plight and applying the ABCs to remedy it. First, in the evolution of the primate brain, the superior sense of smell that predominates in lower social mammals (e.g., rodents and canines) has been replaced by a sense of sight that predominates in monkeys, apes, and man. The primacy of binocular vision allows our primate "cousins" to dwell among trees, and allows us hominids to inhabit open ground— and to drive across it and fly over it at speeds unattainable via nature alone. But vision's emergent supremacy also causes severe problems, both inhibiting recognition of our own species, and impairing cognitive development, as we will see in chapter 10.

Second, the primate brain had to modify itself to accommodate this emergent priority of vision over smell. In the process, the olfactory bulb shrank while the visual cortex enlarged. However, in the lower social mammals, olfaction was the key sense that allowed them to distinguish among family, friends, and foes, as well as allowing males to know when females were "in heat" (i.e., ovulating), and thus sexually receptive. In lower mammals, the olfactory bulb interfaces with the more ancient module of the reptilian limbic system, which allows the sense of smell to control behaviors such as fighting, fleeing, or mating.

But in primates, the bulb has drastically shrunk, and has lost most of its contact with the limbic system, while the emergent visual cortex itself has no such contact. In consequence, humans have lost their olfactory capacity to distinguish among family, friends, foes, and receptive sexual partners, and in its place have evolved the capacity to confuse all the different behaviors that encounters with these different categories of conspecifics would normally elicit. So benign visual (and verbal) cues can and do elicit malignant behaviors. Vision and sound stimulate strong emotions, but there is no olfactory bulb to ensure the most appropriate responses. The chief problem here is that dominance, violence, and sexuality are all commingled in the primate brain. This is the root of all sexual abuse, as well as sexual violence, which is mostly (but not wholly) directed by males against females. It is also the root of human sex serving every possible purpose under the sun except reproduction—including domination, humiliation, recreation, prostitution—and both sexes are parties to this. I repeat that the primates alone suffer from this problem, and humans suffer from it more than any other primate species.[18]

Sigmund Freud had brilliantly but controversially excavated the psychological foundations of this conundrum without being aware of their evolutionary, ethological, and sociobiological roots. He saw no cure and, therefore, harbored no hope for human beings. Freud expressed the belief that we humans are living "psychologically beyond our means" to suppose that we can ever mend our most malevolent ways.[19]

Third, in the evolution of humans specifically, nature has practiced a few "economies" that prove lethal to our species, because they exacerbate the design flaw in the primate brain. Humans differ from all other animals in the vast variety of our tools and weapons, and differ too in the deleterious effects that some of our tools and weapons have on the biosphere—but humans are not the inventors of tools and weapons themselves. Nature herself has anticipated many of the scientific and technological breakthroughs that have allowed humans to mimic her vast array of implements and arsenals of weapons. Aristotle remarked on this long ago: "For other animals have each but one mode of defense, and this they can never change . . . But to man, numerous modes of defense are open, and these, moreover, he may change at will."[20] Some examples are instructive.

In terms of physical weapons, numerous flora and fauna alike sport needles, thorns, spines, spikes, and quills. These, as in the porcupine and stingray, may be barbed. Felines slash with razor-sharp talons; canine teeth stab as daggers; horns, antlers, and tusks gore as short sword and spear; while swordfish and narwhal brandish long sword and pike, respectively. The mandible of the soldier ant, the claw of the crustacean, and the beak of the bird function as powerful pincers and shears. Roman snails throw calcium carbonate darts at each other's feet (as part of a sadomasochistic courtship ritual).[21]

Chemical weapons abound among plants, insects, arachnids, and reptiles, not to mention the skunk. Plants synthesize a wide range of alkaloids, terpenes, and other compounds for protection against insects. The most ingenious of plant chemicals are juvenile hormones of insects synthesized by trees which, if ingested by insects at an inappropriate time of their life cycle, prevents them from reaching maturity.[22] Furthermore, the insects cannot acquire immunity to their own hormones, as they can to chlorinated hydrocarbons of human manufacture.

Slave-taking ants make use of so-called "propaganda substances" (e.g., decyl and polydecyl acetates), some of which cause the defenders of a nest to attack each other while the invaders carry off the brood.[23] The venom of snakes, injected through their fangs, is the natural poisoned dagger or arrowhead. The *Formica rufa* ant and the spitting cobra can accurately project their venom.

For purely defensive purposes, nature is the armorer *deluxe*, boasting the keratin "chain mail" of reptiles, the suit of the armadillo, the shell of the turtle, and a simply enormous variety of invertebrate carapaces. Other defences include the smokescreen of the bombardier beetle, whose aqueous equivalent is the ink cloud of the octopus and squid. Body camouflage is doubly ubiquitous, "both in all parts of the world, and within all groups of animals."[24]

As to special tools and weapons, nature has also anticipated man. The pit trap is used by the antlion and wormlion. Bridges are built by ants. The tunneling animals preceded the sapper. Nets are spun by spiders. Electric shock is administered by the eel *Electrophorus electricus*, which generates six hundred volts of electromagnetic force. The archer fish fires water bullets at insects. The internal navigation systems of migratory animals continue to surpass human understanding. Sound navigation ranging, or "sonar," is used by bats and porpoises. The snake's tongue, which contains infrared sensors, allows its head to function as a close-range heat-seeking missile.

In short, humans did not invent weapons: They reinvented them, as a continuation in nurture of their natural embodiment of five thousand animals. But here is the catch: Most species that come equipped with a deadly weapon are also equipped with a program for limiting its use—especially against conspecifics. For example, mantis shrimp batter each other at the point of their heaviest armor, the tail. Venomous serpents wrestle instead of biting one another. Wolves roll over on their backs and bare their throats as a gesture of submission, a signal that actually prevents dominant wolves from tearing out the jugulars of their more subordinate pack members. Domesticated dogs have inherited this behavior, which you can elicit when you play with them (unless they dominate you). Darwin rightly observed that animal instincts are not lost under domestication.

Recognized gestures of submission or appeasement abound throughout the animal world, having evolved as remarkable behavioral "lock-and-key" mechanisms that ritualize or limit conspecific violence. What about humans? Alas, nature has played a small economy on us, with large consequences. Humans are born so utterly helpless and dependent, and remain so for so long, that they surely pose no threat to anyone or anything. They have no natural weapons of any kind, and so (nature rightly reasons) have no need of biologically implanted programs to limit their use. So follows a grand irony: Helpless infants, whose big brains equip them with means to invent weapons of increasingly unprecedented lethality but no instinctive mechanism for limiting their use, become the deadliest predators on the planet when they reach maturity. Unlike every other species, we require cultural conventions—chivalry, white flags, red crosses, theories of Just War,

Geneva and Hague conventions, strategic arms limitations treaties—to act as a brake on our naturally unrestrained use of weapons. Much human history is a history of failed brakes. Combine that with a brain that also lacks the natural capacity to reliably recognize its fellow humans as fellow humans, and also lacks the natural capacity to reliably regulate its behaviors toward family, friends, and sexual partners, and you get a being that is born—but not condemned—to sow the wind and reap the whirlwind. Amazingly, and thankfully, this being can also exercise some choices in the matter.

We are fortunate indeed to have evolved the ABCs, for only The Middle Way is powerful enough to counteract the "stacked deck" from which biological evolution deals its human hands.

Humans can and must be guided and encouraged to behave more often in fuller awareness of their humanity. By mindfulness of the ABCs and the practice of their virtues, humans can spend more time mimicking better animal states, and spend less time inhabiting worse ones. Again, and via the ABCs, humans can find more constructive and productive interpretations of their situations. And perhaps most important, the inexhaustible ABCs help humans discover and celebrate the most profound aspects of their own humanity, in both themselves and in others, and so bridge the deep divides of tribe and totem, over which they habitually howl, and worse.

Insofar as humans have merely extended biological behaviors into cultures, have amplified them with technologies, have justified them with political ideologies, and have sanctified them with religious doctrines, we are no more than exquisitely complicated—and deeply conflicted—social and tribal animals. However, unlike all other animals, humans have another avenue perennially open to them, which is the realization of their uniquely human potential to attain states of awareness and benevolence that do not belong to any one culture, but to all of humanity.

The human being is a producer and consumer not only of goods and services, but also of paradoxes. That man is a social animal has been known from time immemorial, and our ABCs knew it well. Aristotle said that "He who is unable to live in society, or who has no need because he is sufficient for himself, must be either a beast or a god."[25]

Much later, Nietzsche could not resist adding a third, sardonic possibility: that to live alone a man must be either a beast, a god, or a philosopher. Even so, Aristotle is telling us something vital about being human: that our humanity cannot be properly nurtured or sustained in a social vacuum. People need other people; hence we coalesce in groups. Buddha agreed about the importance of community. On his own deathbed, instead of appointing a successor, he instructed his disciples to maintain the sangha (the community) as the vehicle for propounding his teachings (the dharma). And of course Confucius also supports the legitimate claims of the group—be it family, community, or polity—over the private interests of the individual. Centuries after these ABCs we finally encountered a D—namely Darwin—whose scientific works underpin the sociobiological (not the social Darwinistic) view of why groups are so important to humans. The key is found in his insights on our relation to the apes, and our dispersion as a species.

Human beings frequently flock or herd together, as part of their natural tendency to mimic other animal forms. Most people feel comfortable in a flock or a herd, which in human terms translates into a community, a congregation, a crowd, an assembly, a throng, and so forth. The human flock also needs to be tended by shepherds, one of whose tasks is to protect the flock from wolves and other predators. It sometimes happens that the wolves disguise themselves as shepherds and convince the flock (by propaganda, brainwashing, and similar means) that the actual shepherds are wolves. Then the flock demonizes the shepherds and follows the wolves to its doom. Hitler was a wolf disguised as a shepherd. So was Stalin. So was Pol Pot. So were the Taliban. So is Osama bin Laden. So are many serial killers, who lull their victims with charming lies in order to destroy them. If, for example, you follow a Way that leads to inculcation of hatred, unprovoked aggression, premeditated murder, and exhortation to premature death, then you follow a wolf and not a shepherd.

Buddha cautioned, "Believe nothing, no matter where you read it, or who said it, no matter if I have said it, unless it agrees with your own reason and your own common sense." In spite of his warnings, the human flock is rarely able to penetrate such deceptions until it is too late, and even very intelligent people fall prey to them. So distinguishing between the shepherds and the wolves is not just a matter of mind; it is also a matter of heart and spirit. Buddhist theories and practices are very potent at removing veils of ignorance. Among Buddha's last and most important words are these: "Work out your own salvation. Do not depend on others."

Thus nature bequeaths to human beings a terrible paradox of nativity: We are born needing to belong to a social group, yet we also need to separate smaller social groups from larger ones and from the universal one. We understand intellectually that "All men are brothers," as every humane religion and philosophy teaches, yet we are evolutionarily almost incapable of living together as brothers. To do so, we must diminish or nullify the repulsive forces between one group and another: the xenophobic hatreds of racism, the ruthless prejudices of ethnocentrism, and the demonizing myths of tribalism.

How can The Middle Way reconcile extreme conflicts between groups? Here are the ABCs. Aristotle would ask us to consider the purpose of a human life, which is to become happy and fulfilled by the pursuit of excellence and the practice of virtue. As he asserted in his *Ethics*, "Happiness, then, is at once the best and noblest and pleasantest thing in the world." People who harbor prejudices and hatreds are not happy, and neither do they become happy by acting on their prejudices and fears. Thus they are missing the point of being alive. As Aristotle observed, "People regard themselves as noble everywhere, and not only in their own country; but they deem foreigners noble only when at home." We must learn to see human nobility in each and every person, for the global village is our shared home.

Even more strongly, Buddha's teachings unify humankind by reminding us that the opportunity to lead a human life is a great gift. All human beings have the potential to become awakened to their true nature, which has nothing to do with race, sex, gender, ethnicity, or tribe—including religious or political affiliation. Beneath our skins and beyond our myths, we are all capable of becoming happy at nobody else's expense. Buddha said, "In the sky, there is no distinction of east and west; people create distinctions out of their own minds and then believe them to be true." Divisive thoughts lead to divisive speech, which leads to divisive acts. Thus your thoughts are supremely important.

Confucius would concur that humanity is common to all, but that we become divided by our institutions. In the *Analects* he says, "Men are near to each other at birth: the lives they lead sunder them." The ABCs can help repair the sundered chains of our common humanity, and enable us to produce peace and share prosperity in the global village. In the service of that mission, we will next address some burning questions associated with extremes afflicting women. Just as the substance of this chapter—human sociobiology—is essentially a banned subject in American universities, some of what I am going to discuss next is more than banned on the deconstructed campuses, and in the politically correct climates of the West—as you will discover in chapters 9 and 11—it is taboo.

# 9

## PANDORA'S EXTREMES
### The Politicization of Sex Difference

*And what could be more sacred than this, or more desired by a man of sound mind, than to beget by a noble and honored wife children who, as shepherds of their old age, shall be the most loyal and discrete guardians of their father and mother, and the preservers of the whole house?*
—Aristotle

*What is the appropriate behavior for a man or a woman in the midst of this world, where each person is clinging to his piece of debris? What's the proper salutation between people as they pass each other in this flood?*
—Buddha

*In vain have I looked for one whose desire to build up his moral power was as strong as sexual desire.* —Confucius

### Male Chauvinism versus Gender Feminism

NATURE CHALLENGES HUMANS with extremes at a fundamental level: sexual dimorphism. God or nature (or both) have decreed that humanity will manifest in two different forms: female and male. All reasonable people agree that there are biological differences between the sexes—for example in anatomy, physiology, endocrinology, and brain function. Most will also agree that these biological differences—starting with XX versus XY—give rise to emotional, behavioral, psychological, socioeconomic, political, and archetypal differences. However, two extreme viewpoints about the significance of these differences clash in the global village.

The male chauvinist viewpoint—shared by many religiously or socially orthodox women—asserts that biological sex difference gives rise to inevitable and irremediable social consequences (or gender differences), and that a modified Stone Age manual of best practices for the sexual division of labor among other facets of society is still appropriate for the twenty-first century and beyond. The gender feminist viewpoint—shared by many neo-Marxist or deconstructed men—is that women have been oppressed by men since the dawn of time, and that once women become fully emancipated all social differences will be seen as nothing more than social constructs.

These days, the word *gender* itself is on the front lines of the gender wars, and it is used in two completely different ways: the traditional and the radical. Traditionalists, including equity feminists like Christina Hoff Sommers, distinguish between sex and gender. Sex is a biological term (e.g., there are male and female structures and functions); gender is a cultural term (e.g., there are masculine and feminine aspects of personality and behavior). Equity feminists believe that as women become more fully emancipated, they will be able to accomplish more or less everything that men can accomplish, but will still retain their essential feminine characteristics. Hence, equity feminists seek equality of opportunity for women but still recognize that there are differences between women and men. One important implication of equity feminism is that equal opportunities for women and men do not necessarily or always lead to equal outcomes between women and men. Why? Because sex differences and gender preferences both exert influence on our behaviors and our choices.

But so-called "gender feminists" have deconstructed the equity feminist position, and have replaced it with a cluster of views that range from radical to delusional. The gender feminist position is sanctioned as the official, politically correct one in the postmodern West. Gender feminists have eliminated the word "sex" altogether, and use "gender" to represent both biological as well as social traits. They then claim that all gender differences are social constructs which, being completely arbitrary, can be changed at will. For example, as taught by professors Lucy Gilbert and Paula Webster at Hunter College in New York:

"Each infant is assigned to one or the other category on the basis of the shape and size of its genitals. Once this assignment is made, we become what culture believes each of us to be—feminine or masculine. Although many people think that men and women are the natural expression of a genetic blueprint, gender is a product of human thought and culture, a social construction that creates the 'true nature' of all individuals."[1]

In other words, gender feminists claim that being feminine has no connection with being female, and being masculine has no connection with being male. Although this delusional view is falsified by much objective evidence, it has the decisive advantage of working perfectly in Marxist-feminist-postmodern theory, whose openly avowed political objective is not equal opportunity for women, but rather the elimination of patriarchy. In the words of Kate Bornestein, a man who underwent a sex change (and is therefore an "expert witness" for the Party): "Women couldn't be oppressed if there was no such thing as 'women' . . . doing away with gender is key to the doing away with patriarchy."[2] Gender feminists will also have to "do away with" the vast majority of moderate women, who not only appear to enjoy being women, but also seem to believe that women and men should partake of their shared humanity as coequals. But the vast majority of moderate women have an inadequate conception of the oppressive damage done to Western civilization by the dehumanizing and deluded Marxist politics of gender feminism. They, and you, will be further edified in chapter 11.

Meanwhile, Pandora's extremes are polar opposites: Male chauvinists suppose that sex difference means everything in terms of social function; gender feminists believe that sex difference means nothing in terms of social function. Let us seek The Middle Way.

## The Reconciliation in Brief

Neither extreme represents an accurate approximation of reality. As usual, each contains some truth and some falsehood. Each disregards the other's truth, and trumpets its own falsehood. More than one billion women on this planet are still disadvantaged by dictates emanating from the chauvinist extreme; while Western civilization itself (another billion people) is being undermined, thanks partly to the relentless connivance of the gender feminist extreme. As usual, The Middle Way is required to reconcile them.

I can explain the reconciliation right now. It goes like this: There are human sex differences. They give rise to some social consequences—and "some" means less than all but more than none. According to Buddhist theory, all differences between human beings are manifested throughout the lower levels of consciousness, but not at the highest. All humans, of any sex or gender, can attain a state of awareness and compassion unclouded by sex difference and gender orientation alike. But that requires practicing The Middle Way. Those who stray off its moderate pathways may become casualties of one extreme or another: male chauvinism or gender feminism. That's the short story.

But since the "war of the sexes" appears eternal, we have time for the longer story too. So here it is. Once upon a time, throughout nature and nurture alike, structure ordained function. Human sexual structure is not as polarized as many cultures have made it out to be. Every human embryo passes through a hermaphroditic phase, manifesting both male Wolffian and female Müllerian reproductive structures. ("Wolffian" refers to the Russian embryologist Caspar Friedrich Wolff, who described the male reproductive organs in 1759. "Müllerian" is derived from the German physiologist who described female embryogenesis in 1830.) But our species is not evolved to be functionally hermaphroditic; hence one set of these structures is normally slated for fuller development. Yet there are no "pure" male or "pure" female types; just like their archetypal yang and yin, each is infused with the other. Some cultures, mainly in the developing world, reflexively treat men and women like polar opposites on the basis of their sex differences alone, but that extreme fails to take into account our most important commonalities. At the other extreme, some cultures in the developed world now deny that there are any social consequences at all of sex difference, but their need to enforce that falsehood likewise makes them fail to take into account our most important commonalities, especially our moral dimension as human beings. In both cases, the result is fruitless conflict and needless suffering. And just what are these commonalities? The ABCs inform us very well.

From Aristotle, we know that each person has the potential for fulfillment, which can be attained by refining and expressing their talents via the golden mean. From Confucius, we know that harmonious social order is also necessary for humans to attain fulfillment via Tao. The chauvinistic extreme does not permit women to express their human excellence beyond motherhood and domesticity, while the feminist extreme deconstructs the social order itself, attempting to make the sexes "equal" by eliminating both femininity and masculinity. In other words, the chauvinists take Confucius to one extreme, imposing an overly rigid social hierarchy, while the gender feminists take Aristotle to another extreme, politicizing then deconstructing the very differences that make society possible. Buddha's Middle Way is able to reconcile these extremes through its nine-level model of consciousness, an alternative to traditional Western psychology and deeper even than ancient Chinese metaphysics.

In reviewing these nine levels, I will summarize the Nichiren Buddhist view, as expressed for example by Dr. Yoichi Kawada in a recent lecture in New York.[3] Dr. Kawada, a learned Buddhist scholar as well as an immunologist, has been director of the Institute for Oriental Studies in Tokyo since 1985.

The first five levels of consciousness pertain to the five external senses. Whatever we see excites the visual cortex, whatever we hear excites the auditory cortex, and so forth. The phenomenal world stimulates our brains via sensual pathways, sometimes crossing over into what psychologists call "synesthesia"—experiencing one sense via another. (If you have ever heard the sound of a sunrise, or felt the tinkling of a bell on your skin, you have experienced synesthesia.) The sixth level is mentation: the exercise of reason and will, the level on which we evaluate what our senses are telling us (e.g., the music is too loud) and what we are going to do about it (e.g., turn the volume down). The seventh level corresponds to the Freudian subconscious and unconscious, where thought processes and emotions (as well as dreams, memories, and fantasies) influence our conscious reason and will, even though we are unaware of their presence. The eighth level corresponds to Jung's collective unconscious, and also to Plato's world of ideas:

Herein reside the primordial archetypes and idealized forms that all humans cognize in common. The ninth level is Buddha consciousness, which is attainable by all human beings who are willing to free themselves from the fetters of the other eight levels. The Middle Way is nothing else than the royal road to the ninth level.

Only at the ninth level are we free from the dualities and dimorphisms manifest at the other levels, all susceptible to the deluded cravings that cause human suffering. The psyche suffers when its reason and will are held hostage by the appetites—whether drives, desires, emotions, needs, wants, wishes, fantasies, or expectations—that afflict every level but the ninth. The ninth level alone is empty of cravings, and full of unselfish love, compassion, awareness, and a boundless willingness to help others in distress. At the ninth level, there is no sex difference and no gender difference.

You can do only three things with an appetite: sate it wholesomely, sate it unwholesomely, or not sate it at all. Guess which one is The Middle Way? That's right: Sating it wholesomely is the virtuous Middle Way; the other ways lead to vicious extremes. For example, we all have appetites for food. This is normal; we need to ingest all kinds of nutrients to maintain healthfulness. Those who eat too much food become obese, an epidemic that afflicts American and, increasingly, all globalized cultures. At the other extreme are those who, even in the presence of abundant food, starve themselves to death. Westerners call this condition anorexia. The broad Middle Way means getting enough to eat, and enough good things to eat, on a daily basis. The human appetite for food, in and of itself, is simply part of nature's larger food chain. It is neither a sin nor a crime nor "bad karma" to hunger for food every few hours. However, you can control what you end up eating, along with how you obtain it and how you prepare it. The effects of ingestion partially determine how well or how poorly you live. Eating healthful food contributes to a wholesome life; eating junk food, to an unwholesome life. You are what you eat, as you are what you think.

Most human appetites are similar in this respect, whether appetites for food, drink, shelter, clothing, constancy, change, possessions, myths, legends, totems, relationships, sex, babies, status, money, power, you name it. Extreme denials and extreme indulgences confer little pleasure, and produce great suffering, even when practiced with right reason and goodwill. Working hard, for example, might be your duty, and you might also love to do it. Yet at some point "workaholism" becomes an extreme—when it starts to harm you and diminishes your capacity to help others—even if your work does good. Even good things can be taken to harmful extremes.

Normal expression of these appetites can diverge so much in men and women that we sometimes perceive one another as different species, or aliens from different planets (Mars and Venus, as John Gray explains so well[4]). The human spiritual journey is the same for all people with respect to its destination, namely the ninth level, but we are assigned different vehicles to take us there. Some vehicles are male, others female. Their differences should be acknowledged, valued, honored, cherished, and respected, not utilized as a basis for oppression or deconstruction.

As we will see at the end of this chapter, ordinary morality transcends deeds too. A good deed is neither a male nor female deed. It is neither masculine nor feminine. It is a human deed. Women and men both try to make themselves happy at the expense of others, which only leads to unhappiness. Mahayana Buddhism teaches that we can become happy—men and women—only by working for the happiness of others. Yet the tasks that women and men perform, for themselves or for others, for good or for ill, are not necessarily the same.

Both male chauvinism and gender feminism visit gross injustices upon human beings through the politicization of sex differences. Male chauvinists extend sex differences too far into culture so they can retain political power, thus unfairly excluding females from opportunities for fulfillment that they richly deserve. Gender feminists extend antirealist and neo-Marxist ideologies too far into nature, also for political gains, denying sex differences that reemerge inevitably in cultural contexts, and that no amount of social engineering or wishful thinking will eradicate. The conflicts produced by these contending extremes give rise to much suffering by both sexes and genders. The polarization of people, whether by the overassertion or denial of sex difference, is inimical to a shared sense of humanity, and therefore also to human happiness.

The Middle Way offers a balanced, realistic, and humanistic approach. It asserts that until we get to the ninth level of consciousness, sex differences do exist. But such differences are quite irrelevant to the deeper and overarching purpose of human existence, which is awareness and expression of the Buddha nature in yourself and others. Men and women can partake equally in their common humanity and the awakened state of consciousness accessible to all humans, which underlies and unifies the divisions produced by chromosomes and/or cultures. I will offer a compelling illustration of this point, drawn from Dr. Kawada's lecture, toward the end of this chapter.

## The Main Question

The main question that divides observers of sex difference, from Genesis to Plato, from suffragettes to postmodernists, from feminists to chauvinists, is the extent to which biology influences culture. In other words, where do we draw the line between nature and nurture? How much equality can we expect between the sexes? When we see unequal outcomes, to what extent are they a product of natural difference (which cannot easily or at all be changed), and to what extent are they a product of cultural conventions (which can be changed by moral or political will)?

At one extreme is a widespread traditional doctrine, which still holds sway in more than half the world, that asserts women are by definition inferior to men in many significant respects, and therefore that woman's place is subordinate to man's. That's the male supremacist account. At the other extreme is the neo-Marxist ideology that has pervaded the West since the 1960s, and has now attained the status of an unchallengeable dogma. It asserts that all the significant differences between men and women are "socially constructed"—that woman is historically enslaved by man, or is an exploited and oppressed social class, who needs only to be liberated in order to become his equal. Every cultural manifestation of sex difference is viewed as a political problem that can be solved by social engineering. The proponents of these two extremes have been openly at war for several generations (known in North America as gender wars), and their main casualty is humanity.

Here's an anecdote that paves the way to the heart of the debate. In 2005, Harvard president Larry Summers mused that innate sex differences may be responsible for the disparity between male and female achievement in natural sciences and mathematics. The repercussions of this statement were extreme. Male supremacists snorted, "So what? It's obvious." Radical feminists wanted Summers's head on a platter. Governed not by its motto (*Veritas*, or Truth), but by dictates of political correctness, Harvard University swiftly mobilized a regiment of publicists, diplomats, and political commissars to apologize for Summers and quash the debate.

Harvard has the largest endowment ($25 billion at this writing) and the greatest number of Nobel laureates on faculty (forty at this writing), among numerous other factors that contribute to its greatness. However, the Tao reminds us that the inevitable complement of greatness is terribleness. Harvard University's greatness—its history of academic success and prestige—is severely compromised by the present terribleness of its alterego: The People's Democratic University of Harvard, whose political commissars have systemically replaced higher education—starting in the liberal arts and metastasizing throughout the academy—with political indoctrination.

I had an opportunity to challenge one of Harvard's most senior political commissars—an influential man at the JFK School of Government who has advised both Democratic and Republican presidents—on the shameful suppressions of freedom of thought, speech, and inquiry that are hallmarks of campus culture, coast to coast. Shortly after Summers's pronouncement, this political commissar was dispatched to a private dinner party where the guests were debating the issue of sex differences in the human brain and their cultural consequences. He interrupted our debate to make what sounded like a paid political announcement—his "apology" for Summers. He began by reassuring us that he himself didn't know anything about science, but that he was convinced that President Summers should never have said what he said. We at the dinner party—male and female scientists, philosophers of science, public intellectuals, and business leaders—had two large problems with this utterance. First, if he didn't know anything about science, then how could he possibly judge whether Summers's claim had any merit? Second, universities should be committed to discussing, researching, and clarifying issues, to testing hypotheses and discovering scientific truths, instead of censoring politically incorrect questions and promulgating politically correct ideologies.

My argument to Harvard's political commissar was this: Maleness or femaleness, or sex difference, is innate and resides in the sex chromosomes. You are conceived, gestated, and born either male (XY) or female (XX). The first words uttered about you pertain to your sex: "It's a girl!" or "It's a boy!" To be sure, there is a continuum of sex difference, with rare hermaphrodites in the center, but there is also a concentration of characteristics at each pole. So the human species itself is heir to the most widespread "bipolar disorder" of all time: sexual dimorphism. Yet each sex contains vestiges of the other, too. Males and females are not polar opposites in the sense of positive and negative magnetic poles; rather, they are Taoist complements that spring from the common ground of humanity. Nonetheless, there are significant differences between males and females that have been either politically exaggerated or politically deconstructed.

Mary Wollstonecraft poignantly and succinctly observed that "either Nature has made a great difference between man and woman, or that civilization which has hitherto taken place in the world has been very partial."[5] Since it is now politically incorrect to assert "a great difference" between men and women (i.e., one owing to nature), every problem that arises from sex difference is currently blamed on civilization (i.e., on nurture). "Fix" culture, postmodernists claim, and you will "fix" sexual inequality. There's only one problem with this approach: "fixing" culture to account for biological sex differences goes against the very way that makes culture endure. The radicals who are trying to socially engineer male and female sameness are succeeding only in destroying our civilization. Equality is one thing; sameness is quite another.

Wollstonecraft is correct, of course, but more than she realized. It is true that nature "has made a great difference" between males and females, yet it is forbidden by political edict to say this throughout the extreme left culture. It is also true that civilization has been "very partial" toward males and against females for a long time in the West and remains "very partial" toward males and against females in the developing world, but chauvinists do not wish this to be said.

Fairness demands that we eliminate cultural bias. But in every century of human history we see the same mistake being made over and over again, a mistake that leads to constant conflict and victory only for extremists. The mistake is to create present and future unfairness in a futile attempt to "compensate" for past unfairness. Rousseau's spiteful revolutionary road has always led, and will always lead, not to Buddha's serenity, but to Robespierre's guillotine.

For a very long time, Western women were politically, economically, and socially disempowered. Sex difference was extended and expressed unfairly as culture difference. As with baboons and apes, anatomy was destiny. Then, during the twentieth century, Western women became politically, economically, and socially empowered. Today they are exercising their own power (which is a good thing) and they are also being "given power" to compensate for their past lack of empowerment (which is not a good thing). Now the pendulum of injustice has swung too far in the opposite direction. Instead of sex difference being used to exclude women unfairly, it is ignored in order to include them unfairly. And no one within our political or educational institutions is "allowed" to mention sex difference or its cultural effects, because that's not "with the program." (Let's ignore the craters and mountains on the moon, said the Jesuit political commissars. After all, Galileo's not "with the program.") Unfortunately, when "the program" subscribes to unchallengeable dogmas, it is not the truth that suffers. It is people and civilizations who are deluded and destroyed. Schopenhauer said, "The truth can wait, for it lives a long time." But comparatively speaking, we humans do not live a long time. Yes, we can experience "eternity in an instant," but an instant can also seem an eternity when one is suffering. And lies—no matter whom they're directed toward—make people suffer.

Masculinity is a cultural extension of maleness; femininity, of femaleness. There are objectively real cultural consequences of objectively real biological sex differences. I stand by this. It is a plain truth, whether "politically incorrect" or not. Do you disbelieve me? If you drive a car, you can confirm this truth for yourself in just a few minutes.

If you are a female living in a culture whose norms persist at the male chauvinist extreme, you are forbidden to drive at all. This prohibition reflects a Stone Age model of sexual division of labor. As I write these very words (in late 2005), the Saudi Arabian government is just now preparing to allow women to obtain driver's licenses. This is undoubtedly an important reform, one of many to come, some long overdue, that will together help usher the Arab world into the twenty-first century. Forbidding women to drive merely because they are female—like forbidding them literacy, education, and careers—is an unjust denial of their humanity. But males and females exhibit statistically significant differences in the ways that they drive. So equal opportunity to operate motor vehicles (which is good) still gives rise to observable differences in large populations of drivers: many males and females do not drive in the same way (which is undeniable). This example is holographic: Driving is only one among myriad human behaviors in which social consequences of sex difference are obvious to all but those blinded by dogmas. Throughout all mundane levels of existence, equality is not sameness.

## Cultural Evolution Illustrated

We in the (formerly) free West know this story well, for we have witnessed what women can accomplish when liberated from the fetters of second-class citizenship. The conventions of Victorian womanhood, for instance, confined affluent women to playing the roles of dolls in dollhouses. While many women undoubtedly relished and still relish certain aspects of being "dolls," others obviously chafed at the restrictions and constraints of their confinement.

For example, prior to World War I, British women were forbidden to drive buses and trucks, because such activities were deemed to be "unfeminine." By the same token, most women today do not aspire to be bus drivers or truck drivers, yet that is not a just reason to forbid the ones who do. Today, a century later, many women drive buses and trucks, and these professional women drive just as well as men, yet their proportions are much smaller. More than zero, but much less than 50 percent. I wonder whether Larry Summers would have ruffled the feminists' feathers had he asserted that natural sex differences might help explain why fewer women become truck drivers than do men.

During World War I, as the trenches of Europe became slaughterhouses of a generation of able-bodied men, British women were suddenly needed to do all kinds of "men's work" that had formerly been forbidden to them. American women experienced this during World War II as posters celebrating "Rosie the Riveter" attracted women to all kinds of occupations—like riveting and welding—that had previously been all-male by cultural convention, and not by any iron laws of nature.

British women experienced ongoing cultural evolution to a pronounced extent during the Battle of Britain, when they (along with handicapped male World War I veterans) were conscripted to ferry new fighter aircraft from the factories to the airfields, where male fighter pilots desperately awaited the planes. Thus, in barely one generation, British women evolved from being forbidden to drive buses, to being needed to ferry fighter aircraft. No Darwinian in his right mind would attribute this transformation to a favorable genetic mutation in British women. It is transparently a case of the cultural evolution of egalitarian social norms, ironically precipitated (like so many developments in science, technology, and social policy) by warfare—waged by dominant male hierarchies, often with the complicity of women.

So in late 2005, as our Saudi Arabian neighbors begin to frame their revolutionary policy of allowing females to drive cars, we see that they are more or less one century behind the West in this particular area of women's liberation. And while biological evolution typically requires millions of years to do its work, cultural evolution can ring in momentous changes—for better or worse—in a single generation.

The transformation of women from Victorian house dolls to blue-collar workers became most pronounced in the United States during World War II. As the U.S. Department of Transportation's Federal Highway Administration reports:

"From 1940 to 1945, the number of female workers rose by 50 percent, from 12 million to 18 million. In 1940, women constituted 8 percent of total workers employed in the production of durable goods. By 1945, this number increased to 25 percent. During the war years, women became streetcar conductors, taxicab drivers, business managers, commercial airline checkers, aerodynamic engineers, and railroad workers. Women operated machinery, streetcars, buses, cranes, and tractors. They unloaded freight, built dirigibles and gliders, worked in lumber mills and steel mills, and made munitions. In essence, women occupied almost every aspect of industry."[6]

The developing world—including many parts of Africa as well as large swaths of Islamic and Asian civilizations—still lag far behind the most developed nations, whose vibrant economies depend more than ever on women's full integration in the workforce, not only as manufacturers of goods but increasingly as providers of services.

At the same time, we should not lose sight of another fact. Although women of Rosie the Riveter's generation were willing and able and needed to perform all kinds of labor that had previously and chauvinistically been classified as "male," most women were still excluded from wartime combat. They assembled weapons but did not fire them; built warships but did not sail them into battle; ferried fighter aircraft but did not fly combat missions. From prehistory to 1976, women became wartime combatants only in the most desperate circumstances. Courageous women joined and fought and perished with the French Resistance, the Yugoslav partisans, the Warsaw ghetto uprising, the Viet Cong insurgency, and similar desperate causes, but only when circumstances had become so dire that all possibility of hearth and home, marriage and motherhood, liberty and opportunity, had been denied them.

In 1976, the American military establishment capitulated to feminism, and with the passage of the Stratton Bill opened its premier military academies for the first time to women, which has created a legion of controversies, sex scandals, lawsuits, debates, and opportunities for social scientific research (where not politically prohibited). The issue of women in combat is a thorny one indeed, and has been since the time of Plato. It divides men and women, and there is no consensus on the horizon. U.S. admiral Elmo Zumwalt (among others) has observed that, in many respects, women make finer soldiers than men—just as they often make finer students and finer workers. I happen to agree with him, and we shall revisit this point anon. But by the same token, women may also make "finer" terrorists than men, and that is surely a cause for concern.

Women can make crueler torturers than men as well. Consider the Jesuit martyrs of Lower Canada, who were caught and tortured to death by the Iroquois. When the braves had finished with them, they were turned over to the women, who prolonged their agonies and death throes much more ingeniously than the men. To be egalitarian, we must give credit wherever it is due. Just as women are often much kinder than men, so they can also be more cruel.

On the one hand, proponents of social justice applaud the integration of women into the workplaces of the developed world, which, for the first time in hominid and human history, grants them full participation as providers in precisely the same ways as men had evolved as providers. But on the other hand, the hope that the world will automatically become a more peaceful place because of women's liberation—which supposedly allows her "nurturing" and "caring" nature to extend itself into political arenas and international relations—is demonstrably false. This hope, based on the misguided notion that "violence is male,"[8] was held out by men as well as women, and enjoyed its heyday during the 1970s and 1980s.[9] But the 1960s and 1970s saw a spate of urban terrorism in Western Europe, whose most notorious exponents were the Baader-Meinhof gang (Red Army Faction) in Germany and the Red Brigades (*Brigate Rosse*) in Italy. Their members were neo-Marxist urban guerrillas, some well educated and from affluent backgrounds, who kidnapped and murdered white male politicians, bankers, military officers, and industrialists. The "crimes" of these victims were their contributions to the highest standards of liberty and prosperity in European history. The terrorists styled themselves as urban equivalents of Che Guevara, emulated the emergent terrorism of the Palestinian Liberation Organization (PLO), traded on the weakness of Western European security and its political appeasement of PLO terrorism, and earned their income by kidnapping, extortion, robbery, and narco-trafficking. At the height of their violent urban crime spree in the seventies and eighties, fourteen of twenty-two of Europe's most wanted terrorists—that is, 63 percent—were women.[10]

For all human beings, men or women, liberation does not mean exchanging one yoke of bondage for another, nor does it mean reversing the roles of oppressor and oppressed. The cycle of human suffering is broken neither by extremes of chauvinism nor of radicalism, but only by The Middle Way.

Even peaceful revolutions have a price. Indeed, the decline of macrocosmic Western civilization is in no small measure attributable to the demise of its microcosm, namely the nuclear family, which cannot, has not, and will not survive the condition of having two breadwinners but no homemakers. Women seem to know this too, and are learning the hard way that their integration into developed economies does not guarantee them human fulfillment or personal happiness. In my practice as a philosophical counselor, I have seen a steady stream of young, intelligent, and successful professional women who do not derive fulfillment or happiness from producing impressive business cards, or even from earning decent wages. Their American higher educations subjected most of them to political indoctrination by radical feminists, who brainwashed them into imagining that they would become fulfilled and happy by living and working, more or less, after the fashion of men. But the human female biological clock obliges these young women to acknowledge a deeper truth: Motherhood is not a social construct, rather the fulfillment of a woman's natural purpose, and her passport to lasting satisfaction. But the pressures of trying to be both a good careerist and a good mother are truly formidable. Some exceptionally talented women can juggle both, and can even manage to be good wives on top of that, but they often end up sleep-deprived and stressed, which causes other problems. Ironically, many of these young women say that they envy their mothers or grandmothers, who were "unliberated" housewives. This is exactly what women in the former Soviet Union said, after having experienced "coerced liberation," and working alongside men as "equal" comrades: They envied the American housewives of the golden age of capitalism. Insofar as feminism has mutated from the well-intended emancipation of women to a vicious war of matriarchy against patriarchy, it has swung, like an overenergized pendulum, from one extreme to another. Is it possible to liberate women without devaluing or demonizing men? Not in the West, at any rate.

It appears that human beings find satisfaction difficult, and dissatisfaction easy. And women may experience more ways of being dissatisfied than men. In the developing world, women suffer from a lack of equal opportunity. But in the developed world, they suffer from a surfeit. Equal opportunity does not automatically lead to happiness for anyone, except when they reach the ninth level of consciousness.

## Equal Opportunities Spell Unequal Outcomes

Equal opportunities for women and men often lead to disparate outcomes between them. If a disparity is due to social convention, then it can be corrected by cultural evolution. If a disparity is due to natural difference, then it cannot be corrected by cultural evolution, and especially not by social engineering. Yet these two facets of humanity, nature and nurture, are intertwined. So cultural corrections can also serve to highlight natural differences. Thus equal opportunities for women and men to become truck drivers, theoretical physicists, or heads of state does not necessarily translate into equal numbers of women and men becoming truck drivers, theoretical physicists, or heads of state. In the twentieth century, Western women have come a long way: from confined Victorian house dolls to elected leaders. But just as it was extremely unfair to deny women equal opportunity, so preventing them from manifesting their excellence, it is also extremely unfair to establish quota systems that compel arbitrary outcomes, which only empower mediocrity or incompetence in place of excellence.

And this is what our Saudi Arabian neighbors will discover if they correct the social convention that prohibits females from driving.

Allowing women to drive does not turn them into men; rather, it turns them into female drivers. Sex differences are plainly evident behind the wheel, and as usual at both extremes.

If you live in a culture whose norms are more egalitarian and in which women have been driving cars (and other vehicles) since the early to mid-twentieth century, you know perfectly well that sex difference manifests as gender difference in driving behavior. The majority of drivers—male and female alike—are statistically in the middle of a normal distribution: We don't notice much difference, because they drive "normally"—men a little faster than average and women a little slower. But at the extremes, males tend toward aggression and recklessness; females, toward indecision and fearfulness.

It is patently obvious that these gender differences in driving behavior are the reflections of sex differences in the brain, entrenched by millions of years of primate evolution. Aggressiveness in male primates was favored as their best way to ascend a male dominance hierarchy, and to attract females. Submissiveness in female primates was favored as their best way to invite the protection and paternity of dominant males. Giving humans cars and drivers' licenses—a cultural development a century or so old—does not override fifteen million years of primate evolution. Women holding driver's licenses does not alter sex differences or gender differences, but does provide social scientists the opportunity to study the differences with a view to reducing accidents. Most traffic accidents happen at the extremes: too much recklessness or too much hesitancy. Too much yang, or too much yin. The best drivers, male and female alike, balance yin and yang behind the wheel.

If the People's Democratic Universities of America did not impose a monolithic culture of political correctness, prohibiting freedom of thought, speech, and academic inquiry, it would be interesting to open an experimental driving academy, and see to what extent reckless aggression and fearful hesitancy alike can be modified by learning. It would be useful to ascertain to what extent cultural reprogramming can override biological hardwiring. Perhaps Harvard should undertake the research, and maybe the Saudis would care to fund it. But we can never discover such things if we are governed by extremist cultures that use sex difference as the basis of exclusionary social policy, or by extremist cultures that deny sex difference altogether because of politicization.

## Equality Is Not Sameness

Current gender conflicts are inflamed and escalated by ideological confusions of gender feminists, and their male apologists, who dogmatically but mistakenly insist that equality means sameness. But equality is not sameness. Two plus three equals four plus one, but they are not the same. I like apples and oranges and pears and bananas equally well, but they are not the same. I hope you love all your children equally, and yet can tell them apart—because they are not the same. Having equal rights and opportunities does not make everybody attain the same outcomes. Giving political or social equality to women does not make women the same as men. Confusing equality with sameness is one of a few widespread but monumental errors of "postmodern thought" (pardon the oxymoron) committed by women and men alike, which along with confusing "right" with "privilege" and "offense" with "harm," have sanctioned measures that are eroding the foundations of Western civilization. Beyond that, confusion makes people more unhappy than they need to be, and more deluded than is good for them.

Males and females see many things differently, starting with what it means to be male or female. Since men and women are equal in their humanity, but different in their mundane ways of manifesting it, they can easily choose to demonize one other. Men have demonized women for centuries. For example, European Inquisitions burned one in ten women at the height of their deranged persecutions, and the Inquisitors were convinced they were doing God's work. Viewed in terms of Buddhist psychology, their self-righteous violence was a manifestation of their ignorance and fear—ignorance of the way the world works in reality, and fear of women whom they ignorantly accused of witchcraft. Their ignorance and fear together produced anger, one of three toxins (envy and greed are the other two) that poison the human mind with deluded cravings and lead to the commission of heinous acts. When men are angry they tend to lash out, because that is the first reflex of their primate heritage. So-called "witch hunts"—as such sustained outbursts of persecution have since become known—can only be carried out by those possessed by the very "devils" they claim to be exorcising in others. These "devils" are the by-products of their own intoxicating anger.

That said, women are equally capable of becoming poisoned by anger, which they tend to express differently than men. That's obviously and demonstrably true, even if we're forbidden to say it or even think it at Harvard. Whereas men tend to lash out in anger, women tend to internalize their anger, transforming it into depression or vengefulness. In the West, where politicization of sex difference has inhibited wholesome sexual expression and fomented a lot of anger in the general populace, acute and chronic depression have skyrocketed, to the delight of pharmaceutical companies that encourage depression and sexual dysfunction, and profit from these afflictions. Unhappy males tend toward sadism—inflicting pain and suffering on others in futile attempts to become happy themselves; whereas unhappy females tend toward masochism—inflicting pain and suffering on themselves in equally futile (but distinctively different) attempts to become happy themselves. These are behavioral consequences of biological sex difference. They are not social constructions.

Here are two more sex differences, which turn out to be correlated. We observe larger proportions of male leaders than female ones, and larger proportions of female depressives than males. These two phenomena correlate with at least one biological common denominator, namely serotonin levels. Serotonin is secreted into and reabsorbed by the brain in a regular cycle. Its levels are strongly correlated with happiness, confidence, and self-esteem. It is well documented and widely observed that women are often less happy, less confident, and less self-esteeming than men. This is undoubtedly related to at least one sex difference in neuroendocrinology: Females tend to have lower serotonin levels than do males. Formulations like Prozac are "serotonin reuptake inhibitors"— they inhibit the reabsorption of serotonin by the brain, thus enhancing its presence, which supposedly promotes more happiness, confidence, and self-esteem. At the same time, recent primate studies show that as monkeys ascend their dominance hierarchies, their serotonin levels climb correspondingly high.

This is undoubtedly an interactive process. To ascend a dominance hierarchy, a primate must be able to sustain higher-than-average levels of serotonin. In turn, the ability to sustain such levels would express itself in the capacity to ascend a dominance hierarchy. Human females who become leaders by ascent (rather than by "empowerment") manifest the same leadership qualities of confidence and self-esteem that male leaders manifest, but perhaps statistically fewer women sustain sufficient serotonin levels to compete as effectively in male dominance hierarchies. Male chauvinist cultures have erred unjustly in excluding all women from politics. In fact, some women can lead as effectively as men, and many women can hold elected office and undertake political work just as well as men. Leadership is a human quality, not a male or female one. The history of Western civilization, with its emphasis on individual liberty, is sprinkled with women who have excelled as leaders, from Joan of Arc to Catherine the Great, from Queen Elizabeth I to Queen Isabella; from Margaret Thatcher to Catherine de Medici.

Even so, proportionately fewer women than men have attained such greatness to date. Canada and the United States lead the world in women's liberation. In 2004, both nations conducted populist, TV-driven polls to identify the "greatest" Canadians and the "greatest" Americans. Not one woman made the Canadian top ten, and only one woman (Oprah) made the American top ten. BBC then conducted its own poll of America, whose number-one pick (Homer Simpson) reflects BBC's animus as well as America's precipitous decline in international opinion, but whose top ten contains no women.[11] Naturally, all these "great" men had "great" mothers, just as many had "great" wives, who derived contentment from being the "power behind the throne." No man can become great without the corresponding greatness of women—either by their presence as partners or in their absence as muses—but this correspondence of greatness may still come to be expressed in different ways.

If similar polls were conducted to identify the most "terrible" Canadians and Americans, men would dominate those lists as well. What does this mean? Among other things, it suggests that men are more extreme than women, in terms of their capacities for greatness and terribleness alike. Said another way, women are more average than men in certain respects, and therefore less prone to populate the extremes of greatness and terribleness.

Feminists may be correct to assert that it will require some time for women to make up for the "deficit" of female greatness owing to "historical disadvantage." But they may also err in seeking equal proportions of female leaders, because they neglect to take into account that female primates many not possess the brain chemistry of leadership (among other attributes) in the same proportions as do males. Yes, women can equal men in the quality of their leadership, but women may or may not produce great leaders in the same proportions as men. Equality is not necessarily sameness. And that is why the myth of "female underrepresentation" must be debunked: We cannot assess the quality of social justice on the basis of sophomoric head counts alone. Different proportions of men and women in different fields may be indicative of natural divergencies in ability and preference. Equal opportunities do not necessarily lead to equal outcomes; unequal outcomes do not necessarily arise from social injustice.

Male primates become fulfilled by ascending to their fitting stations as protectors and providers in the dominance hierarchy. Female primates become fulfilled by winning the protection and provision of dominant males, and mothering their progeny. These differing means of fulfillment are observable across the primate spectrum, from monkeys to apes to humans. Ask the average man to define himself, and he starts by producing his business card, or stating his occupation. Ask the average woman to define herself, and she starts by telling you her marital status and whether she has children. Even the most successful and powerful women in the world, who have ascended human dominance hierarchies on the basis of being liberated to express their natural abilities (as opposed to being "socially engineered" to ascend to positions they could not otherwise reach) will tell you about their marriages and children.

As we will see, one pervasive effect of women's liberation is a precipitous decline in birth rates in the affluent world. This suggests that even the evolutionarily ancient female primate operating system called "motherhood" can be reprogrammed by cultural evolution. However, the price of this reprogramming—the deconstruction of motherhood—is the imminent demographic collapse of Western civilization itself. So motherhood is hardly a social construct; rather, a precondition for the existence of society itself.

Like all primates, human males and females are equal in their capacities to experience biological and social fulfillment, but far from the same in the strategies and goals they have evolved, over millions of years and via the first eight levels of consciousness, for doing so. Unlike the other primates, and according to Buddhist psychology, human males and females are equal in their capacity to experience the ninth level of consciousness, have exactly the same experience of it ("one taste"), and moreover come to experience it in exactly the same way: The Middle Way. Here and here alone are human equality and human sameness conjoined. Male chauvinism and gender feminism succeed only in distorting or denying human sex difference, and thereby perpetuating needless human suffering.

## Mutual Demonization of the Sexes

It is easy and tempting but also counterproductive to use sex differences—and the gender differences that arise from them—to demonize one sex or gender from the standpoint of the other. Men and women are mutually desirous, and hunger for each other, but at the same time they are mutually aversive, and repel one another. From time out of mind, men have demonized aspects of womanhood that they find infuriating or irritating; and since becoming "liberated" and politicized, women have likewise demonized aspects of manhood that they find repugnant or abhorrent. Men and women need to spend time together to explore their mutually inclusive capacities for romance, love, affection, and parenting; yet they also need to spend time apart—males bonding with other males and females supporting other females—in order to experience their mutually exclusive manifestations of sex and gender difference.

Only in Buddhist sanghas do I see men and women coming together in search of their common humanity. There, sex difference and gender difference alike are transcended—and not, as in so many theistic religions, demonized or segregated. In Buddhist communities, the lower levels of consciousness are renounced for the highest. There, men and women resemble Plato's Guardians, and could (but need not) do exactly what Plato envisioned of the most trustworthy citizens in his Republic; that is, wrestle naked in the Gymnasium without Eros intruding on their exercise. There, in the sanghas, we can even discuss sex differences and their social consequences. Unlike Harvard's political commissars, most Buddhists are unafraid of free speech.[12]

My top-ten list of greatest aphorisms contains the following one coined by a woman, Anaïs Nin. She said, "We don't see things as they are; we see them as we are." How perceptive of her to notice this. Men and women have equal capacities to see. There is no sex difference in the parts of the eye itself, and the internal images relayed to the visual cortex are probably similar if not identical as well. But after that the similarity ends. When Anaïs Nin says that we "see" things as "we" are, she means that we interpret the same images differently, according to structural differences in our brains, functional differences in our neuropsychology of perception, and gender differences in our behavior—all of which arise from sex difference itself. Only at the ninth level of consciousness, which transcends sex difference, do men and women alike see "that which is." At every other level, they see "as they are"—equally in eyesight, but differently in interpreting the images. Placed in the same social setting, or contemplating the same social phenomena, men and women tend to notice different things.

Let me give you an example. Many of my friends, male and female, are authors. Let's call one of them "John Smith." One day I mentioned John to a female colleague—call her "Jane Doe"—a savvy and professionally successful woman. Jane also knows several other women who know John, and when I mentioned John to her, Jane's immediate reaction was, "John Smith? He's a little devil."

What did Jane mean by this? I interpreted it in one way, but as it turns out she intended it in quite another. The meaning I attributed is essentially male; the one she intended, essentially female. When Jane called John a "little devil," at first I couldn't believe it, because I know he is a spiritual warrior in the service of good. Nevertheless, John has a dark side. We all do. I also know that there's usually only one way for a man to become a little devil: by making a deal with a bigger devil. This is the story of Faust and Mephistopheles, Adam and the forbidden fruit of Eden, C. S. Lewis's *The Screwtape Letters*, Frank Sinatra and the Godfather. It is an archetypal story, rooted in the eighth level of consciousness, and thus reflected in every culture's myths and legends. People barter their souls to the devil (or his local sales rep) in exchange for some transitory pleasure or power, then pay a heavy price—perhaps for all eternity. So my immediate interpretation of Jane's remark was that John Smith had bartered his soul in exchange for fame and fortune. He would not be the first, nor the last, to strike that nefarious bargain. I felt sorry for John, if this were the case.

All that flashed through my mind as I formulated my question to Jane: "What makes you call him a little devil?"

Without hesitation, she replied "He has a woman in every port."

At that, I laughed aloud. This is a perfect illustration of seeing things "as we are." Many men have had, or have, or aspire to have, "a woman in every port." Maintaining an international harem is a cultural extension of our primate heritage, which amounts to little more than furnishing a dominant male gorilla with a passport. Likewise, every port seems to harbor a sufficient number of women who play the complementary role. From a male point of view, having a woman in every port is a sign of a man's fame, or wanderlust, or being a sailor, all of which women generally find attractive. And also from a male point of view, having a woman in every port could be one of the "payoffs" for making a deal with the devil. But in that case, John Smith is not a little devil because he has a woman in every port (the female view); rather, he has a woman in every port because he is a little devil (the male view). There is a monumental sex difference at work here: It has the power to reverse the way in which cause and effect are perceived, up to and including all the causes and effects that move the world. Throughout the eight levels of consciousness, we see things as *we* are—and this fuels endless quarrels between the sexes, who see them differently. At the ninth level, we see things as *they* are.

So which is "the cause" and which is "the effect"? One might be tempted, like postmodernists and moral relativists, to suppose that each way seems right to its respective perceiver, and that nothing "privileges" either way over the other.

The Middle Way declares differently. There are causes and there are effects, and they should not be confused. Suffering is removed by removing its causes, not its effects. It is likewise terminated by removing one's consciousness from the realm of cause and effect together, which is done by making cause and effect simultaneous, at which point they mutually annihilate. It is akin to stepping outside space-time. Without cause, suffering cannot arise. Without effect, it cannot propagate. The Middle Way not only elaborates such elegant theories, it also teaches practices that confirm them by experience. The human moral in this case is: If you see a devil in someone else, make sure you didn't put it there yourself.

### Unequal versus Equal Opportunities, and Different Outcomes

If we look at some large-scale outcomes of human civilization, we can see that men and women have attained extremely disparate results. These disparities indeed support both of Wollstonecraft's contentions: that nature has made significant differences between males and females, and that (until the twentieth century) civilizations have tended to favor men, and disfavor women.

Literacy is one of the biggest indicators of a culture's partiality or impartiality. While oral traditions once served a vital purpose, and while small isolated tribes managed to survive without a written tradition, since the advent of modernity literacy has become a prerequisite for and passport to a decent life in the global village. Those who learn to read and write at an early age have a considerable and lifelong advantage over those who do not. And regrettably, females in the developing world have been excluded en masse from becoming literate, and so have been excluded from all the opportunities that literacy confers. Illiterate women comprise about 70 percent of the world's poorest people. They are less likely to look after their children as well as literate women, less likely to send them to school, and thus more likely to perpetuate their poverty trap. Female illiteracy is truly a vicious circle that can be broken only in conjunction with related socioeconomic, religious, and political reforms. As UNICEF asserts, "Gender inequality is evident in virtually every country, rich or poor. But inequality in education is particularly important because it undermines the struggle for equality in almost all other fields."[13] (We will look at educational extremes in the coming chapters.) Female illiteracy is also an ironic vicious circle, because one well-established sex difference is greater verbal facility among girls than boys.[14]

In cultures where girls have equal access to literacy, they will read on average more than boys, and this tendency continues into adulthood. In the world's largest book publishing markets, women read more than men. They do not, however, read the same things. Equality of literacy does not produce sameness in literary taste. Both sexes appreciate classics, but their mundane tastes are radically divergent—as reflected in the completely different contents of mainstream "women's" versus "men's" magazines.

Sex difference and gender difference are not eradicated by equal opportunity. Women can become pregnant; men cannot. Men can impregnate; women cannot. Women can become mothers; men cannot. Men can become fathers; women cannot. These roles are biologically different, and will always be different, regardless of whether men and women have equal rights to education or employment. And these different roles mandate corresponding cultural differences in attitudes, preferences, tastes, and interests.

I have spent decades in universities, teaching and learning on campuses all over the world. I've taught students from more than 150 countries on the campus of the City College of New York alone. It is empirically clear to me that, given equal literacy and freedom to choose courses, males are on average more interested in natural sciences (physics, chemistry, engineering) and mathematics than are females; and females with scientific inclinations are on average more attracted to the biological, social, and behavioral sciences (biology, psychology, sociology). There is much more equality of interest in professions such as medicine, law, or journalism—essentially applied sciences and performing arts—in which women and men excel much more equally.

I have seen feminist educators try time and again to influence more women to study mathematics and natural science, by persuasion and coercion, until the proportions of female students in such programs reach one-quarter or one-third that of males. What happens next is influenced by gender difference, not politics. Time and again, significantly more females than males drop out of math and natural science courses, opting instead for social sciences, medicine, law, or humanities. Since the 1960s, radical feminists have at the same time loudly and persistently criticized science and mathematics (along with men who excel at them), because these radicals are caught in their own trap of untruth. They are committed to the false premise that if women and men are given equal opportunity to pursue higher education, they will automatically evidence equal interest in every subject. At the other extreme, male chauvinists do not wish to acknowledge that some females are perfectly capable of doing mathematics, physics, and engineering.

Between these two extremes, we see the empirical truth: More men than women are attracted to mathematics and natural science, and more women than men are attracted to social sciences, professions, and performance arts. Natural difference surely accounts for some of the disparity in numbers of male versus female geniuses in theoretical science. Consider the 1927 Solvay Conference, attended by the most brilliant theoretical physicists of the era (including some of the greatest who have ever lived.) One woman—Marie Curie—qualified to participate on her merits.[15] But as Larry Summers discovered, merely to hypothesize that this empirical disparity owes something to natural differences is to commit "thoughtcrime" against the tyranny of political correctness.

Women are perfectly capable of learning calculus, just as men are perfectly capable of learning knitting. As an undergraduate student, I used to tutor women in mathematics and physics, and was sought out because I specialized in cases of "math neurosis." All my female students passed. They were all capable of solving math and physics problems, and most of them simply needed extra encouragement and clear explanation. It was also clear to me that most of them didn't *love* math or physics, or find it *thrilling* to prove a theorem or solve a problem, as many men do. Women are certainly capable of exercising dispassionate logic, but most have little interest in making a career of it. Human relationships interest them much more, and for a very good reason: They have evolved this way. By contrast, abstract relations of ideas interest men much more, and for a very good reason: They have evolved this way. These differences are not "social constructs"; they are normally distributed social manifestations of sexual dimorphism. Equality of opportunity does not lead to sameness of outcome.

Male chauvinists assert that females are incapable of mathematical and scientific genius by reason of their sex alone. Gender feminists cite an "historical conspiracy" of "male oppression" of females, "preventing" them from displaying mathematical and scientific—as well as literary—genius. The Middle Way can resolve this clash of extremisms, but only for those who are willing to abandon their prejudices on both sides of the issue.

### Where Have All the Female Geniuses Gone?

Before the senior political commissar from Harvard arrived at the dinner party to admonish us on behalf of Big Sister and to insure that we would all celebrate "diversity" by thinking only preapproved thoughts, the assembled company of accomplished women and men had managed to agree on some important points, and to disagree on others.

For example, we had agreed that gender disparities in the developing world are mostly due to cultural suppressions of women, and not to sex differences in the brain. We had agreed that women's liberation in the West has enriched women's lives, but has also complicated their lives and made women prone to new kinds of unhappiness—possibly and partly because of ancient sex differences in the brain. We even agreed that disparities of income between men and women are not primarily (or not at all) caused by a universal male conspiracy to pay women less than men, but that women tend to value themselves less than men, to ask for less than men, and to settle for less than men—and that this may be partly due to sex differences in the brain. We had also agreed that the ubiquitous phenomenon of female underachievement needs to be studied more closely. Time and again, we have all seen brilliant female students and talented female professionals turn down gilt-edged career-enhancing opportunities that might have jeopardized their relationships with less-accomplished boyfriends, strained their marriages, or deprived them of time to mother their families. Human social priorities are heavily influenced by primate evolutionary programs, whose operations entail sex differences in the brain.

The women at this dinner had also expressed their horror at the unbridled promiscuity of the current teenage female generation, whose practice of "hooking up" (i.e., indulging in casual sex without any emotional content) seems to contradict the "eternal" female preoccupation with "relationships." Indeed, if women's liberation and radical feminism have led to this pass, then they have succeeded only in unraveling the very social fabric that makes relationships possible.

The last question we were debating, before being instructed in the politically correct answer ("It is forbidden to ask this question"), was a difficult one indeed. It was Larry Summers's question: How do we account for the preponderance of male over female genius in creative arts and sciences? As usual, extremists of the right claimed that women are by nature intellectually inferior to men, and therefore cannot be geniuses. As usual, extremists of the left claimed that an oppressive conspiracy of "white male heterosexual patriarchal hegemonists" has, from time immemorial, prevented women from displaying their genius, which they possess in equal measure to men.

I will offer you my own inimitable answer, which endeavors to uphold truths and reject falsehoods from both extremes. I would like you to bear in mind two ideas. First, most sciences are divided into theoretical and experimental (or "pure" and "applied") branches. Second, we similarly divide the arts into creative and performing branches. Since becoming emancipated in the twentieth century, Western women have very swiftly demonstrated all kinds of excellence in experimental and applied sciences, such as medicine and engineering, as well as across the spectrum of performing arts—including music, dance, theater, film, law, and politics. Even though women may not be as well represented as men in some of these areas, they nonetheless show equal capacity to perform at the highest levels. From such copious evidence, we must surely acknowledge that woman's historical absence of contributions in these areas were a result of cultural biases against them, as opposed to any natural deficit of talent or indeed of genius. I have learned much from many brilliant women, who have excelled in fields too numerous to name since being afforded equal opportunities.

Then again, women have not (or have not yet) demonstrated the same capacities for achievement in the most austere echelons of theoretical sciences and creative arts. Pure mathematics, symbolic logic, theoretical physics, and rigorous philosophy, as well as music composition, poetry, painting, and architecture of immortal quality, continue to be created mostly by men, albeit with noteworthy exceptions. Freud had surmised that attaining the summit of creative insight requires (among other things) the sublimation of sexual energy, and he observed that women do not sublimate sexual energy in the same ways as men. In any case, it is this conspicuous absence of female genius in theoretical sciences and creative arts that prompted Larry Summers's comments, and that became the focus of our dinner debate until the political commissar intruded to dictate the Party Line.

I digress to identify one apparently creative field in which women have enjoyed considerable success since being permitted to express themselves in it, and that of course is writing. Female authors, and some gifted ones indeed, have proliferated under their own names following the Victorian prohibitions that suppressed talents like George Eliot's. Yet even within the vast field of writing, males comprise larger proportions of immortal bards, playwrights, novelists, and historians. Virginia Woolf penned a compelling condemnation of cultural bias against female authors,[16] claiming that if Shakespeare had been born a woman, that is to say born with his literary brain housed in a woman's body, she would never have been permitted to write and produce plays. A female Shakespeare, opines Woolf, would have been misunderstood, mistreated, abused, ostracized, slandered, persecuted, and mostly likely driven to early suicide instead of great renown.

I believe that Virginia Woolf's claim is meritorious, although perhaps not quite as she intended. She is saying that a female literary genius would not have been accepted by society, and so would have perished of persecution, neglect, or suicide. From an historical point of view, however, it is clear that male geniuses have not been readily accepted either, often not for decades and frequently not in their lifetimes, and precisely because the nature of genius itself is utterly nonconformist. Its allegiance is to unorthodox or even heterodox ideas, to discovery of novel truths, or to creation of original works; and not to mere conformity with entrenched norms, lip service to received untruths, or recitation of popular catechisms, all for the sake of being "accepted" by society.

One of the most significant social consequences of sex differences, observed since antiquity and confirmed by modern psychology, is that women are statistically much more conforming than men to prevalent social norms of all kinds, whereas men are much more likely to rebel, to reform and reshape norms to suit their visions. Moreover, the emotional support that women draw from groups is dependent on their conformity with the group itself—conformity to its opinions, tastes, fashions, behaviors, and lifestyles—in a word, to all its norms. Even Rousseau— the archenemy of liberty, humanity, and Western civilization, and so the patron saint of deconstructionists—took considerable pains to describe in terms of virtues and vices exactly what postfeminist Phyllis Chesler reconfirms with social science: Autonomy of thought, and not caring a fig what others think of one, are virtues in a man but vices in a woman; whereas conformity of thought, and caring above all else what others think of one, are virtues in a woman and vices in a man.[17]

So my reply to Woolf is this: Most females were evolved to conform to norms, and not to flout them. The Galileos, the Beethovens, the van Goghs, the Cantors, the Dostoyevskys, the Einsteins of this world had to be geniuses to accomplish what they did, but they also needed to be men in order to survive the vicissitudes of genius long enough to create their mature and lasting works. They had to endure torments, persecutions, inquisitions, isolations, rejections, impediments, imprisonments—not to mention envies, hatreds, cruelties, calumnies, and neglects of their peers, and also had to stave off or quarantine the condition of madness that so often accompanies and ultimately encroaches on such creative minds. All this became grist for their mills. Even so, many succumbed to suicide. Virginia Woolf is absolutely right to observe that most women could not survive the "gifts" that so often accompany such creative genius, but not just because society would ostracize them (that goes without saying);

more so because women were evolved to be embraced, loved, and cherished by families, support groups, and communities, not banished from them. Moreover, if there were a female Pythagoras, Euclid, Newton, Gauss, Gödel, or Ramanujan, no power on earth could keep such women from bearing the fruits of their mathematical genius and delivering them to the world. On balance, "oppression" alone is not a meritorious excuse.

Time will tell whether women of immortal genius emerge from women's liberation and feminism's corrupted revolution, and in what proportion compared with men. My guess is: more than zero (contra the male chauvinists), and less than half (contra the gender feminists). When important universities like Harvard start researching the matter, instead of dictating politically correct dogmas, we'll do better than guesswork.

At one extreme, Western civilization is crumbling from the politicization of sex difference, and denial of its social consequences. At the other extreme, the developing world is struggling to embrace Western civilization, and to free itself from the pervasive injustice and dire poverty that ensue from overasserting the social consequences of sex difference. You see, Mary Wollstonecraft was correct on both counts: Nature has made a difference and nurture has been too partial. So where's The Middle Way?

## Aristotelian and Confucian Views of Woman

When it comes to Woman, Aristotle and Confucius each contribute a vital perspective concerning extremes to be avoided. Buddha is the most humanistic of the ABCs, and so we will give him the last word.

Aristotle's view of women, in general, was much the same as the global view that prevailed until the twentieth century: He emphasized the obvious differences, and proffered the usual excuses, as a rationale for sustaining what amounts to a male dominance hierarchy.[18] Women were excluded from Aristotle's Lyceum, as they were excluded from higher education for subsequent centuries and millennia. Even archenemies of Aristotelian civilization such as Rousseau took it for granted that boys and girls should have different educations, as a preparation for their different adulthoods.[19]

Speaking as a professor who has taught in sexually integrated classrooms for decades, I can assert from experience that women make finer students than men, on average, in several respects. Here are two. First, young women possess on average greater verbal skills than do young men (a sex difference), and reading and writing are essential to learning. Second, the female archetype is yin, the Receptive: hence women in the classroom are more receptive to ideas, and less confrontational, than are men. This is also quite consistent with Aristotle's vital notion of individual excellence, which he elaborated for men but failed to extend to women because of his emphasis on differences. Women have all kinds of human excellences that must be developed virtuously for them to become fulfilled as human beings.

But at the same time, Aristotle was the first philosopher to warn us that the human being is a political animal. As such, any human endeavor under the sun can become politicized—as has sex difference in the American gender wars. If Aristotle could witness the absurdity of the politicization of sex difference, and if he could behold much of the cant and hatred of men, and of science, that passes for feminist "scholarship"—which is politically immunized from quality control at Harvard and throughout the American Gulag of higher education—he might be tempted to say, "I told you so." All this only exacerbates gender conflicts, and does not resolve them. Nonetheless, he told us so.

Similarly, we find wisdom but also limitations in the Confucian picture. Confucius is right to uphold the importance of the family, and woman's place in it—and most women who are not spiteful Marxists or vengeful gender feminists implicitly endorse Confucius, by assiduously seeking husbands, babies, and the emotional fulfillments of motherhood and family life. Jobs remain second priority to a majority of women, even to women who are professionally successful. The "motherhood" program is the most powerful feature of the female operating system, and the hierarchy of the family is essential to its proper function. Woman most naturally and most happily fulfills her role as a mother when, simultaneously, Man most naturally and happily fulfills his role as a protector of and provider for his family. Confucian cultures have long understood the inviolability of balanced order in the maintenance of social harmony, and so they have also understood (as have Vedic cultures) the importance of service. The immutable order of nature, as clearly reflected in such cultures, is this: Woman fulfills herself by serving her man; Man fulfills himself by serving his sovereign; sovereign fulfills himself by serving the Mandate of Heaven. As long as each one dutifully follows the Way (Tao), everyone can attain peace and prosperity.

The Japanese code of Bushido, alloyed as it was with Confucianism and Buddhism, produced an elegant and elaborate version of this order, in which men and women respected, honored, and valued one another by seeing things as they are, and by surrendering to the doctrine of service. As Inazo Nitobe explained to Westerners in his classic work, *Bushido*:

"Woman's surrender of herself to the good of her husband, home and family, was as willing and honorable as the man's self-surrender to the good of his lord and country. Self-renunciation, without which no life-enigma can be solved, was the key-note of the loyalty of man as well as of the domesticity of woman. She was no more the slave of man than was her husband of his liege-lord . . . I say the doctrine of service, which is the greatest that Christ preached and was the sacred key-note of His mission—so far as that is concerned, Bushido was based on eternal truth."[20]

What truth? That we are all born equally to serve, yet no two persons serve in exactly the same capacities. We are equal, but different.

The liberation of Western women from familial hierarchies has made many women professionally successful but personally unfulfilled. Economies boom, but social orders implode. The disintegration of the nuclear family itself, along with the precipitous decline in birthrates among the most affluent Western nations, has bequeathed the West a phase of unprecedented short-term economic prosperity, but at the possible longer-term cost of its inability to sustain its own civilization. Like a supernova that heralds the death of a star, the full integration of women into Western economies has made these economies perform vibrantly and brightly; and yet this may signal a larger civilizational collapse. The fundamental underlying structure that makes enduring civilization possible, namely the balanced order of the family, is disintegrating. And this is why the other three great civilizations—Islamic, Indian, and East Asian—want to accept globalization on their own terms, yet seek to avoid embracing what they see as Western extremism's self-destructive tampering with natural orders of social stability and cultural longevity.

Yet at the same time, we see that an excess of balanced order produces too much social rigidity, and especially condemns women to roles that delimit or inhibit their fulfillment as human beings. Is there a Middle Way between these two extremes? Yes there is, and Buddha revealed it long ago.

## Woman as The Middle Way of Humanity

We have seen that Aristotle and Confucius both extolled the virtues of marriage and mutual respect between the sexes—not only as good in themselves, but also as harmonious with nature and necessary for the maintenance of civilization. Yet we have also seen how extremes of politicized gender feminism deny and deconstruct the cultural consequences of human sex difference, while extremes of Asian chauvinism exaggerate and overemphasize their cultural consequences. Both extremes produce injustice, preventing women and men from attaining their fullest potential within a shared humanity.

Buddhism by its very definition and practice eschews both extremes, and advocates instead a Middle Way that liberates the human being from suffering by eliminating the causes of suffering. These causes invariably arise in and permeate the lower eight states of consciousness, where they manifest as deluded cravings. Because of sex difference, these cravings are manifest differently too. For example, man evolved to view woman as an end in herself—a plaything, a possession, a pleasure giver—and so he supposes that by conquering this woman or that woman, he will become happy. His cravings are real, but his notion that sating them in this way will bring lasting happiness is deluded. And for example, woman evolved to view man as a means to her end, a protector and provider, for her children and family, and so she supposes that by marrying this man or that man she will live happily ever after. Her cravings are likewise real, and likewise deluded.

Acting upon their differently manifested but equally deluded cravings, men and women alike seek to complete themselves through the Other, but selectively so: only through those parts and aspects of the Other which each needs or wants. When this fails to confer lasting happiness—and it always fails, for it never recognizes the Other as fully human in herself or himself, only as a provider of parts and aspects— then suddenly each one becomes aware of the Other's imperfections and differences, which give rise to arguments, disaccords, conflicts, quarrels, recriminations, demonizations, psychological warfare, violent abuse, and irreconcilable mutual despite. Such are the wages of confusion.

Buddhism detoxifies minds, dispels delusions, and opens the way to the ninth level of consciousness. At this level, we do not perceive men or women, only human beings in various stages of awareness. Sex and gender differences are no more than garbs of embodied minds, mere cosmetic effects that may allure or irritate the lower levels of consciousness, but which can and must be transcended in order that suffering end. Any mind free of deluded cravings can relate to others in this mode: as awakened beings in their own right. Rather than harping on the basest human differences, Buddhism focuses on the noblest human commonality, namely the highest level of consciousness. That is where fulfillment lies, for men and women alike, and it is attainable in this very life and even in this very instant, by following The Middle Way.

For two thousand and more years, men have written of the countless ways in which women are beautiful and lovable and adorable on the one hand, and insatiable and irrational and impossible on the other. Nowadays any man who criticizes women will be branded a "sexist" or a "misogynist," and will be either favored or denounced, depending on prevailing political fashion. Many men have held their tongues and checked their pens, before crossing that ever tempting but always treacherous Rubicon. Tolstoy wavered on the brink, but retreated to safety.[21] Schopenhauer and Nietzsche crossed over, and thereby condemned themselves to perdition.

Since the twentieth century, liberated women have written of the countless ways in which men are powerful and lovable and admirable on the one hand, and unfeeling and uncaring and unchangeable on the other. Any woman who critiques men will be branded a "bitch" or a "witch," or granted tenure and accorded prestige as a feminist scholar, depending on prevailing political fashion. So Edmund Burke condescended to respond dismissively to Wollstonecraft's entreaty for liberation, while Sandra Harding and other liberated "feminist scholars" have hysterically repudiated the finest works of Newton.

As promised, I will conclude this chapter with a Buddhist anecdote that shows clearly how we can respect and honor the social consequences of sex difference, while avoiding the extremes of exaggerating or deconstructing them. In his lecture on the nine levels of consciousness, Dr. Kawada noted that people who recover from near-death experiences, or who regain consciousness from deeply comatose states, are often impelled to awaken by the voices of their attending loved ones, who call to them or—as Nichiren Buddhists do—chant for their recovery. By their own testimony, comatose men are most frequently awakened by the voices of their wives; comatose women, by the voices of their children. This bespeaks social consequences of sex difference, but not for the purposes of politicizing either extreme. Rather, it illuminates the precious gift of consciousness itself, and the universal human goal of attaining a state beyond those conditioned by, and suffering from, lower manifestations of sexual dimorphism. It makes little difference who awakens us, as long as we awaken.

So when Schopenhauer wrote, "Women are . . . a kind of intermediate stage between the child and the man,"[22] he may not have envisioned a Buddhist interpretation of his words. "Ladies and gentlemen" and "women and children" are phrases repeated daily and ubiquitously; whereas "men and children" is rarely heard. In her wifely role, woman nurtures man as cocreator of her children, and as protector and provider for her family. In her maternal role, woman nurtures children as their primary caregiver during the critical periods of gestation, infancy, and early childhood. In this sense, woman is truly The Middle Way between man and child, the one who links with both: one Ring to bind them. Yet she is neither a man nor a child herself.

This is reflected in Dr. Kawada's illuminating disclosure that men are awakened from comas by the voices of their wives; women, by the voices of their children. Woman arouses man; child arouses woman. She is the link between them and, in this linkage, she is indeed intermediate between man and child. She is The Middle Way of humanity. But this balanced order of The Middle Way does not discriminate for or against anyone on the basis of their sex or gender. Rather, it values human consciousness above all else, and encourages all humans to attain the ninth level, no matter whose voice beckons them from slumber to arousal, from coma to consciousness, or from waking sleep to full awareness.

Perhaps the ultimate social consequences of sex difference lie not in life, but in death itself. Women live longer than men, on average by about four years. Given the boundless joy or sorrow we can experience in any instant, four years can seem a long time indeed, although it is fleeting, and nothing beside eternity. More pronounced is a phenomenon you can observe in your local cemetery: Widows are much longer-lived, on average, than are widowers. Wherever you see husband and wife lying buried side by side, conjoined at last in peace, their presumably undying love preserved by death, examine the life spans on their markers. Where the man has died first, his widow often endures for years and frequently decades more, fulfilled by the family she has created with him, for he was only her means to that end. Where the woman has died first, her widower often dies soon after, within mere months or years. Why? Perhaps he is rendered inconsolable by her passing. Maybe he is less able to care for himself alone. These tombstones may be "social constructs," as are their coldly chiseled trails of warm but brief embrace, and yet the tales they tell are nature's truths, not human fabrications.

The Middle Way, which is also a way between life and death itself, suggests that we close Pandora's box, and open our minds instead.

# 10

## COGNITIVE EXTREMES
### Oral, Written, Visual, and Digital Traditions

*Without an image thinking is impossible.* —Aristotle

*A disciplined mind brings happiness.* —Buddha

*By three methods we may learn wisdom: first, by reflection,*
*which is noblest; second, by imitation, which is the easiest;*
*and third, by experience, which is the bitterest.* —Confucius

### The Greatest Instrument on Earth

THESE DAYS, POLITICAL, BUSINESS, CULTURAL, and religious leaders in every part of the world emphasize or at least pay lip service to the importance of education. Indeed, the future of our global village is being partly determined, right now, by what our future leaders and their followers are learning while they are still children. But educational systems are subject to extremisms of various kinds, ruining young minds through neglect or poisoning them with venomous doctrines. Before looking at some of these extremes in more detail in chapter 11, and suggesting how The Middle Way can help reconcile them, I need to restate some basics about education itself.

First, our big brains make us fundamentally a learning animal. Almost all life-forms on earth are capable of "learning" at some level, if by this we mean that they can modify their behaviors at least, or their cognitive processes (if they have any) at most, in response to their environments. But instinctive behaviors, even sophisticated ones such as ants following scent trails to food sources, or bees communicating the location of flowers, are inherited. These animals do not learn from each other; rather, they execute programs that were genetically implanted in them. Generally speaking, the bigger-brained an animal, the more it needs to learn in order to survive and reproduce. Among lions, for example, stalking and pouncing are instinctive behaviors, while hunting is not. Hunting is a skill with both instinctive and acquired components, an interplay of Darwinian and Lamarckian elements. Humans need to learn more than any other animal in order to survive and reproduce successfully, hence the importance of education and lifelong learning. For example, we are all born with the innate capacity to learn one or more languages, but the language(s) we are exposed to when young are the ones we will learn best. If we are not exposed to any language at all, we will never activate this innate capacity, and our brains will not develop along optimal or even normal cognitive pathways.

It is by cognitive development that we progress from one level of consciousness to the next, or by lack of it that we fail to progress at all. The purpose of our earliest learning, which begins in the womb and continues in infancy, is to further neurological and cognitive development in the immature brain. Many neural pathways are actually established and grown in response to stimuli from the environment. All "inputs" from human and environmental sources alike—visual, verbal, musical, tactile, olfactory, emotional—are accepted by the infant's immature brain, and will influence its growth and development, for better or worse. Early education, roughly during the first seven years, lays a cognitive foundation for human learning. If that foundation is deep and strong, it can support a tall edifice later; if it is shallow and weak, it cannot. Each of the first three cognitive traditions—oral, written, visual—provides a different kind of foundation. The strongest of these three is written; the next strongest, oral; the weakest, visual. The digital tradition incorporates all three and magnifies their strengths and weaknesses many times over. Given the benefits of hindsight, it is easier to observe and understand the net effects of the oral and written traditions, which are relatively ancient, on cognitive development. That said, the effects of the more recent visual tradition—which began with the spread of television in the 1950s—are so powerful and so pronounced that they can be assessed as well, even though that tradition is obviously much newer.

The digital tradition is something else again. The personal computer, its array of software applications, and its networking capacities via the Internet, are civilization-changing and paradigm-defining developments, comparable in their impact to the invention of the printing press by Gutenberg, yet incomparably more powerful. The World Wide Web itself emerged only in the 1990s, yet it has entirely reshaped and retooled the ways in which data are exchanged, interactions are mediated, identities are evolved, and lives are led. The digital tradition is redefining the daily routines, transactions, and lifestyles of hundreds of millions of people—on one side of the "digital divide" that afflicts the global village.[1] In so doing, the digital tradition is fundamentally altering humanity itself—and this tradition has only just begin to evolve. Even so, those of us who were born and reared in the written tradition, and who remember (and who possibly resisted) the encroachment of the visual, are the only people in the world who can begin to appreciate the enormity of the digital tradition's impact on the global village, and human civilization. So my assessment of the digital tradition necessarily remains woefully incomplete. Yet even an incomplete assessment will suffice to convey a sense of the impact of the digital revolution on cultural evolution. Since the digital tradition is the last of the four to emerge, I will leave it for last.

So let us begin with the first three traditions—oral, written, visual— and assess their effects, for good and ill, on human cognitive development. The chronological order in which these three traditions emerged is not the ascending order of their cognitive benefits: the visual tradition is the latest but also the most damaging of the three, and that does not bode well for us as a species. Each tradition has its strengths and weaknesses, yet among them too there is a Middle Way. As we will see, the oral tradition limits cognitive development, while the visual tradition impairs it. The written tradition is The Middle Way, and the best way, for human beings to develop cognitively, and thus to benefit from further and higher education, with the digital tradition as the ultimate learning environment and mental tool kit.

The matter of education lies very close to my heart, because I have been involved in it for most of my life—as a student and teacher, graduate student and professor, tutor and mentor, lifelong learner, educational innovator—and all over the world. Responsible parents know the importance of education: In the United States many parents search exhaustively for the best schools for their children, and the location of schools often becomes the determining factor for the location of the home itself. Many parents will sacrifice much for their children's education—enduring longer commutes, higher property taxes, expensive tuition fees—to send their children to the best possible schools. Yet too many parents pay little or no attention to their children's cognitive development, which makes education possible or impossible, independent of schooling itself.

The best overall education involves a partnership between parents and schools. Parents are primarily responsible for their children's cognitive development and good study habits, while schools are primarily responsible for curriculum and content, as well as for reinforcing good academic and social habits alike. Countries like Japan are educationally successful because both partners are expected to assume responsibility for their child's learning; countries like the United States are in educational free fall because often both partners eschew that responsibility. And too many countries in the developing world are in educational limbo because both partners are too ill prepared and ill equipped even to begin to assume adequate measures of responsibility.

The importance of cognitive development was well known to the Jesuits, who famously said, "Give us the child until the age of seven, and we will answer for the man." Indeed, the first seven years of life are critical. A child will be strongly influenced, emotionally and intellectually, by the values and prejudices instilled in him or her during this period. The music they hear at this point in their life remains most faithfully in long-term auditory memory; emotional attachments to religious or mythical beliefs ingrained during this period last a lifetime. The child's neurological system matures for years after birth, but whether a child's cognitive potential is reached or not depends on the earliest stimuli it receives.

Humans have been gifted (and burdened) with big brains, making pregnancy, childbirth, and motherhood more arduous experiences for females of our species than for any others, including our primate relatives. Among social mammals that browse, forage, or graze in herds—such as deer, antelope, giraffe, elephant—the young are normally born without much fuss and without any assistance to the mother. These neonates have about an hour to get on their feet, find their balance, and move with the herd, albeit shepherded and suckled by their mothers. Among monkeys and apes, the young must cling to their mothers for a much longer time—typically months, while their nervous systems mature enough for them to become independently and securely mobile. Human babies still have the "grasping reflex" of monkeys: Stick your finger into a newborn's palm, and it will grab your finger so tightly that you can safely hoist the baby into the air. But in general, the human baby needs about a year to take its first tottering steps, and needs several years of constant care to reach a state of neuromuscular maturity sufficient for periods of relative independence that baby ungulates must attain in hours, and baby primates in months. Why do humans need so many years to mature?

The evolutionary answer is clear: Our big brains, the most amazing instruments on earth, require years of neurological and cognitive development to mature, and require constant fine-tuning thereafter. So nature had to effect a compromise to allow human births to take place at all. As Stephen J. Gould has pointed out, if human neonates were as neurologically mature as newborn monkeys or apes, our gestation period would be eighteen months instead of nine, and very few mothers would survive childbirth.[2] The bigger the baby's brain, the more the mother's pelvis has to be reshaped and angled to accommodate its gestation and birth. Said another way: the bigger the baby's brain, the less mobile the mother will become during pregnancy. (Human females are also less mobile than males, even when not pregnant). The strongest muscle in a woman's body is uterine, evolved for expelling the oversized fetus at birth. The strongest muscle in a man's body is his quadriceps, evolved for hunting big game and defending a large territory. That's nature's compromise: The human baby is helpless for months and years after birth, and the human mother is barely mobile during the late stages of pregnancy, and has a more difficult time birthing than any other animal on earth. Why? To service the big brain.

And what do we do with our big brains? Ideally, we learn. Just think about how much learning some of us do. In the developed world, there is a K-12 system of primary and secondary schools, then the possibility of attending four years of college or university, then additional years of graduate or professional schools. An M.A. alone can take twenty years of schooling; an M.D. or J.D., twenty-four; a Ph.D., twenty-eight. So you might spend one-fourth to one-third of your life in formal educational settings, just preparing to "hunt" the big game of paychecks and career opportunities. That's a lot of learning, but it's just the beginning. You can learn to drive a car; learn a musical instrument, another language, or a game, sport, or hobby. You can learn to court a partner, parent your children; go through a divorce, property settlement, and custody battle. You can learn about promotion and career change; about life's unexpected joys and certain disappointments; to reinvent yourself; to cope with or recover from serious illness. You learn many things every time you read a book or newspaper, listen to the radio, browse a Web page, take a trip, or make a friend.

If you are a professional, then you must continue to learn as your profession evolves. If you use a computer, you must continue to learn about new hardware and software. If you acquire any new technology, you must ascend the associated learning curve. The global village functions increasingly as a "knowledge economy," and citizens of its most prosperous regions are committed to lifelong learning. This is the legacy of our big brain, and no other animal on earth makes learning its fundamental means to so many ends.

The big human brain allows us to use and evolve language in highly nuanced ways, which, if the capacity is activated, separates us from the other apes. There are documented cases of feral children—i.e., wild and savage children, whose behavior is just like that of other wild animals.[3] A few such children had wandered into the vast forests that used to carpet Europe prior to the Industrial Revolution, and became lost but managed to survive like wild animals. Lacking nurture and acculturation, they never acquired language. Never acquiring language, they never developed human cognition, and remained in apelike states. If a child is not properly nurtured and acculturated, and fails to acquire fluency in a first language prior to the age of seven or so, it will never attain its full human potential. The inverse of the Jesuit maxim is also true: "Neglect the child until the age of seven, and it will never become a man." If it does not acquire at least a first language during the period of neurological "plasticity" in the years following birth, the child becomes a wild animal, not a human being.

This process is irreversible, and highlights one of the fundamental and critical asymmetries of human cognitive development. It is now well established that learning begins in the womb itself, so the mother-to-be can do much to help, or to harm her baby, while it is gestating. Once born, it must be acculturated to acquire fluency in a first language at least. During the "plastic period" of the first seven years, it can acquire several more languages easily and without confusion. After that, linguistic acquisition slows down. The first language is the foundation upon which the edifice of lifelong learning can be built. Language is the first window of understanding; if it never opens, the big brain is wasted. Without a first language, the human being is little more functional than an ape. If da Vinci, Bach, Newton, or Einstein had been lost in the woods and become feral children, they would never have fulfilled their potential for genius. This is true of us all. Whoever fails to acquire a first language cannot fulfill their human potential. So this is the asymmetric moral: We do not fashion geniuses via education, but we fail to attain normalcy through lack of it.

So how is a first language best acquired? With the benefit of hindsight, we can see how the first three traditions—oral, written, and visual—compare in managing this essential task.

## The Oral Tradition and the Four Pillars of Cognition

Imagine, if you will, our hunter-gatherer ancestors, living about fifty thousand years ago, in bands a few dozen strong. They ranged over territories of a few hundred to a few thousand square miles, ate whatever the men could hunt and the women could gather, knew how to light fires, used Stone Age tools and weapons, buried their dead along with prized possessions (feathers or furs or flints), and communicated with rudimentary gestures and speech. Undoubtedly they danced and sang, and made music on skin drums and bone flutes. They sat around campfires and told stories. And they invented myths to explain the world around them and their place in it. They evolved an oral tradition, a story of themselves and the world, which they narrated from generation to generation.

For a story to be told and retold, understood, embellished and handed down, three things are necessary. First, there needs to be a shared language between and among generations, with a vocabulary and a grammar that the children begin absorbing at birth. Second, there have to be storytellers, narrators who are invested with the lore of the band or tribe, who remember and who pass on the myths and the legends. Third, there have to be listeners, who understand and absorb the lore, and from among whom will emerge the next generation of storytellers.

Peoples immersed in oral traditions develop four vital human skills which conduce to their cognitive development and socialization. I call them "the four pillars of cognition." They are: attention span, linguistic acuity, imaginative capacity, and cultural memory. In order to follow, understand, and remember a story, you need all four. I want you to remember (or write down) these four pillars, and see what becomes of them as we progress through the initial three learning traditions, from oral to written to visual, and beyond them into the digital tradition.

It is easy to gain an appreciation of these attributes in action. All you need to do is tell a story to your young children at bedtime. (If you're not a spellbinding storyteller, you can "cheat" and read to them: They still receive it aurally.) Observe your child while you tell or read a bedtime story, and you will realize how these four attributes come into play. First, attention span: Children love stories, and will pay more attention to them than to most other things. You can observe attentiveness being exercised by the child as he or she absorbs a story.

There is a period of relaxed but unbroken concentration, focus, and stillness. This is nothing other than attention span. Moreover, such spans of attention are lengthened by exercise. The more stories your child absorbs, the greater his or her capacity to absorb more becomes. This is a positive feedback loop. Attention span is crucial for effective engagement with other vital activities in life, too: study, play, work, and awareness of the human condition. The oral tradition—that is, storytelling—is a major pathway via which young children develop and exercise their attention spans. And it is a very pleasant and loving way, for all concerned, provided that the stories themselves are not laced with prejudices, hatreds, and other toxins that so readily poison open but credulous young minds.

Second, now that your child is paying attention, what exactly is he or she paying attention to? Primarily, to the language in which the story is recited. If the story is too boring, too predictable, or too incomprehensible, then her attention will wane. If it is exciting, meaningful, and challenging enough, her attention will wax. We all understand many more words than we utilize, and this applies to children as well. The oral tradition helps children to acquire new vocabulary, to reinforce grammatical patterns, and thus to master a first language. The first language and its stories become a window onto their culture and, if universal enough in their scope, a window onto humanity and the world. Human languages and their narratives further understanding in children and adults.

Third, beyond attention span and linguistic acuity is the precious human capacity for imagination—literally the visualization of images. Any of our senses can provoke imaginative response, but since vision is the primary human sense, mental images most naturally arise as a response to external stimuli. The word *imagination* itself reflects the human capacity to generate internal images in response to external stimuli (and in response to internalized or unconscious stimuli, in the case of dreams). So when you're telling a story to your child, he or she is not merely a passive recipient being bombarded with language. On the contrary, his or her imagination actively generates images, creatively producing an internal but dynamic visual representation of the words.

Just as you "picture" telling a story to your child as you read these words, so your child "pictures" the story itself as you tell it. This is an amazing capacity. Every human being is, in essence, a producer and director of their own internal movies, engendered by the "script" that they are hearing aloud.

This is also why it was possible, before the advent of TV, to broadcast sports on the radio—and also why TV has not made radio broadcasting obsolete. If the commentators are sufficiently skilled narrators, they can "tell the story" of a football or baseball or a hockey game to millions of listeners, whose imaginations are avidly engaged producing and directing the internal images engendered by the oral broadcast. The capacity to visualize—that is, to generate internal images—is extremely important for other purposes too, beyond entertainment and cognitive development. The oral tradition is very good at fostering this capacity. And for this very reason, the oral tradition of radio broadcasting has not been rendered obsolete by products of the other traditions. In addition, cell phones have become a huge industry worldwide—and they are based squarely on the oral tradition. Marshall McLuhan characterized oral media as "hot," and their cognitive fires are not extinguished by "cold" media such as TV.

It is also vital to note that music is received aurally—via the ear—and as such is intimately bound up with the oral tradition. Every culture has music, and music *enchants* our minds and hearts to resonate with fundamental vibrations that sustain the universe itself. This is why TV and movies utilize music too: The visual tradition is itself incomplete without this auditory component. One must never underestimate the force of words, the power of mantras, the magic of music—all of which are rooted in the oral tradition.

Fourth, when you tell a story to a child, that narrative may have ramifications far beyond the three aspects of individual cognitive development just mentioned—attention span, linguistic acuity, and imaginative capacity. The narrative itself becomes a lens through which the child will interpret the world around him, as well as events that happen to him and others whom he knows. All enduring narratives offer a moral, embody a meaning, teach a lesson, or sound a cautionary note. When you tell your child a bedtime story, be it a fairy tale from Wilhelm and Jacob Grimm, a fable from Jean de la Fontaine, a nonsense rhyme from Edward Lear, a parable from scripture, a myth from Hesiod, a legend from the Mayas, or a reverie from Aboriginal dreamtime, you are giving your child a way of looking at and understanding herself and others, her culture and the world. The images that the child generates in her mind when listening to a story are private, in that she alone can "see" them, but their meanings are public, because they invariably address universal aspects of the human condition.

At the same time, every tribe, every culture, every religion, every ethnicity, every nationality, and every cult has its definitive set of stories, which give its members their collective identity, but too often at the price of regarding other collectives as "alien" or "foreign" or "infidel" or "demonic." Time and again, the human condition becomes fractured by the limitations of a given story, which includes some people but excludes others, or dehumanizes others, or which seeks to annihilate others, or to convert others—but not to tolerate their stories. Stronger cultures can impose themselves, colonize, and destroy weaker ones. Stronger cultures can also incorporate weaker cultures more or less tolerantly, or intolerantly. Weaker cultures can resist or assimilate to stronger cultures more or less successfully, or not at all. It is the content and intent of a given set of myths, legends, and lore that strongly conditions its culture's ability—or lack of ability—to evolve constructively in its inevitable encounters with other cultures, be they weaker or stronger.

So we confront a paradox of the oral tradition. We saw in another context (chapter 8) that culture is a binding force of the human group, and saw moreover that incompatible or competing cultures were necessary for dispersion and flourishing of the human species across the face of the earth. But now that we all inhabit one village—the global village—it has become necessary to reconcile and recombine cultural forces that once divided and drove us apart. This is no mean feat, especially when the storytellers of one group incite hatred for the stories or the peoples of another group. Nietzsche wrote that "a happy people have no history." Unfortunately, many people make themselves unhappy by dwelling too much on their history.

Chimpanzees need families and bands to be normal. Human beings need families and communities too, but we also need cultural memories, which were originally transmitted via the oral tradition. Gradually, as some hunter-gatherers evolved into permanent settlers, and as some permanent settlements evolved into civilizations, their stories evolved too: from campfire legends into world religions, for example. But that could not have taken place without the written tradition.

## The Written Tradition

The invention of written symbols, whether alphabetical or pictorial, that stand for letters and words or objects and concepts makes progressive and enduring human civilization possible. Human beings appeared one hundred thousand to two hundred thousand years ago, and possibly longer if you count Neanderthals as human too. But written traditions are only about five thousand to ten thousand years old, more or less. When we speak of the "ancient world" or of "antiquity," we are speaking only of this latter period of a few thousand years, when stories were first recorded. Throughout most of human existence, nobody read; in the ancient world, only a relative few could read and write; in the contemporary world, as we will see in the next chapter, literacy is at extremes, with some populations almost wholly literate; others, grossly illiterate. In 1969, the leading edge of the written tradition produced flight plans to the moon. But at the trailing edge, in that same year, half the world's people had never seen a phone book, nor could they read one.

Our ABCs straddle this chasm between oral and written traditions. Aristotle, like his teacher, Plato, wrote significant works whose contents helped shape and forge Western civilization. But Plato's teacher, Socrates, wrote nothing, relying upon Plato to record or reconstruct their dialogues. Similarly, the teachings of Confucius contributed mightily to the civilizations of East Asia, yet Confucius himself wrote nothing down: His *Analects* were recorded by his students, and their descendents. Buddha, whose teachings have influenced many civilizations, including lately the West, also wrote nothing down. His students (or disciples) recorded the sutras. We see this pattern over and over again in the formation of major world religions. Abraham wrote nothing. Jesus wrote nothing. Mohammed wrote nothing. But their disciples and heirs wrote books that came to influence billions of people—peoples of "the Book." That book might be the Torah, Bible, Koran, Mahabharata, *Analects*, Pali Canon, or Lotus Sutra. The written tradition and its "Book" allow for unlimited spreading of the message and expansion of the tribe.

Of the three main linguistic functions—speaking, reading, writing— only speaking comes naturally. All infants of all cultures babble instinctively, rehearsing the phonemes ("ba-ba," "da-da," "ma-ma") that become the building blocks of words. As long as they are exposed to a natural language, children will acquire verbal facility without long hours of structured and prodigious effort. But reading is more difficult, and needs to be taught, learned, and practiced. Writing is more difficult yet, and must also be taught, learned, and practiced. Fluent speakers can appreciate great oratory, while fluent readers can appreciate great literature as well. This point underscores the damage done to cognitive function by postmodern deconstructions of meaning. Those who have deconstructed language and literature fail to appreciate greatness of linguistic expression, and thus fail to reach their own potentials for cognitive development.[4]

So how does the written tradition affect the four pillars of human cognition—attention span, linguistic acuity, imaginative capacity, and cultural memory? Compared with the oral tradition, it improves upon them all. Let us briefly see how.

First, while people can pay attention (e.g., to hunting or gathering or praying or meditating) without knowing how to read or write, the studious habits and focused mind-states that come from exercising reading and writing skills develop the greatest attention spans for the greatest number. Hence the written tradition is utilitarian in this respect. These habits, states, and skills also allow individuals to contemplate new thoughts, with the benefit of the perspective gained from knowledge of previously recorded thoughts. So creative individuals imbued with a written tradition can refocus their attentions on producing new works of poetry, literature, music, mathematics, science, and philosophy. These delectable fruits of human contemplation and inspiration can be harvested by creators and performers, and tasted and appreciated by students and audiences across generations, only via well-developed attention spans. The written tradition is superior to the oral one in this respect: It requires less time, but more attentive powers, to read a story than to hear one or tell one aloud. The written tradition has the power to compress and to compact thought, making it highly dense, thereby demanding and inculcating more intense cognitive functionality when reading than when speaking or listening. Reading boosts brain power.

And of vital importance, children who learn how to read and write properly will not only speak more intelligibly, but will also be capable of paying better and longer attention than those who don't learn these things. The so-called epidemic of attention deficit disorder that afflicts millions of American schoolchildren is a culturally induced cognitive deficit produced by a lack of proper reading and writing lessons in the schools, combined with an excess of exposure to television and other visual stimuli at too young an age, along with atrocious diets and other poor living habits. We will return to this cultural catastrophe later in this chapter.

Second, nothing improves linguistic acuity like reading and writing. To begin with, reading is the best way to learn new words, and a rich vocabulary helps one to think more clearly, more abundantly, more creatively. If you know only five hundred words of a given language, as you may find in a pocket guide for travelers, you can communicate only in the most rudimentary ways, perhaps enough to meet your basic needs. Most people know about twenty thousand words in their native tongues, and use about half of them in daily thought and conversation. The English language, which became the international lingua franca of both science and commerce, contains about 250,000 words. So most English speakers are using only 5 to 10 percent of the linguistic resources available to them. Similarly, most people use only about 5 to 10 percent of their brain power too. And since words are not merely tokens of speech, but also the building blocks of thought, most speakers (of any language) are similarly thinking far less richly, precisely, and elegantly than they would if they simply had more blocks at their disposal. What can you construct with a "starter" LEGO set?

Basic things, with limited possibilities. What can you construct with an "advanced" set? Many more elaborate and interesting things, as your imagination will allow. The same is true of language—any language. The more advanced your vocabulary, the more elaborate and interesting thoughts you can construct. Reading and writing are the best ways—and maybe the only ways—of improving your thoughts and advancing your mind.

Third, if you read and write, then you will surely fire your imaginative capacity. If you read with attentiveness and understanding, you envision what is being narrated or described or conjectured, and you reenvision yourself as part of it, and so it becomes part of you. All who read and understand the great works of literature from any culture's written tradition also partake of greatness: that is, the greatness of their own minds, for being able to appreciate these works.

The canon of great books is the story of humanity itself. Whoever cannot read that story, or at least important parts of it, runs a greater risk of failing to appreciate his or her own humanity. Why then, given the precious gift of a human life, would some not wish to enrich it with greatness, partly by reading and understanding the world's great literature?

There are two extremes which divert people from such enrichment. I call them "extreme Zero" and "extreme One" (also known as the "One True Extreme.") Extreme Zero occurs either when a culture has no books at all, as with purely oral traditions of hunter-gatherers isolated from civilization, or occurs when it deconstructs the books it has, thus rendering them useless. Extreme One occurs when the culture has one book only, or one book which it exalts above all others—as with all religious fanatics who consult one book only to explain absolutely everything—and from which adherents derive most of their collective stories, histories, and explanations of things. The Middle Way is the vast road between no books and one book only, wide enough to include all books and deep enough to value some more than others, depending on their purpose. Physicians value the Hippocratic Oath, but they study and practice modern medicine. Daisaku Ikeda values the Lotus Sutra, but he reads and studies everything under the sun. He also exhorts his students—and children everywhere—to read everything too.[5] The more one reads the great books of the great cultures of the world, the more one visualizes the genius and richness and accomplishments made possible by the human mind. We are all born with brains; minds, however, need to be acculturated. The Middle Way means: read everything. Do not be afraid to visualize something new or different. Grow your mind by reading. There are no unthinkable thoughts, no unreadable words, no imaginable boundaries of the imagination.

Fourth, the written tradition is incomparably superior to the oral one when it comes to cultural memory. How many stories can you memorize verbatim? Ten? A hundred? A thousand? There's an upper limit, and you have to keep rehearsing them to retain them in memory. By contrast, how many storybooks can a library contain? Thousands, tens of thousands, hundreds of thousands. If these stories are digitized, then millions can be stored in one library space. If a culture has a written tradition, its memory can become indefinitely large. There's no upper limit. And nobody has to remember anything at all, except how to read and write. Like storytelling, reading and writing are developed and maintained by practice. The more one practices, the better one becomes. The better one becomes at reading and writing, the more one can learn.

A salient difference between oral and written traditions lies in preservation of cultural memory. In an oral tradition, if the storytellers die out, the stories die with them. For example, a richly beautiful oral tradition of the Mayas was about to become extinct, through the unsustainability of their way of life in the face of globalization and Latin American political corruption. So a venerable Mayan shaman named Nicolas Chiviliu summoned a literate acolyte named Martin Prechtel, to whom he orally transmitted the teachings. Prechtel published some of these teachings in books, in English, preserving them for future generations.[6] Ancient cultures that leave a written record—from Babylonian cuneiform to Egyptian hieroglyphics to Indo-European alphabets to Chinese ideograms—can transmit their irreplaceable cultural memories to future generations of humanity, even if the original storytellers, cultures, and languages themselves die out. As long as there is hard copy, we can decode it, translate it, and add it to our collective human cultural memory.

The Lotus Sutra, for example, represents the ultimate teachings of Buddha. It was originally delivered orally by Gautama, in northern India, and recorded in Sanskrit. It made its way to Tibet, China, Japan, and the United States (among a host of countries), and was successively translated from Sanskrit into Tibetan, Chinese, Korean, Japanese, and English (among dozens of languages). Without the written tradition, this invaluable teaching would probably have been lost. Given the written tradition, it has been added to the cultural memory of humanity, where it is preserved and can benefit millions. The same is true of Euclid's *Elements*, Bach's *Well-Tempered Clavier*, and Dostoevsky's novels. These works survive, among myriad others, because they are written down.

When I was a graduate student in London, I used to read primarily at the British Library (BL), which was then housed in the British Museum on Montague Street. One of the world's great libraries, it contained about six million volumes on site, plus another six million in outlying warehouses that could be retrieved within a day or two. I used to walk from the British Library past Senate House, headquarters of the University of London, whose library housed another four million volumes. That walk continued past my college, University College London, whose library contained a modest two million volumes. I would sometimes cut over to the Strand, where the library at our sister college, the London School of Economics (LSE), contained another four million volumes. On the way back from LSE, I would sometimes visit the BL's science library in Chancery Lane, or its Oriental reading room, or the LSE's law library on Russell Square. In about one hour, I could walk in a path that encircled some twenty-five million books, and read anything on any subject under the sun—thanks to the amazing power of the written tradition. As a storehouse of accumulated learning, and a platform on which to build new learning, the written tradition is incomparably more powerful than the oral one.

But reading and writing confer an even deeper advantage over narration, that is, when things are written down, they free up our active memory, and so we can participate more fully in each moment. This is analogous to computer memory, in terms of hard drive versus active

RAM (random access memory). Typical data storage space on hard drives is many gigabytes (soon to be terabytes), but active RAM is always much less—typically megabytes (soon to be gigabytes). Your computer's operating system—plus software applications—are loaded into RAM. The more RAM, the better your system runs. But if you started to fill up RAM with stored data from your hard drive, its capacity would soon be exhausted, and your operating system would be very limited in its functionality.

Your active memory is like RAM. The oral tradition fills up active memory with stories, and of course with the "application software" to understand them (i.e., spoken language). The oral tradition has no other way to "save" stories, except by "burning" them into long-term memory via laborious repetition, and has no other means to retrieve or understand them, outside of spoken language. This is very limiting. By contrast, the written tradition fills up active memory with "application software" for speaking, reading, and writing, and "saves" the stories themselves in books and in repositories full of books—in libraries, bookstores, and on your own bookshelves at home. The written tradition gives us unlimited storage capacity. At the same time, it frees up active memory from rote memorization to reading and to visualizing ideas, to reinterpreting existing ones and to imagining novel ones. Such a flexible and powerful operating system makes the human being much more functional, much more able to learn, and much more likely to develop his or her full cognitive potential.

And one more thing: The written tradition preserves not only enormous quantities of data, but also preserves the blueprints for regenerating what the data stand for. If you wanted to become a house builder in an oral tradition, you'd have to copy existing houses by learning construction techniques from a builder, or by figuring them out for yourself by painstaking trial and error. If you want to become a house builder in a written tradition, you can read books on every aspect of house building, and build your own house from a blueprint. Blueprints are templates for turning imagined things into substantive things.

Similarly, Euclid's *Elements* is a blueprint for geometry. In an oral tradition, very few people could imagine or remember, let alone understand, plane geometry. In a written tradition, millions or even billions of people can understand plane geometry once they can read Euclid. And without plane geometry, we'd have no science, poor technology, and primitive architecture. In other words, the written tradition preserves the blueprints for human civilization. A few hundred books (out of those twenty-five million you can stroll around if you have an hour in London) changed the course of human thought and human history. The oral tradition is static; the written tradition, dynamic.

## The Visual Tradition

Because of the unprecedented success of the dynamic written tradition, both in its ability to preserve existing ideas and to free up the mind to conceive new ones, humans have evolved out of recognition culturally in a very short biological time. The human being today is more or less the same biological animal as he was one hundred thousand or more years ago—it is said that if you gave Neanderthal man a shave and a haircut, dressed him in a suit, and put him on a subway at rush hour, he would pass for a contemporary urbanite. It would be another matter entirely to teach Neanderthal man how to do the many things that you do every day: make breakfast, read the newspaper, answer the phone, commute or telecommute to work. The difference is that you inherited a few thousand years of cultural evolution in the form of a written tradition and its blueprints, whereas Neanderthal man did not. Even so, if Neanderthal babies were reared in a written tradition, they could make up for one hundred thousand years of cultural lag in one generation. Such is the power of the human brain.

Cultural dynamism, through invention and innovation, is the hallmark of the written tradition. Yet in the twentieth century, that very tradition gave rise to an invention that has changed—and ironically reversed—the course of cultural evolution itself. That invention was the cathode ray tube, or CRT. It made possible the further inventions of television, computer monitors, and video games. Very rapidly, and within a few decades, these inventions in turn have largely displaced books, and to that extent have replaced the written tradition with a visual one. The visual tradition has fundamentally altered the ways in human beings learn, remember, and think, and not at all for the better.

American children are at the forefront of a tendency that is sweeping the developed world: a tendency to become acculturated primarily through visual media as opposed to print media. While the written tradition was a vast improvement on the oral one, the visual tradition represents a vast impoverishment of the written one. What I am going to say in the coming pages of this chapter may shock you, but it is better to be shocked into opening your eyes wide than lulled into keeping them tightly closed. Just bear in mind that American children on average watch 4.5 hours *per day* of TV, and on top of that play video games and surf the Internet for several hours more. Their primary mode of learning is through a CRT—or its descendent, a flat (or plasma) screen. This is true from preschool right through to high school graduation.

As a professor, I inherit such students in the public university system. The vast majority of them cannot think, speak, read, or write coherently. Overexposure to the visual tradition, and underexposure to the written one, has irreversibly deprived them of language and acculturation, and has cognitively stunted them—many of them, for life. To understand this, let us briefly reexamine the four pillars of cognition in terms of the visual tradition: attention span, linguistic acuity, imaginative capacity, and cultural memory.

First, watching television erodes attention span. Worse still, watching television also erodes the capacity to develop attention span. What do many adults like to do after a hard day at the office? They like to "veg out" in front of the TV. That's a well-chosen expression. "Vegging out" means becoming like a vegetable. Those who make a career out of this become "couch potatoes"—another well-chosen expression. What do these expressions mean? They mean that watching too much TV turns you mentally into a vegetable or a tuber. Vegetables and tubers are passive. They lack locomotion; they manifest no active consciousness; they cannot learn. The worst cases of human brain death are called "persistent vegetative states." Vegging out in front of the TV does not cause brain death, but it does cause mind death. The more time your mind spends in a vegetative state, the more time it wants to spend in a vegetative state. By eroding attention span, the visual tradition has made human beings passive recipients of visually imposed images and background narratives, instead of active imaginers and interpreters of oral or written narratives in the foreground of consciousness. This in turn is contributing to the mind death of Western civilization.

If you think I'm exaggerating, consider this: Television narrators routinely take what they earnestly but pathetically call "in-depth looks" at topics of interest, in segments that last about ten minutes. Indeed, ten minutes is an eternity on television. By contrast, in the written tradition, an academic researcher might spend ten months taking an "in-depth" look at the same subject, while a philosopher might spend ten years thinking about it "in depth." So what's ten minutes? Next to nothing. Calling such a segment "in-depth" is Orwellian. In fact, it could hardly be shallower. It appears "in-depth" only if your attention span is correspondingly short. Ten minutes seems like a long time on TV, precisely because TV severely erodes attention span.

When children with near-zero attention spans (and sugar-loaded diets) are asked to sit still in classrooms and concentrate on a written curriculum they have not been acculturated to absorb, they are obviously incapable of doing so. This is why they are "diagnosed" with attention deficit hyperactivity disorder (ADHD): an accurate diagnosis, all things considered. Given the massive "epidemic" of ADHD that afflicts American and increasingly other schoolchildren, such that twelve million to fifteen million kids in the United States are daily drugged with Ritalin, why has hardly anyone asked about the causes of the unprecedented outbreak?[7]

Wherever there's an epidemic, there's an epidemiology. Epidemic diseases are incubated, transmitted, acquired, reincubated, retransmitted, and so on. Many are highly contagious. So what's the epidemiology of ADHD? ADHD was "voted in" to the DSM by psychiatrists in the 1980s, when widespread effects of the visual tradition's mind death were first appearing the classrooms. The epidemic has worsened because what's causing it has worsened— increases in TV, video-game, and computer usage by young children, combined with deconstructed language, incoherent curricula, poor diet, and utter lack of discipline at home and at school—all of which unfortunately preempt the cure: a return to the written tradition.

History records massively lethal epidemics of flu, polio, smallpox, yellow fever, plague, and other biologically contagious diseases that have afflicted children and adults since time immemorial, although many have been brought under control by advances in medical science (thanks to the written tradition). While there have always been individual cases of hyperactive children, mostly caused by particular *and noncontagious* problems with brain function, "epidemics" of ADHD have never occurred in cultures that relied on oral or written traditions. Why? Because, as we have seen, oral traditions develop attention span up to a point, while written ones extend it even further. Only the visual tradition erodes it, and only recent generations of children reared in the visual tradition have succumbed to this culturally induced "epidemic."

The visual tradition is culturally contagious too, as well as highly addictive. Just ask Nintendo how many units they've sold. Then ask tens of millions of parents how many times for how many hours for how many years on end they have allowed TV, video games, or the Internet to become their children's baby-sitters and tutors. Have you ever seen a child voluntarily walk away from a video screen of any kind in order to read a book or do written homework? Of course not. They can't. Human beings are evolutionarily adapted to be stimulated and mesmerized by visual stimuli. As we saw in chapter 8, the preeminence of the visual cortex over the other sensory processing centers in the brain is the hallmark of primate evolution, and lately it has become our Achilles heel.

Literate adults are also vulnerable to the allure of visual media. Vision remains the primary sensing mechanism for all primates, including adult humans. I saw this mechanism assert itself at a conference of highly intelligent and well-read adults, who were browsing a book exhibit during coffee break. Absent other stimuli, these literate adults would have picked up, perused, and bought many books. But one of the book exhibitors had set up a TV monitor and VCR machine, and was playing an endless cassette featuring an interview with an author. Everyone who entered the book exhibit immediately crowded around the TV, attracted and mesmerized by the visual stimulus. No one picked up, perused, or bought any books at all—not even the book being advertised in the interview—as long as the TV was playing. If literate adults can succumb so quickly and completely to the visual tradition, what chance do small children have? The difference is, adults who were reared in a written tradition can still pick up a book and read it, whereas children reared in a visual tradition can barely read at all. So much for the catastrophic effects of the visual tradition upon the first pillar of cognition: attention span.

Second, the visual tradition impairs linguistic acuity. It is well known to fluent English speakers worldwide—in Australia, Britain, Canada (the ABCs of English), and throughout the British Commonwealth—that American English suffers from a number of impairments, worsened by recent deconstructions of language. On the one hand, Americanization of the English language is tragicomic; on the other, many Americans have enormous difficulty understanding English outside the United States, or wherever it is spoken fluently. In the worst cases, many Americans (including prominent ones, and even some presidents) seem barely to possess a first language at all—they speak English almost as a second language. Europeans routinely speak four or five languages fluently, yet so many Americans struggle with one.

Where does linguistic acuity come from, and why is Americanized English so impoverished? Linguistic acuity is developed during the "plastic period" of childhood, from birth to about age seven, when children rapidly and readily mimic the speech patterns they hear around them. If they hear their native language spoken well, they will speak it well; if they hear it spoken atrociously, they will speak it atrociously. But linguistic acuity comes also from reading and writing, which are more difficult than speaking and so require more attentive practice, and sometimes guidance. But the visual tradition has already produced deficits in the attention spans of American children, and increasingly among children of other Western nations whose oral and written traditions are being supplanted by visual ones. Those who cannot speak a language well have more difficulty reading, and those who cannot read well have more difficulty writing. If you compare the number of hours that children spend in front of TVs, video games, and computer monitors with the number of hours they spend reading and writing, you will find that exposure to the visual tradition correlates with impairment of linguistic acuity. Since Americans spend more time than any other people in the world transfixed by visual media, their linguistic acuity is also the most impaired.

Third, the visual tradition severely limits imaginative capacity. Why? Because visual media impose external images on the mind, preempting imagination, whereas oral and written media stimulate the creation of images by the mind, though visualization of words as pictures. When you read a novel, your mind is actively engaged, not only in processing the language and understanding the story, but also in generating a rich tapestry of internal images: literally, using your imagination. When you watch TV, your mind is passively bombarded and imprinted with external images, which exert a hypnotic effect. Language is pushed into the background; it becomes a recessive "soundtrack," a mere accessory to the images. The visual tradition focuses your attentiveness on the very thing that erodes your attention span—a sequence of images—while it neglects your linguistic acuity and preempts your imaginative capacity.

Fourth, the visual tradition's damage to the mind culminates in the eradication of cultural memory. Many contemporary American university students, lacking attention span, linguistic acuity, and imaginative capacity, also lack cultural memory. They have little conception of history, geography, politics, civics, science, mathematics, arts, literature, or any of the subjects that form the core curriculum of Western civilization. Those who cannot read simple words are functionally illiterate, while those who can read simple words but who do not understand their meanings are culturally illiterate. To counteract widespread cultural illiteracy, three American educators published a best-selling *Dictionary of Cultural Literacy*, which contains about five thousand items of basic information about culture and civilization that used to be common knowledge, assimilated from the written tradition.[8] That knowledge is no longer in the culture, thanks to the displacement of the written tradition by the visual one, in tandem with the totalitarian and Kafkaesque deconstruction of the written one by universities themselves.

The vast majority of contemporary American children and students inhabit a timeless, placeless world of shopping malls, television, and

Web pages. They have little conception of how anything came to be as it is, because they have not assimilated a written tradition in which to orient the cultural evolution that makes us human, and that gave us shopping malls, television, and Web pages. The visual tradition has bred a generation of culturally feral children, who have inherited a civilization they do not understand and will not be able to sustain.

Since the advent of commercial television in the 1950s, the visual tradition has swiftly and thoroughly undermined a written tradition stretching back several thousand years, and an oral one stretching back tens of thousands of years. This problem could have been contained, assessed, and corrected, if not for the neo-Bolshevik revolution that took place in American universities in the 1960s. As we will see in greater detail in the next chapter, the extreme left has itself denigrated and destroyed the written tradition in the humanities from within the very sanctuary supposedly dedicated to its preservation and study: the Academy.

Adults who have been reared and acculturated in the written tradition can withstand mild exposure to the visual tradition without eroding their cognitive capacities—watching the occasional television program will not do any harm. But children reared and acculturated exclusively or predominantly in the visual tradition suffer so much cognitive impairment that their capacities to acquire a written tradition are probably diminished for life. That is why a small number of greatly concerned and conscientious American parents either do not have TVs in their homes or limit their children's TV viewing to an hour or two on weekends. These children will probably not acquire ADHD, and will have a chance to develop fully as cognitive beings. They will also be "out-of-place" in an entire generation of cognitively impaired American children.

As one who values creativity, I am not demeaning the artistic possibilities latent in any medium—including the visual. Far from it. Television and film can also become conveyors of great art, and can also serve many other purposes—from social commentary to educational documentary, from entertainment to escape. The people who make the best TV and movies are creative geniuses, without a doubt. Yet Hollywood's golden age, along with most of the greatest movies ever made, arose from the foundation of the written tradition, which supplied the substance for adaptation to the silver screen. The downward spiral of contentless productions that characterize the contemporary visual tradition—from gratuitous sex and graphic violence, from vacuous special effects to reality TV—are all correlated with the erosion of the written tradition itself.

Classic television and classic film are admirable art forms, but only as adjuncts to the written tradition, and not as substitutes for it. So many movies are derived or adapted from books, yet very rarely indeed is a great movie as good as the great book from which it is copied. The same is true of theatrical productions adapted from stage to screen. Transposition from an oral tradition to a visual one, or from a written to a visual tradition, almost always impoverishes the art that is being transposed, and rarely improves upon it. Even if such transpositions are huge box office successes, they represent the bread and circuses of the global village, and not its enduring contributions to civilization-sustaining culture.

## The Digital Tradition

The foundations of digital computing ironically predate the visual tradition, by decades if not centuries. Binary numbers were invented by the ancient Chinese, and reinvented by Gottfried Leibniz, while Charles Babbage built a digital computing machine (the Babbage engine) in the nineteenth century. But William Shockley's 1949 invention of the transistor led to rapid evolution of radio, television, and computing technologies. I remember my first transistor radio, from the early 1960s. It was a "deluxe" model, because it had eight transistors—each one the size of a thimble. Shockley won two Nobel prizes and, along with other 1950s luminaries such as Alan Turing, paved the way for the digital tradition and the information revolution. By the 1990s, computer engineers had figured out how to place millions of microscopic transistors on a single computer chip smaller than a thimble.

Most human tools, as well as technologies, can be viewed as extensions of our limbs, our senses, and our faculties. Bicycles and cars are extensions of our legs, cutlery and chopsticks of our fingers. Telescopes, microscopes, and cameras are extensions of our eyes;

parabolic receivers and other antennae, of our ears; telephones and radios, of our faculty of speech. Personal computers are extensions of our minds. They not only incorporate, but also amplify, all the virtues and vices alike of the oral, written, and visual traditions. Personal computers turn us all into multidimensional producers and consumers of goods and services, and beyond that allow us to create and evolve virtual identities, to network in unlimited virtual communities, to manipulate data on colossal scales, to embark on exploratory voyages in cyberspace.

Computers have also added new dimensions to the perennial power struggle between man and machine. Do you command your computer, or does your computer command you? Is your computer a multitasking digital tool that serves your human ends, or are you a multitasking human tool that serves as a node in a digital network? These days, we are all a combination of both master and slave, alternating between commanding our digital devices, and being commanded by them.

Aside from all the novelties stemming from the computer revolution, it is vital to realize that the digital tradition incorporates and enhances the three prior traditions: oral, written, and visual. Your PC and associated peripherals can function as a radio, jukebox, music library, recording studio, CD player, voice-message system, text reader, and more—replicating all the functions of the oral tradition. In addition, your PC and associated peripherals can function as a word processor, typesetter, printing press, graphing calculator, post office, text-messaging system, and more—replicating all the functions of the written tradition. And, your PC and associated peripherals can function as an image processor, a photo lab, an animation studio, a movie studio, a TV, a video game arcade, a DVD player, and more—replicating all the functions of the visual tradition. Beyond this, a Web page is nothing but a digital montage of these three traditions: HTML (hypertext markup language) supports sounds, texts, and images, as well as programs that further manipulate sounds, texts, and images (e.g., applets). The digital tradition seamlessly folds all three previous traditions into one and adds its own novel dimension to reality, namely virtuality. Virtuality itself is "smoke and mirrors" of a very high order: layer upon layer of representations of data, whose ultimate substance is nothing more, or less, than strings of zeros and ones. Thus the digital tradition ingeniously combines extremes of simplicity and complexity, and makes them an extension and a mirror of our minds.

In virtual domains, e-mail and ecommerce have fundamentally changed the ways in which we communicate, buy, and sell. The Internet supersedes ordinary constraints of space and time, eliminating them as barriers to human interconnection. Cyberspace links any would-be communicator with any other and facilitates not only information exchange but also instantaneous browsing, buying, and selling across the global village. These aspects of the digital tradition strongly reinforce the Buddhist precept that all phenomena are interconnected. Nothing could be truer of cyberspace. And digital media unfailingly remind us, as does Buddhism, that all phenomena are transitory. Consider these Zen error messages, which will resonate with anyone who works in cyberspace—which increasingly means everyone in the developed world:

*Out of memory.*
*We wish to hold the whole sky,*
*But we never will.*


*A file that big?*
*It might be very useful.*
*But now it is gone.*


*The Web site you seek*
*cannot be located but*
*countless more exist.*


*Chaos reigns within.*
*Reflect, repent, and reboot.*
*Order shall return.*[9]

All my Buddhist teachers, past and present, have their own Web sites. Why? Because cyberspace is a perfect place for Buddhism. Soft copy is transitory, Web sites ephemeral. Hence there is no more apt way to illustrate interconnectedness and impermanence than via the Internet. Nagarjuna's teaching that "All dharmas are empty" is reemphasized when the teaching itself appears on a Web page.

The so-called "digital divide" is the virtual chasm that separates the developed and the developing world. People who still lack a written tradition are falling ever further behind the accelerated pace of global cultural evolution, which is driven by the digital tradition. Consider how many hours per day people spend at their computers, or wired to other digital devices, whose net effect is that each person becomes a single unit—a mind cell of an enormous and amorphous cyberorganism—networked with all its other mind cells via all the layers, textures, links, and hypertexts of cyberspace. In this sense, everyone's Web pages reflect the most cherished contents of their minds: the sounds, images, and texts that they most exuberantly display to the entire global village, and for whatever purposes. In fact, their missions are usually made clear by their Web pages as well. Viewed in this way, cyberspace is a vast and virtual public meetingplace where one can encounter the contents of people's minds and the purposes in their hearts. Cyberspace, in other words, is the town hall of the global village.

Being a full citizen of the global village now requires a gateway to the Internet and a virtual identity—ranging from a Hotmail address to an interactive Web site to a Second Life avatar. So computers function not only an extensions of our minds, they funnel the contents of our minds themselves into cyberspace, which then acts as a repository for all the contents of the other three traditions—oral, written, visual—continuously updated, augmented, uploaded, browsed, downloaded, reprocessed and renetworked.

## The Digital Tradition and the Four Pillars of Cognition

Since the digital tradition incorporates the three prior traditions—oral, written, and visual—it is important to ask how this revolutionary tradition fares at fostering the four pillars of cognition.

First, as regards attentiveness, the digital tradition can both heighten and diminish it. People who have been reared in the visual tradition will tend to use digital media as platforms for yet more visual stimuli: television, movies, videos, and games. Insofar as computers are used to replicate the experience of television, they affect attention span in the same way as television: by destroying it. Video games and computer games are another matter entirely. Playing games of any kind demands a certain level of performance, which in turn requires attentiveness. This is undoubtedly the evolutionary significance of game playing, which children of every culture love to do, and need to do. Playing childhood games boosts their cognitive development, while playing games in adulthood and old age also maintains cognitive fitness, and demonstrably delays or prevents the onset of diseases such as Alzheimer's.

So people who play chess against computers, or against one another over the Internet, are just as attentive as they would be playing chess against one another in person. Children who play computer games for hours (and years) on end are also developing and practicing attentiveness, but to what? To two things: to their hand-eye coordination, and to their participation in interactive animated milieus. Their hand-eye coordination is refined by mastering certain digital instruments—miniature keypads and joysticks. If you can play one Nintendo game well, you can play them all well.

Once manipulating the digital instruments is mastered and relegated to lower levels of consciousness, attentiveness is focused on the player's participation in the game. But the content of video games is uniformly primitive and usually juvenile, unfailingly appealing to the most dangerous and the most alluring capacities of human existence, violence and eroticism respectively. These twin tendencies are so deeply rooted in primate evolution, as we have seen in chapter 8, that it is hardly surprising to see them mirrored so extensively by the digital tradition. From an educational perspective, your children will encounter more than enough violence and sexuality in the real world, so perhaps their excursions in the virtual world could offer more enlightening content for their young minds. Attentiveness is a good thing, but overattentiveness to animations of violence and Eros, at the expense of more challenging content, becomes an extreme thing enlisted in a less-than-optimal pursuit.

The second pillar of cognition is linguistic acuity. Once again, the digital tradition can either enhance this faculty, or permanently impair it. The World Wide Web contains resources for boosting linguistic capacity via all the traditions it incorporates—as well as resources for making instantaneous translations from many languages into many others. It also features increasingly good "text readers," allowing the oral tradition to reemerge for those who wish to partake. All this can support linguistic acuity, although it seems not to provide as sound a basis as "old school" activities in the real world—reading books, learning grammar, and writing compositions. And once again, linguistic content in visual domains of the digital tradition—TV, videos, games—is appallingly poor.

The third pillar is imaginative capacity. Once again, the digital tradition can either enhance or diminish it. The World Wide Web is an increasingly vast repository of images, as well as images of images. All the world's great art and architecture, pop art and architecture, and personal art and architecture are warehoused and displayed in cyberspace. Computer imaging allows us to behold things we never saw prior to the digital tradition, from telemetric images of distant stars and galaxies, to tomographic images of the brain in different states, to chaotic images from Mandelbrot sets among other improbable objects of modern mathematics. All of this can only stimulate imaginative capacity. Then again, if the digital tradition is mostly used to replicate the visual tradition, it will reduce human consciousness to vegetative states just as quickly and easily as does television.

The fourth pillar is cultural memory. This is perhaps the strongest pillar to date of the digital tradition. Hume was the first Western philosopher to seal the connection between personal identity and memory.[10] Your egoistic persona is largely the sum of the memories (both short- and long-term) that you choose to hold in active consciousness, along with those you have repressed (in Freud's terms) or imprinted (in Buddhist psychology) into your unconscious. Either way, without memories you would revert to more primordial states of consciousness and unconsciousness alike. This can have wholesome or unwholesome manifestations. On one hand, Alzheimer's erases memory, along with other cognitive functions, reducing human beings to a helpless state. On the other hand, Buddhist practices typically sustain cognitive states that notice memories, but are not inflamed or otherwise impaired by undue attachment to them. But insofar as you "possess" a personal identity, it is largely made of memory. Yet I cannot forbear from adding that memory can serve you well or ill, and that all humans share a much more fundamental as well as a more transcendent identity, which does not depend on personal or cultural memory, but rather upon liberating the mind from its chains of memories—good and ill alike.

Similarly, insofar as there are discernable cultural identities, they are also largely made of collective or shared memories. These memories are passed on from generation to generation, evolving through a process of synthetic selection into what Richard Dawkins called "memes"—the cultural equivalent of genes.[11] Just as your physical identity is built initially from your inherited genes, drawn from a vast human gene pool, your cultural identity is built initially from your inherited memes, drawn from a vast human meme pool. The World Wide Web is a reflection of that very rich human meme pool.

The sheer amount of accumulated data on the Web is staggering. The twenty-five million books that you can stroll around, in an hour in London, amount to about 8.4 billion pages—if we allow an average of 336 pages per book. However you approximate them, there are billions of pages of hard copy in the great libraries of the world, and these billions of pages took about five thousand years to accumulate. At this writing, there happen to be just over eight billion Web pages in the public domain of the World Wide Web—around the same number of soft copy pages in cyberspace as there are hard copy pages in a great library. But these eight billion Web pages have accumulated in a mere decade, and their rate of accumulation is greater than that of hard copy. This highlights a significant difference between reality and virtuality.

In reality, there are far more readers than authors, and far more authors than publishers. In virtuality, every cybernaut is a reader, author, and publisher rolled into one. In short order, an astronomical amount of data—sounds, images, and texts—have accumulated on the Web, and there are no foreseeable limits to how much data cyberspace can hold. The number of Web pages, and the amount of data accumulated by the digital tradition, will soon eclipse that of all other cultural storage facilities combined.

So in terms of storing cultural memory, intercultural memory, and global human memory, the World Wide Web is the medium of choice, and the digital tradition appears extraordinarily powerful in this light.

## A Virtual Caveat

Mesmerizing though it may be, television did not put radio and theater out of business. The visual tradition operates in and on a different domain of consciousness than the oral. Similarly, Web pages did not put books out of business, for the digital tradition operates in and on a different domain of consciousness than the written. As those who work with both soft and hard copy know, there is something inherently satisfying about holding and reading a book—it's just not the same experience as reading soft copy from a screen. As a reading medium, books are still more advantageous than laptops, and in several respects. Books are more durable. Books make affordable gifts. You can take books to the beach, and not worry about exposing them to sand. You can lose and replace books cheaply. Books don't consume power. Books don't need repairs. You can sit, stand, or recline more comfortably while reading a book than while working at a computer. Authors can sign their books for you. Most important of all, a few hundred books have changed the shape or altered the course of human civilization. I do not know of a single Web page of which that can be asserted.

Cyberspace is egalitarian, to be sure. Most of us cannot afford the cost of expressing ourselves publicly on highway billboards or urban marquees, while standing on a soapbox at Speaker's Corner is affordable but unlikely to reach a wide (or a sane) audience. But everyone with access to the Internet can afford to publish a Web page. Moreover, you don't need to pay a fortune to Web designers to build a presentable Web site; the tools and expertise are increasingly accessible and affordable. The design and content of your Web pages are largely a matter of your taste and style, and not your budget. Your Web site reflects the structures and contents your mind, nonintrusively, to any and all who are interested.

Moreover, the advent of blogs has also made journalism more egalitarian, by siphoning power away from monolithic multinational event manipulators and empowering the consumers themselves. Major media have become intoxicated with their own power, creating frenzies that rage out of control, inventing, distorting, and sensationalizing news to service their agendas instead of reporting news to serve the public interest. Blogging acts as a brake on media run amok. For better or for worse, outraged bloggers took down no less a figure than Dan Rather, and that is food for thought. From one perspective, blogging itself could get out of hand, resembling a virtual lynch mob. From another perspective, major media have become so irresponsible and corrupt that blogging may exert the effect of keeping them (somewhat) honest. While conventional media have bequeathed to countless ordinary citizens what Andy Warhol famously called "fifteen minutes of fame," cyberspace is bequeathing its virtual equivalent to countless ordinary bloggers—fifteen million hits, or fifteen megabytes of bandwidth. Anyone with a timely or relevant message might find his or her blog inundated by snowballing hits. If you like egalitarianism, you have to love cyberspace.

Yet this leveling feature of the digital tradition has its own disturbing facets. Cyberspace is highly connected and resistant to preconceived or imposed hierarchies. Any page can link to any other page; a trail of links can lead from anywhere to anywhere. One must applaud this openness. At the same time, it also engenders a new kind of cultural chaos. In a traditional hard-copy library, a uniform and preconceived conceptual hierarchy—namely, a cataloguing system—awaits everyone who enters. You may read whatever you please, but you track down books according to a hierarchy that is designed for you, not by you. In cyberspace, there are preconceived conceptual hierarchies only in the shallow sense of search engines. They turn up what they are paid to turn up, or what is driven by popular demand. Yet a search engine is only a portal into cyberspace, a departure point and not a destination. You remain free to wander from any page, to any page, without a preconceived or intervening hierarchy.

Yet the danger of this openness is also plain. In a hard-copy library, you would find, for example, books of "History" as well as books of "Revisionist History." Yet you would presumably know the difference, because the written tradition housed by a great library provides a uniform map of its own works: a catalogue. But in cyberspace, you can browse two (or many) different Web pages that offer competing and incompatible views of a given historical event, yet you may find no means for assessing which page is "History" and which is "Revisionist History." There is no uniform catalogue of Web pages. So, for example, one set of Web pages claims that al-Qaeda planned and executed 9/11, while another set claims that Mossad (Israel's intelligence service) planned and executed 9/11.

Which of these pages is "History," and which is "Revisionist History"? Most people in Western civilization believe that 9/11 was al-Qaeda's doing, while a great many people in Islamic civilization believe it was Mossad's doing. Most people in Western civilization also believe that anyone who believes that Israelis (and/or Americans) perpetrated 9/11 is completely out of touch with reality. Unfortunately, that means nothing in cyberspace, because—by definition—virtuality *is* completely out of touch with reality. Precisely because the digital tradition is instantaneous and open, accounts of history and revisionist history alike coincide. They appear instantaneously and simultaneously, and there is little opportunity, and no cybercatalog, for disentangling them. In this respect cyberspace is Orwellian. For as Orwell revealed so chillingly in *Nineteen Eighty-Four*, "Who controls the past, controls the future; who controls the present, controls the past." Cyberspace clearly controls the immediate present, as every Web page instantaneously tries to command the assent of anyone who browses it. But no one controls cyberspace itself, and most cybernauts (like most lovers of liberty) find the idea of central control repugnant. But this in turn means that truth finds little purchase in soft copy. Anything or nothing might be true in cyberspace, and once again there is no preconceived map, compulsory catalog, or intervening hierarchy to contextualize what is being browsed.

Cyberspace is the global melting pot for data of every conceivable (and inconceivable) kind, instantaneously commingling plausible truth and patent falsehood, yet offering no way of distinguishing between them. This produces an anarchy of undifferentiated data, a recipe for fragmentation and chaos in the mirrored mind of the global village.

If the digital tradition is to help unify humanity, then what must emerge is a shared version of history, among many other things. There cannot be an enduring new world order in the absence of an emergent new virtual order—a way of honoring truth and disparaging untruth, a way of faithfully mirroring reality with virtuality. This is the challenge that confronts the digital tradition, if it is to become a foundation of global civilization in the way that the written tradition became a foundation of the West.

The implications for cognitive development and education alike are clear. Throwing a computer at every infant will guarantee neither their cognitive development, nor their education as useful and productive citizens of the global village. Then again, given prior exposure to a written tradition, the digital tradition can evolve cognition into new domains, appropriate for forging a new and shared human identity in the global village.

### Report Card on the Four Pillars
As an educator to the global village, I have filled in its "report card," as regards how well or poorly each of these four traditions—oral, written, visual, and digital—have affected each of the four pillars of human cognition. The report card is depicted in fig. 10.1. I hope it helps you ponder the question of how best to further your own cognitive development, and that of your children.

Among the three original traditions, the written one is clearly The Middle Way between the oral and the visual. Overall, the oral tradition alone is too limited in its capacities to develop full human cognitive function, while the visual tradition alone erodes cognitive function itself. Learning to read and write a language well, by means of the written tradition, is the main pillar of cognitive development. The digital tradition can make things better, or worse. It can enhance the strengths

| Cognitive Pillar →  Cultural Tradition ↓ | ATTENTION SPAN | LINGUISTIC ABILITY | IMAGINATIVE CAPACITY | CULTURAL MEMORY |
|---|---|---|---|---|
| Oral  | Very Good | Very Good | Good | Fair |
| Written  | Excellent | Excellent | Excellent | Excellent |
| Visual  | Very Poor | Poor | Very Poor | Very Poor |
| Digital  | Any of the Above | Any of the Above | Any of the Above | Superlative |

Figure 10.1 Report Card on Cutural Evolution and Cognition

of the written tradition, or exacerbate the weaknesses of the oral and visual ones. Since throwing a computer at every infant is not the answer to global education, the advent of the digital tradition highlights the need for a global curriculum and content.

Those who have learned and mastered a written tradition can derive enormous convenience, power, and performance from digital media, as for example in digital versus manual typesetting, in digital versus physical engineering simulations, in digital versus chemical image processing, or in digital versus mechanical word processing. But in each case, the digital tradition of computing either enhances capacities already acquired via the written tradition, or else inhibits these capacities if they have not been acquired via the written tradition. Thus American university students who have learned to read and write fluently can utilize digital word processing and can mine the vast veins of data on the World Wide Web, to produce essays worthy of formerly state-of-the-art educational systems and standards. By contrast, many American university students have been reared in a visual tradition alone, and moreover were never obliged to learn to read and write during what passed for their "education" in the failing American system itself. Such students, from the prestigious Ivy League to the anonymous community college, can barely read or write or comprehend at all, and so they abuse the visual tradition to download, print out and hand in essays purchased from www.essays.com. The professorial art and craft of teaching the canon of civilization degenerates from creative and constructive exploration and exposition of written ideas to "forensic pedagogy" in detecting and exposing essays plagiarized from cyberspace. In what direction is such a civilization headed? Either toward Star Wars, or back to Plato's cave, or possibly a combination of both.

If the human sojourn in and voyage through this galaxy turns out to resemble Star Wars, then the oral tradition of the Jedi masters coupled with the visual tradition of video games, in tandem with the archetypal struggle of good versus evil and the warrior who rescues the princess, will together suffice for the fulfillment of human purpose in the galaxy. We will then resemble our own video games. But if the force is not with us, then assuredly the farce will be. The farcical aspects of the visual and digital traditions will triumph over the force of the written one, as the farce of a deconstructed "higher education" is perilously close to triumphing over the force of a classical one. In that case, we will need a very large cave to accommodate humanity, and that would be Plato's cave.

## The ABCs of Cognition

The ABCs are crystal clear. Aristotle himself was the first philosopher to write systematically across a curriculum of cultural interests, and in many ways his complete works cemented the written tradition into the Hellenic strand of Western civilization, where it reinforced the Abrahamic commitment to "The Book." For Aristotle, the noblest life is a contemplative one, and contemplations are fashioned of thoughts. When Aristotle asserted that "without an image thinking is impossible," he understood that thought requires imaginative capacity. Einstein, one of the most profound thinkers in human history, realized his theories by "imaging" both physical reality and mathematical forms, and then selecting or deriving those forms that best matched his images of reality. Both men were steeped in a written tradition that optimized their imaginative capacities and also made them accessible to future generations. Confucius said, "By three methods we may learn wisdom: first, by reflection which is noblest; second, by imitation, which is the easiest; and third, by experience, which is the bitterest." If Confucian reflection is at all equivalent to Aristotelian contemplation, then it is an endorsement of the written tradition. Imitation is clearly second best to Confucius, and is also a hallmark of the oral tradition. It is second best for a good reason. Those who are able to reflect will eventually see what is mirrored by reflection, and so will discover the Way. Those who are able to imitate and nothing more may learn wise and helpful things thereby, but may also learn foolish or harmful things. Absent the power of reflection, they can distinguish neither wisdom from folly, nor help from harm, nor shepherds from wolves. Among five thousand animals in human nature, the ape is closer to us than any other, and so people will easily revert to aping others without paying sufficient human heed to exactly what they are doing, unless they mobilize their human power of reflection. And worst of all, when we both imitate a harmful lesson and fail to reflect on its harmfulness, we condemn ourselves to learn a bitter lesson in the future, when the fruits of that harm inevitably ripen. This is also where Tao and karma intersect.

And so we move to Buddha, who said, "A disciplined mind brings happiness." Young minds are best disciplined when schooled in the written tradition. No one appreciates this better than Daisaku Ikeda, from whom we will hear momentarily.

Meanwhile, the fruits of the harms done to American higher education since the late 1960s, by an unwitting "one-two" punch—a combination of the visual tradition and the deconstruction of the written one—are more than ripe. As we shall next see, they are quite beyond rotten. Unless American universities are willing and able to reinstate the written tradition, along with its standards and content, the K-12 system has no incentive to do anything but succumb to forces that have made a mockery of education. The vital importance of education to civilization cannot be overemphasized. Most people are born neither geniuses nor cognitively challenged. The vast majority of us start attaining our potential, if at all, via formal education, or else fail to start through lack of it. The American system has failed an entire generation, and a rotten fruit of that failure will be its inability to sustain its own civilization.

So many Americans—including prominent ones—seem not to grasp the extent of their nation's self-inflicted cultural disabilities, which is of course precisely why the slide continues unabated. American cultural deficits also contribute heavily to the increasingly negative image that America herself conveys to the rest of the world. The deficits themselves are exacerbated if not produced by the two political extremes that we saw in chapter 6. The right-wing extreme fails to make adequate funding commitments to cultural refinement, such as endowments to the humanities, while the left-wing extreme deconstructs refinement itself, from within the universities. The resulting cultural image that America conveys to the rest of the world is anything but refined. America's turbines of hard power (its dominant military might) are driven by an evaporating reservoir of soft power (its diminishing cultural assets). As Kishore Mahbubani (dean of public policy at Singapore's National University and a leading public intellectual) has astutely observed, America forged a world in the twentieth century that Americans themselves are increasingly ill-prepared to inhabit in the twenty-first.[12]

I encounter something quite different when I visit Soka Gakkai schools, whether in Japan or the United States. The oral and visual traditions are not discounted, but neither is the written tradition deconstructed. Reading, writing, thinking, speaking, and musical skills are inculcated as The Middle Way of a well-rounded and excellent education, whose youthful beneficiaries are being prepared to carry the torch of pacific and progressive human civilization into the twenty-first century and beyond. I asked Daisaku Ikeda about his philosophy of education, since the schools he has founded contrast so sharply with the educational extremes of widespread functional illiteracy in developing nations, and of pervasive cultural illiteracy in the most developed ones. He replied:

"Education is an endeavor that deals directly with the most essential aspects of what it means to be human. It is not too much to say that it is only through education that we become genuinely and fully human. The purpose of education is to form, shape, foster, deepen and polish our humanity. In my view education must serve to empower people with the ability to engage in the work of creating value for oneself and for society as a whole. It must stimulate, bring forth and unleash the hidden possibilities within people. In this sense, education is very deeply related to the Buddhist idea of human revolution.

"It was based on this ideal, and with the determination to realize the vision and dreams of my predecessors, Presidents Makiguchi and Toda, that I founded the comprehensive Soka education system, spanning the kindergarten to the university levels. Needless to say, I have taken great personal interest in these schools, and have done everything in my power to create the kind of educational environment that encourages the development of all the nascent gifts of the students; one that fosters strength, depth and expansiveness of character; one that gives rise to people of talent able to make a real and lasting difference in the world.

"The goal and objective of education must always be the learners. Students or pupils must always be kept center stage in any educational effort, and anything that ignores their individuality, force-feeds them knowledge or pushes them into a uniform mold must be rejected."[13]

Now let us see what becomes of human potential and individuality where that center stage still needs to be erected—in the developing world that lags so far behind—and where it has been dismantled—in the American Gulag. Perhaps Daisaku Ikeda's philosophy of education will help illuminate more clearly what must be followed—The Middle Way—and what must be rejected, namely the extremes.

# 11

## EDUCATIONAL EXTREMES
### Global Lag and the American Gulag

*The educated differ from the uneducated
as much as the living from the dead.* —Aristotle

*All wrong-doing arises because of mind.
If mind is transformed can wrong-doing remain?* —Buddha

*Those whose measures are dictated by mere expediency
will arouse continual discontent.* —Confucius

### Teach Your Children Well

AS WE HAVE JUST SEEN, a distinctive if not defining feature of humanity is our capacity for cognitive development. This capacity is best actualized by a combination of influences, ideally a partnership between parents and schools. The four pillars of cognition—attention span, linguistic acuity, imaginative capacity, and cultural memory—are erected during the earliest days and years of sentient life, and so the primary caregiver, whether mother, father, or nanny, bears the first and foremost responsibility. But for those children who are fortunate enough to receive formal education as well, schooling must begin during the critical first seven years in order to be most effective. And as we have also seen, the written tradition is by far the most powerful for constructing the four pillars of cognitive development. So the challenge of good parenting is to help a child fulfill its cognitive potential, as well as to support a functional formal education system.

In this chapter, we will look at two educational extremes. At one extreme is the global lag in literacy, which affects billions of people worldwide by excluding them from formal education and preventing them from acquiring any written tradition at all. Absent formal education and the acquisition of a written tradition, very few human beings can attain their full potential, and most will languish in conditions of deprivation that put our global village to shame. At the other extreme is the American Gulag, which has transformed the world's premier liberal arts educational system into a totalitarian imposition of politically correct and often inane ideology. In the process, the apparatchiks of the American Gulag have deconstructed and defamed that which is finest, noblest, and best in our written tradition, replacing great works with celebrations of mediocrity, and inculcations of hatred toward Western civilization itself—woven warp and woof with a spiteful mantra blaming all the world's ills on "white male heterosexual patriarchal hegemony."

If ever a Middle Way were needed, it is in the educational sphere. My Buddhist friends teach how to "make good cause" from adverse conditions, so at the end of this chapter I will propose a way of "making good cause" from both these wasted extremes.

That said, education cannot and does not take place in a vacuum. It is one vital strand of an intricate tapestry woven of socioeconomic, religious, and ultimately political strands as well. In earlier chapters, we have seen the kinds of damage done to children and adults alike by oppressive religious and political systems, and in the next chapter we will look at some of the gross economic disparities of the global village, which leave half the world's peoples bereft of the barest necessities of life, let alone the luxury of an education. For children subsisting in the shantytowns that surround sprawling megalopoli from Latin America to Asia, the daily routine is to scrounge for food, beg for money, or worse. Young boys in the failing or failed states of Africa, Asia, and Latin America find more opportunity in soldiering than in schooling. They learn to wield firearms, not to read books. Young girls in many fundamentalist Islamic states are utterly excluded from what grimly passes for education there, while young girls in Southeast Asia are being sold as sex slaves instead of being sent to schools. India alone has two hundred million rural poor, whose families subsist on one or two dollars per day. Meanwhile, predator capitalists "save" impoverished children all over the developing world, by employing them as slave labor in sweatshops.

Add to this the additional and lethal burdens of malaria, HIV, flood, famine, and political dislocation, and the mosaic of childhood suffering in the developing world assumes proportions that most of us in the developed world are unequipped to process, let alone to help redress. From the time of Buddha's parable of the mustard seed to the present, the death of a child strikes inconsolable grief into the heart of a family. What then must the deaths of forty thousand children per day in the developing world, of mostly preventable causes, strike into the hearts of the human family? Gandhi righteously observed that a society can be morally gauged by the way it treats its animals. Is it no less true that the global village can be morally gauged by the way it treats its children?

So lack of education in the written tradition, which drives low literacy levels and correlates with a web of human suffering and unfulfilled potential, also translates into short life expectancies and diminished quality of lives. The global village has the technology and the money to redress the planetary problem of dying and endangered children, and has all the manuals of best practices and good governance to boot; but it does not possess the political will to redress it. That is because, with notable exceptions, humanity has yet to subscribe to a shared human paradigm for the global village of the twenty-first century.

## Some Numbers to Conjure By

Let us contrast some telling statistics from two democracies, Canada and India.

If we look at Canada, a country among those with the highest standards of living in the world, we can immediately see the relevance of literacy. Among new jobs being created by the Canadian economy, about half require at least sixteen years of schooling. That amounts to K-12 plus three to five years of college or university, at minimum. Canadians at the lowest literacy levels have an unemployment rate of

26 percent, compared with only 4 percent unemployment among those with the highest literacy levels. So while literacy is clearly a passport to employment, remember that education is a partnership between parents and schools. In Canada, 34 percent of children from the lowest income families do not complete their high school education. Thus a significant fraction of these lowest income families fail as educational partners for their children, trapping them in a cycle of illiteracy and diminished opportunity. Although Canada has a generous social "safety net" for its least successful citizens, about 60 percent of those receiving social assistance have not completed high school. Across the board, literacy and higher education correlate with socioeconomic mobility; lack of literacy and incomplete education, with socioeconomic immobility. Amazingly, even though Canadians are among the best-educated and most affluent peoples in the global village, 22 percent of Canadian adults have "serious problems" dealing with printed materials, while almost three-quarters of Canadian companies report problems with functional illiteracy in some sectors of their organizations. So even in a highly successful country like Canada, which has done more than most nations to enhance public education, increase literacy, and reduce poverty, the Gaussian distribution reasserts itself. In any nation, there will always be some segments of the population that require more social assistance, who are less well equipped to acquire the rudiments of literacy, and less able to encourage their children to become literate themselves. For all that, Canada remains one of the best places on earth in which to inhabit the nether regions of Gauss's curve.[1]

In India, the statistics are much grimmer. Overall male literacy is 64 percent, while for females it is only 35 percent. Almost 100 percent of Canadian children complete fifth grade, while 62 percent of Indian children reach fifth grade. Only 30 percent of Indian adults have completed eight years of schooling. Among Indian children aged six to fourteen, one-third do not attend school at all: that amounts to some twenty-three million boys and thirty-six million girls. These data help explain why, as of the year 2000, half the world's illiterate people lived in India. The South Asian pattern of low overall literacy, a pronounced literacy gap between male and females, and perpetual dire poverty for huge segments of the population, is repeated all over the developing world. The South Asian adult literacy rate (49 percent) lags behind that of sub-Saharan Africa (57 percent) and the "Arab world" (59 percent). In India and Nepal, 40–59 percent of all children are now considered "at risk" (in terms of mortality, illiteracy, malnutrition, and risks of HIV/AIDS and armed conflict). Forty-seven percent of Indian people and 50 percent of Nepalese people live on less than one dollar a day. Outside of Sri Lanka, which has taken some positive strides, South Asian women are the least schooled in the world, averaging 1.2 years of school per woman. The average for the developing world is three years. Nepal's female literacy rate is the lowest in the world, at 13 percent; and its overall adult literacy rate is the fourth lowest in the world, at 28 percent.[2]

Worldwide, close to one billion adults are illiterate, and nearly two-thirds of them are women. In 1969, when mankind took its "giant step" on the moon, 80 percent of African women were still illiterate. This has improved to about 50 percent today, but that cup remains half empty. Worldwide, more than one hundred million children—sixty million of whom are girls—still lack primary schooling.[3]

In 1990, in eighteen countries the literacy rates of males were more than twice as high as those of females (see fig. 11.1). The lowest ratios of female-to-male literacy are invariably in African, South Asian, and Islamic countries. Female illiteracy is a correlate both of high infant mortality (see fig. 11.2) and of population explosion. The less education women receive, the more babies they have. Babies born to illiterate women are more at risk for a host of reasons, and those who survive—especially the females—are also more likely to remain trapped in this pitiless cycle of illiteracy, poverty, and overpopulation. The plight of such females is not only appalling, it represents an unconscionable extreme and a compelling challenge for globalization.

Throughout such developing nations and regions, where lack of schooling proceeds from overarching norms of political or religious corruption, poor governance, failed statecraft, or rogue statehood, there is also an increasing and disturbing preponderance of child soldiers. Young boys who have no parents, few prospects for schooling, or little taste to languish passively in poverty are able to find guns, bullets, and

Figure 11.1 Adult Literacy, 1990

| COUNTRY | MALE% | FEMALE% | MALE/FEMALE RATIO |
|---|---|---|---|
| Afghanistan | 42 | 11 | x3.8 |
| Burkina Faso | 26 | 7 | x3.7 |
| Niger | 18 | 5 | x3.6 |
| Nepal | 37 | 11 | x3.4 |
| Sierra Leone | 40 | 14 | x2.9 |
| Liberia | 49 | 18 | x2.7 |
| Mozambique | 52 | 19 | x2.7 |
| Guinea | 45 | 18 | x2.5 |
| Burundi | 45 | 19 | x2.4 |
| Gambia | 48 | 20 | x2.4 |
| Benin | 42 | 19 | x2.2 |
| Bhutan | 51 | 23 | x2.2 |
| Pakistan | 46 | 21 | x2.2 |
| Senegal | 39 | 19 | x2.1 |
| Bangladesh | 47 | 23 | x2.0 |
| Djibouti | 55 | 27 | x2.0 |
| Morocco | 52 | 26 | x2.0 |
| Togo | 61 | 30 | x2.0 |

Source: http://www.unicef.org/pon95/chil0011.html

Figure 11.2 Infant Mortality

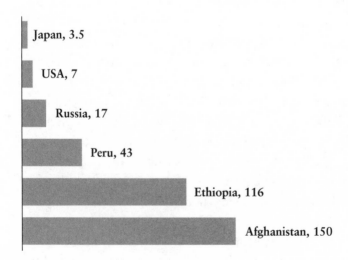

Japan, 3.5

USA, 7

Russia, 17

Peru, 43

Ethiopia, 116

Afghanistan, 150

Figure 11.3 Child Soldiers Around the World

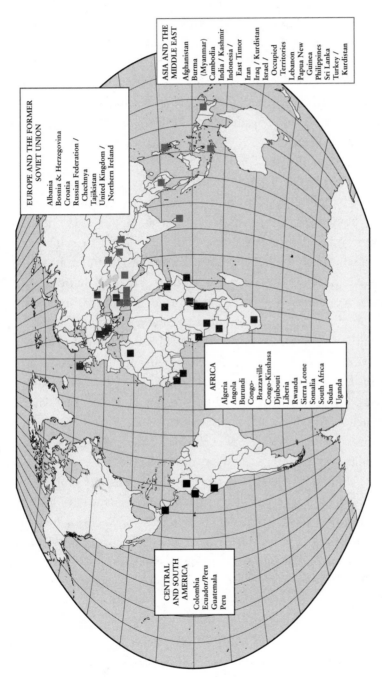

EUROPE AND THE FORMER
SOVIET UNION

Albania
Bosnia & Herzegovina
Croatia
Russian Federation /
    Chechnya
Tajikistan
United Kingdom /
    Northern Ireland

ASIA AND THE
MIDDLE EAST

Afghanistan
Burma
    (Myanmar)
Cambodia
India / Kashmir
Indonesia /
    East Timor
Iran
Iraq / Kurdistan
Israel /
    Occupied
    Territories
Lebanon
Papua New
    Guinea
Philippines
Sri Lanka
Turkey /
    Kurdistan

AFRICA

Algeria
Angola
Burundi
Congo-
    Brazzaville
Congo-Kinshasa
Djibouti
Liberia
Rwanda
Sierra Leone
Somalia
South Africa
Sudan
Uganda

CENTRAL
AND SOUTH
AMERICA

Colombia
Ecuador/Peru
Guatemala
Peru

http://hrw.org/capaigns/crp/crp-map.htm

conflicts aplenty, in stark contrast with a scarcity of books, teachers, and classrooms. While it takes a village considerable time to rear a child, a doomed economy or a failed polity can rapidly arm one. Such neighborhoods of the global village have degenerated into literal Hobbesian states of nature—wars of all against all—which have dispossessed these children of their precious childhoods, substituting in their stead a life immortalized by Hobbes as "solitary, poor, nasty, brutish, and short." Fig. 11.3 shows the nations and regions most sorely afflicted by this horrific condition.

If globalization's dynamics, monies, powers, and manuals of "best practices" cannot ameliorate this extreme, in which young girls and young boys are reduced to daily survival in the most inhumane of circumstances, then globalization will have failed to achieve its own conspicuous promise. Yet it is not a coincidence that nations whose girls are slaves and whose boys are soldiers are also nations in which globalizers themselves can barely find footholds for laying the foundations of modernization. If the people who go in to help are going to be blown up, shot, kidnapped, robbed, tortured, beheaded, or demonized, then we are better off sending in Cabalists, Jesuits, and Buddhists, rather than the marines.

We educators reflexively recite the perennial truism that education is so much better for children than enslavement and warfare, and is moreover astronomically less expensive. Education seems to occupy a perennial and central position in any Grand Solution to the world's problems, and especially to the problems facing children in the developing world. If you want the dollars and sense of it, read this passage from Aldous Huxley's *Encyclopedia of Pacifism*. The question is: What could we have done with all the money spent on World War I, if instead we had diverted it entirely to education? Huxley drew upon Nicholas Murray Butler, an outstanding American educator, philosopher, and Nobel laureate (Peace, 1931) to reply as follows:

"The cost of the Great War has been reckoned at about four hundred thousand million dollars, or eighty thousand million pounds. According to figures quoted by Dr. Nicholas Murray Butler in his

1934 report to the Carnegie Foundation this sum would have sufficed to provide every family in America, Canada, Australia, Great
Britain and Ireland, France, Belgium, Germany and Russia with a
five hundred pound house, two hundred pounds worth of furniture, and a hundred pounds worth of land. Every town of twenty
thousand inhabitants and over in all the above mentioned countries, could have been presented with a library to the value of a million pounds and a university to the value of two millions. After
which it would have been possible to buy the whole of France and
Belgium, that is all the land, houses, factories, railways, churches,
roads, harbors, etc., in these countries."[4]

Now bear in mind that the cost of World War I was utterly negligible
compared with that of World War II. Beyond this, the cost of averting
World War III—the nuclear arms race, the space race, deterrence,
mutual assured destruction, plus the thirty to forty conventional wars
fought simultaneously in the world every year since the end of World
War II—has undoubtedly eclipsed all previous military expenditures in
turn. In that case, we could have fed, clothed, housed, and educated
everyone on the planet, several times over, for a fraction of the cost of
the twentieth-century wars. But we didn't. Instead, we have produced
extremes: inadequate education in the developing world, and
deconstructed education in the developed one.

The better interests of peoples in the developing world will be served
by better education. Delivering that education to them however, is easier
said than done. How can we deliver an education to places where DHL
can't deliver a package? How can one empower good shepherds, and
disempower wolves, when the wolves never voluntarily relinquish
power? How does one emancipate illiterate girls, disarm illiterate boys,
and coax them into schoolrooms? By grassroots reform? By regime
change? By chanting? I wish I knew. I do know that the extreme of
illiteracy and ill-education is an affront to human decency, and that
somehow this global lag must be corrected, and guided into The Middle
Way. Then tens of millions of children will suffer less, live better, and
become more fulfilled as human beings.

## The Other Extreme

What, you may well ask, does the other extreme look like? Is there such a thing as "too much" education? I think not. Recall, we are made to be lifelong learners. If the predominant extreme in the developing world is the conspicuous absence of a viable educational system, then the corresponding extreme in the developed world is the deconstruction of the global village's formerly premier educational system—that of the free West—and its replacement with a totalitarian regime of political correctness, racial and sexual quotas for hiring and admissions, elimination of academic standards, mandatory indoctrination, identity politics; speech codes, mind control, and toxic hatred of Western civilization itself. I call this entire system the "American Gulag." Gulag is a Russian acronym[5] that signifies a ruthless punitive system whose overall purpose is the brutal repression of dissenting political thought, speech, and deed.[6] In the American Gulag, the political dissidents are none other than the defenders of Western civilization itself—including yours truly.

We have already reviewed the Marxist roots of the neo-Bolshevik revolution that took place in the Western universities during the late 1960s. Moreover, we have also glimpsed how French postmodernism—bundled by definition with antirealism and deconstructionism—has destroyed the Aristotelian curriculum of higher education, replacing it with political indoctrination. We will now look at some examples of daily life in the twilight zone of the American Gulag, glimpsing events and processes that lie beyond the imagination of readers who are not themselves subject to its obscene and absurd political dictates. These events and processes have gradually sapped and eroded Western civilization from within, yet have also been exposed and opposed by a small, indefatigable but thus far relatively powerless resistance, with which I am proud to be associated. Some important works by Canadian and American dissidents, refuseniks, and counterrevolutionaries alike are listed in the Suggested Readings section at the back of this book, and I urge you to consult them.[7]

Before surveying the political terrain of the Canadian and the American Gulags, I wish to remind you of the twin totalitarian models from which their ideologies are copied: Nazism and Stalinism. Please place what I am saying in perspective. The Canadian and American Gulags do not command the power to annihilate human flesh. They murder nobody physically. However, they both command and exercise the power to destroy careers, to annihilate the human mind, and with it the life and culture of contemplation—vital to any civilized community— that Aristotle prized above all else. And as Antonio Gramsci knew, and taught his neo-Marxist minions, one can foment a revolution and destroy a polity without firing a shot, if only one can take over its cultural institutions from within, and like a pernicious political retrovirus mutate its cultural DNA to self-destruct. Then the culture— and the civilization it sustains—collapses without ever realizing that it was deathly ill. Meanwhile, those of us who refuse to succumb to this malady—a form of political madness, a collective delusion not found in any DSM[8]—continue to defend what is noblest and best in Western civilization, even though by doing so we are committing "crimes" against the administrations of the universities themselves. Does all this sound mad? It should. It is mad. But it is also true.

## Madmen, Frogs, and Boiling Water

Elie Wiesel is a survivor of Auschwitz and Buchenwald, and a witness to the horrors of Nazism, which killed his mother, father, sister, native village, and their peaceful way of life. The story of how the Nazis rounded up his secluded Jewish community in the remote Carpathian Mountains of Hungary, deported them to Auschwitz, and gassed his mother and little sister, among so many others on arrival, is revealed in his book called *Night*.[9] (Oprah has called attention to this book of late, her way perhaps of showing solidarity against the rising tide of anti-Semitism emanating from hotbeds of hatred in European and Islamic civilization.) In the beginning of the book, Wiesel recounts his last idyllic days of boyhood, when he, his family, and his village assumed that life would go on as it always had. Buddhism, of course, teaches us never to make such assumptions, and reminds us constantly of the impermanence of all phenomena, but Nazism reached the Carpathian Mountains in advance of dharma.

However, Wiesel's tale also introduces someone who might have played the role of a Buddhist, whom his village mistook for a madman. He was a penniless wandering Jew who warned them about unbelievable Nazi atrocities in faraway places. Comfortable in their ways, and not wishing to acknowledge even the possibility of change for the worse—let alone the unimaginable—the villagers ridiculed him, and dismissed his dire warnings as lunacy. Even as rumors and news of Nazism's encroachment on Hungary and its occupation of Budapest reached their ears, they dismissed it. "It won't come here," they rationalized. "It will pass," they temporized. But they were incorrect. Tragically and mortally incorrect. Of course I am not blaming the victims for what befell them, and neither is Elie Wiesel. The Nazis were guilty of committing genocide, among many other crimes against humanity. The Jews of the Carpathian Mountains, like so many others, erred minutely yet fatally on the side of omission: They failed to believe it could happen to them.

The madman who visited Elie Wiesel's village is a real-life archetype. He appears throughout human history, in many cultures and contexts. He is the biblical prophet, often reviled or persecuted—not for issuing dire warnings, but for speaking unpopular truths. He is the Sufi poet, simultaneously irreverent and righteous beyond belief. He is Shakespeare's fool, ridiculed or discredited for his ability to pierce the veils of delusion that shroud and blind the other characters. He is the inmate of an American psychiatric facility, who intuitively penetrated a deception in which ethicists were pretending to be patients in order to study abuses by staff, and who declared to one of the ethicists, "You're not crazy; you're checking up on the doctors."[10] Sometimes the madman is an unassuming German high-school teacher, like Oswald Spengler, who was granted a terrible vision of the West's decline. Sometimes the madman is a Japanese Buddhist monk, like Nichiren, who was savagely persecuted, nearly executed, and eventually exiled for exposing corruption, for warning the rulers of corruption's inevitable costs, and for improving the human estate. Sometimes the madman is a Mayan shaman, like Martin Prechtel, who had a bounty on his head, was hunted like an animal, and barely escaped Guatemala with his life for practicing the healing arts of an ancient culture slated for extinction by the blind cutting edges of globalization. Sometimes he is a fearless leader, like Winston Churchill, who was roundly booed and ostracized by Parliament for denouncing Chamberlain's appeasement of Hitler in Munich as "an unmitigated defeat." And sometimes this archetypal madman is even a professor of philosophy, who claims to be a political refugee from Canada, and a political dissident of the American Gulag.

A popular metaphor for failing to recognize looming danger is that of the frog in water. Drop a frog into boiling water, and it immediately leaps out of the pot. Drop a frog into tepid water that is gradually but inexorably heated, and it boils to death without ever realizing its plight. This is a metaphor for the failure of human imagination. More than a pillar of cognition, imagination is one of humanity's greatest gifts; its failure, one of our worst afflictions. By refusing to envision what lies just beyond the threshold of our experience, in exchange for the false security granted by the illusion of permanence, we may fail to realize magnificent opportunities just beyond our grasp, and may also fail to recognize mortal threats that rise incrementally, like the incoming tide or the slowly boiling water.

And so, by the time Elie Wiesel's village took the threat of Nazism seriously, it was far too late. They were what Americans call the "walking dead"; the waters of the Holocaust had gradually heated up around them, by increments, and inexorably killed them.

Another witness to Nazism, German-American journalist William Shirer, experienced both the incremental and the instantaneous effects of Nazism's heat. Stationed in Berlin during Hitler's transformation of the democratic Weimer Republic into the totalitarian Third Reich, Shirer witnessed the incremental horror of what was transpiring all around him. Step by step, with each edict and proclamation, cloaked and veiled by propaganda, Hitler gradually but inexorably eradicated democracy. He suspended civil liberties, foreclosed academic freedoms, disenfranchised German Jews, and rearmed the military, all in preparation to carry out the plan he had published in *Mein Kampf*, a book that everyone was compelled to read but which apparently nobody believed. Yet immersed in this relatively tepid phase of Nazism, life in Germany seemed normal to enough. As Shirer recounted:

"I myself was to experience how easily one is taken in by a lying and censored press and radio in a totalitarian state . . . a steady diet over the years of falsifications and distortions made a certain impression on one's mind and often misled it. No one who has not lived for years in a totalitarian land can possibly conceive how difficult it is to escape the dread consequences of a regime's calculated and incessant propaganda."[11]

Shirer also recounts how swiftly the German universities capitulated to national socialism, how few professors opposed or fled the tyranny, and how many supported it and its subversions of higher education in order to retain their jobs. One professor later wrote, "It was a scene of prostitution that has stained the honorable history of German learning." Another professor lamented, in 1945, "The German universities failed, while there was still time, to oppose publicly with all their power the destruction of knowledge and of the democratic state. They failed to keep the beacon of freedom and right burning during the night of tyranny."[12]

Meanwhile, behind the Iron Curtain, another kind of totalitarian state had emerged—not from the extreme right, but from the extreme left. Stalin was more than a match for Hitler. To those who value (or devalue) human life by head counts alone, Stalin was the greater butcher, murdering, starving, or enslaving to death twenty to thirty million of his "comrades" during a reign of terror that outlasted the Third Reich. Like Hitler, Stalin built a vast network of concentration camps, some for manual slave labor, others for intellectual slave labor, some for hard slave labor unto death, others for imprisonment pending execution. This system of prison and labor camps was called the gulag. The gulag housed a variety of inmates: common criminals, political dissidents, anyone merely suspected of being politically incorrect, innocents denounced by paranoid or vengeful or tortured informants, hoping to spare themselves by condemning others, and returning

Russian prisoners-of-war whose heroic survival in Nazi Germany led to their conviction as "traitors" to the Soviet Union.

Just as many so-called "good Germans" knew, one way or another, about Hitler's extermination camps yet feigned ignorance or floated denial for the sake of their consciences or their personal safety, so too did most Russians know about the gulag, and similarly feigned ignorance or floated denial, in fear of vanishing into its monstrous labyrinth. Yet as I have pointed out before, there is one significant difference between totalitarianism from the right and totalitarianism from the left, and it is this: Totalitarianism from the right is truthful and candid in certain significant ways, whereas totalitarianism from the left is untruthful and secretive in just those ways. For example, in Hitler's Germany, if you were an Aryan, a member of the Nazi Party, and if you vocally supported the führer and vociferously denounced the Jews, then you were deemed to be a "good citizen" of the Reich, and you enjoyed whatever privileges and protections the Reich had to offer. By contrast, in Stalin's Russia, even if you were a member of the Communist Party, and even if you vocally supported Stalin and vociferously denounced capitalism and all the "enemies" of communism, you could readily be accused and convicted of concealing counterrevolutionary treachery behind a mask of zeal, and could vanish at any instant into the gulag, never to reappear, and never to have existed.

So Nazi extremism bred hatred; Soviet extremism, paranoia. Bigots and racists at least have the candor to hate their victims openly, whereas Stalinists and Maoists harbor hatred of humanity itself, which they conceal beneath the "noble" guise of revolutionary idealism. When bigots and racists murder you, it's because they hate themselves and blame you for their inadequacies. But when Stalinists and Maoists murder you, it's because you are somehow "interfering" with the "greater good" of their Marxist revolutions. Hitler murdered Jews and Gypsies because he hated himself and blamed them for his hatred; Stalin "purged" Bolsheviks, Mensheviks, Trotskyites, Kulaks, Red Army officers, freed Russian POWs, engineers, doctors, intelligentsia, ordinary Soviet citizens of every kind, and even purged the purgers themselves (the NKVD), because they were all somehow "interfering" with the revolution. Stalin hated himself too, and blamed his victims for his hatred, but for the sake of "the revolution" *everyone* became a potential victim. Nazism is sadistic; it demonizes and preys on others. Stalinism is masochistic; it demonizes and preys on itself.

Shirer observed how easily people allowed themselves to be seduced by the tepid phase of Nazism. One saw healthy Aryans at work and at play, happy Aryan families, and a vibrant Aryan economy. No one paid much heed to what lay in store for non-Aryans. This was not the case in Stalinist Russia, however. Russian workers were not healthy, and did not play. The inherently flawed Marxist economy could never be vibrant. Moreover, Soviet families could not be happy, because children were encouraged to denounce their own parents and cause them to vanish into the gulag, all for the sake of "the revolution." Meditate on that.

The family is the most fundamental unit and microcosm of the state, on which the state's very health and prosperity depend, and this has been known from the days of Aristotle, Buddha, and Confucius. Yet extremism from the left destroys the family, allegedly for "the sake" of the state.

So in theory, it's easier to rehabilitate extremists of the right than extremists of the left. Why? It is more direct to awaken the humanity of those whose inadequacies assume the form of hating others outright, than it is to awaken the humanity of those whose inadequacies assume the form of hating others beneath the guise of helping them. That is why Marxists are more resistant to "deprogramming" than Nazis, and why Marxism—as a global cultural virus—has proved a more persistent and ubiquitous threat to humanity, whereas Nazism is (mercifully) more discontinuous and containable. Neo-Nazi groups still thrive in the United States, the United Kingdom, and Germany, but pose no serious threat today to any nation or civilization. That cannot be asserted of Marxism.

## The Soviet Gulag

The Western public initially learned of the Soviet gulag's existence from an inmate, Aleksandr Solzhenitsyn, who wrote and smuggled out a now-classic "novel," *A Day in the Life of Ivan Denisovich*, that afforded his own firsthand account of a Siberian node in Stalin's network of domestic penal colonies. This was followed by *The Gulag Archipelago*. Later, Solzhenitsyn's masterpiece, *The First Circle*, depicted a completely different facility in the same system, this one in the heart of Moscow. As the book's title implies, this facility houses the elite among the far-flung gulag's inmates: the politically incorrect engineers and scientists. These prisoners, typically serving ten to thirty years for the crime of having opinions, or thinking unauthorized thoughts, are nonetheless "privileged" to be allowed to practice their professions, albeit not as human professionals, rather as goods to be disposed of at Stalin's whim. Unlike his totalitarian twin Hitler, Stalin wrote no books informing the world of his grand designs. Instead, he simply went over the death lists every day, picking and choosing thousands of victims personally, in addition to the tens and hundreds of thousands who were starved or murdered by the large-scale systemic purges he instituted.

But within *The First Circle*, the political prisoners at least have the opportunity to fulfill their personal excellence and, in the usual Aristotelian way, this greatly satisfies them. As well, there is a Confucian order in their communal life, unharmonious though it may be at times, and yet this is preferable to chaos. (Buddha makes an appearance too, in a delightful and surprising digression.[13]) Being politically incorrect, these prisoners are also politically aware, and so they know that many millions more of their "equal" comrades are enduring hideous conditions of cold, starvation, hard labor, and a gauntlet of kindred privations. So the prisoners of The First Circle have the good sense to be cynically and even humorously appreciative of their predicament. The Russians have a delightfully ironic and sardonic sense of humor. Engrossed in their work, the political prisoners of *The First Circle* often seem happier than today's free Americans who hate their jobs.

The existence of this facility is secret, and travelers through the streets of Moscow see no sign of it except for the meat wagons that regularly ply certain routes. As Solzhenitsyn remarks, a naive visitor to Moscow would infer from the frequency of meat wagons that Muscovites are pretty well fed. In fact the meat wagons were the prison transports in disguise. It was an ironic and sardonic Russian disguise, given that everybody in Soviet Russia was nothing but a piece of meat, terrorized instead of tenderized, and awaiting his turn—which would come without warning, at any time or place—to be devoured by the Dog of State. And so a naive visitor to Moscow might be seduced by the facade and propaganda—meat wagons and *Pravda*—of this Marxist-Leninist-Stalinist worker's paradise, just as many were seduced by national socialism's full employment and happy families with rosy Alpine complexions and crisp lederhosen.

That is why Aristotle's teacher, Plato, warned us so strongly not to mistake appearance for reality. We are all naive visitors wherever we go on this earth, even if it be to places and people we think we know. Glimpsing reality is like hitting a bulls-eye in archery, or serving an ace in tennis, or executing a musical passage perfectly. It happens only when, in the space of a short time, you manage to do everything exactly right, and effortlessly. It also comes as a result of many years of constant practice, during which (if you're like most of us) you probably managed many moments of doing everything exactly wrong, and strenuously.

Glimpsing reality also means knowing when you are better off disregarding your village and heeding the archetype of the itinerant madman. For if he bears a tale that seems impossible to you, then perhaps your notion of the possible is overdue for an upgrade. If you lead your life without regularly refreshing your conception of what is possible, you not only deprive yourself of liberty, opportunity, and hope, but also make it easier for those who may hate themselves and blame you to dispossess you of those gifts, and maybe of your life itself. You are always better off glimpsing reality than succumbing to appearances.

## The Canadian Gulag

Canada's gradual transformation from a colony to a dominion of the British Empire, and then to an autonomous sovereign nation, was completed by one of its great statesman, Pierre Elliot Trudeau. This flamboyant, modish, Jesuit-schooled, fluently bilingual and bicultural prime minister was the only politician of the 1960s to merit the suffix "mania"—usually reserved for The Beatles. His landslide election victory in 1968 was won with the slogan "Trudeaumania." The crowning achievement of his distinguished career came during his final term, when in 1982 Trudeau repatriated the Canadian Constitution from Britain. However, this historic move was accompanied by the enactment of the Canadian Charter of Rights and Freedoms, a document whose laudable title conceals an Orwellian shift from individual entitlements to "group rights."

As we have seen over and over again, Western civilization has been characterized by an emphasis on individualism and on attendant entitlements that are said to belong to individuals, such as "inalienable rights." Granted, the history of Western civilization is also a history of struggles to win individual rights from political or religious or commercial establishments reticent to grant them. And yet such struggles could not even have been initiated, let alone won, without a strong and deep undercurrent of sympathy for and commitment to the moral ascendancy of the individual over the collective. Wherever they exist, human rights provide a political shield to protect the individual against predations and other injustices of the state, whether wrought by its servants or its tyrants. Human rights are inseparable from individual entitlements. So-called watchdog groups that monitor abuses of human rights are invariably seeking to safeguard the entitlements of individuals, not of groups, whether at home or abroad. The UNESCO Charter of 1945 similarly recognizes the rights of individuals, not of groups. The civil rights movement was focused squarely on applying the protections and entitlements of the American Bill of Rights to African Americans as *individuals*—recognizing that although they had been collectively disenfranchised by slavery and segregation, their political salvation lay in their collectively securing the same *individual rights* that whites enjoyed under the aegis of the Constitution. And similarly, women's liberation was originally conceived in just this spirit, according to *individual* women all the political entitlements that had been accorded and restricted to *individual* men. As a protestor and hippie during the 1960s, I enthusiastically supported civil rights and women's lib as well, and did so expressly on the understanding that individuals, and not collectives, were the intended recipients and ultimate beneficiaries of the invaluable gift of human rights.

You, the individual, have a right to vote. You, the individual, have a right to own property. You, the individual, have a right to privacy. You, the individual, have a right to freedom of expression. You, the individual, have a right to a fair trial and legal representation. You, the individual, have a right to life, liberty, security, and pursuit of happiness. These and kindred entitlements are accorded to you as an individual human being, and not as a member of any group whatsoever—except the human race. Human rights belong to all humans, and the fundamental "unit" of humanity is the individual.

The noble Western aspiration of securing universal human rights via individual entitlements met its demise in Canada in 1982, killed by the very Charter that supposedly guaranteed them.[14] The execution began promisingly enough. Section 2, for example, is called "Fundamental Freedoms," and declares that "everyone has the right" to a number of things that are familiar to and expected by any Westerner: "freedom of conscience and religion; freedom of thought, belief, opinion and expression, including freedom of the press and other media of communication; freedom of peaceful assembly; and freedom of association." So far, so good. Every one of these is an *individual* entitlement: your conscience, your religion, your thought, your belief, your expression, your association with others. But then, in the heart of the Charter, we encounter Sections 15(1) and 15(2), under the notorious heading "Equality Rights":

"15(1) Every individual is equal before and under the law and has the right to the equal protection and equal benefit of the law without discrimination and, in particular, without discrimination based on race, national or ethnic origin, color, religion, sex, age or mental or physical disability."

Bravo. This is a succinct and state-of-the-art rendition of the fundamental thesis of human rights: That they pertain to persons, not to groups. But then comes 15(2):

"15(2) Subsection (1) does not preclude any law, program or activity that has as its object the amelioration of conditions of disadvantaged individuals or groups including those that are disadvantaged because of race, national or ethnic origin, color, religion, sex, age or mental or physical disability."

This is an equally succinct and state-of-the-art rendition of the fundamental thesis of collectivism's hijacking of individual rights: That they pertain to groups, not to persons. George Orwell could not have penned a better parody. In effect, 15(1) says "All persons have equal rights"; while 15(2) says "Some persons and groups have more equal rights than others." Having legislated *Animal Farm*, Canada swiftly procured the livestock. Section 15(2) became the choice instrument of oppression for neo-Marxist enemies of individual entitlements, used to further their collectivist agenda of identity politics, quota systems, retributive justice, and—specifically—the exclusion of white and Jewish males from employment (Canadian Jews are considered "white" for the purposes of exclusion). Unlike the United States, Canada has no history and legacy of slavery and segregation, and so is spared the cathartic clashes of race that obtrude into every facet of American life. So in Canada, women were first in line for cashing in their "group rights." Militant feminists began a mad dash to capitalize politically on all possible suppressions of individual entitlements mandated by section 15(2). They swiftly replaced universal individual rights with feminist identity politics, erecting cultural edifices of monumental hatred and rabid intolerance of individuals—especially white males, whom they blamed for all the world's ills, including the "greatest ill" of all, namely Western civilization.

To mobilize the full weight of 15(2), feminists had to become victims of sexual disadvantage, which they were quick and eager to do. Cults and cultures of victimhood raged feverishly in Canada (and the United States) during the 1980s and 1990s, as everyone who wasn't a white male sought to reap compensations offered to the "historically disadvantaged." But in Canada, feminists established a virtual monopoly on victimhood, consolidated by outcome-oriented studies like CanPan's (the Canadian Panel on Violence Against Women's) ten-million-dollar "Changing the Landscape." The term *outcome-oriented* is a euphemism. It means that politically desired results of a social scientific "study" are determined in advance, then the "study" sets about confirming these predetermined findings. Of course this is the antithesis of science. But as we saw in chapter 7, truth and science stand no chance, in the short run, against ideology. So CanPan's outcome-oriented study, written by feminists for feminists, found that Canadian women are trapped in "lives few in the world would choose to lead." Canadian women are "in bondage, bound by inequality and gagged by fear"; Canadian society as a whole is allegedly waging "war against women." In fact, CanPan found that "Virtually all Canadian institutions are organized around hatred for women and hostility against women."[15]

Do you recall the comparison between Canada and India with which this chapter began? Based on literacy and education, and their correlates of liberty, opportunity, and hope, Canada is surely one of the most successful countries in the world in terms of offering advantages to all its citizens while India is surely one of the least developed in this respect. All the available objective evidence suggests that millions of Asian women—for example in India and Nepal—are certainly and sadly trapped in "lives few in the world would choose to lead," whereas Canadian women lead lives that are the envy of the world. That is, they do so in the real world, which is nowhere on the mental map of the most militant feminists.

CanPan's grotesquely distorted accusation of ubiquitous institutional sexism and "war against women" was nothing but a shallow pretext to establish reverse-sexist institutions from coast to coast. The CanPan study and its sisters spawned nationwide collectivist initiatives, designed to purge white males by attrition and replace them with women: not on the basis of individual merit, but rather on the basis of quota systems informed by identity politics, justified by "group rights," and enforced by section 15(2) of the charter of so-called "Rights and Freedoms."

John Fekete is a Canadian professor of humanities whose parents fled Hungary after having endured occupations by both the Nazis and the Soviets. Professor Fekete is therefore no stranger to totalitarianism from both extremes, and so he rightly deplores the CanPan study as "an extreme example of biopolitics . . . obsessively self-dramatizing, fixated in gender-thinking, and bristling with hostility."[16]

The Canadian Gulag plumbed new depths with the 1990 election of Bob Rae as Ontario's premier. Ontario is Canada's largest, wealthiest, and most politically correct province. Rae's government, which swiftly earned the moniker "Rae-cists," passed an "Employment Equity Act" (Bill 79) based on section 15(2) of the Charter. Article 2.2 of the Act stated: "Every employer's workforce, in all occupational categories and at all levels of employment, shall reflect the representation of Aboriginal people, people with disabilities, members of racial minorities, and women in the community." In other words, every employer was obliged to conduct a local demographic survey, and hire according to the quotas stipulated by the numbers. Not even Soviet central planning ever attained the patent absurdity of such a "paint-by-number" workforce.

In chapter 8, we glimpsed the ancient evolutionary origins of the primitive human predisposition to xenophobia and hostility toward others of different appearance—whether garb, pigment, or chromosomes. So extremists of the right discriminate unjustly *against* Aboriginal people, people with disabilities, members of racial minorities, and women—because they do not view them as human coequals. Now extremists of the left discriminate unjustly *for* Aboriginal people, people with disabilities, members of racial minorities, and women in the community—because they do not view them as human coequals, but as statistical conveniences. Justice is never done by substituting one kind of injustice for another. When will they ever learn?

To be just, we should hire the person who is most qualified to do the job, while recognizing the coequal humanity of every single job applicant. Martin Luther King's supremely important utterance, about our children being judged not by the color of their skin but by the content of their character, has been purged from the social consciousness of the West by vapid and feckless extremists of the left under whose dehumanizing political regimes *everybody* is judged first and foremost by the color of their skin, and second by their degree of slavish devotion to the dogmas that drive dehumanization.

To discriminate for or against people is not to see them as human. If you are an employer interviewing candidates for a job, you should be primarily interested in their qualifications and their characters. These are the important things. Now, plenty of well-qualified people of reputable character happen also to be Aboriginal people, people with disabilities, members of racial minorities, women—or even occasional white males.

Why can't we just hire human beings? Because Marxist-Leninist-Stalinist-Maoist-feminist identity politics outlaws the existence of the individual, and views persons only as representatives of racial, ethnic, and gender clusters. This is Marxist "justice." Read Boris Pasternak's *Dr. Zhivago*, or Arthur Koestler's *Darkness at Noon*, and rediscover through historical fiction how the Bolshevik revolutionaries in historical fact prohibited the very thing that Western civilization has prized above all: the private lives of individuals, including eternal love and epic romance, free of politicization from humorless and heartless fanatics who politicize absolutely everything.

To enforce Bill 79, Premier Rae set up an Employment Equity Office, which had the power to monitor the workforce composition of every employer in Ontario, and insure hiring according to demographic data alone. Merit became irrelevant, qualifications suspect, quotas compelled. Yet when an independent researcher attempted to discover the workforce composition of the Office of Employment Equity itself, which was empowered to oblige exactly this disclosure from any and all employers in the province, he was stonewalled.[17] The Office was finally compelled by Canada's "Freedom of Information Act" to disclose its own workforce composition. The 1991 census indicated that women constituted 46.6 percent of the Ontario labor force; they constituted 90.5 percent of the Office of the Employment Equity's staff. Racial minorities constituted 13 percent of the provincial labor force, but 53 percent of the Office staff. What of able-bodied white males? "The Office reported that 0 percent had identified themselves in this category."[18] This is quite consistent with section 15(2) of the Canadian Charter: Some groups are indeed "more equal" than others.

At that same time, a white male philosopher friend of mine was a finalist for a position at an Ontario university. The other finalist was a woman, who was conspicuously less qualified, but who eventually got the job. Two members of the hiring committee objected to her appointment on the grounds that it had been politically orchestrated. The committee had been ordered to "hire a woman" to satisfy the quota system, and not to hire the best candidate who satisfied the job requirements. These two committee members were prepared to testify before the Ontario Human Rights Commission, whose mandate, in effect, was to uphold the Charter. Recall, section 15(1) compels exactly what section 15(2) prohibits: "equal benefit of the law, without discrimination based on race, national or ethnic origin, color, religion, sex, age or mental or physical disability." I guess that includes white males, too.

So the white male philosopher appealed to the Ontario Human Rights Commission, charging that his rights had been violated. His appeal was summarily dismissed. He was told that it was impossible, by definition, for anyone to discriminate against him. Why? Because he was a white male. Welcome to the Canadian Gulag, where everyone has equal rights except for white males, who cannot possibly be discriminated against because they have "historically" oppressed every other Canadian, and moreover have trapped Canadian women in "lives few in the world would choose to lead." Therefore everybody else needs more-than-equal rights, including the right to discriminate against white males who, by definition, cannot be discriminated against. Even Orwell would be impressed. As I continue to assert, ideological hatred from the left is much more twisted than mere bigotry from the right.

Section 15(2) of the Canadian Charter of Rights and Freedoms, the CanPan study, and Ontario's Bill 79, are just a few stars in the galaxy of Canadian political correctness. Since the neo-Marxist ideology of these initiatives is rooted in the universities, it is not surprising that the universities themselves are at the "leading edge" of the implosion of Western civilization. After all, their tenured radicals are the demolition team.

For example, in 1993, the Canadian Philosophical Association adopted a notorious set of hiring recommendations, based on another feminist "outcome-oriented" *Report*, which this time discovered (to its horror) that philosophy was, and had always been, a "male-dominated" activity devoted primarily to excluding females.[19] By means of sophisticated "social science"—that is, head counts—feminists found that 13 percent of Canadian philosophers were female. They concluded that this represented a "situation" that needed "to be rectified." Why? Because women represent about 52 percent of the general population. Therefore, according to the philosophy of justice that informs political correctness—namely quotas—every difference in raw numbers becomes incontrovertible "proof" of institutional injustice. The *Report* concluded that there are "too few" female philosophers both because females have been allegedly excluded from philosophy, and because the putative "political agenda" of male-dominated philosophical inquiry apparently "socially constructs" a subject matter, tradition, and climate hostile to the interests of women.

The *Report* ordained explicit quotas for female philosophers (40 percent by the year 2020), such that that *every* female with a Ph.D. in philosophy would be guaranteed an academic job, whether competent to hold one or not. In practice, the pool of qualified females was (and still is) quickly exhausted, so unqualified females were (are still are) vaulted to the front of the hiring queue. This means that women who have not yet completed their doctorates, who have not acquired postdoctoral experience, who have published little or nothing, and who have taught little if at all—in other words, applicants who should rank at or near the bottom of any list of candidates for professorships compiled on the basis of objective merit—are preferentially hired in the place of male applicants who have doctorates, postdoctoral experience, significant publications, and evidence of outstanding teaching ability.

The *Report* declared that "being female is itself an academic asset in a job candidate." This blithe disclosure reiterates nothing but the sum and substance of Hitler's Nuremburg Laws, which excluded Jews from German universities on the grounds that being Aryan was itself an academic asset in a job candidate.[20] The grand irony is that German Jews were excluded from employment for being "non-Aryan"—that is, not white enough. Canadian Jewish males, including yours truly, were now excluded from employment for being "too white." My question is, when will the world learn to be inclusive on the basis of humanity, instead of exclusive on the basis of dehumanization? As you can see from Canada, a relatively "advanced" nation, not anytime soon.

Just as the Nazis demonized "Jewish physics," so militant feminists have demonized "male philosophy." The CPA *Report* continued, "Do we mistake traditional male social roles (particularly those associated with aggressiveness) for philosophical skill? Many women are simply not comfortable with the social behaviors associated with adversarial philosophy . . . Hiring policies at the faculty level cannot possibly succeed in achieving their goals unless female undergraduates can be convinced that philosophy provides a hospitable climate for women." So 2,500 years of rigorous philosophical (including mathematical and scientific) inquiry, whose consistent purpose has been to deepen human understanding and discover natural truth—all in the cause of ameliorating the human estate—has been politicized and debased by female fanatics. The mission of philosophy is no longer to furnish a foundation for the edifice of higher education; rather, it is to make women "feel good" by providing them with "a hospitable climate."

Now perhaps you grasp the fuller force of one of chapter 8's main themes. Recall that primitive hunting and gathering tribes worldwide practiced strict sexual division of labor: the men hunted, while the women gathered. Women were excluded from primitive male hunting parties, and moreover were probably grateful. Human females evolved to be mothers and gatherers, not warriors and hunters. Most women who hunted with men would have experienced extreme discomforts that they were not evolved avidly to seek or happily to endure. But cultural evolution has shifted the hunting grounds, from savannas to symbolic structures, and has transformed the quarry, from flesh-and-blood creatures to electronic numbers. And so there are myriad symbolic structures within which women can hunt as well as men—from selling real estate to arguing lawsuits to practicing medicine—as long as they are afforded the liberty, opportunity, and hope of doing so.

Among the most elusive "big game" pursued by the human mind are philosophical insights, mathematical theorems, and physical laws: Such transcendent ideas are glimpsed and stalked and trailed and sometimes caught by the "top predators" in the stratosphere of rarefied mind, who happen to be mostly but not solely men—and for very good evolutionary reasons, as we have seen in chapters 8 and 9. Hunting big game of the mind can be as strenuous and arduous as hunting the big game of the field. And by their very own testimony, militant academic feminists feel just as uncomfortable on this intellectual hunt as they would have felt on the physical one: Mathematics, logic, and theoretical physics do not satisfy their emotional needs, which clearly, by their own testimony, take precedence over their intellectual ones. (Recall Prof. Betty Johnston from chapter 7: "We found that much of our mathematical experience had been of a dominating practice that alienated us from our own knowledge and the everyday world, separating mind, body and emotion, and prioritizing abstraction and generalization over meaning.") To make themselves feel better, these feminists have obliged the universities to provide "hospitable climates" instead of intellectual foundations. As a result, the culture and civilization that the universities support have become utterly debased.

We briefly glimpsed how the role of science in Nazi Germany was politically degraded from a noble search for universal laws to a debased endorsement of racial mythology. It provided a "hospitable climate" for Aryans by demonizing and excluding Jews. Similarly, philosophy in the Canadian Gulag has been politically degraded by militant feminists, from a noble love of wisdom to a debased endorsement of feminist mythology. It provides a "hospitable climate" for women by demonizing and excluding males.

The *Report to the CPA* met with intrepid but futile resistance from a small handful of academics—human beings (of both sexes and assorted colors) to whom this fascism of the new left represented an affront to the cherished fundamental freedoms, rights, and human dignity that were now a dead letter in Canadian philosophy departments, from coast to coast. But this infamous *Report* was only one wavelet in a rising totalitarian tide, hardly confined to philosophy departments, which has transformed "the true North strong and free" (lyrics from Canada's national anthem) into a People's Femocratic Republic.

There has been a steady exodus of well-qualified but unemployable white (and Jewish) males from the Canadian Gulag to many parts of the world. We are united in exile because we carry a politically banned chromosome—XY. I was fortunate to find an academic position in the

United States, and so I thank the Canadian feminists for excluding me. I guess I love Big Sister after all (at a safe distance).[21] But many of Canada's best and brightest minds, which happen to be housed in white or Jewish men's bodies, are denied individual rights, deprived of equal opportunities, and excluded from employment by Canada's constitutionally mandated liberal fascism. Michael Moore forgot to film that part of Canada. Like far too many "good liberals," he's in total denial of the totalitarian extremes of the illiberal left.

## The American Gulag

So in 1994, I relocated from the feminist frying pan into the racialist fire, from the minor-league Canadian Gulag to the major-league American Gulag. And not to any ordinary political prison—I was vaulted to the American First Circle: The City College of New York. Repugnant to freedom and malignant to liberty though it may be, Canadian political correctness seems mildly astringent beside its corrosive American counterpart. In sporting terms, it's like softball compared with hardball.

The feminist component of American political correctness is just as rabid as its Canadian version, but its totalitarian powers are shared by more "diverse" interests. The militant feminist departure point for Canadian and American gender relations is that of Marilyn French: "All men are rapists and that's all they are. They rape us with their eyes, their laws, and their codes." Alas but true, not everyone loves Big Sister. But American feminists have had to take a backseat to something that doesn't exist in Canada: the politically correct legacy of the African slave trade. The highest card in the American playing deck of identity politics is the Ace of Race, followed by the King of Class, the Queen of Gender, and the Knave of Victimhood. American feminists generally stand after the poorest of the poor (single teenage mothers, thanks partly to feminism) in "class warfare"; and aligned if not allied with gays and lesbians in "gender warfare." The measure and therefore the power of their grievances, based on "historical disadvantage," is strictly graduated. The enslavement and segregation of Africans, as well as the socioeconomic distinctions loathed by

Marxists, are tacitly conceded by feminists to have been more appalling than the "enslavement of women by men"—otherwise known as marriage, which has been also been known to sustain master-slave dynamics in both directions (especially the other one).

Playing the race card has become a refined art, as far as it goes. When reporter Jayson Blair of the *New York Times* was caught red-handed—as it were—filing stories from places he had never been, which for some strange reason violates journalism ethics, he played among other things the race card: He's not responsible for fraudulent reporting because his great-great-grandfather was a slave. He learned this mantra from guilt-ridden white liberals, who try to make themselves feel better by claiming that making a black man accountable for his actions is racism. It is sad beyond measure to descend from a legacy of slavery. I share Jayson's grief over the tragedy of his forebears. But the abdication of individual responsibility has been drummed into his head since birth, or earlier, by the political commissars of the American Gulag, who seek only to perpetuate the tragedy through Jayson and his descendents, rather than to liberate Jayson and his descendents from it. My point is, if a feminist is caught committing professional fraud, she (perhaps in tandem with her lawyer and her psychologist) could certainly formulate a defense based on victimhood, but she could not credibly deny responsibility on the grounds that her great-great-grandmother was a hausfrau. And that's why race trumps sex in the United States.

Coast to coast, the American Gulag is committed to one proposition above all: that the entire world is oppressed along the lines of race, class, and gender by a ruthless conspiracy of white male heterosexual patriarchal hegemonists, whose "texts" and "narratives" were fabricated by dead white Eurocentric males. Bring down Western civilization, the political commissars and tenured radicals assert, and all will be well. Sure it will. Just like it is in Africa, the Middle East, and South Asia. The flagrant antirealism, hatred of reason, and contempt for liberty that have governed campus cultures, deconstructed the Western canon, and debilitated generations of young American minds since the 1960s, have come a long way toward achieving their goal. That goal is to sap the intellectual vitality of Western civilization with toxic doctrines, so that the flocks cannot discern the wolves from the shepherds, distinguish truths from falsehoods, tell liberty from enslavement.

If you want to learn the identities of the wolves, as well as their doctrines, you can read all about them. While militant Canadian feminists were having a protracted field day with the Charter, their American counterparts were equally busy during those decades, deconstructing the republic and replacing it with a gulag. It was well-educated Europeans—Communist Herbert Marcuse at Berkeley, ex-Nazi Paul de Man at Yale, and master deconstructionist Jacques Derrida—who, coached by Italian Marxist Antonio Gramsci, cynically sewed the first seeds of institutionalized American self-hatred. Nowadays, flocks whom these wolves have fleeced of their civilization graduate from today's Poison Ivy Leagues, bleating accusations like "Eurocentric" at the very civilization that spawned, nurtured, and educated them—and gave them the liberty and opportunity to bleat.

The totalitarian agendas of European fascists and Marxists alike were defeated by America and her allies—that is, were defeated politically, militarily, economically, geostrategically. But they were not, nor can they ever be, completely defeated culturally. Determined Marxists smuggled totalitarianism's cultural DNA out of Europe and into North America itself, via the Trojan horse of the 1960s. That decade was one great mare, and I'd ride her any time; but she was also karma's mule, having been used to smuggle a deadly cultural virus—totalitarianism—into the very brain of Western culture, the universities. Leading homegrown totalitarians soon joined the fray: the communist-fascist hybrid Noam Chomsky at MIT, deconstructionist Stanley Fish at Duke, Jew-baiting African Americans like Leonard Jeffries at CCNY, WASP-baiting Cornel West at Yale, and man-hating feminists like Sandra Harding, whose "contributions" to "higher education" include denouncing Isaac Newton's *Principia* as a "rape manual."[22]

Storied institutions whose mission had once been to study and enlarge the canon of what Matthew Arnold called "the very best that has been thought and said" have been converted into the American Gulag, dedicated to the wholesale destruction of Western civilization from within. In the words of Roger Kimball, who has traced the course of this rot firsthand:

"What we are facing today is nothing less than the destruction of the fundamental premises that underlie our conception of both liberal education and of a liberal democratic polity. Respect for rationality and the rights of the individual; a commitment to the ideals of disinterested criticism and color-blind justice; advancement according to merit, not according to sex, race, or ethnic origin: these quintessentially Western ideas are bedrocks of our political as well as our educational system. And they are precisely the ideas that are now under attack by *bien pensant* academics intoxicated by the coercive possibilities of untethered virtue. Just how bad have things become? Alas, it is virtually impossible to overstate the case."[23]

## Groupthink and Thoughtcrime

Like all institutions in the American Gulag, the University of Pennsylvania is committed to "diversity," a word whose dictionary synonyms include "assortment, mixture, multiplicity, variation, difference, unlikeness, distinctiveness." In the Orwellian language of the Gulag, however, words most frequently denote their opposites. So "diversity" actually means ruthlessly enforced mind control of students by administrations, which compel conformity to monolithic doctrines *du jour*. One female student at Penn dared to challenge the "Diversity Follow-Up Program" that monitors and rectifies students' attitudes, bringing them into compliance with "groupthink." She objected to its contempt for individualism, to its desire "continually to consider the collective before the individual." She complained that to "dictate what to think regarding groups or individuals" was "merely a process of thought homogenization" that actually destroyed "intellectual diversity."[24]

The political commissar (that is, university administrator) who read her memo underlined the word "individual" and wrote, "This is a 'red flag' phrase today, which is considered by many to be racist . . . Arguments that champion the individual over the group ultimately privileges [sic] the 'individual' belonging to the dominant group . . . in a pluralistic society, individuals are only as significant as their groups."[25]

Just so. And indeed, not all groups are equal: Some are more equal than others. For example, an Ivy League university's Office of Student Life annually prints a handbook lauding "tolerance" and extolling the virtues of cultural "diversity." The office also compels attendance at freshman orientation films, one of which illustrates methods of contraception and abortion. When a Roman Catholic student tried to exit the cinema, asserting that she had no need to watch these practices because her religion forbade them, she was physically prevented from leaving, coerced, in the name of "tolerance" and "diversity" to watch the entire film. Rank hypocrisy is another face of political correctness.

One must learn to decode the convoluted meanings of words like "diversity" and "pluralism" in the American Gulag. In the words of Prof. Alan Kors, a champion of individual liberty at Penn, "An individual is not an autonomous moral being, but a member of a racial and historical group that possesses moral debt or credit. There is only one appropriate set of views about race, gender, sexual preference, and culture, and holding an inappropriate belief, once truth has been offered, is not an intellectual disagreement, but an act of oppression or denial. All behavior and thought are 'political,' including opposition to politicized 'awareness' workshops."[26] In his classic *Nineteen Eighty-Four*, Orwell called such opposition "thoughtcrime." Indeed, in the American Gulag, holding individual opinions or thinking for oneself has become a crime against university administrations. For students, such "crimes" are punishable by suspension or expulsion; for faculty, by firing, denial of promotion or tenure, or other administrative sabotage of their careers.

## Speech Codes

Since freedom of thought is intolerable in the American Gulag, freedom of speech must be ruthlessly suppressed. Speech codes are enforced on campuses from coast to coast, and here is what they typically forbid. The University of Maryland at College Park prohibits "idle chatter of a sexual nature," "graphic sexual descriptions, sexual slurs, sexual innuendoes," "comments about a person's clothing, body, and/or sexual activities," "comments of a sexual nature about weight, body shape, size, or figure," and "pseudo-medical advice such as 'you might be feeling bad because you didn't get enough.'" Nonverbal communication is also thoroughly regimented. Prohibited gestures include "movements of the body, head, hands, and fingers, face and eyes that are expressive of an idea, opinion, or emotion." Unacceptable gestures also include "holding or eating food provocatively."[27] Above all, speech codes are put in place to prevent the creation of a "hostile learning environment"—that is, saying something that any sufficiently "diverse" person finds in the least provocative or disagreeable. The punishments for violating speech codes are the same as those of committing thoughtcrime: suspension or expulsion for students, firing or career destruction for faculty.

What is consistently tolerated, encouraged, sponsored, and celebrated by the Gulag is open hostility and overt hatred toward white men, heterosexuals, Christians, conservatives, and any individuals (i.e., "political dissidents") whose thoughts, opinions, or actions fail to conform to "diversity." As Kors and Harvey Silverglate attest, "On virtually any college campus, for all its rules of 'civility' and all of its prohibitions of 'hostile environment,' assimilationist black men and women live daily with the terms 'Uncle Tom' and 'Oreo' said with impunity, while their tormentors live with special protections from offense. White students daily hear themselves, their friends, and their parents denounced as 'racists' and 'oppressors,' while their tormentors live with special protections from offense. Believing Christians hear their beliefs ridiculed and see their sacred symbols traduced—virtually nothing, in the name of freedom, may not be said against them in the classroom, at rallies, and in personal encounters—while their tormentors live with special protection from offense. Men hear their sex abused, find themselves blamed for all the evils of the world, and enter classrooms whose very goal is to make them feel discomfort, while their tormentors live with special protections from a 'hostile' environment."[28]

## No Due Process
Throughout the American Gulag, a vast and sprawling network of political commissars and apparatchiks monitor the thought, speech, and behavior

of students and faculty alike, from Orwellian Offices for Affirmative Action, Equal Opportunity, Student Life, Cultural Diversity, Sensitivity Training, Sexual Harassment, and the like. Their powers are broad, sweeping, and secretive. Anyone accused of violating any prohibition in the copious manuals of political indoctrination and dehumanization that have replaced higher education in America is prosecuted, convicted, and sentenced in absentia, without any recourse to due legal process. True to its totalitarian form, the American Gulag dispenses not only with the presumption of innocence, but also with the right to know the identity of one's accusers, and even with the specific nature of the accusations themselves. As we have seen, charges of "racism" or "sexual harassment" or "creating a hostile learning environment" can mean expressing a dissenting opinion, eating food in a disapproved way, or quoting from an unauthorized (i.e., insufficiently "diverse") version of history.

Trials by ordeal and courts of Star Chamber with secretive proceedings and arbitrary rulings are the order of the day. The fortunate few find lawyers to defend them in federal courts of law, or journalists to publicly expose the egregious persecutions of the Gulag. These are the only two things that the political commissars fear: judgment by higher authority, and light of public scrutiny. But the courts are often loath to "poach" on academic preserves, ironically because of their misplaced respect for academic freedom, while many inmates of the Gulag are understandably terrified to talk to the press, for fear of retaliation by the commissars. Until the injustices of the American Gulag are addressed and reversed by the three branches of U.S. government—Supreme Court rulings, Senate hearings, and Executive Office measures, the American taxpayers will continue—wittingly or not—to fund the most monumental educational fraud in the history of Western civilization, and beyond that to proudly consign their own children to the Gulag. Journalist Arnie Silverstein covered a particularly vindictive Inquisition of a Jewish male student at Penn, who was convicted of "racism" for calling a bunch of drunken students carousing under his dormitory window at three A.M. "water buffalo." After filing his story, the journalist remarked, "I can't wait to get off Penn's campus, and back to the United States of America."[29]

Punishments reserved for dissenting faculty are more severe, but less publicized. And the Bill of Rights does not apply on the precincts of private universities. At a New Hampshire university, a faculty majority voted to suppress freedom of speech on campus. New Hampshire's state motto is "Live Free or Die." On the West Coast, a male professor was fired for saying what Jean-Jacques Rousseau and Larry Summers said: that natural differences may help account for women's lesser interests in theoretical sciences. In a private southern university run by a religious order, a Latino male professor was censored for wanting to teach a course on humanism in classic film. He was compelled by the administration to strike the word *humanism* from his course description and materials, on the grounds that "humanism" is an "offensive" doctrine disseminated by "Eurocentric elites." If he refused, he would be fired. He supports a wife and children. That professor, ironically, is the son of Cuban refugees who fled Castro's totalitarianism for freedom in America, only to see their son's life of contemplation crushed by the American Gulag.

### Confusion of Offense with Harm

One of the pillars of political correctness is the readiness to take "offense" at any utterance or gesture that violates, or appears to violate, the monolithic requirements of "diversity." Anyone who is officially "offended" by anything whatsoever—provided they belong to the privileged groups protected by speech codes, who themselves offend daily against so-called "privileged" white and Jewish males, Christians, conservatives and heterosexuals—anyone who is officially "offended" can accuse the so-called "offenders" with complete impunity, and can bring to bear against them the entire weight of the Gulag, which after all exists only to exacerbate the very tensions it pretends to rectify.

The confusion of offense with harm, and the invocation of remedies (i.e., compensations, punishments, and retributions) normally restricted to cases of harm, is a hallmark of political correctness. This confusion is rooted in the Gulag, but has metastasized like a malignant cancer throughout Western civilization. I have published many pieces that clarify and debunk this confusion, and that identify the damages that ensue from confusing offense with harm, and in several genres: scholarly articles, magazines, a pop-philosophy book that devotes an entire chapter to it.[30] The New York publisher of that book, herself a zealous graduate of the American Gulag, attempted to censor that very chapter, because it "offended" her. At the same time, I have received more thanks for that chapter than for any other, by readers in America and around the world who were helped by it. Helped how? By relearning an invaluable moral lesson that political correctness willfully prohibits—the assumption of personal responsibility for one's state of mind.

If someone harms your body by doing violence to it, you are not normally responsible for the harm that is done. The one who harms you is responsible, whether they harmed you by accident or not. You probably did not seek to be harmed, and you possibly could not prevent it. Every civilized society has laws designed to protect its citizens from harms done to them by others, and to provide legal remedies against the perpetrators of such harms if they can be brought to justice. In fact, you have a right not to be harmed: not to be assaulted, injured, battered, raped, murdered, and so forth. Once again, this right belongs to you as an individual human being—independent of your race, class, sex, gender, ethnicity, or religion, or political views. Moreover, even a licensed professional, such as a nurse, dentist, or doctor, must obtain your informed consent before performing any procedure on you that may result in unintended harm. It is a duty of every good government to protect its citizens from harms and so to limit the liberties of any who would perpetrate harms, whether intentionally (as in premeditated violence) or unintentionally (as in driving while intoxicated). John Stuart Mill, the British champion of individual liberty (who ominously no longer ranks among the top-ten philosophers in the United Kingdom), asserted this fundamental precept in what has come to be known as the Harm Principle: "That the only purpose for which power can be rightfully exercised over any member of a civilized community, against his will, is to prevent harm to others."[31]

By contrast, no one can possibly offend you against your will. They can assault, injure, batter, rape, or murder you against your will; but offense can only be offered to you, and you can never be compelled to accept it against your will. If someone calls you a name, or offers you an insult, or simply expresses a view you don't share, you have not been harmed in any way. You may have been proffered an offense, and it is your responsibility to accept it or refuse it, to take it or leave it. But if you have been politically indoctrinated to accept offense at every possible turn; and if you have been ideologically conditioned to experience agitation every time you hear a certain word or phrase, or see a certain gesture or symbol; and if you have been behaviorally reinforced to seek compensation or retribution every time you feel offended, by a system that has robbed you of your individuality and humanity and transformed you into a collective victim—then you will inhabit a state of perpetual agitation and suffering, always blaming others and never mobilizing your individual power to become fulfilled as a human being.

So welcome to the American Gulag, where everyone constantly takes "offense," then blames their state of mind on others by claiming they have been harmed, and demanding a remedy. The Gulag affords its "empowered victims" a surfeit of counterfeit "remedies"—powers of persecution, intolerance, hatred, exclusion, of their "enemies"—that renders them ever more vulnerable to self-inflicted suffering. The racialization and feminization of the American universities have resulted in the infantilization of their students, faculty, administrations, and through them, of Western civilization itself.

Just as in Canada, a few clarion American voices of freedom and reason have spoken out against this tyranny, but to little avail. Some of their works are listed in the suggested readings for this chapter. If you care a fig for Western civilization, I urge you to read them. If ever afforded an opportunity to reconstruct American higher education on its ruins, I would gladly do so. Believe me, I know exactly what must be done, and just how to do it.

Meanwhile, strange as it may sound to you, I have been a political prisoner of the American Gulag since 2000, when I was denounced for practicing philosophy at the City University of New York (CUNY). Denounced by whom? I am forbidden to know, by order of the Gulag.

Evidence points to clinical psychologists, who were "offended" or "felt threatened" by the idea that philosophy helps people too. They apparently convinced CUNY's political commissars that people who receive philosophical counseling are likely to become mentally ill and commit suicide. Their evidence? They have none, and require none. In the Gulag, you are always presumed guilty if accused, but you are permitted neither to confront your accusers, nor to know their identities, nor to defend yourself against their accusations, nor even to know the nature of the accusations themselves. In the American Gulag, accusation alone is sufficient grounds for conviction and sentencing, in absentia and without trial. The convicted student or professor is later sent a memo, informing him of the sentence that has been passed. This is Franz Kafka's *The Trial*, made flesh in the American Gulag.

As Kors and Silverglate know all too well, having seen this transpire from coast to coast, "There is virtually no place left in the United States where kangaroo courts and Star Chambers are the rule rather than the exception—except on college and university campuses."[32]

As far as I can ascertain, I was convicted of the charges of practicing philosophy without a license, and of thoughtcrime; specifically, of aiding and abetting clients to think thoughts not preapproved by the University, and perhaps even disapproved by some psychologists. (You can well understand how unfashionable it has become to think unauthorized thoughts on a university campus.) Mind you, no state of the United States and no country in the world requires or issues a license to practice philosophy. No matter. The American Gulag is a law unto itself. So, since 2000, CUNY has prohibited my philosophical practice on campus. The orders apparently emanate from the offices of CUNY's Big Brother himself: Chancellor Matthew Goldstein. I am clearly privileged to merit such attention. Imagine John Glenn, the first American in space, getting pulled over by the interplanetary police, who demand to see his license to orbit the Earth. Now imagine a pioneer of philosophical counseling getting busted by the Gulag's thought police, who demand to see his license to orbit philosophical space with clients.

Forbidden to practice on the campuses of my university, I have been invited and encouraged to practice philosophy all over the global village, with corporations, governments, and world leaders—everywhere except in the American Gulag. So I thank my Buddhist friends and mentors for helping me make good cause with this prohibition, and likewise thank Chancellor Goldstein of CUNY (or whoever issued the orders) for cocreating so much opportunity. Just as I learned to love Big Sister (from a distance), so have I learned to love Big Brother (from even greater distances). All you need is love.

Yet many of my American colleagues have not been so fortunate. Careers have been destroyed, minds crushed, and humanity devalued by this Gulag. When I speak of these matters with my Russian and East European friends, they recognize at once that Stalinism is alive and well, now terrorizing the mind politic of the very nation that defeated Stalin's body politic. So the wisdom of The Middle Way is demonstrated yet again: By harboring ideas of "an enemy," we run the risk of becoming that enemy ourselves, even by defeating him. Wrongs must be righted, but can never be righted by wrong itself.

Among many letters and e-mails that I receive, from people helped by my work in practical philosophy, one brief hand written note has moved me the most. It came from an eighteen-year-old African-American girl in Los Angeles. She wrote not to me directly, but to the philosophical association I cofounded:[33] "Dear APPA, Thank you for what you are doing for our civilization." I only wish I could do more. More for her and her entire generation, who have been betrayed by the American Gulag, and more for the young women and men all over the developing world, who desperately need the educational "best practices" of a civilization that the American Gulag has prohibited.

## Diversity Revisited

Off campus, I speak to many different kinds of groups across the United States—business people, professionals, civil servants, investment managers, industry leaders, among others. Sometimes they invite me to give after-dinner talks on the role of philosophy in their walks of life, and in the global village. I raise with them many of the issues that I am raising with you in this book, and in much the same voice. As you can tell, I am a thought provoker, able to stir people from their complacent mental habits, to challenge them to think more carefully about what they believe and why, to exhort them to lead the examined life—at least for an hour or two after their annual banquets. I very much enjoy this kind of interaction with people, and they enjoy me too. These audiences are full of sincere and hard-working Americans, most of whom have, and would like to maintain, a firm handle on reality. So it always strikes me as bizarre when I hear them say, as they do over and over again at these functions, "You don't sound like an academic," or, "You don't sound like any of the professors I know." They say this in a surprised but relieved way, because to many of them I represent an unexpected breath of fresh air.

Still, isn't this odd? I have been based in the academy for most of my adult life, and have been professing philosophy in universities since the 1980s. Dogs bark; cats meow; ducks quack; cows moo. What sound does an academic make? What is a professor supposed to "sound like"? It is beyond merely odd, and more perversely tragic, that every academic and professor that they have met or heard sounds exactly like all the others. That's "diversity" at work.

My colleague Daphne Patai became a professor in order to express her humanity more fully. As things turned out, in her case at the notorious Amherst campus of the American Gulag, she couldn't have picked a worse career path for that laudable purpose. Here's what she published in a magazine called *The Liberal*, in a moving article called "Speaking as a Human." Brace yourself, because Professor Patai doesn't "sound like" an academic either.

"I have always wanted to be able to speak as a human, but over the years this aspiration has become ever more difficult to achieve. I became a professor because of my desire to engage with ideas. I then became a Feminist Professor, and had about half my academic appointment moved to Women's Studies. And about the time I was being classified as a privileged white, heterosexual, European-American woman—and realized that our teaching was specifically intended to steer students into feminist activism—I became an ex-feminist professor and returned full-time to my original department

[Romance Languages] . . . What happens when one writes or speaks 'as' a member of this or that identity group? . . . When I speak as a woman, men had better shut up. When I speak as a heterosexual woman, lesbian women can trump me, but if they're white, they in turn can be trumped by non-white women, lesbians or not . . . But it is my conviction that this is no way to conduct academic life or teaching, and that identity politics has a pernicious effect on education . . . as revealed by my University's recent hiring in the social sciences of a lesbian professor (whose supporters also acknowledged that she wasn't the best candidate for the job), on the grounds that 'our students need a lesbian teacher.' . . . Evidently I'll have to wait for another life to be able to speak as a human."[34]

Do you understand Professor Patai? She is not permitted to be human in this life, by edict of the American Gulag. It has revoked her liberty, denied her opportunity, and crushed her hope of being human.

Recall that Aristotle valued a life of contemplation above all others as being most conducive to one's fulfillment *as a human being*. This too was Daphne Patai's aspiration: to "engage with ideas" as a way of experiencing her humanity to the fullest.

Recall Aristotle's assessment, that "the educated differ from the uneducated as much as the living from the dead." Well-educated human beings who work in milieus of ill-educated collectives indeed feel like they are living among the dead—the mind-dead, dead to their own humanity.

Recall Daisaku Ikeda's Buddhist philosophy of education: "Students or pupils must always be kept center stage in any educational effort, and anything that ignores their individuality, force-feeds them knowledge or pushes them into a uniform mold must be rejected." The American Gulag places identity politics and dehumanizing ideologies at center stage of its educational efforts. The American Gulag not only ignores the individuality of its students; it "red flags," demonizes, and prohibits their individuality and its wholesome expression. The American Gulag does not force-feed its students knowledge; even worse, it deconstructs knowledge, and in its place force-feeds them revisionist history, reverse-racist and reverse-sexist mythology. The American Gulag is to be rejected and replaced—as Daisaku Ikeda has done—with schools and universities that value the individual student, and transmit the liberal arts tradition.

Recall that Confucius also viewed himself as a transmitter of culture, and taught his students to honor their traditions, to venerate their forbears, to respect their teachers, and to practice benevolence and righteousness amongst themselves. Where in the American Gulag is there honor, veneration, respect, benevolence, or righteousness? Confucius observed, "Those whose measures are dictated by mere expediency will arouse continual discontent." Such is the American Gulag: a hell world whose measures are dictated by the most naked expediency—the Emperor's New Expediency—and whose indoctrinated minions seethe with perpetual discontent at themselves, at history, and at the whole wide world around them.

## The ABCs

To anyone who values humanity, and who sees education as vital to each individual's fulfillment, cannot but be dismayed by these two educational extremes in the global village. In the developing world, as we have seen, young girls are barred from literacy while young boys tote assault weapons. These children have no opportunity for a decent education. Their young minds will be stunted and wasted. In the developed world, as we have seen, education has been replaced by widespread cognitive impairment and political indoctrination. These children have every opportunity for an indecent education. At neither extreme does the individual count for much. At neither extreme do children have an opportunity to learn and extend "the very best that has been thought and said"—by individual human beings, for the benefit of other individual human beings. Neither in the global lag, nor in the American Gulag, can persons flourish as the ABCs have advocated. This does not augur well for the global village.

# 12

## ECONOMIC EXTREMES
### Overabundance and Dire Dearth

*Thus it is manifest that the best political community is formed*
*by citizens of the middle class, and those states are likely*
*to be well-administered in which the middle class is large.* —Aristotle

*"I have children, I have wealth"; thinking thus, the deluded*
*torment themselves. But when they are not the possessors of their own*
*selves, how then of children? How then of wealth?* —Buddha

*In a country well governed, poverty is something to be ashamed of.*
*In a country badly governed, wealth is something to be ashamed of.* —Confucius

### Geometries of Parity and Disparity
GLOBALIZATION HAS CREATED opportunity for many people, and holds
out similar prospects for many more. For people and organizations who
are already wealthy, globalization opens new vistas for investment, and
allows them to risk and possibly multiply their wealth manyfold. Well-
educated middle classes can also prosper, especially those in the
developed world who make the shift from producing goods to
delivering services. There is also an increasing brain drain out of the
United States and toward Asia, especially in high-tech sectors. Asians
refer to it as a "brain gain." This flow of brain power operates in at
least two dimensions: the physical and the virtual. Physically, many
people with talent and ability are simply packing and leaving for Asia,
where economic dynamism and cultural growth values them, and offers

exciting opportunities. Foreign students continue to flock to American universities, whose "brand names" still have cachet, but increasingly these students graduate and return home to build their careers, instead of remaining in the United States. In Beijing, they say "Better to be the head of the chicken than the tail of the ox." America is the ox: big and powerful, but also dumbed down and lumbering toward decline. In virtual domains, all kinds of intellectual work is being outsourced from American to Asian bases, where the high-tech workforce is typically better motivated, more efficient, and less costly.

But at the same time, globalization is outsourcing manufacturing and similar jobs to developing nations—where labor is far cheaper, benefits to workers far fewer, safety standards far lower, environmental protection far less (if at all) mandated, and thus profits are much higher. Working classes in the developed world are becoming an endangered species except at the most menial levels, where wages are so low that such workers can barely afford to live. Meanwhile, workers in the developing world are happy to have their jobs, because the "slave wages" they earn at Wal-Mart in countries like Mexico (Wal-Mart is Mexico's biggest employer) are a vast improvement over no employment at all. Nonetheless, there is no question that such workers are exploited, and that this aspect of globalization resembles nothing if not the Industrial Revolution writ large, across the very face of the planet.

And at the same time, in nations or regions where corruption is excessive, where crony capitalism or predator capitalism is endemic, where bad governance has discouraged or retarded development, where infrastructure is eroded or nonexistent, or where government has utterly failed and degenerated to a Hobbesian state of nature—such nations or regions are falling further and further behind the developing world, and their peoples are becoming even more impoverished. As journalist Robert Kaplan chronicles, the peoples in the "failed states" of Africa, Asia, and the Middle East have correspondingly diminished liberty, opportunity, and hope.[1] But if "global governance" fares no better than triage in an emergency room, then many of these states will be left to expire, and their populations to subsist, in their tens of millions, in a condition resembling the movie *Soylent Green*—if they are fortunate.

Baldly stated, more people in the world are living better than ever, while increasingly many are living worse than ever. Parts of the developed world have attained standards of living, replete with luxuries and amenities enjoyed by the middle classes, that few in human history would have conceived possible on such scales. At the same time, half the world's people still subsist on two dollars a day or less, have never read a book, have never made a phone call, have never watched television, have never sent an e-mail, have never eaten in a restaurant, have never flown in an airplane, and have never shopped at Wal-Mart. So the gap between rich and poor is growing, and narrowing that gap represents the greatest challenge to globalization. As the gap widens, so the extremes between "haves" and have-nots" become more pronounced. This in turn engenders boundless human suffering, destabilizes the global village, and menaces mankind's common aspirations for peace, prosperity, and security.

There are underlying geometries of wealth distribution too, which can be represented as variations on a shape we have already encountered, a shape that is highly favored by nature and nurture alike. It is none other than Gauss's normal distribution. It can be used to depict three different kinds of wealth distributions: grossly inequitable, moderately inequitable, and reasonably equitable.

Fig. 12.1 illustrates a grossly inequitable distribution, which has three modes (hence "trimodal"). A very small number of people own most of the wealth. A somewhat larger number of people own moderate wealth—the middle classes. But the vast majority of people own almost no wealth, and in fact live below the poverty line. These three modes are separated by class, caste, or other kinds of barriers to shared wealth and socioeconomic mobility—such as theocracy, feudalism, predator capitalism, failed statehood, or Marxist command economy. Many different political arrangements can give rise to this grossly inequitable distribution. However it arises, its net effect is invariably the same: vast numbers of impoverished people—and their children—have little or no chance to improve themselves socioeconomically.

Fig. 12.1 shows a grim picture. Yet half the world's peoples are trapped in its crushing poverty. Three billion human beings, mostly in

Figure12.1 Trimodal Distribution of Wealth (not to scale).
This is the global picture.

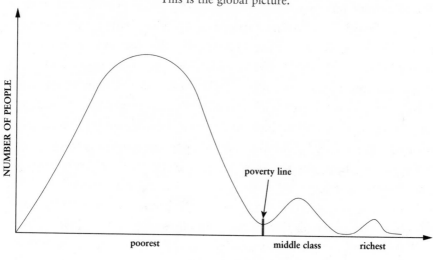

Figure12.2 Skewed Normal Distribution of Wealth (not to scale).
This is the American picture.

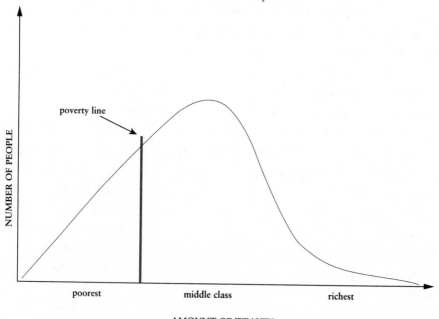

Africa, the Middle East, Asia, and Latin America are living on less than two dollars per day, with little or no prospect for improvement in their lifetimes. Fig. 12.1 is globalization's—and humanity's—biggest challenge. How can this grossly inequitable distribution be improved? As Aristotle knew in antiquity, the remedy is the golden mean, which is why he contended that a strong middle class is essential to the viability of any state. Wealth must be generated but not excessively hoarded: It must be allowed to "trickle down" to those beneath the poverty line—not solely as charity or philanthropy, but also as opportunity—so that they can progress sufficiently to form a numerous and prosperous middle class. As Aristotle wrote, "Great then is the good fortune of a state in which the citizens have a moderate and sufficient property; for where some possess much, and the others nothing, there may arise an extreme democracy, or an extreme oligarchy, or a tyranny may grow out of either extreme."[2]

Fig. 12.2 illustrates a moderately inequitable (and therefore also a moderately equitable) distribution of wealth. A relatively small number of people still control enormous wealth, but that wealth has "trickled down" to create sufficient opportunity for the emergence of a large and strong middle class—most of whom live above, not below, the poverty line. There is socioeconomic mobility, along with volatility, such that even the poorest can aspire to become rich, while even the richest remain vulnerable to ruin. Even so, there are disproportionately more people at the impoverished extreme than at the wealthy one, the majority of whom will never rise even above the poverty line, and into the thriving middle classes. This is a skewed normal distribution of wealth. It is a vast improvement upon fig. 12.1, but is still afflicted by an excess of poverty.

Fig. 12.2 happens to be the picture of America, the world's richest country and leading economy. The most attractive economic feature of America has long been the opportunities it affords to penniless immigrants to work their way into the middle classes, and for middle class people to work their way into the wealthier echelons. Yet at the same time, tens of millions of Americans live in poverty, both urban and rural. They lack decent food, housing, health care, and education. Tens of millions more are illegal immigrants, mostly from Mexico, and they cannot even be tracked for the purposes of socioeconomic assessment. Fig. 12.2 is the approximate shape of many developed countries, less wealthy overall than the United States but able to distribute their wealth to a similar extent.

While poverty produces suffering, it is also far better to be poor in a rich country than poor in a poor country, because the poverty line in a rich country is far above that in a poor one. If we compare the fates of the poorest survivors of the tsunami that inundated South Asia in December 2004, killing two hundred thousand people and leaving millions more with nothing, with the fates of the poorest survivors of hurricane Katrina, which destroyed New Orleans and killed about 1,500 people in September 2005, we will see a stark contrast. Notwithstanding the legendary corruption that afflicts many countries in Asia, and corruptions that afflict the state of Louisiana, the survivors of Katrina have far better prospects than the survivors of the tsunami. This is not Job's comfort. Why? Because the shape of fig. 12.2 indicates

Figure 12.3 Normal Distribution of Wealth (not to scale). This is the Canadian, Scandinavian, Japanese, and Singaporean picture.

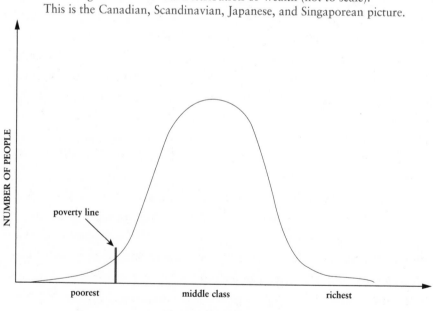

that more assistance and opportunity will flow to disaster-stricken people in New Orleans than will flow to disaster-stricken people in Bangladesh or Aceh (the generous donations of many people and nations to aid tsunami victims notwithstanding). Yet poverty is poverty, whether in Asia or America, and precious few nations in the global village have succeeded in reducing it to minimal levels.

Fig. 12.3 depicts the shape of wealth distribution in the most successful social democracies—Canada and the Scandinavian nations. Fig. 12.3 is a normal distribution, neither skewed nor multimodal, and many economists claim that it represents the very best result that can be achieved on a national scale. This distribution reduces excessive wealth and excessive poverty alike, and encompasses the vast majority of people in a vibrant middle class, which enjoys the highest average standard of living in the world. High taxation of the wealthy and middle classes alike helps maintain a generous social safety net, such that relatively few people indeed fall below the poverty line. Social democracy is not the only way to attain such a distribution; authoritarian but compassionate Confucian democracies, like those of Singapore and Japan, have attained equivalently equitable distributions of wealth without becoming "welfare states" in the bargain.

Regardless of how it is achieved politically, the distribution of wealth depicted in fig. 12.3 remains an ideal approximated only by about 2.5 percent of the world's peoples, and mostly by nations that have relatively small or even tiny populations. Another 35 percent or so of the world's inhabitants live in nations whose distributions of wealth resemble fig. 12.2, while the vast majority of the world's population has yet to evolve economically beyond the poverty trap of fig. 12.1.

While it is painfully obvious that grotesque inequities persist in the global economy, and that globalization can ameliorate as well as exacerbate them, the measurement of wealth, or more generally of economic well-being, is by no means a simple or objective matter. Physicists can determine physical properties of bodies or systems with far more ease and objectivity, at least in the everyday Newtonian world, where mass, length, charge, and time are fundamental and universal dimensions of measure. Similarly, chemists and biologists work with "observables" that exist objectively, and so can be measured objectively. The "observables" of social scientists, including economists, are not so objective, and as such are far less amenable to universal dimensions of measurement. The mass of a proton is an objective property of the proton, whereas the wealth of a human being is partly a subjective conception of the economist. All physicists will arrive at the same value for the rest mass of the proton, however they measure it; but every economist will arrive at a different value for the wealth of a human being, depending on their conceptual models of wealth itself. Does wealth mean income, or net worth? Does it mean equity, or capacity to service debt? Do you calculate an individual's income before taxes, or after taxes? Do you correct for other factors, such as age, gender, demographics, and future earning potential? How do you measure quality of life? How do you balance quantitative factors with qualitative ones? Because these questions cannot be answered uniquely, there is no unitary conception of wealth per se. Each economist builds his or her own conceptual model, and so does not measure the wealth of a human being, but rather measures his or her conception of what it means for a human being to own wealth.

So I am speaking of wealth and poverty on an ordinary common-sense basis, not on a conceptual economic one. Figs. 12.1, 12.2, and 12.3 convey the essential and objective disparities in global wealth distribution, without getting bogged down in the variable and conceptual nuances of economic models. You need not be an economist to know whether you are richer or poorer than your neighbor, whether your community is more or less affluent than the neighboring one, whether your nation is more or less prosperous than its neighbors in the global village.

## Does Wealth Cause Poverty?

This question is often asked, especially by those who are agitated into believing that "white male heterosexual patriarchal hegemonists" are responsible for all the world's ills. To what extent is poverty in the developing world a function of affluence in the developed world? Are half the world's people so poor *because* so many others are so affluent?

This question will admit of different answers, depending on conflicting political agendas, as well as on varying interpretations of statistics. Economists are pretty much agreed about two ways in which affluence in some places drives poverty in others, and I will summarize both momentarily. Most generally, however, there is an overarching factor that always needs to be taken into consideration; namely, that economics is a not a "zero-sum game." Let me explain.

Poker is a zero-sum game, because the net winnings (among all players who win) equals the net losses (among all players who lose). So if you win a hundred dollars playing poker, some player (or some combination of players) must have lost a hundred dollars. However, wealth creation is not zero-sum. Wealth can be created, and destroyed. If someone earns a hundred dollars, it does not mean that someone else (or some combination of others) has necessarily lost a hundred dollars. They may have bought goods for a hundred dollars which they can resell for more than a hundred dollars, or purchased services that will enhance their capacity to provide other goods or services in turn. Because wealth creation in general is not zero-sum, one cannot simplistically assert that some people are poor just because other people are rich.

Then again, wealthier nations (and individuals) can use their wealth to leverage profits out of poorer nations (and people), and in this sense economists, business leaders, and politicians know perfectly well that extremes of wealth in the most affluent neighborhoods of the global village can and do contribute to perpetuating extremes of poverty in the least affluent ones. First, subsidized agriculture in the developed world, notoriously in the EU (and especially France), where dairy farmers are paid subsidies of more than eight dollars per cow, artificially lowers the price of their produce, which can be sold cheaply at home and "dumped" on developing markets at lower cost to consumers than indigenous and unsubsidized produce. So money is sucked out of poor economies by rich ones. Second, poorer nations are prevented from competitively marketing their own produce in developed markets by an intricate system of protective tariffs, which make it unaffordable for poorer nations to gain a foothold in the most lucrative markets. Taken together, these two factors—subsidies and tariffs—subject developing nations to forms of economic imperialism, and to this extent it is undeniable that wealthier nations profit from the poverty of poorer ones. This led to the well-known and sardonic observation, by food analyst Devinder Sharma, that a subsidized European cow enjoys a better standard of living than a landless Asian peasant.[3]

Beyond the subsidies and tariffs that regulate the flow of goods in the global village, there are also processes that regulate the flow and ownership of information, such as intellectual property rights. The British philosopher Francis Bacon first observed that knowledge is power, and he was of course correct. By regulating the flow and ownership of intellectual property—such as patents on pharmaceutical drugs—governments and corporations can foster inequities between haves and have-nots. Some critics call this "information feudalism."[4] Just as with trades and tariffs, excesses of information feudalism are regarded as a form of economic imperialism.

Then again, it must be emphasized that not every shortage, shortfall, or shortcoming in the developing world is the "fault" of affluence in the developed world. For example, India has sixty million urban poor and more than two hundred million rural poor—crushing poverty on a scale and magnitude incomprehensible to citizens of affluent nations. There are regions of India, such as Rajasthan, which boast the highest levels of annual monsoon rainfall in the world, yet whose inhabitants pay seven rupees for a liter of water during the dry season, which is trucked in from outside the region. Since India has the atomic bomb, we can safely infer that Indian engineering is more than advanced enough to build reservoirs and cisterns to catch and store the abundant monsoons, and so could spare its poorest people the necessity and cost of buying water during the dry season. These same people who are deluged in annual monsoons, yet must buy water during annual droughts, also suffer from an appalling lack of education, such that they pray annually to their gods to "cause" the monsoons to come. None of this is the fault of the developed world. It is the Indian system that underexploits a vital natural resource (rainfall), which in turn impedes the economic development of its human resources.

Overexploitation hurts Indians too. Entire regions of India have been utterly deforested, not by the logging industry, but by the religious custom of cremation. It takes two trees to cremate a corpse, and India is a vastly populous nation—with few reforestation programs. Recently, a solar-powered crematorium was introduced to India. It is inexpensive, reusable, and inexhaustible when the sun shines. Yet corrupt Brahmins, jealously retaining their traditional religious control over the masses, resist the implementation of this technology, and so the deforestation continues. It is not the fault of the affluent West that Indians lack firewood.

At the other extreme, in the heart of the developed world, we encounter cities like Phoenix, Arizona. Built in a desert, whose arid climate enhances respiration and whose sunshine benefits the spirit, Phoenix has expanded into a sizeable metropolis: a locus of urban development and a popular retirement region besides. All this has severely strained the water supply. Nonetheless, Phoenix daily pumps more water to irrigate its more than two hundred golf courses than is pumped by all its other industries combined. In consequence, Phoenix is now in the process of tapping its deep aquifers, nature's unreplenishable wells that even monsoons cannot refill. When Phoenix runs dry, water will have to be trucked there too. Since it cannot be trucked from India, Phoenicians will have to pay a lot more than seven rupees per liter. Phoenix will become one of the best developed ghost towns in the West, through overexploitation of its most vital natural resource: water.

As always, the ABCs teach that underexploitation and overexploitation of resources are both vices, whereas moderate exploitation—otherwise known as "sustainable development"—is the virtuous course. But there is another factor at work in the human being, which makes it difficult if not impossible for people to limit their consumption. This factor has dire implications for human conservation of nature's resources, and it militates both against the sustainability of synthetic exploitations of the natural environment, and against the equitable distribution of wealth generated in the process of cultural evolution. This factor is thus a two-edged socioeconomic sword. One sharp edge is the absence of any natural check on human population density. The other sharp edge is the absence of any natural check on the amount of wealth that humans seek to accumulate. The first edge induces people to overexploit and ultimately to desecrate the very environment that sustains them—up to and including the terrestrial biosphere of Earth itself. The second edge induces people to accumulate evermore, and to share ever less, as their primary means of ascending the human dominance hierarchy. This double-edged sword, which humans are utilizing to ritually disembowel themselves as a species, is a legacy of natural selection's little economies. In the process of evolving this magnificent creature called man, natural selection clearly exceeded its "budget," and so became obliged to cut a few corners during the production phase.

In chapter 8, we saw the result of one such economy, a "cost-cutting" measure that fails to furnish human beings with any instinctive mechanisms for sending and receiving gestures of appeasement or surrender—for the compelling reason that we are born so helpless and harmless that we do not need such instincts. Given that nature did not arm us innately with any deadly weapons, we hardly need any natural safeguards against their use. This is nature's exquisitely ironic version of the "French Question": It works perfectly in theory, but not at all in practice. The conventional arms industry is the world's second-largest, a behemoth ten times bigger than microelectronics, and smaller only than the Leviathan of petroleum. This is what comes of making man so helpless and harmless at birth.

Two more of nature's little "economies"—no natural checks on human population density or their acquisitiveness—give rise to the socioeconomic disparities that cause so much suffering, and to the unsustainable developments that now threaten planet Earth herself.

## The Population Bomb

If you recall some of the ironies about human evolution that we have mentioned, early human beings were very weak and vulnerable creatures, not designed to survive the rigors of biological evolution. Look at the female reproductive cycle, for example: The human female ovulates about once per month, from early adolescence until her late forties. This does not make much sense in affluent societies, where women on average now bear fewer than two children each. Why does she ovulate more than four hundred times in her life, to produce fewer than two offspring? On the one hand, this is nature's way of "stacking the deck," to increase the odds of conception, live birth, and survival into adulthood. On the other hand, if you think back one hundred thousand years, the earliest humans had a life expectancy comparable to that of their simian cousins, about thirty-five years. On top of that, their infants had huge mortality rates, and very little chance of surviving long enough to become reproducing adults. So the human female was designed or evolved to bear ten or twenty offspring by age thirty-five, many or most of whom would not survive into adulthood.

So how did we ever arrive at this present stage of overpopulation? As we saw in chapter 8, we got this far because of ingenuity and dispersion. Our big brains "told" us to live in small hunting and gathering bands, as remote from one another as possible, and so we did. Throughout most of our prehistory, humans were probably an endangered species. There were precious few of us, dispersed over vast areas, for many millennia.

As we have seen, every species in nature has an "optimum number"—that is, a characteristic population density that allows the species to husband its food resources and not overexploit the land or sea or air space that contains the food which that species needs to survive. An animal population will expand until it reaches its optimum number. If that number is exceeded, then the population will fission and disperse, in order to reduce the density. If the population cannot fission and disperse, then "normal" social behaviors for that species will degenerate into abnormal antisocial ones, until the population density is reduced to the "optimum number." Then normal behaviors resume.[5]

Fig. 12.4 illustrates some typical optimum numbers for various species, including prehistoric man. As you can see, primitive human hunting and gathering bands had about the same population density as wolves. For tens of thousands of years, humans inhabited a veritable Garden of Eden, replete with abundant fish, game, fruits, nuts, berries, and tubers.

It was only during the late Neolithic revolution, roughly twelve thousand years ago, that humans began to learn to inhabit large and somewhat defensible permanent settlements. So too they learned to domesticate animals, cultivate crops, develop conceptions of property,

| GROUP TYPE | TYPICAL NUMBER | TYPICAL AREA (SQ. MILES) | OPTIMUM DENSITY / SQ. MILE |
|---|---|---|---|
| ant formicary | 1,000,000 | 0.05 | 20,000,000 |
| gibbon family | 4 | 0.1 | 40 |
| baboon troop | 40 | 15 | 3.35 |
| gorilla troop | 17 | 17 | 1.0 |
| human band | 30 | 1,000 | 0.03 |
| wolf pack | 10 | 1,000 | 0.01 |

Figure 12.4 Natural Population Densities

and evolve more specialized societal functions. That allowed population centers to grow, and civilizations as we know them to emerge. From that time on, human population densities departed radically from nature's original "design" for us, and began to increase exponentially. Feudal extremes of wealth and poverty began to emerge. If we compare the prehistoric human population density of about .03 persons per square mile to modern microstate and urban densities, the difference is staggering. Fig. 12.5 shows typical microstate population densities; fig. 12.6 shows typical urban population densities.

People living in microstates have achieved population densities ten thousand times higher than hunter-gatherers, while people in crowded urban areas have achieved densities one hundred thousand to one million times higher than hunter-gatherers. These staggering densities are all relatively recent. Fig. 12.7 illustrates the human population curve, which was almost flat during most of our existence on earth, and which only in the twentieth century began to explode. This explosion is not normal, and will not be tolerated by nature herself.

Despite the carnage of World War I, which took five million lives; despite the pandemic of influenza in 1918 which took twenty million

| MICROSTATE | POPULATION | AREA (SQ. MILES) | POPULATION / SQ. MILE |
|---|---|---|---|
| Liechtenstein | 34,000 | 62 | 548 |
| San Marino | 24,000 | 29 | 827 |
| Barbados | 180,000 | 166 | 1,084 |
| Tuvalu | 12,000 | 9 | 1,333 |
| Malta | 400,000 | 122 | 3,278 |

Figure 12.5 Typical Microstate Population Densities

lives; despite the global slaughter of World War II, which took sixty million lives; despite the genocide of six million Jews by the Nazis, of three million Armenians by the Turks, of three million Cambodians by Pol Pot, of tens of millions of Russians by Stalin and more tens of millions of Chinese by Mao Tse-tung; despite dozens of other twentieth-century wars that took tens of millions more lives; despite the AIDS epidemic in Africa that has also taken millions; despite the tens of thousands per day in the developing world who die of malaria and famine and other avertable causes; despite falling birth rates among the

| METROPOLIS | POPULATION / SQ. MILE |
|---|---|
| London | 10,500 |
| Hong Kong | 17,333 |
| New York | 25,600 |
| Tokyo | 34,132 |
| Mumbai | 41,984 |

Figure 12.6 Typical Urban Population Densities

429

affluent; despite China's "one child" policy; despite all this, human population continues to soar into the billions. This means that wars, famines, epidemics and genocides—which have caused unimaginable suffering to humanity—even these grotesque excesses of human self-slaughter and vulnerability to contagion have exerted no significant dampening force on the population explosion.[6]

This partly explains why so many people in the twentieth century believed that an apocalypse was nigh. The biggest Cold War fear was of course a nuclear holocaust, which would have depopulated the planet in a hurry. When that specter faded with détente, many have since believed that AIDS, Ebola, SARS, or some other emergent biological agent will bring about massive depopulation. Apocalyptic novels by Stephen King became all the rage, describing in horrifying and lurid (but obviously compelling) detail various scenarios for the demise and rebirth of humankind.

Freud had earlier postulated that each of us has an individual death wish or death instinct, which he called *Thanatos*, a supposed counterbalance to *Eros*, the appetite for life's pleasures. In the 1960s, Bob Dylan wrote a song about each of us having a death wish for humanity itself, expressed in dreams or nightmares in which the dreamer and a few friends survive, and everyone else perishes, in a man-made or

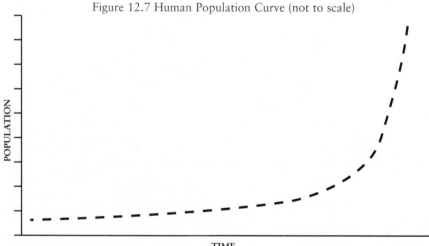

Figure 12.7 Human Population Curve (not to scale)

POPULATION

TIME

natural cataclysm. "I'll let you be in my dreams if I can be in yours," sang Dylan, expressing a cynical awareness that we can multiply our fantasies about survival, without necessarily increasing our odds.

The discovery that the dinosaurs were probably wiped out by a massive meteorite strike and a subsequent Ice Age loaned weight to the twentieth-century apocalyptic view of things. Religious beliefs, from Hindu cosmology's Kali-Yuga (Age of Kali, the goddess of destruction) to Christianity's Book of Revelations, also fueled twentieth-century fears of apocalypse. Others view the end of the Mayan calendar in 2012 as apocalyptic. Let's hope that the Mayas miscalculated. Rachel Carson's book *Silent Spring*, which marked the inception of environmentalism, gave grounds for serious concern that we humans will do ourselves in by gradually poisoning the very biosphere that sustains us. So while the twentieth century witnessed the greatest growth of awareness in human history of the fragility of our existence on this planet, it also produced the population explosion and depletion of nonrenewable resources. Ironically, the many triumphs of human cultural evolution have also sewn abundant seeds of disaster, for our planet and therefore our species itself. This might be termed "the failure of success."

### Population and Predation

Humans are the top predators on the planet, and we are omnivores. If something grows, we will harvest it; if it serves, we will husband it; if it moves; we will hunt it. Being rapacious and omnivorous as well as strategic hunters, we humans rapidly ascended to the summit of the food chain, which "freed" us from the cyclical codependencies and other constraints that shape all specialized predator-prey relations, and which ultimately govern their population dynamics. Fig. 12.8 illustrates the generic population curves of predators and their prey. These are nonlinear but cyclical equations, that reflect predator-prey dynamics throughout nature. For example, the arctic fox eats only the arctic hare. When hares are plentiful, foxes multiply accordingly. As the number of hunters increases, the number of prey decreases. This decrease in prey results in a decrease in hunters, which then allows the prey to become plentiful again.

Figure 12.8 Predator-Prey Population Dynamics (Lotka-Volterra Equations)

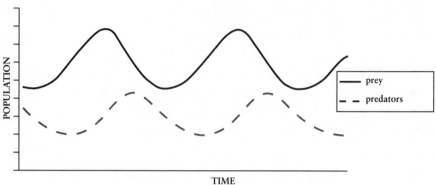

Such are the cycles of life throughout the planetary food chain, and the overall shape of all these food chains, woven together, is essentially a pyramid. Prey tend to outnumber their predators, and every predator itself is a prey to some other predator, which stands higher in the pyramid. The pyramid of food is a natural hierarchy (and not a "social construct"). At the apex of this pyramid stands man. He eats everything else voraciously, and is eaten by nothing else on any significant scale. Philosopher Mary Midgely has ably debunked some media-driven myths concerning the "world's deadliest predator," which popularly grant that title to sharks.[7] As she points out, sharks kill fewer than one hundred humans per year, on average. Humans, however, kill on average millions of sharks per year, deliberately or inadvertently. So who is more deadly to whom? Humans are by far more deadly, even to the "world's deadliest" predators.

Clearly, the human population curve in fig. 12.7 does not resemble any of the "standard" predator-prey population dynamics that are observable throughout the animal kingdom. If you are thinking ahead, you have probably realized that our exponential increase in human population comes at the inevitable cost of an exponential overexploitation and depletion of all the natural resources upon which we have preyed so rapaciously and unrestrainedly. That is illustrated in fig. 12.9. As a direct consequence of overpopulation, water tables and deep aquifers are being depleted. Fish and game are being depleted. Forests, fossil fuels, and the ozone layer are being depleted. The ice caps

Figure 12.9 Overexploitation and Depletion of Natural Resources (not to scale)

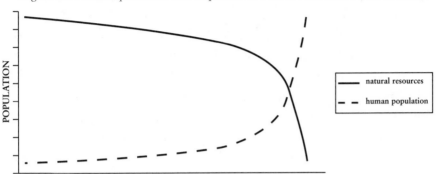

and glaciers are being depleted. Thousands of species are becoming extinct, as their ecosystems and habitats become overexploited, overdeveloped, paved over, polluted, and depleted. The biosphere itself is becoming depleted, thanks to its top predator: man.

The self-reliance of hunter-gatherers was predicated on intimacy with their natural environments, from desert to jungle. By contrast, the other-reliance of urban and, increasingly, of rural populations alike, is predicated on their estrangement from nature, and their intimacy with synthetic environments, from McDonald's to Wal-Mart to the Home Depot. In this sense, globalization represents the optimization and integration of technocratic networks that provide synthetically selected substitutions for all the naturally selected resources that we have depleted by overpopulation. Water used to be drawn and carried by the drinkers themselves; now they buy it in bottles. Wood used to be cut and hewn and fashioned and finished by skilled carpenters; now preboxed "furniture" made of pseudowood and designed for efficiency of packaging and shipping, is waiting to be loaded into SUVs and assembled by the consumer, with disposable tools.

The abundant and variegated fish stocks of all the great oceans and seas are gone, depleted by the rapacious fleets of the great fishing nations of the twentieth century: Japan, Norway, Portugal, Russia, and the rest. Our postmodern hunter-gatherer buys his fish from the retailer who buys them from distributors who buy them from markets serviced by fish farms. You want wild fish? You pay more, but you get more:

They come laced with mercury and DDT and PCPs—toxins that everyone should avoid, and that even hippies didn't imbibe at the height of the sixties. You want farmed fish? They're genetically reliable, but they also acquire brand new diseases, and harbor a new generation of toxins as a result of overcrowding in their aquatic pens.

Extreme human overcrowding has forced us to replicate the same fulsome phenomenon in our food stocks—animals whose parts we "hunt" in the meat section of the supermarket are fattened for slaughter in the most appallingly cruel conditions. Their swamps of concentrated waste matter, as with pigs in the Carolinas, become toxic waste sites that pervade and poison the entire ecosystem surrounding the farms. What we have done to ourselves, we have done to our food supply. Food is produced, hunted, and gathered by entirely synthetic means: Organic things have been stripped away from their natural habitats and processed entirely by synthetic technologies, in order to feed human beings who have been stripped away from their natural habitats and processed entirely by synthetic technologies. (Part of chickens and pigs and cows are all fed to one another, then fed to people. Dogs and cats eat one another as pet food.[8]) Once everything immediately useful to man has been stripped away, the habitat itself collapses from depletion of its vital links, and can then be exploited as landfills, strip malls, motels, used car dealerships, and cookie-cutter housing developments—from executive RV parks to McMansions. Of course it's all quite hideous and tasteless and ghastly in its uniformity, but it's also "globalitarian": "The greatest good for the greatest number" has evolved into "The biggest brands for the greatest number of consumers."

These vast networks of systems, and systems of networks, are increasingly based on dynamic models of production, consumption, and market evolution, and on strategic partnerships among transnational corporations, sovereign governments, world religions, media leaders, and other stakeholders in planetary management. Manuals of "best practices" have evolved for efficiently feeding, clothing, and housing the world's swelling urban, suburban, and exurban populations.

At grassroots levels, it is still possible to resist or opt out of globalization, for example by going back to the land and forming communes or cooperatives of biodynamic agronomists, free-range farmers, organic bakers, and the like. Such people can and do live lives of far greater health and quality than the affluent masses caught up in the urban congestion of the globalized rat race, which has evolved into a Mr. and Ms. Pac-Man race. But the vision of Thoreau and Emerson, and their community of New England Transcendentalists—infused with the humanistic spirit of the Enlightenment and the perennial wisdom of Indian philosophy, effused with an uncompromising love of man and nature, diffused from a stultifying herd mentality by self-reliance and self-government—that epoch is relegated to memory.

Remember my paraphrase of Trotsky: You may not be interested in globalization, but globalization is interested in you. Its interest has become almost inescapable in the developed world. The rest of the world, with the exception of some die-hard fanatics, rogue governments, and failed states, is desperately trying to close the gap between haves and have-nots. That gap is partly technological and technocratic—the digital divide, the cyber chasm, the Internet interstice, on the wrong side of which half the world's people are falling even further behind—if downloading upgrades for the Pac-Man race amounts to human progress. But that gap also bespeaks acute and chronic dearths of liberty, opportunity, and hope, such as can be offered only by modernized secular governments, progressive religious sects, and compassionate (as opposed to predatory or protectionist) capitalism. The so-called "digital divide" is only one prominent aspect of a systemic developmental divide, which can be widened by poor governance, intolerant theocracy, and crony capitalism, and which can be narrowed by best practices of cultural evolution.

One trend is clear. As congested human populations deplete, despoil, and destroy the once-bountiful natural resources on this planet, they become increasingly dependent on globalized networks and systems to produce and distribute their living necessities, as well as whatever luxuries they can afford. The hundreds of millions who subsist outside this loop are plainly and daily bereft even of the most basic necessities—such as clean water and minimal nutrition—let alone the catalogs and credit cards that hundreds of millions of others take for granted. The developmental divide is depicted in fig. 12.10.

Figure 12.10 The Replacement of Natural Resources by Synthetic Ones, and the Developmental Divide (not to scale)

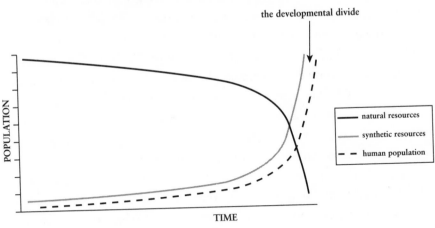

If I may wax more optimistic for a moment, I will reemphasize the potential that that cultural evolution holds for bridging this divide. Two brief examples will serve: tourism, and cell phones. Travel and leisure industries are booming worldwide, for globalization efficiently repackages remote and exotic destinations as reachable and affordable. Tourists and their vacation monies pour into ports, airports, and hinterlands, and do good in all kinds of local economies, especially in the developing world. Leave aside the absurdities afforded by the spectacle of adventurous tourists who voyage into the once-forbidding Stone Age realm of New Guinea's Mudmen, only to find them drinking Coca-Cola, wearing Nikes, longing for Big Macs, and selling replicas of shrunken heads manufactured in China. Ironies abound, yet if this is what it takes to unite formerly disjointed peoples in awareness of their shared humanity, albeit by a common denominator of branded peace and prepackaged prosperity, so be it. Headhunting warfare and colonial serfdom are both trumped by Pax Nabisco.

Second, the example of cell phones illustrates how the developmental divide can be bridged, rapidly and cheaply, by emergent technologies. It is not necessary for developing nations and regions to modernize by stepping in each and every agonizing footprint left on the convoluted trail of human progress. Newer technologies enable cultures to "leapfrog" over older ones, sparing them decades or even centuries of arduous catch-up. In the 1970s, the Finnish company Nokia was a small manufacturer of rubber boots. Some visionary genius coaxed them into microelectronics, and Nokia currently commands a substantial global market share of cell phones. Their Indian market alone is absorbing two million new units per month, with no saturation in sight.

What does this mean to Indians? They can now communicate and network without landlines, fiber optics, power grids, and all the associated infrastructures that daunt the developing world. One small generator can recharge cell phone batteries for an entire village. Indian fishermen are now carrying cell phones on their boats, and so can be forewarned of approaching bad weather, and apprised of better markets for their catch in neighboring villages or ports. Their lives and lifestyles are immediately improved. This emergent and affordable technology offers them more liberty, opportunity, and hope than ever before. It also makes them more self-governing. And while Thoreau's serenity on Walden Pond would have been sorely tested by incessant ringing, chiming, buzzing, and bleating of cell phones, he surely would have approved of their liberating potential in the developing world. So globalization has the power both to deepen and to bridge the developmental divide.

## Inevitability of Unequal Outcomes

That said, there remains the economic question of unequal outcomes. Nations and regions which offer the least liberty, opportunity, and hope to their citizens, also feature the most grotesque extremes of socioeconomic inequality. The Gini coefficient—a measure of wealth or income distribution—illustrates this well. A perfectly egalitarian distribution would occur if everyone controlled exactly the same amount of wealth, in which case that nation's Gini coefficient would be zero: total equality, which is totally impossible to achieve in densely populated states. A perfectly inegalitarian distribution would occur if one person controlled all the wealth, in which case that nation's Gini coefficient would be unity: total inequality, and all-too-easily approached in too many places. In practice, the most developed European nations tend to have Gini coefficients between 0.24 and 0.36, while the United States is above 0.4, denoting its greater extremes of wealth and poverty. Parts of Africa, Latin and South America, the Middle East, and Asia are well above 0.5 or even higher, which indicates gross disparities between their richest and poorest citizens. Fig. 12.11 depicts Gini coefficients, worldwide.[9]

One must be careful not to interpret Gini coefficients politically. Democracies can manifest the same Gini number as authoritarian regimes. One must also be careful not to infer measures of absolute prosperity from Gini coefficients. For example, Greenland has a much more "utopian" Gini number than Canada, but this indicates Greenland's more even distribution of incomparably less wealth per capita.

My reason for mentioning the Gini coefficient is to illustrate the practical impossibility of achieving perfectly equal outcomes. Tocqueville, for example, astutely observed that Americans would have to choose between liberty and equality. In socioeconomic terms, liberty inevitably gives rise to inequality, while equality requires social engineering, which inevitably gives rise to loss of liberty. Developed nations have learned to balance these values, more or less; developing ones have not.

Prehistoric hunting and gathering bands had Gini coefficients near zero, but only because their net economic wealth was near zero: It's easy to share nothing. Yet measured another way, their wealth was near infinite—the abundant natural wealth of unspoiled Earth. But in order to sustain large permanent settlements—the precursors of civilizations—people needed to recognize, define, and own property. Wherever everything (and everyone) is owned by a pharaoh, an emperor, a führer, a despot, a dictator, or tyrant, there the Gini coefficient soars wildly close to unity, and correlates with limitless suffering. Where the greatest wealth is dispersed throughout a strong middle class, there the Gini coefficient is correspondingly tamed, and correlates with liberty, opportunity, and hope, which in turn reduce many kinds of suffering.

Even so, there will always be inequalities of socioeconomic outcome, and this is not because of any iron law of economics. Rather, it is because

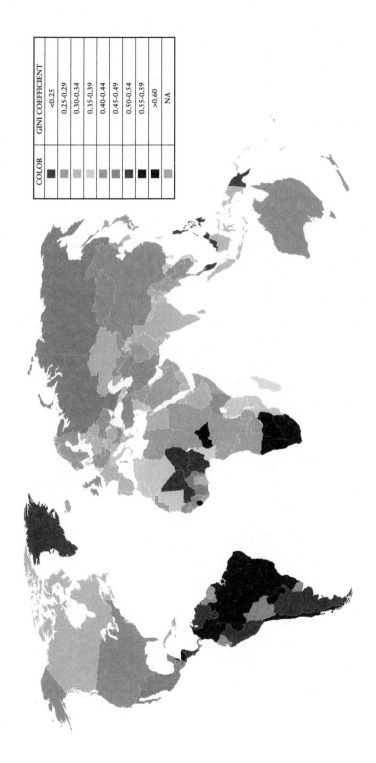

Figure 12.11 Gini Coefficients, world-wide

of underlying geometries of nature. While pyramidal wealth can be reshaped and reformed into more normal distributions via cultural evolution, neither the political art of good governance nor the social science of economics has the power to alter nature's dominance hierarchies, including the pronounced forms that evolved among the primates. Rather, cultural evolution provides human primates with new arenas, such as politics and socioeconomics, in which they can upgrade the roles they play in the process of running their evolutionarily ancient operating systems. This inevitably entails the articulation of dominance hierarchies. So wealth itself becomes a measure of political power and socioeconomic standing. There are inevitably unequal distributions of wealth in every society, precisely because there are innately unequal distributions of ability, desire, will, and opportunity to ascend the ladders of political and socioeconomic dominance. Those born into circumstances of wealth or power, but who lack the ability, desire, and will to sustain themselves there, will surely slide down the slopes of ill fortune. Those born into circumstances of poverty or powerlessness, if vouchsafed the ability, desire, and will to achieve, will surely climb the ladders of fortune. But nowhere in the human world is there equality of outcome—except in the potential for awakening our inner wealth and power via The Middle Way (and also in the cemetery, where all former beings are eternally and equally dead).

These disparities of income and outcome, that have manifested since the dawn of civilizations, arise most fundamentally because nature herself has practiced another ironic economy with us. We have already seen the cause and effect of one such ironic economy: Because as humans we are born completely helpless and harmless, and bereft of innate weapons, we have no instinctive check on our capacity to inflict violence and murder on one another. Similarly, it is clear that humans have no instinctive check upon our acquisitiveness, because we are evolved to live in small and highly dispersed bands as hunter-gatherers, owning nothing but relishing everything. We are not evolved to contend in congested metropoli as commingled tribes, owning everything but relishing nothing.

We are biologically evolved to occupy and defend territories, but not to own them; to bond with others in hierarchical relationships, but not to own them; to hunt and gather our foodstuffs, but not to own them; and even to exercise stewardship over our abundant natural resources, but not to own them. Yet we are culturally required to do many things that nature, a practitioner of small economies, omitted from our evolutionary operating systems. Peace, prosperity, and sustainability require that we live amicably in large numbers, that we rein in our rapacity, that we adhere to self-imposed limits on our fecundity, and that we accommodate diversity of custom and belief. Yet nature has decreed that we should live otherwise, and so we did, for tens of thousands of years—humans lived xenophobically in disparate tribes; gave full rein to their rapacity; set no limits on their acquisitiveness, and were intolerant of one another's customs and beliefs. Cultural evolution, and especially the ABCs, can supersede these natural tendencies. But wherever cultural institutions, traditions, values, and practices are not sufficiently enlightened to override our biological inheritance, there economic inequalities will be greater rather than lesser, opportunities lesser rather than greater, and human suffering will increase rather than decrease.

The problem of acquisitiveness looms largest in economic contexts, for it is plain that many people have not enough, while others have more than they can ever use. At one extreme, radical attempts to "socially engineer" economic equality, such as Marxist command economies, have not proved viable. They impoverish everyone, except for ruling party elites. At the other extreme, social Darwinism and imperialism, which express primatological dominance hierarchies in socioeconomic and political terms, engender grotesque inequities. The political art of tempering these extremes and evolving a strong middle class is greatly abetted by The Middle Way. Why? Because The Middle Way teaches us to live amicably in large numbers, to rein in our rapacity, to impose limits on our acquisitiveness, and to accommodate diverse custom and belief.

Let me ask you a fundamental question: Will you get enough to eat today? This week? This month? This year? If you are reading this book, then you will probably answer affirmatively. Most people who can afford the luxury of reading books have already solved the more fundamental problem of getting enough to eat. Yet half the world's people would answer this question negatively, if anyone asked them.

Now let me ask you another question: Do you have enough money? It seems clear that all the people who have not enough to eat do not have enough money, for if they had enough money they could presumably buy enough food. Then again, I am willing to wager that most people in the developed world, who have more than enough to eat, would still say that they don't have enough money, or perhaps that they have enough but could always use more. In fact, if I phrased the question in this way, "Could you use some more money?" most people in the world would answer "Yes!" whereas if I asked, "Could you use some more food?" at least half the people in the world would answer "No, we have enough." By now my point should be clear. If most people in the world can use more money—even those who have sufficient food, clothing, and shelter—then most people in the world are acquisitive.

This is not surprising, because humans are cultural as well as biological beings. Our biology demands that we satisfy recurrent short-term appetites; our culture demands that we achieve nonrecurrent medium-term and long-term goals. Culture allows us to create value. Creating value usually requires devoting time and committing resources. Devoting time and committing resources usually requires spending money. Spending money usually requires earning it. So almost everyone can use more money, which means that almost everyone is acquisitive. No matter how rich or poor, most people seek more and not less. And since our abilities, desires, and wills to acquire are manifestly unequal, as well as our external circumstances and subsequent experiences, we can hardly expect anything but unequal distributions of wealth, no matter how we measure it.

Since economists are measuring concepts (wealth, income, welfare) as opposed to things (moons, planets, stars), there will always be room for dispute concerning economic equity and social justice. Nonetheless, it is clear that the shape of the most equitable and just distributions of wealth, or of income, resemble a normal distribution. So not only does nature adore the Gaussian function, cultures that have simulated it economically adore it too. It is not accidental that the economies that most closely simulate this shape have adopted some version of the ABCs in their political and other cultural institutions—arts, sciences and technology (the Aristotelian component), compassionate society (the Buddhist component), balanced social and political order (the Confucian component). Nor is it accidental that the economies that most widely deviate from this shape have rejected one or more of the ABCs in their political and other cultural institutions. They lack either arts, sciences and technologies, or compassionate society, or they lack lawful and stable social and political order. Failed and failing states lack all three.

Moreover, "throwing" food or money at such economies, as the affluent tend to do, does not help in the medium or long terms. We need to "throw" some version of the ABCs at them as well, so that they can reform their political and cultural institutions, and thus make the best possible use of their own resources as well as ours.

## The Hottentots and the Urban Jungle

To speak of "the village" (the kind it takes to rear a child) is to conjure images of pastoral charm, natural simplicity, and moral decency. One of the last communities to achieve celebrity for philosophical and literary works emanating from such an ethos were the New England idealists. Nowadays, Emerson's celebration of "Self-reliance" and Thoreau's sojourn on Walden Pond are relics of a bygone age; a scant century and a half in the historical past, but separated from our present by the gulf of globalization, in which virtuality and technology displace mere chronology. The villages of yesteryear were knitted by the spirit of community. Such villages have all but vanished, transformed out of recognition in the developed world by successive waves of progress—the Industrial Revolution, utilitarian and democratic reforms, the golden age of capitalism, the information revolution, the postmodern exurban sprawl. Community is superseded by technology, and moral consciousness is eroded by technocracy.

In his forthright 1905 rebuttal of social Darwinism, Peter Kropotkin wrote: "And while in a savage land, among the Hottentots, it would be scandalous to eat without having loudly called out thrice whether there is not somebody wanting to share the food, all that a respectable citizen has to do now is to pay the poor tax and to let the starving starve."[10]

Kropotkin's critique bears substantial weight today, save that our taxes are paid to a more complex array of inefficient, unaccountable, and technocratic governments, while more people than ever starve.

In New York City, the quintessential urban jungle cum central hub of the global village, yet hardly a savage land—at least to all appearances on Fifth Avenue—the Hottentot custom is all but impossible to practice. Ride the New York subway system, and you will regularly observe the following succession of events. First, a charity worker enters the subway car with a hamper of sandwiches, fruits, and beverages, announces his or her mission, and asks whether anyone is hungry or thirsty. There are no takers, so he moves on to the next car. Second, and before long, a beggar enters the car and recites a compulsory tale of woe, which may gild truth with exaggeration because of fierce competition (even in this tragic sector, where beggars are "selling" their dire need). There are no givers, so he or she moves on to the next car. In decades of riding the New York subway, I have never seen the food donor and the food seeker in the same car at the same time. Apparently, they have evolved a pattern of perfect mutual avoidance. If the Manhattan chapter of the global village can finesse the Hottentot maxim so deftly, imagine how many more people, across much greater distances, it can also fail to feed.

The inapplicability of the maxim of the Hottentot village to the global village becomes starker in the context of Emmanuel Levinas's "other-centered" ethics. Levinas observes that the very existence of others imposes inescapable moral obligations on us all. He asserts that "justice remains justice only, in a society where there is no distinction between those close and those far off, but in which there also remains the impossibility of passing by the closest."[11] To those who sustain virtual selves in that unbounded e-Commons known as cyberspace, the former distinctions of time and space "between those close and those far off" no longer apply. In principle, any two people anywhere on the planet can communicate instantaneously. But in reality, for instance in the New York subway, there remains a probability approaching certainty of "passing by the closest," especially while speaking on a mobile phone to "those far off." And if one can so easily "pass by the closest," then one can even more easily forget the existence of billions of "those far off" who have never used phones or e-mail, and who are just as hungry as "the closest" whom everyone passes by. Levinas would (and did) conclude that such a system is utterly unjust, and that in consequence it is accumulating an incalculable moral debt. The question is, who will pay?

## Political, Religious, and Corporate Extremes

In many respects, globalization is driven by an unprecedented phenomenon—the supersession of economic forces over political and religious ones. The great architecture of the world tells this story well. Formerly, the grandest architectural monuments attested to the power of political rulers and of religions. From the pyramids of Giza to the Taj Mahal to the palace of Versailles, we see incontrovertible evidence of the vast wealth and power once concentrated in the hands of monarchs. Similarly, the ornate cathedrals of Christianity and the glittering mosques of Islam, along with innumerable Hindu temples and Buddhist shrines throughout Asia, testify eloquently to the wealth and power wielded by organized religions. But since the turn of the twentieth century, the definitive features of all modern metropoli are their skylines. The skyscraper has become the preeminent symbol of economic power, and great cities vie for prestige and wealth-attraction by erecting ever-taller buildings. Taipei, Kuala Lumpur, Chicago, Shanghai, Hong Kong, Guangzhou, Shenzhen, and New York are home to the world's tallest inhabitable structures. (Toronto's CN tower draws two millions visitors annually, but is not otherwise inhabited.) Note the increasing predominance of tall buildings in Asia. Dubai—the Singapore of Arabia—is slated to erect the world's newest tallest building, which will dwarf all the others, and is a vital symbol of the Arab world's potential for modernization. Shanghai is overtaking New York as the metropolis with the most impressive skyline, and that owes more to the economic growth of China than to the destruction of New York's World Trade Center on 9/11.

Even so, it is important to observe that 9/11's main attack—two of the four hijacked aircraft—was focused on the twin towers. Insofar as al-Qaeda also attacked the Pentagon, and probably intended to attack the White House with the fourth plane, 9/11 amounted to a declaration of war on the United States of America by nonstate Arab-Islamist actors, with the support and sympathy of many Arabs and Islamic states, but at arm's length from them politically. But insofar as al-Qaeda's primary target was the World Trade Center—and a follow-up from the 1993 bombing planned by Arab fanatics across the river in Jersey City—9/11 was an attack on the de facto chamber of commerce of the global village, and hence a declaration of war on globalization itself.

This represents the violent tip of a seething iceberg. Transnational economic forces that drive globalization cannot operate locally (e.g., within nation-states) without the cooperation of sovereign governments and predominant faiths. Nor can predatory capitalism (which we will treat in the next chapter) operate locally without the complicity of corrupt leaders, whether political or religious. But whereas corrupt politicians and other government officials can easily be bribed or bought by multinational corporations, many religious leaders view economic development with suspicion or hostility. Why? Because modernization implies secularization, and its benefits of education (as well as its drawbacks of moral decay), all of which threaten to emancipate the cowed masses, liberating them from their addiction to the opiates of dogma, and making them more self-determining. Autocrats fear losing their political power to the democratizing side effects of modernity, but they can be compensated by sufficiently fat Swiss bank accounts. Theocrats, on the other hand, fear losing their religious authority to the secularizing effects of modernity, and they can prove much more resistant to compensation, because the source of their power lies not in the bodies of the faithful, but in their souls. Hence the fulminating ayatollahs and malevolent mullahs of the Islamic world are far more implacable than are its despots. The Saddam Husseins rule their subjects by instilling in them fear of arrest, torture, and murder, not only of themselves but also of their loved ones. But the ayatollahs rule their subjects by instilling in them fear not only of this world, but also of the next.

Hence even the despots who wish to modernize and join the global village must strike a nefarious compromise with their indigenous religious leaders, who hold the power to agitate the masses and foment violent revolution against governments themselves. So the price of maintaining political power is often perfect duplicity—outward acceptance of globalization to placate the power brokers and economic developers of the new world order, and internal rejection of globalization to appease fanatical religious leaders and to allow their media to hemorrhage toxic hatreds that poison the minds of the masses against secular modernity. The ensuing convulsions will take decades, if not centuries, to settle down.

So globalization unfolds from the interactions of a complex triangular dynamic, composed of economic, political, and religious forces. Where they act in concert, much can be accomplished. Multinational corporations and allied financial institutions have the economic power and expertise to modernize and develop any nation or region on earth, if governments and religions will cooperate. Governments have the power to ensure that their human resources are not cruelly exploited, and that their natural resources are developed in sustainable pathways. Religions have the power to reform themselves, and to allow their adherents greater opportunities for modern education, material prosperity, and personal fulfillment, without relinquishing their vital missions as shepherds of the spiritual and moral dimensions of their flocks.

But wherever these forces conflict rather than cooperate, people suffer. And they conflict worldwide. Predatory multinational corporations join forces with corrupt sovereign governments to strip peoples and nations of their wealth, instead of helping them create it. Despots join forces with religious fanatics, promoting obscene hatreds, and blaming economic backwardness on everything but their own dysfunctional ways of life. Tribalism itself resurfaces in the form of sovereign government, preempting economic development and spiritual welfare alike, and preying on rival tribes through the facade of statecraft.

At the wealthy end of the developmental spectrum, the nations that offer the most liberty, opportunity, and hope to their citizens—from social democracies like Sweden to Confucian democracies like Japan—have the following three features in common. First, their secular governments protect religious freedoms but prohibit theocratic tyrannies. Second, their secular governments stimulate economic growth but guard against predatory capitalism. Third, their secular governments are framed by constitutions—a rule of law, not a rule of man—and their leaders are answerable to the electorate. When the developing world is better able to emulate these three features, its peoples will benefit economically, and in many other ways.

### Religions and Poverty

If we assess the roles that organized religions play, both in wealth creation and poverty perpetuation, we are faced with contradictions aplenty. All religions extol the virtues of charity, yet they also perpetuate the conditions that make charity necessary. Even so, these contradictions are helpful, because they cast the roles of organized religion into a useful perspective.

It seems that every major religion enters a phase during which it exerts near-total control over the political, social, and educational dimensions of the lives of its adherents. This phase can last for centuries. Whatever spiritual benefits it confers, this phase also maintains large masses of people in a state of abysmal ignorance, impedes or arrests their socioeconomic mobility, and so prevents them from attaining their full human potential. In such phases, massive poverty is a direct effect of religion's suppression of human potential, its control over human life for the sake of exercising power, and not for improvement or enlightenment of its flocks.

In the West, the best-known example is the Roman Catholic Church, which harnessed itself to great imperial powers like Spain. Although the Spanish empire forged by the Conquistadors is long gone, its two great aftereffects are the twin influences of Roman Catholicism, and the Spanish language. That language—spoken by the peoples of Spain and Latin America (Brazil excepted), and increasingly in the United States—has the third-largest number of native speakers in the world, after English and Mandarin. The prominence of the Spanish language in today's global village owes much to the Roman Catholic Church. Matters of religious faith and doctrinal dispute aside, one cannot fail to be impressed by the scale and scope of Christianity as a world religion, and by its largest denomination, Roman Catholicism.

The Roman Catholic Church, which rose like a phoenix from the ashes of the Roman Empire, has proved far mightier than that empire itself, in terms of geopolitical reach, numbers of adherents, and longevity as an institution. That said, it remains true that all empires wax and wane—even religious ones. The secular modernity and nihilistic postmodernism that accompany globalization (and against which Islamist extremists are fomenting civil riots) are also affecting the Catholic Church of late, and in several dimensions. In North America, the Church is besieged by scandals arising from allegations of decades of sexual abuse, and is selling off prime real estate to raise cash for hefty out-of-court settlements. At the same time, faith is waning among adherents, even within monastic religious orders, who (as we saw) are importing Zen Buddhism and other philosophical modalities to rekindle guttering spiritual flames. In Europe, centuries-old Catholic strongholds—from Ireland to Spain, from Poland to Italy—are evaporating by attrition, as populations decline from plummeting birth rates. Feminist president Mary Robinson legalized abortion in Ireland, while Italy leads the way in depopulation (currently 1.1 children per family). Thus even the Roman Catholic Church, the leading bastion of Christianity for so many centuries, is experiencing undeniable weakening of many of its vital signs.

In retrospect, the Catholic Church grew so vast, and has lasted so long, precisely because of its conservatism—including its resistance to reform. But this very tendency has also made it brittle, and unable to accommodate the evolving spiritual needs of increasingly sophisticated and affluent masses, whom globalization has emancipated politically and socioeconomically, but whom the Church has failed to emancipate theologically. The absence of a Middle Way between devout medieval Catholicism and lapsed postmodern Catholicism is resulting in the erosion of the Catholic Church's population base—the reversal of a centuries-old pattern that may signal the beginning of the end of the Catholic Church itself.

A distinguishing feature of fervently religious fundamentalist populations—notably Jewish, Christian, Muslim, and Hindu—persistent over many centuries, is the number of babies they produce, and the corresponding poverty in which they live. Said another way, fundamentalist religious faith is often negatively correlated with socioeconomic dynamism, a tension between the City of God and the City of Man. This tension is still characteristic of India and much of Islamic civilization, and has until recently been true of Roman Catholic populations from Mexico to Ireland, from the Philippines to Canada's province of Quebec.

I grew up in Quebec, where there is centuries-old and sometimes bitter conflict between the French Catholic majority and the English Protestant minority. Throughout my decades in Quebec, I witnessed on a daily basis the religious dimensions of that conflict. For a long time the English-Canadians ("Anglophones") monopolized banking, insurance, commerce, management, higher education, the professions—the lifeblood of urban culture and the economy—while the French-Canadians ("Francophones") comprised the uneducated urban working classes and the overpopulated rural poor, with few or no prospects for advancement in life. The socioeconomic culture gap between anglophones and francophones became so pronounced that, during the 1960s, an imprisoned French-Canadian terrorist named Pierre Vallières wrote a landmark book of protest in which he referred to French-Canadians as the "white negroes" ("les nègres blanches") of North America.[12]

Vallières's analogy with American slavery and civil rights was accurate in some respects, but distorted in others. The main impediment to the political liberation and socioeconomic progress of French-Canadians was not English-Canadian prejudice; it was Roman Catholic dogma. On one hand, the incredible hardiness and enduring fortitude of French-Canadian pioneers in the New World owe a great deal to the depth of their spiritual faith. On the other hand, the Roman Catholic Church made sure that the majority of French-Canadian families would have as many children, as much catechism, and as little education as possible, thus preparing them for a life of spiritual servitude to Rome, and socioeconomic servitude to anglophones. During World War II, the Church opposed conscription of French-Canadians, teaching its flock that their "enemy" was English Canada, not Nazi Germany. Even so, many French-Canadians fought and served with distinction (just as many African Americans fought and served with distinction, even though the United States segregated them) because they recognized the greater threat to their liberty, opportunity, and hope.

When large-scale French-Canadian political consciousness began to emerge in the 1960s, Francophones were able to cast off their shackles of religious dogma, harness their passionate Gallic temperaments to political self-determination instead of spiritual servitude, bear fewer children per family, acquire modern education instead of medieval indoctrination, and remedy their socioeconomic deficiencies instead of blaming them on Anglophone Protestants and—as usual—on Jews.[13] By accepting responsibility for their fates instead of blaming others, Francophones have emancipated and transformed themselves, in mostly nonviolent ways and by democratic political process, into a vibrant culture.

Religion per se imposes no limitations on what can be accomplished by any human being. On the contrary: Just look at the unparalleled artistic achievements of the Italian Renaissance, the musical ones of the Late Baroque, the intellectual and scientific ones of the Enlightenment, so many of whose immortal works were conceived by Catholics, or by artists patronized by Catholic cultures. I myself have been blessed by numerous mentors, guides, and friends who are also Roman Catholics. But at the other extreme—mass conformity to rules and repressive social control—religious cultures are infamous for keeping their minions overpopulated, undereducated, and in abject poverty.

My point is simple. As democratization and modernization take hold in traditionally Catholic countries, from Spain to Poland, from Chile to Ireland, we see common features emerge: increased economic productivity, better education, more affluence, smaller families, greater emphasis on individualism and self-determination, enhanced quality of life. Providential religion has diminished influence, making room for secular concerns about a good life now. That's a pattern. And that pattern needs to be instated and repeated throughout other parts of the world as well, where poverty is even more crushing and human potential even harder to attain.

Christianity is a vital strand of Western civilization, and the Roman Catholic Church is a pillar of Christianity. Yet The Middle Way suggests, with respect, that Christian communities fare better when they balance the City of God with the City of Man, instead of using one to suppress the other.

## Islam and Poverty

There is a natural evolution in the birth and development of great religions, which includes recurrent patterns that can be readily perceived. One such pattern is the emergence of rival and even hostile sectarian factions within a given religion—e.g., the Pharisees and the Sadducees in biblical Judaism, the Catholics and the Protestants in Christianity, the Sunnis and the Shiites in Islam, the Mahayanists and the Theravadans in Buddhism. Secular religions such as Marxism show similar but shorter-lived patterns, having featured rivalries between Bolsheviks and Mensheviks, Leninists and Trotskyites. Rival Buddhist factions, as well as rival Jewish factions, have generally refrained from conspicuously violent expressions of doctrinal difference, but they can be bitterly if clandestinely divided as well. Human history chronicles long-standing, oft-recurring and large-scale slaughters of Christians by Christians, and Muslims by Muslims. Why? Primarily because Christianity and Islam are the world's two most aggressive proselytizing faiths. Aggressive proselytization produces blinded, tormented, and debilitated believers, who in the worst cases pervert God's love to justify the demonization and slaughter of fellow human beings.

A second pattern that one can perceive in major religions is the gradual movement from orthodoxy toward reformation, which often precipitates a violent schism followed by a period of reform. Hinduism was reformed peacefully by Buddha around 500 B.C.E., but Nichiren's reforms of corrupt Japanese Buddhism in the thirteenth century were met with violence against him and the murder of some of his followers. The attempted reform of Judaism by Jesus around 30 C.E. led him to a violent end at the hands of the Romans, whose empire nonetheless converted to Christianity three centuries later. Martin Luther reformed Papal Christianity in the sixteenth century, precipitating a far-reaching historical movement that resulted in the Enlightenment—along with science, technology, democracy, human rights, globalization, and the highest standard of living ever enjoyed by human masses in the entire history of our species. Judaism was reformed many times, for example in Europe and America in the nineteenth century, as a consequence of the Enlightenment project. It is noteworthy that the reform of Judaism allowed Jews—where not persecuted by others—to join society in secular endeavors such as science. In the twentieth century, this resulted in 18 percent of Nobel prizes being won by Jews, who comprised only $1/24$ of 1 percent of world population. This highlights the importance of religious reforms, in terms of freeing human cognitive function from stultifying dogmas, and liberating noetic space for creative questioning and discovery.

In contrast with orthodox Hinduism, Catholicism, and Judaism, Islam still—and desperately—awaits widespread reform. Being the newest of the world's great religions, founded only in the seventh century C.E., relatively recently compared with the others, it stands to reason that Islam will also be the last to undergo reform. Because Islam lags about five hundred years behind Protestant reform, it provides a useful "snapshot" in which we can see how socioeconomically and intellectually stultifying are the effects of religious dictatorship over human life.

Many Arabs themselves imagine that they inhabit a different world than the rest of humanity—they constantly refer to the "Arab world" in major media broadcasts to the West and to each other, reinforcing the idea to themselves and everyone else that they are somehow separate. There is no other group on the planet that makes such strident claims of separateness; we never hear of the "American world" or the "British world" or the "French world" or the "Spanish world"; nor do we hear of the "Hindu world" or the "Buddhist world" or the "Christian world" or the "Jewish world." We certainly speak of the "developed world" and the "developing world," but these are socioeconomic terms, which designate huge cross-sections of people, of every conceivable race, creed, ethnicity, and color.

It is clear that the Arabs are an ancient and extremely proud people, and by tradition also a very hospitable people, who have learned to survive in incredibly harsh and inhospitable desert climes.

But the harsh political and social controls that Islam has exerted over their lives, for unbroken centuries, has impoverished them economically and intellectually. This in turn has mightily embarrassed Arab leaders and intellectuals alike, who have too often rehearsed the common human habit of blaming others for their own deficiencies, instead of taking steps to remedy them. Thus many Arabs, confronted by postmodern cultures that are centuries ahead of their premodern cultures, tend to withdraw even further into the cocoon of Islam, and fall even further behind, instead of metamorphosing and emerging from that cocoon. Arab leaders know perfectly well, and Americans learned to their horror on 9/11, that the "Arab world" is not separate from the global village. Now many Arab leaders themselves are making "good cause" in the aftermath of 9/11, trying harder to become more constructively integrated.

For example, it is heartening to read the words of His Excellency Amre Moussa, secretary-general of the League of Arab States, who in 2005 said, "I would like to affirm that we are all in the same boat: East and West, North and South, Muslims, Christians and all others. What we need is to build a new international order that would steer our ship through the first decade of the twenty-first century and beyond."[14] This enlightened and inclusive perspective needs to percolate throughout all Arab states, where it may help to stimulate the religious reforms required to enhance economic productivity, and reduce the isolation, privation, and desperation that help spawn terrorism.

But the plain truth is that the Arabs have a lot of catching up to do. In economic terms, the GDP of the entire "Arab world"—twenty-two countries with an aggregate area and population (three hundred million) comparable to the United States—is smaller than that of Spain, a country of only forty million that reformed itself politically only in the 1970s. The "Arab world" has one of the global village's highest rates of female illiteracy, which contributes mightily to its lack of economic productivity. A primary cause of this economic underperformance is unreformed Islam, whose sharia (religious law) does not recognize any separation between mosque and state. History teaches clearly that socioeconomic progress and a strong middle class follow only on the heels of separating temple from state, church from state, ashram from state. And these processes always require a reformer.

Intellectual deprivation is another consequence of religious bondage. Consider this stark comparison between the two Semitic peoples, Jews and Arabs. Reformed Judaism allows the fuller participation of Jews in the intellectual life of Western civilization—whenever and wherever they were not being excluded, persecuted, or exterminated by their "host countries." As a result, a population of twelve million Jews has produced 164 Nobel laureates. By contrast, unreformed Islam denies the fuller participation of Arabs, and Muslims in general, in the intellectual life of Western civilization—a civilization their former Caliphs ironically helped safeguard during the Dark Ages of Europe. As a result, a population of 1.4 billion Muslims—117 times the number of Jews—has produced six Nobel laureates. This disparity is a result of the stultifying and crippling effects of unreformed religious indoctrination upon the minds of young people.

A well-educated Palestinian friend of mine is mightily embarrassed by the "Arab world's" failure to produce scientists, even in proportion to the rest of the developing world. He is also embarrassed that institutions such as the World Youth Orchestra contain talented young musicians from across North America, South America, Europe, and Asia—and not one from the "Islamic world." Like many Arab and Islamic intellectuals, trained in the West and versed in modernity, he knows full well that underdeveloped Islamic cultures are all but bereft of Aristotelian sciences and arts, and that their captive citizens cannot fulfill themselves as human beings as long as they remain enslaved by crippling, debilitating and spiteful dogmas.

An Arab-American psychiatrist, Dr. Wafa Sultan, understands this very well. As he said in an interview with al-Jazeera: "The clash we are witnessing . . . is not a clash of religions, or a clash of civilizations. It is a clash between two opposites, between two eras. It is a clash between a mentality that belongs to the Middle Ages and another mentality that belongs to the twenty-first century. It is a clash between civilization and backwardness, between the civilized and the primitive, between barbarity and rationality."[15]

As Islam reforms itself, and affords its young men and women modern educations instead of purely religious indoctrinations, the economic poverty and intellectual impoverishment of the "Arab world" will rapidly reverse itself. I see encouraging signs of such transformation already, for example among many Arab and other Muslim students at City College, where I teach philosophy. Just like Jews and Christians, Muslims are a "People of the Book." This predisposes them to the written tradition, instills in them respect for the written word, and inculcates in them studious habits that lay strong foundations for cognitive development and intellectual enrichment. When such students are exposed to the Western canon, they immediately begin to absorb its liberal arts and sciences, and reintegrate them into Islamic cultural contexts. This process is producing a gradual but deep groundswell of intellectual reform, that will slowly but inevitably percolate through the "Arab world" as well as through other Muslim cultures. This exercise of "soft power"— transformation through education—will bridge the gap between Islam and the West more effectively than any military invasion or political imposition. It may even lead to the unimaginable: that is, the reunion of Islamic and Western civilizations, and a new golden age of tolerance and cooperation, from which the entire global village would reap economic among many other benefits.

The events of 9/11 precipitated worldwide awareness of the necessity of political and religious reform in the "Arab world," both for the sake of regional prosperity and world peace. We will soon turn to the Middle East itself—a region that can take dubious credit for being a cradle of extremism.

Before doing so, let us summarize this chapter on wealth and poverty, and recapitulate the wisdom of the ABCs on the matters of material possessions, and what is valuable in life.

## The ABCs

People who have much money are not necessarily wealthy in terms of life's treasures, while people who have little money are not necessarily poor in terms of those treasures. We've all heard the saying, "Money won't buy happiness," and that is true. At the same time, excesses of poverty, such as we see among millions of people in the developing world, and among the homeless in the developed world, are far more widespread and crushing than excesses of wealth. To find The Middle Way, we must ask, "How much is enough?" and "How should wealth be shared?"

Many forms of political economy have been tried since the dawn of humanity, and all of them are imperfect. Winston Churchill said famously of democracy that "It's the worst form of government . . . except for all the others." One could well echo his words in terms of democratic capitalism: "It's the worst form of economics . . . except for all the others." John Locke's defense of private property, in his *Second Treatise on Government*, is the best justification yet provided for private property. Karl Marx's theories are the worst justification ever invented for its abolition.

Nature has ordained the pyramid as one of her fundamental structures. In myriad species (e.g., reptiles, amphibians, fishes, cephalopods), multitudes of young are hatched at once, but progressively fewer—the strongest, smartest, luckiest—survive the rigors of maturation: a pyramid. All social insects (ants, bees, wasps) are organized in absolute monarchies ruled by queens only (female hegemony), with all subservient classes beneath her: a pyramid. Among the so-called "tournament species" of ruminants (e.g., deer, elk, moose), 5 percent of the males emerge victorious from seasonal combats (the "rut"), to inseminate 95 percent of the females: a pyramid. Human organizations, from corporations to educational institutions to military forces, are structured with one leader, under whom we find increasingly broad subordinate layers: a pyramid. And in all human societies, the greatest wealth is invariably concentrated in the fewest hands, the least wealth, in the most hands: a pyramid. Malthus was the first to notice the tendency toward geometric increase in human populations, and the inevitable social inequities to which they give rise. In his 1798 *Essay on Population*, he wrote "Our ability to produce children will always exceed our ability to secure food for their survival." That's the poverty pyramid.

So we must either find a force that checks the growth of human populations (affluence in the West has accomplished this well, perhaps too well, and so has the policy of one-child families in China), or we will face the unhappy alternative of constantly trying to feed hungry masses (as we see in much of the developing world).

Marxism subverted the natural pyramid, and in empires like the former Soviet Union replaced it with something infinitely worse: a "People's Democratic Pyramid," in which the party made everybody poor. Similarly, organized religions wielding political power are recipes for widespread poverty, plus ignorance, which completes the trap. The poorest countries in the world are also among the most fervently religious. Theocracies keep their minions chained in states of political apathy, theological fatalism, cultural paralysis, and dire poverty.

In areas of the world where tribalism, feudalism, despotism, or theocracy still hold sway, the contrast between excess for the fewest at the top, and dearth for the majority at the bottom, is staggering. Parts of Africa, Latin America, the Middle East, and Asia offer the most ghastly inequities for the greatest numbers.

Varieties of democratic capitalism, as practiced in the United States, Britain, Australia, Canada, Western Europe, Scandinavia, Israel, Japan, Singapore, South Korea, Taiwan, exert a corrective force on such pyramids, turning them into bell-shaped curves (Gaussian distributions) that elevate the bottom layers into a middle class. This provides the greatest good for the greatest number. There will always be disproportionate wealth at the top, but there need not be disproportionate poverty at the bottom. Moreover, the existence of a vibrant middle class in a socially dynamic system that permits upward mobility always offers opportunity for the poor, via education.

A large question looms: What kind of social safety net (if any) should we allow? Here the social democracies like Canada and Sweden part company with more purely capitalistic republics like the United States. Socialism is more compassionate, but is also a slippery slope toward collectivism and totalitarianism. "Free" health care and education are great ideas, but in the end somebody has to pay for them, usually the middle class. Most Americans like the idea of socialized medicine, justice, education, and welfare, until they find out how much this costs taxpayers, and how inefficient socialized democracy can become.

Aristotle's prescription still stands: a vibrant middle class is the best possible solution to the economic equation. And while Aristotle insisted that a life of contemplation is more noble than a life of commerce, it is commercial interests that must subsidize and champion the powers of contemplation, nowadays through higher education. Buddha reminds us that all attachments are potential causes of suffering: whether to material possessions or to proprietary knowledge. And the Confucian tradition counsels us, through the Tao, not to accumulate wealth or learning merely for their own sakes, but as means to a greater end—understanding of the Way.

Poverty inflicted upon masses of people will always make them suffer; whereas individuals may always choose to renounce material possessions in order to accelerate their spiritual development. Similarly, seeking riches for their own sake is a recipe for misery, while making wise and compassionate use of money is a powerful way of doing good in the world.

# 13

## TOTEMIC EXTREMES
### McFoods, McDrugs, and Brave New McWorlds

*And the avarice of mankind is insatiable . . . for it is in the nature of desire to be unlimited, and most men live only for the gratification of it.*
—Aristotle

*Every human being is the author of his own health or disease.* —Buddha

*Those who do nothing but cram themselves with food and never use their minds are difficult.* —Confucius

## McFoods

AMERICA IS AN INCREASINGLY fractured society. As we have seen, it is politically polarized, deeply divided between Red states and Blue states—the result of decades of unremitting cultural civil war. It is racially polarized, subject to unrelenting waves of white guilt and black racism, black rage and white racism. It is religiously polarized, divided by fundamentalist Christianity on one hand and postmodern moral anarchy on the other. It is sexually polarized, between chauvinistic suppressions of women's liberation and militant feminist deconstructions of civilization itself. It is cognitively polarized, with a growing rift separating literate but politically indoctrinated "elites" from televisually impaired, culturally and functionally illiterate masses. It is economically polarized, with a widening socioeconomic chasm separating the well-off who are sheltered in gated communities, and the tens of millions of disenfranchised who subsist in projects and ghettoes, RV parks and rust belts.

This congeries of seething polarizations is still the world's leading military power, thanks to its leading edge of Aristotelian science, and still the world's mightiest economic engine, thanks to its traditions of liberty, opportunity, and hope. But America's lead in science is waning, and its economy resembles a gargantuan bubble, ripe for bursting, as debt-rich and cash-poor consumers strive to stay a step ahead of soaring costs and diminishing returns of the American Dream.

Against this fractured backdrop, the main "common good" to emerge in contemporary America is consumerism. Americans love to consume, both in reality and online, to the extent that consumption—and overconsumption—has become a way a life. One of the first things visitors to America notice is the epidemic of obesity, which has transformed adults and children alike from fulfilled and productive beings into hypoglycemic and chronically ill people who are barred, along with their children, from the pale of normalcy. Latin Americans, Europeans, and Asians are increasingly and justifiably concerned as American brands of junk foods, predigested thoughts, and cookie-cutter lifestyles permeate global markets, pervade local cultures, and compromise quality of life.

Another thing that foreign visitors notice is the size of American portions. The quantities that Americans consume, whether of decent food or of junk, are simply indecent. Americans daily overstuff themselves, consuming double, triple or quadruple the amounts required to sustain a healthy body; millions who fail to attain obesity are nonetheless severely overweight, as are their children. Bulk food outlets pander to such "tastes" selling FDA-approved foods laced with sugar, salt, bad cholesterol, and trans fat, in oversized boxes and jumbo bags that consumers cram into their gargantuan SUVs. The most important features of SUVs are the capacities of their beverage holders, the amount of extra space they can take up on America's overcongested roads, and the quantity of gas they can guzzle. Americans comprise 5 percent of the world's population, yet consume about 25 percent of its energy resources on a daily basis, in addition to their caloric overdose. Americans have little idea how they are regarded by the rest of the world: as a nation of selfish and self-indulgent beings, whose bloated bodies and stupefied minds are ample testaments to the drawbacks of a "culture" based on gluttonous overconsumption.

Even Buddha, whose teachings are temperate and gentle for the most part, condemned gluttony in surprisingly stark terms: "If a man is torpid, gluttonous, slumberous and rolling to and fro like a huge hog which has been fattened by pig wash and podder, that indolent and stupid fool is born again and again."

En route to the American Dream, many newcomers experience nightmares. When immigrants manage to get a foothold in America, they can swiftly succumb to prevailing market forces. To me, the most shocking aspect of overconsumption is the sight of obese children from cultures in which one rarely sees overweight people at all, let alone grotesquely corpulent ones. Obese Arab children, obese Indian children, obese Southeast Asian children, obese Latino children, obese African children—some of their parents emigrated from destitute places to spare their children premature death by starvation, only to condemn them to premature death from juvenile diabetes and heart attacks.[1]

America's obesity is not just the result of massive daily overdoses of sugars, fats, salts, and bad cholesterol, in tandem with a chronic lack of mental and physical exercise and too much television. On top of this, the dairy industry daily poisons hundreds of millions of Americans with bovine growth hormone, which humans metabolize and which lends them the physique of cows.[2] We are what we eat and drink, more than most people realize. Add to this the battery of growth hormones that saturate the feeds used by intensive animal husbanding industries, which accelerate the time between the birth, adulthood, and slaughter of these tortured animals, but which remain in their carcasses and accumulate in the humans who overconsume them. These growth hormones are accelerating the puberty of American children, making them biologically capable of sexual activity at increasingly and shockingly young ages, a tendency reinforced 24/7 by the prurient and decadent culture of MTV and other mass media.

This downward spiral of overconsumption, obesity, hedonism, promiscuity, and amorality, tinged with violence and etched with the absence of family, education, literacy, and attention span, are together producing a nation of culturally feral savages who have lost their capacity to acquire or carry on the legacy of Western civilization. American "culture" is synonymous with shopping for brands in megastores, outlets, and Web sites. But where, in this vast marketplace, do you "get a life"?

Never have production and consumption, as well as their conspicuous absence, attained such pronounced global extremes. At one extreme people are starved materially yet force-fed and overstuffed spiritually. In many underdeveloped Islamic regions, whose rates of production and consumption are exceedingly low, the totem of religion is used to distract people's attention from their lack of material necessities and cultural amenities. It is also used to foment hatred of Western civilization, which makes those comforts and necessities possible. At another extreme, American consumers are overfed and overstuffed materially, and starved spiritually. So, for example, throughout the United States, where rates of production and consumption are among the world's highest, the totem of consumerism is used to distract people's attention from their lack of spirituality. It is also used to foment a sense of superiority toward developing civilizations. Adherents to Islam pray five times per day; adherents to consumerism shop 24/7. Each appears extreme to the other. Benjamin Barber aptly and presciently described this phenomenon, during the decade before 9/11, as "Jihad versus McWorld."[3] Indeed, Americans live in McMansions, eat McFoods, drive McTrucks, work McJobs, attend McSchools, and lead McLives. The entire McCulture is prepackaged, and increasingly monolithic. Brands are the new totems. Welcome to Brave New McWorld.

## Just Waiting

And yet there's still this difference: Americans allow mosques, and other houses of worship, to coexist with Wal-Mart. When more Islamic nations allow Wal-Mart to coexist with mosques and other houses of worship, their respective totems will cease to impel violent conflicts. But this is no easy matter. It took decades of hatred, violence, and bloodshed before two Arab-Islamic states—Egypt and Jordan—made peace with Israel. The tribes of that region have warred since time immemorial, and the magnitudes of their conflicts are literally biblical. They will not readily give up their grievances. They dread any influence that could reshape their historical and spiritual touchstones.

In Aristotle's era, the Persians very nearly conquered Greek civilization. Alexander quieted their ambitions for a few centuries at one stroke, but a pacified Persian civilization remained intact. Today's Iranians are descended from those Persians, a highly cultured people with redoubtable prophets, poets, philosophers, scholars, and warriors. Depending on the regime that governs them, Iranians can be as highly cultured or as mob-driven as anyone. But lately they have been fanatically Islamicized, and the poisonous hatred of Jews, Israelis, and the West that spews from Teheran is as toxic to the mind as the poisons that spew from McDonald's are toxic to the body. The totem of intolerant Islamist hatred collides head-on with the totem of ignorant American overconsumption. Inflamed by hypocritical intolerance of a satirical Danish cartoon about Islam, Islamic mobs have rampaged from Syria to Indonesia, burning McDonald's and Kentucky Fried Chicken franchises to protest the West's freedom of expression, and to demonstrate once again how many centuries they lag behind the West in political maturity, social satire, and sense of humor.

America is so polarized internally that her citizens' animosities are largely consumed domestically. Thus many Americans remain grossly ignorant of the wide world over which they exert so much influence—only 20 percent of Americans have passports—yet are remarkably good natured and unxenophobic toward it. America's proverbial and moderate moral majority is still somehow alive—if unwell and underrepresented in so many vital arenas: politics, education, media. But on the ground, and in the heart of the people, where so much of America's true greatness still survives, nourished by its Whitmanesque spirit, I find not one iota of hatred, or even ill-feeling, toward Islamic civilization. Western universities have accepted enormous endowments from Arab-Islamic sources, to build centers, establish chairs, and fund programs for the study of Islamic civilization—and all too often, to be used as hotbeds of vilification of their American hosts. The West has given Islam a home, as it has done for countless peoples of innumerable cultures. Most middle Americans—and for that matter most Jews and Israelis—do not hate Arabs or Muslims at all. On the contrary, Muslims are welcomed into the melting pot just as everyone else. When will Islamic universities accept Western endowments from non-Islamic sources, to build centers, establish chairs, and fund programs for the study of Western civilization?

Moderate, well-educated, assimilated Arab Americans are caught, like everyone else, between two extremes. Their long-standing knee-jerk response to Arab terrorism has (regrettably) not been to condemn it vociferously, but to ring shrill alarms about their own civil rights so as to counteract "racial profiling." Then again, many moderate Arabs have been afraid to speak out against terrorism, because they themselves are both terrorized and terrified. Only recently, as hordes of frenzied Muslims are rampaging on a massive "war path" from Europe to Indonesia, trashing totems of globalization, committing acts of vandalism and arson, has the contrast with North American Muslims become glaringly obvious. Canadian and American Muslims are not going on the rampage. Why not? Because they have better lives by far in what remains of the free West than do their brethren in the "Arab world" and other developing Islamic nations, and because they understand that a source of their betterment is tolerance. Now that things are getting out of hand, moderate Arab Americans are waking up to their own responsibilities, which include defending the West, which has given them liberty, opportunity, and hope, not only to thrive and prosper as Muslims, but also to live in peace with non-Muslims.

If a Muslim in New York City—or any American city—wanders through the wrong place at the wrong time, he or she might get mugged, just like anyone. Such violence is criminally, not religiously or politically, motivated. In the aftermath of 9/11, and for several days thereafter, all the Arab shops in Jersey City, New Jersey—right across the river from the twin towers—were shuttered, their sturdy steel doors festooned with American flags. (Some of these flags hung upside down, casualties of hasty patriotism.) Islamist terrorists living in Jersey City had built, warehoused, and driven the truck bomb in the 1993 attack on the World Trade Center. So on 9/11 Jersey City's Arab merchant community—who operate bodegas, cafés, and other small businesses—feared murderous reprisals from American vigilantes.

Murderous reprisal is a routine policy in much of the "Arab world," to be sure. But these merchants were safe and sound in Jersey City, where there is no law against flying the flag upside down. As the debris settled across the river, their shops gradually reopened. None were torched or looted. In an isolated incident, a Sikh American was murdered on Long Island by some local vigilantes who mistook him for an Arab. But in general there was little vigilantism, because there was little hatred. Whereas you may have noticed that Westerners meet with a very different reception in many parts of the "Arab world."

The hater is always wrong to hate. And yet it is easy to see why the "Arab world" in particular fears and rejects so much of American "McCulture." Millions of Arabs have now settled in Europe, but a majority are neither well adapted nor well received. They first arrived mostly as immigrant laborers, but their children are cultural hybrids whose political identity is a result of feeling unwelcome in their new homelands. In England, France, Holland, Germany, and Denmark, the same phenomenon is manifest: One sees swelling hordes of marginalized Islamic youths, ticking demographic time bombs. Two forces above all have conspired against them: unreformed Islam, which does not prepare them to swim in the mainstream currents of EU culture; and the tolerant freedoms of EU culture itself, which ironically allows them to be born and reared in fundamentalist Islamic isolation, without a cultural architect—neither political nor corporate nor religious nor educational—to help bridge the gap. Architects have built dwellings for them—in low-cost "housing projects" that African Americans would immediately recognize as urban ghettoes—but a house is not a home. Their children do not fit in, and yet they are citizens. They are ripe for resentment, hatred, and violence against their hosts, who ironically offer them liberties, opportunities, and hopes that they are poorly equipped to handle.

At the same time, these disenfranchised Muslims have aroused dormant European xenophobia and racism, of both nationalistic and religious tribal varieties. Indigenous Muslim discontents that lead to violence and vandalism are reawakening and innervating European national identities, which will politically splinter the EU if the violence and vandalism intensify, and as each nation closes ranks to quell its own internal unrest. This is an eminently satisfactory state of affairs to the radicals, the fanatics, the agitators, and the terrorists, among other parties who have interests in the West's demise, but it is preeminently a tragic failure of the human spirit to transcend its primate origins.

Too many Arabs have forgotten for too long that Jews are their cousins, and that Jews suffered horrible persecutions, intermittently for centuries, throughout Europe. The European racism that Arabs are now encountering in their own adopted homelands is nothing new. The virulent anti-Semitism that has haunted European civilization for two millennia is just as readily directed against Arabs as against Jews.

There is another viewpoint too. Europe is a battleground of the New Crusades. The Crusaders were Western knights who sought to capture Jerusalem—if not the Holy Land itself—from Islam, in the name of Christianity. The New Crusaders are Muslim immigrants to Europe and their demographically burgeoning descendents, who may well succeed in capturing European capitals (starting with Amsterdam) from post-Christianity in the name of Islam. Europe has been a soft target for Islamicization: de-Christianized, debellated,[4] open bordered, its divisive nationalist sentiments temporarily numbed by economic unification. The EU is economically strong, but bureaucratically hamstrung and politically impotent—ripe for Islamic insurrection via sheer weights of numbers of discontented and unassimilated Islamic populations.

But America is very different—a bastion of evangelical Christianity and a military superpower, even if politically polarized and culturally degenerate. America remains a hard target. She is unconquerable by invasion, yet all who seek to conquer her by immigration run the risk of succumbing to her polarizations and degeneracies themselves. Everything that happens in America becomes grist for her neo-Roman mills of bread and circuses: junk food, trash TV, mass McCulture. For the

American McDream functions just like cultural paint stripper: Its timeless and placeless shopping malls are also full of obese Arab-American kids in blue jeans and sweatshirts, habituated to junk food, wired to the digital tradition, and addicted to the visual one.

## Time is On Whose Side?

The greatest resource and most formidable "weapon" of peoples who have survived since ancient times, is time itself. Peoples whose collective cultural memory spans thousands of years of history can project as far into the future. Such are the Semitic peoples, Jew and Arab alike. Such is Indian civilization, and such is East Asian civilization too. Europeans share a remote antiquity, if a less foreseeable future. But America is still a very young nation. Founded in 1776, the United States is a mere "adolescent" among nations, and a "juvenile" empire in both senses of the word. A day looms long in the life of a child, as a summer seems eternal. Not so for mature adults, whose accelerated sense of time makes months and years slip through life's grasp like so many grains of sand. Even so, the impetuousness and impatience of youth are ironically harnessed to youth's momentary eternities; while the equanimity and patience of maturity are equally bound to maturity's fleeting moments. Hence American McCulture pervades an endless present, but may also have a short life expectancy.

Well beyond the outskirts of Cairo, an hour or so from the suburb of Heliopolis, lies a large biodynamic farm, founded in the 1970s by Ibrahim Abouleish and his family. Dr. Abouleish is a scientist and CEO, a humanist and visionary. He has won an "Alternative Nobel Prize" for his great achievements. He has drawn eight hundred biodynamic farms into his network, and his group of agricultural and pharmaceutical industries, part of a unified corporate entity called "SEKEM," exports organic produce, natural remedies, and other goods to the "Arab world" and the EU. Dr. Abouleish is also founding SEKEM University, which will graft Western science and technology onto Islamic tradition. I had the honor of helping him craft its mission statement, in the company of its first president-to-be: a distinguished professor who happens to be a woman. Dr. Abouleish knows how to twist the Islamist tiger's tail. The main farm, where he and his family still live, is one of the few places in the entire "Arab world" where Jews, Christians and Muslims alike live and work in peace, goodwill, and harmony. Dr. Abouleish is a model for the "Arab world" and the global village. Why is he not featured on CNN and al-Jazeera?

As we were driving from the farm toward Heliopolis one morning, to SEKEM's corporate headquarters, I beheld a spectacle of stunning simplicity yet profound depth, which seared an indelible image in my mind. Between the farm and the highway to Heliopolis lies a jumble of partly cultivated fields, semi-inhabited structures, and half-deserted Bedouin encampments, all awash in a sea of scalding sand, eroded by burning wind, baked by relentless sun. As we flashed past this unforgiving landscape in Dr. Abouleish's very forgiving Mercedes, I beheld a Bedouin man standing motionless by the side of the road. Tall, erect, and proud, his hawklike countenance sculpted and bronzed by the elements, his piercing gaze fixed unblinkingly on the horizon, his flowing robes stirred by swirling wind, his ebony fingers curling a gnarled wooden staff. Thus he stood, in the middle of nowhere, going no place, surrounded by nothing.

"What is he doing there?" I asked my friend and host.

"He is waiting," Dr. Abouleish replied.

"Waiting for what?" I inquired, from the shadow of the Puritan work ethic.

"Just waiting," came the ancient Egyptian reply.

When we drove back to the farm toward the end of the day, to my astonishment the Bedouin man was still standing in the same place, unbent, and unmoved: a veritable sculpture, a monument to something that may remain standing long after America falls.

Most people who wait are awaiting something. Jews await the Messiah. Christians await the Second Coming. Existentialists are waiting for Godot. But a great many Americans have reached a pass where they cannot wait for anything. They want everything now; and moreover, it must be "quick" and "easy." These are the two watchwords of American consumption: quick, and easy. If it is not quick, people have insufficient patience to consume it. If it is not easy, people have insufficient learning capacity to absorb it. Patience is a virtue that (like all virtues) requires habitual exercise and constant practice. Aristotle and Confucius both explicitly emphasized its importance, while Buddha exemplified it beyond measure. Patience and learning capacity have a common denominator: attention span. To learn, you must be able to pay concerted attention for hours on end. To be patient, you must remain attentive yet unhurried for even longer stretches of time—sometimes years and decades. We have already seen that American attention spans have been reduced to near zero by overconsumption of the visual tradition, in tandem with deconstruction of the written one. As a result, Americans can hardly wait for anything. They can hardly wait to shop. They can hardly wait to watch every channel on TV at once. They can hardly wait to overdose on junk food. They can hardly wait for anything that isn't "quick" or "easy." Because they can hardly wait for anything, they can scarcely wait for nothing. And because they can scarcely wait for nothing, the Bedouin can outwait them—quickly, and easily.

Thus do extremes obtrude. If you really want to understand something about the essence of a nation, or a civilization, you should avoid the extremes of urban congestion and sophistication on the one hand, and the extremes of rural sparseness and rusticity on the other. For every New York, there is an Appalachia. Every nation has rich urban tourist attractions, and impoverished rural tourist repellents. My rule of thumb is this: I like to travel one or two hours beyond the cultural black hole of a definitive metropolis, and see what life is like just outside its event horizon. There, in a zone between its urban and its rural extremes, you can usually catch a glimpse of the essence of a nation.

Extremes abound. Egyptians cannot produce enough foodstuffs, even for subsistence consumption, primarily because their civilization has stagnated for centuries—whether by Allah's will, or man's unwillingness. By contrast, Americans produce and consume more pseudofood than they know what to do with. When it comes to the twin totems of production and consumption, one has to hand it to the Americans: They have outdone everyone on the planet. However, 90 percent of the foodstuffs that overflow American supermarkets and overstuff American gullets are largely the nutritional equivalents of toxic waste. So the

Bedouin who waits for nothing begins to look prudent, precisely because he is not waiting for McFood, McShelter, McMovies, or McLateNite TV. Nor is he waiting, like so many millions of Pac-Manauts running the infinite maze of cyberspace, for a download or an upgrade.

On balance, one would still be bound to say that if extremes are evil, then the American extreme of too much materialism is still, and by far, a lesser evil than the Islamic extreme of too much minimalism. The American way of paving roads and cookie-cutting suburbs and stocking shelves is of course neo-Roman in its efficiency and deplorable in its incessant lowering of the common denominator, but is also based on the utilitarian premise of the greatest good for the greatest number. So America is still a destination of choice for any number of immigrants, worldwide. A deeper strength of America, and of Western civilization, is that one has the liberty, opportunity, and hope of eating more nutritionally than do the McMasses of consumers, at the affordable price of awareness and effort. By contrast, only a very tiny fraction of Egypt's population—the wealthiest—can improve the quality of their food consumption by an act of will alone, be it theirs or Allah's.

The American extreme of overproduction and overconsumption of pseudofood is a lesser evil than the Egyptian extreme of underproduction and underconsumption of subsistence food, if only because those who wish to pursue a moderate way have more liberty, opportunity, and hope of doing so in America than in Egypt.

The question remains, why don't they? Perhaps they have been badly informed about what conduces to quality of life. Their informants are predatory capitalists who profit from impairing the health of a consuming class that is too ill educated and too spiritually malnourished to know what is good for them. Even though these consumers are of majority age, deemed legally and morally responsible for their own well-being, and the well-being of their children, the sheer quantities of junk food and junk culture that they overconsume debilitate their qualities of life. Their "life condition," as my Nichiren Buddhist friends call it, is greatly diminished and severely impaired, compared to its potential.

Their diminishment of life condition is caused partly by overdoses of nutritional and televisual toxic waste, resulting in chronic inability to imagine and to will things. If you somehow manage to deprive people of their ability to imagine and to will, and habituate them to diets and lifestyles that deform their bodies and impair their health, they are likely to become unhappy and disturbed in the bargain. But there is a panacea for these ills, too. Lately it is known as Prozac. If you're going to overeat McFoods, you may as well overdose on McDrugs.

## McDrugs

The word "drugs" is loaded with ambiguous meaning. It broadly describes two different kinds of substances, with different purposes and different effects on anyone who ingests them. The drugs prescribed by doctors—licit or legal or prescription drugs—are widely accepted by most modern cultures and are generally considered to be good for you and your health. On the other hand, illicit drugs—barred, banned, and prohibited by some governments, yet grown, manufactured, and distributed with the compliance of others—are sold by drug dealers and are supposed to be bad for you. Both views are deeply flawed. To trace a Middle Way through the seemingly impenetrable thicket of claims and counterclaims, we must first identify extreme prejudices on both sides of the drug issue.

The Cambridge dictionary illustrates the difference nicely. On the licit or legal side, it defines a drug as "any natural or artificially made chemical which is used as a medicine"—meaning (in the United States) used with the prior approval of the Food and Drug Administration, and available over-the-counter (like aspirin) or via prescription by a licensed physician (like Prozac). On the illicit side, it defines a drug as "any natural or artificially made chemical which is taken for pleasure, to improve someone's performance of an activity, or because a person cannot stop using it." That includes recreational drug use (from cannabis to ecstasy), sports doping (like steroids), and pure addiction (such as heroin and crack cocaine).

These two opposed views are derived from two contrasting but ultimately complementary philosophies of medicine: the allopathic or scientific view, and the holistic or naturalistic view.

The first, which justifies the use of licit drugs, is derived from a Newtonian picture of the world and its inhabitants as machines, whose parts and systems need to be regularly replaced or adjusted. In this view, drugs are like engine oil or new tires, keeping the automobile functioning and useful. At their best, licit drugs such as vaccines and antibiotics have saved millions of lives and increased life expectancy wherever they are available and affordable. Clearly medical science can be a great boon to humankind.

But at the extreme end of this allopathic or scientific philosophy, every possible human complaint is viewed as some kind of disease to be treated with prescription drugs. The medical profession has been colonized by the pharmaceutical industry, and so, as we saw in chapter 10, fraudulent "epidemics" (such as ADHD—attention deficit hyperactivity disorder) have been created so as to legalize the drug-pushing of Ritalin onto millions of children worldwide. Adults are similarly "diagnosed" en masse with so-called "diseases" (like generic "depression" or "social anxiety disorder"), and are drugged by the millions with concoctions like Prozac and Paxil. As we saw in chapter 10, it is my contention that most of these so-called "diseases" have resulted not from medical malady, but from cultural dysfunction.

The other view—the holistic or homeopathic or naturalistic view—of drugs comes from a spiritual picture of the world as a giant interconnected organism. It supposes that many so-called "maladies" in this world (like post-traumatic stress disorder and social anxiety disorder) are really maladjustments, and that nature herself contains most of the remedies that we need for physical wellness. The holistic view is very respectful of the power of nature, of her wisdom as a biochemist, and attentive to a host of natural ways of regaining equilibrium: including neglected recuperative powers of human beings themselves.

While science has improved our understanding of the world beyond measure, and while technology has enhanced both quantity and quality of human life in numerous ways, human relations with the plant Earth are becoming very strained—past the breaking point. This is partly because of an excess of human population, partly because of instinctive human rapacity, and partly because we have chosen unwise models from which to construct global human civilization. In deforesting the planet to build cookie-cutter housing developments, humans are annihilating more biodiversity than was lost in the two previous mass extinctions that were caused by cataclysmic forces. And for example, when humans started introducing pesticides such as DDT to curb insect damage to crops, they had no idea that they were poisoning the entire food chain. But nature is in many ways a more sophisticated chemist than man. For example, there are trees that synthesize the juvenile hormones of their insect pests, so that insects that feed on these trees never reach maturity and never reproduce. At the same time, there are no cumulative damages to the food chain. In this scenario, the tree is the master biochemist and alchemist alike, while man is a mere blundering amateur. Nature contains myriad undiscovered remedies, for all kinds of diseases that afflict humankind—remedies for illnesses known and as yet unknown. The rapacious burning and logging of the great forests of the earth is a crime against nature, and a folly of which the whole human race will soon enough repent.

Said another way, I believe that a great many diseases that afflict humankind—from cancer to heart disease to Alzheimer's—are partly caused by leading spiritually unhealthy lifestyles, and dissociating ourselves from nature. By destroying biodiversity and synthesizing inferior drugs, by deforesting the planet and turning it into a giant parking lot, and by replacing healthy nutrition with McFoods, we rob nature and ourselves of enormous potential.

Professor Dominique Belpomme is one of France's leading oncologists. He is a physician and a professor of medicine at the University of Paris. He has written a pair of ground-breaking books, as yet untranslated into English, that strongly corroborate my hypothesis.[5] Belpomme—whose name fortuitously means "good apple"—has studied the steady increases in French mortality rates from cancer, which began to rise dramatically after World War II, and which continue to rise today. He claims, in no uncertain terms, that most cancers are not genetic "time bombs"; rather, they are the result of consuming toxic foods, ingesting toxic drugs, inhabiting toxic environments, and leading toxic lifestyles. All these toxicities are man-made. They are engineered products, as well as unintended byproducts, of our Brave New McWorld.

Some of nature's drugs are designed to transcend the physical, and transport the user to dimensions of spiritual growth. Those drugs—from cannabis to peyote—are intended to alter consciousness, to facilitate sacred journeys and shamanistic rites, as well as to increase pleasure. Aristotle said that everything in nature has a purpose. In my view, only a sick society could carry on a crusade against the proper use of her vast cornucopia of amazing substances. Beneficial drugs like cannabis, for example, are made illegal by reason of entrenched prejudice, and fear of greater awareness.

But take a closer look at the extreme end of the holistic model, where science and reason are readily rejected in favor of sympathetic magic and rank superstition. We see this in the so-called "New Age" subculture, which marks a rejection of reliable science and a return to atavism. The same sort of naivete is found at the other extreme, the religious one, from Jehovah's Witnesses (who refuse blood transfusions), to Christian Scientists (who reject medicine wholesale in favor of prayer), to redneck religious rightists (who drown themselves in alcohol, a debilitating back-brain depressant, while condemning cannabis, a mind-expanding and analgesic herb), to ultra-orthodox Hasidic Jews who stone ambulances in Jerusalem on Sabbath (even though the Torah approves life-saving measures whenever necessary).

Looking again to Aristotle, we can hear him saying that every drug needs to be understood, and used according to its purpose, in its proper time and place. Buddhists are divided on the use of intoxicants, as well as medicines; some forbid them entirely, while others view them as part of the karmic path. Confucian cultures often condemn mind-expanding intoxicants like pot, while at the same time endorsing questionable herbal remedies such as powdered bear gall bladder. Such cultures emphasize the collective over the individual; they need society to be integral, so are afraid of individuals "dropping out."

Air and water are also drugs. Let us hope that governments and religions do not overregulate them, in their zeal to control (and stifle) awareness. If you can offer your teenagers a glass of wine with a meal, at home, you can educate them about the proper uses of alcohol. If you can smoke a joint with your teenagers after supper, at home, you can educate them about the proper uses of pot. Among many important thinkers, John Stuart Mill and William James were pot smokers. Medical marijuana also offers tremendous and low-cost benefits to the ill. It is well past the time for ridiculous taboos to be terminated, especially the long-standing prejudice against cannabis. Even the great archconservative thinker and Parliamentarian Edmund Burke, who strongly condemned both the French Revolution and Mary Wollstonecraft's feminism, weakly condoned the use of intoxicants. He wrote, "Under the pressure of the cares and sorrows of our mortal condition, men have at all times, and in all countries, called in some physical aid to their moral consolations— wine, beer, opium, brandy, or tobacco."[6]

## Why Drugs?

Globalization has either already affected, or else plans to affect, every human being on the planet. In the latter half of the twentieth century, globalization has reached out to engulf the last isolated tribes on earth—from the Kung! Bushmen of the Kalahari to the Mudmen of New Guinea to the Yanomamo of the Amazon rainforest. These among other isolated peoples subsisted for thousands of years in a state of nature, in primitive cultures of oral tradition. Suddenly, their children are confronted with MTV, and the rest of the visual tradition. One cynic claimed that the Tuareg (desert nomads) postponed their seasonal migration in order to watch the final episode of *Dallas*. We know that many indigenous peoples do not survive their encounters with Western civilization, and end up on reservations with disproportionate numbers of alcoholics and drug abusers. Indeed, Western civilization's own citizens have conspicuous problems with alcohol and other substance abuse, so why should indigenous peoples whose cultures are stripped away by the American McDream fare any better than us?

Then again, when anthropologists were able to observe indigenous peoples in their "unspoiled" habitats, before they got Coca-Cola and Tupperware and Game Boys, there were still some common denominators spanning tribes and continents, involving alcohol and drugs. These peoples were typically hunter-gatherers, or nomads, or primitive villagers, with high mortality rates, short life expectancies, and few technologies. Even so, you would see the men sitting around a campfire, drinking fermented beverages or imbibing consciousness-altering drugs. The Indians of the American Southwest, for example, knew of dozens of narcotic plants, not to mention hallucinogenic mushrooms. Indigenous natives of Peru chew coca leaves to gain superhuman stamina on forbidding mountainous trails, and are able to trek for days and nights without sleep or food, owing to the stimulating effects of cocaine. In that habitat, the drug makes sense.

Transplanted to urban Western civilization, cocaine is a highly addictive and expensive drug, which earns billions per year for drug lords, causing untold suffering to millions of users and psychosis among addicts. Cocaine abusers inhabit hell worlds, which they entered by trying to use cocaine to escape from some other hell world that they were inhabiting. Drug addiction is not an escape from hell. It is the substitution of one kind of hell for another.

However, it seemed common to indigenous peoples that the men typically imbibed alcohol and drugs after the hunt or the war party, the better to embellish their tales and grow their myths. Substance abuse is more common among men than women. In the West, women are much more afflicted by depression than are men, and also much more prone to severe eating disorders such as anorexia and bulimia. Both substance abuse and eating disorders are symptoms of human suffering. The sexes have different ways of expressing their suffering. Every human being suffers, sooner or later, more or less. The question is not whether we will suffer, nor not even how we will suffer, but what we will do with it.

When men find themselves in an uncomfortable state of consciousness, they often try to escape from it or alter it, and that is why they abuse alcohol, or drugs, or sex, or all of the above. Worse than this, if man's monumental self-regard (i.e., ego) is not tempered with sufficient compassion, then suffering men can wreak enormous havoc on others, multiplying other people's and their own suffering. Sadists, serial killers, and mass murderers are mostly men, although they can be abetted by women. When female "caring" turns to its opposite, namely cruelty, women excel at emotional torture. Still, most of the overt violence in the world is done by males, often as misguided or inappropriate extensions of their evolutionary roles as providers and protectors. At the same time, considerable male violence is also incited by women, provoked by women, or condoned by women. Hence the currently fashionable but utterly deluded dogmas of political correctness, which portray women as victims, blame all the world's ills on men, and empower women to compensate them, are only making matters worse. For better or worse, woman is man's helper or accomplice, mistress or muse, companion or tormentor. The main point is that men try to use alcohol, drugs, and sex to escape from an unpleasant state of consciousness into a more pleasant state. This almost always backfires. And in the worst cases, men use sadism and sadistic violence to try to resolve the additional problems posed by their failed escape attempts. Needless to say, this backfires even more. All these measures increase human suffering, and never decrease it.

In the Confucian model, which stems from Tao, man is creative; woman, receptive. But when misguided or self-deceived, man is also prone to creating destruction; woman, to receiving self-destruction. Man has sadistic potential; woman, masochistic potential. These qualities are not "social constructs": They inhere in human nature as sex differences, and they find cultural expression as gender differences. Yet they can be contained by The Middle Way.

Women too experience unpleasant states of consciousness, and even more: They are afflicted with menstrual and lunar cycles of hormonal surges, which cause physical discomforts and mood swings, all of which make their existence seemingly unbearable at times. Inhabiting a world of appearance, sensation, and emotion, women are on average more prone than men to experiencing discomfort and indisposition. So of course women seek escape from unpleasant states of unconsciousness. But their attempted escapes are different, just as they are different.

Women do not abuse alcohol as much as men do, and that is just as well. Neither do women abuse drugs as much as men do, for the simple reason that women want to intoxicate men, not themselves. She wants to be the drug that turns you on, and so she regards the other drugs you take as competitors. It is her nature ruthlessly to eliminate all competitors for men's attentions and affections. She views alcohol and drugs as competition, not as escape.

So what does she do to escape her own unpleasant states of consciousness? Unlike man, who creates destruction for others, woman receives destruction from others, and ultimately takes control of the process and destroys herself. Man's sadistic tendencies are complemented by woman's masochistic ones. Sadly, such destructive complementarity often assumes the form of abusive relationships, which are lately blamed totally on men but which in fact have two contributing partners. Although women complain incessantly about men and the world, women also blame and punish themselves for being unhappy. This blame and punishment commonly takes the form of depression and eating disorders, from which women suffer abundantly.

So these are the differing roles that intoxicants play: When men suffer, they poison themselves and mutilate others. When women suffer, they mutilate themselves and poison others.

## Medicinal Imbalances in the Global Village

If you look at life expectancies in different countries, and different regions of the world, you will see some obvious tendencies. Life expectancies are longest in the developed world; shortest, in the developing world. Essential ingredients of long life expectancy are potable water, breathable air, hygienic environment, reasonable diet, access to education and health care, rule of law and order, and absence of war. Education itself is vital to the maintenance of most of these other essentials. Medical science has helped bring under control many of the epidemic and pandemic diseases that have ravaged humanity over the centuries: typhoid, cholera, polio, yellow fever, bubonic plague. Western medicine—however mechanistic, invasive, person disregarding, disease-focused, expensive, and profit driven—is still the best way to treat catastrophic illness, contagious disease, and life-threatening emergency. Eastern traditions are much more effective in aesthetic matters, and value-oriented issues: guidance in leading a philosophically balanced and holistically healthy life is their forte. But if something goes drastically wrong, and you need heroic interventions to save your life, then 911, an ambulance and an emergency room are probably your best bets. By contrast, in most of the developing world, there is no "golden hour": If you need state-of-the-art emergency treatment in many parts of Africa, the Middle East, Asia, or Latin America, you won't need it for long.

Overall, the global village is extremely imbalanced in terms of access to medicines, and philosophy of medicine. In North America, at the forefront of the medical pioneering of drugs, medications are plentiful but not cheap, unless one has health insurance. Since about forty million people in the United States have no health insurance, they can't afford prescription drugs either. However much good its products can do, the pharmaceutical industry is also a gargantuan business, which turns physicians into licensed drug dealers. The drug companies are not interested primarily in your health; they are interested primarily in your drug consumption. The medical profession is interested in your health, but is also at the mercy of many powerful forces—insurers, bureaucrats, administrators, governments—who may compromise health care as much as physicians and nurses seek to provide it.

The most-publicized imbalance of drugs to date is in Africa, where the AIDS pandemic has wiped out huge segments of populations—tens of millions of people. Cocktails of antiviral medications can reduce viral loads to near-undetectable levels, allowing HIV-positive patients to live lengthy and productive lives. But these drugs are expensive, need to be taken religiously, and presuppose infrastructures and lifestyles that do not exist in much of afflicted Africa. Thanks to efforts coordinated by the World Economic Forum, among other organizations, prominent people such as Bill Clinton have helped persuade pharmaceutical companies to make antiviral medications affordable to Africans, while Melinda and Bill Gates have committed hundreds of millions of dollars to begin funding the process and to stimulate further fund-raising.

However, given the continued absence of two major ingredients, this recipe for humanitarian relief—a "Marshall Plan" for millions of HIV-positive Africans—will fail to have a large-scale impact. The first missing ingredient is a stable infrastructure in Africa itself. The sub-Saharan African continent is awash in brutal dictators, tribal wars, civil wars, mercenary armies, bandits, failed states, endemic corruption, high illiteracy, crime and unemployment rates, famines, pestilences, dearths of clean water and electricity, bad roads, poor communications, unreliable distribution networks, and lack of secure port and airport facilities. What chance then, do most HIV-positive Africans have of receiving antiviral medications, even if sufficient and affordable quantities are made available? The chances of these lifesaving medications running the African gauntlet, and finding their way into the hands of those who need them, in sufficient quantities and with sufficient regularity to make a significant difference, are slim to none.

The second missing ingredient is prevention. We don't yet have a cure for AIDS, but we do know the causes of HIV infection. Yet African governments and leaders have repeatedly and publicly denied these causes—primarily, widespread unprotected sex, spread to and from prostitutes into the general population—for fear of exposing underlying issues that have exacerbated HIV transmission on such extravagant scales. A typical strategy of some African leaders is to blame AIDS on Western colonialism and its aftereffects. This allows them temporarily to avoid confronting their real problems on the ground: such as unbridled sexual promiscuity without protection, desperate socioeconomic conditions that favor prostitution, and pervasive superstitions that abet the spread of HIV—for, example that HIV-infected men can be "cured" by having sex with a virgin. How much easier is it to blame whites, or politics, or history, rather than to assume a fair share of responsibility at the preventive end of one's problems?

Time and again, governments all over the world perpetuate preventable sufferings among their own citizens for the sake of illusory pride in themselves, or deluded blame of others. The Indonesian government refused to allow American military relief vessels to land emergency supplies on Aceh following the December 2004 tsunami. Why? Because of the territorial imperative: They needed to have Indonesian troops in place and in charge, to chaperone the Americans. Similarly, many Arab and Islamic countries refuse to allow Israeli high-tech rescue terms permission to deploy and to detect and unearth survivors of earthquakes. Why? We will discover some plausible reasons in the next chapter. Meanwhile, emergency care to acutely as well as chronically suffering beings is often stonewalled by the tribal political extremism of their own leaders—invariably, such leaders are wolves masquerading as shepherds.

Meanwhile Africans among myriad others suffer from a dearth of medications. Malaria, for example, claims millions of victims per year in Africa and Asia. Malaria can be prevented by aggressive mosquito control and protective netting, and can be treated by antimalarial drugs. But by definition, the undeveloped world is unable to adopt such measures to a sufficient extent to alleviate mass suffering. And even if wealthier Western nations offer to intervene with preventions or treatments, they will encounter similar political, cultural, and technological obstacles, which must be overcome before those who suffer most can be helped.

## Drugged to Death in America

Contrast the dearth of medications in the developing world, at one extreme, with the overabundance of medications in the developed world, at the other. America's laissez-faire economy and pioneering spirit gave rise early on to "snake oil" vendors of every kind, artfully peddling dubious remedies and fashionable concoctions for every conceivable ailment. Then as now, the American marketplace is governed by one rule above all: "Caveat emptor" ("Let the buyer beware"). The process has come not full circle, rather full spiral. In the idyllic Wild West, mustachioed men in string ties hawked home-brewed panaceas from horse-drawn wagons, from one frontier town to the next. Nowadays, their equivalent is the endless stream of drug-ad spam that clogs the e-mail servers of cyberspace. It used to be claimed that "snake oil" cured common ailments; now it's claimed that the drugs you can buy on Web sites—Ambien, Valium, Cialis, Viagra, Soma—cure common ailments too. Except that "common" has changed. It was formerly gout, rheumatism, and fever. Now it's depression, anxiety, and sexual dysfunction.

The American people, and people all over the developed world, have been psychologized and medicalized to an unwholesome extreme. Life's normal human problems are diagnosed and drugged as though they were illnesses. It is the culture that is ill. Meaning, value, and purpose in life are discovered and attained chiefly by philosophical, spiritual, yogic, or shamanistic practices, not by diagnoses and prescription drugs. Colonized and manipulated by the pharmaceutical and insurance industries, too many psychologists and psychiatrists now regard the vast majority of Americans as "mentally ill," and seek simply to diagnose them via paint-by-numbers questionnaires and drug them with designer mood-enhancers. How's that for "quick" and "easy"? The twentieth century has seen the emergence of a new human paradigm, a psychological and diagnostic paradigm that views the human being as a psychologically sick animal by default. This is a monumentally myopic and tragic view. Mythologically, it constitutes the replacement of Augustine's "original sin" with Freud's "original neurosis."

In the early fifth century C.E., Augustine declared in *City of God* that Adam and Eve were sinful by nature, and that all human beings have inherited, and are born with, their sin. Augustine's doctrine, called "original sin," has perhaps one billion Roman Catholic adherents. Attached to this doctrine are strings of terrible guilt, such that some people spend their entire lives consumed by feeling guilty about having been born and being alive. Viewed behaviorally, and without disrespect, this is a crippling and debilitating burden, an impediment to the attainment of human potential. Contrast this with the Buddhist view that a human birth and a human life are precious gifts, for which we should feel enormous gratitude. Augustine's doctrine, that human beings are fundamentally sinful animals, was courageously repudiated by Thomas Hobbes in 1651, in his *Leviathan*. We have seen that Hobbes's landmark book was banned by Rome, and burned in Oxford. Catholics and Anglicans alike tried to burn Hobbes himself for heresy. Hobbes's "crime" was to contradict Augustine, and to assert that "the natural desires, and other passions of men, are in themselves no sin."[7] In other words, it is natural (and not sinful) for human beings to have desires and passions. It is our human challenge to manage and to express these natural drives and appetites wisely, and not to spend our entire lives wracked by guilt for having them in the first place.

The twentieth century in America has seen the wholesale replacement of Augustine's theological doctrine, that man is a fundamentally sinful animal, with Freud's psychological doctrine, that man is a psychosexually sick animal. But whereas Freud would have had you spend a decade or so in psychoanalysis (supposedly to discover the psychosexual roots of your "sickness"), the contemporary "mental health" industry is heavily influenced by time-saving, paint-by-numbers diagnoses, followed by prescription drugs. After all, if you're any kind of a sick animal, you ought to be medicated. Daily. For the rest of your life. So that's the other extreme: overmedication in America, as opposed to undermedication in Africa. Every possible human problem and complaint is viewed by regnant psychological and medical paradigms as a sickness, or a symptom of one. Life itself becomes a disease, for which daily medications of every possible kind are prescribed.

This is also a deeper reason why clinical psychologists apparently manipulated CUNY's political commissars into banning philosophical counseling on campus. They clearly feel threatened by anyone who might expose their colossal and lucrative fraud, which depends on gullible and ill-educated consumers buying into the notion that every problem in life is a "symptom" of a "mental illness." Philosophical practice empowers people, and helps them mobilize their inner resources. This is clearly intolerable to those who derive prestige and profit from diagnosis and disempowerment.

## Licit versus Illicit Drugs

Not only are some regions and peoples undermedicated while others are overmedicated, but there are also extreme discrepancies in the ways that different political and cultural systems distinguish between "licit" versus "illicit" drugs. Some alcohols—beers, wines, spirits—are recreational drugs. Where legal, their sale is both controlled by permits and often restricted to users of majority age. Western civilization in particular has "pioneered" the uses, and abuses, of alcoholic beverages. The Germans are famous for beer, the British for gin, the French for wine, the Spanish for sherry, the Scots for whiskey, the Russians for vodka, the Mexicans for tequila, the Jamaicans for rum, the Americans for cocktails. The "Singapore sling" is a Western invention. Sake is an indigenous Japanese specialty, one of the few world-renowned alcoholic beverages that is non-Western in origin. Globalization has spread the manufacture and use of alcohol to many new markets—for example, Australian, Californian, and Chilean wines are now highly competitive with the French—but the daily consumption of alcohol in immoderate quantities remains a Western tradition. For centuries, until the 1960s, alcohol has been the "drug of choice" among Westerners, and particularly among Europeans and North Americans. It is not an accident that these peoples, in general, have the highest tolerance for alcohol.

By contrast, Asians, Middle Eastern peoples, and indigenous peoples of North America (e.g., peoples of Indian and Inuit descent) have very low tolerance, which makes it easier for them to abstain from alcohol on the one hand (as in Islamic cultures), or become alcoholics on the other (a terrible disease afflicting many indigenous peoples). Among its milder deleterious effects, alcohol consumption dehydrates the body, which also helps explain why it is not abused in desert climes like the Middle East. Nor is alcohol abused in Confucian cultures, because individual inebriation interferes with teamwork, while public drunkenness and its unrestrained and unpredictable behaviors are anathema to Asia's culture of shame, and to its strict social etiquette.

In moderation, fine alcohol enhances the taste of fine food, just as coarse alcohol enhances the taste of coarse food. So alcohol contributes to our experience of taste. At one extreme, there are many places where alcohol is forbidden—for instance in Saudi Arabia, where Westerners are allowed to drink only in their own homes, or in the special housing compounds reserved for Western workers. In Cairo, a city of more than twenty millions, there's only one small "Bohemian" quarter where you'll find restaurants that serve beer or wine. At the other extreme, in the French Quarter of New Orleans, around-the-clock inebriation is a norm. Roam around central London on a Friday or Saturday night: Normally overreserved and ultrapolite Britons embark on sprees of public drunkenness, featuring rude, lewd, obnoxious, violent, and destructive behaviors not seen during the working week.

Lest we forget, alcohol was forbidden even in America during the "Prohibition" years, when a small handful of extremists (the "Temperance League") leveraged the political power to impose a nationwide ban on its consumption. One irony of Prohibition was that "temperance"—a classic virtue from Aristotle's time—means moderation, not abstention. Another irony is that Prohibition merely drove the manufacture, sale, and consumption of alcohol underground, vastly profiting organized crime, enriching gangsters like Al Capone and earning subsequently respectable fortunes for dynastic families. Western beer barons are a unique cultural breed. But governments were, and still are, slow learners. When legislators criminalize a behavior (like drinking alcohol) that merely needs to be regulated, they only drive it underground, enriching organized criminals, and endangering ordinary citizens who are going to engage in such behaviors no matter what the law forbids, or enjoins.

The ABCs are fairly clear on the question of alcohol. Aristotle would say that it's fine in moderation—except for alcoholics who, being unable to moderate, must abstain. Used moderately, the purposes of alcohol include enhancing the taste of food, promoting loquacity (*in vino veritas*), and loosening inhibitions of those who are too closed and fearful. One of Plato's most endearing dialogues, *Symposium*, treats the topics of love and beauty, and unfolds at a party where philosophers drink and debate all night long. Aristotelian cultures are the ones that "evolved" alcohol to its current state, following his own prescription of attaining excellence in one's endeavors. Presumably, beer brewers, winemakers, and bartenders are also eligible for improvement, excellence, and fulfillment.

Confucian cultures also drink, but not to debilitating excess. Since individual intoxication is anathema to group cohesion and teamwork, Confucian cultures frown on excessive self-indulgence, leading to the detriment of self and others, that characterizes substance abuse. But in proper settings, alcohol consumption is not only permitted but encouraged.

Buddhists are divided on the issue of intoxicants. The Tibetans tend to eschew alcohol completely, but among them are some "party animals" as well. Similarly, the austerities of Zendos do not conjure images of Munich beer halls, but then again I have seen western Zen practitioners hold their own at Irish weddings. And, I know many

Nichiren Buddhists who drink in moderation. Daisaku Ikeda—whose general views on intoxicants I will quote at the end of this chapter—has this to say about drinking:

> "Alcohol is a drug that can be both used and abused. In Japan it has since ancient times been referred to as first among medicines and first among poisons. Taken in moderation, alcohol can be a mild relaxant; the benefits of encouraging blood circulation and promoting sweating have been medically recognized. On the other hand alcoholism or severe alcohol dependence is profoundly destructive of mental and physical health, bringing terrible suffering to the alcoholic, their family and loved ones . . . While I myself do not drink alcohol—it simply doesn't agree with me—I understand the feelings of those who do. I think what is crucial is, in the Japanese expression, to consume sake and not be consumed by it."[8]

So once again excesses are bad, and at both extremes. Anyone who has lived with an alcoholic or otherwise endured the alcoholic's lifestyle knows that alcohol abuse is one of the worst forms of excessive consumption. Then again, at the other extreme, Islamist terrorists abstain from alcohol, but are willing to bomb restaurants or hotels or nightclubs, often committing suicide in the process of their murderous carnage. Maybe they should try getting bombed on alcohol, for a change.

### All the King's Drugs

Just as with alcohol, there is very little uniformity—and many extremes—when it comes to criminalizing or regulating consumption of other drugs. I am a child of the 1960s, so many of my views on drugs were shaped (or possibly bent out of shape) by that Magical Mystery Tour of a decade. As a recovering hippie, I have views that are certain to win friends in some places, and detractors in others. So be it.

I was recently in India. One night I fell ill and began to run a fever. I asked the hotel concierge if they had a doctor on call, and within a few minutes a very friendly Indian physician rang me up in my room. "What kind of drugs do you want?" he asked me over the phone.

I couldn't believe my ears. He sounded like a neighborhood drug dealer in the United States, except that he was a doctor practicing completely within the laws of India. The hippie in me was tempted to reply "First cure my fever, then ask me what kind of drugs I want." In fact, the philosopher requested an examination and a diagnosis, not drugs. So he came over, diagnosed me with a viral fever, and gave me some drugs anyway, which actually helped.

The point is that possession of narcotic drugs, which are available over the counter in counties like India or Mexico, might get you a death sentence in Singapore or China, or a long prison term in the United States or Europe. Western travelers to Asia, who often carry their own prescription drugs from the United States or Europe, are sometimes liable to having them confiscated, or even to being arrested and charged with smuggling illicit substances. For the most part, governments are concerned about narcotics—heroin, morphine, cocaine—along with barbiturates and addictive painkillers like Quaaludes. Narcotic drug trafficking is one of the great tragedies of universal human cravings for both intoxication and money, and of the slowness of governmental learning. Because of outdated and barbaric laws, substances that could be legally regulated are criminalized, as alcohol was during Prohibition, with the same predictable results: As an encore to Al Capone among other whiskey bootleggers, our system created Pablo Escobar and the Medellin drug cartel.

But there's a difference. The "street value" of a bottle of whiskey during Prohibition was a few dollars at most. The "street value" of an equivalent volume or weight of cocaine or heroin is hundreds of thousands of dollars. The international drug trafficking trade is worth tens to hundreds of billions annually. At the height of his infamy, Pablo Escobar was listed by *Forbes* magazine (1989) as one of the world's ten wealthiest men. Escobar's empire was not built by supplying hundreds or even thousands of North American crack whores with dime bags (i.e., ten-dollar fixes). It was built by supplying millions of affluent middle-class and upper-class inhabitants of North America and Europe with ounces of cocaine, to be consumed at parties and orgies, or to help turn parties into orgies.

Addictive personality types and addictive drugs make a bad combination, so naturally many addictive users will snort or freebase or inject as much cocaine as they see in front of them—just as an alcoholic will empty your liquor cabinet if you invite him to. By the same token, it is possible for nonaddictive personality types to snort a few rails of cocaine at a party—and have a few drinks, and smoke a few cigarettes—without becoming habituated to any of these substances. Escobar's biggest customers were Hollywood celebrities, rap music moguls, Wall Street brokers, and a generation of yuppies[9] and dinks[10] up for a good time. Cocaine empires are built on recreational users, not addicts. Of course they turn addictive personality types into addicts—and so does cigarette smoking, drinking, and gambling. How many people on welfare spend their food money (and their children's food money) on tobacco, alcohol, and lottery tickets? Too many, no doubt.

People need to be reminded that, in the United States, not only was alcohol criminalized during Prohibition: Gambling was criminalized (Las Vegas excepted) until the introduction of state-run lotteries in the 1970s. If you wanted to buy a "lottery ticket" prior to that, you had to "play the numbers" with the Mafia, which had monopolized the so-called "numbers racket." This highly popular form of gambling had been driven underground, and straight into the arms of organized crime, for the usual reason: political fear of embracing a publicly "unpopular" issue, which has clandestine support but which offends prevailing (and usually hypocritical) moral opinion. Once Western morality became degenerate enough, and the "Protestant work ethic" was sufficiently debunked or deconstructed, it became "safe" for governments to legitimize and monopolize the lottery business.

Government lotteries are also called "voluntary taxation." They are sources of such vast and unaccounted-for revenues that governments don't even have to pay prize money out of their accumulated principal: They dole out installments, which are more than covered by the interest they earn on revenues from ticket sales. When was the last time any government disclosed to its tax-paying citizens how much money it collected in any given year from lotteries, and what became of that revenue? Governments are no more accountable for their lottery revenues than organized crime was for its "numbers rackets," and governments regard the habituated citizens who support their legalized racketeering with the same indifference, bordering on contempt, that organized criminals reserve for the suckers and marks who once played the numbers, and who now lose their mortgage payments in Las Vegas.

Gambling is fueled by the vice of greed, by the fantasy of getting something for nothing, and by the desperate hope for sudden wealth among people who have discovered no surer means for fulfillment in their lives. It is also affordable entertainment for a great number of consumers who enjoy the hypnotic experience of pouring coins into humming, blinking, whirring slot machines. Yet it is better that governments rather than criminals profiteer from these vices, hopes, and escapes. Governments provide wider distribution of tickets, more and bigger prizes, and less fraudulence than does organized crime. At the same time, extremes of greed, fantasy, and desperation are not particularly wholesome states of mind, but governments don't care about the states of mind of voluntary taxpayers. Just like the pharmaceutical drug and alcoholic beverage industries, they care primarily about revenues. The American political process is market driven. Lotteries are about business, not about virtue.

So it's only a matter of time before some Western governments get into the drug business too, and monopolize the multibillion-dollar traffic in cocaine and heroin. They'll start by decriminalizing softer drugs like cannabis, then they'll begin to manage psychedelic substances, and will eventually figure out how to regulate narcotics too. Canada is on the verge of legalizing marijuana, which Holland decriminalized years ago. America lags decades behind, even though some states have downgraded possession of cannabis from a felony to a misdemeanor. Yet pot is still regarded as a "narcotic" in some parts of the United States, and U.S. federal agencies are particularly slow to understand the world of difference between cannabis and heroin, for example. Most parents know better. Many baby-boomer parents will smoke a joint with their grown children, at least once in a while, just as they will drink alcohol with them. Very few baby-boomer parents, however, would sit down and shoot heroin with their children. So why do so many governments continue to classify cannabis as a narcotic drug, especially when (as in the West) about 95 percent of their children have smoked pot long before they graduate from high school?

## The Altered States of America: Legacy of the 1960s

Widespread recreational drug use among the affluent—especially psychoactive drugs—along with interest in cultures that cultivate altered states of brain and mind, was a signature phenomenon of the 1960s. Cultural shockwaves from epicenters in Chelsea, London; Greenwich Village, New York; and Haight-Ashbury, San Francisco, propagated around the world. The baby boom generation entered its adolescence to the chant of Timothy Leary: "Tune in, turn on, drop out." Millions of youth did just that: tuned in to The Beatles, turned on to LSD, and dropped out of Lyndon Johnson's "Great Society." They also saw some of their most beloved rock stars, guitarists, and poets—from Elvis Presley to Brian Jones to Jimi Hendrix to Janice Joplin to Jim Morrison, and much more recently Kurt Cobain—die of drug-related causes. But that deterred no one from experimenting with drugs. On the contrary.

During its brief heyday, hippie culture was a harmonious blend of philosophy, poetry, music, spirituality, psychedelics, individualism, communalism, creativity, nonviolent political protest, cosmic awareness, reverence for nature, celebrations of peace, and expressions of free love—along with plenty of sex, drugs, and rock 'n' roll. It was the decade of Woodstock nation, astronauts on the moon, and freaks on every street corner. The consciousness of the free West was truly transformed by that decade. Even those enslaved behind the Iron Curtain's and the Bamboo Curtain's brutal totalitarian regimes sampled freedom in black market blue jeans, or smuggled rock music.

The Heaven of Hippiedom was counterbalanced by the Hell of Vietnam, the first war in history to be televised nightly in America. The images from Vietnam became the front lines of the Culture Wars back home, a civil war that the mainstream media helped wage against its own civilization. The media coverage of Vietnam was characterized by willful imbalance, distorted perspective, and relentless sensationalism. The fifty-eight thousand Americans who died there, in an undefined and unpopular war that was neither won nor lost, were mourned but not revered by their own culture, which neither understood nor appreciated their sacrifice. Those who returned from service in Vietnam endured the additional trauma of this mixed reception, and the difficulties of reintegrating into a society that did not greet them as returning heroes, rather as warriors who had somehow dishonored their own cause. That added insult to their injury. In fact, their cause—and the cause of the free world—had been so badly misrepresented by the radicalized American media that the ultimate victors in the Vietnam war were not the Viet Cong or the North Vietnamese, and not Richard Nixon's "peace with honor," but the American television networks themselves.

The American nation of the 1960s became a seething hotbed of contending cultural forces, a sometimes violent clash of unprecedented cultural extremes, a polity bitterly divided not only by the uncertainties and chaos of Vietnam, but also by the victories of Northern civil rights integrationists over Southern segregationists, of revolutionary student radicals over conservative university administrations, of "free love" (thanks to the Pill) over monogamy and chastity, of psychedelic mind expansion over black-and-white mental constipation, of unique and authentic "freaks" over a canned culture of mass conformity, and of cosmic consciousness over personal prejudice.

In retrospect, however, many of these "victories" were clearly and sadly Pyrrhic. Vietnam became a worse hell for the Vietnamese in the decade after the American withdrawal. The "domino theory" that had lured America into Southeast Asia to check the spread of communism, a theory that the naive American media loved to discredit, soon toppled Cambodia. Pol Pot and his chief strategist had been educated by French Marxists, whose policies worked perfectly in theory, but led to the "killing fields" in practice. The "victory" of the civil rights movement was not the end of racism in America, only the beginning of its metamorphosis into many new and convoluted forms, including black hatred of whites, much of it sponsored by guilt-ridden liberal whites themselves. The "victory" of the student radicals—and I was one of them—did not end in curricular reform, but in the Stalinization of North American universities, by the same neo-Bolsheviks who had wrested power from craven administrators, in the name of "liberation." The "victory" of free love has resulted in neither love nor freedom, but in the disintegration of the nuclear family, the feminization of western institutions, and the demonization of white males. The "victory" of psychedelic mind expansion did not fundamentally alter the American way of life, as Madison Avenue's idea of a "trip" (namely a shopping trip) resulted in pastel tissue paper, floral bedsheets, and colored kitchen appliances, all of which came only in white prior to LSD. The victory of "freaks" and "heads"—unique individuals being authentic to themselves and not harmful to others in their manner of life—did not result in a Renaissance of individualism; rather, it resulted in globalization, and with it the most gargantuan imposition of mass-marketed conformity in human history, which has coincided with the coming of age of the "freaks" and "heads" themselves.

To me, the main lasting victory of the 1960s was that of cosmic consciousness over personal prejudice. East met West in the 1960s. We exported The Beatles and imported Ravi Shankar; exported Coca-Cola and imported Afghani hashish; exported the *Wall Street Journal* and imported the Bhagavad-Gita; exported Super Bowls and imported martial arts; exported telecommunications and imported Tao; exported yo-yos and imported yogas; exported backpacks and imported Buddhism. Mostly, we exported Aristotelian science and technology and economic development, and imported the great wisdom traditions of the East: Hindu, Buddhist, Confucian, Taoist.

We children of the 1960s lived under constant threat of nuclear annihilation. It was called "MAD" (mutual assured destruction), and it was mad—a madness that compelled us to be sane. We lived life to the fullest, precisely because a nuclear sword of Damocles dangled over our heads. In response, we became "heads"—acidheads, potheads, you name it. Political borders were frozen solid during the Cold War, but cultural boundaries dissolved. Personal prejudices were transcended by cosmic consciousness, by awareness of the interconnectedness of beings, by realization of the oneness of humanity. Hippie horizons expanded largely under the influence of recreational and sacred drugs—pot, hash, mescaline, psilocybin, peyote, ayahuasca, LSD, STP, DMT, DET, MDA,

Alice B. Toklas brownies, and spiked punch. The peace, love, honesty, openness, and integrity that formed the heart of hippiedom were outgrowths of expanded consciousness. Insofar as drugs contributed to that, they were good. Drugs did a lot more good in the West than napalm did in the East, to be sure. And if Aldous Huxley's experiences with mescaline and LSD helped him envision and write *Island*, his allegory on Mahayana Buddhism, then hallucinogenic drugs are instruments that can be used for betterment.

And let me remind you of another truth, albeit uttered by a man whose misguided philosophy has done much more harm than good in the world: Karl Marx. Yet when Marx described religion as "the opiate of the people," he was correct. Religion is also a potent and addictive drug, with potentially harmful side effects. For example, people who get too high on Jesus try to convince everybody else to take the same drug in the same quantity, and don't understand why anyone would refuse. From time to time, a few Christians got way too high on Jesus, and burned people at the stake merely for disagreeing with their theology, let alone for refusing to convert to it. Nowadays it's fanatical Islamists, high on Allah, who commit heinous acts of terrorism, while their intoxicated and agitated masses are provoked to riot by a mere cartoon. Marx's opiate has this terrible side effect: It robs people of their sense of humor.

In contrast please take note, all my zealously religious brothers and sisters: If a hippie or a freak offered you a hit of acid, or passed you a joint, he wouldn't kill you or terrorize you for refusing it. He'd say, "That's cool, man," whatever you decided. Hippies were "far out"—*far enough out of prejudices* to leave others in peace, respecting their choices. That was righteous, and not self-righteous. No hippie would ever dream of hijacking an airplane: that would be the ultimate "bad trip."

So tell me about "drugs." Whenever some inane American billboard or subway advertisement asks me, "Is your child on *drugs*?" I sometimes think, "I sure as hell hope so." Good drugs may be his best chance of getting off all the bad drugs—the cigarettes, the alcohol, the Ritalin, the lottery tickets, the McFoods, the McDrugs, the evening McNews, the televangelism, the suicidal martyrdom, and the Starbucks coffee.

## The ABCs

Consulting the ABCs on the issue of drugs, we obtain divergent prescriptions from them too. In general, as we have seen, the Aristotelian view is purposive: The purpose of the human being is to become happy through the development of individual excellence. In this picture, drugs have their purposes—whether in medicinal, recreational, or sacred contexts. As usual, the Aristotelian key lies in moderation, a path between abstention and addiction. By contrast, as we have seen, Confucian cultures tend to subordinate the individual to the collective. The individual's purpose is fulfilled by finding his or her proper way to serve the larger interests of society. So Confucius would applaud medicinal drugs, for these help maintain or restore the individual's health, and so enable him or her to continue serving society. But Confucius would condemn the use of mind-expanding or recreational drugs, for these could make creative individuals too aware to remain mere cogs in a societal machine, and would make those susceptible to addiction useless as workers. Hence strict Confucian cultures (like Singapore) maintain the death sentence for hard-drug smugglers.

So if Aristotle votes "for" and Confucius votes "against" the use of mind-expanding drugs, how will Buddha break the tie? Buddhism offers arguments on both sides, but ultimately recommends and teaches practices that lead to more awakened mind-states than can be experienced with drugs. At one extreme of Buddhism, religious Buddhists like the Tibetans avoid the use of intoxicating substances, and practice yogas which elevate and purify consciousness, rather than inflate and distort it. At the other extreme of Buddhism, Western intellectual Buddhists from Aldous Huxley to Alan Watts integrated psychedelic drugs into their individual credos, and managed to become highly evolved beings who did very much good (and correspondingly little harm) to the human estate.

The Middle Way within The Middle Way goes something like this. Most people take mind-expanding or recreational drugs to experience pleasurable states of being, or to avoid painful ones. While such activity may not appear particularly harmful in the short run, and may even be necessary as part of experimentation that conduces to personal growth, in the long run it is a cul-de-sac. You can get high every day, but you will reach a "ceiling" of consciousness beyond which drugs cannot climb. If you really want to get as high as you can, absolutely without risks or side effects, then Buddhist practices are the best way. But because Buddhists do not generally proselytize, they aren't going to ram dharma down your throat, or sell it on street corners. They will let you discover it on your own, and that way you will really accept it.

Daisaku Ikeda understands all this better than I, and here is what he has to say about drugs in general:

"It is first important to distinguish among the various purposes for which drugs are used: whether medicinally to treat illness or recreationally for the pleasurable sensations they may produce. Buddhism regards the former as appropriate and necessary; the Buddha is sometimes compared to a skilled doctor capable of treating people's illnesses and referred to as the king of physicians.

"The parable of the skilled doctor that appears in the Lotus Sutra demonstrates the deep parallels between Buddhism and the medical arts. In this parable, the skilled doctor prepares and gives excellent medicine for his children who are suffering as a result of having taken poison. Likewise, Bodhisattva Medicine King is often portrayed holding a vessel containing medicine symbolic of the function of the Buddha to alleviate living beings of their suffering.

"On the other hand, Buddhism seeks to implant in people's lives an experience of indestructible happiness, one that is not dependent on outside forces or influences. From this perspective, the use of intoxicants—which can easily inflict permanent physical and psychic damage on the user—as a means of gaining a momentary, fleeting sense of pleasure is something that Buddhism must reject. The fact that, in establishing The Middle Way, Shakyamuni denied extremes both of asceticism and hedonism is reflective of his profound insight into the nature and sources of genuine and enduring human happiness.

"It is true that certain drugs can induce states that may seem to offer glimpses of a world beyond everyday reality. But in the end, this is a drug-induced state and thus illusory. The experience of such a state cannot provide the power and energy required to transform the realities of daily living, opening the path to real happiness. Repeated use or dependence on such drugs can have severely deleterious impacts on physical health and can undermine a person's vitality and will to live."[11]

The will to live is a great gift. Its complement, however, is the will to die. And that leads us to the next two chapters: the Middle East and terrorism.

# 14

## MIDDLE EASTERN EXTREMES
### Stinging Scorpions and Free Figs

*It is ridiculous to lay the blame of our wrong actions*
*upon external causes, rather than on the facility with*
*which we ourselves are caught by such causes.* —Aristotle

*Through hatred, hatreds are never appeased; through non-hatred*
*are hatreds always appeased—and this is a law eternal.* —Buddha

*Pleasure not carried to the point of debauch;*
*grief not carried to the point of self-injury.* —Confucius

### Locating the Middle East

Suppose you spun a globe of the earth and randomly threw six darts at
it, each one representing the birthplace of a major world religion:
Judaism, Christianity, Islam, Hinduism, Buddhism, and Confucianism
(the latter being a kind of secular religion). What would be the odds of
two of these darts landing in the same tiny region, namely Israel, with
an area smaller than New Jersey? What would be the odds that a third
dart would land in a nearby state, namely Saudi Arabia? Improbably or
not, the Middle East has given rise to three of the world's great religions.
In all, half the world's people adhere to an Abrahamic faith—either the
Judeo-Christian strand, or the Islamic one. The historical, political,
theological, and economic rifts between these two strands, and the lack
of bridges between them, have permitted extremisms not only to

flourish in a region whose norms are themselves extreme, but also to spread worldwide in the wake of the Cold War's end.

From the outset, I must caution you that no debate is more slippery, and no conflict more intractable, than that between Islam and the West. It represents a vicious circle in the worst sense. The conflict is real, and the goals of Islamist extremists are plain, but the West itself is bitterly divided over both the nature of the problem and its conceivable resolutions. Islamist extremists represent only a small fraction of the world's Muslims, a majority of whom are probably willing to live in peace, both with one another and with the global village itself. But many Muslim nations are violently fanaticized by belligerent despots, fulminating imams, and incendiary mass media. From a Western perspective, Islamist extremism is the antithesis of globalization: It seeks to maintain its peoples in retrograde states of intolerance, bellicosity, backwardness, and isolation. This is more or less what Europe looked like when it was terrorized by Christian fanatics, with the complicity of monarchs, prior to the scientific revolution and the Enlightenment.

Middle Eastern conflicts are multifaceted and almost intractable, having unfolded in four broad dimensions: biblical, imperial, theological, and commercial. First and oldest is the ancient biblical wrangle between Jews and the Arabs, who are feuding cousins in an epic tribal saga that splits into parallel branches, engendering mutually incompatible histories: the Jews of Israel versus the Arabs of Palestine and adjacent lands. They are both descended from sons of Abraham and Sarah: the Jews from Isaac; the Arabs from Ishmael. According to the book of Genesis, God said to Abraham: "Sarah your wife shall bear you a son, and you shall call his name Isaac; I will establish My covenant with him for an everlasting covenant, and with his descendants after him. And as for Ishmael, I have heard you. Behold, I have blessed him, and will make him fruitful, and will multiply him exceedingly. He shall beget twelve princes, and I will make him a great nation."[1] Thus did two great peoples descend from Abraham and Sarah: Jew and Arab. Their quintessential sibling rivalry is as ancient as Genesis itself, and was most recently rekindled by the rebirth of Israel in 1948, which most Jews view as a long-overdue fulfillment, and many Palestinians view as a catastrophic dispossession.

Israel's Independence Day, May 15, is celebrated by the singing of its national anthem, "Hatikvah"—meaning "Hope." That day is also mourned by Palestinians, who call it "al Nakba"—the Catastrophe.[2] Yet the "Arab world's" decades of opposition to Israel's existence made the Palestinian problem unsolvable, while the Arab-Israeli conflict has mutated out of control, and now engulfs the global village at civilizational levels, with Islam pitted against the West.

The second dimension of this conflict is the centuries-old string of imperial and colonial invasions and occupations of Middle Eastern and West Asian Islamic territories by Western powers—the Macedonians, the Romans, the Crusaders, the French, the British, the Soviets, the Americans. The Crusades in particular are constantly in the minds and on the lips of Islam's most ardent extremists, who seize upon battles of a thousand years ago as today's and tomorrow's rallying cries against the contemporary West. The Islamic world would be incomparably better served by recalling its golden age of tolerance and learning under the caliphs, and by equipping its youth with educations conducive to good citizenship in the global village, not with hateful propaganda, high explosives, and suicide missions.

Third is the religious dimension of these invasions and occupations, which since the Crusades have loaned particular acrimony to the Muslim view of the invaders as unbelievers, infidels who must at all costs be chastised by the wrath of Allah and driven from "Muslim" lands. It is this dimension more than any other that mobilized the Arab-Afghani mujahideen against the godless Soviets, armed and encouraged by the CIA in order to turn Afghanistan into a "Soviet Vietnam." This strategy worked all too well, but also animated the "Frankenstein" of Osama bin Laden, who eventually turned on his American creators. It is this third dimension, more than the other two, that resulted in 9/11, that provoked American regime change in Afghanistan and Iraq, and that engenders any number of apocalyptic scenarios—especially now that Iran is threatening to obliterate Israel with nuclear weapons.

And just in case these three dimensions of conflict are not enough, Allah or irony saw fit to locate the planet's largest and most accessible fossil fuel reserves in the Persian Gulf—obliging these historic feuding parties to become partners in the world's biggest business.[3] As a result, the twentieth century's politics of petroleum have added highly flammable fuel to an already overheated multidimensional conflict. It is emblematic of this fourth dimension of conflict that the World Trade Center was destroyed by jet fuel, refined in whole or in part from Middle Eastern crude.

Historically, it appears that Islamic civilization in general, and the "Arab world" in particular, desired above all to be left alone by the West—notwithstanding the earlier spate of Muslim conquests in Iberia and Asia, and their golden age during which they were willing custodians of and contributors to Western civilization.[4] During four hundred years of indolent Ottoman rule (1517–1917), Palestine and the surrounding area became an historical and cultural backwater. The Ottomans cared little for the region, save to deforest and denude Lebanon of its once-renowned cedars, from which Herod had built his palace. From the malarial swamps of the Galilee to the arid wasteland of the Negev, Palestine itself was a neglected and underpopulated province, where Turkish administrators served reluctantly, as if in exile from their own Empire. Jerusalem had no political importance whatsoever, and Western travelers to the "Holy Land," such as Mark Twain in 1867, were astounded by its barrenness. He described Palestine as: ". . . [a] desolate country whose soil is rich enough, but is given over wholly to weeds—a silent mournful expanse . . . A desolation is here that not even imagination can grace with the pomp of life and action . . . We never saw a human being on the whole route . . . There was hardly a tree or a shrub anywhere. Even the olive and the cactus, those fast friends of the worthless soil, had almost deserted the country."[5]

This changed dramatically after World War I, when the British and French divided the "spoils" of the defeated Ottoman Empire between them, and assumed colonial mastery over Syria and Lebanon under French mandate, and over Palestine (today's Israel, Gaza, West Bank,

Figure 14.1 Palestine in 1918

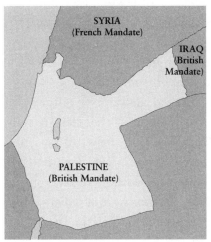

British and French Mandates

and Jordan) and Iraq under British mandate.[6] This is illustrated in fig. 14.1.[7] Meanwhile, nineteenth-century emancipations of European Jewry, and the successes of emancipated Jews, had also inflamed backlashes of virulent anti-Semitism—from the Dreyfus affair in France to pogroms in Russia—and so Theodore Herzl and his colleagues founded the modern Zionist movement: an aspiration to return Jews to their biblical homeland, after almost two thousand years of Roman diaspora. The British Balfour Declaration of 1917 held out the promise of a Jewish homeland in Palestine, but at the same time the British also gave the Arabs—including those of Palestine—contradictory assurances concerning their own self-determination.[8]

As Russian and European Jews began to immigrate to Palestine—to pioneer, to farm, to produce, to modernize—they were received by the "Arab world" with a mixture of receptivity and hostility. Palestinian and other Arabs prospered from their presence, but agitators soon got the upper hand, and violence began to flare. Smoldering embers of biblical rivalry, historical enmity, religious intolerance, and nationalist ambition were fanned into flames of resentful resistance to the immigration of Jews in general, and to the founding of a Jewish state in particular.

The Nazi Holocaust, which systematically murdered six million Jews, also unleashed a tide of Jewish desperation among survivors for a homeland in Palestine. Prior to Hitler, Zionism had been opposed by many Jews, whose faith decreed that only the Messiah could resurrect Israel, and that any man-made attempt to do so would constitute an abomination in the sight of God. After Hitler, surviving Jews questioned their faith in God, doubted the viability of their continued existence in diaspora, and avidly supported the reestablishment of Israel. The British, meanwhile, toyed with maps of a partitioned Palestine, but bowed to Arab pressure and restricted Jewish immigration to a trickle, thus ensuring the uninterrupted flow of oil from the Gulf states to the West. Even though the British were nominal victors in World War II, their own empire crumbled rapidly in the late 1940s, almost faster than they could redraw the maps.

Amid a whirlwind of international diplomatic activity, along with flaring violence between both Jews and Arabs, and Jews and British troops in Palestine, the United Nations approved a British partition plan in November 1947, by a vote of 33–13, with ten abstentions.[9] U.N. Resolution 181 recognized two states: the Jewish state of Israel, and the Arab state of Palestine. Israel was officially reborn in May 1948. The United States and the Soviet Union were among the first nations to recognize the renascent Jewish state, but the Middle East would soon become a theater of "managed conventional conflict" in their bitter Cold War.

As fig. 14.2 shows, the British had already carved Transjordan (today, Jordan) from their original Palestinian mandate, leaving Palestine as a tiny rump territory. This, as shown in fig. 14.3, is what they finally partitioned into Israel and Palestine, with an international zone surrounding Jerusalem, a holy city to all the Abrahamic faiths.

The Palestinians could have established their own state in 1948, then and there, alongside Israel. The Jews had gladly accepted this partition of a partition. But rather than accepting two states side by side, the "Arab world" rejected Israel, rejected Israel's right to exist, rejected United Nations Resolution 181 that recognized Israel's right to exist, and rejected the affirming votes of all the nations that recognized Israel's

## Figure 14.2 Palestine in 1922

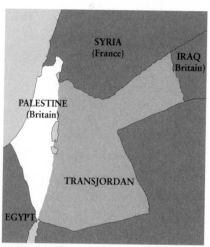

Palestine in 1922, after the first British partition

## Figure 14.3 Palestine in 1947

This British partition was approved by United Nations Resolution 181 (November 1947).

Resolution 181 was accepted by Jews, but rejected by Arabs.

☐ Jewish State

■ Palestinian State

☐ International Zone

existence. Five Arab armies (Egypt, Syria, Transjordan, Lebanon, and Iraq) invaded the Jewish state on May 14, 1948, as David Ben-Gurion read Israel's Declaration of Independence. Their intentions were declared by Azzam Pasha, then secretary-general of the Arab League: "This will be a war of extermination and a momentous massacre which will be spoken of like the Mongolian massacres and the Crusades."[10] Lest we forget the Crusades.

Somehow, Israel won that war. The result is depicted in fig. 14.4. Israel's war of independence yielded slightly larger borders than U.N. Resolution 181, while the Palestinians inhabiting the West Bank and the Gaza strip, along with those who fled or were driven out of Israel (there are proportions of both) became refugees and stateless persons. Why? Not because of the re-creation of Israel, but because of the "Arab world's" refusal to recognize Israel and Palestine alike. To be sure, the Palestinians have endured a combination of cruel tragedies over several decades, each new tragedy compounded by the previous ones, and each seemingly destined to produce new ones. In fact, the belligerence and intransigence of the "Arab world" thrust both Israel and the Palestinians into impossible political positions from 1948 onward. Every Arab-Israeli war thereafter— 1956, 1967, 1973—was provoked by the "Arab world," and every Israeli victory (Israel cannot afford to lose a single war) has only compounded Israel's problems, afflicted Israel with more terrorism, and added to the tragedy and suffering of the Palestinians.

Figure 14.4
Israel in 1948

The "Arab world" that refused to accept Israel's and Palestine's coexistence in 1948 is depicted in fig. 14.5. It comprises some two dozen nations, with an area and population comparable to the United States (three hundred million), a dominant monolithic religion (Islam), a dominant common tongue (Arabic), and the world's largest oil reserves. The average GDP of the Arab world is $3,250. Israel, no matter how you partition it, is a minuscule country, with a population of six million, no oil reserves, and a GDP of $18,000. At this writing, Israel is the only democracy in the region.

Why, for so many decades and to its own detriment, has the vast and sprawling "Arab world" been violently obsessed with the annihilation of this tiny Jewish state? Why, given the endless catalogue of troubles in the world between 1948 and 1991, did the U.N. Security Council devote 97 of its 175 resolutions to condemning Israel? Why, for so many decades and to their own detriment, have the Palestinian people been unwilling to accept Israel, and unready to build their own state of Palestine alongside it? The large regional conflict that pits the Goliath of the "Arab world" against the David of Israel also gave rise to the nested local conflict that pits the "Israeli pharaohs" against the "Judeo-Palestinians." For the Palestinians have annexed the history of Judaism to their own purposes, in their quest to "out-Jew" the Jews by remaining homeless, stateless, and scattered in a diaspora born of Israel's rebirth. Palestinian

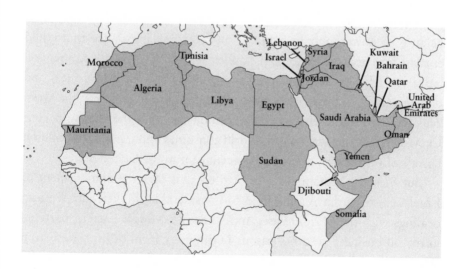

Figure 14.5 The "Arab World" and Israel

extremists seek their ingathering at the price of Israel's destruction, and envision the recreation of Palestine on the ashes of annihilated Zion. Palestinian moderates seek coexistence with Israel, but their voice has yet to prevail in the long-playing Middle Eastern chorus of violent extremism that is so endemic and detrimental to the region.

These two concentric rings of unresolved conflict—the outer Arab-Israeli one and the inner Israeli-Palestinian one—eventually propelled PLO terrorism into Europe, where Islamist terrorists learned a great deal about Western civilization, in terms of using its own virtues—liberty, opportunity, hope—to work its ruin. The Arab-Israeli conflict, and the Israeli-Palestinian conflict that it spawned, have directly influenced two other dimensions of Middle Eastern cooperation and conflict with the West: the petroleum industry, which is the world's largest business, and Islamic civilization, which has stepped wholesale into the political vacuum created by the collapse of the Soviet Empire.

The insatiable Western thirst for Arabian oil has two post-1948 branches. First, Persian Gulf crude was desperately needed to confront the Soviets by conventional means during the Cold War. Stalin had ten thousand or more tanks poised to overrun Western Europe. NATO countered with its tanks, poised to check Stalin's. They needed an assured oil supply from the Persian Gulf to maintain their conventional balance of power, and to avoid at all costs any imbalance that could escalate into nonconventional (i.e., nuclear) conflict. Second, Arabian oil has also fueled decades of unrestrained consumption, for business and pleasure alike, by the world's most affluent nations—mostly in the West. This trend was "driven" by the auto industry: "See the U.S.A. in your Chevrolet." At this writing, the world consumes about eighty-six million barrels of oil per day, almost 25 percent of it in the United States.

But Western addiction to Arabian oil plus Western commitment to Israel's existence have amounted to considerable duplicity in Western dealings with the Middle East. And while our Middle Eastern partners in the oil business need no lessons in duplicity from us, not even from Western imperialists, they took many of their cues from us.

So, as the West enriched the oil-rich Arab states beyond imagination, pumping their black gold for cash on the barrel, to the tune of millions of barrels per day for decades, and at the same time supported Israel's defense against wave after wave of Arab aggression, war, and terrorism, all of which exacerbated the Palestinians' impossible position, Saudi Arabia emerged as the "Arab world's" most visible dichotomy: The home of Mecca and Medina and orthodox Wahabi Islam on the one hand, and partner of the infidel West in the world's biggest business on the other. Against whatever odds, or by Allah's decree, this soon formed the epicenter of the "perfect Islamic storm," a collision of sacred and profane extremes.

The astronomical amount of Western money that flowed to Arabia during the twentieth century in exchange for oil—trillions of dollars by any estimate—could have been used to enrich immeasurably the lives of all Middle Eastern Arabs. A tiny fraction of those trillions of dollars would have sufficed to build and grow a prosperous Palestinian state, as modern and well developed as Israel. Recall (or reread) the excerpt from Aldous Huxley, in chapter 11, as a reminder of the staggering sum of economic and cultural development that could have been implemented in Europe for the cost of fighting World War I. The "Arab world" has had even more cash than that at its disposal, but has shown incomparably less political will to generate peace and prosperity with petrodollars. This has been accomplished on comparatively small scales, by states such as Dubai—the "Singapore" of Arabia, a model for modernizing the Middle East—but it needs to be done on vastly larger scales to resolve the regional conflicts that now implicate the global village entire.

Petrodollars have instead sponsored much Arab terrorism, initially against Israel but increasingly against the West. During the Cold War, Arab terrorism was confined to Israel and Europe. But the collapse of the Soviet Union has allowed the flexing of pan-Islamic political muscle, along the entire civilizational interface between Islam, East Asia, India, and Europe. Fig. 14.6 illustrates the magnitude of these interfaces. Arabian terror has now expanded into Islamist terror, which operates anywhere and everywhere in the global village, spawned from a contiguous front that stretches from Morocco to Indonesia. Moreover, new acts of terror are now being perpetrated by "homegrown"

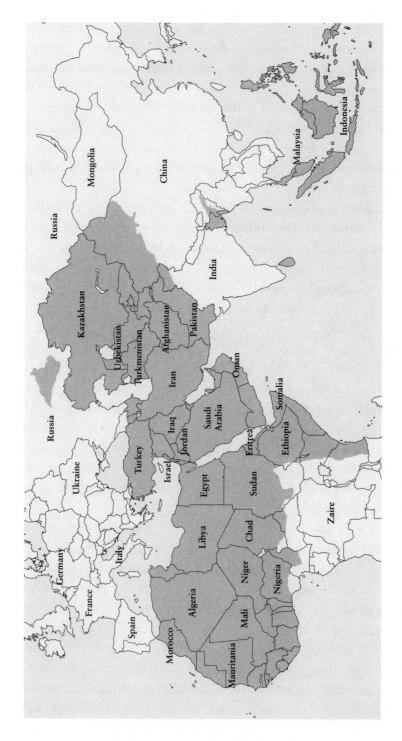

Figure 14.6 The "Islamic World," Israel, and the Civilizational Interface between Islam, East Asia, India and Europe

terrorists drawn from unassimilated but swelling Islamic populations in Europe, the United Kingdom, and elsewhere.

Piggybacking on the opportunities afforded by globalization, and leaving a digital trail that can be detected but cannot be used to predict what they will do next, Islamist terrorists have learned to operate throughout Europe and America. 9/11 was not only a sacking of contemporary Rome by neobarbarians, not only an attack on the chamber of commerce of the global village by religious fanatics opposed to secular globalization, not only a continuation of jihad against the unwitting inheritors of the Crusades, not only an escalation of Arab terrorism of the kind that Israel has endured unremittingly since 1948: In addition, 9/11 was an attempted political coup against the Royal House of Saud, by the Saudi renegade, Osama bin Laden. Saudis, not Palestinians, hijacked the planes on 9/11.

Welcome to the Middle East, where extremism is the norm.

## Ferrying Frogs and Free Figs

Two factors above all need to be borne in mind by those who wish to explore the unfathomable depths of Middle Eastern extremes. First is the suicidal zealotry that infects the entire region, and which sometimes seems embedded in its very sands. Second is the region's habitual transformation of truth, reality, reason, and beneficence into deceit, fantasy, irrationality, and maleficence, which entangles dialogue, inflames debate, and compromises good-faith negotiation. I will shortly illustrate these factors with a couple of parables.

As concerns suicidal zealotry, the region centered about the heart of the Middle East—Israel, Gaza, Sinai, the West Bank, Jordan, Syria, Lebanon—is historically and geostrategically unstable and volatile. The Old Testament is in part a chronicle of endless wars among countless tribes and contending civilizations that inhabited, invaded, and crisscrossed this land bridge spanning West and East. Israel perches midway between the southern arm of Western civilization (counting Turkey), lying across the entire northern shore of the Mediterranean, and the western arm of Islamic civilization, lying across the entire southern shore of the Mediterranean. Israel is geopolitically situated so as to bear the continuous brunt of their intermittent but centuries-long collisions, like a nut in the jaws of a geopolitical nutcracker. Israel is caught between the rock of the West and the hard places of Arabia. It is a land bridge which armies have crossed since time immemorial, en route to imperial conquest and ignominious oblivion alike. The price of maintaining a foothold in this extremely precarious region is all too often a kind of suicidal extremism: not a will to live, rather a will to die.

The region's suicidal zealotry is captured by the parable of the scorpion and the frog. A scorpion wanted to cross the Jordan River, and asked a frog to ferry it across on its back. The frog replied that it would gladly do so, except that it could not trust the scorpion: "This is the Middle East. We'll get halfway across, then you'll sting me, and we'll both drown." But the scorpion persisted, importuned, and gave every assurance that it would do no such thing. So the frog finally relented, and breasted the river with the scorpion on its back. Sure enough, when they were halfway across, the scorpion stung the frog. As they were about to sink, the frog turned to the scorpion and asked, "Why did you sting me? Now we will both drown." The scorpion shrugged and said, "That's the Middle East." Everyone who has lived in this region comes to realize how greatly it differs from the West in this respect: Its hostilities are not only murderous, but often also suicidal.

We know that truth is the first casualty of war.[11] But the wars of the Middle East have been waged for so many centuries, and in so many dimensions, that in this region we encounter not only wars, but also wars over wars, wars about wars, wars within wars, and wars on top of wars. We encounter wars over who fought whom and why, over who is fighting whom and why, over who will fight whom and why. Haggling over goods in the souk is an age-old Semitic custom, dear to Arab and Jew alike, and prone to turn any routine shopping trip into a theatrical extravaganza, replete with histrionics and exaggerations, feigned umbrages, and true deceits. But haggling over history in this hotspot of the global village automatically converts any routine war into a miracle, a myth, or a wrathful deity's vendetta. All proportions are biblical by default, and apocalyptic by popular demand. Any peace is frightfully difficult to negotiate, because the resolution of conflict in one dimension—whether tribal, civilizational, theological, or economic—tends to provoke conflict in another.

If you doubt me, just consult (for example) the cornucopia of controversies surrounding the life, words, and deeds of the prominent Palestinian-American scholar, the late Professor Edward Said (1935–2003). If you attempt to find straightforward answers to any of the following questions, you will be immediately and irretrievably lost in a labyrinth of heated dispute: Where was he born? Where was he schooled? Was he a Palestinian refugee? What was his position on Palestine? On Israel? On Jews? On the Middle East? On America? Did he endorse anti-Semitic publications? Did he oppose terrorism? Did he participate in the intifada? Why were his books banned by the Palestinian Authority? Wikipedia, the online encyclopedia whose entries address these questions and more, features this strident disclaimer: "The neutrality and factual accuracy of this article are disputed. Please see the relevant discussion on the talk page."[12] Such is the Middle East, a region in which neutrality is often difficult and factual accuracy is sometimes impossible. If we cannot attain consensus on the salient details of a leading Palestinian-American's well-documented life and works, what prospects do we have of attaining consensus on a shared history and collaborative vision of the region from which he sprang?

The Middle East's exquisite convolutions of truth and reality are illustrated by the parable of the free figs. A Middle Eastern elder's afternoon repose—customary during this fiercely hot time of the day—was interrupted by a throng of children, who were playing boisterously beneath his window. So the elder called out to them, "Children, why are you playing here? Don't you know that they're giving away free figs in the marketplace?" This was a fib, but the credulous children believed it. So they scampered off to the marketplace, in search of free figs, leaving the elder to resume his nap in tranquility. But the elder could not fall back asleep. Tossing and turning, he ruminated, "Why am I lying here, trying to sleep, when they're giving away free figs in the marketplace?" This epitomizes the Middle East: a place where truth and untruth, reality and fantasy, sometimes mesh so seamlessly that it can become impossible to disentangle them. Anything might be the case, or come to be believed as such.

Here is what a Libyan friend and neighbor professed to me in the 1980s, when we were graduate students together in London. He said that as a devout Muslim, he also accepted the truths of Judaism and Christianity. He believed, as Jews do, that the Messiah will one day come for the very first time. He also believed, as Christians do, that the Messiah has already come, and will one day come a second time. And he believed, as a devout Muslim, that Mohammed is the one true prophet of the one true God, Allah. With a confident smile, he concluded, "So you see, no matter who is right, I will go to heaven." Just so. Welcome to a mindscape in which no belief is inconsistent with any other. While there are "Messianic Jews" in the West (e.g., Jews for Jesus) who manage to believe both that Jesus was not the Messiah (the Jewish position) and that Jesus was the Messiah (the Christian position), it takes a far more nubile mind to believe both of these things, and at the same time to deny them both, by asserting that Mohammed and Allah are their true successors. "Ordinary" Western believers, who adhere to just one doctrine, are not accustomed to a world in which anything might be believed in conjunction with anything else. In characterizing totalitarianism, Orwell only went so far as "doublethink." That sufficed for the West. But if you want to understand the Middle East, you need "triplethink, quadruplethink, . . . n-tuplethink." That's because the supply of free figs is inexhaustible.

From a Jewish standpoint, zealotry has been a consequence of persecution and besiegement. If you stand atop the mountain fortress of Masada, you can still clearly discern the rectilinear outlines of the Roman encampments, etched starkly in the arid, saline verge of the Dead Sea. Looking at the adjacent mountain built by the industrious Romans, whose slaves dragged their siege engines up the far slope to breach the defenses of this last enclave of the Jewish revolt against their empire, you can better understand why nine hundred "zealots"—men, women, and children—put themselves to the sword rather than surrender and be carted off to slavery, or worse, in Rome. (In a way, it was very Japanese.)[13] The memory of Masada is etched not only in the surrounding terrain, but also in the minds of contemporary Jews of the Roman diaspora.

The Warsaw ghetto uprising against the Nazis was a reenactment of Masada, a last desperate attempt to give life meaning through suicidal combat. And this is also the mentality of the Gush Emunim ("The Bloc of the Faithful"), a sect whose adherents inhabit, among other places, hilltop settlements south of Jerusalem. Many of these settlers are American Jews, relatives of families massacred by British-led Jordanian troops that overran this area during Israel's 1948 War of Independence. These settlers will not leave their villages voluntarily or alive: They will fight to the death against any who threaten to displace or evict them—Arab or Jew alike. They would fire on the IDF (Israel Defense Forces) itself rather than resettle. And a few million Jews clinging to a tiny sliver of land called Israel, the rump of a twice-partitioned state, surrounded as they are by hundreds of millions of hostile Muslims in dozens of countries—Arabs and others, who for decades have invested their energies in hating Jews, Israelis, and the West, and have committed so much time and energy to Israel's destruction—cannot but live in a state of siege, and be perpetually ready to die in suicidal defense of their nation.

From an Arab standpoint, the improbable rebirth of Israel in 1948 represents not a miracle, but a catastrophe: a reinvasion by the West, neither as a crusading army that can be driven out, nor as a colonial government that can be outwaited but as something far more personal—the fulfillment of a biblical promise to one branch of cousins in a feuding family. Arabs and Jews have longer collective memories than most peoples on earth. For although Israel's very existence is rooted in biblical history, in Jehovah's promises to Abraham and Moses, and in the continuous presence of Jews in the Holy Land since those days, so do Arabs' grievances against Jews boast a similar antiquity, of the same continuity, and have for centuries been inflamed by a diametrically opposed reading of that same history.

So the Arabs did not exactly welcome the Jews "home," nor did they countenance the recreation of Israel. The Arabs did not revolt against the French mandate in Syria and Lebanon. They did not revolt against the British mandate in Iraq and Palestine. They did not revolt even when

Britain carved Transjordan (today, Jordan) out of Palestine—ceding about 80 percent of Palestine's area to this spontaneously generated kingdom, and transforming its Palestinian inhabitants into Jordanians and subjects of its Hashemite Bedouin monarch, with one stroke of the pen. Why? Because neither the Middle Eastern Arabs in general, nor the Palestinians in particular, possessed aggressive national consciousness. That didn't happen until 1947–48. Ironically and tragically, Arab national consciousness—and Palestinian national identity—emerged only with the rebirth of Israel itself, when the entire Arab world rejected the British partition of the remaining sliver of Cisjordan into the twin states of Israel and Palestine.

Palestinian national consciousness emerged on the heels of the Palestinian refugees of Israel's War of Independence. They could have had their own neighboring state, then and there, if they themselves had been politically organized at the time—which they were not—and if the "Arab world" had accepted the partition, and helped to resettle them in their own state, which it did not. So the rebirth of Israel came twinned with the birth of the Palestinian refugees, who were caught, in their own tragedy, "between a rock and a hard place": the rock of Zion, and the hard place of a hostile and belligerent "Arab world." The tragedy of the Palestinians was not manufactured by them, but rather for them and against them. Their own leaders and the "Arab world" refused to accept the state that was offered them, and instead sought to destroy Israel and reclaim "all" of Palestine (except 80 percent of it, namely Jordan). They opted for "double or nothing" and got nothing, which only increased their suffering, as the "Arab world" was delighted to keep these refugees festering in subhuman conditions, the better to inculcate their hatred for Israel, for Jews, for the West—and to transmute that hatred into a weapon of terror.

"The duped children returned, disconsolate and hungry, from the marketplace. 'There were no free figs,' they complained to the elder. So the elder pointed beyond the barren hills, toward the horizon, to a neighboring land flowing with milk and honey, and said, "The Jews stole them." And thus the children were taught, not how to plant fig trees themselves, but how to hate others for having planted their own."

Any two states can coexist peacefully, side by side. No two states can exist congruently, one atop the other. Jews and Israelis alike have accepted the partition of a partition that created Israel and Palestine, side by side. Palestinians and the "Arab world" rejected it, and sought instead to recreate Palestine atop the ashes of the Jewish state, to whose annihilation they have been overwhelmingly committed for decades. Most Jews, Israelis, and Westerners do not hate Palestinians, the "Arab world," or Islamic civilization, but are subject to much unrequited hatred from these sources. Yet within the West, a generation of radicalized illiberals from the extreme left, and culturally illiterate graduates of the deconstructed universities, have been taught to hate Western civilization itself, and thus to hate Israel and Jews in the bargain. Hatred of Israel is a pillar of "diverse" American campus culture.

This is another result of the disintegration of the West from within, whose radicalized postmodern culture has seen its "immune system" become so compromised by amorality, unreality, and untruth that it is vulnerable to every kind of deceit—the more preposterous, the better. The tipping point of the West's increasing ignorance of the causes and cures of Islamist fanaticism, and of the self-hatred of hapless Western masses who can no longer distinguish between ideas that further civilization and doctrines that destroy it, came in the late 1960s. We have seen the results of these campus revolutions, when Western civilization itself was guillotined by postmodernist Jacobins, themselves the stooges of their neo-Marxist Robespierrian masters.

## All the King's Wars

After 1948, the "Arab world" regrouped, and prepared to renew its quest to annihilate Israel. The Palestinians, subsisting in the no-man's-land between Israel and Jordan, were governed by privation and coercion. Held captive by the "Arab world"—and by their own corrupt leadership—they endured festering poverty and exploitation as transient laborers, receiving support from the "Arab world" mainly as pawns in the war against Israel, and never as genuine candidates for political self-determination.

The more astute Palestinians, in essence, became the "new Jews." They fled to freer parts of the world, seeking liberty, opportunity, and hope in diaspora. Unlike so many other Arab peoples, they intermarried and assimilated, especially in the free West. They and their children became more attuned to Western ways than most other Arabs, and in this lies their greater promise and mission. Given their superior understanding of and familiarity with the West, gained through adaptation to it instead of violence against it, descendants of the Palestinian diaspora could help reform the entire "Arab world" from within. They are already accomplishing this in Jordan. But diaspora can be a long story, and insofar as Palestinians hoped to build their state by emulating Jews, they were bound to experience persecution, setback and suffering. Insofar as the Palestinians remaining in the territories have subscribed to terror instead of statecraft, they have brought, and continue to bring, suffering upon themselves.

While the world has heard and felt much of the post-1948 Palestinian plight, it must also be observed that almost a million Jews were subsequently driven out of the "Arab world" in the aftermath of Israel's rebirth. Israeli Arabs have prospered; Jews in the "Arab world" have been demonized and expelled. Most Arabs have never met a Jew, yet are remorselessly propagandized to hate and revile the Jewish people. During a week in Cairo, I was more or less accepted as an American, yet was appalled at the ordinary speech patterns of so many well-educated Egyptians, which were laced with venomous anti-Jewish sentiments, reinforced daily and nightly by Egyptian mass media. And Egypt is a "moderate" Middle Eastern country, and only one of two (along with Jordan) to have made peace with Israel. Even so, a lingering price of that peace is widespread and deep-seated hatred of Jews and Israel. Such hatred is reflected throughout the "Arab world" and the "Islamic world," and beyond that is mirrored on the campuses of American, British, Australian, and Canadian universities.

## The 1956 War

In 1956, Egyptian President Gamal Abdel Nasser nationalized the Suez Canal. This rang alarms in Europe, because at that time—prior to the introduction of supertankers—Persian Gulf oil was shipped to the West via Suez. In addition, and in violation of international law, Nasser not only closed the Suez Canal to Israeli shipping, but also blockaded the straights of Tiran, sealing off the Gulf of Aqaba and Israel's Red Sea port of Eilat. At the same time, Syria and Jordan also mobilized for a new war against Israel, and placed their armies under Nasser's overall command. Lest any doubt remained as to his intentions, Nasser announced in October 1956: "I am not solely fighting against Israel itself. My task is to deliver the Arab world from destruction through Israel's intrigue, which has its roots abroad. Our hatred is very strong. There is no sense in talking about peace with Israel. There is not even the smallest place for negotiations."[14]

Do yourself and the global village a favor, and look again at the map of the "Arab world" depicted in fig. 14.5. How in the name of truth and reality can anyone seriously believe that the aim of Israel's existence has been to destroy the "Arab world" by intrigue—or any other means? The aim of the Jewish state was, and is, to ingather survivors of the descendants of the Children of Israel who were scattered by the Babylonians and Romans, expelled by the Spanish and Portuguese, persecuted by innumerable nations, mass-murdered by the Nazis, and held hostage by the Soviets. Yet Nasser's speech reinforced a pervasive delusion in the "Arab world"—that the insignificant State of Israel had the power or the will to destroy her neighbors, whereas in fact she has at every opportunity sought to live peaceably among them. It was the "Arab world" that was overcome with a blinding hatred of Jews and of Israel, and that was bent on Israel's destruction. Thus the assassin accuses his victim of being an assassin, in order to justify assassinating him.

In a preemptive attack in November 1956, later joined by France and Britain, Israel routed the Egyptian forces. This was followed by Israeli withdrawal from captured Egyptian territory in an uneasy truce compelled and brokered by the United States. For by the 1950s, France and Britain were spent imperial forces, having given way to the United States and the Soviet Union, whose Cold War increasingly dictated policies of "conflict management" in the Middle East. The post–World War II roles of former imperial powers in this region—such as France and Britain—were relegated to those of arms dealers, a demotion from kingmakers to be sure. Indeed, much of the contemporary anti-Semitism in Britain, including the BBC's frequent and flagrant demonizations of Israel, stem from smoldering resentment of Britain's own loss of power, pomp, and circumstance in the Middle East and the world. At one time, the sun never set on the British Empire; now the sun never rises on it. The Jews, as usual, are the scapegoats of choice.

So in 1956, the United States stuffed a Cold War cork into the bottle of fuming Arab hostility and belligerence, but did not impose a political settlement on the region. By the early 1960s, the Cold War itself had heated up: the Bay of Pigs, the Berlin wall, the Cuban Missile Crisis, the space race, Vietnam—Armageddon was the order of the day. Westerners and Soviets became too preoccupied with mutual assured destruction (MAD) to be much concerned over the perennial suicidal zealotry and abundant free figs of the Middle East. But the Palestinian refugee problem had not been solved, nor could the volatile hatreds of the "Arab world" remain bottled up indefinitely. By 1967, mounting Middle Eastern pressures popped the cork of 1956, and in so doing opened a dual-chambered Pandora's box: Israel's occupation of the West Bank and Gaza, and Palestinian terrorism in Europe. The first chamber exacerbated Middle Eastern extremes of strife, yet also furthered the emergence of a Palestinian state, albeit through a gauntlet of oppression; the second chamber expanded the unresolved Middle Eastern conflicts into Western Europe, paving a highway of hijacked airplanes that led to straight to 9/11.

## The Six-Day War

By May 1967, the "Arab world" had goaded itself into another total war on Israel, spurred into action by a new Palestinian leader, Yasser Arafat. By now the Arab armies were equipped with the latest Soviet warplanes and heavy tanks. Analysts still gave Israel the edge, even against overwhelming odds and with grossly outdated equipment. Once again, Egypt blockaded the Straits of Tiran, and on May 16, Nasser ordered U.N. secretary-general U Thant to withdraw U.N. troops from the security zone between Egypt and Israel. Radio Cairo announced "The existence of Israel has continued too long. The battle has come in which we shall destroy Israel."[15] On May 30, King Hussein of Jordan stated "The armies of Egypt, Jordan, Syria and Lebanon are poised on the borders of Israel . . . while standing behind us are the armies of Iraq, Algeria, Kuwait, Sudan, and the whole Arab nation." On May 31, Iraq President Abd al-Rahman Aref announced, "This is our opportunity to wipe out the ignominy which has been with us since 1948. Our goal is clear—to wipe Israel off the map."[16]

The world stood by and watched, prepared to let the Arabs continue Hitler's work. President Lyndon Johnson toyed with the idea of sending a U.S. fleet to open the Straits of Tiran, but in the end he stood by and watched as well. On June 5, Israel launched a preemptive air strike against Egypt, destroying more than four hundred aircraft on the ground, thus achieving total air superiority. Israel then routed the massed Arab armies, driving them back and capturing Gaza, Sinai, the West Bank, the Golan Heights, and the Old City of Jerusalem—all within six days.

But Israel's stunning victory in the Six-Day War delivered into Israeli hands a Palestinian refugee population that had been systematically disenfranchised, brutalized, and propagandized by the "Arab world" since 1948. So was born the dilemma of the "occupied territories," and the dramatic role reversal of Israel from besieged state to occupying power.

From 1967 until 9/11, increasingly distorted Western media reversed the entire historical process of cause and effect, blaming Islamic civilization's increasingly burning hatred of the West, along with unrelenting Arab belligerence against Israel, on Israeli rule over the Palestinian people. The Israeli-Palestinian conflict was portrayed as the cause of the larger Arab-Israeli conflict, whereas in fact it has been the unfortunate and avertable effect. Israel's 1967 occupation of the Palestinian territories, combined with a Palestinian government by terrorists (the PLO) whose avowed policy was the destruction of Israel, and the infiltration of countless other terrorist organizations (including Black September, Hamas, Hezbollah) into the region, placed the Israelis and the Palestinians alike in an impossible political predicament.

Instead of understanding that a peaceful and lasting resolution of the localized Israeli-Palestinian problem would come only with a resolution of the larger regional Arab-Israeli conflict—and ultimately of the global

Islamic-Western civilizational conflict—Western universities and Western media conveniently (and to the delight of Islamist terrorists) blamed everything on the Israelis. A myth of terrifying and debilitating proportions quickly captivated the deconstructed West. The Palestinians eagerly became the new "Jews," "denied" a homeland by "Israeli Nazis." While Arafat's PLO was terrorizing Europe, murdering Israeli Olympic athletes at Munich, hijacking planes and murdering Jews and Americans on board, the U.N. was charmed by Arafat's rhetoric, and passed a 1975 resolution equating Zionism with racism. Jews and Israelis became both victims and scapegoats for every act of Arab and Islamist terror. Western public opinion embarked on an extravagant and exotic voyage through the Arabian looking glass, which was shattered for some Westerners only by 9/11.

But in 1967, only two prominent voices in all of Israel raised alarms about the status of the "Occupied Territories"—the West Bank and Gaza—and the possibility that Israel's victory in the Six-Day War could turn Pyrrhic. These voices were the well-known author Amos Oz, and the respected intellectual professor Yeshayahu Leibowitz. Both of them warned that Israel could not "police" the peoples of the West Bank and Gaza without serious moral and political backlash, but no one listened to these "madmen" in the jubilation of the moment.

Israelis conditioned by, and to, a harsh and unforgiving Middle Eastern ethos saw the annexation of these territories as an opportunity, but so did their implacable enemies. From a strategic Israeli perspective, the capture of the Golan Heights put a stop to the incessant shelling and rocketing of northern kibbutzim by Syria and her Lebanese lackeys, while the capture of the Gaza strip sealed a favored corridor of invasion by Egypt. Most important, the capture of the West Bank gave Israel a badly needed buffer zone to protect against the cutting of the nation in half, at her precariously narrow waist, in any future invasion from the East. From an economic perspective, the occupied territories gave Israel access to a substantial population of Palestinians who were exploitable as cheap labor, and who—as stateless persons exploited no less cruelly by the "Arab world"—became dependent on jobs in Israel, but as permanently disenfranchised laborers. This combination of exploitation and oppression, framed by the unwholesome mutual interdependence of the master-slave dialectic and dynamic, was further inflamed by Israeli arrogance, and constantly exacerbated by PLO and other terrorism.

Given the Palestinian unreadiness for statehood, there were only two possible political models for governing the territories: oppressive apartheid as (formerly) in South Africa, or a Hobbesian state of nature as would soon prevail in Lebanon. Israelis chose the lesser of two evils, the South African model. This left Palestinians relegated to roles of slaves, either in Israel or elsewhere in the Arab world, where they were also severely disadvantaged, as well as despised—despised by Arab governments that wanted them to remain stateless, to be used as agitated and explosive pawns in the unending regional chess match against Israel.

Israelis and Western Jews alike soon became deeply divided by the issue of the occupied territories. After two thousand years of homelessness in diaspora, Jews had learned to regard themselves as strangers in strange lands, either thriving at the mercy of their hosts, or enduring their persecutions with long-suffering Messianic resolve. Western Jewish identity had been forged by this experience, and was unable to accommodate itself to the notion of Jews (in this case, Israelis) as occupiers and pharaohs. Many Western Jews became disenchanted with Israel's occupation. This disenchantment has been cleverly exploited by Arab propagandists—who are lionized by politically correct North American campus cultures—not to advance the political maturity of the Palestinian people, but to promote hatred against Israel.

The vicissitudes of statehood had descended upon Israel in any case, just as the vicissitudes of a lack of statehood had descended on the Palestinians. The stereotype of the Sabra—the native-born Israeli—began to evolve an Israeli identity different from that of its ingathered diasporans—the Ashkenazi Jews of Europe and America, and the Sephardic Jews of Iberia and North Africa. The Sabra (an Israeli born in Israel), like the cactus after which it is named, is tender inside but prickly outside. The Jews of the Ashkenazi diaspora had evolved by being malleable outside but immutable inside. This set the stage for the polarization of Jewry itself, which the occupation quickly exacerbated. It became more pronounced during the intifadas, and in the twenty-first century is being fed to the deconstructed West, by opportunistic and clever Islamists, as an ideology. The doctrine is: "Good Jews hate Israel; bad Jews support Israel." The Western world has become so Orwellized that substantial numbers of New York City's deconstructed Jews—typically Upper West Side liberals—applaud this slogan. Their minds have been so weakened by exposure to all the malign influences gnawing at Western civilization that they have become infected with hatreds formerly confined to the "Arab world."

At the same time, Israelis themselves became polarized in ways that did not ameliorate the situation. The political left tended to be dovish, calling for unilateral withdrawal, which unfailingly invited more aggression from the Arabs; the right tended to be hawkish, calling for further Jewish settlement in and de facto annexation of the territories, which was bound to provoke more aggression from the Arabs. As Israel's conscript army became an occupying police force, Israelis who were morally opposed to the occupation served reluctantly or not at all in the territories—and yet they would have made the best "front-line ambassadors," even in this politically impossible scenario. Their reluctance to be party to the occupation opened the door to more oppressive and sadistic personality types, some of whom sought to serve in the territories in order to exercise abusive power over a hapless Palestinian populace.

Despots are despots, and every state has them. Israel is no exception. Palestinians who have suffered cruelly under the lash of Israeli occupation may not realize that there are ex-patriot Israeli despots in the West too, who treat their subordinates in some organizational cultures—Jew and non-Jew alike—with similar cruelty. For that matter, the Israeli mafia is as feared and fearsome as any other. But just as Arab peoples should not be judged by a minority of terrorists, neither should Israelis be judged by a minority of despots or gangsters.

If circumstances conspire to make sadists policemen, they will seek out masochistic criminals. A culture in which parents are paid cash rewards for sending their explosive-laden children to destroy themselves and as many innocent civilians as possible is indeed a culture of masochists, and they in turn attract the harshest possible reprisals, in the form of targeted assassinations and the like. The media mantra for this is a "cycle of violence." Gandhi prepared Indians for self-government by teaching and practicing nonviolence against their British occupiers. Arafat maintained the Palestinians in self-enslavement by teaching and practicing terrorism against their Israeli occupiers.

But because the Middle East is always convoluted, every instance of Israeli brutality or abuse in the territories—whether real or invented—actually earned Israel respect in the wider "Arab world"— although of course no Arab would admit this publicly. Privately, however, a good many Arabs began to regard Israel as a "respectable neighbor"—perversely but precisely because of Israel's willingness to oppress and exploit the Palestinians.[17] So Israel's loss of moral ascendancy in the West was clandestinely but finely balanced by a gain of immoral ascendancy in the Middle East—unfortunately at the expense of the Palestinians.

Even so, a considerable part of the Palestinian tragedy had little or nothing to do with the post-1967 occupation. It had more to do with the regional dimensions of the wider Arab-Israeli conflict, with the persistent unwillingness of the "Arab world" to make peace with Israel, and their unwillingness to cultivate peace—along with statehood— among the Palestinians. Instead, the "Arab world" geared up for yet another war—the 1973 Yom Kippur War—whose aftermath inflated the price of Persian Gulf oil, causing Western consumers to hemorrhage hundreds of billions into Arabian Swiss bank accounts, and galvanizing the Middle Eastern ayatollahs into escalating the regional Arab-Israeli conflict into a clash of Islamic versus Western civilizations.

## The Yom Kippur War

The 1973 War of Attrition almost got out of hand. In a well-coordinated surprise attack, which followed many months of feints against which Israel could not afford to mobilize her citizen army at every provocation, and on the eve of the holiest day in the Hebrew calendar (Yom Kippur), the armies of Egypt and Syria attacked Israel, swiftly breaching her unready and undermanned defenses. Thanks to the Cold War and the space race, military hardware had evolved quantum leaps beyond 1969, and so by 1973 the Arabs were equipped with Soviet-made SAM ground-to-air missiles. They shot down dozens of Israeli jets over Syria alone, and without air superiority Israel's ground forces could have been overwhelmed by the sheer numbers of the invaders' tanks and troops. In addition, Israeli pilots were not only trying to dodge Soviet heat-seeking missiles: They may also have been dogfighting East German and North Korean pilots flying Syrian MIGs. The long fingers of the Cold War stirred the cauldron of the Middle East in 1973, making the region a flash point for World War III.

Back in the White House, Nixon and Kissinger agonized over how and when to intervene if things got too far out of hand. They decided to let Israel bleed before resupplying her air force, perhaps to help justify later and harsher countermeasures against Syria and Egypt, should they be required. Israel took heavy casualties in an Alamo-like defense of their state, and yet the region—and the world—was spared a dreaded United States–Soviet Union confrontation. A belatedly resupplied Israel eventually turned the tide of battle, repulsed the Syrian armies, and put the Egyptians to rout. That marked the "Arab world's" last attempt of the twentieth century to annihilate the State of Israel by classical Clausewitzian war, "a continuation of policy by other means."[18] Hereafter they would change their policies, but much of the "Arab world" would nonetheless continue the war by other means.

### Warriors for Peace

However, in a subsequent act of visionary statesmanship, demonstrating the formidable courage of a warrior for peace, Egyptian president Anwar Sadat made peace with Israel. Egypt is the most populous nation of the Middle East, and a very influential one. When he signed the treaty with Israel in 1979, Sadat must have known that he was also signing his own death warrant. Middle Eastern treaties are signed in blood, not ink. Sure enough, Islamist fanatics within the Egyptian Army assassinated Sadat in Cairo, in 1981. His monument presides over the site of his murder, across from the reviewing stands not far from al-Azhar university. Egyptians are proud of Sadat, and rightfully. He unlocked the door to regional peace in the Middle East, setting a much-needed example of Arab willingness to live in peace with Israel. Jordan made peace with Israel in 1994, thanks to its enlightened monarchy, and Jordanians (most of whom are of Palestinian origin) have continued to modernize and prosper ever since. Of five states that attacked Israel in 1948—Egypt, Jordan, Syria, Lebanon, and Iraq—it took four wars and four decades for two of them to make peace.

Syria needs to make peace too, which would also enable Lebanon finally to free itself from client statehood, and rid itself of malign influences—emanating largely from Syria and Iran—that have worked its tragic ruin. But neither Lebanon nor Iraq are currently in any position to make peace with Israel, because both are riven by violent internal faction. The tragedy of Lebanon was not manufactured by the West, rather by a constellation of contending regional forces opposed to Lebanon's Western inclinations and pluralistic profile.

Neither was the current tragedy in Iraq manufactured by the West. Saddam Hussein was a Hitlerian despot, who murdered more Iraqis (including genocide of Kurds and Marsh Arabs) than insurgents are murdering in the upheaval following his demise. Saddam imposed structural and actual violence—law and order enforced by brutality and murder—on Iraqis. In his absence, Iraqis are afflicted by anarchy: lawlessness and disorder, enforced by insurgency and terror. Saddam posed dangerous threats to the Persian Gulf and Israel alike, but ironically also helped hold Iran's ambitions in check. The Middle East was volatile with Saddam, as it is volatile without him.

Peace in the Middle East requires warriors for peace, not warriors for war. The Arab world's normalization of relations with Israel requires warriors for peace, not warriors for war. The Arab world's acknowledgement of its historical responsibility for exacerbating the Palestinian tragedy, as well as its willingness to help craft a Palestinian state, requires warriors for peace, not warriors for war. And the Arab world's political evolution, from tyranny, theocracy, and insurgency toward twenty-first-century statecraft, requires warriors for peace, not warriors for war. Beyond this, the Arab world's ability to ward off toxic clouds of hatred that currently envelope and spew from Iran, and to resist succumbing to Iran's ambition to infect Arabia with virulently hostile Islamism, likewise requires warriors for peace, not warriors for war.

But even if all this came to pass, prospects for greater peace in the Middle East may come with increasing unrest in Europe, in Central Asia, or in any place where Islamic civilization and globalization collide. Children in Indonesia, the most populous Islamic nation in the global village, are being taught that Americans and Israelis hijacked the planes on 9/11, in order to give the warmongering West a pretext to invade peace-loving Muslim lands. These are free figs of a very dangerous kind. This tale is also told, and sponsored, on the campuses of American universities, from coast to coast. But what transpires on those campuses matters increasingly less, and what transpires in the Indonesian madrasas matters increasingly more to the well-being of the global village. If Middle Eastern hatred of Jews, Israelis, and Americans is successfully transplanted all over Islamic civilization, then the conflict will become even more global than it is now, and a conflagration could result. So it is good that the Arab and Muslim worlds are themselves becoming divided over the issue of civilizational conflict. Many brilliant young Arab and Muslim intellectuals are demanding fundamental freedoms that would reform their cultures and draw them into the global village as willing partners and good neighbors. Meanwhile, the Middle East needs a Middle Way more than most places on earth.

## Israel's Extremes

Israel is a pluralistic democracy, with dozens of parties vying for seats in her Parliament (the Knesset) in each election. No party is permitted to use hatred as the basis of its policies. For example the Kach Party, founded by Rabbi Meir Kahane (who in a more benign phase of militancy also founded the Jewish Defense League[19]) preached unadulterated hatred of Arabs. Hatred toward any group is repugnant to the Israeli Constitution, so Kach was banned as a political contender in the 1980s. Yet the UN declared Zionism to be racism, under the influence of one of the twentieth century's most accomplished hatemongers, Yasser Arafat. As a matter of fact, Israeli Arabs are regularly elected to the Knesset, and serve as political equals beside

Israeli Jews. Women are elected too, and serve as political equals beside men. Israel is one of the few Western democracies to have had a female Prime Minister: Golda Meir.

Ultraorthodox Jews are elected to the Knesset as well, even though they do not officially recognize the State of Israel itself. They do not salute the flag of Israel when it is raised, nor do they sing the national anthem when it is played. They do make one important concession, however: They cash their parliamentary paychecks, accepting the shekels while rejecting the state that mints them. The Jesuits did not invent casuistry.

By contrast, not one Arab nation is a functional democracy. Not one Arab nation has a Jew serving in its government. Not one Arab nation has had a female leader. Yet the hateful anti-Jewish and anti-Israeli propaganda that has emanated from the "Arab world" since 1947, and which has been echoed and reinforced on the deconstructed campuses of Western universities, paints Israel as an enemy of liberty, opportunity, and hope. The Middle East is rife with contradictions, but sometimes seems quite sane compared with the postmodern West, whose inhabitants are ever more easily induced to eat free figs.

Israel must be far more powerful that it realizes: a nation of six million, inhabiting a sliver of land smaller than New Jersey, has apparently prevented the entire "Arab world"—twenty-two nations, three hundred million people, a cumulative area comparable to the United States, plus the world's largest oil reserves—from modernizing and joining the global village. Want some free figs? Sorry, the Jews took them all. "There is nothing new under the sun," said Ecclesiastes. Not under the Middle Eastern sun, apparently.

## From Regional Peace to Civilizational War

Egypt's 1979 peace with Israel did much to stabilize the Arab-Israeli conflict, and paved the way to Jordan's peace and economic joint ventures with the Jewish state. But 1979 also saw the overthrow of the shah of Iran, and the regression of Iran into a state of medieval fundamentalism under the ayatollahs. At the same time, the Soviet nightmare in Afghanistan prepared the ground for its takeover by the

Taliban, a regressive band of Stone Age mullahs who stoned women to death for visiting beauty salons. Syria, a dangerous wild card in the Middle Eastern deck, became more bellicose toward Israel, even as Egypt and Jordan waxed more pacific. The Syrians were major instigators of the destabilization, terror, civil war, and anarchy that descended on Lebanon during the 1980s, tearing that once-progressive Arab nation—whose capital, Beirut, was the "Paris of the Mediterranean"—into pieces. No fewer than a dozen rival factions destroyed Lebanon, which Syria then controlled as a client state until the 2005 assassination of former Prime Minister Rafiq Hariri.

In 1982, Israel restored the Sinai Peninsula to Egypt, but also embarked on an invasion of Southern Lebanon, in an attempt to establish a security zone to neutralize the terrorism that Syria unleashed, or sponsored, from Lebanese bases. As always, the Palestinians were caught in the middle, perpetrating acts of terror on the one hand, and enduring massacres on the other, for example at the hands of the Christian Phalangists in the camps of Sabra and Shatilla. The suicidal cyclone of zealous Middle Eastern warfare, which in the 1980s spared Israel from attack by conventional Arab armies, now ravaged Lebanon, proliferated terrorism, and entrenched Syria as a die-hard rogue state. Even as I write these words, in late 2005, the Syrians have just accorded a VIP welcome to David Duke, who spewed his vicious hatred of Jews and Israel into mainstream Syrian media. His venomous words were broadcast to resounding ovations from the politicized masses, most of whom have never met a Jew in their lives, and never will.

The 1980s saw the growth and spread of Arab and Islamist terrorism, and a global increase in religiously motivated Arab and Islamist hostility against "infidels" of all kinds: Jews, Christians, atheists, Israelis, Americans, Europeans, Soviets. Within the region, Iran and Iraq waged a bitter, eight-year World War I–style conflict, killing millions and resolving nothing. Twenty-six nations, including the United States and leading European powers, sold arms to both sides— as the Nigerians say, "Business more than usual." Meanwhile, the unresolved Palestinian refugee problem entered its fifth decade. The Israelis found no credible Palestinian partner with whom to negotiate peace, while the Palestinians themselves were trapped between their own government of terrorists and encroaching Israeli settlements in the occupied territories. A bumper crop of hostile mullahs and fulminating ayatollahs threatened the West in increasingly incendiary tones, while the U.N. passed resolution after resolution condemning Israel, blaming all these problems and more on the Jewish state, and its increasingly isolated ally America. Europeans began to condemn Israel and America too, in attempts to appease their own growing populations of unassimilated, unemployable, and disenfranchised Muslims—such as the ones who recently rioted across France.

Reaganomics allowed America to recover from the hyperinflation of the 1970s, triggered by OPEC's hijacking of oil prices, and Americans recommenced their orgiastic consumerism. The 1980s was also the decade during which American campus radicals consolidated their power by eliminating the core literature of Western civilization from humanities curricula coast to coast, and replacing the classics that celebrated liberty, opportunity, and hope with a collage of contemptuous, fatuous and ultimately suicidal critiques of the declining civilization that sponsored them. So the closing of the American mind, and the deconstruction of the torch bearer of Western civilization, unfolded in earnest, at a time when Arab and Islamist hatred of Western civilization began to proliferate worldwide, and to flourish on the campuses of American universities. All this abetted the establishment of active Arab and Islamist terrorist cells far beyond the Middle East, and well beyond Islamic nations—such as the Arab cell in Jersey City, New Jersey, that planned and executed the first bombing of the World Trade Center in 1993. (I felt quite safe living in Jersey City during the 1990s, knowing that all the bombs being built and warehoused there would never be detonated there, except by accident or Allah's will.)

Then, during the 1990s, the Clinton administration actively attempted to improve matters regionally on the one hand, but retreated in the face of expanding terrorism against the United States globally. The late, great diplomat Abba Eban once quipped that the Palestinians "never missed an opportunity to miss an opportunity" for peace and statehood, and this could not have been truer of the Oslo accords, along with Clinton's "bridging proposals." Clinton's last-ditch efforts in 2000, before relinquishing the Oval Office to Bush, brought the Israelis and the Palestinians closer to peace, and the Palestinians closer to statehood, than at any time since 1947. Clinton must be commended for that. But Palestinian terrorism against Israelis continued unabated, and the scorpion of Arafat stung the frog of peace at the proverbial eleventh hour, drowning Oslo and Camp David II in a river of suicidal zealotry.

The year of 1995 saw the assassination of would-be peacemaker Yitzhak Rabin by an Israeli extremist. At a memorial dinner held in November 2005, President Clinton said that Yasser Arafat had made a "colossal historical blunder" in refusing the terms of peace and statehood in 2000.[20] But Clinton and his administration also failed to recognize and respond to growing threats of international Arab and Islamist terrorism. Long on diplomacy and charisma, but short on lines in the sand, the draft-dodging Clinton cut and ran wherever terrorists struck at American targets abroad, which they did with increasing frequency and boldness during the 1990s. Without a doubt, his failure to take a decisive stand emboldened al-Qaeda and others, and gave them the confidence to proceed with 9/11. Clinton's hindsight is as good as anyone's, and he has privately admitted as much. At the same time, the disintegration of the Soviet Union has allowed for Islamist expansionism along and into its entire former southern flank, and beyond.

The recent troubles of the Middle East, fomented by hostile Arabs particularly since 1947, and spread worldwide by intolerant Islamists, have also been exacerbated by a half century and more of Western cowardice, complacency, and appeasement in the face of Arab aggression against Israel. And now that the larger genie of international Islamist aggression against the West itself is out of the bottle, it remains to be seen whether the remnants of Western civilization are willing and able to defend themselves at all. The EU is politically impotent, and may be commandeered outright by Islam in a matter of decades, or may fracture over resurgent nationalisms, as each European nation struggles to assimilate its unassimilated, and possibly unassimilatable Muslims. America remains internally fractured, and hardly able to attain consensus on any important issue, except consumerism.

The meek may one day inherit what is left of the earth when the clash of Islamic and Western civilizations subsides, but if Middle Eastern extremes prevail then that earth will be scorched and barren. The ferrying frogs will become extinct, and the scorpions will starve amid abundant free figs.

## Small Peace

Emerging from behind these clouds of hatred, warmongering, and intolerance, are a new generation of well-educated and tolerant Arabs and other Muslims, who want nothing more than to modernize, to cast off their self-afflictions of so many centuries, and to join the global village as benevolent and productive neighbors. It is their voices that need to be heard, and heeded, before the escalations get completely out of hand. During these tumultuous decades in and around the Middle East, I have managed to make friends from all over the Arab and Muslim worlds, from North Africa to the Middle East, and from Central Asia to South East Asia.

Many Arab and Muslim friends have shown me kindness, hospitality, friendship, love and respect, and I know how pained they are not to have a greater voice in the Arab and Muslim worlds. Their voices are small now, but they are growing, and I hope they will soon be vastly louder. My friend Ibrahim operates a biodynamic farming and manufacturing community in Egypt, on which Muslims, Christians, and Jews live and work in peace and harmony. When will his vision become the rule, instead of the exception? My friend Mazin is a Saudi businessman well schooled in Western ways, as well as in those of Wahabi Islam. He is urbane and affable, tolerant and well read—and, without contradiction, an observant Muslim. He is a thoroughly modern Saudi, if there ever was one. Yet he encounters hatred in Saudi Arabia because of his affinity for the West, and suspicion in the West because of his Saudi identity. He is a bridge to the future, a bridge that must be strengthened and widened. My friend Karim is a Palestinian who lives in the West. Such Palestinians know more about the West than do all other Arabs, and indeed have become strongly assimilated to it, much like the Jews. Karim is a vibrant intellectual who aspires to see more Palestinians become scientists instead of suicide bombers. His own children are being taught to develop their minds so as to make constructive contributions to the global village. They are not being taught, and will not be taught, to hate Jews or anybody else, nor to commit atrocities of terrorism as a "meaningful" way of premature death. My friend Hamzaa is an Arab American and pacifist who deplored the carnage on 9/11 and who works incessantly to build good relations, including tolerant understanding, between Muslims and non-Muslims.

I could continue these anecdotes indefinitely. I have Muslim friends in Malaysia and Indonesia too, who want to distance themselves from Arabian Islam, if not break away entirely, the better to reform. But their voices of peace, reason, and modernity do not yet predominate, and indeed are barely audible over the tirades against Jews, Israel, and the West that spew from their governments and their media, and that are officially taught in too many of their schools. Nor are the voices of small peace always audible over the bombs of al-Qaeda.

Even between the Israelis and Palestinians, there were and are great initiatives of small peace—the peace between cousins and neighbors that is crucial to cementing the larger peace between nations. Yet how many Christian Arabs dare speak out for peace in today's volatile Middle Eastern climate? For that matter, the Arab and Muslim worlds sorely need some Buddhists to chant for peace in their own midst: In Cairo, in Beirut, in Khan Yunis, in Amman, in Damascus, in Baghdad, in Riyadh, in Teheran, in Islamabad, in Kabul, among myriad troubled cities. I wonder why the U.N. neglects to arrange it. There is no shortage of Buddhists in America; Bodhisattvas are more sorely needed in Arabia than Marines.

So do great people make small peace. It may be the only kind of peace that can slip through the cracks of the large wars of the Middle East, which like untreated malignant tumors have now grown to civilization-threatening proportions.

## The "Arab World" and the ABCs

The "Arab world" is a phrase that one sees and hears throughout the "Arab world"—and it lies near the root of all the contemporary problems that gush, like oil, from the Middle East. We have seen again and again in this book that the global village is one place, not many;

that the earth is one planet, not many; that human beings comprise one species, not many; that reality is one thing, not many. When we speak of the "developed world" or the "developing world" we refer to vast numbers of peoples and cultures, and in doing so highlight a chasm in economic development with a view to bridging it. But when Arabs speak of the "Arab world," they do so as though it were another planet, remote from this one, on which they choose to live in isolation from the rest of us. The very concept of the "Arab world" suggests a self-imposed and xenophobic separation from all the other peoples of the global village. It also reinforces a widespread unwillingness to join the global village, and sustains incapacitating hostilities against it. I repeat that there is only one world—this one—and it will welcome the Arabs, whenever they are ready to join it.

And so it is heartening, at last, to hear universally inclusive humanitarian sentiments echoed by Amre Moussa, secretary-general of the League of Arab States, whom I quoted in chapter 12. Recall, he said, "I would like to affirm that we are all in the same boat: East and West, North and South, Muslims, Christians and all others."[21] Beyond this, it is even more uplifting to hear Moussa reiterate Crown Prince Abdullah's peace proposal from the Beirut Summit of 2002, in which numerous Arab leaders indicted their readiness to normalize diplomatic relations with Israel, if at the same time a Palestinian state can be formally established. While this is more easily said than done, at least it is now being said. This is what the Middle East has needed since 1947: a comprehensive agreement that both recognizes Israel and establishes a neighboring Palestinian state. Secretary General Moussa's declaration that "security has to be guaranteed for Israel and Arab counties as well"[22] is a welcome change: a far cry from the invective of predecessors like Azzam Pasha, who in 1947 called for the extermination of the Jewish state.

The sooner they open their minds to the ABCs, the sooner the Arabs of the Middle East and elsewhere will begin to partake more fully of the blessings of this world, including its ferrying frogs. But there are no free figs, just as there are no free lunches. Abundant harvests of fruits come only to those who plant and tend the trees. Among many messages that the ABCs could send to the "Arab world," I have chosen three that need to be delivered most urgently.

First, from Aristotle: "It is ridiculous to lay the blame of our wrong actions upon external causes, rather than on the facility with which we ourselves are caught by such causes." In other words, it is ridiculous if not sublime for the "Arab world" to continue to blame the Jews and Israel, America and the West, for its own debilitating hatreds, self-inflicted backwardness, and delusional versions of reality. Aristotle would say that the "Arab world" is caught in a trap of its own fabrication, from which no one else can extricate it except itself. He would observe that the "Arab world" will not make progress as long as it remains destitute of science and arts, and enslaved by political despotism and religious fanaticism alike. The greatness of the Arab peoples will be unchained and unleashed, to everyone's benefit and to no one's detriment, once they allow themselves the luxury of emancipation from their self-imposed cultural confinements.

Second, Buddha would surely bemoan the needless suffering of the "Arab world," which in generation after generation arises from adherence to harsh and hateful doctrines concerning selfhood and society, and by deluded cravings for the destruction of others as a supposed means to self-realization. To the extent that the "Arab world" is afflicted with ill will, and has sought to escape the necessity of love and compassion, it is miserable indeed. As Buddha said: "Through hatred, hatreds are never appeased; through non-hatred are hatreds always appeased—and this is a law eternal." This message sounds very close to one preached by a man named Jesus, some six hundred years later in the Middle East. And that's the other extreme for you: This region has produced so much hatred that it had to be capable of producing that much love—and so it did. In fact, the deepest and noblest spiritual traditions of all the Abrahamic faiths—Judaism, Christianity, and Islam alike—cultivate human capacities for universal love, compassion and goodwill that are indistinguishable from the benevolence of Buddhism. When imbued with the radiant love of their Gods, adherents of all Abrahamic faiths can illustrate the greatness of spirit that sprang and still flows from this region of Abrahamic extremes. Perhaps Buddhism can help emancipate them, from their entrenched divisiveness and toward their unmanifested munificence.

Third, Confucius cautions: "Pleasure not carried to the point of debauch; grief not carried to the point of self-injury." This alludes to the Book of Songs, and is Confucius's injunction that lovers should neither overindulge nor self-destruct. Yet it applies just as well to the "Arab world." At one extreme, too many Arab dictators, ayatollahs and oil sheiks indulge in debauchery of every conceivable kind: from excesses of the flesh that make Las Vegas look like Sunday school, to excesses of power that culminate in orgies of oppression. At the other extreme, too much of the "Arab world" is afflicted with sublime grievances, not only to the point of self-injury through cognitive and socio-economic paralysis, but well beyond the point of self-injury, to suicidal terrorism.

## A Fig-free Diet

Clearly, one of the greatest challenges confronting humanity in the twenty-first century is to convey The Middle Way to the Middle East. In particular, in the wake of 9/11 and its wide-ranging aftermath, solving the problem of terrorism is central to resolving Middle Eastern extremes. But just as with alcoholism or any physical malady, along with terrorism or any cultural malaise, acknowledging the problem is always the first step toward recovery. And so, as Arab leaders veer toward the brink of saying what must be said and doing what must be done to resolve the conflicts they initiated in 1947, they are still in danger of succumbing to free figs. Amre Moussa himself, for all his visionary statesmanship, balks on this crucial issue. Aware that Islamist terrorist groups are responsible for a part—but not for the whole—of terrorist activity worldwide, he wonders "how and why this association between Islam and terrorism came to be," particularly in the Western mind. So let me take this opportunity to edify him.

As British empiricist David Hume explained so clearly, our ideas about the world are copied from our impressions of it.[23] Our impressions are none other than the sum of our perceptions of the world: what we see, hear, taste, touch, smell, and (later) remember. Hume's thesis informs our quotidian prudence of "making a good impression," and the importance of "first impressions" alike. Thus the associations we forge in our minds depend upon the impressions we form, and these impressions depend upon what we perceive in the world.

So *how* and *why*, Amre Moussa apparently wonders, do so many Westerners come to associate Islam with terrorism? Hume would say that we do so because of the impressions we have formed from the events we perceive, at first hand or via the media, and later remember. Here are a few examples from my perception and memory. In 1972, at the Munich Olympics, Israeli athletes were kidnapped and massacred by terrorists who happened to be Muslim. In 1976, an Air France flight was hijacked to Uganda, by terrorists who happened to be Muslim. An audacious and desperate Israeli commando operation rescued one hundred Jewish and Israeli civilians, who had been segregated and held hostage—while the non-Jewish passengers were freed—by terrorists who happened to be Muslim. In 1979, the United States embassy in Iran was stormed by terrorists who happened to be Muslim. During the 1980s, a number of Americans were kidnapped and murdered in Lebanon—including a President of the American University in Beirut— by terrorists who happened to be Muslim. In 1983, the United States Marine barracks in Beirut was blown up by terrorists who happened to be Muslim. In 1985, the cruise ship *Achille Lauro* was hijacked, and a seventy-year-old American passenger was murdered and thrown overboard in his wheelchair, by terrorists who happened to be Muslim. In 1985, TWA Flight 847 was hijacked at Athens, and a U.S. Navy diver trying to rescue passengers was murdered, by terrorists who happened to be Muslim. In 1988, Pan Am Flight 103 was bombed out of the skies over Lockerbie, Scotland, by terrorists who happened to be Muslim. In 1993, the World Trade Center was bombed, by terrorists who happened to be Muslim. In 1998, the U.S. embassies in Kenya and Tanzania were bombed, by terrorists who happened to be Muslim. On September 11, 2001, four airplanes were hijacked, the World Trade Center was destroyed, the Pentagon was attacked, the White House was targeted, and thousands of civilians were killed, by terrorists who happened to be Muslim. In 2002, the United States invaded Afghanistan to replace a rogue regime established by terrorists who happened to be Muslim. In 2002, reporter Daniel Pearl was kidnapped and murdered by terrorists who happened to be Muslim.

Subsequent to this, dozens more Western civilians have been kidnapped and murdered, some beheaded in front of video cameras, by terrorists who happened to be Muslim. Hundreds more civilians worldwide—from a Balinese nightclub to Madrid's Atocha train station, from the London Underground to Egyptian tourist hotels—have been murdered by terrorists who happened to be Muslim. And in the state of Israel, for whose security His Excellency Moussa kindly expresses concern, more than 1,000 civilians have been killed and more than 7,500 others were wounded during the second intifada alone, by terrorists who happened to be Muslim.[24] Every single day of the year, millions of air travelers pass through elaborate, expensive, time-consuming, and space-congesting security measures at airports all across Western civilization, as necessary precautions against terrorists, many of whom apparently happen to be Muslim.

Thus many Westerners have formed an association between Islam and terrorism. That link has been forged, not coincidentally, by terrorists who happen to be Muslim. However, as Hume took pains to explain, there is no necessary connection between the things we come to associate through our experience. So Hume would say, and rightly, that Muslims are not necessarily terrorists, and terrorists are not necessarily Muslims. At the same time, among all the diverse groups of terrorists operating in the global village, Islamist terrorists have made by far the strongest impression upon the Western mind. I was shelled by terrorists, during the 1960s, on an Israeli kibbutz near the Lebanese border. More recently, on 9/11, I watched the twin towers implode. That made a Humean impression, to be sure.

Let me say unequivocally that I grieve for all victims of terrorism, and for their bereaved loved ones. I also grieve for the image of Islam, which has been badly tarnished by terrorists who happen to be Muslim. When the overwhelming majority of the world's peace-loving Muslims speak out vociferously and act out persistently against terrorism, then the West's associations with Islam will no doubt change accordingly, and for the better.

Terrorism poses a serious threat to the well-being of the global village. It persistently and viciously attempts to scuttle that boat in which, as Amre Moussa says, we all sail together. Leaders in every civilization—Western, Islamic, Indian, East Asian, the lot—agree that terrorism is a problem. So does Amre Moussa. I hope by now he better appreciates *how* Islam and terrorism came to be associated in the Western mind.

In the next chapter we will take up his more difficult question: *why?* I will also pose an even tougher one: what, if anything, can we do about it? To that end, we now take up the topic of terrorism, and ask whether The Middle Way can temper such suicidal zealotry.

# 15

## TERRORIST EXTREMES
### Bombed If We Do, and Bombed If We Don't

*In Mesopotamia, a region of Syria, and at Istrus, they say that
there are certain little snakes, which do not bite the people of
the country, but do great injury to strangers.* —Aristotle

*The hatred of those who harbor such ill feelings as "He reviled me,
assaulted me, vanquished me and robbed me" is never appeased.*
—Buddha

*He who will not worry about what is far off will soon find
something worse than worry close at hand.* —Confucius

### A Terrible Dilemma

WHILE THERE IS WIDESPREAD consensus among civilized world leaders
that terrorism is a grievous problem,[1] there is little or no consensus—
and considerable disagreement—as to what should (or should not) be
done to contain it. In addition to preventive security precautions that
everyone is obliged to take, two extreme options also present
themselves, in response to terrorist attacks that cannot be prevented.
These options are two horns of a dilemma: appeasement and retaliation.
Neither seems to work very well, or for long. Israelis have tended to
retaliate against Islamist terrorism, yet Israeli civilians have suffered
from increasingly severe bouts of terrorist attacks. Europeans have
tended to appease Islamist terrorists and governments which sponsor
them, yet European civil strife involving Muslims is conspicuously on

the rise. Americans tried appeasement (during the Reagan and Clinton administrations), but the problem only worsened. Americans also tried retaliation (under both Presidents Bush), but the problem worsened further. So it looks like we'll get bombed if we do retaliate, and bombed if we don't. Is there a Middle Way? Yes there is, but it entails neither cowardly appeasement nor violent retaliation; rather, effective transformation of the conditions that spawn terrorism: through dialogue, education and emancipation.

## What is Terrorism?

Following much debate within the United Nations, and too much bloodshed in the global village, the U.N. has managed to condemn terrorism in very broad terms, without agreeing on how to define it. Kofi Annan suggests that "any action constitutes terrorism if it is intended to cause death or serious bodily harm to civilians or noncombatants with the purpose of intimidating a population or compelling a Government or an international organization to do or abstain from doing any act."[2] The U.S. Department of Defense defines terrorism as "the unlawful use of—or threatened use of—force or violence against individuals or property to coerce or intimidate governments or societies, often to achieve political, religious, or ideological objectives."[3] There are myriad definitions of terrorism, partly because terrorism itself assumes many forms. It is also clear that many preventive, preemptive, or retaliatory acts against terrorism attract accusations of fitting some definitions of terrorism themselves.

Like any crime, and like all crimes against humanity, terrorism can be contained but never completely eliminated. Every nation has its own domestic terrorists, psychopaths or sociopaths bent on the murder of innocents. But beyond this, and of graver concern to the peace, prosperity, and security of the global village, are the emergent networks of international terrorism, operating on every continent. While the most prominent global terrorists are currently Islamist, they exert no monopoly on this ubiquitous form of violent murder. To minimize terrorism, we must transform the political, religious, economic, and other cultural conditions that spawn it. Yet bringing about such widespread change presents us with dire difficulties. The "soft power" (i.e., beneficent values) of The Middle Way alone may not accomplish this task, for such values find little purchase in cultures hardened by extremism. Yet the exercise of "hard power" (e.g., militarism) also fails, for even though it may succeed in quarantining terrorism, it cannot by itself defeat the conditions that spawn terrorism. If out of cowardice we appease terrorists instead of standing up to them, we may embolden them and become their victims. But if out of boldness we attempt to eliminate them by targeted assassination, we run the risk of becoming terrorists ourselves, and of fueling everyone's appetite for violence and vengeance.[4] It looks like we're bombed if we do, and bombed if we don't.

From time out of mind, human wars and their aftermaths—famine, disease, looting—have typically wrought terrible consequences on noncombatants. Civilian populations have been plundered, slaughtered, or carried off into slavery, for reasons of custom, caprice, or revenge. Yet even so, there has often prevailed at least a tacit recognition of "civilians" per se, as distinguished from combatants. While civilians have found themselves in every circle of hell during the conduct and aftermath of wars, they were often protected by some defenders—a standing army, a sovereign government, at least a band of resisters—who had to be defeated before havoc could be wreaked among women, children, and other noncombatants. Until World War I, European noncombatants could pack picnic hampers and spread blankets on hilltops overlooking battlefields, and watch the carnage with impunity. Artillery put an end to that. If ants can spoil a picnic, imagine the effects of artillery shells.

Starting with Nazi Germany and Imperial Japan, the twentieth century witnessed the harnessing of the entire technological power and workforce of the state, consigned to "total war" on unprecedented scales, including aerial bombardment and wholesale enslavement of civilian populations. Among the first "guinea pigs" to have such horrors inflicted on them were the civilians of Guernica, during the Spanish Civil War, who were bombed by Franco's air force under the tutelage of the Nazis. Picasso painted a work (*Guernica*) commemorating this new horror. The blitz of London and the razing of Coventry by Hitler, followed later by Allied firestorms in Dresden,

Hamburg, and Tokyo, and ultimately by the atomic bombings of Hiroshima and Nagasaki, placed large, noncombatant, urban civilian populations in the front lines of combat. "Combat," in the cases of massive aerial bombardment or nuclear annihilation of civilians, is obviously one-sided in the extreme.

Such civilian populations typically had little or no chance to defend themselves (except, when forewarned, to seek refuge in bomb shelters), yet were viewed nonetheless as legitimate targets. Why? Because conditions of "total war" prevailed: That is, the human and material resources of entire nation-states were pitted against one another, under direct command and control of their governments. In this era of total war, which included the Cold War, every single citizen—man, woman, and child—become a combatant, in the very real sense of being a potential target of all-out militarism. Similarly, terrorism makes every civilian—man, woman, and child—a potential target of murderous violence, and only rarely do terrorists' intended victims have any chance to defend themselves or fight back.[5] Most civilian victims of terror attacks are defenseless, as are civilian victims of total war: They perish violently en masse, and without warning.

Yet there is one significant difference between total war and terrorism. Civilian populations caught up in total wars know definitively that they are at war, and against whom, and know moreover that they may become targets of militarism. However, terrorists prey on civilian populations whose governments are not necessarily—or not at all—at war against anyone. Beyond this, terrorists prey on civilians whose own governments sustain diplomatic relations, commerce, trade, and cultural exchange with governments that also spawn or sponsor terror. So civilian populations caught up in terrorist attacks do not necessarily (or do not at all) conceive themselves to be at war with anyone. On the contrary, civilian victims of terrorism may even be engaged in pacific and benevolent efforts to help peoples or nations that spawn or sponsor the terror itself. Thus, in addition to murdering civilians, terrorists offend against chivalry. That makes terrorism intolerable to many Americans among other Westerners, and at deep levels.

## Chivalry and Terrorism

Chivalry is a Western concept that attained its zenith in medieval courtly myths like Malory's *Morte d'Arthur* (the original legend of Camelot), but it is rooted anciently and deeply in the Western psyche. When the Spartan commander Archidamus first saw a dart hurled from a catapult, he mourned, "The valor of man is at an end." From David and Goliath to the Roman gladiators, from jousting in the lists to showdowns at high noon, ritual face-to-face and hand-to-hand combat between brave warriors has been the noblest and most ideal form of Western warfare. The Olympic Games themselves are the "moral equivalents" of chivalrous war. The martial arts of East Asia, along with the Bushido code of the samurai, have also captured this idea, albeit with a different underlying philosophy, as we shall see. Brave warriors from myriad human cultures refrain from hiding behind the weak or preying upon the defenseless. On the contrary, they are the protectors of the weak and the defenders of the defenseless, and are the first to fight and die to protect their hearths and homes. This defines chivalry.

From what we saw of primate social orders in chapter 8, it is clear that the protection of females and their young by dominant males is an evolutionarily ancient social strategy, evolved by many monkey and ape species, as well as by later human cultures. Thus the primate origins of chivalry are millions of years old. However, we have also seen that cultural evolution is capable of overriding ancient biological differences, for example in the liberation of women to pursue careers formerly regarded as exclusively "male." This applies no less to the questions of conventional armed combat and terrorism alike. Ever since World War II, women have fought bravely in resistance movements (e.g., in France and Yugoslavia) or in national defense forces (e.g., Israel). The Stratton Bill of 1976 integrated women into America's elite military academies (not without ongoing controversy and sex scandal). All this has reopened the heated debate, which had been closed from Plato's time until the twentieth century, on the role of women in combat. This chapter's concern is not that women are serving as conventional combatants, which poses one set of problems, but that women have also begun to "distinguish themselves" as terrorists too, which poses quite another.

The emergence of total war, Cold War, and terrorism in the twentieth-century warfare have conspired not only to eradicate the distinction between "combatant" and "noncombatant," but also to affront deeply ingrained conceptions of chivalry. Terrorism has killed fewer civilians than has total war, and threatens fewer civilians than does Cold War, but terrorizes entire populations nonetheless. Terrorists turn everyone—men, women, and children—into potential victims of sudden, violent and lethal international crime. Every act of terrorism is a crime against humanity, and must be condemned in no uncertain terms.

### Precursors of Terrorism: Guerilla and Kamikaze Warfare

Twentieth-century Arab warfare against the West presents a study in extremes: the ineffectiveness of their armies and the overeffectiveness of their terrorists. Arab armies have in general been swiftly put to rout in the face of concerted Western-style confrontation. This pattern has repeated itself since the battle of Poitiers in 732, through to the Second Gulf War of 2003, when the Americans routed Saddam's vaunted Republican Guard in a matter of days. Indeed, this is exactly how Israel has consistently defended herself against numerically overwhelming Arab forces—by characteristically Western organization, discipline, defense, preemption, and counterattack. But the Arabs have demonstrated beyond a doubt that they are death-defying and suicidal warriors when it comes to individual acts of terrorism.

If we step back and gain perspective, we can understand this phenomenon as part of a much bigger picture, which partially explains why the empires of Western civilization gradually conquered and colonized the rest of the world, and have not yet been successfully invaded or colonized by the rest of the world. The same pattern repeats itself again and again, all over the planet. Relatively small but well-equipped, highly disciplined, and superbly motivated Western armies have defeated numerically overwhelming opponents, who often fought with courage and valor, but who were sometimes badly equipped and often ill disciplined or poorly motivated. Among legion examples, this was true of the Greeks and the Macedonians against the Persians, the Romans against the Carthaginians and the Gauls, the Franks against the

Moors, the Spanish against the Aztecs, the British against the Zulu, the Americans against the Sioux, and the Israelis against the Arabs.

A horrific corollary of this phenomenon is the massive slaughter that ensues when sizable Western armies themselves clash in the field. The battles of the Napoleonic wars, the American Civil War, World War I, World War II, and the Korean War provide catalogues of ever-increasing carnage, resulting from the massive shock-collision of two or more equally well-equipped, well-disciplined, and highly motivated armies. Indeed, the immense difficulties America faced in defeating Imperial Japan and, soon after that, North Korea, stemmed largely from the adoption of Western-style militarism and warfare by the Japanese, and later by the Chinese and the Koreans.

Victor Davis Hanson fleshes out a deep philosophical point that has pervaded military history in his bestseller *Carnage and Culture* (in the United Kingdom, *Why the West Has Won*).[6] Part of the superior motivation of Western forces has always resided in the measure of individual liberty that each man enjoyed, and was fighting to preserve. This invariably contrasted with the conspicuous lack of liberty, or condition of outright slavery, that prevailed (and still prevails) among masses ruled or owned by despots. Slaves have much less incentive to fight than do free men. A slave gains little by victory, and forfeits little by defeat. A free man preserves much by victory, and loses much by defeat. This Western notion of individual liberty goes back to the Greeks and their unprecedented experiments with democracy. Aristotle sums it up as well as any philosopher, and better than most: "A man should be free to live as he pleases."[7] This Aristotelian notion is quintessentially Western. Neither Islamic nor Indian nor East Asian civilizations have ever ensconced such a premise in their political foundations. Historically, it is a source of the West's uniqueness, and of its ability to prevail in conventional conflicts against opponents who boasted numerical superiority but lacked the personal incentives of politically emancipated men—and these days, women.

## What Is a Terrorist?

One way to counter overpowering armies is by refusing to meet them head-on; by weakening their morale, disrupting their logistics and eroding their power instead, through the practice of guerrilla warfare. Sun Tzu revealed this in his classic *The Art of War*, which (along with Marcus Aurelius's *Meditations*) is late-night reading for many a philosophically inclined political leader or CEO. In legend, this is how Robin Hood foiled the sheriff of Nottingham. In reality, it is how American militiamen and Dutch Boers disrupted the British redcoats; how the French Resistance and the Greek partisans harassed the Nazis; how Fidel Castro undermined the Batista government; how the Viet Cong demoralized the Americans; how the Afghani mujahideen thwarted the Soviets. To greater or lesser extents, all these guerrilla warriors were successful, either defeating or helping to defeat incomparably larger and better-equipped forces, by refusing to meet them head on.

With gross exceptions such as the Viet Cong (VC), who inflicted widespread premeditated atrocities on South Vietnamese civilians to dissuade them from cooperating with the Americans, guerrilla fighters have traditionally and primarily attacked military targets and military personnel only. This has allowed guerrillas around the world to enjoy folkloric stature as popular heroes. To this day, Che Guevara remains an icon of that image. But when guerrillas cross this critical threshold, and start attacking civilians, they become terrorists. So the VC fought as guerrillas against the Americans, but as terrorists against Vietnamese civilians.

Combatants not wearing uniforms are not necessarily terrorists either. Wearing civilian clothing allows a combatant to be camouflaged among the local civilian populace, which facilitates attacking military targets or personnel. This is precisely the problem that uniformed law enforcement officers face: Their uniforms, badges, and insignias make them conspicuous targets of opportunity for would-be cop killers—who themselves may be indistinguishable from the general civilian populace until too late. So nonuniformed combatants are justly regarded, by their uniformed opponents, as criminals, spies, or guerrillas, and are liable to be summarily shot if captured in war, even by signatories of the Geneva Convention, which guarantees humane treatment only to uniformed prisoners of war. So, guerrillas are either freedom fighters or criminals, depending which side you're on. But as long as guerrillas are attacking military targets or personnel, they're not terrorists.

Similarly, the Japanese kamikaze pilots were by definition suicidal warriors: They were terrifying, but not terrorists. Why? Because they attacked only military targets and personnel; specifically, U.S. warships in the Pacific. After the battles of Midway and the Coral Sea, Japan lost its naval supremacy, and the United States began to recapture—at great loss of life to both sides—Pacific islands held by the Japanese military. The Japanese high command deemed it only a matter of time before the Home Islands themselves were invaded by the United States, so they tried to deter the Americans with a last-ditch form of psychological warfare: suicide pilots, crashing planeloads of high explosives into warships. This was extreme warfare, but not terrorism. Not only did the kamikazes attack only military targets, but most of the warships had a chance to shoot the planes down before being struck by them. "You get them or they get you" was the challenge of combating kamikazes. But at least you saw them coming.

This contrasts sharply with suicide bombers. Unlike the military targets of kamikazes, the civilian targets of suicide bombers have little or no chance to defend themselves. When suicide bombers guide vehicles laden with explosives into military barracks or bases—as they did against a U.S. Marine base in Lebanon in 1982, killing 250; or against the warship Cole in Yemen in 1999, killing 17—then their behavior is analogous to kamikazes. If you're vigilant, you can see them coming. But when suicide bombers hijack and crash civilian airplanes, or blow up public buses and trains, or detonate high explosives in public restaurants, cafes, or nightclubs, killing civilian men, women, and children who have no chance to defend themselves, as they have done all over the world, they perpetrate despicable acts of terrorism in the eyes of the defenders of Western civilization. These are not acts of war, but rather, crimes against humanity.

Not one of the 100,000 Japanese Americans interned in the United States for the duration of World War II, following Imperial Japan's attack on Pearl Harbor, ever perpetrated an act of terror against civilian Americans on U.S. soil. Nonetheless, because martial law trumps civil law in every polity at war, Japanese Americans were temporarily stripped of their civil rights and incarcerated. Yet they were not physically harmed: They were interned, but provided for. By contrast, Imperial Japanese militarists treated captive civilian populations—in Korea, Manchuria, Indonesia, Malaysia—as subhuman slaves. Moreover, because of the extreme version of Bushido (warrior code) ingrained in the Japanese military, according to which surrender was dishonorable, Japan was not a signatory of the Geneva Convention. As a result, captured Allied troops were also treated as subhuman slaves, without a shred of humanity or compassion. They were beaten, starved, tortured, or murdered on a whim. The survivors of the Bataan march, and similar crimes against humanity, reminiscent of the Nazis, never forgot the cruelty and sadism of the Japanese militarists.

And because Bushido forbade surrender, Japanese troops fought to the death on every Pacific Island they held—Iwo Jima, Okinawa, Saipan, the lot. American strategists estimated that if the United States had to invade and occupy the Japanese Home Islands in order to bring the war to a conclusion, and if they met with similar suicidal resistance, they would incur about 2.5 million casualties. This was an unacceptably high number, which contributed strongly to Truman's decision to drop atomic bombs on Hiroshima and Nagasaki. The Americans reasoned on a utilitarian basis. What was preferable? Two and a half million U.S. troops wounded and dead, along with several million more Japanese wounded and dead, civilians and military both, as a result of a conventional invasion; or no U.S. casualties, and a hundred thousand Japanese wounded or dead, as a result of dropping one or two unconventional bombs? This is the raw calculus of war, indifferent though it is to the suffering and death of its victims. Only the Japanese can tell us what it feels like to be on the receiving end of a nuclear weapon, a horror and a sorrow that they as a people bear in unimaginable solitude.

Japan remains the first and only nation ever to be bombed with nuclear weapons, and let us hope the last. Theirs is a tragic and horrific distinction. Nonetheless, it must be fairly said that the Japanese Imperialists did their part to "earn" this distinction, because of their extreme militarism that entailed suicidal defenses of Pacific islands, kamikaze attacks on U.S. vessels, and criminal atrocities against civilian populations and POWs alike. Imperial Japan's extreme brand of aggressive warfare brought extreme consequences home to the Japanese people. Led by wolves, they met with slaughter. Yet to this day, many Japanese still have difficulty admitting their former regime's culpability in colonizing and brutalizing Asia.

I am mentioning the Japanese for a very important reason. They were bombed with nuclear weapons, and obliged to surrender unconditionally, primarily because they would not cease and desist from all-out suicidal warfare. Many Americans view 9/11 as analogous to Pearl Harbor. Both were unprovoked attacks on American soil, by belligerent powers hostile to the freedom, reason, and democratic political process that characterize Western civilization, more or less. Americans are rightly concerned that if Islamist extremists ever took possession of nuclear weapons, or of enough radioactive material to fabricate "dirty bombs," they would use these weapons against American civilian populations. Whereas America's response to 9/11 was swift "regime change" in Afghanistan and Iraq, with similar threats and incentives to Pakistan, Iran, Syria, and other state sponsors of Islamist terrorism who refuse to cooperate in bringing terrorists to justice. Some have wondered: What would America's response to nuclear terrorism be? I hope we never have to answer that. I know some Americans who would favor swift and massive nuclear retaliation against urban populations of terror-friendly governments. I also believe that a credible threat of nuclear retaliation will not deter Islamist terrorists, as it did the former Soviet Union. In the Middle East, deterrence theory might be just one more ferrying frog, to be stung by the scorpion of suicidal zealotry.

Deterrence worked against the Soviets because they genuinely did not wish to see their nation destroyed. The same was true of Americans. Hence mutual assured destruction (MAD) kept everybody sane. That was the logic of the Cold War. I didn't like it, but—like everyone else—I was obliged to live it. It was strange, stranger than *Strangelove* and "Strange Brew," but it worked. I digress to express my dismay that Pakistan and India not only possess nuclear weapons, but both seem enthusiastic about coauthoring "the next chapter" in the book on nuclear deterrence. Pakistan, a non-Arab Muslim nation that harbors considerable hostility against both Indian and Western civilizations, and whose latest fad is burning Christian churches, is also a prime candidate for supplying Islamist terrorists with nuclear weapons or radioactive material.

But even if deterrence works for India and Pakistan, it might fail spectacularly in the Middle East. Osama bin Laden, for example, appears to court the destruction of his home country, Saudi Arabia. His masterminding of 9/11 was an intended blow to the ruling House of Saud, as much as an actual blow to America. As we have seen, the Middle East is a phenomenally complicated and convoluted region; so much so that Cold War deterrence theory may simply not apply there. Israel has possessed nuclear weapons for a long time, but has also been committed to deterrence: which means never being the first to use them. But Islamist terrorism might just be "indeterrable," in which case the sands might one day glow.

## Political Partition and Terrorism

At the end of the nineteenth century, in the last year of Queen Victoria's reign, the British Empire had reached its zenith. Within fifty years, it would all but vanish, leaving an invaluable cultural legacy—the British Commonwealth—but passing the torch of global dominance to America. The British showed a great fondness for partitioning their colonies, and their partitioning of Palestine was but one of several such divisive maneuvers that invariably gave rise to terrorism. As we saw in the previous chapter, the inherent extremism of the Middle East resulted in Palestine being partitioned twice—with the "Arab world" accepting the 1922 partition that created Cisjordan and Transjordan, but rejecting the 1947 repartition of cisjordan, which recreated Israel and Palestine. In all the other British adventures with map making, one partition was sufficient to entrench divisiveness and mutual isolation between cultures, ideal breeding grounds for opportunistic terrorists. Palestine needed an extra partitioning to turn this trick, but the British were certainly up to it.

The British had long since partitioned Canada into anglophone Upper Canada (Ontario) and francophone Lower Canada (Quebec)— and the FLQ terrorists emerged in the 1960s and 1970s. The Front de

Liberation du Quebec planted bombs in royal mailboxes in the well-heeled WASP municipality of Westmount. In 1970, the FLQ kidnapped British High Trade Commissioner James Cross, and Quebec Education Minister Pierre Laporte. Cross was later released, but Laporte was murdered by his abductors.[8] He left a widow and children. His "crime"? He served the people of Quebec as a minister duly appointed by its democratically elected government, in accordance with federal and provincial rules of law.

In 1976, when folk hero and journalist Rene Levesque was elected premier of Quebec on a Separatist Party platform, Quebecers began to realize many of their most cherished cultural and political ambitions, which gave them civic parity with English Canada. Terrorism did not further that political process; it impeded and imperiled it. The FLQ did not liberate Quebec: Quebecers liberated themselves by learning to utilize and participate in a constitutionally democratic political process that the British—in their wisdom—had left in place. A rule of law, not of terror. The British folly was the folly of all imperialists: not bothering to understand the cultures of the peoples they think they have conquered until it is too late. But that neither exculpates nor exonerates terrorists.

The British and the Irish have a centuries-long history of conflict. The British partitioned Ireland—Northern (Protestant) and Southern (Catholic)—and "the troubles" of the 1920s saw the emergence of the IRA. Their spate of violence, which lasted decades, left a trail of cruelly murdered people—most of them civilians. The catalogue of vendetta-driven atrocities in cities like Belfast, where men, women, and children were bombed by Protestants or Catholics for being Catholics or Protestants, is a tragic reminder that Christianity is not far removed from, and may never become immune to, its Abrahamic inheritance of wrathful violence. "Vengeance is mine," said their Lord, while Jesus said "Turn the other cheek." But scripture cannot check terror. The IRA used to plant bombs in Harrods around Christmas time, to transmute the shoppers' acts of love, in choosing gifts for loved ones, into heinous acts of carnage.

Such acts of terrorism were not the alchemical transmutations of the soul that Aristotle and Newton sought in the fabled "Philosopher's stone"; they were political statements made by violent means using the most innocent and cherished victims—women and children shopping for Christmas—as "political fodder" in their campaign to make terror sovereign over law. The so-called "political arm" of the Irish Republican Army, namely Sinn Fein, could have advanced its cause more rapidly and smoothly without the terrorist violence.

The British partitioned India in 1947, dividing it into Hindu India and Muslim Pakistan, later dividing Pakistan into East and West dominions, separated by the subcontinent herself. It was Gandhi who, by practicing Satyagraha, a militantly nonviolent hybrid of Thoreau's civil disobedience and the Bramacharya's spiritual purification, drove the British out of India by mobilizing an army of teachers, armed only with moral truths, who gradually but also aggressively educated the British into realizing that India was ripe for release into her own political custody. Nonetheless, looming clashes among Hindus, Muslims, and Sikhs, with centuries-old grievances and tribal enmities always simmering in regional pots, encouraged the British to try partition as a way of avoiding civil war or anarchy.

Whether British partition inhibited or exacerbated India's indigenous anarchy, it did produce dislocations of ten million people—Hindu, Muslim and Sikh refugees, fleeing communal massacres of one by the other, with the Sikhs caught in the middle, but sadly not in The Middle Way. Two million people died in that British partition of India and midwifery to the birth of Pakistan, and mostly civilians. In the past, Gandhi's fasting unto death and spiritual force had prevented exactly this scale of violence from erupting in the rich but volcanic matrix of subcultures that populate the subcontinent. But neither King Canute nor Gandhi could arrest the tides. In this case, Gandhi had himself unleashed the tide of partition in the wake of British departure.

Then, in 1947, the British repartitioned Palestine. That helped restore Israel, but also helped inflame a region renowned for its acute and chronic political inflammations, going back millennia, all the way back to Genesis, and to Abraham himself. The Jews and the Arabs are Semites and cousins, tribes of close and ancient relation. They know how to get along, and they know how to quarrel. They are proud and stiff-necked peoples of long memory and ancient lineage, and they are living descendants of the original peoples of Genesis, the survivors of epic Biblical clashes, in which a wrathful deity smites infidel foes. This was clearly no ordinary place to partition.

The PLO, led by Yasser Arafat, and its subsequent and increasingly violent spin-offs throughout the "Arab world"—Hezbollah, Hamas, al-Aqsa, al-Qaeda—are by far the most virulent form of terrorism ever spawned by a British partition. Arab terrorists pioneered the hijacking of European civilian airplanes, the massacring of civilian travelers in European airports, the kidnapping and murder of Israeli athletes at the Munich Olympic Games, along with a catalogue of suicidally murderous horrors inflicted on Israeli civilians.

Europeans appeased the PLO in exchange for being terrorized, and for a variety of reasons. To fight the Cold War and to prosper economically, they needed Arabian oil. The Europeans all had (and have) growing Arab and Muslim populations at home, whom they were—and are—increasingly afraid to antagonize by condemning Arab and Islamist terrorism. Then again, many Arab leaders were and are themselves potential targets of terror, and walk a tightrope between placating and restraining their own fanatical terrorist factions at home. Among those who fell off the rope, King Abdullah of Jordan was assassinated for trying to make peace with Israel; while Anwar Sadat of Egypt was assassinated for making that peace. Just east of Arabia, the staunchly pro-Western Shah of Iran was deposed by the rabidly anti-Western Ayatollah Khomeini. And Yitzhak Rabin of Israel, another peacemaker, was assassinated by a militant Jew. Rafiq Hariri, rebuilder of a Lebanon shattered by more than a dozen rival factions, and occupied by Syria for twenty-nine years, was assassinated by Islamist fanatics or their Syrian supporters. For every frog who ferries peace across the region, legions of suicidal scorpions await their chance to sting.

Have there been Jewish terrorists too? Yes. The Irgun and the Stern Gang were the two most notorious. They operated during the expiration of the British mandate and the run-up to partition. Since they attacked primarily British military targets, they might be classified as guerrillas rather than terrorists, but their strategy and tactics were those of terrorists. In 1946, the Irgun blew up the King David Hotel in Jerusalem, which had been appropriated by the British High Command. Ninety-one people died: British officers, Jews and Arabs alike. This and other heinous acts of Jewish terrorism were denounced by David ben Gurion and Israel's provisional government, and their strong stance against terrorism gained allies abroad for Israel's legitimate government.

Although terrorism emerged as a political by-product of British partition, in Canada, Ireland, India, Palestine, and other former British colonial possessions, it has also emerged in many other places, and independent of British rule. The Spanish people are painfully aware of ETA, the Basque terrorist group. The Peruvian people are painfully aware of the Shining Path, a Maoist terrorist group founded by a neo-Marxist professor, Abimael Guzman, which claimed thirty thousand victims during its reign of terror. The Colombian people are painfully aware of terrorists from both the political left ("guerrillas") and the political right ("paramilitaries"), both of whom engage in kidnapping, extortion, assassination, and narco-trafficking. The Sri Lankan people are painfully aware of the Tamil Tigers, a "liberation" group of guerrilla fighters that also use terrorist tactics in their armed insurrection against Sri Lankan rule of law. The German people were terrorized by the Bader-Meinhof gang in the 1960s and 1970s; the Italians by the Red Brigades in the 1970s and 1980s. These "urban terrorist" copycat groups featured narco-trafficking, kidnapping, and murder of civilians. Americans remember the SLA, or Symbionese Liberation Army, which kidnapped and brainwashed heiress Patty Hearst, who helped them rob a bank at gunpoint.

Finally, advocates of feminism and critics of "male violence" should also take note: As we saw in chapter 9, during the height of European urban terrorism, more than half of Europe's "most wanted" terrorists— fourteen of twenty-two—were females. Margaret Mead had warned of the dangers of awakening the demonic powers of women by separating them from their natural place at hearth and home. Extremes of women's liberation in the West, and neo-Marxist egalitarianism in Asia, produced a generation of female terrorists who were more "wanted" in Europe and more feared in Vietnam than their male counterparts. It was Mao's wife who instigated the Cultural Revolution, in which between forty and seventy million Chinese intelligentsia and others were murdered, by a terrorist apparatus that held the reins of government itself.

And this is the final goal of most terrorists: to win political power, so that their slaughter can begin in earnest. The political aspirations of terrorists are not to liberate human beings, but to enslave and destroy them. Terrorism does not engender human flourishing, compassion, or appreciation of the value of life; rather, it promotes dehumanization and destruction, vengeance, hatred, depreciation of life, and veneration of death. The worst political excesses in human history are inextricably linked to the terrorization of civilian populations by their own rulers, wherever and whenever the subjective rule of cruel men (or women) overpowers the objective rule of just law. Adolf Hitler, Joseph Stalin, Fidel Castro, Idi Amin, Pol Pot, Slobodan Milosevic, Saddam Hussein—among a pantheon of twentieth-century gangsters and mass murderers—held their own populations in check by reigns of terror, instituted and unleashed through reins of government itself.

## The Value of Life

Aggressive suicidal warfare—whether emanating from Asia or the Middle East—is essentially intolerable to defenders of Western civilization. The last children of the West to die in suicidal warfare were the products of Adolf Hitler's insatiable mania for death and destruction—the remnants of Hitler Youth, defending a ruined Berlin against the savage Red Army. But at the turn of the twenty-first century, young children across the Muslim world are being taught to revere what Palestinian terrorists have condoned: Turning their own children into human bombs, for the purpose of killing and maiming Israeli men, women, and children.

So I ask you to ponder one significant difference between cultures that have produced aggressive suicidal warfare in its most extreme forms—such as Japanese militarism and Islamist terrorism—and cultures that are willing to fight back in defense of their fundamental freedoms. The difference is that one kind of culture values death; the other, life. Suicidal terrorists place no value on their lives, other than on sacrificing themselves in order to kill more people. By contrast, defenders of Western civilization value their lives, and the lives of their citizens, very greatly. In Imperial Japan, all lives by definition and from birth belonged to the emperor, to do with as he saw fit. In the majority of Islamic cultures worldwide, there is little if any separation of mosque and state, so all lives similarly belong to Allah, and suicidal terrorists are Allah's "martyrs." By contrast, most Western nations are governed according to secular constitutions which underwrite a fundamental "right to life" of all citizens.

Most Western nations (the majority of U.S. states excluded at this writing) have also abolished the death penalty, even for the most heinous crimes. The EU makes this a condition of membership, and other Western democracies, from Canada to Israel to Australia, have similarly done away with capital punishment. Note too that most mass murderers in these countries, whether serial killers or domestic terrorists, are not usually suicidal themselves. Even if they don't value other people's lives, they still value their own. Timothy McVeigh was a domestic terrorist, born and bred in the United States. Waging a psychotic war against the U.S. government, he blew up the Federal Building in Oklahoma City in 1995, killing and maiming more than one hundred civil servants, and many of their small children in the building's day-care center. Yet McVeigh didn't kill himself. He had to be apprehended, tried, and convicted by the justice system. The same is true of American serial killers—they are rarely suicidal. Even the worst domestic criminals of free Western civilization valued their own lives: Charles Manson and his cult, Richard Speck, Ted Bundy, Son of Sam, Jeffrey Dahmer, none of these ghastly murderers was suicidal. The exceptions who commit suicide are invariably either religious zealots—such as the Jonestown cult and the Hale-Bopp comet cult—or disturbed teenagers—such as Eric Harris and Dylan Klebold at Columbine.

This stands in stark contrast to suicidal warriors and terrorists reared in cultures based on slavery, not freedom, cultures in which the rulers are proprietors, and not protectors, of their own citizens' lives. As long as Western civilization values freedom and life, it will be targeted by those who value enslavement and death. Even stanch Buddhist pacifists, such as Daisaku Ikeda, recognize that terrorists are criminals who must be brought to justice. As he said after 9/11, "Terrorism, which so cruelly robs people of life, can never be excused or justified by any reason or cause . . . it is vitally important that all efforts be made to identify responsibility for this heinous act and bring those involved to justice."[9] But when such criminals enjoy the provision and protection of sovereign governments, they cannot be apprehended unless the governments that protect them can be convinced, or compelled, to surrender them.

There is no better evidence for the distinction between life-valuing and life-devaluing cultures than the "gradient of defection" that one observes in the aftermaths of violent conflicts. For example, in the last days of the Third Reich, Nazis and Wermacht (regular army) troops surrendered en masse to American, British, and Canadian forces in the West. Very few indeed surrendered to the Soviets in the East. Why? Because the West treated German POWs humanely, even when some of these POWS were themselves callous mass murderers. The totalitarian Soviets, who sentenced liberated Russian POWs to the gulag for "collaboration with the enemy," took brutal revenge on German POWs—for the Nazis had treated Slavs as slaves, and worse.

Similarly, during the Cold War, the gradients of defection were overwhelmingly from behind the Iron and Bamboo Curtains toward the free West, and almost never the other way around—with a few exceptions such as British double agent Kim Philby, who defected to the Soviet Union. Where did the Cubans try to flee to? Miami, not Moscow. Where did the Vietnamese boat people try to wash up? The free West, safe from the mass murderers who devastated and decimated Southeast Asia in the name of communism. How many Mexicans have crossed the U.S. border illegally, preferring to take their chances as stateless persons in the United States rather than remain citizens in Mexico? No one even knows how many: tens of millions at the very least. How many Americans have similarly fled to Mexico? Tourism and retirees aside, very few. Similarly, tens of millions of Muslims from the Middle East and North Africa have emigrated to the EU. How many citizens of the EU have emigrated to North Africa and the Middle East? Very few, and for the same good reasons. They prefer cultures that value life to cultures that devalue it. Cultures that value life also value liberty, opportunity, and hope. Cultures that value death also value enslavement, oppression, and despair.

## The Gradient of Liberty

During World War II, and deep within the interstices of militarized Imperial Japanese culture, two extraordinarily courageous and visionary men embarked on a path parallel to that of Gandhi in India, but with potentially greater repercussions on the global village. They were both humble educators, and Nichiren Buddhists. Their names were Tsunesaburo Makiguchi and Josei Toda. They were also the first two presidents of Soka Gakkai, which in English means "Society for Value Creation." Makiguchi and Toda were apparently the only two people in Japan who were fully mindful that the incumbent culture of aggressive suicidal warfare represented a destruction of value, beginning with the widespread destruction of life itself—the most precious phenomenon of all. These two men therefore defied the emperor, the military, and the culture by declaring themselves conscientious objectors to Japanese imperialism and militarism. I doubt that the concept of "conscientious objector" existed in the Japanese mind or language of that day. At any rate the two men were imprisoned, and Makiguchi later perished behind bars. After the war, Toda was freed, and he continued to nurture Soka Gakkai. Soon he attracted an able successor, President Daisaku Ikeda, under whose leadership Soka Gakkai International (SGI) is flourishing and creating value worldwide.

Whether Tibetan or Zen or Nichiren or of any other school, sincere Buddhists personally renounce and peacefully resist violence in every conceivable form. And where does the Buddhist gradient of migration flow? Once again, to the West. After Buddhism's long journeys and sojourn within Asia, it migrated from Japan to the United States and Europe in the forms of Zen and SGI—to the free West, where it could take root and flower. And where did the Dalai Lama go, after the communist Chinese occupied Tibet in 1951, exiled his government, and ruthlessly suppressed Tibetan culture? The Western democracies did not lift a finger to save Tibet, but they gave Tibetan exiles refuge. The Dalai Lama established a base in Dharamsala, India, the world's most populous democracy. The Tibetans quickly founded cultural centers in Britain and the United States, built universities and monasteries, translated and published their books, and generally made a gift of their culture to the West. Why? Because the West was free enough to receive it.

In towns and cities across the United States, Jews, Christians, Muslims, Hindus, Buddhists, atheists, agnostics, and their children—adherents of all religions and of none—are free to worship any God or none, free to read any book or none, free to revere any prophet or none. They are largely tolerant of one another's different beliefs, and cognizant of one another's humanity. Scenes like this are possible in many places, but not in all. What makes them possible? Secular political authority, productive economy, civil liberty, and tolerant education.

## Total War and Technological Hygiene

This question has been asked repeatedly: How can Western nations like the United States justify aerial bombardments that kill innocent civilians, and at the same time deplore terrorist beheadings of kidnapped civilians from the West? Isn't that inconsistent? It certainly appears so. From a Buddhist perspective in particular, it is always wrong to kill. So let us probe the origins of this inconsistency. Its main sources are total war and technological hygiene, with ever-present vestiges of chivalry.

As we have seen in passing, the twentieth century was the first century of total war, with the entire resources of nations consecrated to war effort. During the mechanized slaughter of World War I, when young men of military age were being massacred by machine guns and artillery, women worked in the factories to supply them with arms and other materials. As we saw in chapter 9, women did "men's work" en masse, for the first time. Yet these women and other civilian workers, so essential to the war effort, were still not regarded as combatants. Even the men in the opposing trenches at the front lines, living and dying courageously in conditions of unimaginable horror, retained enough vestiges of chivalry to exchange gifts and sing carols to one another across no-man's-land during Christmas truces, in the first years of that "war to end all wars." However, once the Germans violated standing conventions and started using mustard gas, the gifts and carols stopped. The warfare could not have become more brutal, but it did become less forgiving.

Even so, POWs were generally well treated. Pilots shot down behind enemy lines were especially well treated, even if captured by men they had been bombing or strafing moments earlier. Pilots were officers, and chivalry demanded that they be accorded respect. Chivalry is a theme that courses through Western civilization, and is the West's equivalent of Bushido—ethics for warriors. Chivalry prescribes valiant effort in combat, but also distinguishes between combatants and noncombatants, and allows for humane treatment of captured or vanquished combatants. Chivalry once dictated the rules of engagement for medieval knights, but its core precepts were still enshrined in twentieth-century codes of ethical warfare, most famously the Hague and Geneva Conventions.

One way of telling the "good guys" from the "bad guys" in any game, including warfare, is to see who obeys the rules of engagement and who breaks them. The Germans were regarded as rule breakers, since they had violated Belgian neutrality and used banned chemicals (e.g., phosgene and other gases) as weapons. These may seem trifling charges in the contexts of later wars, but such violations of standing conventions struck deep moral chords among the Allies at the time. And while the governments of the day would have continued to slaughter each other's conscript armies indefinitely, annihilating the young men of each other's nations according to their rules of engagement, few if any World War I generals would ever have conceived of harming one hair on the head of any civilian noncombatant—man, woman, or child alike.

The rules changed in World War II, but even then chivalry did not die— it just contrasted more starkly than ever with total war. As mentioned earlier, the Nazis helped Franco to bomb the Basque town of Guernica in 1937. About 1,600 civilian noncombatants perished in a three-hour bombardment by high explosives and incendiaries. That was a turning point in modern warfare, not only in terms of establishing the importance of air superiority, but also in setting the precedent of treating unarmed, urban, civilian populations as front-line combatants. Hitler soon adopted this practice during the razing of Coventry and the blitz of London. Not only Luftwaffe bombs, but also V1 (and later V2) rockets with explosive warheads rained death upon the noncombatant citizens of London. There is little doubt that, once the tide of World War II finally turned, the Allied firestorms that consumed Dresden, Hamburg, and Tokyo—killing more people than the atomic bombs—were acts of reprisal for the cruel and inhumane treatment of civilian populations and POWs, by the Nazis in Europe and the Imperial Japanese in Asia. The Western Allies still practiced some forms of chivalry, including humane treatment of POWs—which again is why so many Nazi war criminals surrendered to the West rather than to the Soviets—but civilian populations were no longer exempt from being treated like front-line troops. This was not because chivalry had waned, but because technological hygiene had waxed.

To appreciate how technological hygiene works, ask your small children where hamburgers come from. In their experience, hamburger is a raw red foodstuff that comes from the supermarket, neatly wrapped in cellophane on Styrofoam trays, or comes cooked and boxed in a fast-food outlet. Young urban children have no idea how beef cattle are intensively farmed, drugged, fatted, transported, slaughtered, butchered, packaged, and presented for public consumption. All the overcrowding, force-feeding, suffering, and pain, plus the death, blood, guts, and gore of the abattoir—all the unbelievably cruel treatment of these animals by the meat industry, culminating in their engineered slaughter and butchery—is completely concealed from the end users (the consumers) by technological hygiene. All they see is the end product: a tidy little package of hamburger. It is almost impossible for children, and adults alike, to follow the trail of that package, back to its origins as a cow. Technological hygiene obliterates the trail, and so the beef is never understood to be the end product of a process of engineered slaughter of sentient beings.

When the Nazis did exactly this to Jews, Gypsies, and others, they were regarded as having perpetrated the greatest crimes against humanity in the blood-soaked annals of history. Yet the stationmasters who made the death trains run on time to Auschwitz, like all the bureaucrats of that engineered slaughter of humans, were also blinded by technological hygiene. Making a train run on time becomes dissociated from the act of killing, even when it's a vital link in a chain of engineered mass murder. Whether the sentient beings aboard the transports are humans or cattle, technological hygiene puts space and time between the accomplices to mass murder and the actual murderers, so that the accomplices don't feel like accomplices at all. Heinrich Himmler, who was in charge of the Nazis' so-called "final solution" (the extermination of the Jews), could not bear to witness a single execution, let alone pull a trigger himself. Yet technological hygiene permitted him to orchestrate the mass slaughter of millions of human beings.

Similarly, technological hygiene facilitates the bombing of civilian populations. The men in the bombers have wives and children at home, and most bomber crews would never harm a hair on the heads of the women and children they obliterate from far above, if only they encountered these women and children in person, on the street. But technological hygiene transforms murdering defenseless civilians into completing a mission, or hitting a target, or obeying orders, thus allowing bomber crews to dissociate themselves from the act of taking human lives, just as it allows women and children buying hamburger in supermarkets to think of themselves as "shopping for supper," and similarly to dissociate themselves from the act of taking bovine lives.

Appreciating and respecting the value of *all* sentient life lies near the core of Buddhist philosophy. Appreciating and respecting the value of human life, at least under certain conditions, lies near the core of chivalry and Western civilization. This is why Buddhists have sought and found refuge in the West, but not yet in the Middle East.

Valuing life means respecting life. Among other things, valuing life means valuing human beings for being human, and not devaluing them because of their religious beliefs or cultural origins. And this is also why Westerners are appalled when Islamist extremists behead kidnapped civilians in front of video cameras. War is hell, killing is wrong, and violence begets violence; this we know from time out of mind. And while the armed forces of Western civilization are deadly in face-to-face combat, they—unlike terrorists—recognize the value of the lives of noncombatants, prisoners of war, and other civilians. Terrorism is an unacceptable behavior not only in the West, but increasingly in the global village.

Let me be clear: There is no moral superiority in violently destroying human life, however it is done. Bombing people via technological hygiene is not morally superior to beheading them in front of video cameras. However, it is morally superior to value human life rather than to devalue it. Knights who practice Arthurian chivalry—like gentlemen who practice Confucian arts—align themselves neither with persons nor tribes nor ideologies, but only with Right. Knights and gentlemen lay down their own lives for the sake of Right, in contrast to terrorists who take others' lives for the sake of Wrong. Knights and gentlemen protect the weak, the innocent, the careless, the carefree, the unarmed, and the defenseless, instead of preying on them as do terrorists. Practitioners of knightly and gentlemanly arts clearly value human life more than do practitioners of terrorism, and are therefore morally superior to them.

Fortunately, the virtues of knighthood and gentlemanliness belong to all humanity, not just to the West or East Asia, and so reside within the hearts and minds of Islamic and Indian civilizations too. It is Buddhism—India's greatest of great philosophies—that might help stimulate the reawakening of these virtues throughout Islam. In fact, it is already happening. Muslims all over the world are manifesting chivalry, serving Right by speaking out against the Wrong of terrorism.

## Chivalrous Muslims Speak Out

Peace-loving Muslims the world over also value human life, and so are beginning to denounce vociferously Islamist terrorists who devalue it. Muslim scholars and public intellectuals have the authority to disavow and repudiate religious justifications so glibly offered by terrorism's suicidal zealots. One among many examples is Mohammed Abu-Nimer, professor of international peace and conflict resolution at American University's School of International Service in Washington, D.C. Professor Nimer writes:

"Attacking and terrorizing civilians, human rights advocates, relief workers, and peace advocates has never been an Islamic way of resisting occupation or fighting oppression . . . there is no religious justification within Islam for brutal and ruthless actions like beheading, randomly attacking Mosques, or terrorizing civilians of any nationality."[10]

Another prominent Islamic proponent of moderation and tolerance is Imam Feisal, founder of American Society for Muslim Advancement (ASMA). He writes:

"The Qur'an warns us not to succumb to such provocation, counseling us that 'if an incitement to discord is made to you by the force of evil, seek refuge in Allah.' This verse teaches us that 'good and evil are not alike'; and urges us to respond to evil by doing what is more beautiful in behavior, so that the person with whom one bears enmity transforms into a close friend [41:34–36]. This is the Islamic ethical imperative, to transform hatred into compassion, and we call upon all our fellow Muslims to meet this Quranic directive."[11]

These are courageous and laudable sentiments. Yet to some Westerners, passages like the following from the Koran seem to imply a religious justification for brutality: "I shall terrorize the infidels. So wound their bodies and incapacitate them because they oppose Allah and His Apostle."[12]

So, just as Western civilization is divided over responses to Islamist terrorism, from appeasement to retaliation, so Islamic civilization is becoming divided over responses to such terrorism itself, from condoning to condemning it. Professor Abu-Nimer understands what Gandhi asserted: that each one of us must become the change we wish to see in the world. So Islamist terrorism will cease to be a driver of international conflict only when a sufficiently large proportion of moderate, peace-loving Arabs and other Muslims condemn it, repeatedly, insistently, and publicly. In Professor Abu-Nimer's words:

"Arabs and Muslims must take to the streets and mobilize all of our social, cultural, and political institutions to fight these groups and their messages of hatred, exclusion, and blindness. When all those who oppose such actions and strategies, such as teachers, pharmacists, journalists, imams, housewives, and shopkeepers, claim the public space and call for their end, the credibility and legitimacy of such ideology and terrorism will become a religious, cultural, and political taboo."[13]

These sentiments hold out great hope for the global village that 9/11 is backfiring on its perpetrators, and has opened a door to the modernization of Islamic civilization itself. Indeed, as Lee Kwan Yew, among other political visionaries, has observed, the real "war on terror" must be fought peacefully but persistently, by the Islamic moderate moral majority itself. My Buddhist friends call this "making good cause." We cannot undo 9/11, but we can derive better as opposed to worse outcomes in its wake.

### The War on Terror

Joseph Nye observed that "the democratization of technology has led to the privatization of war." Terrorists are private citizens—nonstate actors, often helped by states sympathetic to terrorism—waging war against other private citizens whom they deem representatives of their enemies. Like other kinds of crime, terrorism can be kept to a minimum by effective cooperation of legitimate authorities. Many problems arise in such cooperative ventures, not the least of which is that these authorities may be in competition or in uneasy peace with one another.

Minimizing municipal, state, and federal crime requires the cooperation of government, military, paramilitary, police, intelligence services, communities, and individual citizens. Minimizing terrorism, a species of international crime, requires the cooperation of many more agencies, many of whom, such as sovereign governments, may also be in dire competition with one another. This complicates counterterrorism, and raises a crop of controversial measures—

including threats, bribes or replacement of sovereign governments to elicit cooperation in the struggle to control terrorism.

Moreover, terrorists prey on our virtues, not our vices. This makes them even more dangerous, because the more virtuously we behave the greater their opportunities for terror become. And if we sink to their level and fight terror with terror, or targeted assassination, we verge on becoming the very thing we oppose. So it looks like we're bombed if we do, and bombed if we don't.

In the wake of 9/11, the World Economic Forum did an unprecedented thing. In a show of concern and solidarity, not only for New Yorkers but for all citizens of the global village, the WEF moved its annual meeting from Davos to New York. This was the first and only time in its history that the WEF had ever done such a thing. So 2,500 of the world's business, political, and cultural leaders congregated in the Waldorf-Astoria Hotel, and of dozens of speeches and briefings and meetings that unfolded there during late January of 2002, a good many focused squarely on, and a majority of others were influenced by, the causes, effects, and remedies of the complex conditions that had given rise to 9/11.

As analyses unfolded from every quarter of the global village, on every conceivable aspect of the problem and from every plausible perspective, almost everything I heard suggested a long and difficult road ahead—not merely for months or years, but for decades and perhaps even centuries to come. All this stood out in relief, in the foreground of that annual meeting. But in the background, something else was transpiring. Two things, really. First, a rift was opening between America and Europe, even as Europeans expressed solidarity with Americans over the terror attacks on 9/11—the largest single-day loss of life on American soil since the 1862 Civil War battle of Antietam. The rift has grown much larger now, following American regime change in Iraq. America too is fractured over Iraq, as we saw in chapter 6. Second, many signals indicated to me that Western civilization has grown too affluent, myopic, and effete to sustain itself in a long-term struggle for power against Islamist terror, insurgency and incursion alike.

Western Europe and North America were once closely bound and tightly knit in their Cold War standoff against the Soviet Union. The

Soviet empire played the classic Hobbesian role of a "power to keep them all in awe." At the same time, however, their demographic and immigration patterns could not have been more divergent. The affluence and proximity of the United States to Latin America has attracted tens of millions of illegal Mexican immigrants, along with a great many other peoples of Latin America. Caucasians are essentially ceasing to replace themselves in the populations of Western civilization; their breeding rate is under two per couple in North America and declining, while in Western Europe it is even lower. I can only paraphrase the sentiments of Martin Luther King yet again: What counts for any civilization is not the color of its people's skins, but the contents of their characters. Will those who inherit Western civilization also sustain the principles—liberty, opportunity, and hope—that once made it the light of the world? Absent educational reform in America, our successors of every shade and hue will have insufficient appreciation of these principles to sustain them. If our successors fail to ripen as stewards and champions of liberty, then Western civilization itself will rot.

In Europe, the demographics are even more graphic: Indigenous Western Europeans are vanishing by self-imposed attrition. The Italians "lead" the way with 1.1 children per couple, while many other EU nations cluster around 1.6 or 1.7. At the same time, European affluence has attracted millions of Arabs and Muslims from throughout Islamic civilization. They immigrated largely in order to accept menial work and manual labor—careers for which their appallingly poor educational systems had prepared them admirably. On top of this, their social eruptions have activated class sentiments and racial prejudices that lie ever dormant in the European psyche.

What is common to both sides of the rift is a dramatic increase in populations of largely unassimilated immigrants, who are trapped by their lack of assimilation in the marginalized classes, where they are swiftly outbreeding the ruling majorities. As this process unfolds across decades, it lies well beyond the event horizons of democratically elected politicians and quarterly-report-driven CEOs alike. Nonetheless, it is transpiring. Consider Holland, whose Muslim population approaches 20 percent of the whole, and which is outbreeding the Dutch by far. All things remaining equal, Dutch Muslims will attain a majority within this century, at which time Holland will become the EU's first—but not last—Islamic Republic. No one can object, since this will have been accomplished by entirely democratic means. But will the Islamic peoples who take over Holland respect and preserve the liberty that lies at the heart of Dutch democracy? Will they sustain the indomitable and centuries-long Dutch commitments to freedom of thought and expression, which attracted the likes of Spinoza when no other country in Europe would tolerate him? Most of the current evidence suggests that no Islamic Republic is prepared to tolerate Dutch liberty and Dutch culture. But for how long can tolerant democracies like Holland tolerate intolerance from within, and still preserve their essential characters?

A conspiracy theorist might even assert that the Islamic peoples who will take over Holland came there for the very purpose of *not* assimilating. Holland's original Muslims were Indonesian, and had flowed back there through the channels of reverse colonialism. They learned Dutch, became Indonesian-Dutch, did not harbor hostile anti-Western prejudices, and more or less assimilated. But the vast majority of Muslims in Holland today are not from Indonesia, are not becoming "hyphenated" Dutch, do harbor hostilities toward the West, and have not assimilated. They are from North Africa and the Middle East, and their unassimilated communities are as terrorized by Islamist despotism as are their native lands.

Everyone who visits Amsterdam regularly, as I have done for years, has noticed the change. The streets have become more dangerous, the people more surly. Hordes of unemployed and unemployable Muslim youths are taught to hate the West, instead of learning its ways. They comprise a seething hotbed of counterculture, draining the resources of the mainstream economy that supports them to work its own ruin. The Dutch phenomenon Pim Fortuyn, a new breed of politician who, as an openly gay conservative, cut across stereotypical dividing lines, was a leading candidate for prime minister in 2002. One of his planks was restriction of immigration to Holland, but he was assassinated by a Dutch environmentalist for his policies on agriculture. This passed unnoticed in America, but it was a shock to the Dutch.

Unemployed and unassimilated youths pose problems in any polity. In Amsterdam, some deal hard drugs on the streets, fund-raising for terrorist cells, whose former financial supply lines have been fouled or cut by post–9/11 global initiatives. Others glare at or openly threaten tourists, especially Americans and Jews. One murdered a Dutch filmmaker—Theodore van Gogh—for portraying Muslims in an unfavorable light. That murder was a signature Islamist "hit," inspired by Hollywood's glorifications of Mafia-style murder. Vincent van Gogh's brother's great-grandson was gunned down in the streets, then had a quote from the Koran pinned to his corpse by a dagger. In retaliation, Amsterdam mosques were burned by Dutch youths. In revenge for that, Amsterdam churches were burned by Muslim youths. (In a show of solidarity, churches were burned in Pakistan.) I can scarcely believe that all this is happening in Holland, and neither can the Dutch. Yet it is.

What is true of Holland is true of Europe. France was recently set ablaze as well, by rampaging hordes of unassimilated North African Muslims. Every Western European nation, including Britain and Scandinavia, faces declining birth rates, deconstructed values, and increasingly large and disaffected Islamic populations. Europe is once again a battleground, as of old, but its current form of warfare is unprecedented: dazed Europeans are seeing their declining cultures colonized by unassimilated Muslims.

In 2005 I walked into a Middle Eastern fast-food restaurant in downtown Copenhagen, dressed in blue jeans, a leather jacket and a baseball cap: the unofficial "uniform" of Americans. I love Middle Eastern food (except for free figs), and wanted some for lunch. A dozen youths sat idly around a long table, smoking cigarettes, drinking Coca-Cola, and speaking Arabic. They fell silent when I entered, and they glared at me. I stared back and said, "Salaam." They said "Salaam" and resumed their conversation. I wished I knew enough Arabic to understand it. The man behind the counter, having "made" me for an American, shot me a defiant look and said, "Welcome to Iraq." I glanced outside. It was snowing, and the storefront signs were in Danish. I was definitely in Copenhagen. Thanks to my "Eurocentric" education, I had always thought that Copenhagen belonged to the Danes, and not to the Iraqis. At least—to quote Saint Augustine—"not yet." So I rose to the challenge, and replied to my disputatious cousin behind the counter, "Welcome to New York." He laughed sardonically, and served up a delicious platter of Middle Eastern food.

Europe is undergoing a slow-motion invasion and conquest by its Islamic minorities, who may within decades or will within a century become majorities in many nations. This is what Joseph Nye would call "soft power"—immigration and nonassimilation—and it contrasts sharply with the "hard power" of their eighth-century invasion, which won them Iberia for a while, but nothing beyond the Pyrenees. This scenario is different. Unassimilated Islamic minorities have little to lose in Europe, and much to gain. In this slow but irrevocable demographic way, they may effect more regime change in Western civilization than America and her allies will effect in Islamic civilization. Compared with this long-term strategic view, terrorism is but a short-term distraction, a mere tactic designed to harass and terrify, and perhaps to wrest concessions or repressions that will further the long-term process in any case. Meanwhile, we're bombed if we do, and bombed if we don't.

What is true of Europe is true along the entire southern flank of the former Soviet Union, whose collapse created a political vacuum that is being filled by expanding and encroaching Islamic cultures. Nobody is in charge of this process. It represents the waxing of Islamic civilization, and the waning of the European branch of Western civilization, according to complex but apparently irreversible global dynamics.

America's decline is different, because her geopolitics and demographics are different. The Muslim population in the United States is relatively small—about 2 percent. The Muslim political lobby is proportionately small, but growing. In America, militant Islam is ideologically sponsored by the Academy, whose hatreds of Israel and America itself, as required tenets of campus culture, make it a natural ally of militant Islamic ideology, and an enthusiastic sponsor of anti-Western Islamic rhetoric and dialectic.

This is where the rift between Europe and America opens widest. Every European ally of American regime change in the "Islamic world" fears backlash from its indigenous Muslims: Bombed if we do. Terrorists bombed Madrid, which brought down the Aznar government, and the Spanish pulled out of Iraq. Americans fear no such thing. On the contrary, post–9/11, many fear only that doing nothing will encourage yet more terrorism: Bombed if we don't.

But my experiences in "Davos in New York" convinced me of something else, and I was far from alone. U.S. senators, members of Congress, policy advisors, and the intelligence community all heard what I heard. Representatives from many spheres of Arabian and Islamic civilization, whose dispositions toward the West ranged from humanistically empathic to blatantly hostile, assured us—each in his and her own way—that Islamist terrorism will continue for a very long time, no matter what the Americans or anybody else do, or don't do about it. We'll be bombed if we do, and bombed if we don't.

Terrorism is now dividing Islamic civilization as well, and that is probably a good thing. Hundreds of millions of peace-loving Muslims would like nothing better than to join the global village as productive and constructive partners in global civilization. To do so, they will need to achieve reforms of several kinds, in political, religious, economic, and educational dimensions. The establishment of stable constitutional democracies, the separation of mosque from state, and the introduction of secular educational curricula, are all necessary steps toward the modernization of Islamic civilization. Wherever taken, these steps will act as disincentives to terrorism.

As mentioned earlier, many leaders in the "Arab world" are walking political tightropes: to retain political power, and to stave off assassination by fanatics, they must directly support broad-spectrum Islamic fundamentalism, and indirectly condone its fanatical extremes. But that support impedes modernization, tolerates virulent anti-Western propaganda, sustains widespread ignorance and poverty, deprives people of liberty, opportunity, and hope, and creates breeding grounds for terrorism. This is true not only in Islamic states, but also among populations of unassimilated Muslims in Europe. Increasingly, Islamist terrorist acts are being perpetrated by young and disenfranchised Muslims who were born and raised in Europe itself.

But the primary terrorist models, and role models alike, are still centered in Islamic nations, and it is there that they must be deprogrammed and transformed.

For decades, Israel has had no choice but to endure Arab-Islamist terror attacks. Whether they occupied post-1967 buffer zones, or whether they retreated to 1947 partition boundaries, Israelis have been surrounded by hostile influences committed to their destruction. Up to 9/11, Europeans and Americans alike were content to let Israelis suffer, bleed, and die from terrorist attacks, in return for placating OPEC, appeasing Arab despots and indigenous Islamic populations, and ensuring the flow of oil from the Persian Gulf to the West. Between 1948 and 1999, some 1,795 Israelis were killed by Arab terrorists. These men, women, and children were blown up on buses, or in cafés or restaurants, or were shot on the street, or were murdered in their own beds. During the 1990s, 428 Israelis were victims of terrorism. That represents about 0.01 percent of the population. If the same proportion of Americans had been killed by terrorists, the number would have been about thirty thousand. America lost three thousand people on 9/11, and that loss precipitated two military invasions (Afghanistan and Iraq), and possibly more to come. I had been saying for years that Americans would not abide living as Israelis as have been forced to live: with terror as a daily fact of life. Since 9/11, New Yorkers, Americans, and all Western peoples have become Israelis.

If America and Europe had stood up to Islamist terrorism in the 1970s, 1980s, and 1990s, 9/11 might have been averted. And because the West is still divided in its response to 9/11—divided between extremes of Europe's political impotence and America's military might, and within America divided between extremes of naked power and deluded appeasement—the West is likely to endure more, and worse terrorism in the future. We'll be bombed if we do, bombed if we don't, and bombed if we can't agree between "doing" and "don'ting."

## Arab Strongmen

Many Westerners exhibit a great deal of difficulty, or reluctance, in grasping the realpolitik of the Middle East. Free figs aside, the "Arab world" has habitually coalesced around a "strongman"—preferably a belligerent warrior, who oppresses his own people by default, but who also defies the West with bellicose words and violent deeds. Gamal Abdul Nasser of Egypt was such a man. He overthrew the British-backed and fleshpot-ridden Farouk regime in 1952, made an alliance with the Soviets, and mobilized the "Arab world" to destroy Israel, both in 1956 and in 1967. Sadat played that same role in 1973, before performing a dramatic volte-face and becoming a warrior for peace.

Sadat's "heir" was Muammar Ghadafi of Libya, a formerly defiant dictator whose terrorist escapades ended, along with his taste for the limelight of infamy, only after the Americans bombed his palace in Tripoli, very nearly killing him. The mission was flown by U.S. warplanes that took off from British bases with the backing of Margaret Thatcher, but which were denied permission by the French government to fly over French airspace en route to Libya. (The French undoubtedly surmised that the air strike would produce the desired effect in practice, but that it would never work in theory.) I listened to the subsequent debate in the House of Lords, broadcast by BBC, which took only twenty minutes to resolve all differences of British opinion, and dissatisfaction with Thatcher, by blaming the entire affair on Israel.

After Ghadafi, the leadership model shifted from the defiant dictator to the fulminating ayatollah. The revolution in Iran, which replaced pro-Western Shah Palavi with anti-Western Ayatollah Khomeini, was and remains a significant setback to the modernization of Islamic civilization. The Islamic and "Arab world" marveled as this renegade cleric and his ragtag mob of religious fanatics stormed the American embassy in Teheran, and held 250 Americans hostage for more than a year. Jimmy Carter and his administration—brilliant peacemakers with willing partners but weak in the face of naked aggression—were humiliated by their inability to resolve the crisis in a timely and decisive fashion, and the entire "Islamic world" was further emboldened by this triumph of terrorism over international law. The Iranian nuclear threat is ever more grave, while the Khomeini leadership model inspired the Taliban, whose involvement with Osama bin Laden and 9/11 made them the very first candidates for American regime change.

Against this backdrop, Saddam Hussein came into his own, reinstating himself as the Arab strongman of the belligerent despotic type, and impressing the "Arab world" with his defiance of the West in general, and of the United States in particular. He attempted to undo the coalition of President Bush senior, which drove him from Kuwait in the first Gulf War, by launching Scud missiles against Israel. Had Israel retaliated, Egypt and Saudi Arabia would have withdrawn from and fractured the U.S.-led anti-Saddam coalition. The United States supplied Israel with Patriot antimissile defenses, prevailed upon Israel to take hits from Iraqi Scuds without retaliating, and so more Jews bled for the West's oil. The Palestinians, who at this time still chafed under the implacable despotism of Arafat, viewed Saddam Hussein as their hero and liberator for attacking Israel, and vociferously sided with him—and against the U.S.-led coalition—to their profound political detriment. But throughout the 1990s, Saddam did not desist in his saber rattling and berating of the United States; and that, along with Clinton's weakness in the face of widespread Islamist terrorism abroad and the first bombing of the World Trade Center in 1993, almost certainly emboldened al-Qaeda and invited the catastrophe of 9/11.

This is what George W. Bush inherited. His regime change in Afghanistan was a direct response to 9/11, and a clear message to the "Islamic world" that the tyranny of ayatollahs is incompatible with the well-being of the global village. His regime change in Iraq was an indirect response to 9/11, and a clear message to the "Arab world" that its belligerent despots have essentially two choices: Either work with the United States and the international community in rounding up terrorists and preventing terrorism, or run the risk of being deposed and replaced by a government that will do so. Thus, after the fall of Saddam, when hostile Syria began to allow thousands of insurgents to diffuse through its porous borders into Iraq, the Americans warned Syrian President Bashar al-Assad to seal his borders or face regime change himself. Hosni Mubarak made an urgent visit to Damascus, possibly to convince Assad that the Americans were serious.

The United States and the West did not seek, and did not provoke, the chronic metastasization of Middle Eastern terrorism that led to 9/11—

just as Israel did not seek, provoke, or declare the wars she has had to fight for her survival, and the terror she has endured for decades. Rather, the "war on terror" was sought, provoked, and declared by retrograde governments and the nonstate terrorist actors these governments both fear and support. By confronting such governments with a greater fear and greater hope alike—the fear of swiftly enforced regime change and the hope of prosperity for their peoples—the United States elicits both cooperation and hostility. Indigenous extremist groups of all kinds will ruthlessly exploit the vulnerabilities of such cultures-in-transformation, destabilizing them with insurgency, trying to make the people yearn for a new tyrant to keep the civil peace—at the familiar price of retarding modernity. One can only feel empathy and sorrow for the plight of the Iraqi people, who were tyrannized by a brutal despot, and are now plagued by violent anarchy. The familiar cyclone of suicidal zealotry that afflicts the Middle East is wreaking daily havoc in Iraq. Yet the sacrifices of Iraqis and Americans alike may yet promote peace in the wider region, as neighboring governments scramble to modernize of their own accord, which they wisely prefer to having modernity thrust upon them. Meanwhile, Middle Eastern and other Islamist suicide bombers remain bent on committing murderous acts of terrorism against innocent civilians. They have done so for decades against Israel, and increasingly against America and the wider West. Anyone who blames this on Israel, America and the wider West has overdosed on free figs, and has been temporarily rendered morally insensible.

While the extreme of hard power can change regimes, it is minds and hearts that must be transformed. Minds and hearts cannot be changed by force, but neither can they be changed by appeasement. One regnant delusion among liberal extremists is that if you appease terrorists, or apologize to them, or ignore them, they will simply go away, or will bomb somebody else. But on no account, in the politically correct mindscape of the illiberal left, may you ever confront terrorists, or even worse, *offend* them by denouncing their heinous acts.

The newest and most dangerously deluded doctrine du jour, currently making the rounds of the deconstructed West and the global village entire, asserts that if someone hates you, then you are to blame for their hatred. It asserts that if someone hates Jews, then Jews are to blame. It asserts that if someone hates America, then America is to blame. It asserts that if someone hates Western civilization, then Western civilization is to blame. The tactic of "blaming the victim" has been inflated to global proportions, as reporter Gersh Kuntzman discovered in the wake of 9/11: "All across the world, credible newspapers and columnists are unleashing a second attack on America, claiming that we are to blame for world terrorism and, for that matter, all the other problems in the world today."[14]

This debilitating doctrine proliferates as unchallengeable dogma on the campuses of the American Gulag, in the politically correct media of the deconstructed West, and in the madrasas of militant Islam. It also flies in the face of the ABCs, for it repudiates individual responsibility and thus affronts the very essence of liberty. If your emotions are utterly controlled by others, such that they can "compel" you to hate them, it is because you have abdicated your responsibility for your own state of mind. Just as nobody can offend you without your consent, nobody can make you hate without your complicity. If you feel hatred toward something or someone outside yourself—regardless of what they said or did to you, whether in fact or in fantasy—that hatred is yours. It rose within you and by you, and must be extinguished within you and by you. To blame someone else for your hatred is to drink the poison of delusion in a vain attempt to cure the fever of malice. Buddha said: "The self is master of the self. Who else can that master be?" Good question. If someone else is master of your emotions, then you have consented to be enslaved.

## Who Started It?

Venerable Confucian Grandmaster S. M. Li taught that when two students fight, they are both wrong. Why? Because in Confucian terms, students are like siblings, while their master is like a parent. Students should honor their master and venerate his teachers, just as siblings should honor their parents and venerate their ancestors, through mutual cooperation and not via conflict. Moreover, students are ignoramuses compared with their master, and so—win or lose—fighting proves nothing. The ethics of Chinese martial arts are unequivocal: Two students who fight, like two brothers who fight, are both wrong. And yet the aggressor is more wrong, for one always has the right to defend oneself against attack. And that is the purpose of the martial arts: never unprovoked attack; always self-defense. Yet even in self-defense, one should adopt "a back-to-the-wall" policy, using force only as a last resort. And even when using force as a last resort, one should adopt a conservative policy, and never generate too much of one's own force if it is possible to deflect or reflect the force that has already been directed against one. This is invariably true of all one-on-one combats: When two masters encounter one another, the one who moves first loses. If neither aggresses, they both win. The aggressor is always wrong; the defender always right. All systems of Asian self-defense share this premise, and their whole purpose is to ensure two things. First, that you, as a student of martial arts will never aggress against anyone; and second, that you will acquire sufficient mastery such that you can defend yourself against an aggressor.

So, for example, World War II was a tragic cataclysm of death and destruction, yet was also a justifiably necessary defense against Nazi and Imperial Japanese aggression.[15] Similarly, the Israeli War of Independence brought tragic results to the Palestinians, yet was also a justifiably necessary defense against aggression by five nations of the "Arab world."

When one is confronted by multiple simultaneous threats, the situation differs from one-on-one combat, and the Confucian strategy of justifiable self-defense differs too. If two or three or five people threaten to attack you at the same time, then your inaction carries a heightened risk. In such cases the best defense—and a justifiable one—may lie in preemptive attack. If the threat is credible, then preemption is defensive and so justified. If a master is threatened by several attackers, and decides to use preemption as a defense, he will invariably attack and disable the biggest and strongest of the threatening parties: the bully who inevitably leads them. The expected result is that the other would-be attackers will lose heart, and abandon their aggressive intentions. In practice, once their "leader" is disabled, they usually turn and flee, so as not to share his fate.

This is exactly the strategy Israel followed in 1967, when faced with credible threats from Egypt, Syria, Jordan, Iraq, and other Arab states. By preemptively disabling Egypt—the leader of the aggressive Arab coalition—Israel won the war speedily, and with relatively few casualties sustained by all parties. Similarly, this is what the United States did by invading Iraq in 2003, when faced with credible threats from nonstate terrorist actors, who were and are nonetheless sponsored by a host of Arab and Islamic states. By preemptively toppling Saddam—the most belligerent aggressor of the day among Arab leaders—Bush sent a message to all the others, enjoining their cooperation in the war against terror. Indeed, this is precisely why Islamist terrorists have struck in Egypt, Jordan, and Saudi Arabia: They wish to threaten, destabilize, and if possible topple Arab regimes that cooperate with the United States, and increasingly with the international community, in curtailing terrorist activities.

Bruce Hoffman of RAND has characterized terrorism metaphorically as a shark: It is constantly hungry, persistently moving forward, relentlessly seeking unwary prey. If we prevent it from preying on one quarry, it attacks another. And so a new tendency is emerging among those for whom terrorism has become a way of life and death. Instead of preying on our virtues, terrorists groups are now feeling the restrictions and constraints that have been put in place against them since 9/11, including international cooperation in cutting off their traditional sources of funding and money laundering. This has had the effect of obliging terrorist groups to become more financially independent, a problem they have solved by moving wholesale into narco-trafficking. Heroin and cocaine are being produced and trafficked by terrorists in ever-increasing quantities, holding subsistence agricultural communities hostage to narcotics (as drug cartels have done for decades in Colombia, and in the golden triangle of Asia), and preying on the vices of affluent users and addicts throughout the developed world. The vast profits, in turn, fund renewed terror operations worldwide.

## The ABCs

The ABCs are unequivocally clear about terrorism.

Aristotle would deplore it, both because it celebrates the extreme vice of premeditated murder, and because it depends on vicious indoctrinations of young minds to sate its twisted thirst for blood. It is the Aristotelian nations of the West that have been hardest hit by Arab and Islamist terrorism—Israel, Western Europe, the United States—and they will also be among the last nations on earth to condone it, precisely because it presents a mortal affront to Aristotle's and the West's fundamental political premise: that man should be free to live pretty much as he pleases—with J. S. Mill's caveat, that he should not be free to harm others in the process. Insofar as terrorism does not allow one to live as one pleases, and in fact compels one to die as others please, it is a polar opposite of Western political philosophy, and utterly repugnant to anyone who cherishes the intrinsic value of an individual human life.

Buddhists also deplore terrorism in no uncertain terms, and likewise deplore violent retaliation against it. Daisaku Ikeda writes:

"It is because we cherish and admire the values and ideals of Western civilization that we urge humanity to resolutely pursue the path of nonviolence, which is truly worthy of the civilized world. We insist that a just and equitable international tribunal be established to try those responsible for acts of war and terrorism. We insist that every effort be rendered so as to transform distrust into trust. I believe this is the most effective and fundamental antidote against terrorism and its repugnant worship of violence."[16]

Thanks to their long-standing identification of the three mental poisons—anger, greed, and ignorance—and to their steadfast devotion in developing effective nonviolent remedies against them, Buddhists also understand, better than most, the intoxicated states of mind from which terrorists suffer. Again, in Daisaku Ikeda's words:

"We must not allow ourselves to fall captive to perceived differences. We must be the masters of language and ensure that it always serves the interests of humanity. If we force ourselves to review the nightmares of the twentieth century—the purges, the Holocaust, ethnic cleansing—we will find that all of them have sprung from an environment in which language is manipulated to focus people's minds solely on their differences. By convincing people that these differences are absolute and immutable, the humanity of others is obscured and violence against them legitimized."[17]

Buddhists not only recognize the humanity of every human being; they also express compassion for the suffering of every human being. From that perspective, one might view 9/11 as a enormous cry of distress, emanating from minds so poisoned, and from beings suffering such torment, that they could not even call out for help, except by self-destructing in a conflagration that precipitated even more suffering. Terrorism is tragic, wasteful, and futile. Individuals must end suffering in themselves; they can never do so by causing it in others.

Confucius gave this lucid and prescient warning: "If a man takes no thought about what is distant, he will find sorrow near at hand." Indeed, for decades Europeans took insufficient account of "distant" Arab terrorism against Israelis, yet soon enough they encountered it on their own soil. Americans also took insufficient account of "distant" Arab terrorism against Israelis, against Europeans, and even against American targets abroad, yet soon enough they encountered 9/11 and its myriad sorrows, as near at hand as their morning commute.

As this book has emphasized from the outset, thanks to globalization no place on earth is distant anymore. And although Aristotelian science and Western democracy made globalization possible, Buddha and Buddhists know full well that all phenomena are interconnected. So, because of globalization's myriad pathways through Buddha's interconnected manifold of a single reality, human suffering in one place can cause more human suffering in another—for every place has become near at hand to every other.

Buddhists will take Confucius's warning to heart in one way (The Middle Way), and will work to alleviate suffering wherever they encounter it. Confucians will take Confucius's warning to heart in a different way, and will work to weed terrorism from their cultural gardens before it takes root and flowers.

Lee Kuan Yew is a consummate contemporary Confucian. He expressed these pragmatic and prescient sentiments on terrorism in *Foreign Affairs*: "Man needs a certain sense of right and wrong. There is such a thing called evil, and it is not the result of being a victim of society. You are just an evil man, prone to do evil things, and you have to be stopped from doing them."[18] To this end, I heard him say clearly, if privately, in Singapore, that he (if he could) would reform all the madrasas run by militants. Madrasas are schools for children, the majority of which are operated by moderate and peace-loving Muslims. But tomorrow's suicide bombers are brainwashed in today's militant madrasas: It is there, at the heart of militant Islam, that terrorism is legitimated, and it is there that future terrorists are indoctrinated with hatred of the West, and intoxicated with the prospect of martyrdom. In the wake of globalization, Confucian cultures are aspiring more than ever to turn their young children into Nobel laureates, not suicide bombers.

Meanwhile, The Middle Way remains open to all: to the overwhelming moral majority of human beings who simply want to lead decent lives, and who are not preoccupied with winning Nobel prizes (at the extreme of creative genius) or hijacking airplanes (at the extreme of destructive malice). The Middle Way is the best way to deal with terrorism. Appeasing terrorists does not work, while fighting terror with terror doesn't work either. Given that we are bombed if we do and bombed if we don't, then the only choice is The Middle Way, which you have the power to practice at any time and place. No terrorist on earth can prevent you from embarking on The Middle Way, and no terrorist can hijack it or blow it up. In turn, practicing The Middle Way immunizes you from feeling terrorized, whether you are bombed or not. And as soon as a majority of human beings becomes immune to feeling terrorized, then terrorism will have lost its grip on the global village. Only then will terrorists cease and desist from terrorism: When terrorism loses its power to terrify. The more people practice The Middle Way, the sooner terrorism's power will ebb.

When terrorists hijack airplanes, you must continue to fly. When terrorists bomb trains or buses or subways, you must continue to ride. When terrorists bomb restaurants and cafes and markets, you must continue to eat and drink and shop. When terrorists bomb hotels, you must continue to vacation. When terrorists bomb embassies, you must continue to practice diplomacy. When terrorists take lives, you must continue to live. You have the power to do all these things, and no one can prevent you but yourself.

And so we arrive at the final chapter of this book, which is a reminder of some more things you can do here and now, as soon as you finish reading, to practice The Middle Way—not only to help disempower terrorism, but also to help reconcile all the other extremes upon which we have touched. The Middle Way lies within you, awaiting activation. Do not delay. Read on, and activate it now.

# PART III
## The ABCs
## Here and Now

# 16

## IMPORTING THE ABCs INTO YOUR LIFE
### Exporting Them into Your Environment

*If each man is somehow responsible for the state he is in, he will also be himself somehow responsible for how things appear.* —Aristotle

*Work out your own salvation. Do not depend on others.* —Buddha

*The good man does not grieve that other people do not recognize his merits. His only anxiety is lest he should fail to recognize theirs.* —Confucius

### Import-Export

OUR SWEEPING TOUR of the global village and its civilizational dynamics, as viewed from philosophical orbital space, is winding to a close. Before long you will lay down this book, and pick up the threads of your daily life. Perhaps, in light of our tour, you will henceforth view your personal situation in a new light, too—one of deeper awareness of our human interconnectedness, of the impermanence and fragility of all our endeavors, of the wastefulness and needless suffering caused by adherence to extremisms, and of the greatness of the human spirit's capacity—your capacity—for understanding, compassion, and beneficence. For the ABCs, like The Middle Way they advocate, cannot apply to the global village unless they apply to you. As Gandhi said, "You must be the change you wish to see in the world."

Bearing that in mind, putting down this book marks but the beginning of your engagement with the ABCs, and hardly the end. If you can manage to import just one lesson from each of the ABCs into your daily affairs, not only will your life become more enriched and fulfilled, it will also become a radiant beacon, creating conditions whereby others in your environment will experience enrichment and fulfillment, too. And your "environment"—our shared environment—is none other than the global village. The ABCs, along with their golden mean, Middle Way, and balanced order, teach us how to create value for ourselves and others alike, making "good causes" that promote liberation and happiness, instead of "bad causes" that perpetuate bondage and suffering. The ABCs all teach that you are the captain of your soul, you are the cultivator of your mind, and you are the keeper of your virtue. So it is not my place, but rather yours, to determine how and where you will import the ABCs into your life and export them into your environment. I can only remind you what they offer; it is for you to receive and transmit their offerings as you best see fit.

Those of you who are acquainted with my pop-philosophy books know that I help people apply ideas of great thinkers to the management and resolution of their daily problems. In my journeys throughout the global village, I encounter fellow travelers who, in our routine exchange of greetings and pleasantries on airplanes among other places, are prone to ask what I do. If I tell them that I am a philosopher or an author, this often opens doors to interesting dialogue. But sometimes I don't feel like talking. At such times, if people ask about my line of work, I usually tell them, "I'm in import-export." That sounds innocent enough, and of course it can mean anything. If they pursue this line, asking what I import and export, I reply, "Ideas." That is usually followed by a pregnant pause or a protracted silence, as they "import" the idea of importing and exporting ideas, and ponder what to ask next. Ideas, after all, are not publicly traded on Wall Street. Who could possibly be interested in them? What price do they command? What value do they have?

If you think more carefully about it, you'll realize that we're all in the "import-export" business. Whether we're breathing, thinking, eating, drinking, helping, harming, producing, or consuming, we are constantly importing and exporting things—from goods to services, from molecules to machines, from traditions to technologies, from idioms to ideologies—from and to our surroundings.

So, in light of the ABCs, it might do you some good to think about what you import from and export into your environment, especially since your environment is the same as mine, along with everyone else's: nothing less than the global village itself.

## Importing and Exporting Aristotle

To me, Aristotle's greatest lesson comes in three parts. First, your fulfillment as a human being lies within you, and is not dependent on external things. Second, each and every human being has a particular excellence or individual talent, a special gift or unique capacity, which when cultivated, refined, and polished gives rise to fulfillment. Third, the surest way for each of us to perfect our gifts, and thereby to become fulfilled, lies in acquiring virtuous habits via the golden mean—avoiding extremes and adhering to proportions that are good, right, and just.

So how do you "import" Aristotle? By applying each part of his lesson to your life. It may be easier for you to do this in reverse order.

First, make a list of your habits, virtuous and vicious alike. Which habits are most helpful to you and others? Strive to reinforce them by daily practice. Which habits are most harmful to you and others? Strive to reduce them by daily practice. What good or helpful things do you do, but too infrequently? Strive to do these things more often. What bad and harmful things do you do, and to excess? Strive to do these things less often. What good or helpful thing have you always wanted to do, but somehow never managed to? Start doing it today. What bad or harmful thing have you always wanted to stop doing, but somehow never managed to? Start abstaining from it today. In these ways, you will direct yourself via Aristotle's golden mean.

Second, make a list of your excellences, talents, gifts, or capacities. Which ones are you perfecting? Which ones are you neglecting? If you are perfecting your gifts, you will feel a sense of worthiness and accomplishment, meaningfulness, and purpose, which over time becomes enduring happiness, i.e., Aristotelian fulfillment. If you are neglecting your gifts, you will feel a sense of unworthiness and failure, meaninglessness, and purposelessness, which over time becomes chronic unhappiness, i.e., absence of Aristotelian fulfillment.

Third, if you are experiencing fulfillment, understand that it comes from within you. It is first a general result of your preponderance of virtuous over vicious habits, and second a special result of cultivating your particular gifts in these virtuous pathways. Aristotle understood what the Stoics realized, namely, that no one can take your virtue from you. You may change or relinquish your principles, but nobody can coerce you to do so. Similarly, others may damage or destroy your house, your car, your career, or your idols; but nobody can damage or destroy your fulfillment—except you yourself. In sum, by importing Aristotle into your life, you assume responsibility for your lasting happiness.

If you are able to import these vital ingredients from Aristotle's philosophy into your life, thus becoming more fulfilled, then you are also able to export them into the lives of others, thus helping them to become more fulfilled as well. For example, if you are a parent, teacher, coach, or employer, or a professional caregiver of any kind, then you are responsible for shaping pathways in which others may experience greater or lesser fulfillment themselves. So whatever you do for yourself in an Aristotelian sense, you can do for them as well, and by the exactly the same three means.

First, are you encouraging them to acquire virtuous habits, or vicious ones? Second, are you helping them to discover and refine their excellences, talents, gifts, or capacities—or are you hindering them from doing these things? Third, are you facilitating their experience of self-sustaining fulfillment, or are you inculcating unwholesome dependencies that inhibit the development of their autonomy and responsibility? Insofar as Aristotle can be a model for you, you too can be an Aristotelian model for others. Thus, importing Aristotle into your life is tantamount to exporting him into your environment.

### Importing and Exporting Buddha

Since Buddha is already within you, you do not need to "import" your Buddha nature, but rather awaken and activate it by importing The

Middle Way. Speaking as a friend of Buddhism, and a beneficiary of Buddhism's friendship to me, I heartily encourage you to meet this friend yourself. Aristotle, too, extolled the virtues of friendship, recognizing it as one of life's greatest treasures. In turn, Buddha is not only the best friend that any human being can make—but also one whose friendship guarantees that you will have no enemies.

To me, what sets Buddhism apart from all other religions and philosophies on earth is its compassionate and indefatigable insistence that you yourself contain all the resources necessary for your emancipation from suffering, and for helping fulfill the cosmic mission of similarly emancipating all sentient beings alike. While pleasures and pains, comforts and discomforts, triumphs and tragedies, are experienced naturally and necessarily in the course of our life cycles as embodied beings, suffering is something else again. According to classic as well as contemporary Buddhist teachings, all human suffering arises from our deluded cravings and the unwholesome attachments they invariably spawn: the products of a blind ego, a selfish heart, and a grasping mind. Such a being desperately seeks only to gratify its senses, heedless of the inevitable karmic costs to itself and others.

By means of classic as well as contemporary Buddhist practices—The Middle Way—all human suffering is dispelled through opening the inner eye, tapping the selfless heart, and taming the wild mind. Such a being extinguishes its cravings, attains and reflects serenity, transcends the sorrows of existence, crosses the sea of suffering, helps all and harms none, and realizes the limitless potential of that most precious gift: humanity. Hatred, greed, and envy—among other poisons of the mind—are dissolved by daily Buddhist practice, just as they are accumulated by its neglect.

Neither faith in God nor power of prayer alone redeems one from these poisons, for a self-righteous mind cannot but radiate toxic thoughts and rationalize hurtful deeds. Invoking the names of sacred and loving deities while perpetrating hateful and profane acts is hypocrisy, not religion. It is better to doubt God and do good, than to profess faith and cause harm. Buddhism is a friend to agnostics, atheists, pagans, Jews, Christians, Muslims, Hindus, all human beings—even though members of these groups are sometimes loving friends, and sometime hateful foes, to one another. I know many deeply religious people whose spiritual devotions have been purified by Buddhist practice; I know few Buddhists whose clarity and compassion have been compromised by spiritual devotions. Buddhist theory and practice offer a refuge from hatred, intolerance, and corruption alike, wherever they are found.

So how do you import Buddha's Eightfold Path into your life? If you are reading these words, then you are doing it now. Remember, Buddha himself essayed and later eschewed extremes of indulgence and asceticism, declaring that neither extreme conduces to "the norm"— that is, to The Middle Way. Whatever your mission, stage, or station in life—young or old, male or female, student or teacher, employed or unemployed, rich or poor, believer or nonbeliever, your humanity is your passport to the benefits of The Middle Way, which you accrue as soon as you begin to practice. Just as suffering has one taste, independent of the hour, day, or season of its experience, so does liberation from suffering have one taste, independent of the time and place and person who experiences it. There are many ways to practice The Middle Way, many teachers and guides to demonstrate these ways—yet only you can choose to walk this Way of ways.

Just as Aristotle insisted that your lasting fulfillment lies within you, so Buddha insisted that your liberation from suffering lies within you. Those who suffer are wronging themselves, and they often commit the further error of blaming others for those wrongdoings. You can liberate yourself from suffering only when you accept that you have imprisoned yourself in suffering, and only when you confront and dissolve your unwholesome attachments and deluded cravings. For they and they alone comprise the bars and cells, the walls and wardens of your prison. Liberty is inseparable from responsibility. Yet assuming responsibility requires a degree of emotional and philosophical maturity. Suffering can also be a teacher and a guide, a demanding but enlightening guru who furthers one's capacity to accept responsibility for utilizing liberty to dispel one's suffering. Is this convoluted? Yes. It surely needs to be in order to plumb the depths of our convoluted beings. Just as it sometimes takes a thief to catch a thief, it sometimes takes a convolution to dispel one.

When, on his deathbed, Buddha told his followers to be "lamps unto yourselves," he reinforced this very notion: We are each the ultimate source of our sorrows, as well as the ultimate resource for their dispellment.

Yet all of us need help from time to time, that is, help in helping ourselves, and this is the deeper and further purpose that Buddhist practice serves. As we have seen throughout this book, globalization makes our interconnectedness plain, and in the process reinforces Buddha's message that we are all interconnected and interdependent. Thus lasting fulfillment (in an Aristotelian sense) and personal liberation (in a Buddhist sense) cannot endure as long as sentient beings are suffering in this universe. So the ultimate goal of Mahayana Buddhist practice is not to free yourself alone from the chains of suffering, but to help unfetter all sentient beings alike—for only then can "you" (who are connected to all "others") be truly free.

So ultimately there is no distinction between helping yourself and helping others. Trying to maintain this distinction—that is, attempting to help yourself without helping others, or by disregarding others, or through harming others—always backfires, and results in self-induced suffering. It likewise follows that there is no distinction between importing Buddhism into your life, and exporting it into your environment. Just as inhalation and exhalation together comprise respiration, so what you receive from and what you give back to your environment, along with what you receive from and what you give back to others, together comprise your karma. You cannot import Buddhism into your life without exporting it into the lives of others, any more than you can inhale without exhaling. And for that matter, you cannot export Buddhism into the lives of others without importing it into your own life, any more than you can exhale without inhaling.

The ancient Chinese knew this too, and hence their saying, "When the student is ready, the teacher will appear." When you are ready to receive a lesson, a teacher will always appear for the purpose of transmitting it to you. But this also applies to you as a transmitter. For when other students are ready, it is you who will appear to them as a teacher. And this is the link between Buddha and Confucius.

## Importing and Exporting Confucius

Just as Aristotle's golden mean is rooted in geometry, the underlying structure of cosmos and chaos alike; and just as Buddha's Middle Way is grounded in karma, the universal moral law of cause and effect; so Confucius's balanced order is embedded in Tao, the way of unified and harmonious relations among complements. Recall that Confucius identified himself as a transmitter, not an innovator. What did he mean by this?

First, Confucius knew of a legendary and enlightened ruler of Chinese antiquity (circa 1300 B.C.E.), namely the Duke of Chou, who governed his realm according to Tao (the Way), using moral force rather than physical coercion as his guiding instrument of leadership and governance. However, the duke's successors among other warlords did not persevere in following Tao, which resulted in a gradual but relentless disintegration of Chinese moral, social, and political orders in the ensuing centuries. The subsequent and turbulent period of the Warring States, during which Confucius and Lao Tzu both were born and lived, was to both of these sages a direct consequence of their civilization's straying from Tao. When leadership loses the Way—the Way of moral authority rooted in balanced order—human society flounders and implodes, self-destructing through uncontained and uncontainable conflict. We too have seen this time and again in subsequent world history: When flocks are led by wolves, their path is strewn with terror, privation, and slaughter. By contrast, when leadership aligns itself with the Way, and encourages its manifestation in society, then balanced order prevails over unbalanced strife. When flocks are led by shepherds, their path is garlanded with security, prosperity, and harmony.

So Confucius touted a return to the Way as a panacea for the plethora of ills and injustices of his time—a return to a secular Eden, from which humanity was not expelled by divine edict, but had banished itself by dint of rapacious leadership, collective negligence, and moral decline. Hence Confucius conceived his role as that of a transmitter, not an innovator: a transmitter of the ancient precepts and practices conducive to restoring The Way, and in its wake, to reinstating balanced order for humanity.

Thus importing Confucius into your life means aligning yourself first and foremost with The Way. How? By implementing precepts, observing rituals, and exercising virtues consonant with Tao, and by relinquishing precepts, rejecting rituals, and eschewing vices dissonant with it. Confucius emphasized the vital importance of cultivating a universal disposition of benevolence toward others, of ranging oneself with what is right independent of egoistic gain or loss, of doing good without regard to personal advantage or disadvantage—all for the sake of upholding the Way itself. So from the outset, Confucius subordinates each individual's interests to those of the larger society. The measure of our worthiness as human beings is not how well we serve ourselves, but how well we serve others. Moreover, the higher one ascends in the Confucian social order, the greater becomes one's responsibility to serve others—as opposed to one's opportunity to serve oneself. This represents a key intersection of Confucian and Buddhist thought.

Everybody has a place in the Confucian system; everyone has a role to play. Nobody is superfluous, nobody is unimportant, nobody is neglected. Everyone serves in their appropriate capacity, and each one is valued. Everyone's role is accounted for, and each one is accountable to others. So, to import Confucius into your life, think of yourself as a single cell in a vast social organism, and ask yourself these questions: "What role(s) am I supposed to play? What is the appropriate Way for me to do so? How best can I serve the social organism of which I am an inseparable part? Who depends on my service(s)? How graciously can I offer my service(s)? On whose service(s) do I depend? How graciously can I accept their service(s)?

So you import Confucius into your life in general by reflecting on your duties toward others, and specifically by understanding how to express your benevolence most appropriately through the various social channels that link you to the organism of humanity. The five basic human relationships that Confucius defined—parent-child, husband-wife, friend-friend, younger-elder, subject-ruler—are the main types of channels by which you are connected to others, and through which your benevolence must flow. From this it follows that importing Confucius into your life is not strictly separable from exporting him into your environment. If your benevolence flows through your social channels, in tandem with others' benevolence flowing through theirs, then import and export unfold in cooperative unison. Enlightened self-interest mandates and necessitates our service to others, as a condition of furthering ourselves by participating in a harmoniously balanced order. Unenlightened self-interest rationalizes short-term and myopic personal gratification at the expense of others, at the inevitable cost of disadvantaging ourselves and others by fomenting a discordantly unbalanced disorder.

## The ABCs Together

As we have seen, the Confucian position on the relation of the individual to society is juxtaposed by Tao to the Aristotelian one. Aristotle saw individual fulfillment as a necessary condition of societal harmony; Confucius saw societal harmony as a necessary condition of individual fulfillment. These are not contradictory positions, but rather complementary ones. As we have seen, if either is taken to an extreme, then both break down. If Aristotelian emphasis on the individual is permitted to degenerate into anarchy, society cannot sustain its balanced order. If Confucian emphasis on the collective is permitted to ossify into rigidity, individuals cannot attain their unique potential.

We have also seen that Buddhism defines not only The Middle Way for humanity, but also a golden mean and balanced order among the ABCs themselves. By apportioning your attentions, consecrating your efforts and distributing your energies among Buddha, dharma, and sangha—the role model, the teachings, the community—you cannot fail but to respect the ABCs in their entirety, and to honor them in their unity. To become fully human yourself, and to serve humanity as fully as possible, make the ABCs your closest friends and trusted confidants.

Be Aristotelian in your unrelenting commitment to improving your mind. Be Buddhist in your unstinting effort to deepening your heart. Be Confucian in your unselfish devotion to serving your fellow beings. You possess these precious keys to the betterment of the human estate; you wield awesome powers to make a difference for the good; you hold the lamp that illuminates The Middle Way. You also command the genie who inhabits that lamp, and who makes all things possible, including the ABCs themselves. That genie is your will. Exercise it wisely; for as you will, so shall you become.

# Endnotes

## Introduction

1. http://www.loumarinoff.com/global%20agenda.pdf

## Part I. The ABCs
## Chapter 1. Globalization and Its Discontents

1. Kwame Anthony Appiah, *Cosmopolitanism: Ethics in a World of Strangers* (New York: W. W. Norton, 2005).

2. In case you skipped Philosophy 101, Plato's theory of the forms is found in Book VII of his *Republic*, embedded in his celebrated Allegory of the Cave. It turns out that Plato's theory is highly compatible with Christian theology. This forged a powerful link between the two strands of Western cultural DNA.

3. I have the distinction of authoring a book that has been "banned" by Western civilization: a novel so politically incorrect that not one house in New York, London, or Toronto has dared to publish it.

4. As we will see in chapter 7, the alliance is between neo-Marxists, feminists, and postmodernists.

5. Erik Erikson, *Gandhi's Truth: On the Origins of Militant Nonviolence* (New York: W. W. Norton, 1960).

6. Elie Wiesel, *Memoirs: All Rivers Run to the Sea* (New York: Schocken Books, 1996).

7. Pandit Rajmani Tigunait, *Seven Systems of Indian Philosophy* (Honesdale, PA: Himalayan Institute Press, 1983).

8. Gurdjieff, Ouspensky, and Madame Blavatsky are classified as "theosophists," Western mystics who blended theology and philosophy in their quest for spiritual awakening.

9. The chakras are energy centers, activated and regulated by yogic practice.

10. Montesquieu advocates what can be termed "psychoclimatology" in his *Spirit of the Laws* (see http://plato.stanford.edu/entries/montesquieu/#4.3). So does Tsunesaburo Makiguchi, *A Geography of Human Life*, ed. Dayle Bethel (San Francisco: Caddo Gap Press, 2002).

11. R. Linton, *The Study of Man* (London: Peter Owen, 1965), pp. 326–327.

## Chapter 2. Aristotle's Golden Mean

1. http://www.nobelprizes.com/nobel/peace/MLK-jail.html

2. http://www.philosophyarchive.com/person.php?era=400BC-301BC&philosopher=Aristotle#biography

3. Aristotle, *Nicomachean Ethics*.

4. This led to the French jest: How many aspirins does an Englishman take for a headache? Four: one for each corner.

5. Aristotle, *Nicomachean Ethics*.

6. Those readers familiar with my earlier popular books, *Plato, Not Prozac* and *The Big Questions*, know that philosophical counselors help people resolve or manage everyday problems that are not mental illnesses.

7. Aristotle, *Nicomachean Ethics*.

8. Daisaku Ikeda, personal communication, 2005.

## Chapter 3. Buddha's Middle Way

1. Daisaku Ikeda, personal communication, 2005.

2. Ibid.

3. Nagarjuna, *The Fundamental Wisdom of the Middle Way*, trans. Jay Garfield (London: Oxford University Press, 1995).

4. Thomas Hobbes refuted Augustine in the seventeenth century, placing his very life in jeopardy—for Roman and Anglican Church doctrines were then unassailable dogmas. Hobbes wrote that "the desires, and other passions of men, are in themselves no sin." In other words, they are part of our nature, and not susceptible to moral judgment on that basis alone. Then again, Hobbes was not a believer in "free will" either: He called human will "the last appetite" prior to action, anticipating Freud's theory that our thoughts and behaviors are largely determined by unconscious psychological factors.

5. A clear explanation of this teaching is given by Geshe Michael Roach, *The Diamond Cutter* (New York: Doubleday, 2000).

6. Daisaku Ikeda, *The Flower of Chinese Buddhism*, trans. Burton Watson (New York: Weatherhill, 1986).

7. All by W. Evans-Wentz: *The Tibetan Book of the Great Liberation* (London: Oxford University Press, 1954); *Tibetan Yoga and Secret Doctrines* (London: Oxford University Press, 1935); *Tibet's Great Yogi Milarepa* (London: Oxford University Press, 1928); *The Tibetan Book of the Dead* (London: Oxford University Press, 1927), with a foreword by Carl Jung.

8. E.g., by Lobsang Rampa: *Doctor from Lhasa* (London: Corgi Books, 1959); *The Third Eye* (London: Secker and Warburg, 1956); *The Hermit* (London: Corgi Books, 1971).

9. See, e.g., Roger Kamenetz, *The Jew in the Lotus: A Poet's Rediscovery of Jewish Identity in Buddhist India* (San Francisco: HarperCollins, 1995).

10. One also hears "Bujus," short for Buddhist Jews.

11. E.g., D. T. Suzuki, *Zen Buddhism*, ed. William Barrett (New York: Anchor Books, 1956); D. T. Suzuki, *An Introduction to Zen Buddhism* (1934; repr., New York: Grove Press, 1964) with a foreword by Carl Jung.

12. E.g., Alan Watts, *This is It: and Other Essays on Zen* (New York: Vintage, 1973); *The Way of Zen* (New York: Vintage, 1957).

13. Roshi Philip Kapleau, *The Three Pillars of Zen* (New York: John Weatherhill, 1965).

14. By Roshi Robert Kennedy, S.J.: *Zen Spirit, Christian Spirit* (New York: Continuum, 1997); *Zen's Gifts to Christians* (New York: Continuum, 2000).

15. *The Lotus Sutra*, trans. by Burton Watson (New York: Columbia University Press, 1993).

16. See *The Writings of Nichiren Daishonin*, ed. and trans. The Gosho Translation Committee (Tokyo: Soka Gakkai, 1999).

17. For a social scientific analysis of details of this transplantation, see Phillip Hammond and David Machacek, *Soka Gakkai in America* (Oxford: Oxford University Press, 1999).

18. See Suggested Reading for this (and other) chapters.

19. Daisaku Ikeda, personal communication, 2005.

# Chapter 4. Confucius's Balanced Order

1. For an excellent brief overview of Chinese philosophy, see Hyun Höchsmann, *On Philosophy in China* (Singapore: Thomson-Wadsworth, 2004). For a classic in-depth treatment, see Fung Yu-Lan, *The Spirit of Chinese Philosophy* (London: Routledge and Kegan Paul, 1962).

2. Many editions of the *I Ching* have come out in recent years, but I still recommend the Richard Wilhelm translation (into German) retranslated into English by Carey Baynes (Princeton, NJ: Princeton University Press, 1950), with a foreword by Carl Jung. A recent and noteworthy edition is *The Complete I Ching*, by Master Alfred Huang (Rochester, VT: Inner Traditions, 2004).

3. Again, of many editions of Lao Tzu's *Tao Te Ching*, my favorite is by Ch'u Ta-Kao, (London: George Allen and Unwin, 1937). A very good and more recent edition is by Stephen Mitchell (New York: Harper and Row, 1988). A classic English edition of the *Analects of Confucius* is translated and annotated by Arthur Waley (New York: Vintage Books, 1989).

4. Confucius, *Analects*.

5. Representative selections of paradoxes stemming from rationality are *Paradoxes of Rationality and Cooperation*, ed. Richmond Campbell and Lanning Sowden (Vancouver: University of British Columbia Press, 1985); R. M. Sainsbury, *Paradoxes* (Cambridge: Cambridge University Press, 1987); Michael Clark, *Paradoxes from A to Z* (London: Routledge, 2002). For example, consider this pair of sentences, S1 and S2: (S1) The following sentence is true. (S2) The preceding sentence is false. Suppose S1 is true. That means S2 must also be true. But if S2 is true, then S1 is necessarily false. But if S1 is false, then S2 must also be false. But if S2 is false, then S1 must be true. This is an infinite regress. The point is: If we assume that every sentence is either true or false, then we immediately encounter paradoxes.

6. In addition to Bohr's coat of arms and Jung's foreword to the Wilhelm/Baynes *I Ching*, see Raymond Smullyan, *The Tao is Silent* (New York: HarperCollins, 1977).

7. See Höchsmann, *On Philosophy in China*.

8. My editor informs me that radical feminist readers may "bristle" at the Confucian notion that Woman is the quintessential homemaker. As we will see in chapters 9 and 11, they are already bristling without my help. The liberation of women in the West, and their full integration in the workplace, has also led to the disintegration of the nuclear family, and may well lead to the collapse of Western civilization itself. By contrast, the longevity of East Asian civilization owes much to the Confucian division of power and of labor between women and men, in accordance with Tao. The only home Man finds on this Earth, for the brief time he is here, is that which Woman makes for him and their children. In turn, he provides for and protects them. As we will also see in chapters 9 and 11, militant feminists bent on destroying patriarchy, hearth, and home have also destroyed community, family, and matriarchy itself.

9. Daisaku Ikeda, personal communication, 2005.

10. See Plato's dialogue *Crito*: "I only wish it were so, Crito; and that the many could do the greatest evil; for then they would also be able to do the greatest good—and what a fine thing this would be! But in reality they can do neither; for they cannot make a man either wise or foolish; and whatever they do is the result of chance." http://plato.thefreelibrary.com/Crito/2-1.

## Chapter 5. ABC Geometry

1. Bolyai, Lobachevsky, and Riemann would later rediscover and formalize the geometry of curved spaces, which revolutionized mathematics and physics.

2. The discovery of non-Euclidean geometries also resolved a formidable problem latent in Euclid's work itself, a problem that had gained notoriety across centuries as a number of mathematicians succumbed to frustration or worse in their doomed mission of trying to solve it. The problem was to prove Euclid's infamous Fifth Postulate, that parallel lines meet at infinity. Mathematical, philosophical, and theological treatments of the infinite are all fraught with paradoxes of the most fiendish kind, which sometimes lethally afflict minds already plagued by more than the average quota of demons. One such suicide was Russian George Cantor (1845–1918), whose work on transfinite numbers was and remains so controversial that opinion among mathematicians is fiercely divided to this day. David Hilbert thanked Cantor for creating "a paradise from which we will never be banished," while Poincaré called Cantor's work "a disease from which mankind may one day recover." Cantor succumbed to madness, but his work lives on—and reappears in twentieth-century chaos theory, which (as we will see) is also relevant to The Middle Way. My point here is that non-Euclidean geometries and Cantorian transfinite arithmetic are products of unsolved problems embedded in Euclid's *Elements*.

3. In any right-angled triangle, the square of the hypotenuse equals the sum of the squares on the adjacent sides.

4. J. Aubrey, *Aubrey's Brief Lives*, ed. O. Dick (London: Secker and Warburg, 1958).

5. This notorious problem is known as "squaring the circle"—constructing, with a straight edge and compass, a square of equal area to a given circle. For convenience, choose a unit circle, whose radius (r) is by definition 1 unit. The circle's area ($\pi r^2$) is then equal to $\pi$. To "square the circle," we must construct a square of area $\pi$. To accomplish that, we must construct a square whose sides are $\sqrt{\pi}$ length. For more than two thousand years, every philosopher and mathematician worth his salt devoted a few hours per day to the attempted solution of this problem. Hobbes left us an entire volume of cleverly inspired but ineluctably flawed constructions. The number $\pi$ turns out to be transcendental, which means it can neither be expressed as a ratio of two integers nor constructed by Euclidean means nor be a root of an algebraic equation.

6. Construct a unit square, ABCD. Bisect the side AB at E, then join EC. Pythagoras's theorem tells us that EC = $\sqrt{5}/2$. With center E and radius CE, draw an arc AF, such that F lies on the extension of line AB. You're done. AF = $\varphi$, and AFGD and BFGC are golden rectangles.

7. Daisaku Ikeda et al., *The Wisdom of the Lotus Sutra*, Volume III (Santa Monica, CA: World Tribune Press, 2000), chapter 8: "A Cultural History of the Lotus Flower."

8. Revealing works on sacred geometry include Matila Ghyka, *The Geometry of Art and Life* (New York: Dover Publications, 1977); Robert Lawlor, *Sacred Geometry, Philosophy and Practice* (New York: Thames and Hudson, 1989); Rudolf Taschner, *Der Zahlen Gigantische Schatten* (Wiesbaden: Vieweg Verlag, 2004).

9. David Bohm, *Wholeness and the Implicate Order* (London: Routledge and Kegan Paul, 1980).

10. E.g.. see Robert Devaney, *Chaos, Fractals and Dynamics* (Menlo Park, California: Addison-Wesley, 1990); Manfred Schroeder, *Fractals, Chaos, Power Laws* (New York: W. H. Freeman, 1991).

11. Benoît Mandelbrot, *The Fractal Geometry of Nature* (New York: W. H. Freeman, 1982).

12. Nāgārjuna, Mūlamadhyamakakārikā, or *Fundamental Verses on the Middle Way,* e.g. see http://en.wikipedia.org/wiki/Nagarjuna.

# Part II. The Extremes and the ABCs
# Chapter 6. Political Extremes

1. Aristotle, *Politics.*

2. Confucius, *Analects.*

3. Walker Percy, *Lost in the Cosmos: The Last Self-Help Book* (New York: Farrar, Straus, 1983).

4. Viktor Frankl, "Reductionism and Nihilism," in A. Koestler and J. Smythies, eds., *Beyond Reductionism* (London: Hutchinson, 1969).

5. Daniel Yankelovitch, "Poll Positions," *Foreign Affairs,* September/October 2005: 2–16.

6. Among many sources, see http://mideasttruth.com/forum/viewtopic.php?t=3667.

7. Kishore Mahbubani, *Can Asians Think?* (Singapore: Time Books International, 1999).

8. Provincetown, at the tip of New England's touristic Cape Cod, has attracted a large gay community in recent decades.

9. E.g., see http://www.arlingtoncemetery.net/kachanawongse.htm.

10. Many Web sites offer graphic demonstrations that generate the normal distribution in real time, most commonly by simulating balls bouncing randomly through an array of pins. A snapshot of such a process is depicted in fig. 6.1. You can watch the process unfold by visiting the indicated Web site http://webphysics.davidson.edu/Applets/galton4/intro.html.

11. E.g., see Mark Gerzon, *A House Divided* (New York: Putnam, 1997).

12. Francis Galton, "Statistical Inquiries into the Efficacy of Prayer," *The Fortnightly Review* 12 (1872): 125–35.

13. Sometimes attributed to Mark Twain as well. E.g., see http://www.ucpress.edu/books/pages/9358/9358.intro.html.

14. David Brock, *Blinded by the Right* (New York: Crown Publishers, 2002).

15. In King's words: "I have a dream that my four little children will one day live in a nation where they will not be judged by the color of their skin but by the content of their character." From his celebrated "I Have a Dream" speech, e.g., http://www.usconstitution.net/dream.html.

16. Pema Chödrön, *When Things Fall Apart* (Boston: Shambhala, 2000).

17. See, e.g., Richard Herrnstein and Charles Murray, *The Bell Curve* (New York: The Free Press, 1994); and Dinesh D'Souza, *The End of Racism* (New York: The Free Press, 1995). See also http://www.afsc.org/pwork/1200/122k05.htm.

18. http://www.afsc.org/pwork/1200/122k05.htm

19. For specific examples, see, e.g., Roger Kimball, *Tenured Radicals* (Chicago: Ivan R. Dee, 1998); Alan Kors and Harvey Silverglate, *The Shadow University* (New York: HarperCollins, 1999); James Traub, *City on a Hill* (Reading, Massachusetts: Addison-Wesley, 1995).

20. E.g., Thomas Sowell, *The Vision of the Anointed* (New York: Basic Books, 1996).

21. http://en.wikipedia.org/wiki/Jared_Taylor

22. http://www2.davidduke.com/index.php?p=30

23. As is the case with journalists, I cannot reveal all my sources. These things have been disclosed to me by African-American friends and acquaintances from coast to coast.

24. http://www.okayplayer.com/dcforum/DCForumID1/24328.html

25. http://www.gakkaionline.net/soka/strand.html

26. Applicants are obliged to identify themselves from among the following choices: "Race/Ethnic Identification: American Indian or Alaskan Native, Black (not of Hispanic Origin), Asian/Pacific Islanders, Hispanic/Latino, White (not of Hispanic Origin). Gender: Male or Female." I myself cannot comply with this questionnaire. First, I am a human being. There is no category for human beings. Second, I am of Jewish origin. There is no category for Jews. Third, my gender is masculine; my sex is male. But there is no category for sex, because sex and gender have been deliberately confused by political correctness. We will examine these issues in greater depth in chapters 9 and 11.

27. Daisaku Ikeda, personal communication, 2005.

# Chapter 7. Sacred and Profane Extremes

1. From Aristotle's *Fragments*, quoted by Seneca.

2. Aristotle, *On the Heavens*.

3. http://www.skepticfiles.org/atheist/virginjc.htm

4. http://www.law.umkc.edu/faculty/projects/ftrials/scopes/menk.htm

5. Anonymous, *The Cloud of Unknowing* (Harmondsworth, UK: Penguin, 1961).

6. See, e.g., Robert Jungk, *Brighter Than a Thousand Suns* (London: Victor Gollancz, 1958).

7. http://www.bbc.co.uk/pressoffice/pressreleases/stories/2005/07_july/13/radio4.shtml

8. Isaiah Berlin, *Freedom and Its Betrayal: Six Enemies of Human Liberty*, ed. Henry Hardy (Princeton, NJ: Princeton University Press, 2002).

9. Mikhail Gorbachev and Daisaku Ikeda, *Moral Lessons of the Twentieth Century: Gorbachev and Ikeda on Buddhism and Communism* (London: I. B. Tauris, 2005), pp. 147–48.

10. Cited by S. Stanley, *The New Evolutionary Timetable* (New York: Basic Books, 1981), p. 205.

11. http://www.gnxp.com/MT2/archives/001952.html

12. "Empires wax and wane" are the first words of Lo Kuan-Chung's epic Chinese novel, *Romance of the Three Kingdoms*, trans. by C. H. Brewitt-Taylor (Rutland, VT: Charles E. Tuttle, 1959).

13. See, for example, Walter Isaacson's excellent biography, *Benjamin Franklin: An American Life* (New York: Simon and Schuster, 2003).

14. Alexis de Tocqueville, *Democracy in America* (1840, repr.; New York: Vintage Books, 1990).

15. http://www.egs.edu/faculty/lyotard-resources.html

16. Ibid.

17. Ibid.

18. Afghanistan, Burundi, Cote d'Ivoire, Democratic Republic of the Congo, Georgia, Haiti, Iraq, Liberia, Pakistan, Papua New Guinea, Russia (Chechnya), Somalia, Sudan, Zimbabwe.

19. http://www.forbes.com/lifestyle/travel/2006/02/16/dangerous-travel-destinations-cx_sb_0216feat_ls.html

20. Kevin Kumashiro, " 'Posts' Perspectives on Anti-Oppressive Education in Social Studies, English, Mathematics, and Science Classrooms," *Educational Researcher* 30, no. 3 (2001): pp. 3–12.

21. Among many such findings, by female researchers themselves, see E. Maccoby and C. Jacklin, *The Psychology of Sex Differences*, (Stanford, CA: Stanford University Press, 1975).

22. http://www.nottingham.ac.uk/csme/meas/papers/johnson.html

23. Ziauddin Sardar and Merryl Wyn Davies, *Why Do People Hate America?* (New York: The Disinformation Company Ltd., 2002).

24. "We don't need any geniuses in our Republic."

25. http://www.physics.nyu.edu/faculty/sokal/

26. Francis Fukuyama, *The End of History* (New York: The Free Press, 1992).

27. George Orwell, "Politics and the English Language," 1946; see http://www.orwell.ru/library/essays/politics/english/e_polit.

28. *The Philosophers Magazine*, Autumn 1999.

29. Cited by Abe Peck, *Uncovering the Sixties* (New York: Pantheon Books, 1985).

30. http://www.americanpoems.com/poets/eecummings/11881

31. *Moral Lessons of the Twentieth Century*, p. 44.

# Chapter 8. Tribal Extremes

1. E. O. Wilson, *Sociobiology* (Cambridge, MA: Belknap Press/Harvard University Press, 1975).

2. See, for example, Al Gore, *Earth in the Balance* (London: Earthscan Publications, 1992).

3. Johan Huizinga, *Homo Ludens* (London, Maurice Temple Smith, 1970).

4. Overall data for 224 tribes yielded the following percentages (male%/female%) for various activities: combat 100/0; metalworking 100/0; hunting and trapping 97/3; fishing 86/14; trade 74/26; agriculture 48/52; fire making and tending 30/70; pottery making 18/82;

clothing manufacture and repair 16/84; cooking 9/91. Source: A. Scheinfeld, *Women and Men* (New York: Harcourt, Brace, 1944).

5. Jane Goodall, *In the Shadow of Man* (London: Fontana Books, 1973); and *The Chimpanzees of Gombe* (Cambridge, MA: Belknap Press/Harvard University Press, 1986).

6. I digress to observe that the female of our species is also a formidable huntress in her own right, highly specialized to prey on one quarry above all: the human male. And the human female has evolved a unique strategy for hunting the male: She is the huntress who disguises herself as prey. Accustomed to his evolutionary role as a predator, man imagines that he hunts woman too; yet on this hunt he is just as likely to be the unwary and hapless quarry.

7. http://www.pubmedcentral.nih.gov/articlerender.fcgi?artid=65549

8. http://www.straightdope.com/columns/010420.html

9. Richard Wrangham and Dale Peterson, *Demonic Males: Apes and the Origins of Human Violence* (Boston: Houghton Mifflin, 1996).

10. Ibid., chapter 10: "The Gentle Ape."

11. Robert Sapolsky, "A Natural History of Peace," *Foreign Affairs*, January/February 2006: 104–20.

12. I. de Vore and S. Washburn, "Baboon Ecology and Human Evolution," in F. Howell and F. Bourliere, eds., *African Ecology and Human Evolution* (London: Methuen, 1964).

13. Robert Ardrey, *The Territorial Imperative* (London: Collins, 1967).

14. But many contemporary feminists blithely ignore biological precedents that contradict their ideologies, and instead "legitimate" their ideologies to deny the reality of biology.

15. Auguste Forel, *The Social World of the Ants Compared with that of Man*, vol. II, trans. C. Ogden (London, G. P. Putnam's Sons, 1928), p. 336.

16. Auguste Forel, *The Social World of the Ants Compared with that of Man*, vol. I, trans. C. Ogden (London, G. P. Putnam's Sons, 1928), p. 60.

17. Hans Zinsser, *Rats, Lice and History* (New York: Bantam Books, 1960), pp. 146–55.

18. See Arthur Koestler, *The Ghost in the Machine* (London: Hutchinson, 1967).

19. Sigmund Freud, "Thoughts for the Time on War and Dearth," *The Complete Works of Freud*, vol. 14 (London: The Hogarth Press, 1955).

20. Aristotle, *On the Parts of Animals*.

21. D. Carr, *The Sexes* (London: William Heinemann, 1970).

22. D. Carr, *The Deadly Feast of Life* (London: William Heinemann, 1972).

23. Wilson, *Sociobiology*, p. 370.

24. H. Friedmann, "The Natural History Background to Camouflage," *Smithsonian Institution War Background Studies* 5 (1942): 17. See also J. Huxley, "Evolution, Cultural and Biological," in *New Bottles for Old Wine* (London: Chatto and Windus, 1957), pp. 137–54.

25. Aristotle, *Politics*.

# Chapter 9. Pandora's Extremes

1. Babette Francis, "Is gender a social construct or a biological imperative?" *Family Futures: Issues in Research and Policy*, 7th Australian Institute of Family Studies Conference, Sydney, July 24–26, 2000. http://www.aifs.gov.au/institute/afrc7/francis.html.

2. Ibid.

3. SGI Culture Center, New York, October 12, 2005.

4. John Gray, *Men Are from Mars, Women Are from Venus* (New York: HarperCollins, 1992).

5. Mary Wollstonecraft, *A Vindication of the Rights of Woman* (Boston: Peter Edes, 1792), from her introduction.

6. http://www.fhwa.dot.gov/wit/rosie.htm

7. Margaret Mead, "Alternatives to War," in M. Fried, M. Harris, M. Murphy, eds., *War: The Anthropology of Armed Conflict and Aggression* (Garden City, NY: Natural History Press, 1968).

8. Brian Easlea, *Fathering the Unthinkable* (London: Pluto Press, 1983).

9. E.g., "an overall increase in the percentage of powerful positions held by women might tend to buffer political systems against violence." M. Konner, *The Tangled Wing* (Harmondsworth, UK: Penguin, 1982).

10. See, e.g., J. Laffin, *Women in Battle* (London: Abelard-Schuman, 1967); M. Binkin and S. Bach, *Women and the Military* (Washington, DC: Brookings Institution, 1977); R. Smyth, "Daughters of the Gun," *Observer* magazine, December 11, 1977.

11. Discovery Channel top ten: Ronald Reagan, Abraham Lincoln, Martin Luther King Jr., George Washington, Benjamin Franklin, George W. Bush, Bill Clinton, Elvis Presley, Oprah Winfrey, Franklin D. Roosevelt. (http://dsc.discovery.com/convergence/greatestamerican/greatestamerican.html). Canadian Broadcasting Company's top ten: Frederick Banting, Alexander Graham Bell, Don Cherry, Tommy Douglas, Terry Fox, Wayne Gretzky, Sir John A. Macdonald, Lester Pearson, David Suzuki, Pierre Trudeau (http://www.cbc.ca/greatest/top_ten/). British Broadcasting Corporation's top ten: Homer Simpson, Abraham Lincoln, Martin Luther King Jr., Mr. T, Thomas Jefferson, George Washington, Bob Dylan, Benjamin Franklin, Franklin D. Roosevelt, Bill Clinton (http://news.bbc.co.uk/1/hi/programmes/wtwta/2997144.stm).

12. Gender equality is a thorny subject in some Buddhist communities, particularly the Tibetan, where nuns have a lesser standing than monks.

13. http://www.unicef.org/pon95/chil0011.html

14. Maccoby and Jacklin, among other female researchers, have established four primal gender differences, statistically speaking, between boys and girls. First, boys have superior spatiotemporal skills. Second, girls have superior verbal skills. Third, boys establish more competitive and rigid social hierarchies than do girls. Fourth, girls are more socially supportive and conforming than are boys. These data (obvious to philosophers since antiquity) strongly support Larry Summers's observation and also explain disparities in male versus female leaders.

15. The participants included Bohr, Born, Compton, de Broglie, Debye, Dirac, Einstein, Heisenberg, Planck, Pauli, and Schroedinger. See, e.g., http://www.alwaysbeta.com/wp-content/uploads/bshih/016.jpg.

16. Virginia Woolf, "A Room of One's Own," a 1929 essay that has become a classic.

17. "By the law of nature women, for their own sakes as well as for the sake of their children, are at the mercy of the judgment of men. Worth alone will not suffice, a woman must be thought worthy; nor beauty, she must be admired; nor wisdom, she must he

respected. Their honor is not only in their conduct but in their reputation, and it is not possible that one who lets herself be seen as disreputable can ever be good. When a man does the right thing he only depends on himself and can defy public judgment, but when a woman does the right thing she has done only half of her task, and what people think of her is not less important than what she in effect is. Hence her education must, in this respect, be the contrary of ours." Jean-Jacques Rousseau, *Emile* (1762), sect. 1278. See also Phyllis Chesler, *Woman's Inhumanity to Woman* (New York: Nation Books, 2002).

18. "Woman is more compassionate than man, more easily moved to tears, at the same time is more jealous, more querulous, more apt to scold and to strike. She is, furthermore, more prone to despondency and less hopeful than the man, more void of shame, more false of speech, more deceptive, and of more retentive memory." Aristotle, *History of Animals*, Book IX.

19. "Once it is demonstrated that men and women neither are nor ought to be constituted the same, either in character or in temperament, it follows that they ought not to have the same education. To cultivate the masculine virtues in women and to neglect their own is obviously to do them an injury." Rousseau, *Emile*.

20. Inazo Nitobe, *Bushido: The Soul of Japan* (Boston: Tuttle Publishing, 1969), p. 147.

21. "When I have one foot in the grave, I will tell the whole truth about women. I shall tell it, jump into my coffin, pull the lid over me and say, 'Do what you like now.' "—Leo Tolstoy

22. Arthur Schopenhauer, "On Women," in *Essays and Aphorisms*, trans. R. Hollingdale (Harmondworth: Penguin, 1970).

## Chapter 10. Cognitive Extremes

1. The "digital divide" refers to the technological gap between populations with computers and Internet access, and populations without them. Those on the "wrong side" of the digital divide are falling behind the accelerated pace of globalization.

2. S. J. Gould, *Ever Since Darwin* (London: Burnett Books, 1978).

3. E.g., see L. Malson, *Wolf Children*, and J. Itard, *The Wild Boy of Aveyron*, trans. E. Fawcett, P. Ayrton, J. White (London: N.L.B., 1972).

4. Compare the greatest use of language, which we find in the classics of any written tradition, with the poorest, which we find in postmodern writings. For example, see the "winners" of Professor Denis Dutton's "bad writing contest": http://www.aldaily.com/bwc.htm.

5. Daisaku Ikeda's advice to young people includes this about books: "Reading gives you access to the treasures of the human spirit—from all ages and all parts of the world. Someone who knows this possesses unsurpassed wealth. It's like owning countless banks from which you can make unlimited withdrawals. And those who have tasted this joy, who look on books as friends, are strong." Beyond this, he says: "Reading is essential to thinking . . . To build a humane society where people live with dignity requires leaders who are acquainted with great literature." Daisaku Ikeda, *The Way of Youth*, (Santa Monica, CA: Middleway Press, 2000), pp. 74–76.

5. There are four books by Martin Prechtel listed in Suggested Reading for this chapter. I recommend them all.

7. One physician's exposé of the ADHD fraud is Lawrence Diller's *Running on Ritalin* (New York: Bantam Books, 1998).

8. Ed Hirsch Jr., Joseph Kett, James Trefil, *The Dictionary of Cultural Literacy* (Boston: Houghton Mifflin, 1993).

9. http://buddhism.kalachakranet.org/resources/zen_fun.html

10. David Hume, "We Have No Substantial Self with Which We Are Identical," from *A Treatise of Human Nature*, 1738.

11. R. Dawkins, *The Selfish Gene* (Oxford: Oxford University Press, 1976).

12. Kishore Mahbubani, *Beyond the Age of Innocence: Rebuilding Trust Between America and the World* (New York: Perseus, 2005).

13. Daisaku Ikeda, personal communication, 2005.

## Chapter 11. Educational Extremes

1. http://www.worldlit.ca/facts.html

2. Ibid.

3. Ibid.

4. Aldous Huxley, *An Encyclopedia of Pacifism* (London: Chatto and Windus, 1937), p. 32.

5. Gulag is an acronym for "Glavnoye Upravleniye Ispravitelno-trudovykh Lagerey i kolonii," which translates to "The Chief Directorate [or Administration] of Corrective Labor Camps and Colonies" of the NKVD.

6. http://en.wikipedia.org/wiki/Gulag

7. The Canadian resistance includes: Grant Brown, John Fekete, John Furedy, Bill Gairdner, Andrew Irvine, Jan Narveson, Karen Selick. The American resistance includes Stephen Balch, Allan Bloom, John Frary, Barry Gross, Paul Gross, Susan Haack, David Kelley, Roger Kimball, Noretta Koertge, Alan Kors, Michael Levin, Norman Levitt, Daphne Patai, Harvey Silverglate, Christina Hoff Sommers, Thomas Sowell.

8. The DSM is the *Diagnostic and Statistical Manual*, published by the American Psychiatric Association. It is the "bible" of mental illnesses, which psychiatrists and licensed psychologists consult to make their diagnoses.

9. Elie Wiesel, *Night, Dawn, The Accident: The Elie Wiesel Trilogy* (New York: Farrar, Straus and Giroux, 1987).

10. D. Rosenhan, "On Being Sane in Insane Places," *Science* 179 (January 1973): 250–57.

11. William Shirer, *The Rise and Fall of the Third Reich* (London: Book Club Associates, 1959), pp. 247–48.

12. Ibid., 251–52.

13. One day, for no apparent reason, a handful of prisoners are bathed, clothed, and well fed. Their cells are furnished with books, magazines, and other knickknacks. After several days of this heavenly treatment, they learn the reason: An International Red Cross team has been given permission to visit the prison. What the Red Cross sees convinces them that the prisoners are well treated. Once the visit is over, the prisoners are stripped and forced to don their old rags. Their horrible diet is reinstated, and the books, magazines, and

knickknacks are removed from their cells. But in one prisoner's cell, a little figurine remains, tucked into a crack in the wall and overlooked by the guards: a smiling Buddha.

14. *Canadian Charter of Rights and Freedoms* (1982), Part 1 of the Constitution Act, 1982.

15. Canadian Panel on Violence Against Women, *Changing the Landscape: Ending Violence—Achieving Equality* (Ottawa: Minister of Supply and Services, 1993).

16. John Fekete, *Moral Panic* (Montreal: Robert Davies, 1994), p. 23.

17. M. Loney, "The Politics of Race and Gender," *Inroads* 3 (Summer 1994): 84–85.

18. Ibid.

19. B. Baker et al., Report to the Canadian Philosophical Association from the Committee to Study Hiring Policies Affecting Women (Ottawa: Canadian Philosophical Association, 1991).

20. http://www.mtsu.edu/~baustin/nurmlaw2.html

21. The name of Orwell's totalitarian despot in *Nineteen Eighty-Four* is Big Brother.

22. For a revealing account of the militant feminist attack on science, see Paul Gross and Norman Levitt, *Higher Superstition* (Baltimore: Johns Hopkins University Press, 1994).

23. Roger Kimball, *Tenured Radicals* (Chicago: Ivan R. Dee, 1998), p. xii.

24. Alan Kors and Harvey Silverglate, *The Shadow University: The Betrayal of Liberty on America's Campuses* (New York: The Free Press, 1998), p. 213.

25. Ibid.

26. Ibid, p. 215.

27. Ibid, p. 154.

28. Ibid., p. 103.

29. Ibid, p. 31.

30. For free readings of my work exposing political correctness, see http://www.loumarinoff.com.

31. John Stuart Mill, *On Liberty*, first published 1859.

32. Kors and Silverglate, *The Shadow University*, p. 276.

33. The American Philosophical Practitioners Association (APPA), http://www.appa.edu.

34. *The Liberal* (September-October 2005), 28–30.

# Chapter 12. Economic Extremes

1. Robert Kaplan, *The Coming Anarchy* (New York: Vintage Books, 2000) and *The Ends of the Earth* (New York: Vintage Books, 1997).

2. Aristotle, *Politics*.

3. A representative sample of Devinder Sharma's work is archived at http://www.indiatogether.org/agriculture/opinions/dsharma/faminecommerce.htm.

4. Peter Drahos with John Braithwaite, *Information Feudalism* (London: Earthscan Publications, 2002).

5. This is the brilliant insight of V. Wynne-Edwards, *Animal Dispersion in Relation to Social Behaviour* (Edinburgh: Oliver and Boyd, 1962).

6. See, for example, Pitirim Sorokin, *Man and Society in Calamity* (New York: E. P Dutton, 1943).

7. Mary Midgley, *Beast and Man* (Sussex, UK: Harvester Press, 1978).

8. See, e.g., Eric Schlosser, *Fast Food Nation* (New York: HarperCollins, 2002).

9. http://en.wikipedia.org/wiki/Gini_coefficient

10. Peter Kropotkin, *Mutual Aid* (London: William Heinemann, 1902).

11. Emmanuel Levinas, *Otherwise Than Being or Beyond Essence*, trans. A. Lingis (The Hague: Martinus Nijhoff, 1978).

12. Pierre Vallières, *White Niggers of America* (Toronto: McClelland and Stuart, 1969).

13. Some members of my family—Russian Jewish immigrants—lived in a small French-Canadian town, whose citizens made the sign of the cross whenever they passed a Jew in the street, having been taught by the Church that Jews are devils. Harboring medieval prejudices does not help people assimilate to modernity.

14. Speech at the Second International Roundtable on Constructing Peace, Deconstructing Terror, Brussels, June 26, 2005, archived at http://www.strategicforesight.com/index.htm.

15. From an interview by Al-Jazeera, quoted by Thomas Friedman, *New York Times*, March 15, 2006, p. 8.

## Chapter 13. Totemic Extremes

1. The harms of fast food are graphically illustrated by Morgan Spurlock's film, *Supersize Me*, http://www.supersizeme.com.

2. Robert Cohen, *Milk: The Deadly Poison* (Englewood Cliffs, NJ: Argus Publishing, 1998).

3. Benjamin Barber, *Jihad versus McWorld* (New York: Ballantine Books, 1995).

4. "Debellated" literally means "de-warred": that is, militarily exhausted by centuries of unremitting warfare.

5. Dominique Belpomme, *Ces Maladies Créées Par l'Homme* (Paris: Albin Michel, 2004); and *Guérir du Cancer ou S'en Protéger* (Paris: Fayard, 2005).

6. http://en.wikiquote.org/wiki/Edmund_Burke

7. Leviathan, chapter 13.

8. Daisaku Ikeda, personal communication, 2005.

9. Yuppie stands for "Young urban professional"—the evolution of "hippie."

10. "Dink" stands for "Dual income, no kids"—such couples have disposable cash for expensive amusements.

11. Daisaku Ikeda, personal communication, 2005.

## Chapter 14. Middle Eastern Extremes

1. Gen. 17:15–20.

2. Imagine the effect on Anglo-American relations if every July 4, when Americans celebrate their Independence Day, the British populace went into public mourning.

3. See, e.g., Robert Baer, *Sleeping with the Devil: How Washington Sold our Soul for Saudi Crude* (New York: Three Rivers Press, 2003).

4. See, e.g., Bernard Lewis, *What Went Wrong? The Clash between Islam and Modernity in the Middle East* (New York: HarperCollins, 2002).

5. From Mark Twain's *Innocents Abroad*. See also Alphonse de Lamartine's *Recollections of the East* (1835): "Outside the gates of Jerusalem we saw no living object, heard no living sound. . . ." See also http://www.danielpipes.org/comments/1727.

6. The British experience in Iraq during the 1920s and 1930s is parallel to the American experience there today: The nation is torn by rival factions—for example, Sunni and Shi'ite Muslims—who cannot or will not collaborate for the good of all, and who apparently require a Hobbesian dictator, whether benevolent or malevolent, "to keep them all in awe." See Andrew Krepinevich, "How to Win in Iraq," *Foreign Affairs* (September/October 2005): 87–104.

7. http://www.mideastweb.org/briefhistory.htm

8. "His Majesty's Government view with favor the establishment in Palestine of a national home for the Jewish people, and will use their best endeavors to facilitate the achievement of this object, it being clearly understood that nothing shall be done which may prejudice the civil and religious rights of existing non-Jewish communities in Palestine, or the rights and political status enjoyed by Jews in any other country." See http://en.wikipedia.org/wiki/Balfour_Declaration_1917 and http://www.mideastweb.org/mebalfour.htm.

9. The thirty-three countries that voted in favor of UN Resolution 181: Australia, Belarus, Belgium, Bolivia, Brazil, Canada, Costa Rica, Czechoslovakia, Denmark, Dominican Republic, Ecuador, France, Guatemala, Haiti, Iceland, Liberia, Luxembourg, Netherlands, New Zealand, Nicaragua, Norway, Panama, Paraguay, Peru, Philippines, Poland, Sweden, South Africa, Ukraine, Uruguay, Union of Soviet Socialist Republics, United States, Venezuela. The thirteen countries that voted against UN Resolution 181: Afghanistan, Cuba, Egypt, Greece, India, Iran, Iraq, Lebanon, Pakistan, Saudi Arabia, Syria, Turkey, Yemen. The ten countries that abstained: Argentina, Chile, China, Colombia, El Salvador, Ethiopia, Honduras, Mexico, United Kingdom, Yugoslavia. One state was absent: Thailand. See http://en.wikipedia.org/wiki/UN_General_Assembly_Resolution_48/181.

10. http://en.wikipedia.org/wiki/Israel_and_the_United_Nations

11. See, e.g., Phillip Knightley, The First Casualty (London: André Deutch, 1975).

12. http://en.wikipedia.org/wiki/Edward_Said

13. Two books that illustrate commonalities between the Japanese and the Jews are: Ben-Ami Shillony, *The Jews and the Japanese* (Rutland, VT: Charles E. Tuttle, 1991); and Isaiah Ben-Dasan, *The Japanese and the Jews* (New York: Weatherhill, 1972).

14. http://www.jewishvirtuallibrary.org/jsource/History/Suez_War.html

15. http://en.wikipedia.org/wiki/Arab-Israeli_conflict

16. Ibid.

17. This point is also made by Thomas Friedman, in *From Beirut to Jerusalem* (New York: Anchor Books, 1990).

18. C. von Clausewitz, *On War*, trans. by J. Graham (1832; repr., Harmondsworth, Penguin, 1968).

19. Meir Kahane, *Never Again!* (New York: Pyramid Books, 1972).

20. http://www.haaretz.com/hasen/spages/644510.html

21. Speech at the Second International Roundtable on Constructing Peace, Deconstructing Terror, Brussels, June 26, 2005, archived at http://www.strategicforesight.com/index.htm.

22. Ibid.

23. David Hume, *A Treatise of Human Nature*, 1738.

24. In Israel's case, these are shocking numbers for such a small population. Were the United States to suffer proportionately, there would be 50,000 dead and 300,000 wounded.

## Chapter 15. Terrorist Extremes

1. "Terrorism is a threat to all that the United Nations stands for: respect for human rights, the rule of law, the protection of civilians, tolerance among peoples and nations, and the peaceful resolution of conflict. It is a threat that has grown more urgent in the last five years. Transnational networks of terrorist groups have global reach and make common cause to pose a universal threat. Such groups profess a desire to acquire nuclear, biological, and chemical weapons and to inflict mass casualties. Even one such attack and the chain of events it might set off could change our world forever." http://www.un.org/largerfreedom/chap3.htm

2. http://www.un.org/largerfreedom/chap3.htm

3. http://www.pbs.org/wgbh/pages/frontline/teach/alqaeda/glossary.html

4. For examples of arguments both for and against targeted assassination, see, e.g., Daniel Byman, "Do Targeted Killings Work?" *Foreign Affairs* (March-April 2006).

5. For example, the heroic 9/11 passengers on hijacked Flight 93, knowing via their cell phones what had already happened in Manhattan, and surmising that their plane too was a weapon of terror, perished trying to wrest control of it from the hijackers. We do not know, and may not find out for some time, whether Flight 93 crashed because of the onboard struggle or whether it was shot down to make sure it did not reach Washington, D.C.

6. Victor Davis Hanson, *Carnage and Culture* (New York: Anchor Books, 2002).

7. Aristotle, *Politics*.

8. One of his murderers was Pierre Vallières, whom we encountered in chapter 12.

9. http://www.sgi.org/english/Features/quarterly/0201/feature1.htm

10. http://www.monitor.upeace.org/archive.cfm?id_article=331

11. Press release, February 24, 2006. See also www.asmasociety.org.

12. Qur'an 8:12.

13. http://www.monitor.upeace.org/archive.cfm?id_article=331

14. http://www.msnbc.msn.com/id/3067717/site/newsweek/#storyContinued

15. At one time, Gandhi believed that the Nazis could be defeated by his brand of militant nonviolence. I disagree. A Gandhi in Nazi Germany would have been murdered immediately. Gandhi's nonviolent protests against British colonialism, like King's nonviolent protests against American segregation, needed to take root in and activate the moral sensibilities of the oppressors. While all oppressors have moral sensibilities, not all moral sensibilities can be activated in this way.

16. http://www.sgi-usa.org/publications/wtexpress/WTE-092801preview-No130.htm

17. Ibid.

18. From Fareed Zakaria, "A Conversation with Lee Kuan Yew," *Foreign Affairs* (March-April 1994).

# Suggested Readings

## Chapter 1. Globalization and Its Discontents

Anonymous. *The Yellow Emperor's Classic of Internal Medicine*. Translated by Ilza Veith. Berkeley: University of California Press, 1949.

Appiah, Kwame Anthony. *Cosmopolitanism: Ethics in a World of Strangers*. New York: W. W. Norton, 2006.

Augustine. *The City of God*. Translated by J. Healey. London: J. M. Dent and Sons, 1942.

Bhagavad-Gita. Translated by S. Purohit, London: Faber and Faber, 1969.

Bucke, R. M. *Cosmic Consciousness*. New York: The Cidatel Press, 1975. First printed in 1901.

Capra, F. *The Tao of Physics*. London: Fontana/Collins, 1975.

Carlyle, T. *On Heroes, Hero-Worship, and the Heroic in History*. London: J. M. Dent and Sons, 1940. First printed in 1841,

———. *Past and Present*. Oxford: Clarendon Press, 1918. First printed in 1843.

Erikson, Erik. *Gandhi's Truth: On the Origins of Militant Nonviolence*. New York: W. W. Norton,1960.

Freud, S. *The Complete Psychological Works of Freud*. Vol. XXI, Civilization and Its Discontents (1927–1931). London: Hogarth Press, 1955–1961.

Fuller, R. Buckminster: *Operating Manual for Spaceship Earth*. Carbondale: Southern Illinois University Press, 1969.

Gandhi, Mohandas. *The Story of My Experiments with Truth*. Ahmedabad, India: Navajivan Press, 1929.

Hanson, Victor Davis. *Carnage and Culture: Landmark Battles in the Rise of Western Power*. New York: Doubleday, 2001.

Hobsbawm, Eric. *The Age of Extremes: A History of the World, 1914–1991*. New York: Vintage, 1996.

Huntington, Samuel. *The Clash of Civilizations: Remaking of World Order*. New York: Touchstone, 1997.

Kaplan, Robert. *Warrior Politics: Why Leadership Demands a Pagan Ethos*. New York: Vintage, 2003.

Kipling, Rudyard. "The Ballad of East and West," in *A Victorian Anthology*. Edited by Edmund Clarence Stedman. Cambridge: Riverside Press, 1895.

Koran, translated by E. Lane, S. Lane-Poole, A. Sarwar, Crescent Books, N.Y., undated.

Lamb, Harold. *The Crusades: Iron Men and Saints*. Garden City, N.Y.: International Collectors Library, 1930.

Lewis, Bernard. *What Went Wrong? The Clash Between Islam and Modernity in the Middle East*. New York: HarperCollins, 2003.

Linton, R. *The Study of Man*. London: Peter Owen, 1965.

Makiguchi, Tsunesaburo. *A Geography of Human Life*. Edited by Dayle Bethel. San Francisco: Caddo Gap Press, 2002.

McLuhan, Marshall. *Understanding Media: The Extensions of Man*. Cambridge: MIT Press, 1994. First printed in 1964.

New Testament. The Gideons International. New International Version. Cambridge: Lutterworth, 1981.

Old Testament (according to the Masoretic Texts). Philadelphia: Jewish Publication Society of America, 1960.

Patanjali. *Yoga Sutras of Patanjali*. Translated by Mukunda Stiles. San Francisco: Weiser Books, 2001.

Pirsig, Robert. *Zen and the Art of Motorcycle Maintenance*. New York: Bantam, 1984.

Plato. *Republic*. Translated by B. Jowett. Oxford: Clarendon Press, 1908.

Rumi, Jelaluddin. *The Essential Rumi*. Translated by Coleman Barks. Edison, NJ: Castle Books, 1997.

Thoreau, Henry David. *Civil Disobedience*. New York: Dover Publications, 1993. First published in 1849.

Tigunait, Pandit Rajmani. Seven Systems of Indian Philosophy. Honesdale, PA: Himalayan Institute Press, 1983.

Toynbee, Arnold. A Study of History. Abridged by D. Somervell. London: Oxford University Press, 1963.

Upanishads. Translated by J. Mascaro. Harmondsworth: Penguin, 1985.

Wiesel, Elie. Memoirs: All Rivers Run to the Sea. New York: Schocken Books, 1996.

Zukav, Gary. The Dancing Wu-Li Masters. New York: William Morrow, 1979.

## Chapter 2. Aristotle's Golden Mean

The following books by Aristotle were consulted and/or quoted in this book. The version used was The Complete Works of Aristotle: The Revised Oxford Translation, Bollingen series, vol. LXXI, ed. Jonathan Barnes. Princeton, NJ: Princeton University Press, 1984.

Categories; Economics; Fragments; Generation of Animals; History of Animals; Nicomachean Ethics; On Marvelous Things Heard; On Memory; On the Heavens; On the Universe; Parts of Animals; Physics; Politics; Problems; Rhetoric; Rhetoric, to Alexander

Hobbes, Thomas. Leviathan. Oxford: Basil Blackwell, 1957. First published in 1651.

King, Martin Luther, Jr. "Letter from Birmingham Jail," in Why We Can't Wait. New York: Harper and Row, 1963.

Plato. Crito. Translated by B. Jowett. Oxford: Oxford University Press, 1892.

Popper, Karl. The Open Society and Its Enemies. Vol. 1, The Spell of Plato; Vol. 2, The High Tide of Prophecy. London: Routledge and Kegan Paul, 1957.

## Chapter 3. Buddha's Middle Way

Boethius, Anicius. The Consolation of Philosophy. Translated by V. E. Watts. London: The Folio Society, 1998.

Causton, Richard. The Buddha in Daily Life. London: Rider, 1995.

Dhammapada: Wisdom of the Buddha. Pasadena, CA: Theosophical University Press, 1980.

Emerson, Ralph Waldo. Nature, Addresses and Lectures. Boston: Houghton, Mifflin, 1891 (includes The Method of Nature, 1841).

Evans-Wentz, W. The Tibetan Book of the Dead. London: Oxford University Press, 1927.

———. The Tibetan Book of the Great Liberation. London: Oxford University Press, 1954.

———. Tibetan Yoga and Secret Doctrines. London: Oxford University Press, 1935.

———. Tibet's Great Yogi Milarepa. London: Oxford University Press, 1928.

Hammond, Philip and David Machacek. Soka Gakkai in America. Oxford: Oxford University Press, 1999.

Harrer, Heinrich. Seven Years in Tibet. Translated by Richard Graves. New York: E. P. Dutton, 1954.

Hochswender, Woody, Greg Martin, and Ted Morino. The Buddha in Your Mirror: Practical Buddhism and the Search for Self. Santa Monica, CA: Middleway Press, 2001.

Ikeda, Daisaku and Arnold Toynbee. Choose Life: A Dialogue. Oxford: Oxford University Press, 1976.

Ikeda, Daisaku. A New Humanism: The University Addresses of Daisaku Ikeda. New York: Weatherhill, 1996.

———. The Flower of Chinese Buddhism. Translated by Burton Watson. New York: Weatherhill, 1986.

Ikeda, Daisaku et al. The Wisdom of the Lotus Sutra. 6 vols. Santa Monica, CA: World Tribune Press, 2000.

Kamenetz, Roger. The Jew in the Lotus: A Poet's Rediscovery of Jewish Identity in Buddhist India. San Francisco: HarperCollins 1995.

Kapleau, Roshi Philip. The Three Pillars of Zen. New York: Anchor Books, 1989.

Kennedy, Roshi Robert. Zen Spirit, Christian Spirit: The Place of Zen in Christian Life. New York: Continuum, 2001.

———. Zen's Gifts to Christians. New York: Continuum, 2000.

Lotus Sutra. Translated by Burton Watson. New York: Columbia University Press, 1993.

Nagarjuna. The Fundamental Wisdom of the Middle Way. Translated by Jay Garfield. New York: Oxford University Press, 1995.

Nichiren. The Writings of Nichiren Daishonin. Edited and translated by The Gosho Translation Committee. Tokyo: Soka Gakkai, 1999.

Roach, Geshe Michael. The Diamond Cutter. New York: Doubleday, 2000.

Sogyal Rinpoche. *The Tibetan Book of Living and Dying*. San Francisco: HarperCollins, 1994.

Suzuki, D. T. *Zen Buddhism*. Edited by William Barrett. New York: Anchor Books, 1956.

———. *An Introduction to Zen Buddhism*. New York: Grove Pres., 1964.

Thoreau, Henry David. *Walden*. New York: Book-of-the-Month Club, 1996. First printed in 1854.

Trungpa, Chogyam. *Shambhala: the Sacred Path of the Warrior*. Boulder, CO: Shambhala Publications, 1984.

Watts, Alan. *The Way of Zen*. New York: Vintage, 1957.

———. *This Is It: and Other Essays on Zen*. New York: Vintage, 1973.

## Chapter 4. Confucius's Balanced Order

Campbell, Richmond and Lanning Sowden, eds. *Paradoxes of Rationality and Cooperation*. Vancouver: University of British Columbia Press, 1985.

Chuang Tzu. *The Book of Chuang Tzu*. Translated by Martin Palmer, London: Penguin Books, 1996.

Clark, Michael. *Paradoxes from A to Z*. London: Routledge, 2002.

Confucius. *Analects of Confucius*. Translated by Arthur Waley. New York: Vintage Books, 1989.

Fung Yu-Lan. *The Spirit of Chinese Philosophy*. London: Routledge and Kegan Paul, 1962.

Höchsmann, Hyun. *On Philosophy in China*. Singapore: Thomson-Wadsworth, 2004.

*I Ching*. Translated by Richard Wilhelm and Carey Baynes. Princeton, NJ: Princeton University Press, 1950.

*I Ching (The Complete I Ching)*. Translated by Master Alfred Huang. Rochester, VT: Inner Traditions, 2004.

Ivanhoe, Philip and Bryan Van Norden. *Readings in Classic Chinese Philosophy*. New York: Seven Bridges Press, 2001.

Lao Tzu. *Tao Te Ching*. Translated by Ch'u Ta-Kao. London: George Allen and Unwin, 1937.

———. *Tao Te Ching*. Translated by Stephen Mitchell. New York: Harper and Row, 1988.

Sainsbury, R. M. *Paradoxes*. Cambridge: Cambridge University Press, 1987.

Smullyan, Raymond. *The Tao is Silent*. New York: HarperCollins, 1977.

## Chapter 5. ABC Geometry

Aubrey, J. *Aubrey's Brief Lives*. Edited by O. Dick. London: Secker and Warburg, 1958.

Bigelow, John. *The Reality of Numbers: A Physicalist's Philosophy of Mathematics*. Oxford: Clarendon Press, 1988.

Bohm, David. *Wholeness and the Implicate Order*. London: Routledge and Kegan Paul, 1980.

Devaney, Robert. *Chaos, Fractals and Dynamics*. Menlo Park, California: Addison-Wesley, 1990.

Euclid. *The Thirteen Books of the Elements*. Translated by Thomas Heath. New York: Dover Publications, 1956.

Ghyka, Matila. *The Geometry of Art and Life*. New York: Dover Publications, 1977.

Hilbert, D. and S. Cohn-Vossen. *Geometry and the Imagination (Anschauliche Geometrie)*. Translated by P. Nemenyi. New York: Chelsea Publishing Company, 1952.

Lawlor, Robert. *Sacred Geometry, Philosophy and Practice*. New York: Thames and Hudson, 1989.

Mandelbrot, Benoît. *The Fractal Geometry of Nature*. New York: W. H. Freeman, 1982.

Rucker, Rudy. *Infinity and the Mind: The Science and Philosophy of the Infinite*. Brighton, UK: Harvester, 1982.

Schroeder, Manfred. *Fractals, Chaos, Power Laws*. New York: W. H. Freeman, 1991.

Smullyan, Raymond. *Satan, Cantor and Infinity*. New York: Alfred A. Knopf, 1992.

Taschner, Rudolf, *Der Zahlen gigantische Schatten*, Vieweg Verlag, Wiesbaden 2004.

## Chapter 6. Political Extremes

Brock, David. *Blinded by the Right: The Conscience of an Ex-Conservative*. New York: Three Rivers Press, 2002.

Chödrön, Pema. *When Things Fall Apart: Heart Advice for Difficult Times*. Boston: Shambhala, 2000.

de Tocqueville, Alexis. *Democracy in America*. New York: Vintage Books, 1990. First printed in 1840.

D'Souza, Dinesh. *The End of Racism: Principles for a Multiracial Society*. New York: Free Press, 1995.

Frankl, Viktor. "Reductionism and Nihilism," in *Beyond Reductionism*. Edited by A. Koestler and J. Smythies. London: Hutchinson, 1969.

Galton, Francis. "Statistical Inquiries into the Efficacy of Prayer." *The Fortnightly Review* 12 (1872): 125–35.

Gerzon, David. *A House Divided*. New York: Putnam, 1997.

Golding, William. *Lord of the Flies*. London: Faber, 1954.

Herrnstein, Richard and Charles Murray. *The Bell Curve*. New York: The Free Press, 1994.

Kimball, Roger. *Tenured Radicals*. Chicago: Ivan R. Dee, 1998.

Kors, Alan, and Harvey Silverglate. *The Shadow University*. New York: HarperCollins, 1999.

Mahbubani, Kishore. *Can Asians Think?* Singapore: Times Books International, 1998.

Makiguchi, Tsunesaburo. *A Geography of Human Life*. San Francisco: Caddo Gap Press, 2002.

Percy, Walker. *Lost in the Cosmos: The Last Self-Help Book*. New York: Farrar, Straus and Giroux, 1983.

Sleeper, Jim. *Liberal Racism*. New York: Penguin, 1997.

Sowell, Thomas. *The Vision of the Anointed*. New York: Basic Books, 1996.

Tillyard, E. M. W. *The Elizabethan World Picture*. London: Chatto and Windus, 1945.

Traub, James. *City on a Hill*. Reading, Massachusetts: Addison-Wesley, 1995.

Yankelovitch, Daniel. "Poll Positions." *Foreign Affairs* (September-October 2005): 2–16.

## Chapter 7. Sacred and Profane Extremes

Anonymous. *The Cloud of Unknowing*. Translated into modern English by Clifton Wolters. New York: Penguin, 1961.

Berlin, Isaiah. *Freedom and its Betrayal: Six Enemies of Human Liberty*. Edited by Henry Hardy. London: Chatto and Windus, 2002.

Darwin, Charles. *On the Origin of Species*. London: Watts, London, 1950. First printed in 1859.

Fukuyama, Francis. *The End of History*. New York: The Free Press, 1992.

Galilei, Galileo. *The Sidereal Messenger (Sidereus Nuncius)*. Translated by Albert van Helden. Chicago: The University of Chicago Press, 1989. First printed in 1610.

Gorbachev, Mikhail and Daisaku Ikeda. *Moral Lessons of the 20th Century*. London: I. B. Tauris, 2005.

Gross, Paul and Norman Levitt. *Higher Superstition: The Academic Left and its Quarrels with Science*. Baltimore: Johns Hopkins University Press, 1994.

Isaacson, Walter. *Benjamin Franklin: An American Life*. New York: Simon and Schuster, 2003.

Jungk, Robert. *Brighter Than a Thousand Suns*. London: Victor Gollancz, 1958.

Kipling, Rudyard. *Just So Stories*. New York: HarperCollins, 1996.

Koestler, Arthur. *Darkness at Noon*. London: Vintage, 1994.

Kuan-Chung, Lo. *Romance of the Three Kingdoms*. Translated by C. H. Brewitt-Taylor. Rutland, VT: Charles E. Tuttle, 1959.

Lamarck, Jean-Baptiste de. *Zoological Philosophy*. Translated by H. Eliot. London: Macmillan, 1914. First printed in 1809.

Maccoby, E. and C. Jacklin. *The Psychology of Sex Differences*. Stanford, CA: Stanford University Press, 1975.

Marx, Karl and Friedrich Engels. *The Communist Manifesto*. New York: Signet, 1998. First printed in 1848.

Mill, John Stuart. *On Liberty*. London: J. W. Parker and Son, 1859.

Orwell, George. *Homage to Catalonia*. London: Secker and Warburg, 1967.

———. *Politics and the English Language: An Essay*. London: Horizon, 1947.

Peck, Abe. *Uncovering the Sixties*. New York: Pantheon Books, 1985.

Rand, Ayn. *Atlas Shrugged*. New York: Random House, 1957.

Rushdie, Salman. *The Satanic Verses*. New York: Consortium, 1992.

Sardar, Ziauddin and Merryl Wyn Davies. *Why Do People Hate America?* New York: The Disinformation Company, 2002.

Shirer, William. *The Rise and Fall of the Third Reich: A History of Nazi Germany*. London: Book Club Associates, 1983.

Sokal, Alan. *Transgressing the Boundaries: Toward a Transformative Hermeneutics of Quantum Gravity*. Durham, NC: Duke University Press, 1996.

## Chapter 8. Tribal Extremes

Ardrey, Robert. *African Genesis: A Personal Investigation into the Animal Origins and Nature of Man*. London: Collins, 1961.

———. *Territorial Imperative: A Personal Enquiry into the Animal Origins of Property and Nations*. London: Collins, 1967.

Carr, Donald. *The Deadly Feast of Life*. London: William Heinemann, 1972.

———. *The Sexes*. New York: Doubleday, 1970.

Chance, M., and C. Jolly. *Social Groups of Monkeys, Apes and Men*. London: Jonathan Cape, 1970.

Darwin, Charles. *The Descent of Man*. London: John Murray, 1901. First printed in 1871.

De Vore, I. and S.Washburn. "Baboon Ecology and Human Evolution," in *African Ecology and Human Evolution*. Edited by F.

Howell and F. Bourliere. London, Methuen, 1964.

Eibl-Eibesfeldt, I. *The Biology of Peace and War*. Translated by E. Mosbacher. London: Thames and Hudson, 1979.

Forel, Auguste. *The Social World of the Ants Compared with that of Man*. Translated by C. Ogden. London: G. P. Putnam's Sons, 1928.

Fossey, Dian. *Gorillas in the Mist*. New York: Mariner Books, 2000.

Freud, Sigmund. "Thoughts for the Time on War and Death." Vol. 14, *The Complete Works of Freud*. London: Hogarth Press, 1955.

Friedmann, H. "The Natural History Background to Camouflage," *Smithsonian Institution War Background Studies* 5 (1942).

Goodall, Jane. *In the Shadow of Man*. London: Fontana Books, 1973.

———. *The Chimpanzees of Gombe*. Cambridge, MA: Belknap/Harvard University Press, 1986.

Gore, Al. *Earth in the Balance*. London: Earthscan Publications, 1992.

Hoffer, Eric. *The True Believer: Thoughts on the Nature of Mass Movements*. New York: Harper, 1951.

Huizinga, Johan. *Homo Ludens*. London: Maurice Temple Smith, 1970.

Huxley, Julian. "Evolution, Cultural and Biological," in *New Bottles for Old Wine*. London: Chatto and Windus, 1957.

Koestler, Arthur. *The Ghost in the Machine*. London: Hutchinson, 1967.

Morris, Desmond. *The Naked Ape*. London: Cape, 1967.

Sapolsky, Robert. "A Natural History of Peace," *Foreign Affairs* (January-February 2006): 104–20.

Schaller, G. *The Mountain Gorilla*. Chicago: University of Chicago Press, 1963.

Scheinfeld, A. *Women and Men*. New York: Harcourt, Brace, 1944.

Tiger, Lionel and Robin Fox. *The Imperial Animal*. New York: Holt, Rinehart and Winston, 1971.

Trotter, W. *Instincts of the Herd in Peace and War*. London: T. Fisher Unwin, 1920.

Wilson, E. O. *Sociobiology*. Cambridge: Belknap/Harvard University Press, 1975.

Wrangham, Richard and Dale Peterson. *Demonic Males: Apes and the Origins of Human Violence*. New York: Houghton Mifflin, 1996.

Wynne-Edwards, V., *Animal Dispersion in Relation to Social Behaviour*. Edinburgh: Oliver & Boyd Ltd., 1962.

Zinsser, Hans. *Rats, Lice and History*. Boston: Little Brown, 1935.

## Chapter 9. Pandora's Extremes

Aristotle, *History of Animals*, Book IX.

Binkin, M. and S. Bach. *Women and the Military*. Washington, DC: Brookings Institution, 1977.

Chesler, Phyllis. *Woman's Inhumanity to Woman*. New York: Nation Books, 2002.

de Beauvoir, Simone. *The Second Sex*. Translated by H. Parshley. London: The New English Library, 1962.

Deutsch, H. *The Psychology of Women*. New York: Grune and Stratton, 1944.

Easlea, Brian. *Fathering the Unthinkable*. London: Pluto Press, 1983.

Gairdner, William. *The War Against the Family: A Parent Speaks Out*. Toronto: Stoddart, 1992.

Goethe, Johann Wolfgang von. *Faust*. Translated by Walter Kaufmann. New York: Anchor, 1962.

Gray, John. *Men are from Mars, Women are from Venus*. New York: HarperCollins, 1992.

Konner, M. *The Tangled Wing*. Harmondsworth, UK: Penguin Books, 1982.

Laffin, J. *Women in Battle*. London: Abelard-Schuman, 1967.

Levin, Michael. *Feminism and Freedom*. New Brunswick, NJ: Transaction Books, 1987.

Lewis, C. S. *The Screwtape Letters*. London: Centenary Press, 1942.

Marinoff, Lou. *The Big Questions: How Philosophy Can Change Your Life*. London: Bloomsbury, 2003.

Mead, Margaret. "Alternatives to War," in *War: The Anthropology of Armed Conflict and Aggression*. Edited by M. Fried, M. Harris, M.

Murphy. Garden City, NY: Natural History Press, 1968.

Morgan, Elaine. *The Descent of Woman*. London: Souvenir Press, 1972.

Nitobe, Inazo. *Bushido: The Soul of Japan*. Boston: Tuttle Publishing, 1969.

Rousseau, Jean-Jacques. *Emile, or On Education*. Translated by Allan Bloom. New York: Basic Books, 1979.

Schopenhauer, Arthur. "On Women," in *Essays and Aphorisms*. Translated by R. Hollingdale. Harmondworth, UK: Penguin, 1970.

Smyth, R. "Daughters of the Gun," *Observer* magazine, December 11, 1977.

Sommers, Christina Hoff. *Who Stole Feminism: How Women Have Betrayed Women*. New York: Simon and Schuster, 1994.

Wollstonecraft, Mary. *A Vindication of the Rights of Woman*. New York: Dover, 1996. First printed in 1792.

Woolf, Virginia. *A Room of One's Own*. New York: Harcourt, Brace, 1929.

## Chapter 10. Cognitive Extremes

Dawkins, Richard. *The Selfish Gene*. Oxford: Oxford University Press, 1976.

Diller, Lawrence. *Running on Ritalin*. New York: Bantam Books, 1998.

Flesch, Rudolf. *Why Johnny Can't Read*. New York: Harper and Row, 1955.

Gould, S.J. *Ever Since Darwin*. London: Burnett Books, 1978.

Hirsch, Ed, Joseph Kett, and James Trefil, eds. *The Dictionary of Cultural Literacy*. Boston: Houghton Mifflin, 1988.

Hume, David. "We Have No Substantial Self with Which We Are Identical," in *A Treatise of Human Nature*. London: Green and Grose, 1898. First printed in 1739.

Ikeda, Daisaku. *The Way of Youth: Buddhist Common Sense for Handling Life's Questions*. Santa Monica, CA: Middleway Press, 2000.

Mahbubani, Kishore. *Beyond the Age of Innocence: Rebuilding Trust Between America and the World*. New York: Perseus, 2005.

Malson, L. and J. Itard. *Wolf Children* and *The Wild Boy of Aveyron*. Translated by E. Fawcett, P. Ayrton, J. White. London: N.L.B., 1972.

Mander, Jerry. *Four Arguments for the Elimination of Television*. New York: Morrow Quill Paperbacks, 1978.

Marinoff, Lou. *Plato Not Prozac: Applying Philosophy to Everyday Problems*. New York: HarperCollins, 1999.

McLuhan, Marshall. *Understanding Media*. London: Routledge, 1964.

Prechtel, Martin. *The Disobedience of the Daughter of the Sun: Ecstasy and Time*. Cambridge, MA: Yellow Moon Press, 2001.

———. *Long Life, Honey in the Heart: a Story of Initiation and Eloquence from the Shores of a Mayan Lake*. Berkeley, CA: North Atlantic Books, 2004.

———. *Secrets of a Talking Jaguar: Memoirs from the Living Heart of a Mayan Village*. New York: Tarcher/Putnam, 1999.

———. *The Toe Bone and the Tooth: An Ancient Mayan Story Relived in Modern Times: Leaving Home to Come Home*. London: Thorsons, 2004.

Sommers, Christina Hoff and Sally Satel. *One Nation under Therapy*. New York: St. Martin's Press, 2005.

## Chapter 11. Educational Extremes

Baker, B. et al. *Report to the Canadian Philosophical Association from the Committee to Study Hiring Policies Affecting Women*. Canadian Philosophical Association, 1991.

Bloom, Alan. *The Closing of the American Mind*. New York: Simon and Schuster, 1987.

Brown, Grant. *The Employment Equity Empress Has No Clothes*. Occasional Paper #2. Edmonton: Gender Issues Education Foundation, 1992.

*Canadian Charter of Rights and Freedoms*, Part 1 of the Constitution Act, 1982.

Panel on Violence Against Women. *Changing the Landscape: Ending Violence—Achieving Equality*. Ottawa: Minister of Supply and Services Canada, 1993.

Fekete, John. *Moral Panic*. Montreal: Robert Davies, 1994.

Hobsbawm, Eric. *The Age of Empire: 1875–1914*. New York: Vintage, 1989.

Huxley, Aldous. *An Encyclopedia of Pacifism*. London: Chatto and Windus, 1937.

———. *Ends and Means*. London: Chatto and Windus, 1937.

Irvine, Andrew, "Jack and Jill and Employment Equity," *Dialogue* XXXV (1996): 255–91.

Kafka, Franz. *The Trial*. New York: Schocken, 1999.

Kimball, Roger. *Tenured Radicals*. Chicago: Ivan R. Dee, 1998.

Koertge, Noretta, and Daphne Patai. *Professing Feminism*. New York: Basic Books, 1994.

Koestler, Arthur. *Darkness at Noon*. London: Vintage 1994.

Kors, Alan and Harvey Silverglate. *The Shadow University: The Betrayal of Liberty on America's Campuses*. New York: The Free Press, 1998.

Loney, M. "The Politics of Race and Gender," *Inroads* 3 (Summer 1994).

Mill, John Stuart. *On Liberty*. London: J. W. Parker and Son, 1859.

Ontario Provincial Legislature. *Employment Equity Act* (Bill 79).

Orwell, George. *Animal Farm*. London: Secker and Warburg, 1945.

———. *Nineteen Eighty-Four*. London: Secker and Warburg, 1949.

Patai, Daphne. "Speaking as a Human," *The Liberal* (September-October 2005): 28–30.

Ravich, Diane. *The Language Police: How Pressure Groups Restrict What Students Learn*. New York: Vintage Books, 2004.

Rosenhan, D. "On Being Sane in Insane Places," *Science* 179 (January 1973): 250–57.

Shapiro, Ben. *Brainwashed: How Universities Indoctrinate America's Youth*. Nashville: WND Books, 2004.

Shirer, William. *The Rise and Fall of the Third Reich*. London: Book Club Associates, 1959.

Solzhenitsyn, Aleksandr. *The First Circle.* Translated by Thomas Whitney. Evanston, IL: Northwestern University Press, 1997.

———. *One Day in the Life of Ivan Denisovitch.* Translated by Ralph Parker. New York: Penguin Group, 1998.

Spengler, Oswald. *The Decline of the West.* London: Allen and Unwin, 1922.

Sykes, Charles. *Dumbing Down Our Kids: Why American Children Feel Good About Themselves But Can't Read, Write or Add.* New York: St. Martin's, 1995.

Wiesel, Elie. *Night, Dawn, The Accident: The Elie Wiesel Trilogy.* New York: Farrar, Straus and Giroux, 1987.

## Chapter 12. Economic Extremes

Brown, Lester. *Plan B: Rescuing a Planet Under Stress and a Civilization in Trouble.* New York: W. W. Norton, 2003.

Carson, Rachel. *Silent Spring.* New York: Fawcett Crest, 1962.

Drahos, Peter with John Braithwaite. *Information Feudalism.* London: Earthscan, 2002.

Emerson, Ralph Waldo. *Self-Reliance.* New York: Dover Publications, 1933. First printed in 1841.

Gore, Al. *Earth in the Balance.* London: Earthscan, 1992.

Hardin, Garrett. "The Tragedy of the Commons," *Science* 162 (1968): 1243–48.

Kaplan, Robert. *The Coming Anarchy: Shattering the Dreams of the Post Cold War.* New York: Random House, 2000.

———. *The Ends of the Earth: A Journey at the Dawn of the 20th Century.* New York: Random House, 1996.

Kropotkin, Peter. *Mutual Aid.* London: William Heinemann, 1902.

Leslie, John. *The End of the World: The Science and Ethics of Human Extinction.* London: Routledge, 1996.

Levinas, Emmanuel. *Otherwise than Being or Beyond Essence.* Translated by A. Lingis. The Hague: Martinus Nijhoff, 1978.

Locke, John. *Two Treatises of Government.* Cambridge: Cambridge University Press, 1970. First printed in 1698.

Lovelock, James. *Gaia: A New Look at Life on Earth.* New York: Oxford University Press, 2000.

Malthus, T. *Population: The First Essay.* Ann Arbor: University of Michigan Press, 1959. First printed in 1798.

Midgley, Mary. *Beast and Man.* Sussex, UK: Harvester Press, 1978.

Schell, Jonathan. *The Fate of the Earth.* London: Cape, 1982.

Sorokin, Pitirim. *Man and Society in Calamity.* New York: E. P Dutton, 1943.

Spencer, Herbert. *Principles of Sociology.* London: MacMillan, 1969. First printed in 1893–96.

Sumner, William Graham. *Social Darwinism (Selected Essays).* Englewood Cliffs, NJ: Prentice Hall, 1963.

Vallières, Pierre. *White Niggers of America.* Toronto: McClelland and Stuart, 1969.

Wynne-Edwards, Vere. *Animal Dispersion in Relation to Social Behaviour.* Edinburgh: Oliver and Boyd, 1962.

## Chapter 13. Totemic Extremes

Barber, Benjamin. *Jihad Versus McWorld.* New York: Times Books, 1995.

Belpomme, Dominique. *Ces Maladies Crées Par l'Homme.* Paris: Albin Michel, 2004.

———. *Guérir du Cancer ou S'en Protéger.* Paris: Fayard, 2005.

Cohen, Robert. *Milk: The Deadly Poison.* Englewood Cliffs, NJ: Argus, 1998.

Huxley, Aldous. *Brave New World.* London: Chatto and Windus, 1932.

———. *The Doors of Perception.* London: Chatto and Windus, 1954.

———. *Island.* London: Chatto and Windus, 1962.

Leary, Timothy. *The Politics of Ecstasy.* New York: Putnam, 1968.

Plato. *Symposium.* Translated by B. Jowett. Oxford: Oxford University Press, 1892.

Schlosser, Eric. *Fast Food Nation: The Dark Side of the All-American Meal.* Boston: Houghton Mifflin, 2001.

Sinclair, Upton. *The Jungle.* London: Heineman, 1906.

Wurtzel, Elizabeth. *Prozac Nation: Young and Depressed in America.* Boston: Houghton Mifflin, 1994.

## Chapter 14. Middle Eastern Extremes

Baer, Robert. *Sleeping with the Devil: How Washington Sold our Soul for Saudi Crude.* New York: Three Rivers Press, 2003.

Clausewitz, C. von. *On War.* Translated by J. Graham. Harmondsworth, UK: Penguin, 1968. First printed in 1832.

Ben-Dasan, Isaiah. *The Japanese and the Jews.* New York: Weatherhill, 1972.

Dimont, Max. *Jews, God and History.* New York: Signet, 1962.

Donovan, Robert. *Israel's Fight for Survival.* New York: Signet, 1967.

Friedman, Thomas. *From Beirut to Jerusalem.* New York: Anchor Books, 1990.

Josephus, Flavius. *The Jewish War (66–70 C.E.).* Translated by A. Williamson. New York: Penguin Putnam, 1959.

Kahane, Meir. *Never Again: A Program for Survival.* Los Angeles: Nash Publishing, 1971.

Katz, Samuel. *Battleground: Fact and Fantasy in Palestine.* New York: Bantam Books, 1973.

Knightley, Phillip. *The First Casualty.* London: André Deutch, 1975.

Krepinevich, Andrew. "How to Win in Iraq," *Foreign Affairs* (September-October 2005), 87–104.

Lawrence. T. E. *Seven Pillars of Wisdom.* Hertfordshire, UK: Wordsworth Editions, 1997. First printed in 1935.

Michener, James. *The Source.* New York: Random House, 1965.

Nutting, Anthony. *The Arabs.* New York: Mentor, 1964.

Peres, Shimon. *The Imaginary Voyage.* Cambridge, MA: Zoland Books, 2000.

Schwartz-Bart, André. *The Last of the Just.* Harmondsworth, UK: Penguin, 1977.

Said, Edward. *Orientalism.* New York: Vintage, 1979.

Shillony, Ben-Ami. *The Jews and the Japanese.* Rutland, VT: Charles E. Tuttle, 1991.

Twain, Mark. *Innocents Abroad.* New York: Penguin Putnam, 2002. First printed in 1869.

Uris, Leon. *Exodus.* New York: Transworld, 1970.

## Chapter 15. Terrorist Extremes

Brisard, Jean-Charles and Guillaume Dasquié. *Forbidden Truth: U.S.-Taliban Secret Oil Diplomacy and the Failed Hunt for Bin Laden.* New York: Nation Books, 2002.

Byman, Daniel. "Do Targeted Killings Work?" *Foreign Affairs* (March-April 2006).

Conquest, Robert. *The Great Terror.* London: Macmillan, 1968.

Inoguchi, Rikihei and Tadashi Nakajima. *The Divine Wind (Kamikaze).* Translated by Roger Pineau. Westport, Connecticut: Greenwood Press, 1978.

Malory, Thomas. *Le Morte d'Arthur.* London: Edward Moxon, 1868.

National Commission on Terrorist Attacks. *The 9/11 Commission Report: Final Report of the National Commission on Terrorist Attacks Upon the United States.* New York: W. W. Norton, 2004.

Power, Samantha. *A Problem From Hell: America and the Age of Genocide.* New York: Basic Books, 2002.

Stevenson, William. *90 Minutes at Entebbe.* New York: Bantam, 1976.

White, T. H. *The Once and Future King.* London: Collins, 1958.

Zakaria, Fareed. "A Conversation with Lee Kuan Yew," *Foreign Affairs* (March-April 1994).

# Image Credits

Page 52, figure 2.3, the Parthenon: photograph from morgueFile.

Page 55, figure 2.7, nautilus: photograph from Shutterstock.

Page 55, figure 2.8, galaxy M100: photograph from NASA.

Page 56, figure 2.9, cauliflower: photograph by Dror Bar-Natan.

Page 56, figure 2.10, shrimp cocktail: photograph from iStock.

Page 57, figure 2.11, female face: photograph from Shutterstock.

Page 146, figure 5.6, stylized lotus flowers: images from Shutterstock.

Page 153, figure 5.11, matryoshka dolls: photograph from Shutterstock.

Page 158, figure 5.16, Mandelbrot sets: 5.16.1, image from Wikimedia Commons; 5.16.2, image from Wikimedia Commons; 5.16.3, image from Shutterstock; 5.16.4, image from Wikimedia Commons; 5.16.5, image from Shutterstock; 5.16.6, image from Shutterstock.

Page 159, figure 5.17, Mandelbrot sets: images from Shutterstock.

Page 160, figure 5.18, higher order Mandelbrot set: background image created by Dror Bar-Natan.

Page 160, figure 5.19, lotus flowers in and around Mandelbrot set: images from Shutterstock (left and center) and Wikimedia Commons (right).

Page 162, figure 5.20, Mandelbrot set as fractal Buddha: images from Shutterstock (top and bottom row) and Wikimedia Commons (middle row).

Page 376, figure 11.1, adult literacy chart: chart from http://www.unicef.org/pon95/chil0011.html.

Page 376, figure 11.2, infant mortality chart: chart from http://www.prb.org/Content/NavigationMenu/P RB/Educators/Human_Population/Health2/Wor ld_Health1.htm.

Page 377, figure 11.3, child soldiers chart: chart from http://hrw.org/campaigns/crp/crp-map.htm.

Page 439, figure 12.11, Gini coefficients: Bob Steimle.

Page 503, figure 14.1, Palestine in 1918: Bob Steimle.

Page 505, figure 14.2, Palestine in 1922: Bob Steimle.

Page 505, figure 14.3, Palestine in 1947: Bob Steimle.

Page 506, figure 14.4, Israel in 1948: Bob Steimle.

Page 507, figure 14.5, the "Arab World" and Israel: Bob Steimle.

Page 510, figure 14.6, the "Islamic World," Israel, and the Civilizational Interface Between Islam, East Asia, India and Europe: Bob Steimle.

# Index

Page numbers in italics indicate maps and tables.

170.44
MAR

Marinoff, Lou.

The middle way.

$24.95

30656014102894

| DATE | | | |
|---|---|---|---|
|  |  |  |  |
|  |  |  |  |
|  |  |  |  |
|  |  |  |  |
|  |  |  |  |
|  |  |  |  |
|  |  |  |  |
|  |  |  |  |
|  |  |  |  |
|  |  |  |  |
|  |  |  |  |
|  |  |  |  |
|  |  |  |  |

10/07